WILLIAM R. DAVIE

As charged by our organizational documents dating from 1783, the North Carolina Society of the Cincinnati exists to promote the memory and ideals of the "vast event" that was the American Revolution. Few North Carolinians were more committed to those ideals than William R. Davie.

We therefore were honored to have sponsored the original publication of this splendid biography in 1957. We heartily support its republication today and offer our special thanks to the Friends of Historic Halifax and the Historic Halifax Restoration Association as well as the Davie descendants for their efforts in bringing this important volume back to light more than sixty-five years later.

Joseph B.C. Kluttz, President, NCSoC
March, 2025

GOVERNOR WILLIAM RICHARDSON DAVIE

Oil portrait of the subject, aged 44, by Charles Xavier Harris, from the original, executed in Paris, 1800, by John VanderLyn (1775-1852). The original has been lost or destroyed. This copy, showing Davie with letter and signature of VanderLyn in his left hand and a copy of the signatories and their seals to the French Convention of 1800 in his right, is now in the possession of Colonel Preston Davie, New York City.

WILLIAM R. DAVIE

by
Blackwell P. Robinson

Original edition copyright © 1957 and was renewed in 1985 by the University of North Carolina Press. This edition copyright © 2025 by the Friends of Historic Halifax, Inc. and the Historic Halifax Restoration Association, Inc. All rights reserved. This America 250th Commemorative Edition has been published with the gracious permission of the descendants of Blackwell Pierce Robinson.

ISBN 978-1-4696-9267-8 (hardcover)
ISBN 978-1-4696-9268-5 (paperback)
ISBN 978-1-4696-9269-2 (ebook)

A limited hardcover edition is available through the Historic Halifax State Historic Site in Halifax, NC. All revenue from sales of the book supports projects at the site.

Published by the Friends of Historic Halifax and the Historic Halifax Restoration Association

Distributed by the University of North Carolina Press

To the Memory of

My Son

PREFACE

A PREFACE to this study of the life of William R. Davie seems superfluous—with the exception of a number of heartfelt acknowledgments. It is intended as a straightforward, chronological narrative of the eventful and versatile life of one of the founders of the state of North Carolina and of the United States.

In an effort to preserve something of the flavor or "feel" of the period, the original spellings, capitalizations, and punctuations have been preserved in all quoted material—without employing the ubiquitous and annoying *sic*. And in an effort to enhance the readability, informational footnotes only are placed at the bottom of the pages; those which cite authorities have been placed in the back of the book.

As far as possible the writer has allowed the man Davie to speak for himself through his writings and actions. If a marmoreal, statuesque portrait emerges, the writer asks indulgence. And if the end-result classifies the writer as an apologist or a Carlylean hero worshipper he offers in rebuttal that a careful check of all available sources has failed to reveal any blemish in Davie's private or public career—except for the superficial indulgences of the men of the world of that day: a well-stocked wine cellar, an interest in horse flesh, and perhaps in cockfighting.

His career was varied and—to paraphrase Mark Antony's appraisal of Caesar—the qualities were so mixed in him that it might rightly be said, "This was a man!"

As a young officer in the North Carolina forces during the American Revolution, along with Marion, Pickens, and Sumter, he achieved an aura of military fame and éclat in his early twenties. This reputation

Preface

contributed to his success in the arduous responsibilities which he was pressed into assuming as Nathanael Greene's interim commissary general and as the state commissary general from December, 1780, until the cessation of hostilities.

Upon the return of peace, Davie took his place among the leaders of Eastern North Carolina at Halifax and married Sarah, daughter of the influential officer and Conservative statesman, General Allen Jones, of Mount Gallant, Northampton County, Attorney General of the Crown, and niece of the Radical aristocrat, Willie Jones, "the Thomas Jefferson of North Carolina." An ardent Conservative, to whom the paper money crowd was anathema, Davie very naturally aligned himself with the Federalist party. As one of their ablest leaders he fought for his beliefs in nine sessions of the House of Commons in the period 1784-1798; served as a delegate to the Federal Constitutional Convention in Philadelphia, where he played an important role in casting North Carolina's vote for the "Connecticut compromise"; and, along with Iredell, fought for the adoption of the Constitution in the two state ratifying conventions at Hillsboro and Fayetteville.

And it was Davie who introduced two of the most important bills ever enacted in North Carolina: one provided for the adoption of the Federal Constitution; the other, for the founding of the University of North Carolina. Not content with the passage of the University charter, Davie performed yeoman service on the building committee, in selecting the faculty, in the drafting of the plan of studies to be followed by the University, and in all the harassing minutiae incidental to its creation and establishment.

His star rose even higher in the next decade, reaching its zenith in his election as governor in 1799 and his appointment as one of the three United States ministers plenipotentiary to France in 1800. After reaching his peak at the turn of the century, his political fall was sudden. He retired in 1805 to his plantation, "Tivoli," in the Waxhaws in South Carolina, where he lived, a successful planter and disillusioned Federalist, until his death in 1820.

This study, begun at the suggestion of Dr. Robert Diggs Wimberly Connor, late National Archivist and history professor at the University of North Carolina, could never have been brought to a con-

Preface

clusion without the continued inspiration and direction of Professor Hugh T. Lefler, under whom the first eight chapters were written.

Among others to whom the writer is deeply indebted for constructive criticism and helpful leads in research are Dr. J. G. de Roulhac Hamilton, Dr. Archibald Henderson, Dr. Elisha P. Douglass, Miss Mary Thornton, Dr. William P. Jacocks, Dr. James Patton, Mr. William S. Powell, Mr. Henry Lewis, and the entire staff of the Southern Historical Collection—all of Chapel Hill, North Carolina. The staffs of the North Carolina Department of Archives and History and of the Duke Archives also rendered invaluable assistance.

The names of others, both in their official and private capacity, would be legion—from California to Edinburgh, but especial appreciation is hereby extended to Miss Nancy Crockett of Lancaster, South Carolina, Mr. Hugh Frank Rankin of Williamsburg, Virginia, and Dr. John A. Crockett of Austin, Texas—a descendant, maternally, of the subject of the biography.

A special note of gratitude is extended to Colonel Preston Davie of New York, a collateral descendant of William R. Davie. For his invaluable collection of Davieana, amassed over a lifetime, for his indefatigable research, and for his discriminating advice and his enthusiastic encouragement, the writer will be eternally grateful.

Deep appreciation is also extended to the North Carolina Society of the Cincinnati, who magnanimously contributed one-half the cost of publication.

To my wife I am indebted, not only for her encouragement and valuable suggestions, but for her ability to decipher and type the entire manuscript.

Blackwell P. Robinson

CONTENTS

	Preface	vii
1.	Why They Came to the Waxhaws	1
2.	Young William Richardson Davie	16
3.	Youthful Patriot and Student of Law	27
4.	The Partisan Leader	37
5.	Subsisting an Army	90
6.	A Conservative under the Constitution	137
7.	A Federalist Star Rises	177
8.	The Father of the University	222
9.	A Federalist Star at its Zenith	277
10.	His Excellency the Governor	302
11.	The French Mission	319
12.	A Federalist Star Falls	359
	Appendices	401
	Notes	411
	Bibliography	456
	Index	477

ILLUSTRATIONS

Governor William Richardson Davie, oil portrait by Charles Xavier Harris, from the original by John VanderLyn   *frontispiece*

facing page

William Richardson Davie, preliminary study by John VanderLyn	192
William Richardson Davie, miniature by Eliza Mirbel	193
William Richardson Davie, pastel portrait by James Sharples	208
William Richardson Davie, original "physionotrace" by Gilles Louis Chrétien	209
Loretta, exterior	336
Loretta, interior	336
The Theatre of War in the Carolinas, 1780-1782	337
Robert Jones, Jr.	352
Brigadier General Allen Jones	352
Bookplate displaying Davie heraldic Arms	353
Hatchment displaying Davie heraldic Arms	353
Tomb of Governor William Richardson Davie	353

WILLIAM R. DAVIE

CHAPTER I

Why They Came to the Waxhaws

INTO the Garden of the Waxhaws, into a new and challenging world, came a young family of five, in the year 1764—the father, aged forty, the mother a year older, with their three children: William Richardson Davie, a lad of eight; his sister Mary, three years younger; and Joseph, aged three. Archibald Davie and his wife, Mary Richardson, had gathered up their children and their household possessions in their home near Whitehaven, in Egremont Parish, co. Cumberland, England, to transplant them to the South Carolina Back Country. To understand why they made such a move involves retracing their long journey and searching out the rural parish in northwestern England where they had lived. Yet journey's end would not be here, but, for the maternal line, farther north in Scotland above the Solway Firth to the parish of Ruthwell (pronounced "Rivvel"); and, for the paternal line, possibly to Argyll, Scotland, or to southern England. Perhaps among the progenitors from whose loins sprang the parents of William Richardson Davie, or among their more immediate relatives, may be found the reasons why a substantial family should uproot itself to begin a new existence across the Atlantic in a region recently inhabited by the red men.

Of William Richardson's paternal line little is known except that his father, Archibald Davie,* was born in the year 1724, probably in

* The orthography of that time was so unsettled that closely related members of this family, as late as 1800, spelled their surname in various ways: Davy, Dave, Davey, and Davie. A notable instance of this different spelling is that

[1]

WILLIAM R. DAVIE

Argyll, Scotland.* Some evidence as to the position of the family in the British Isles may be inferred from the heraldic arms † which Archibald

---

William R. Davie's great-uncle, the first of the family to come to America, William, spelled his name "Davy," but his son Gabriel spelled his name "Davey." For an excellent, well-documented typescript sketch of this branch of the family which settled first in Maryland in 1720 and later moved to what is now Person County, North Carolina, the writer is indebted to Colonel Preston Davie, of New York, a collateral descendant of William R. Davie. This sketch, a copy of which is in the writer's possession, is entitled "The Story of Governor William Richardson Davie and His Times."

* The date of birth is inscribed on his tomb at the Old Waxhaw Presbyterian Meeting House, near Lancaster, South Carolina. The place of birth is inscribed in the Davie family Bible, recently presented to the Louis Round Wilson Library, Chapel Hill, N.C., by the children of William R. Davie Crockett of Austin, Texas. There is recent evidence, however, which points to the conclusion that the Davies were originally from the south of England. The identical heraldic arms used by both the South Carolina and the Maryland branch of the family were not Scottish but English arms and are traceable back as far as the 15th century in several south of England counties. See letter, Preston Davie to the writer, September 19, 1956, in writer's possession. Colonel Davie is at present having research done through the College of Heralds to trace this family. Also tending to corroborate their south of England origin was the location, in the summer of 1956 by William S. Powell of Chapel Hill, N.C., of a number of Davie tombstones in the churchyard of the parish church at Sandford in Devon.

† The armorial bearings of the family are as follows:

> Quarterly, first and fourth sable; a fesse or, between two cinquefoils argent; second third, per fesse, or, and argent in chief three eagles heads couped, issuant proper.
> Crest: A lion sejant proper supporting a column or
> Motto: "*Diu delibera cito fac*" (Deliberate long, act quickly).

These Davie Arms, before being quartered, were recorded in the College of Arms in 1623 by John Davy of Harnham in Wiltshire. These Arms, subsequently quartered, were engraved on the tomb of Archibald Davie's wife, Mary Richardson, and on a silver ewer belonging to the original William Davy, which was, in the 1880's, in the possession of Winston Jones Davie, a member of the Maryland branch of this family. They were also used both on his bookplate and seal by William Richardson Davie and later generations. The original engraved copperplate from which was imprinted Governor Davie's armorial bookplate has been recently presented to the Louis Round Wilson Library of the University of North Carolina Library. This bookplate may also be seen in Davie's copy of Lord Henry Home Kames, *The Gentleman Farmer*, published in Edinburgh in 1788, now in the Carolina Room of that library. Three

Why They Came to the Waxhaws

Davie had engraved on his wife's tomb in Old Waxhaw Presbyterian churchyard, near Lancaster, South Carolina, and on the hatchment used at his wife's funeral there.* It is also known that Archibald's father was the younger brother of William Davy, who was the progenitor of the Maryland branch of this family in America.[1]

There is a tradition that Archibald was educated by the Duke of Argyll and was brought up as a member of his family. This tradition was accepted as fact in 1853 by Mary Fraser Davie, the second wife of William Richardson Davie's third son, Frederick William Davie. She stated that when the Scottish Rebellion of 1745 broke out, the Duke of Argyll did not join the rebels but intimated to his household and clan that if any chose to do so, he would not interfere.† Archibald Davie was one who did join the rebels, and after the battle of Culloden in 1746, sought refuge in Holland, where he was able to support himself by writing in "a very extensive mercantile establishment," where he remained until all concerned with the Rebellion were pardoned. This romantic, apocryphal account further stated that upon his return to Scotland, Archibald paid his addresses to Mary Richardson, whose stern father, an East India merchant, would not consent to the marriage until the young Lochinvar had established himself in a sound business. He strongly advised Archibald to set up an establishment for "the manufactory of damask," a process with which the young man had become familiar in Holland; and he further agreed to contribute a certain amount of capital towards the enterprise as his daughter's dowry. According to this legend, Archibald complied by setting up such a business in Egremont, near Whitehaven, Cumber-

---

other books in this room also bear Davie's bookplate. The impression of Governor Davie's seal showing these Arms is affixed to the original convention of 1800 between France and the United States, in the Library of Congress.— Preston Davie, "The Story of Governor William Richardson Davie and His Times."

* A replica of this hatchment has been placed in the Old Waxhaw Church by Colonel Davie.

† This seems unlikely in the light of the fact that the second and third Dukes of Argyll espoused the Hanoverian side in 1715 and that the latter recommended the formation of the Highland regiments as a means of pacifying the Highlands. See *Dictionary of National Biography* (London: Smith Elderd Co., 1886), VIII, 341.

land County, England, and was wed to the lady of his choice.* The same writer described Archibald (her grandfather-in-law) as "a man of great personal beauty, highly intellectual, fond of literary pursuits and hunting, in which taste he indulged himself." [2]

Archibald's wife, Mary Richardson, mother of William Richardson Davie, was of a family long seated in the parish of Ruthwell, Dumfriesshire, Scotland, as early as the first half of the 17th century, and earlier in Lochmaben parish, Dumfriesshire, where the surname appears as early as the latter part of the 13th century. Records there show that individuals of that surname held lands of and served in the forces of "Robert the Bruis."

Mary's father, David Richardson the younger (1693-1743), resided at "Stank"—an estate he possessed in Ruthwell which overlooked Solway Firth, where it is joined by its estuary, Lochar Water. At his death he left a substantial estate and eight children, three of whom were minors. The three minors, Mary, born in 1723, William, born in 1729, and Joseph, born c. 1730, were placed under the charge of guardians—or "tutors and curators"—until they reached their legal majority.

Mary's mother was Janet (1699-1741), daughter of Walter Johnstone of Dumfries. The Johnstones were one of the numerous septs or branches of that extensive and powerful southeast Scottish border clan. The hereditary chieftains of Clan Johnstone were of the senior line of Johnstones of Lochwood Castle in present Johnstone Parish, Dumfriesshire. The head of the clan, James Johnstone, was created Earl of Annandale by Charles II; his son and successor, William Johnstone, was created Marquess of Annandale by William III.†

---

*Mary Fraser Davie to Sarah [?], Aug. 1853.—Mary DeSaussure Fraser Papers, Manuscript Room, Duke University, Durham, N.C. The extent of the verity of the first part of this account is problematical, but the latter part, in regard to her father's demands, is disproved by the established fact that her father died in the year 1743 and Mary was not married until Aug. 10, 1752.

† The above information is based on the inscription on the tomb of David Richardson in the burial ground of the Presbyterian Church, Ruthwell Parish, and in the Commissariat Records of Dumfriesshire, Scotland, 1733-1738, now preserved in the Historical Room, Register House, Edinburgh. Photostatic copies of these records may be found in a two-volume portfolio compiled by Colonel Preston Davie, entitled "Records Pertaining to Mary Richardson Davie," in the Louis Round Wilson Library, Chapel Hill, N.C. The writer is

Why They Came to the Waxhaws

As regards the children of David Richardson the younger, two of his sons attended the University of Glasgow.* David, the second son, matriculated in 1736, and William, the third son, in 1747. Here the latter became so deeply imbued with the rather grim Calvinism of the period that he spent his Saturday afternoon holidays with a friend and fellow-student, Archibald Simpson, in the vicinity of Glasgow, "in the field, in prayer, praise, and reading God's word"—according to the diary of the latter, whose life and path were to parallel closely those of his friend, until Richardson's death in 1771. So strong was their early friendship that Simpson gave up a visit home in order to stay at the bedside of his friend when he suffered a serious illness in February, 1751, at the University of Glasgow.†

William's sister Mary seems also to have become imbued with a religious zeal equal in intensity and fervor to her brother's. In December, 1751, while living at "Langbogflash," in Ruthwell Parish, she wrote on the fly-leaf of her Bible:

"Mary Richardson bought this bible. God grant her gras to understand it, and to peruse it for the Glory of God and the good of her Soul. O Lord of Heaven and Earth, this is the night I give myself

---

deeply indebted to Colonel Davie, who instituted in Scotland and England a detailed research regarding the antecedents of William R. Davie. His documented research was first incorporated in 1951 in an unfinished typescript sketch, "The Early Years and Antecedents of William Richardson Davie (1756-1820)," a copy of which he kindly presented to the writer. A second valuable sketch (detailed and copiously documented) was compiled by him in 1956, entitled "A Biographical Sketch of Mary Richardson (1723-67), Her Early Environments and Some of Her Antecestors." Copies are in the possession of the writer and in the above-mentioned library.

* Though the exact dates of his matriculation and graduation are unknown, the University of Glasgow records show he was there in 1747.—Preston Davie, "The Story of Governor William Richardson Davie."

† This diary, from which a great deal concerning William Richardson may be gleaned, was begun in 1748, when its author was fourteen years old. A follower of George Whitefield, the diarist sailed for South Carolina March 6, 1753, under an engagement to Whitefield to be employed in his orphan-house at Charleston. His diary, covering the period 1748 to March 24, 1784, is an important source of information for the history of the Presbyterian church in South Carolina. The manuscript volumes are written mostly in a kind of shorthand, with only the consonants being used. They have been used extensively by George Howe in his *History of the Presbyterian Church of South Carolina*, 2 vols. (Columbia, S.C.: Duffie & Chapman, 1870). The original diary is in the Charleston Library Society.

over to thee, entirely and unreservedly. I am no longer my own but the Lord's. I with Joseph say for myself, tho I cannot say for the rest of my House, but Lord they are still in Thy hand, Make them thine I pray for Christ Jesus sake.
"Langbogflash, December 1751." [3]

This dedication of faith seems to reveal a genuine religious fervor rather than the conventional sentiments supposed to animate young ladies of that period. It also shows Mary's solicitude for her younger brother Joseph and suggests that all was not well with her older brothers and sisters.

By this date—December, 1751—Mary was twenty-eight. Thus far she had devoted her life to rearing, under the supervision of their guardians, her two younger brothers. Probably Mary and Joseph both lived at "Langbogflash," where William also resided when not attending the University.

Ruthwell Parish, in the southern extremity of Scotland, was perhaps not unlike the region of the Waxhaws in South Carolina, where Mary was later to live. The soil was, for the most part, arable and of good average quality, and practically the entire population was engaged in activities connected with agriculture and a generally rural economy. Always sparsely populated, the parish had 996 inhabitants in 1801.[4]

Mary Richardson evidently deferred her marriage until her youngest brother had come of age. At all events, on August 10, 1752, she and Archibald Davie were married in Ruthwell Parish. The couple established their residence below the Solway Firth in the parish of Egremont, co. Cumberland, England, sometime before the arrival of their first-born, William Richardson Davie.

Confusion exists among earlier biographers of Governor William Richardson Davie, who did not have access to evidence now available, as to the exact date of his birth; also a misreading by the engraver who carved the epitaph on Governor Davie's tomb, composed by Judge William Gaston of North Carolina at the request of Governor Davie's son, Frederick William Davie, has caused confusion as to Governor Davie's place of birth.

To eliminate both of these confusions the following facts are cited: Governor Davie's date of birth, inscribed by Governor Davie's mother in her own handwriting in her Bible, is stated as June 22, 1756, and his place of birth as "Egremont." In engraving the epitaph on Governor Davie's tombstone, mentioned above, the engraver misread "Egremont" for "Edinburgh." The foregoing appears to establish adequately that Governor Davie was born June 22, 1756, and the place of his birth as Egremont, co. Cumberland, England. Whether the residence of his parents at the time of his birth was within the limits of the small town of Egremont, or outside that town but within the parish of the same name in which the town is situated, is, however, not definitely established by evidence at present available.[5]

Governor Davie's parents were nonconformists and therefore of course no records of the births or baptisms of their children are contained in the Church of England records of Egremont Parish. The nearest dissenter (Presbyterian) church was in the town of Whitehaven, co. Cumberland, England, about five miles distant. In the Record Rolls of that church there is recorded the birth of Archibald and Mary Richardson Davie's daughter, and second child (Governor Davie's sister), Mary Richardson Davie, as December 15, 1759, and her baptism there December 24, 1759; neither William Richardson nor his brother, Joseph, appears in this Record Roll, but in view of the strong religious convictions of their mother, it seems probable they were also baptized, but in the residence of their parents instead of in the church, a not unusual practice.[6]

Meanwhile, about the time of the marriage of Mary Richardson and Archibald Davie, an event occurred which was to influence profoundly this branch of the Davie family. Sometime within the years 1752-1754 Mary's brother, William Richardson, embarked for the New World. According to a letter to his friend, Archibald Simpson, from "his dear comrade, W. R.," William was in Hanover County, Virginia, about twelve miles from the town of Richmond, not later than February 8, 1755. Here he resided in the house of the Reverend Samuel Davies, under whose guidance he prepared himself for ordination as a Presbyterian minister.[7]

William Richardson's mentor and host has been described as the "big-brained and large-hearted" Davies, the father of Presbyterianism in Virginia and one of the most eminent divines the Presbyterian church has produced. The founder of the "Society for Managing the Mission and Schools among the Indians," he was also an orator of such force and inspiration that he was taken as a model by Patrick Henry. In 1758 he became the fourth president of the College of New Jersey, later Princeton University.[8]

It was not until June 9, 1757, that William Richardson "was taken on trial" by Hanover Presbytery and the following January 25 he was licensed by this presbytery to preach "at a meeting at Capt. Anderson's, in Cumberland, Virginia." Later, July 12, 1758, he was ordained as a missionary to the Cherokee Indians. The Reverend Samuel Davies preached the sermon at his ordination. Along with Richardson, another student was ordained, Henry Pattillo, afterward a pastor in Orange and Granville counties, North Carolina, a great friend of education and an admirer of William Richardson Davie.[9]

At this same meeting Richardson was appointed to perform the installation services of Alexander Craighead at Rocky River, in Anson, later Mecklenburg County, North Carolina. Accordingly, on his outbound journey to the Cherokees, he arrived at Craighead's home, November the first. Six days later, he performed the installation ceremony.*

It was perhaps at this time that he first met his future wife, Agnes Craighead,† one of the six daughters of the newly installed pastor of the Rocky River Church. The career of the Reverend Craighead had been eventful. A Scot, born in Northern Ireland, son and grandson of Presbyterian ministers, he had come with his father to New

---

* His manuscript report of this mission to the Cherokees, beginning October 2, 1758, and ending March 17, 1759, and forwarded to the Reverend Samuel Davies, "Secretary of the Society for Managing the Mission & Schools among ye Indians," is found in the Wilberforce Eames Collection, MS Division, New York Public Library. A photostatic copy has been presented to the Southern Historical Collection by Colonel Preston Davie and is in the William R. Davie Papers, No. 2, there. These papers, which include 117 other items, were all presented by Colonel Davie and are to be distinguished from the William R. Davie Papers, No. 1. Hereafter, these Davie collections will be cited as W.R.D. Papers, No. 1, and W.R.D. Papers, No. 2.

† All printed sources, including those of Charles W. Wiltse, Samuel Cole Williams, and Marquis James, probably following George Howe, have given her Christian name as Nancy, but William Richardson's will, her father's will, and other primary sources record her name as "Agnes."—Charleston, S.C., Probate Court, Will Book 1771-1774, p. 44. According to a descendant of Agnes, or Nancy, Craighead, the two Christian names were used interchangeably.—Conversation with Miss Nancy Crockett, of Lancaster, South Carolina, December 31, 1952.

Why They Came to the Waxhaws

England and thence to Lancaster County, Pennsylvania, where he had been ordained minister by the Presbytery of Donegal, of the Synod of Philadelphia, in 1735. Shortly thereafter he fell under the sway of George Whitefield, who was making his first journey in this country. In company with Whitefield, William Tennent, founder of the famous Log College in Neshaminy, Pennsylvania, and Samuel Blair, founder of a similar school at Fagg's Manor, Craighead was reported to have traversed Chester County, and as this foursome rode along "they made the woods ring, most sweetly singing and praising God." No doubt this association led to Craighead's being identified with the "New Side" clergy of the Presbyterian Church. This branch rebelled against the conventional religious practices of the "Old Side" and insisted that personal religious experience and conversion were a prerequisite for every minister and every layman. This departure foreboded trouble. In 1743 a pamphlet, said to have been written by Craighead, was presented (in the name of the governor) to the Synod. Unanimously they decided that it was "full of treason, sedition, and distraction, and grievous, perverting of the sacred oracles to the ruin of all societies and civil government, and directly and diametrically opposed to our religious principles." *

But Craighead remained in Pennsylvania until late in 1751 or early in 1752, when he and some of his parishioners moved on to the frontier county of Augusta, Virginia. There he became minister of the Windy Cove congregation on the Cow Pasture River and a member of the Hanover Presbytery, founded by the Reverend Samuel Davies. Yet as a result of the threatened ravages of the Indians after Braddock's defeat in 1755 and the injustices done to dissenters by the Anglicans in Williamsburg, Craighead again sought freer environment. This time he found refuge in present Mecklenburg County, North Carolina, where he received the call from the Rocky River

---

* Quoted in Alice M. Baldwin, "Sowers of Sedition: The Political Theories of Some of the New Light Presbyterian Clergy of Virginia and North Carolina," *William and Mary Quarterly*, Third Series, V (January, 1948), 65. Dr. Baldwin has made an extensive search for this pamphlet in public and private collections and among the family records of the Craighead family to no avail.—Letter to the writer, January 5, 1953. Also, see Rev. James Geddes Craighead, *The Craighead Family: A Genealogical Memoir of the Descendants of Rev. Thomas and Margaret Craighead, 1658-1876* (Philadelphia: Printed for the Descendants, 1876), pp. 41-42.

Church in the neighborhood of what in a few years would be Charlotte. In accepting this call, he became the first Presbyterian minister with a regular pastorate in Western North Carolina and the third in the state. Here he found the religious and civil freedom he craved. Here he was to become the chief shepherd and spiritual leader of no fewer than seven Presbyterian congregations lying within the present Mecklenburg, Cabarrus, and Iredell counties.[10]

Craighead's future son-in-law, William Richardson, a young man of twenty-nine, must have felt some awkwardness in performing what was presumably his first installation ceremony, for such a patriarch. Perhaps, however, his awkwardness was lessened by the presence of Mistress Agnes.

The day following the ceremony, November 7, young Richardson set out for the Catawbas, "preached to a vacant congregation in the Waxhaws" and reached Fort Prince George in the Cherokee Nation by the last of November.[11] But the laudable mission of converting these Indians to the Presbyterian faith was fraught with almost insuperable difficulties, especially after the decline of British prestige resulting from Braddock's defeat. The following April he was back on the South Carolina seaboard with his old friend and associate at Glasgow, Archibald Simpson. Simpson, who had also been ordained a Presbyterian minister, was at this time serving several congregations in the South Carolina Low Country and was a member of the Charleston Presbytery.[12] In his diary, under the date of April 16, 1759, he reported Richardson's failure and his present situation:

"Dear old comrade, W. R., came to my house. He was licensed and ordained by a presbytery in Virginia. Had gone some months ago a missionary to the Cherokee Indians, but finding no good could be done among them, as they were inclined to join the French, he has laid down his mission and accepted an invitation from a people at the Waxhaws, about two hundred miles beyond Charlestown, is come down to join presbytery and accept their call, this being in our bounds."[13]

The old friends had many long conversations, and Simpson found that Richardson had "not been without his share of troubles, afflictions and sickness." In fact, at that moment he was not only low in spirits but his finances were also low. Simpson sent him to preach at Pon Pon, across the Edisto River from Jacksonborough, and at Port

Why They Came to the Waxhaws

Royal, or Beaufort. Finally, on May 16, Richardson was received as a member of the Charleston Presbytery. Members of his future congregation from the Waxhaws were present at the service and forthwith presented their call, which he promptly accepted. He was accordingly installed in the fall as their minister.[14]

His church, which was located in what was then called St. Mark's Parish, Craven County, was the religious mecca for the inhabitants of the entire region known as the Waxhaws. This region, which derived its name from the Waxhaw Indians, had no specific boundaries and no political meaning, but extended roughly from a few miles below Charlotte, North Carolina, to a point near Camden, South Carolina, and from the Catawba River on the west to a point near present Wadesboro, North Carolina, on the east. It included much of the present Mecklenburg, Union, and Anson counties in North Carolina, and Lancaster, Chester, and York counties in South Carolina. Particularly fertile was the land adjacent to the Waxhaw Creek, which rises in North Carolina, a little north of the point where the state line turns to pass around the old Indian reservation. The creek flows westward to the Catawba and waters a considerable area of bottom land, thereby forming a rich oasis in a region of pine barrens.[15]

The first white settlers, consisting of some six or seven families, had come in May, 1751, followed by a few more in the fall. A considerable number, chiefly from Augusta County, Virginia, and the Pennsylvania Back Country, came the next year. These first settlers, known as the "Pennsylvania Irish," had come down from the north by the Great Philadelphia Wagon Road and the Catawba Trading Path. They were soon joined by the Ulster Scots, or so-called "Scotch-Irish," who came up from Charleston by way of the Charleston-Salisbury Post Road. Here in the Waxhaws they merged. Of the Presbyterian faith, a few had considerable wealth and standing.[16] By the time William Richardson settled among them they probably numbered fifty or sixty families; nine years later they were estimated by one source at one hundred and twenty families.*

---

*This estimate is taken from an enumeration of Dissenters throughout the English colonies in North America in which the Reverend Elam Potter reported to the Reverend Ezra Stiles of Yale College that the Waxhaw settlement consisted of one hundred and twenty families and that the pastor of the settlement was Mr. Richardson.–Howe, *The Presbyterian Church in S.C.*, I, 363.

WILLIAM R. DAVIE

Perhaps a less accurate description was that written by an English clergyman, the Reverend Charles Woodmason, who came up to the Waxhaws to preach in January, 1767. Incidentally, the elders refused to let him preach in the church. This "Settlement of Irish Presbyterians called the Waxaws," he said, was "a very fruitful fine Spot, thro' which the dividing Line between North and South Carolina runs," and "a finer Body of Land is no where to be seen." His further description of the people must be viewed in the light of the prevailing mutual distrust and animosity between Anglicans and Presbyterians: "But it is occupied by a Sett of the most lowest vilest Crew breathing—Scotch Irish Presbyterians from the North of Ireland." [17]

Woodmason's references to William Richardson also throw an entirely different and perhaps erroneous light on his life and on his Anglican proclivities: "They have built a Meeting House and have a Pastor, a Scots Man among them—A good Sort of Man—He once was of the Church of England, and solicited for Orders, but was refus'd —whereon he went to Pennsylvania, and got ordained by the Presbytery there, who allowed him a Stipend to preach to these People, who (in his Breast) he heartily contemns—They will not suffer him to use the Lords Prayer. He wants to introduce Watts' Psalms in place of the barbarous Scotch Version—but they will not admit it—His Congregation is very large—This Tract of Land being most surprisingly thick settled beyond any Spot in England of its Extent—Seldom less than 9, 10, 1200 People assemble of a Sunday—They never heard an Episcopal Minister, or the Common Prayer, and were very curious. The Church people among them are thinly scatter'd but they had a numerous Progeny for Baptism." [18]

By dint of the sanctity of his profession and the superiority of his education, Richardson—as did all Presbyterian ministers in the Back Settlements—held an exalted position among his parishioners, who accepted the leadership of gentlemen as a matter of course.[19]

The log church itself, to which Richardson was called, had been built sometime before 1755 on the plantation of Robert Miller, the ordained minister at the time. Described as "a man of popular talents and lively," Miller unfortunately exercised his talents too freely and was excommunicated for violating the seventh commandment. Despite this sentence, issued at the meeting of the presbytery in Charleston in

Why They Came to the Waxhaws

June, 1758, the disgraced minister before departing deeded to the community the log church and four surrounding acres for a burial ground. The beclouded pulpit had been destitute, with the exception of a "few supplies," until Richardson came to settle among them and to give to the Old Waxhaw Presbyterian Meeting House the distinction of being the only pastorate in the Upper Country to enjoy full Gospel ordinances.[20]

Here he soon organized a school or academy where he taught Latin and Greek. Nor did the new pastor confine his evangelistic labors and ministrations to this particular church, but extended them widely throughout the Catawba region. His preaching tours at times were said to have continued for a month, during which he preached daily from place to place, visited the people, and was instrumental in organizing a number of congregations and churches in Chester, York, and Newberry counties, South Carolina, and in present Union County, North Carolina. As a by-product of these tours he acquired a very substantial holding. His two-story house and his library were the pride of this frontier region, which stood in some awe of its pastor's "literary evenings."[21]

Indeed, material prosperity and success in the secular field characterized Richardson's progress in the New World. Though he had been without funds in the spring of 1759, by 1771—the year of his early death at the age of forty-two—he had acquired a considerable estate for one of his calling in the Upper Country in pre-Revolutionary days. This holding had been acquired, it may be assumed, from two sources. The first was his share of the principal of the legacy which was left in trust by his father, David Richardson of "Stank." By the terms of this will, probated in 1744, the principal of this legacy to his three minor children—Mary, William, and Joseph—was not to be distributed until the youngest, Joseph, became of age, which was in 1751 or 1752.[22] This inheritance may have been used by William to pay his passage and support him in America or it may have been that he did not receive it, because of the law's delay, until after he was established in the Waxhaws. In view of his abstemious traits, it is highly improbable that he squandered his birthright. His second source of income was acquired through his exertions for the Lord. A kinsman, Robert Carr, who lived in the Richardson home, attested to the fact that when Richardson returned from "these itinerant tours" he would bring back a great deal of money.²³ In fact, this large congregation, extending over a fruitful country reaching some twenty miles from his residence in all directions, took a "laudable pride" in supplying a minister so much beloved with everything needed. Moreover, his expenses were small and living was cheap.²⁴

Yet his expenses, no doubt, were greatly increased after he rode back up to the venerable Alexander Craighead's home and brought back as his wife the high-spirited, talented, and beautiful Agnes. The exact date of the marriage is not known, but it was probably soon after Richardson, on August 26, 1760, had purchased from Thomas McIlhenny a tract of 150 acres in St. Mark's Parish, which had been granted McIlhenny April 3, 1752. Five years after this purchase, January 4, 1765, Richardson made another 150-acre purchase adjacent to the first.²⁵ Here the newly-wed couple developed a comfortable residence, "Poplar Spring," only a short distance from the church.²⁶

This new home was probably often enlivened by Agnes's five attractive sisters. One of them, Jean, presumably while visiting the Richardsons, met and married Patrick, the father of John Caldwell Calhoun. The Calhouns lived beyond Ninety-Six, at Long Canes, where Richardson had gone to preach and help organize a church in 1764. A closer connection between the Richardsons and the Calhouns was prevented when Jean died of a miscarriage of twins, September 10, 1766, and Patrick took John Caldwell's daughter as his second wife.²⁷ Another of Agnes's sisters, Rachel, married the Reverend David Caldwell, the prominent, politically active Presbyterian preacher, teacher, and physician of Guilford County, North Carolina.²⁸

Agnes, whose father's wineglasses were reputed to be the finest in the county,²⁹ no doubt brought a vivacity and social grace into Richardson's life which caused not a few of the sturdy frontier folk to lift their eyebrows. And what a contrast she was to her austere husband, who was given to frequent seasons of fasting and prayer! Though he was considered "kind and social in his prevailing disposition," at home and especially in his last years, he was described as morose and melancholy.³⁰

Perhaps this melancholy was the result of a general debility caused by too Spartan a diet. Or maybe its chief source was a keen and bitter disappointment that his attractive wife did not bear him any children.

Why They Came to the Waxhaws

It was no doubt to assuage this emptiness that, by frequent correspondence, he induced his older sister, Mary, to come with her family and join him in this new country. There is also some evidence that Richardson sent the Davies the passage money.[31]

Thus, a year after the termination of the French and Indian War, Archibald Davie and his family sailed, probably from the port of Whitehaven, to join Mrs. Davie's well-established brother in the Waxhaws.*

*For further comment on the date of the family's arrival in America, see Appendix A.

CHAPTER II

Young William Richardson Davie

IT IS probable that the Davies lost little time in proceeding to the Waxhaw settlement, though their port of entry is unknown. Had they landed at Charleston,* the most likely port, their journey would have involved a two-hundred-mile trek up the Charleston-Salisbury Post Road. Yet it is possible that, like so many of the inhabitants of the Waxhaws, they landed in Philadelphia and followed the long, arduous route down the Great Philadelphia Wagon Road. Perhaps Archibald Davie invested in a Conestoga wagon, "the vehicle of the empire," to transport his family and household effects down the long road, which would have led them through Lancaster and York, Pennsylvania, thence across the Potomac to the entrance of the Shenandoah, where it passed through Winchester and Staunton, then crossed the upper waters of the James to the Roanoke, where it turned eastward through the Staunton River Gap of the Blue Ridge, crossed the Dan, and led to the original terminus at Wachovia on a

---

* None of their names appears in the list of the Protestant immigrants from Europe who came through the port of Charleston during the years 1763-1773, on the encouragement of an act passed by the South Carolina General Assembly, July 25, 1761, called the Bounty Act, a copy of which is not available. —Janie Revill (compiler), *A Compilation of the Original Lists of Protestant Immigrants to South Carolina. 1763-1773* (Columbia, S.C.: The State Co., 1939), p. 3. Nor do any of their names appear in the manuscript records of His Majesty's Council Journal for South Carolina, in the office of the Historical Commission of South Carolina, Columbia, South Carolina (hereafter cited as H.C.S.C.). It is possible that all ship lists were not included in the Council Journal.

branch of the Yadkin. From there, they would have followed the Catawba Trading Path, through Salisbury, down to Waxhaw Creek.[1]

After this journey of 550 miles, how welcome must have been the sight of the good dominie, William Richardson, and his comparatively comfortable manse, "Poplar Spring."

The Davies probably lived in the manse at least three years, until Archibald Davie could take advantage of the Bounty Act which had been passed by the General Assembly of South Carolina, July 25, 1761, and which was designed to encourage "Protestant refugees from Europe who come to South Carolina." [2]

He accordingly petitioned the Governor's Council, April 23, 1765, for "200 acres on Poplar Spring joining lands of the Rev. Mr. Richardson," as a result of which the clerk was ordered to issue the warrant for a survey.[3] By July 26, 1766, the requisite survey and plat for this tract were completed.* By September 11 of that year another survey and plat for an additional 150 acres located on Cane Creek were completed.†

The following June 1, formal grants for these two tracts were made in the name of George III, under the Great Seal of the Province of South Carolina by Governor Lord Charles Greville Montague.[4] This plantation was finally rounded out to 570 acres in 1785, when

---

* The surveyor's description, accompanying the plat, recorded in Plat Book, No. 9, Folio 24, H.C.S.C., is as follows:

"Pursuant to a precept from John Troup, Esqr., D. S. G. [Deputy Surveyor General] dated the 6th day of June. A. D. 1766, I have admeasured and laid out unto Archibald Davy [sic] lying and being in Waxhaw Settlement, on the N. E. side of the Catawba River, and on the waters of said river, in Craven County: Bounded on the S. E. side with lands belonging to Rev. Wm. Richardson, and on all other sides by vacant land; And hath such form shape and marks as the above plat represents.
     Certified by me this 26 day of July A. D. 1766.
     John Gaston. D. S."

† The surveyor's description accompanying the plat of this tract, recorded in the same book as the previous one, Folio 25, was as follows:

"Pursuant to a precept from John Troup Esqr. D. S. G., dated the 2d of July A. D. 1766, I have admeasured and laid out unto Archibald Davy a tract of land containing one hundred and fifty acres situate, lying and being in the Waxhaw Settlement, on the waters of Cane Creek, in Craven County: Bounded on all sides with vacant land; and hath such form shape and marks as the above plat represents.
     Certified by me this 11th day of September 1766.
     John Gaston, D. S."

WILLIAM R. DAVIE

Archibald Davie obtained from the State of South Carolina a grant for 220 acres, executed July 4, 1785, by Governor William Moultrie.*

Thus the young William Richardson Davie spent his impressionable and formative years at his father's Cane Creek home, adjacent to his uncle's, located on the northeast side of the Catawba on the waters of Cane Creek in what was then St. Mark's Parish, Craven County, South Carolina.†

The ink had not long been dry on the first two of these grants when his mother died, September 20, 1767, and was buried in the Old Waxhaw Presbyterian burial ground. The ceremony no doubt was performed by his uncle, who was to join her there four years later.‡ Returning from the ceremony, his father, a widower at the age of forty-three, must have felt particularly desolate when he

---

* The surveyor's description, accompanying the plat, recorded in Plat Book, No. 4, Folio 258, H.C.S.C., was as follows:
"South Carolina:
"I have caused to be admeasured and laid out unto Archibald Davie, a tract of land containing two hundred and twenty acres situate in the District of Camden on the waters of Cane Creek on the North side of the Catawba, and hath such form and marks butting and bounding as the above plat represents.
Certified for the fourth day of December 1784.
Ephraim Mitchell
Surveyor General"

Wm. Tate, D. S.
The grant is recorded in Grant Book, Vol. 4, p. 108, H.C.S.C.

† By the year 1785 the plantation lay within the boundaries of what was then called the Camden District of the State of South Carolina. Today these lands lie in Lancaster County.—Preston Davie, "The Early Years and Antecedents of William R. Davie."

‡ Her epitaph is as follows:
> "*Here Lies the Body of*
> *Mary Davie*, wife of Archibald Davie,
> Who departed this life on the
> 20th day of September A. D. 1767,
> aged 44, leaving
> her sons *William* and *Joseph*,
> and a daughter *Mary*."

> "Frail mortal come, approach to me
> And learn what you must shortly be."

In addition to a typical quatrain on the reverse side there appears the heraldic family Arms of her husband.

looked at his three children whose rearing and education were his responsibility. Yet in this respect he was fortunate in having both the moral and financial backing of his brother-in-law in those trying years when he had so many adjustments to make. Perhaps it was to build a home on his new land that Archibald borrowed £200 from his brother-in-law on December 4, 1767.[5]

That a well-established, childless uncle of the calibre of William Richardson should have bestowed a great deal of attention, care, and affection upon the children of his dead sister might well have been expected. It is highly probable that he himself taught them, in his church school, the classics as well as the rudiments of learning. It is also probable that he lavished a little more love and attention on his namesake, realizing his precocity and potentialities. It is known, in fact, as testified to in August, 1780, by William R. Davie, that his uncle had educated him to be his successor as the pastor of the Waxhaw Presbyterian Meeting House.[6]

Yet this guiding inspiration was suddenly and dramatically snatched from the young William shortly after his fifteenth birthday. This incident, with its barbaric sequel, undoubtedly had a profound effect on the boy and may well have been the reason he forsook the ministry and the church of his fathers.

There are several versions of the cause of his uncle's death, the circumstances surrounding which led to what was among the last instances in this country of one of the medieval ordeals or tests of innocence or guilt. According to one version, the forty-four-year-old minister had been visited early in the day, July 20, 1771, by William R. Davie's father, who had seen nothing unusual about him, though he had lately been more subject to fits of melancholy than usual. After Agnes Richardson had gone to a quilting party, her husband retired to his combination library and study on the second floor, which had become his constant resort. Sometime later, an emissary from a group of Ulsterites who had recently settled on Rocky River in Chester District came to request the worthy divine to hold a service among them. Mrs. Richardson, who had just returned, informed him that her husband was probably in his study, to which they repaired. Here they found him dead, in a kneeling position, with a bridle around his neck. Neighbors and friends were immediately called in and apprised of the facts. All agreed that "the interests of religion and the fair fame of so eminent a minister would suffer if he should be known as a *felo de sé*." Accordingly, it was given out that he died at his devotions.[7]

The most damning version of the manner of Richardson's death was that of our Anglican minister, Charles Woodmason, apparently written many years later, which concluded: "... Therefore (to bring no disgrace on the Kirk) they called no Coroner, but buried Him as next day—the Widow following the Corps with Great Sorrow to the Grave. But some that knew the Temper of the Wife and her Relations—made this Affair Public—And it was insisted on that the Corps should be taken up out of the Grave and examined which was done. And Marks of Strangulation found on the Neck—and Bruises on the Breast. On Examination of Persons, it appeared That all the Servants were sent abroad into the Field that Morning and none left in the House but the Wife—And that her Brother had been there in Interim for a short Space. It was found too that no Man could destroy himself by the Manner in which the Bridle was found about his Neck. And it was more than probable that it was put round the Neck, and the Body plac'd in that Posture after he was strangled."[8]

Perhaps all would have been well had not the still beautiful Agnes Craighead Richardson, in the course of the year, married George Dunlap, "a gentleman of worth." Meanwhile, the story of the bridle began to be whispered about, until by embellishment and exaggeration, a suspicion arose that the new Mrs. Dunlap had been instrumental in her first husband's death. To prove her guilt or innocence, an ancient Scottish test was used. The erstwhile widow was haled before the whole community, which had assembled around Richardson's grave. There his body was exhumed and exposed to the view of all. The poor woman was then directed to undergo the cruel ordeal of touching the forehead of her deceased husband, on the theory that blood would flow from her fingers if she were the murderess. When no blood met the eyes of the gaping on-lookers, Archibald Davie, not content with a mere touching by Agnes, pressed down the hand of the hysterical woman, but to no avail.[9]

To the credit of the assembled people, it must be admitted that "the transaction was ridiculed or sadly deplored by the majority as a farce discreditable to those who had been the chief actors in it."

Yet, according to this same source, the belief persisted that other hands than Richardson's had manipulated the fatal bridle.[10]

A more charitable version of the affair appeared in the manuscript history of the Waxhaw Church which was sent to the General Assembly of the Presbyterian Church in 1794: "He continued our minister for twelve years, died an untimely death, by what instrumental cause we cannot determine, and the delicacy of the case forbids a conjecture. His death was most deeply lamented by the people of his congregations. He was a warm and lively preacher, remarkable for his piety and devotion to God, and charity to the poor. His memory is still very dear to those who were the people of his charge."[11]

A final version of Richardson's death was that of his old friend, Archibald Simpson, who recorded it as follows in his manuscript diary under date of August 26, 1771:

"On Friday night... was informed by report of the death of my dear friend and comrade, the Rev. Mr. Richardson, and this day had it confirmed. This has afflicted me much, and is, in many respects, the loudest call I ever met with to prepare for the eternal world. Oh! that I may be ready and may give up my accounts with joy! His death is a very great loss to the part of the country where he lived. He was a burning and shining light, a star of the first magnitude, a great Christian, a most eminent minister of Jesus Christ. He has left a disconsolate widow, but no children. His death was something remarkable. He was of a strong and robust make, and in general healthy, but of a heavy, melancholic disposition, subject from his very youth to vapory disorders. His labors for some years were very great. About three or four years ago he began to decline; his vapory disorders increased, his intellect seemed to fail. He turned very deaf, and lost much of his spirits and liveliness in preaching, but still was very useful to his own people. About three months ago he seemed sickly, but his people and family thought he fancied himself worse than he was, as he did not keep his bed, but appeared as usual, and only kept his house. Some time in June one of his elders was visiting him, and in order to divert him had entered into some argument with him, in which Mr. R. talked with a great deal of spirit, and afterwards went up stairs to his room, but was to be down to dinner as usual. Accordingly, when dinner had waited some time, they went up stairs and found him dead on his knees, one hand holding the back of a chair and the other lifted up as in prayer. So that he seemed to have expired in the act of devotion, and to all appearance had been dead some time: a most desirable death indeed...."[12]

By the terms of his will, William Richardson revealed himself as prosperous, philanthropic, and bibliophilistic. The will corrects an error into which all writers dealing with William Richardson Davie have fallen, when they say that the uncle adopted his namesake and made him his sole heir. On the contrary, in the matter of real estate, the young William received only one-fifth of the amount realized from the sale of his uncle's second plantation, consisting of 150 acres. This plantation was to be sold at public auction as soon as possible "and the monies arising from thence to be distributed equally among these persons now to be named, William, Mary and Joseph Dave's [sic], my sisters Children and William Richardson Foster and William Richardson Carruth." * In the matter of personal property, he, Mary, and Joseph received special bequests which were substantially proportionate in value.

In addition to his two plantations, Richardson owned at least four slaves,† a large number of "Horse Creatures," cattle, hogs, feather beds, and a highly prized "Box of Glass," which was "to be used for the House and no other use." This latter must have been practically tantamount to a patent of nobility in the eyes of the Waxhaw settlers.

His library for that period and place was unusually fine. To his wife he bequeathed "Thirty Volumes of any Books in Octavos and Quartos she chooses" as well as one volume, folio, of Ambrose's Works and one of Flavel's. To his namesake he left all his Latin and Greek books except two, his Hebrew, historical, and philosophical books, "Translations of every nature and kind relating to Literature for his use," and "all the English Books of Divinity except the above

---

* This will is in the Charleston, S.C., Probate Court, Will Book, 1771-1774, p. 44. William Richardson Carruth was the son of Agnes's sister Margaret. —Craighead, *The Craighead Family*, p. 51. William Richardson Foster was the son of his neighbors, Henry and Ann Foster, who were members of Waxhaw Church. William Foster died March 19, 1802, in his 35th year, according to his gravestone in Waxhaw Cemetery.

† His will is not definite as to the exact number. In one place he bequeathed to his wife "the Negroes Sancho, Judah and Rose" and later he stipulated that "a Negro called Joe" was to be hired out "so conveniently that he may see his wife and Children." These latter were probably the ones named in the bequest to his wife.

mentioned to my wife." To his wife's brother-in-law, the Reverend David Caldwell, he ordered that "Pools Synopsis Criticism" be offered for three pounds, the proceeds to go to "William Dave for his education." If the former did not accept it, the book would go to William. He gave four volumes to his brother-in-law, Thomas Craighead, also a Presbyterian minister.[13]

His philanthropy found expression in his bequest to the "Society in London for propagation of Christian Knowledge among the Poor." The "monies arising from the sale of this Plantation... which I order to be sold when my wife marries or dies..." were "to be transmitted in Bills of Exchange to the Secretary of said Society then being and Books sent arising from the said Monies to any Minister in So. or No. Carolina near the Waxhaws, that will faithfully distribute them...." The amount realized from this sale, according to his epitaph, amounted to £340 sterling.*

The young William Richardson Davie was not only the beneficiary of one-fifth of the 150-acre plantation and a large library, but all his uncle's wearing apparel, the monies arising from the public sale of his horse, Bucky, and his watch, and from the four years' hire of a Negro called Joe, "to be employed in his education if he proceeds." His brother and sister were also beneficiaries of specific bequests of a supposedly equal amount.

The whereabouts of the sixteen-year-old William Richardson Davie at the time of his uncle's untimely and mysterious death is uncertain. It seems likely that he had already begun his studies at Queen's College, later Queen's Museum, and still later Liberty Hall, in Charlotte, North Carolina. His uncle might have been sending him, for he had been named an original trustee of Queen's College, established by act of the colonial legislature of North Carolina, January 15, 1771, just six months before his death.[14] Or perhaps his own father was sending him, even though at that time still in debt £100 to his brother-in-law.†

---

* One of the Bibles sent over, as a result of this bequest, is today in the possession of Miss Pauline Neely, Spindale, North Carolina, and another is owned by Mrs. J. D. Glenn, Waxhaw, N.C.
† Richardson's will provided that Mary and Joseph Davie should each have fifty pounds out of a note of one hundred pounds that he had on their father.

WILLIAM R. DAVIE

Actually there is no contemporary evidence that the young Davie ever attended this academy at all. The first available mention of it is by Davie's ante-bellum biographer who said that "at the usual age, young Davie was sent to an academy in Charlotte, North Carolina, where he remained till he was fitted to enter college." *

He probably completed his work there in the spring of 1774, before entering the College of New Jersey, later Princeton, in the fall of that year. If so, he was there at the time of the heroic effort to enforce the Schism Act in North Carolina, by which act the governor was to allow no one to come to North Carolina from England "to keep school" without a license from the Lord Bishop of London, and to see that "no person now there or that shall come from other parts shall be admitted to keep school" there without the governor's license.[15] Though the founders of Queen's College and all members of its Board of Trustees except Episcopalians Abner Nash and Edmund Fanning were Presbyterians, Governor Tryon earnestly urged the King's approval of the act of incorporation, in recognition of the aid he had received from the Presbyterian brethren in the late War of the Regulation. The Board of Trade, however, advised its disallowance by the King on the ground that it would promise "great and permanent Advantages to a sect of Dissenters from the Established Church who have already extended themselves over that Province in very considerable numbers." Despite the King's disallowance of April 22, 1772, the college, which had already opened its doors, continued to operate under the name of Queen's Museum until 1777,

---

* Fordyce M. Hubbard, *Life of William Richardson Davie*, Jared Sparks (ed.), *The Library of American Biography*, Second Series (Boston: Charles C. Little and James Brown, 1848), XV, 3-4 (hereafter cited as Hubbard, *Davie*). For a lengthy review of this book, see the *Southern Literary Messenger*, XIV (August, 1848), 510-17. The reviewer was fulsome in his praise of the book: Davie's "various exploits are graphically recorded, and the traits of his character lucidly unfolded, in a style, simple, chaste, classic, and oft-times powerful.... The hero moves through them [the scenes] with the utmost ease and dignity, passing naturally from one to the other, and showing the greatness of his character in all...." This greatness led the reviewer to ask why so little had been heard of Davie before and why North Carolinians knew so little of their history. His answer was forthcoming: "they have been untrue to themselves and their fathers" and have been "too indolent to undertake the task" of recording their history. The reviewer continued by saying that, as a result of this book and the formation of a Historical Society at Chapel Hill, "Old Rip" was awakening from his slumbers after fifty years.

Young William Richardson Davie

when the General Assembly changed its name again, this time to Liberty Hall.[16]

The first documentary evidence as to the young Davie's formal education is that he entered the College of New Jersey some time in 1774—perhaps in the fall—and that two years later he was admitted to the Bachelor's Degree "of which an authentic parchment" was to be delivered to him at the first meeting of the Board of Trustees. In the meantime he was recommended "to all honors of Religion & Learning as deserving of Encouragement." This certificate, dated October 28, 1776, was signed by Dr. John Witherspoon, the president of that institution. The degree itself was not conferred until the Board met again at Cooper's Ferry, New Jersey, May 24, 1777, but Davie was listed as a graduate in the class of 1776.[17]

Some idea of the value of this diploma may be gleaned from the estimate of Philip Fithian, who wrote to his successor as tutor to the Carters of Nomini Hall in Virginia, that "if you should travel through this Colony, with a well-confirmed testimonial of your having finished with Credit a Course of Studies at Nassau-Hall; you would be rated, without any more questions asked, either about your family, your Estate, your business, or your intention, at about £10,000; and you might come, & go, & converse, & keep company, according to this value; and you would be dispised and slighted if you rated yourself a farthing cheaper." [18]

It was while he was at the College of New Jersey that the twenty-year-old Davie, either from a strong conviction or a youthful desire for martial glory, marched as sergeant of a volunteer company of his college-mates, who embodied themselves, contrary to the wishes of their tutors, and marched off to join a detachment of Washington's army stationed at Elizabethtown, New Jersey. The disapproving faculty recommended expulsion for such willful disobedience, but the understanding and practical-minded Dr. Witherspoon vetoed this action. His solution was quite simple: "Let them alone; opposition to their purposes will only increase their desire to adhere to them; exposure to the fatigue of service will effect all that you desire; it will not be long before we have them all back again." [19]

The prognostication of Dr. Witherspoon was soon realized. Davie and the other youthful enthusiasts were soon back at their books.

There is some evidence that Davie, upon completion of his studies at the College of New Jersey, decided to pursue the course for which his uncle had intended him, and to prepare for the ministry in one of "the Scottish universities." This same source stated that he had proceeded as far as Charleston on his way thither, but was prevented from continuing further "by the troubles of the time."[20] In view of his later latitudinarianism in regard to religion and to his immediate espousal of the study of law, this statement was probably incorrect.

For the study of the law, Davie chose as his instructor, Judge Spruce Macay, of Salisbury, North Carolina,[21] and by so doing he not only embarked on his life's work, but he crossed the border into a new arena for his military and post-Revolutionary activities.

CHAPTER III

Youthful Patriot and Student of Law

IT SEEMS only natural that an intelligent lad, born of Scottish Presbyterian parents, nurtured in his teens in the seething Waxhaws, schooled in the hotbed of rebellion aflame in Mecklenburg, and fired by his youthful contemporaries and equally ardent instructors at the College of New Jersey, should have espoused the patriot cause in the growing tension between the Mother Country and her colonies. Indeed, heredity and environment seem to have worked hand in hand in forging a rebel out of this impressionable young American. It may well be that his opposition to the King's government sprang, not from the impetuosity of youth, but from a deep-seated faith in the righteousness of the American cause. This faith no doubt was partially engendered by Davie's constant association with the Presbyterian clergy, who wielded considerable influence in molding the predominant American political ideas which were antagonistic to those of England.* William Richardson, Alexander Craighead, David Caldwell, Henry Pattillo, John Witherspoon—all had played their part in molding a spirit of resistance in the young man's mind.

Nor did Davie find himself in an uncongenial environment when he came to Salisbury, the county seat of Rowan, to begin the study

---

* No student of the literature of the causes of the American Revolution should ignore the penetrating analysis of Claude H. Van Tyne in his "Influence of the Clergy, and of Religious and Sectarian Forces, on the American Revolution," *American Historical Review*, XIX (Oct., 1913), 44-64; also see Baldwin, "Sowers of Sedition," *loc. cit.*

of law. Not only had the Rowanites played a conspicuous part in the War of the Regulation against what they considered Tryon's tyrannical extortions, but had, since 1774, been in the vanguard of those who were most vocal in asserting their rights as Englishmen. Three years before Davie had come there, the leading citizens, assembled at an extra-legal meeting of the Committee of Safety, had seen fit to declare their spirited convictions to the world in general and to Governor Josiah Martin and George the Third in particular. They unanimously asserted that the right to impose taxes or duties, by the colony of North Carolina, "for any purpose whatsover" was "peculiar and essential to the General Assembly" and that any attempt by any other authority was "an arbitrary exertion of power, and an infringement of the constitutional rights and liberties of the colony." Particularly vehement against "the late cruel and sanguinary acts of Parliament" directed against the Massachusetts Bay Colony, they resolved that *"the cause of the town of Boston is the common cause of the American Colonies"* and that it was "the duty and interest of all the American Colonies firmly to unite in an indissoluble union and association" to resist such "infringement of their common rights and privileges." They further called for an intercolonial non-importation association, a banishment of "every kind of luxury, dissipation, and extravagance," the encouragement of local manufactures, and the raising of sheep, hemp, and flax.[1]

Not only were the citizens of Salisbury advanced in their political thinking, but they possessed a culture far more highly developed than that of the usual back-country town. The rapid growth of the town itself, settled in 1753, was recognized in 1766 by its becoming a borough town with a seat in the House of Commons. Settled largely by Ulster Scots and Germans (or Pennsylvania Dutch), most of whom were artisans, the town by 1774 could boast of three silversmiths and at least eight taverns or ordinaries, which proudly offered "Lodging with clean Sheets."[2]

If the citizens of Salisbury in general were congenial to Davie, even more so was Spruce Macay, who had been educated by the Reverend David Caldwell, a friend and brother-in-law of Davie's uncle.[3] In fact, Caldwell may well have arranged for Davie to begin the study of law in the office of the man who, seven years later, was to take into his office another product of the Waxhaws, Andrew Jackson.[4]

YOUTHFUL PATRIOT AND STUDENT OF LAW

The exact date of Davie's coming to Salisbury to read law in Macay's office is unknown, but it was probably in late 1776 or early 1777. According to a later companion in arms, "Light Horse Harry" Lee, Davie began this study because, upon his return to Salisbury, he "found himself shut out for a time from the army, as the commissions for the troops just levied had just been issued." However, Lee stated that as the war continued, "contrary to the expectation which generally prevailed when it began," Davie could no longer resist "his ardent wish to place himself among the defenders of his country." [5]

At any rate, in December, 1777, Davie again cast aside his books and took up arms in the cause of freedom. This time he joined a detachment of twelve hundred men, under Allen Jones of Northampton County, who had been appointed Brigadier General of the Halifax (North Carolina) District Militia in 1776.[6] Incidentally, seven years later he was to marry the daughter of his commanding officer and was to establish his residence along the Roanoke River, first in the county of Northampton, and then in the borough of Halifax.

The detachment, ordered to aid in the defense of Charleston, which was then threatened with a second attack, advanced as far as Camden. Here, as the alarm had abated, they made an about-face and returned after a three months' service.[7]

It may be assumed that Davie, sometime in the early spring of 1778, returned to his study of law in Salisbury.* But by the following spring he again joined the armed forces. This time, rather than simply volunteering in the nearest available unit, he induced William Barnett, "a worthy and popular friend," who was "rather too old for military service," to raise a troop of dragoons, with Barnett as captain and Davie as lieutenant.[8] Davie received this, the first of his many military and civil commissions, April 5, 1779, under the hand of Governor Richard Caswell, and thus became a "Lieut. of a Company of Horse in the District of Salisbury." [9]

The movements of this newly-organized troop are clouded. According to Colonel Lee, it "joined the Southern army," but soon afterwards its captain, too old to sustain the fatigues of active service,

---

* Proof of his residence in Salisbury and of the fact that he was a property-holder is attested to by his serving as a bondsman on eleven marriage certificates from Dec. 19, 1778, through March 20, 1779.—Rowan Marriage Bonds, Salisbury, N.C.

returned home on furlough, and the command devolved on Davie.[10] Another version is that Davie was ordered with two hundred horse "to quell the insurgents in the back country." After reaching Charlotte, however, he learned that the anticipated uprising had been suppressed and he returned to Salisbury.[11]

After Captain Barnett's resignation, Davie's company, at his request, was annexed to the Legion of Count Casimir Pulaski, which was operating around Dorchester, South Carolina, about fifteen miles north of Charleston.[12] On May 27, 1779, Davie was promoted to Brigade Major of Cavalry.[13]

For the succeeding events, battles, skirmishes, and encounters in which Davie participated, much can be gleaned from his personal experiences and observations contained in his two accounts of the Revolution. Written at different times, the first begins with the battle of Stono in June, 1779, and carries him up to his appointment as commissary general to General Nathanael Greene in December, 1780. The other covers the first few months of his services as commissary general.

Contemporary accounts of the Southern campaign in the American Revolution were written by such American participants as "Light Horse Harry" Lee, General William Moultrie, Dr. Alexander Garden (aide-de-camp to General Nathanael Greene) and Dr. David Ramsay, and by such British participants as Lieutenant Colonel Banastre Tarleton, William Gordon, Roderick Mackenzie, and Charles Stedman.

Davie did not attempt a general history of the Southern campaign, but limited himself to a detailed account of his own engagements. These form an important contribution to the bibliography of the period and are indispensable for a study of Davie.

The numerous engagements he described, although on a comparatively small scale, were part of the over-all strategy of attrition employed by the Americans to defeat the primary purpose of the British to divide the Southern and Northern colonies and subjugate them separately. The end-result of this successful Fabian policy was, of course, the British surrender at Yorktown.

Davie's detailed accounts omit little of his active participation in the Revolution and are therefore followed closely for the remainder of this chapter and the two which follow.*

* See Appendix B for a fuller discussion of these two sketches. Unless otherwise cited, the remainder of this chapter and the two immediately following are based on Davie's "Sketches."

Youthful Patriot and Student of Law

The Southern states had remained free from invasion until December, 1778, with the notable exceptions of Sir Peter Parker's repulse at Charleston, June 28, 1776, a few light predatory incursions from Florida, and the various uprisings of the Tories in their midst. At this time, Colonel Archibald Campbell was dispatched with 3,500 men by Sir Henry Clinton to the Georgia coast, where they landed three miles below Savannah. They completely routed Major General Robert Howe's army of 1,500 American regulars and militia and entered Georgia's capital in triumph. The following month General Augustine Prevost marched up from Florida with 2,000 regulars and took command of the united forces at Savannah. Lieutenant Colonel Campbell was forthwith dispatched into the interior of the state and within one month from the fall of Savannah the conquest of Georgia had been effected.[14]

Meanwhile Major General Benjamin Lincoln, who had superseded Howe in command of the Southern Department, had collected about 7,000 men at Charleston, of whom about one-third were North Carolinians—the militia under General John Ashe and the Continentals under Brigadier General Jethro Sumner. Thus strengthened, General Lincoln decided to take the offensive by detaching General Ashe with nearly 1,500 militia, only 100 of whom were Continentals, with orders to take post opposite Augusta, Georgia. However, on March 3, 1779, at Briar Creek, which rises on the Georgia side about sixty miles below Augusta, they were surprised by Colonel Mark Prevost, the brother of the General. His detachment of 900 men routed the Americans so completely that less than a third of their number succeeded in rejoining General Lincoln. All hope of recovering Georgia at that time was abandoned.[15]

General Lincoln's forces remained encamped along the South Carolina side of the Savannah River at Purysburg, Black Swamp, and the heights opposite Augusta, while the British, with headquarters at Savannah, "foraged and plundered the whole State [of Georgia] without either check or apprehension." By April 19, Lincoln's forces having been augmented to about 5,000 men, the General felt that he had a sufficient force to act with confidence. Accordingly, on that date, he called a council of war, during which it was decided to cross the river and occupy a position enabling them to cut off the enemy's communication with the Indians, intercept their supplies from the upper country, and attempt to circumscribe their operations to Savannah and the seaboard. Four days later, Lincoln left about 1,000 militia, the 5th South Carolina Regiment and part of the 2nd under the command of Brigadier General William Moultrie at Black Swamp and Purysburg and began his march up the left bank of the Savannah. Yet these well-laid plans were suddenly reversed when it was learned that General Prevost, with 2,400 British troops and some Indians, had attempted to surprise the posts at Purysburg and Black Swamp and Moultrie had fallen back to Tulifinny Bridge spanning the river of that name, about sixty miles from Charleston. Later information from Moultrie revealed that the enemy continued to press him back towards Charleston and that his command was diminishing by the desertion of the militia. Abandoning the prospect of menacing the capital, Lincoln recrossed the Savannah in pursuit of Prevost. He pressed constantly forward by forced marches through "a desert barren country in which no arrangement had been made for supply," but the army "supported the oppression of thirst, hunger and fatigue with becoming spirit and cheerfulness."

Moultrie, meanwhile, had allowed himself to be bottled up in Charleston by Prevost on May 11. Two days later, Prevost decided that it was the better part of valor to retreat before he was caught in a vise on Charleston neck, between the Ashley and Cooper rivers.[16] He therefore returned to his baggage at Ashley Ferry, about ten miles up the river, while Pulaski took a position at Dorchester, a small village about fifteen miles west of north from Charleston.

At this point Davie re-entered the picture. Since his attachment to Pulaski, he had devoted his leisure "to the acquirement of professional knowledge" and had risen "fast in the esteem of the general and the army."[17] His troops consisted of his detachment of North Carolina cavalry with a small part of Colonel Daniel Horry's recruits and some mounted volunteers from the Charleston vicinity—"in all not exceeding 100 men." From Dorchester they constantly annoyed the enemy until General Lincoln arrived on May 18 with his army at Bacon's Bridge at the head of the Ashley. Pulaski's cavalry joined them there. Prevost, in the face of these combined forces, evacuated Ashley Ferry and filed off below Charleston to James and then Johns Island, which were separated from the mainland by the Stono River. Here, opposite Stono Ferry, some fieldworks were thrown up to

Youthful Patriot and Student of Law

secure the communication with the mainland. The American army encamped near by. The two armies remained stationary from the last of May until the middle of June, when Lincoln decided to attack the entrenched camp at Stono. A supporting attack was to be made upon the open camp of the enemy on the island.

The defenses at Stono consisted of three redoubts with lines of communication shaped like a half-moon and protected by a common abatis. The intervals were filled by some pieces of field artillery, and the redoubts were mounted with cannonades and howitzers. In front of the works the ground was level and was covered at a short distance by a thick grove of pine trees. The post itself was manned by Lieutenant Colonel Maitland and about 700 men.

According to plan, General Lincoln, at daybreak on June 20, displayed his army about four hundred yards from the enemy's lines, with the South Carolina brigade on his left, the North Carolina brigade under Brigadier General Jethro Sumner in the center, and Brigadier General John Butler's North Carolina militia on the right.* Pulaski's cavalry, of which Davie's detachment was a part, formed the second line, and General David Mason's † Virginia militia formed the reserves. The flanks were covered by the light troops under Colonel William Henderson ‡ of South Carolina and Colonel Francis

---

* This formation is at variance with that described in Lee's *Memoirs* (Robert E. Lee [ed.], *Memoirs of the War in the Southern Department of the United States By Henry Lee*,... [New York: University Publishing Company, 1869]), but inasmuch as Davie was an active participant in the battle, his account is followed. Perhaps this is one of the errors to which Davie was referring when he wrote that he sincerely wished "that General Lee would print another edition of his memoirs, in which the mistakes in point of fact might be corrected and his military reflections enlarged... his mistakes as to facts, are not numerous, and only where he has copied from the other writers." —W. R. Davie to J. F. Grimké, Jan. 24, 1815. W.R.D. Papers, No. 2, S.H.C.

† Mason, though called a "General" by Edward McCrady (*The History of South Carolina in the Revolution, 1775-1780* [New York: The Macmillan Company, 1901], p. 387), was probably "Colonel" David Mason (1740-1820) of Sussex County who had served on the Committee of Safety in Virginia, was a member of the Virginia convention of 1775, and Colonel of the 15th Virginia Regiment.—National Society of the Daughters of the American Revolution, *Lineage Book* (Harrisburg, Pa.: Telegraph Printing Co., 1914), XXXVIII, 130; *ibid.*, LII, 296 (hereafter cited as D.A.R., *Lineage Book*).

‡ Colonel William Henderson was from up-country South Carolina, between the Broad and Saluda rivers, in what is now Spartanburg County. The following year he "greatly distinguished himself during the siege of Charleston,"

[33]

Malmedy, a French officer.*

Thus formed, the army advanced in good order, opposite the entire length of the enemy's front. The British held their fire until their assailants were within about sixty yards, when, by a general discharge of musketry and artillery, they completely checked the Americans, who, however, returned their fire instantly. The bloody affray continued for an hour and fifty minutes before Lincoln ordered a retreat because of a reinforcement of the enemy and the carnage among the Americans. Colonel Maitland seized upon the ensuing confusion in the American front line to make a sally with his whole force. At Lincoln's order, the cavalry charged the advancing enemy, who formed and received them "with so firm a countenance and a fire so well directed that these light and ill disciplined troops were immediately dispersed." Mason's Virginia militia then moved forward and began a heavy fire on the enemy's advance troops, under cover of which the army was again formed, and the retreat effected in good order.†

In the cavalry charge, Major Davie was severely wounded in the thigh and fell from his horse, but managed to retain his hold on the bridle.‡ His dispirited troops had turned in full retreat, and he was about to be overtaken by the enemy when a private from another company saw him standing beside his horse, unable to mount. With

---

was held prisoner at Haddrell's Point, and upon his release saw action at Eutaw Springs, where he was wounded. He was later advanced to brigadier general and elected to the Jacksonborough Assembly, called to meet in January, 1782, by Governor John Rutledge.—Edward McCrady, *The History of South Carolina in the Revolution, 1780-1783* (New York: The Macmillan Company, 1902), pp. 415-16, 452, 559.

* This officer had served early in the war in Rhode Island, which state appointed him a brigadier general. Later, May 10, 1777, Continental Congress appointed him a colonel in the Continental service. Feeling it inconsistent with his previous appointment he complained to Washington, but to no avail. —Benjamin Franklin Stevens (ed.) *Clinton-Cornwallis Controversy* (London: 4 Trafalgar Square, Charing Cross, 1888), II, 444 (hereafter cited as C.C.C.).

† Davie's critique of this battle, contained in his "Sketches," is a scathing denunciation of Lincoln's tactics.

‡ In the official return of "Killed, Wounded and Missing in the Action of Stone [*sic*] Ferry, 20th June, 1779," Davie was listed as a lieutenant of the militia horse.—*S.R.*, XV, 751.

Youthful Patriot and Student of Law

the enemy only twenty yards away, the private quickly placed the major on his horse and led him from the field and then resumed his place in the ranks before Davie had a chance to express his gratitude sufficiently. There was a sequel to this story. Two years later, on the morning of the attack on Ninety-Six, a stranger was said to have come up to the tent of Davie, then commissary general to Greene, and introduced himself as his deliverer at Stono. In the rush of preparations for the assault, Davie had only a brief moment in which to thank the soldier and make him promise to come again if he survived the battle. This was their last interview.[18]

It was also at the battle of Stono that a Waxhaw neighbor of Davie's, Hugh Jackson, Andrew's oldest brother, perished. A volunteer in Davie's cavalry detachment, he had become ill just before the battle and was ordered not to engage in the fight. Perhaps the same vein of iron and the same defiance of authority characterized the older brother: He fought anyway, but after the battle he died of excessive heat and fatigue.[19]

The thigh wound received by Davie confined him in the hospital at Charleston at least two months,* after which he returned to Salisbury. During his convalescence he again took up the study of law, stood his examination, and obtained a license to practice in the Rowan County Court November 2, 1779.[20]

Tradition has it that this license was granted at the special request of Governor Richard Caswell, who was eager to ascertain the political sentiments of the transmontane settlers in what is now Tennessee. He accordingly sent Davie over to attend the courts in Holston Valley, where he might gain the desired information.[21]

His license, signed by Judges Samuel Spencer and John Williams on March 24, 1780, confirmed the fact that William Richardson Davie had resided in the state about two years, that he was "sufficiently recommended... as a person of unblemished moral character," and that upon examination he appeared "to possess a competent degree of knowledge in the law for the purpose aforesaid."[22]

As might be expected, when the war in the South came closer, Davie succumbed to the inevitable: For the fourth time he took up

---

* Lee, *Memoirs*, p. 578, gives the period as five months; Samuel A. Ashe (*Biographical History of North Carolina from Colonial Times to the Present* [Greensboro, N.C.: Charles L. Van Noppen, 1907], VI, 189), as three months.

arms against the British. This time he succeeded in obtaining authority from the legislature to raise a troop of cavalry and two troops of mounted infantry, at the head of which he was placed with the rank of major. To raise and equip this force, he is said to have expended the last remaining shilling of his share of his uncle's estate.[23]

With this newly-authorized cavalry, the youthful major embarked on a service of a year and a half during which he emerged as one of the leading partisan officers of the South and was contemporaneously ranked with Sumter, Marion, and Pickens—the great South Carolina trio.

CHAPTER IV

The Partisan Leader

THE word "partisan," as applied to Revolutionary leaders, seems nowhere to be defined adequately and has therefore been loosely applied to leaders who had varying degrees of authority, varying types of units—some well organized and some woefully disorganized—and varying modes of waging warfare. Webster defines a partisan as "any member of a body of detached light troops, engaged in harassing an enemy," whereas the popular conception of a partisan leader is one of the guerrilla type, who, without a Continental or a state commission, draws around him a group of hardy volunteers who come as the occasion demands, serve without pay, stake their life's blood, and retire to their homes after the danger has passed. Of the latter type were Sumter, Marion, and Pickens. On the other hand, such military officers as North Carolina's Brigadier Generals Griffith Rutherford, Jethro Sumner, and William Lee Davidson have been classified as partisan leaders.* Yet each of these had a bona fide com-

---

* For a scholarly biography of Davidson, see Chalmers G. Davidson, *Piedmont Partisan: The Life and Times of General William Lee Davidson* (Davidson, N.C.: Davidson College, 1951). The author contends that his subject was "North Carolina's most serviceable partisan" and compares him with Rutherford and Sumner (pp. 124-25). Because he was the state-appointed brigadier of the Salisbury District, it is difficult to see how he fits into the category of a partisan either in the literal or popularly-accepted sense. The author, moreover, incorrectly describes the twenty-four-year-old Princeton graduate, lawyer, and major, Davie, as being, in 1780, "the ward of the Presbyterian parson at Waxhaw" and as sharing "the ambition for military glory common to many

mission, either Continental or state, placing him at the head of a definite command or geographical unit, and as such was commander of far more than "a body of detached light troops engaged in harassing an enemy."

Davie, however, though classified as a partisan by all the older historians, seemed to be in the twilight zone of a quasi-partisan. Although he had at this time a state-granted commission to raise "an Independent Corps"[1] he had what might be called a paper commission and certainly his command was a paper command. It was his responsibility to gather about him and equip an effective force of volunteers. And this force of "detached light troops" succeeded nobly in "harassing the enemy."

Yet such activities were treated rather cavalierly by Nathanael Greene, who wrote Sumter that "Partisan strokes in war are like the garnish of a table" and as such "they afford no substantial national security."[2] However, the victimized British then and Revolutionary authorities today agree on their value to the patriot cause. In arousing popular sentiment against the invaders, in organizing partisan bands, and in prosecuting a system of warfare which reversed the plans of the enemy, impeded their progress, harassed their outposts, disrupted their lines of communication and supply, captured their convoys, and at times by sheer brilliance and bravado achieved signal victories, they performed a service to the South and to the nation of incalculable significance.

There is more than an element of truth in the statement of a recent authority that, because of their advantage in mobility and marksmanship, it would not be going "too far to conclude that the war in the South was decided by scores of little combats in which the invaders lost a total amounting to a Revolutionary army."[3] Along the same lines was Lafayette's description of the Revolution to Napoleon: "The greatest interests of the universe were there decided by the skirmishes of picket guards."[4]

In any consideration of the Southern campaign, perhaps we are too detached in point of time and too aloof in point of attitude to appreciate certain features. Cognizance should be taken of several

---

piedmont striplings" (p. 61). Yet he admits that although Davidson "excelled in self-control, stability and reliability," this stripling "outclassed him in brilliance, daring and originality" (pp. 61-62).

factors which differentiated it from campaigns in the North. Not only had Georgia and South Carolina been overrun by the enemy at this time, but the population, more scattered in the South, was also more evenly divided between Loyalists and Whigs, especially in North Carolina.[5] As a result, the fratricidal war in the South, in the words of a professor of natural history at the University of Pennsylvania in 1819, was "more than ordinarily ferocious and sanguinary," a fact which arose from more "embittered resentment and angry passions, than is usually connected with military operations." Particularly "in small partisan affairs, which, from the nature of the contest, were much more numerous, in the South" did they seem "to fight for extermination rather than victory." Yet, he conceded that though the war in the South "was maddened, in its character, by private deeds of more atrocity and blood, it was also, ennobled, by more signal instances of individual and partisan valour and enterprise."[6]

Greatest among many gallant exploits were, according to this same source, those of the "Swamp Fox" Marion, the "Game-Cock" Sumter, Colonel Andrew Pickens, and Davie. The last, however, "possessed talents of higher order and was much more accomplished in education and manners than either of his three competitors for fame."

A certain appreciation of the grandiloquence and hero-worship of our ancestors must be taken into consideration in reading his further eulogism of Davie:

"For the comeliness of his person, his martial air, his excellence in horsemanship, and his consummate power of field eloquence, he had scarcely an equal in the armies of his country. So sonorous and powerful was his voice, so distinct his articulation, and so commanding his delivery, that the distance at which he could be heard was almost incredible. But his chief excellence lay in the magnanimity and generosity of his soul, his daring courage, his vigilance and address, and his unrelenting activity and endurance of toil. So ardent was his attachment to the cause of freedom and so disinterested his efforts to promote it, that in equipping for the field his corps of followers he expended his whole patrimonial estate."[7]

Equally eulogistic, though a little more laconic, was the appraisal of Davie by a participant in the Revolution, Dr. Alexander Garden, who claimed that Davie was "not only distinguished as an intelligent, but an intrepid soldier," and that "his delight was to lead a charge."

With the possession of "great bodily strength," he was "said to have overcome more men in personal conflict than any individual in the service."[8]

A more realistic description of the trials of these four partisan leaders was that of Amos Kendall, early biographer, friend, and adviser to Andrew Jackson, and his Postmaster General:

"All these and others were for a time independent chiefs, receiving neither pay, subsistence, arms, nor stores from government, but fed and clothed by the contributions of friends and the spoils of enemies, armed with such weapons as could be found or made in the country, and as a remuneration for their sacrifices and dangers, looking only to the success of the cause to which their lives and fortunes were devoted. Farming utensils were wrought into rude arms by common blacksmiths, and pewter dishes were molded into bullets for want of lead. Sometimes they went into battle with not three rounds of ammunition as a soldier; and men without arms would watch the progress of a fight, and if they saw a companion fall, rush forward, seize his arms and ammunition, and supply his place in the conflict. Is it not wonderful that such men, in such a country, never could be conquered."[9]

The exact date when Major Davie received his commission is not known, but it was probably shortly after March 24, 1780, because by June 20, exactly a year after his wound at Stono, he was in the field with his troops at the battle of Ramsour's Mill. In the meantime, after collecting his corps of volunteers, he was engaged in protecting the country between Charlotte and Camden from the predatory incursions of the enemy and thereby serving to keep down the disaffected in the western Carolinas.[10]

Davie may not have decided to re-enter the army until after General Lincoln's surrender of Charleston, May 12, 1780, to the forces of Clinton and Cornwallis. But if his decision had not already been made by May 20, an affair of that date at the Waxhaws would have kindled the flames of war in the hearts of all patriotic Carolinians. Here Lieutenant Colonel Abraham Buford with about three hundred Continentals was overtaken by Lieutenant Colonel Banastre Tarleton with some seven hundred horse and foot. After a brief action, Buford begged quarter, though a few of his men, unaware of his action, continued to fire. This accidental firing was Tarleton's excuse to charge the unresisting Americans. Tarleton's official account reported 113 Americans killed, 150 badly wounded, and 53 made prisoners. "Tarleton's quarter" thus became proverbial.[11]

The American wounded were taken to the Waxhaw Presbyterian Meeting House, where they were tenderly cared for by the neighboring people, among whom was the widowed Rachel Jackson with her remaining two sons, Robert and thirteen-year-old Andrew, who were soon fired to such zeal that they offered their fledgling services to Davie.[12]

For the time being, the surrender of Charleston and Tarleton's massacre at the Waxhaws seem to have temporarily subjugated the second Southern state. With the exception of a great number of refugees, among whom were the Jackson family,[13] the South Carolinians in general submitted either personally or by a deputation of commissioners to a formal promise not to take part in the war thereafter. In a confident mood, General Clinton, on the eve of his departure from Charleston, informed Lord George Germain that Buford's defeat had "completed the destruction of everything in arms" against them in South Carolina and that there were few men there who were not "either our prisoners, or in arms with us."[14] South Carolina did not have a Continental officer in the field, her militia was disbanded, and her governor, John Rutledge, had sought sanctuary in Hillsborough, North Carolina.[15] The British, however, realized that such a capitulation was the "effect of panic, and that benumbing stupor consequent on such an impression." They therefore carefully reconnoitered the upper country, examined the minds and principles of the inhabitants, and, to keep the people in awe, established two strong advance posts at Hanging Rock, about eighteen miles away, and at Rocky Mount, on the western side of the Wateree River about thirty miles from Camden. These well-chosen posts, capable of supporting each other, not only covered the northern part of the state, but gave considerable encouragement to the Loyalists in North Carolina to assemble in large bodies.

Such a body of Tories had arisen precipitately in February, 1776, at Moore's Creek Bridge, under Donald McDonald, and had been precipitately crushed. Now they were again led to try their strength. The ensuing battle—Ramsour's Mill—was to be their final one in North

Carolina and as such this fratricidal conflict deserves more than passing notice.

The instigator of this uprising was one James Moore, who had lived with his father and family six or seven miles west of Ramsour's Mill, about a half-mile from the present town of Lincolnton, North Carolina. The preceding winter he had joined the British in South Carolina, but had returned to his father's home June 7th wearing a tattered British uniform with a sword dangling at his side. Announcing himself as Lieutenant Colonel Moore of the regiment of North Carolina Loyalists, commanded by Colonel John Hamilton of Halifax, he succeeded in inciting the Tory element in that vicinity.[16]

By the middle of June he had collected about eleven hundred [17] of the disaffected at Ramsour's Mill, while Colonel Samuel Bryan [18] of Rowan County was assembling about eight hundred Tories in the forks of the Yadkin in the north end of Rowan County adjoining Surry, about seventy-five miles northeast of Ramsour's. Other Tories, embodied in small parties near the South Carolina border, "carried their depredations in every direction." The North Carolina militia were everywhere in arms, but were in a dilemma as to where to strike, because the Tory groups were mushrooming throughout that section.

Meanwhile, after the defeat of Buford in the Waxhaws, Griffith Rutherford, Brigadier of the Salisbury District, hurriedly ordered out the militia en masse. They assembled, about nine hundred strong, near Charlotte on June 3. These included the South Carolina refugees, under Colonels Thomas Sumter * and Andrew Neel, and "some cavalry under Major Davie who had a commission to raise an Independent corps." No sooner were they assembled than intelligence was received that Tarleton had swung back to Camden. The next day, after an exhortation by the president of Liberty Hall, the Reverend Doctor Alexander McWhorter, General Rutherford dismissed them,

---

* For a discussion of whether Sumter was a colonel or a brigadier at this time, see Anne King Gregorie, *Thomas Sumter* (Columbia, S.C.: Press of the R. L. Bryan Company, 1931), pp. 78, 109. At Tuckasegie Ford, on June 15, 1780, he was chosen a brigadier general by a group of South Carolina volunteers—an organization which was "purely voluntary and without legal or military standing," though it was regarded as official by his followers, and, incidentally, by Cornwallis. However, Governor Rutledge and other South Carolinians held to the old title of colonel, until Rutledge issued a brigadier's commission four months later, October 6, 1780.

with orders to have their arms "in good repair and be in readiness for another call." As a precaution, part of Davie's cavalry was ordered to reconnoitre between Charlotte and Camden.[19]

Four days later, June 8, hearing that Lord Rawdon had advanced as far as Waxhaw Creek, some thirty miles south of Charlotte, Rutherford hastily reassembled the militia, which he proceeded to organize on June 14. Davie's cavalry, consisting of sixty-five men, were formed into two troops under Captains Simmons and Martin. A battalion of three hundred light infantry was placed under Lieutenant Colonel, later Brigadier General, William L. Davidson, a Continental officer who fortunately escaped the capitulation of Charleston by hearing of it on his way to join Lincoln. The remainder were under the immediate command of Rutherford.[20]

That same day Rutherford received intelligence that the Tories were embodying near Ramsour's Mill; whereupon he ordered Colonel Francis Locke, of Rowan, Major Robert Wilson, of Mecklenburg, and Captains Falls and Brandon to exert every effort to disperse them. On June 17 Rutherford was informed that Rawdon had retired towards Camden, thus releasing him temporarily to join the forces under Colonel Locke, whom he ordered to join in a concerted attack.[21]

Colonel Locke had succeeded in assembling about three or four hundred men, composed of the Burke, Lincoln, and Rowan militia, and by the 19th of June they had reached Mountain Creek, sixteen miles from Ramsour's. General Rutherford not having arrived, Colonel Locke called a council of his officers and there it was decided to attack the enemy "notwithstanding the disparity of numbers." At daybreak they advanced upon the Tories who were encamped on a high ridge, clear of underwood and covered with large oaks, their right flank protected by a mill pond, their rear by a strong fence. Upon their advance, the enemy drew up behind the trees and baggage. A general action ensued. Though the enemy's fire was "well directed," the militia pressed forward "with great spirit and intrepidity and in about 30 minutes the Loyalists gave way on all sides." *

About an hour after the Loyalist retreat, Rutherford arrived on the scene and immediately dispatched Major Davie's cavalry to pursue the fugitives to "clear that part of the country of all stragling parties."

---

* Davie's version of the battle and of the reason for the Loyalist retreat is at variance with that of McCrady.—*S.C. in the Rev.*, *1775-1780*, pp. 584-86.

William R. Davie

As a result of Davie's action, "many came and surrendered voluntarily" and "a great number were taken prisoners, some flying to South Carolina, others at their plantations, and in a few days that district of country lying between the river, the mountains and their [the South Carolina] line was entirely cleared of the Enemy."

Having thus dispersed the last formidable concentration of Tories on the western side of the Catawba, General Rutherford next turned his attention to Bryan's embodiment of Tories. Upon hearing of their compatriots' defeat at Ramsour's, they began a hurried march to join Major Archibald McArthur, who was stationed at Cheraw Mills, South Carolina.

Before pursuing these troops, Rutherford ordered Davie's cavalry to take a position below Charlotte, near the South Carolina line just opposite Hanging Rock in South Carolina. Here he would be able "to prevent the enemy from foraging on the borders of the state opposite to the Waxhaws and check the depredations of the Loyalists who infested that part of the Country." Accordingly, Davie chose a position on the northern side of Waxhaw Creek, where his corps was re-enforced by some South Carolinians under Major Robert Crawford (the brother of Andrew Jackson's uncle-in-law, James),[22] the Catawba Indians led by their chief or "king," General New River, and a part of the Mecklenburg militia commanded by Lieutenant Colonel William Heaggins.[23]

It was at this time that Davie's corps was augmented by two youthful adherents, Robert and Andrew Jackson, ages sixteen and thirteen respectively. There have been various accounts of Old Hickory's military feats in the Revolution, but according to Jackson himself, in a conversation with Francis P. Blair, he stated he "was never regularly enlisted," but whenever he took the field "it was with Colonel Davie, who never put me in the ranks, but used me as a mounted orderly or messenger, for which I was well fitted, being a good rider and knowing all the roads in that region." He further stated that the only weapons he had "were a pistol that Colonel Davie gave me and a small fowling-piece that my uncle Crawford lent to me."[24]

As a result of his association with Davie in the ensuing affairs at Hanging Rock and Rocky Mount and—if teen-age psychology was then what it is today—as a result of the gift of the pistol, Davie was "the man, above all others, that the Jackson boys admired most." In fact, one of Jackson's better biographers stated that "so far as any man was General Jackson's model soldier, William Richardson Davie of North Carolina was the individual." His further appraisal of Davie was that he was "swift but wary; bold in planning enterprises, but most cautious in execution; sleeplessly vigilant; untiringly active; one of those cool, quick men who apply master-wit to the art of war; who are good soldiers because they are earnest and clear-sighted men."[25]

The position taken by Davie at this time was only eighteen miles from the British post at Hanging Rock. This proximity led to daily skirmishes between the two for some time. The British, however, being "generally well received," soon "became more cautious and respectful." Davie daily sent out small detachments of cavalry to scour the countryside, so that the Tories were driven into their own lines and the enemy prevented from foraging about Hanging Rock.

On one occasion, however, it appeared to Davie as if serious trouble were in the offing. While stationed near Waxhaw Creek, his scouts informed him that a British party was advancing up the road from Camden. An express was immediately sent to Sumter, who had been covering the west side of the Catawba and who joined Davie on July 17. The next day the two forces marched down Waxhaw Creek beyond the Waxhaw Meeting House, still being used as a hospital for those wounded at Buford's defeat, to the plantation of a Dr. Harper, who was said to be "disaffected." Early the next morning the scouts reported that the enemy had marched from below Hanging Rock Creek up towards Charlotte. In order to gain the ford on Waxhaw Creek—the one most likely to be used by the British—Sumter and Davie marched to it briskly. Davie's cavalry and one hundred riflemen were placed opposite the ford on the north side with the idea that the British were to be allowed to pass until they encountered Davie's men, while those under Sumter were to attack them in the rear and flanks. After an all-night vigil, the enemy did not move. Deeming it inadvisable to attack the enemy in camp, the Americans moved back up, Sumter encamping just south of Charlotte and Davie returning to his former camp.[26]

The British, meanwhile, were in a serious situation in regard to supplies. Having "considered the country entirely at their devotion, [they] depended upon collecting their supplies from day to day."

Moreover, "they had improvidently consumed all the grain between that post and Camden and were now obliged to draw their supplies from that place." Therefore Davie's next objective was to cut off these supplies.

On the evening of July 20, with a part of his dragoons and some volunteers, he set out to intercept a convoy of provisions, spirits, and clothing coming up from Camden to Hanging Rock. After an all-night march he turned the enemy's left flank and gained the main Camden road, five miles below the post. They found a good position at Flat Rock, four and a half miles from Hanging Rock, and here they lay in wait. The convoy appeared in the afternoon and was captured "with little trouble." Its provisions, spirits, and wagons were destroyed and, with the escorts and wagoners mounted on the captured horses, the party began its march back to camp.

The march back presented not a few difficulties. One of the men, the preceding night, had straggled off and presumably been taken prisoner by the enemy, who might well have gained from him information of the expedition. In view of such an occurrence, Davie ordered the guides to take "the most unfrequented route" back. This involved a march, in the night, through a country "covered with thick woods and dangerous defiles."

With an ambush ever in mind, Davie formed his men accordingly. The guides and a few mounted infantry under a Captain Petit formed the advance. These were followed by the prisoners, guarded by some dragoons commanded by Captain William Polk of Mecklenburg, who acted as a volunteer. The remainder formed the rear-guard. Thus formed, they again turned the enemy's left flank about two A.M. and reached a plantation on the principal branch of Beaver Creek, which rises in the southern part of Lancaster County, South Carolina, and flows in a southwesterly direction into the Wateree Pond. Here Major Davie ordered Captain Petit and the advance guard to move forward and examine the houses, the narrow lane through which the road led, and the ford of the creek, with express directions to secure the family at the plantation.

The ensuing action may best be described in Davie's own words:

"... the officer of the advance hailed the enemy concealed under the fence and some standing corn; on challenging a second time he was answered by a discharge of Musquetry, which commenced on their right and passed like a running fire towards the rear of the Detachment; the Major who had rode forward to the advance on the halt of the troops, repeatedly ordered the men to push thro' the lane, but by a mistaken instinct they turned back from the fire upon the loaded arms of the enemy; seeing this, and deeming it his duty to bring them off, he repassed the lane under the 2d fire of the ambuscade, and overtook his party retreating precipitately on the same road by which they had advanced; the detachment were caused to file off to the right and halted upon a hill which overlooked the plantation; Colo. Polk with some of the guard had passed through the lane & the detachment was considerably reduced; but as the enemy were plainly observed passing about unguardedly with lights, every effort was used to tranquillize the men, and induce them to return the compliment on the enemy, but their spirits and confidence were dissipated and the ambuscade had produced all the effect of a complete surprise; all that could be done was to avoid another check by a judicious retreat, several of the prisoners were found to be mortally wounded, and were left on the Hill, the guides as usual had fled, and the Major was obliged at first to take a general direction through the woods, but a Tory who was taken from his bed and compelled to serve as a guide enabled him to pass the enemys patroles and regain his camp the next day without any further reverse of fortune. The loss was slight considering the advantage of the British, Capt. Petit and two men wounded and Liet. Elliot killed; the fire fell principally among the prisoners, who were confined two upon a horse and mixed with the guard presented a larger object than a single dragoon; the advance guard with the prisoners nearly filled the lane, it was owin to these circumstances that the prisoners were all killed or wounded except three or four. The object of surprising the convoy was effected the slaughter of the prisoners could not be considered as a loss; but the ambuscade might have been fatal to the whole Detachment; a misfortune solely occasioned by the officer of the advance guard not having executed his orders...."

Davie sententiously ended with a moral to the effect that "this may furnish a useful lesson to the officers of partizan corps who should never forget that every officer of a detachment on command may at some moment have its safety and reputation committed to him, and that the slightest neglect of duty is generally severely punished by an enemy."

No doubt this small affair, the first of any consequence with Davie in complete command, merely served to arouse Davie's spirit for more action. It also refutes the contention that Davie's corps was never surprised or dispersed during the entire war.[27]

Shortly after this, on July 30, Colonels Thomas Sumter and Andrew Neel, "with a number of the South Carolina Refugees," and Colonel Robert Irwin, with three hundred of the Mecklenburg militia, rendezvoused near Major Davie's camp. The officers, eager to utilize their volunteers to advantage before they departed, held a council. They decided that the British posts of Rocky Mount and Hanging Rock, the former of which was garrisoned by Lieutenant Colonel Turnbull with 150 New York volunteers and some South Carolina militia,[28] were "not only the most important at the time but lying within their reach and strength." It was agreed that Sumter, with the refugees and the North Carolinians under Irwin, should march to the attack of Rocky Mount, while Major Davie should make a diversion to engage the attention of the corps at Hanging Rock.* The two detachments marched the same night.

When Sumter arrived at Rocky Mount, he found that the defenses consisted of two log houses and a loop-holed building, all three surrounded by a strong abatis. The site itself was "considerably elevated, and surrounded with cleared grounds." He advanced "some small parties of rifle men" under the cover of rocks and trees, keeping up a fire upon the houses. Although several corps of this detachment marched repeatedly "with great intrepidity" through the old field to the attack, they were repulsed by the heavy fire of the garrison. After various vain stratagems had been employed to set fire to the buildings, they were obliged, through a want of artillery, to retreat, which they did without interception. The casualties were four or five privates killed or wounded and Colonel Andrew Neel, "an influential enterprising officer," who lost his life in one of the attacks.†

---

* According to one account, in the event of Sumter's success, he was to cross the river and make a joint attack on Hanging Rock.—Amos Kendall, *Life of Andrew Jackson: Pioneer, Patriot, Soldier, Politician, President* (New York: Charles Scribner's Sons, 1904), p. 22.

† For a more detailed account, based largely on Davie's "Sketches" (as used by Wheeler), and on Graham's account, see Gregorie, *Sumter*, pp. 87-90.

The Partisan Leader

According to plan, Davie had set out for the post at Hanging Rock, arriving about one o'clock. His detachment consisted of forty mounted rifle-men and about forty dragoons. While reconnoitering the position, he fortunately found out that three companies of mounted infantry, belonging to Bryan's Loyalists, had just returned from an incursion and had halted at a farmer's house, in full view of the post.

The ensuing action, described by Davie, was one of his most daring exploits:

"The House was placed in the point of a right angle made by a lane of staked & ridered fence; the one end of which opened to the enemy's encampment, the other terminated in the woods, the Major advanced on that next to the woods, and as the riflemen were not distinguishable from the Loyalists, they were sent round to the other end of the lane with orders on gaining it, to rush forward & fire on the enemy. The dragoons were divided so that one half could occupy the lane while the other half entered the field. This disposition was made with such promptitude that the attention or suspicion of the enemy was never excited, the rifle company under Capt. Flenniken [Flenchau] * passed the camp sentries without being challenged, dismounted in the lane and gave the enemy a well directed fire, The astonished Loyalists fled instantly the other way, and were immediately charged by the dragoons in full gallop and driven back in great confusion; on meeting again the fire of the infantry they all rushed impetuously against the angle of the fence where in a moment they were surrounded by the dragoons who had entered the field and literally cut to pieces: As this was done under the eye of the whole British camp no prisoners could be safely taken which may apologize for the slaughter that took place on this occasion. They took sixty

---

* This captain, whose name is also spelled Flenchaw, Flencher, Flenchau, Flenchan, defies further identification, but it is possible that he was the David Flennikin of Mecklenburg County, North Carolina, who "served under Col. Irwin and Gen. Sumter at the battle of Hanging Rock, where he was wounded and carried to the hospital at Charlotte."—J. B. Alexander, *The History of Mecklenburg County from 1740 to 1900* (Charlotte: Observer Printing House, 1902), p. 413; David Schenck, *North Carolina, 1780-1781: Being a History of the Invasion of the Carolinas By the British Army Under Lord Cornwallis in 1780-'81* (Raleigh: Edwards & Broughton, 1889), p. 73 (hereafter cited as Schenck, *N.C., 1780-1781*).

valuable Horses with their furniture and one hundred muskets and rifles; the whole camp beat to arms but the business was done, and the Detachment out of their reach before they recovered from their consternation."

Such an encounter gave to Davie a two-fold reputation: the British attached to his outfit the appellation "the bloody corps,"[29] and the patriots were rapidly enveloping him with an aura of glamor and dash, at a time when their cause seemed at its lowest ebb.

The two posts at Hanging Rock and Rocky Mount served as two beacons or challenges, luring Davie and Sumter on. At any rate, their two detachments met on August 5, at Landsford, in Chester County, at Davie's old home, about nineteen miles from the town of Chester. Major Davie had lost no men, and Sumter's strength was little diminished by his first stab at Rocky Mount. Their combined forces numbered about eight hundred effective men, five hundred of whom were under Colonel Irwin and Major Davie, with the remainder under the South Carolina Colonels Sumter, William Hill of York County, Edward Lacey of the Waxhaw country, and others. At a meeting of these officers they discussed the pro's and con's of the two posts, which they calculated were so interdependent that the fall of one would lead to the evacuation of the other. Finally, Hanging Rock was chosen as their objective because it was an open camp. On learning of this projected attack, the rank and file "entered into the project with great spirit & cheerfulness."

The march was begun that same night and by midnight they were within two miles of their objective. A council of war was held to decide on the mode of attack. Information from scouts revealed that the enemy "were pretty strongly posted in three different encampments." The British regulars, about five hundred according to "Light Horse Harry" Lee,[30] commanded by a Major Garden, of the Prince of Wales's American regiment,[31] were stationed on the right. Encamped at some houses in the center were about 160 of Tarleton's Legion, a part of Colonel Browne's regiment, and the Loyalist regiment of Lieutenant Colonel John Hamilton.*

---

* Colonel Hamilton, who, as the British consul at Norfolk after the war, was to have several dealings with Davie, had been "probably the most important merchant in North Carolina, as well as the most valuable Loyalist to the British cause." A colonial merchant of Halifax and the entire Albemarle section, his

The Partisan Leader

At some distance on the left was the regiment of Colonel Samuel Bryan, a part of whose troops were separated from the center encampment by a skirt of woods. In front of the entire British camp ran Hanging Rock Creek and a deep ravine on one side of which there jutted out a great rock. Hence the name "Hanging Rock." [32]

After deliberation, Sumter proposed that the troops be divided into three sections and marched directly to the center encampment, where they were to dismount and each section attack a different camp. All the officers agreed to the feasibility of this plan except Davie. Aware of the confusion in dismounting under fire and the certainty of losing the effect of "a sudden and vigorous attack," he urged that they tie their horses and approach on foot. Davie stated that his wise counsel was overruled; others, that it was followed.*

Colonel Sumter, as senior officer, was given the general command. There is a great deal of uncertainty as to who led the column on the right. Davie, in his own "Sketches," maintained that he "led the column on the right consisting of his own corps and some volunteers Major Winn's regiment and some detached companies of So. Carolina refugees." Major Richard Winn, however, in his "Notes," written about twenty years after the affair, claimed not only that the plan to attack the British at Hanging Rock was determined by "Gen'l Sumter and Col. Winn," but that *he*, supported by Major Davie, led the attack on the right.† Colonel Irwin led the center column, which

---

loyalty to the Crown cost his company £14,834 through confiscation. He is said to have raised and equipped about fourteen hundred Tories, whom he led in numerous engagements in the Carolinas and Georgia. As a merchant he was respected for his honesty; as a Tory leader, for his kind and just treatment of his Whig prisoners—C.C.C., II, 436; Robert O. DeMond, *The Loyalists in North Carolina* (Durham, N.C.: Duke University Press, 1940), pp. 52-53; Lorenzo Sabine, *Biographical Sketches of the Loyalists of the American Revolution* (Boston: Little, Brown and Company, 1864), II, 511-12.

* Dr. Gregorie said that Davie's suggestion was followed, based on the report of Major Joseph McJunkin, Officer of the Day in that action, who said that Sumter left with the horses about forty men, who took no part in the action.—Gregorie, *Thomas Sumter*, p. 92, n. 68.

† Samuel C. Williams (ed.), "General Richard Winn's Notes—1780," *S.C. Hist. and Gen. Mag.*, XLIII (1942), 201, 209-10. The editor, in comparing Winn's account with Davie's, as reprinted in Wheeler, *Hist. of N.C.*, II, 194 et seq., criticized Davie for giving himself "over-credit, and without giving any to his immediate superior in rank and actual commander, Winn"; for not

consisted entirely of the Mecklenburg militia, while Colonel Hill and his South Carolina refugees formed the left column.

The march began at daybreak on August 6 and soon neared the enemy's "picquet and patrole," which they avoided by a turn to the left, intending to surprise it from the rear under cover of a defile near the camp. However, their best-laid schemes went awry, because the guides, "through ignorance or timidity," led them so far to the left that the three sections all came up together before Bryan's encampment. The Tories, "briskly attacked both in front & flank," were soon routed "with great slaughter." The Americans, pressing on in pursuit of the fleeing Tories trying to gain the center encampment, were fired upon by Tarleton's Legion and some companies of Hamilton's regiment which were posted behind a fence. The impetuosity of the Americans "was not checked a moment by this unexpected discharge" and was of such force that the Legion immediately broke and joined the flight of the Loyalists, "yielding their camp without another struggle to the Militia."

At this point, a part of Colonel Browne's regiment almost reversed the fate of the day. Having "passed by a bold and skilful maneuvre into the wood between the centre & Tory encampment," they had drawn themselves up unperceived and began pouring a heavy fire on the Americans. The latter "took instinctively to the trees and bush heaps and returned the fire with deadly effect." So effective was this fire that in a few minutes there was not a British officer standing. One half of the regiment having fallen, the others threw down their arms on being offered quarter.

---

even hinting he was under Winn's command; for not referring to Winn at all except to mention that he was wounded; for degrading Sumter to a colonel; and for calling the South Carolina troops "refugees," when they "were fighting on the soil of their own state and under their own general." Perhaps some of the editor's indignation might have been lessened had he read the original in Davie's "Sketches." In the reprint, Wheeler had misrepresented Major Winn as "Major Bryan." It might be added that no other authorities consulted mention Winn at all in this battle, unless to say he was wounded: Lee, *Memoirs*, pp. 176-78; McCrady, *S.C. in the Rev., 1775-1780*, pp. 625-31. Gregorie, *Sumter*, pp. 91-96, does say in a note that Davie's account cannot be reconciled with that of Wm. D. James, "Battle of Hanging Rock," *New York Spectator*, August 19, 1828.

As to Sumter's rank at that time, see note (p. 42), *supra*. Winn's rank of major at the time is verified by A. K. Gregorie, "Winn, Richard," *D.A.B.*, XX, 390.

Meanwhile the remainder of the British line drew up in a hollow square in the center of the cleared grounds. Unfortunately, after such success, the plunder of the camps threw the Americans into great confusion. The "outmost exertions" of Sumter and others could not induce the men to attack the British square. Finally about two hundred infantrymen and Davie's cavalry were collected and formed at the margin of the woods. They opened "a heavy but ineffectual fire" on the British, consisting of about three or four hundred of the Legion infantry. Moreover, Hamilton's regiment of Tories rallied and formed in the edge of the woods on the opposite side of the British camp.

Davie described the ensuing action: "... and least they might be induced to take the Americans in flank Major Davie passed round the camp under cover of the trees, and charged them with his company of Dragoons. These people under the impressions of defeat were all routed and dispersed in a few minutes by this hand full of men. The distance of the square from the woods and the constant fire of two pieces of field artillery prevented the militia from making any considerable impression on the British troops; so that upon Major Davie's return it was agreed to plunder the encampments and retire; as this party were returning towards the center encampment some of the Legion Cavalry appeared drawn up on the Camden road, with a countenance as if they meant to keep their position but on being charged by the dragoons of Davie's corps they all took the woods in flight & one only was cut down. A retreat was by this time absolutely necessary—The commissary stores were taken in the center encampment, and numbers of the men were already inebriated, the greatest part were loaded with plunder and those in a condition to fight had exhausted their ammunition. About an Hour was employed in plundering the camp, taking the paroles of the British officers, and preparing litters for the wounded; all this was transacted in full view of the British army who in the mean time consoled themselves with some military music & an interlude of 3 cheers for King George, which was immediately answered by 3 cheers and the Hero of American Liberty; the militia at length got into the line of march in three columns, Davie's corps covering the rear, but as they were loaded with plunder, encumbered with their wounded friends, and many of them intoxicated, it is easy to conceive that this retreat could not be performed according to the rules of the most approved tacticks. However under all these disadvantages they filed off unmolested along the front of the Enemy about 1 O'clock."

The exact American losses[33] were never ascertained. Tarleton maintained that about one hundred dead and wounded were left on the field.[34] Colonel Lee asserted that Davie's corps suffered most, but that the British loss exceeded the American. A great many were killed or wounded while they were tying their horses and forming, a situation that would have been averted if Davie's advice had been followed.*

Davie's critique upon the battle is remarkable in its restrained condemnation of Sumter's tactics: "It is an invariable trait in the character of Militia," he said, "that they will only obey their own officers in the line of action, and this battle would certainly have been more decisive had not the militia fallen into confusion in the pursuit of the Loyalists & Legion Infantry; by which means the different regiments & companies became mixed & confounded. or Had the Divisions of this Army disencumbered themselves of their horses and moved in such manner as to have engaged the encampments separately at the same time; a vigorous and unexpected attack might have prevented the British from availing themselves of their superior discipline, the other encampments must have been soon carried &, the corps would have remained distinct, and in a situation to push any advantage that Davie's column might have gained over the British line."

After the retreat Davie immediately returned with the wounded to Charlotte, where a hospital, "by his provident care," had been established. This accomplished, he hastened to join General Horatio Gates's army at the general rendezvous at Rugeley's Mill.

The critical situation in the South, just before the fall of Charleston, had prompted Washington to dispatch from his own army two thousand Delaware and Maryland troops under Johann Kalb, popularly known as Baron De Kalb,[35] to re-enforce Lincoln. Charleston had fallen over five weeks before when Kalb arrived in Hillsborough,

---

* Lee, *Memoirs*, p. 178. Notable among those killed were Captain McCullock, "who commanded the Legion infantry with much personal honor," two other officers, and twenty men of the same corps, while about forty were wounded. Colonel Browne's regiment suffered the loss of many officers and men, who were killed, wounded, or taken prisoner. Bryan's Loyalists suffered least, because of their early flight.

North Carolina. Despite the appalling lack of preparation to meet the advance of the British, his very presence inspired new hope. Major General Richard Caswell, commanding the brigades of Brigadier Generals Isaac Gregory and John Butler, at once put himself under Kalb's command, as did General Edward Stevens, commanding the Virginia militia, and Colonel William Porterfield with four hundred Virginia Continentals. With these troops Kalb was planning an advance into South Carolina when General Horatio Gates, the hero of Saratoga, arrived in Hillsborough July 25 to assume command.[36]

Every schoolboy is familiar with the precipitate, ill-advised, and over-confident haste with which Gates rushed to the battle of Camden, with little knowledge of his or the enemy's troops or of the topography of the country. Yet his haste did not preclude his trying to inform himself on his way down to Hillsborough as to his new command. On July 17, while on the road twenty-five miles from Hillsborough, he wrote Davie as "The Officer Commanding the Cavalry at Halifax," requesting an "exact Return of the Two Regiments under your Command; distinguishing every particular of Men, Horses, Arms & Accouterments; that are present, absent, or deficient." Wishing to receive this information "in the most correct manner possible," he felt "it is immediately necessary, that the whole Army in the Southern District, should be collected to a point." For this reason he demanded that Davie be exact in acquainting him with "how many Officers & Soldiers of the two Regiments under your command will be ready to March at the shortest notice." *

Davie, after escorting the wounded from Hanging Rock to Charlotte, set out to join Gates at Rugeley's Mill. Upon his arrival on August 15, he found that the impetuous Gates had already set out for Camden. Davie's cavalry rode all night to overtake him. Instead, they were met the next morning by the first part of Gates's troops fleeing from the battle of Camden.[37]

It is difficult to reconstruct the succeeding events of that ill-fated morning from the several accounts of Davie's encounters with the various fleeing elements. According to Lee, Davie was within four miles of Camden when he "met the first part of our flying troops."

* W.R.D. Papers, No. 2, S.H.C. This is the first letter written to Davie that the writer has been able to locate.

William R. Davie

Hoping to be of use "in saving soldiers, baggage, and stores," he continued to advance until he met Brigadier General Huger, of the South Carolina line, who was driving his tired horse before him. From him Davie learned that Sumter was probably ignorant of the disaster and promptly dispatched Captain Martin to tell him about it and request him to come to Charlotte where they would exert themselves to the utmost to assemble all the force possible to take the field against the enemy.[38]

A more dramatic version was that advanced by Hubbard, and followed by Wheeler, McCrady, and Schenck. According to these, when Davie was about ten miles from Camden, he met a soldier "flying at full speed." Presuming him to be a deserter, Davie was about to arrest him when the accused announced to him that the entire army had been routed at Camden and declared that, "if he had deserted, he had done so along with the General and the whole army." His statement was soon confirmed by other fugitives who came up "singly and in straggling bands." Shortly thereafter General Gates himself, accompanied by his staff and many of the officers, shattered all doubts as to the rout. Gates reported that the British dragoons were not far in the rear and "desired" Davie to fall back as fast as possible to Charlotte. The Major replied to the General that "his troops were accustomed to Tarleton's Legion, and that he did not fear the result with any thing like equal numbers." With this the General passed on. Davie then asked General Huger, who had been with Gates, how far it would be necessary for him to obey the orders of the commander-in-chief. Huger's reply revealed his opinion of Gates: "Just as far as you choose; for you will never see him again." Still persistent, Davie dispatched a courier after Gates to inform him that if the General wished it, he would go down to the battlefield and bury the dead. General Gates's reply was swift: "I say retreat; and let the dead bury their dead."[39]

A final version, at variance with those preceding, was reported by one Daniel Alexander, an enlisted man of Mecklenburg County, who had volunteered in Captain Martin Fifer's company and was later assigned to Captain Alexander where he "was called out and went under the command of Major Wm. R. Davie...to join Gen. Gates near Camden." Describing Davie as "a tall, sallow-complexioned man with blue eyes," he continued: "On getting as far as Gaston,* which is near the South Carolina line, we met the American Army retreating. Gen. Gates and Major Davie had some conversation. We advanced some distance, when, on meeting some French Officers flying, we also joined in the retreat.

"Gen. Gates had on a pale blue coat with epaulettes, with velvet breeches, and was riding a bay horse. We retreated as far as Charlotte very much fatigued and worn down." [40]

Writing perhaps a quarter-century later, Davie, as might be expected, had his own observations on Gates's defeat, concerning which he rather loftily observed: "Unfortunate Generals are always the subject of observation and undistinguishing censure, success alone bestows either merit or fame upon a Military character; it is however the duty of the Historian who writes for the benefit of posterity, and not for the purpose of flattering the actors in the scenes he paints to expose with equal freedom the truth the blunders of the politician and the mistakes of the General."

Davie began by defending Gates's moving forward to Rugeley's Mill, saying that "its neighborhood contains the strongest ground in that part of the Country." Here his defense of Gates abruptly stopped. He labeled it as "the grossest folly to stake the whole blindly upon one single throw of the die" when the recovery of the two Southern states and the security of the remainder depended upon his army. In the face of an unknown enemy force, "nothing but the most desperate circumstances could warrant a General to stake so much upon a single Hazard."

After a somewhat detailed criticism of the tactics employed, Davie concluded with a censure of Gates's strategy:

"General Gates had joined the army but a few days which time was employed in continual marches, he was entirely unacquainted with the character of the officers or the merits of the different corps which composed his army, and was ignorant of their numbers, having never received a return untill after the orders of the 15th. were issued, the regular troops wanted rest and refreshment, the whole of the militia wanted arrangement and the ordinary preparation for a battle was intirely neglected among them, in Rutherfords Brigade

---

* Probably the present site of Gastonia, North Carolina.

there was scarce a cartridge made up, and their arms were generally in bad order; the consequence of continual marching & exposure. A man must have had more than ordinary good fortune to avoid a defeat under so many unfortunate circumstances."

Davie, about an hour after his encounter with Gates, dispatched "a confidential officer," Captain Martin, with two dragoons, to warn Sumter, who was moving up the west bank of the Catawba, of the rout at Camden.[41] This foresighted action on Davie's part seems justification for the remark of a later South Carolina historian that "Davie appears to have been the only officer at liberty capable of thinking and acting."[42]

According to Lee, after Davie received his final word from Gates he ignored the fleeing General's injunction and continued to advance down the Camden road, hoping to aid in saving the soldiers, baggage, and stores.[43] How far he ventured down the road can only be conjectured, but his biographer credited him with securing "several wagons loaded with clothing and medicines, which had been abandoned by their drivers and guards, who had unharnessed the horses and used them to hasten their own escape." This same source stated that it was only after he had proceeded far enough to ascertain that the British dragoons had pursued the fugitives but a short distance that he retraced his march towards Charlotte.[44] Dr. Alexander Garden also stated that Davie "hastened forward" as soon as he heard of the defeat, and "was essentially serviceable, not only in preventing pursuit, but in recapturing several wagons, one of which, most fortunately, contained the hospital medical chest."[45]

The morning after the battle Davie encountered Major Archibald Anderson, of the Third Maryland Regiment. Anderson was described by a contemporary historian as the "only man whose efforts to rally the men were any way effectual."[46] Davie bore out this testimony in his statement that "he was the only man who did not appear to be affected by the panic of the day." When Davie passed him on the morning of the 17th he was about forty miles from the battlefield and, with a corporal and eight men, was "eating his breakfast with great composure," and had had the good fortune to fall in with his own baggage wagon.

As Davie was proceeding up the road to Charlotte, hoping to join forces there with those of the forewarned Sumter, affairs were not going so well along the western bank of the Catawba. When Captain Martin arrived on the night of the sixteenth, Sumter, with his detachment of one hundred regular infantry, a company of artillery equipped with "2 brass pieces," and seven hundred militia, began a retreat up the river. By the next night they had reached Rocky Mount, where Sumter was informed that Tarleton's Legion had already occupied the banks and fords on the opposite bank of the Catawba. After a few hours' respite, he marched again at dawn and by noon gained an open ridge on the north side of Fishing Creek, about eight miles above Rocky Mount. Here Sumter halted the troops, and, despite the proximity of Tarleton, allowed them to stack their arms and "indulge themselves as they pleased in rest or refreshment." No precautions were taken for their security except the posting of twenty or thirty militia at the creek. The troops, as might be expected, sought various forms of relaxation from fatigue. Some strolled off to a neighboring plantation; some went down to the river to bathe; some took the opportunity to sleep. In this completely disorganized situation, Tarleton descended on the camp.

Giving "a general shout," one hundred cavalrymen and about sixty light infantrymen, formed in a single line, swooped down on the unsuspecting and the slumbering. The ensuing massacre can be imagined. Seizing first the arms and artillery, the Legion then turned to the men, whom they cut down as they started from their slumbers. Of course no regular opposition could be made, "a general panic ensued," and all who were able fled in disorder.

The British loss was small. Captain Charles Campbell, who had commanded the Highland light companies on the right at Camden, was killed, and fifteen privates were killed or wounded.[47] The American loss could ill be afforded: 150 officers and men killed and wounded and ten Continental officers, and one hundred soldiers, a large number of militia officers and two hundred privates taken prisoners. Tarleton had also seized the artillery, one thousand stand of arms, and forty-six wagons loaded with valuable stores.[48]

Davie's censure of Sumter was exceeded only by his condemnation of Tarleton. He praised the latter for his audacity, but rebuked him for the "unfeeling barbarity" of his men "who continued to hack and maim the militia long after they had surrendered," and whose sabres did not spare the "hoary honors" of a great many old men "who had turned out to encourage & animate the younger citizens."

Yet this "boyish Temerity" on the part of Tarleton, wrote Davie, would have cost Tarleton severely if Sumter, duly informed that the enemy was on his rear, had taken "any of the ordinary precautions" necessary to resist an attack. Instead, he had marched only eight miles before he halted upon an open ridge, taking no advantage of the wagons, posting the rear guard so near that it was not distinguished by the enemy from the main body, and resting the entire security of his force upon two videttes "whose fire was disregarded or not heard by a slumbering camp." A proper disposition of the troops and wagons "would have enabled him to have repelled five times the Enemys force." Davie's conclusion seems justified: "The listless and slumbering security in which this Detachment were caught at Midday under the eye of an enterprising enemy admits of neither apology nor explanation."

Davie's wrath must have reached new heights when he was informed that Sumter, "but half dressed,"[49] had been asleep under a wagon when the attack began. "Fortunately," according to Davie, and "unfortunately," according to the historian of the British Army,[50] Sumter, in the midst of the general confusion, made his escape. Two days later he reached Major Davie's camp at Charlotte without a single follower, "riding bare-back, without hat or saddle, or even a servant."

Scarcely more befitting high-ranking officers had been the pop-call paid to Charlotte by Generals Gates and Caswell. A contemporary report stated that Gates arrived there about eleven o'clock on the night of August 16 seventy-two miles from the battlefield. In too much of a hurry to dismount, Gates had "stopped two or three minutes," while Colonel Senf, one of his aides, ran in to tell Colonel Thomas Polk of the disaster and to say that Gates wished to speak to him outside. Before Polk could get out, the General had hurried on to Salisbury.[51] What more could be expected of his officers and men, who pushed on to Salisbury with equal haste?

While military historians all agree in general* on Gates's brief halt at Charlotte, there is a diversity of opinion as to Caswell's actions

---

* With the exception of J. R. Alden (ed.), *The War of the Revolution*, by Christopher Ward (New York: The Macmillan Company, 1952), II, 730.

there. Governor Nash, in writing to the North Carolina delegates to the Continental Congress, August 23, 1780, reported that "General Caswell made a stand at Charlotte and called in upwards of a *thousand* fresh *men* that he added these to Sumpters party of about seven hundred and gave him the command of the whole while he (Caswell) came on to the Assembly." *

To this, Davie took violent exception, maintaining that it was a "*damnable lie*," that Caswell "did not stay to collect one man," but followed Gates, before Colonel Mordecai Gist, Brigadier General William Smallwood, and the other officers abandoned Charlotte. Moreover, Sumter arrived alone several days after Caswell's departure. Davie's animosity towards Caswell is revealed in his justification for correcting "this falsehood," when he wrote: "It becomes the Historian to correct such shameful misrepresentations calculated to screen certain characters from just censure and attribute to themselves and others merit they never deserved." It should be added, in all fairness, that Major Joseph Graham, Adjutant to the Mecklenburg Militia, made no mention of Caswell at all—an omission which tends to bear out Davie's testimony. Also contradictory are the accounts of Caswell's actions related by the editor of the *North Carolina State Records*. In one place he stated that Gates and Caswell "hastened without stopping to Hillsboro, where the former at once set about drawing reinforcements and military stores from Virginia, and began to organize an army." [52] In the previous volume he had stated that Caswell and Brigadier Jethro Sumner "remained at Charlotte, forming a camp of militia there." [53]

South Carolina after Gates's and Sumter's defeats was, of course, entirely at the mercy of the British, while North Carolina, wide open to attack, was in a condition of nervousness and unrest. Particularly

---

* This quotation, taken from Davie's "Sketches," does not appear in the extract of Nash's letter of same date, from Hillsborough, to the North Carolina Delegates in Congress. S.R., XV, 60. Perhaps on the basis of this letter, both Dr. R. D. W. Connor and John Marshall claimed that Caswell did stop long enough to call out the militia of Mecklenburg, Rowan, and Lincoln counties.—Connor, *Hist. of N.C.*, I, 466-67; John Marshall, *The Life of George Washington* (Philadelphia: Printed and Published By C. P. Wayne, 1805), IV, 182.

was this true of Mecklenburg County, which lay in the direct route of the probable march of the enemy. In fact, when news of Sumter's defeat, accompanied with reports of the approach of the British cavalry, arrived in Charlotte, about nine o'clock on the morning of August 19, the officers who had fled thus far "determined precipitately upon retreating to Salisbury." Nor could Davie, who commanded the only American corps which at that time had not been beaten or dispersed,[54] dissuade them by assurances that his patrols "were several miles down the roads and that the British Horse could not be within many miles." He "entreated them to remain, as it wd. give more confidence &c to the militia; and urged the bad consequences of retiring &c to no purpose." Despite his exhortation "in a few minutes there was none left but Gist and Smallwood."

These two brigadier generals also soon left Davie and continued with the sick and wounded to Salisbury, where Smallwood established a camp.[55] Smallwood left orders with Davie "to proceed down on the Main and River roads below the Hanging Rock, to explore the Country and give the earliest Intelligence of the approach of the Enemy, should they be advancing." However, having learned that "the Enemy retreated precipitately after the action with Sumpter," he ordered "Major Davie with his Corps to remain at Charlotte, as also Major Anderson, with Forty of the regular Infantry and such Militia as had arrived there." Later he ordered them to proceed with "as many horse as they could collect, down to the Hanging Rock, to bring off Such of our Waggons and Baggage as they could fall in with." He was pleased to report, in a letter to Gates, August 22, 1780, that he had "just heard they are likely to succeed in this duty."[56]

Davie's report of these occurrences coincides closely with that of Smallwood. After the latter's departure he immediately marched down the road and in a few miles met Major Anderson, whose party had increased to fifteen or twenty. Anderson, on learning of the continued flight of the officers, "could not help expressing his surprise and indignation" and promised to remain in Charlotte until Davie's return. Davie continued down the road below the Waxhaws, where he found the enemy had all fallen back to Camden, whereupon he returned to Charlotte. True to his word, Major Anderson was waiting for him, and, at Davie's instance, wrote to Smallwood for orders to remain there.*

After the departure of all the fugitives from Camden and after Sumter's defeat, not only did Davie lead the only active corps operating between the enemy and the disorganized forces in Salisbury and Hillsborough, but he was the eyes and ears of the resistance. On August 29, a little over a week after Smallwood's departure, he wrote to Caswell, making a detailed report of the situation from Camden, through no-man's land, to Charlotte. This is the earliest available letter written by Davie:

"Charlotte, August 29th, 1780.
"SIR:
"The Enemy's falling immediately back to Camden and making no further advantage of their victory laid me under no necessity of retreating further than *this*. I kept out small parties of Horse to cover the Country and furnish us with regular Intelligence. The number of the Militia in Camp have been so fluctuating that nothing could be done. Last Saturday, with some difficulty, a command of one hundred horse was made up. I proceeded with them down the Country as far as three miles below the Hanging Rock.

"The Tory Militia have returned to their Plantations, but none of them appeared; they have robbed a few houses, and take every opportunity of expressing their designs of plundering the Country and murdering the Whiggest Inhabitants.

"The North Carolina Militia are now reduced to 300 in Camden, and those are detained by the Enemy's solemnly engaging to march into this State between the first and tenth of next month.

"The arrangements the Enemy are making in Camden indicate a disposition of this kind. They are industriously mounting their Infantry on the captured horses, refreshing and showing the Cavalry of the Legion & Getting Barrels made to carry provisions. This looks like a Bush-Country *Trip*. Have sent off some of their Baggage to Charleston, Convinced, I suppose, of the uncertainty of human affairs. Last Monday, Tuesday and Wednesday marched off the Prisoners to Garrison.

* This request was apparently not granted, as Anderson, according to Major Joseph Graham, after collecting about sixty stragglers, went on about the first of September.—Hoyt (ed.), *Murphey Papers*, II, 236.

William R. Davie

"It is said one party were released by the Militia near Sumpter. Two, who left Camden on Sunday, told me it was publicly spoken of there as a fact. Last Friday they called in their best post from Rugley's. Colo. Turnbull has also discharged his militia on the other side the Catawba and marched with the Regular Troops into Camden.

"All the recruits raised in the District of *Ninety-six* and other parts of So. Carolina were furloughed till the 6th or 7th of the next month, when they are to rendezvous at Camden. Our old friend, Mr. B. B. Boot, is Commissary of Prisoners, and Mr. Kerr, who left Salisbury with him is assistant.—

"They talk of reinforcements from Town, but *God* knows whether they are serious or not.

"The Militia in camp are quite inconsiderable, frightened, too, and irresolute, one day in Camp, another day to secure their property, so that one-half will undoubtedly vanish upon the appearance of the Enemy. The Counties of Rowan and Mecklenburg are rich in provisions and strong in men, staunch, numerous and spirited, if they were only encouraged to take the field by timely assistance. These are the facts, as near as I can collect them, respecting the Enemy's conduct and the situation of this distressed Country. A small body of Regulars, with a few Militia, and these Counties would still keep the Enemy at Bay. Our poor wounded in Camden are in a most wretched situation. Colo. Wilson told me Genl. Rutherford had no surgeon but himself, and that many of them had never been dressed. Something should be done for them; 'tis cruel. Capt. Macneal of Hamilton's Regiment, who came up with Colo. Wilson, till he met with our party, mentioned the Legion's returning last Thursday from capturing some provision wagons on their way to Nelson's Ferry.

"I am, Sir, with great respect,
"Your humbl. Servt.,
"William R. Davie." [57]

Davie's characterization of the inhabitants of Mecklenburg and Rowan Counties as "staunch, numerous and spirited" proved to be an apt description. Left to their fate by Gates and company and vis-a-vis with the entire British and Tory army, the officers of the Mecklenburg militia and some of the most influential citizens called a hurried meeting to decide what should be done. Some argued that further resistance would be temerity and would only produce certain destruction to themselves and their families. Others, in fact the majority, stoutly held out for continued resistance. Some cited South Carolina's lamentable plight as a result of capitulating to the enemy. They declared, in a phrase that recalls Churchill's patriotic eloquence over a century and a half later, that "while there was any part of the North American Continent to which the British authority did not extend, they would endeavor to occupy that." [58] It was of such heroic stands of small bands of rebels—a microcosm of the Revolution as a whole—that effective resistance to the mother country was made.

By majority vote these patriots made their decision to remain and resist. It was recommended to the commanding officer, Colonel Robert Irwin, that he encamp "somewhere to the south of Charlotte, retain half the men liable to military duty, and the other half to attend to their farms, but hold themselves in readiness to join, if the Enemy should advance." It was also recommended "that Major Davie's Cavalry (the only corps in service yet unbroken)" patrol the country next to Camden.[59]

Colonel Francis Locke, with a force of Rowan militia, soon joined Colonel Irwin. Being of equal rank, these two, according to Major Graham, came to a deadlock as to who should be the superior officer.[60] The situation was resolved by petitioning the General Assembly, on August 31, to appoint Colonel William L. Davidson, just recovered from a wound at Colson's Mill in July, to fill the vacancy of brigadier general until Rutherford was released. Among the petitioners were the two ranking colonels and Thomas Polk, Adjutant Joseph Graham, and Major William R. Davie.[61] Governor Abner Nash complied with the request and, upon recommendation of the General Assembly, dispatched the commission September 5.

By the same messenger, he forwarded a commission to Major Davie, then only twenty-four years old, appointing him "Colonel & commander of all the militia Horse acting in the Western District." [62]

Both appointments, according to Major Graham, "accorded with publick opinion and settled the difficulty referred to." The new militia general arrived at Charlotte the next day and at once began to use "every exertion to increase his numbers, and improve them in military discipline." The new cavalry colonel kept increasing his corps "as fast as the limited means of the country would admit." The supply of men and swords was limited. The latter deficiency was remedied by "several of the more ingenious blacksmiths," and scabbards and hangings were made by country shoemakers.[63] The finished products were no doubt a far cry from Damascus steel and Cordovan leather.

The general situation in Mecklenburg was greatly improved by the arrival of Brigadier General Jethro Sumner, who took command of the militia, because North Carolina had had no Regulars in the field after Charleston's fall. With him he brought about eight hundred infantry principally from Guilford, Granville, and Orange counties, along with "several troops of Cavalry which were placed under the command of Col. Davie."[64]

While the two Generals were engaged in assembling their militia, Colonel Davie with eighty dragoons and two mounted companies of Major George Davidson's riflemen set up a post at Providence, about twenty-five miles above the Waxhaws. From this advanced position, according to Lee, he was "actively employed in watching the movements of the enemy" and in "repressing their predatory excursions, which, in consequence of the devastation of the country between Camden and the Waxhaws, were extended to the latter district."*

Davie's corps had hardly established itself when, on September 8, Cornwallis began moving up the whole British army from Camden to the Waxhaws, where he soon took possession of the post which had been occupied by Davie in June and July. Here Cornwallis was faced with a serious problem of supplying his troops. Though the neighboring country contained "many rich farms," the crops had, after nine months of "continual devastation & warfare," been "neglected and destroyed, and many of the plantations intirely deserted." Moreover, Sumter's defeat had meant the capture or death "of a large part of the inhabitants of this populous settlement." Although no army could be supported "without foraging to a considerable distance," Cornwallis expected "that his detachments would meet with little interception in collecting supplies." South Carolina "appeared now entirely subjugated, and his Northern neighbour had not recovered from the panic & stupor occasioned by the dispersion of General Gate's [sic] Army, the remains of which were collecting at Hillsboro, near two hundred miles distant."

* Lee, *Memoirs*, pp. 192-93. Lee incorrectly gave Davie's post as the Waxhaws instead of Providence.

The Partisan Leader

Lord Cornwallis's encampment extended along the north side of Waxhaw Creek where His Lordship occupied the house of Major Robert Crawford as his headquarters.[65] The 71st Regiment was posted on the south side about a half mile in the rear. The Catawba River was on their left flank. The Loyalists and light troops were posted on their right. These had already begun "to spread havoc & destruction."

Having procured this information throughout the neighboring country, Colonel Davie, who knew the terrain from boyhood, could not resist the temptation to make a lightning attack on the predatory Loyalists. He conceived the idea of falling on the quarters of these "lawless Marauders" in the night, thus hoping "to check if not entirely disperse" them. With his own corps and Major Davidson's riflemen, making a total of 150, he set out towards his target, making "a considerable circuit to avoid the enemy's patrols." By two o'clock in the morning he had turned Cornwallis's right flank. After reconnoitering three different places where the Tories were said to have been encamped, he was informed at the last one that they had retired within the flanks of the British army to the plantation of Captain James Wauchope* and that "they might amount to three or four hundred mounted Infantry."

Davie pushed—or exhorted—his men on to Wauchope's. They reached the plantation as the sun was rising and at an opportune time. The British party was going out on command. Their sentries had been called in, and about sixty of them with a part of the Legion were mounted near the house, which stood in the middle of a lane covered by a cornfield up to the very door. Davie detached an infantry company through the corn, with orders to take the house and its dependencies and to fire upon the enemy. The cavalry were sent around the other end of the lane to charge the foe, as soon as the infantry opened fire, while Davie with forty riflemen advanced in front.

---

* This plantation was in the southern part of present Union County, North Carolina. The spelling of the captain's name is variously spelled Wahab, Wahub, and Walkup. According to his great-grandson, William Henry Belk, the correct spelling is the one given here.—Legette Blythe, *William Henry Belk: Merchant of the South* (Chapel Hill: The University of North Carolina Press, 1950), p. 18. Yet according to a grandson of this officer, the correct spelling was Walkup, though "the neighbors still frequently miscal us [Wahab]."—Samuel H. Walkup (Monroe, N.C.) to David L. Swain, Sept. 25, 1857. David L. Swain Papers, S.H.C.

William R. Davie

The ensuing encounter between Davie and Tarleton was dramatically described by Davie:

"... the Houses were briskly attacked, and the Cavalry charged at the same moment. The enemy being completely surprised had no time to form and crowded in great disorder to the other end of the lane when a well reserved fire from the rifle men drove them back upon the cavalry and Infantry who were now drawn up at the Houses, & by whom they were instantly attacked; thus pushed vigorously on all sides they fluctuated some moments under the impressions of terror & dismay and then bore down the fences, and fled in full speed. The Colonels situation was too Hazardous to risque any time in pursuit; the horses and arms were ordered to be collected, and in a few minutes, the Infantry were all mounted, and the surplus horses secured: The 71st regiment had beat to arms in the beginning of the action and upon finding this was the only object moved briskly to attack the detachment, but as they entered one end of the lane the Americans were marching out of the other in good order, The British left fifteen or 20 dead on the field and had about forty wounded; they were surprised, pushed off their reflection, & made no resistance so that only one man of the Americans was wounded and that by mistake, being unwarily seperated in the pursuit, and having no regimentals he was not distinguishable from the enemy."

Tarleton then, "out of pique or a mistaken & cruel policy," set fire to the houses, barns, and fences, though there were three families of women and children living there. Captain Wauchope himself, a volunteer under Davie, had been separated from his family for some time. His wife, née Margaret Pickens (a first cousin of General Andrew Pickens), and children had been in the midst of the action. Afterwards they had time only to gather around him "in tears of joy and distraction" before the advance of the enemy forced him to tear himself away. As this detachment moved off, he looked back "to see their only hope of subsistence wrapt in flames."

Davie maintained that this "barbarous practice was uniformly enacted by the British officers in the Southern States," and that "however casual the encounter might be," their remaining in possession of a plantation was "always marked by committing the Houses to the flames."

From this affair with Tarleton, Davie "brought off ninety six horses with their furniture, & one hundred & twenty stand of arms." He boasted—and justly—that he "arrived at his camp the same afternoon, having performed a march of sixty miles in less than twenty four Hours, notwithstanding the time employed in seeking & beating the enemy."

All other accounts of this daring raid conform in general to Davie's description. According to Dr. Alexander Garden, who served in Lee's Legion and was later an aide-de-camp to Greene, "Sixty of the enemy were left on the ground... with the loss of but one man." [66] General Sumner, from his camp at McAlpine's Creek eight miles below Charlotte, wrote General Gates four days later that Davie "fell in with a party of Tories, supposed 130, surprised them, killed 14, & took two prisoners & 46 Horses, sadles, &c. the others dispersed; his party received no damage except one wounded." [67] Writing on the same day to Gates, General Davidson, then eight miles south of Charlotte, reported Davie's exploit as "Killed, 12; on the ground, wounded, by our best intelligence, about 60, and brought off one prisoner, and the Colonel made good his retreat with 50 Horses, as many saddles, 13 guns, etc." He also reported that Cornwallis was still at Waxhaw Creek where he was "collecting reinforcements from the Militia, fattening his Horses, and Carrying off every article valuable to our Army." His strength was estimated at about twelve hundred, "with one piece of Artillery—perhaps near one-half of his number Tories." [68]

When Davie returned to his camp, he found that Generals Sumner and Davidson had arrived that day with their two brigades of militia "both of which However did not amount to one thousand men all on short enlistments, illy armed, and diminishing every day." This body, with Davie's corps of two hundred men, constituted the entire force immediately opposing the advancing enemy.

Lord Cornwallis soon changed his mind as to the supplies to be obtained from the Waxhaws. Finding his supply situation woefully inadequate, he decided to carry the war into North Carolina. Four days after Davie's affair at Wauchope's, the patrols brought back information that the enemy was on the march towards Charlotte.*

---

* According to Davie they marched up the Steele Creek Road, which runs southwest by Charlotte. Contemporary maps will show that this is obviously an error—into which Lee also fell.—Lee, *Memoirs*, p. 196.

WILLIAM R. DAVIE

On the twenty-fifth they encamped between McAlpine's and Sugar creeks, ten miles south of Charlotte.[69] Upon news of their approach, Sumner and Davidson retreated at once towards Salisbury by the nearest route, which led them by Phifers, about twenty miles from Charlotte.* Colonel Davie was ordered "to attend the enemy's motions and skirmish with their front." With a corps of only 150 dragoons and mounted infantry and some volunteers under Major Joseph Graham, this party "hovered round the British army."

At four o'clock in the afternoon, Davie hurriedly wrote General Sumner that the British had halted about one mile on the Charlotte side of McAlpine's Creek, though for how long or in what numbers, he did not know. He further reported that "Small parties are marauding and plundering the Country several miles from the principal Body." His men, on the other hand, had taken four prisoners.† He would "keep parties down every Route and wait here [Charlotte] for further orders." In closing he added: "I think his Lordship takes it as leashurely as a party of pleasure."[70]

No doubt his estimate of his Lordship's "party of pleasure" was somewhat changed by the next morning, for he dispatched a letter to Sumner at eight o'clock, reporting that "The Enemy were in motion at day break and if they march on will reach this place by ten." He wished "about two hundred light Infantry" were detached to him, as "It would perhaps be in my power to check the enemy more considerably," and pleaded for a reinforcement of horse "as the Horse I have are few and fatigued." He confidently closed by promising to send intelligence every five or six hours.[71]

Shortly thereafter, Davie's patrols were driven in by the enemy's light troops. In a few minutes Tarleton's Legion and the light troops were seen advancing towards the town, followed by the entire army.

---

* According to Lee, Sumner kept on towards Salisbury until he crossed the Yadkin at Trading Ford, while General Davidson halted behind Mallard's Creek, where the Salisbury road crosses it, eight miles northeast of Charlotte. —Lee, *Memoirs*, p. 239.

† According to Major Graham, Davie requested him to take his men, as they were "best acquainted with the country," and go down to the enemy's lines and relieve a party which had been out for two days. He relieved them in the afternoon and that night at a nearby farm he seized four stragglers in search of milk and sent them back to Davie.—Hoyt (ed.), *Murphey Papers*, II, 239.

Tarleton himself was indisposed; thus Davie was not to encounter his former adversary face to face. Instead, the Legion was led by the eccentric and profligate Major George Hanger, later a member of the "fast set" which revolved around the Prince of Wales, later George IV.*

The town of Charlotte, as described by Davie, was situated on rising ground and contained "about twenty Houses built on two streets which cross each other at right angles in the intersection of which stands the Court-House." Graham further described this edifice as "a frame building raised on eight brick pillars ten feet from the ground, which was the most elevated in the place. Between the pillars was erected a wall of rock three and a half feet high and the open basement answered as a market house for the town." [72] On the approaching enemy's left was an open common; the right was "covered with underwood up to the gardens."

Relying on "the firmness of the militia" and reinforced by Graham with fourteen volunteers,† Davie "determined to give his Lordship some earnest of what he might expect in No. Carolina." Resolutely and boldly he posted one company under the courthouse where they were covered breast-high by a stone wall. He advanced the other two companies about eighty yards and posted them behind some houses and gardens on each side of the street. Here is Davie's own description of his gallant delaying action: ‡

"... while this disposition was making the legion was forming at the distance of three hundred yards with a front to fill the street,

---

* Charles Stedman, *The History of ... the American War* (Dublin: Printed for Messrs. F. Hogan [et al.], 1794), II, 216; Wheeler, *Historical Sketches of N.C.*, II, 195; McCrady, *S.C. in the Rev., 1775-1780*, pp. 604-5n. Later the author of several books, Hanger prophesied in one of them, *The Life and Opinions of Colonel George Hanger*, that eventually the Northern and Southern states would fight as vigorously against each other as they had done in unison against the British.

† Major Graham, writing in 1832, maintained he had fifty volunteers under his command.—*S.R.*, XIX, 958; *ibid.*, XXII, 122.

‡ For a more detailed account, see that of Major Graham in William H. Hoyt (ed.), *The Papers of Archibald D. Murphey* (Raleigh: Publications of the North Carolina Historical Commission, 1914), II, 240-44. Graham felt that Lee, who had got his account of the action at Wauchope's and other affairs from Davie, had "very imperfectly described" the "rencounter in Charlotte and at the cross roads."—*Ibid.*, p. 239; Gen. Jos. Graham to Judge A. D. Murphey, Nov. 27, 1820. *S.R.*, XIX, 968-69.

and the light Infantry on their flank; on sounding the charge the cavalry advanced in full gallop within sixty yds. of the Court-house when the Americans received orders to fire, This fell with such effect among the cavalry that they retreated with great precipitation, as the light Infantry behaved with more resolution, and were pressing forward on our right flank notwithstanding a warm fire from the volunteers, who were too few to keep them in check, it became necessary to withdraw the two advanced companies and they were formed in a line with those at the Court House, The flanks were hotly engaged with the Infantry but the center were directed to reserve their fire for the cavalry, who rallied on their former ground, and returned to the charge. They were again well received by the militia and galloped off in the outmost confusion, in the presence of the whole British army, the Legion infantry were now beginning to turn the Colonels right flank, and the companies were drawn off in good order successively covering each other and formed in a single line at the end of the street about one hundred yards from the Court-house under a galing fire from the British light infantry who advanced under the cover of the Houses and gardens, The British cavalry soon appeared again, charging in columns by the Court-house, but on receiving a fire reserved for them by a part of the militia, they wheeled off behind the Houses, Lord Cornwallis vexed at the repeated repulses of his cavalry, [rode up in person and said, 'Legion! Remember, you have everything to lose, but nothing to gain'].* The Legion Infantry thus reinforced pressed forward rapidly on their flanks, The ground was no longer tenable by the handfull of brave men, and a retreat was ordered by the Salisbury road; the enemy followed with great caution & respect for some miles, when they at length ventured to charge the rear guard, The guard were of course put to flight, but on receiving a fire from a single company the Cavalry again retreated, The loss of the Americans consisted of Lt. Locke † and 4 privates killed Major Graham and five privates wounded. The British stated their loss at 12 non-commissioned officers killed and wounded Major Hanger, Capts. Campbell & McDonald wounded with about thirty privates."

* This exhortation, omitted by Davie, came from Stedman, *Hist. of the Amer. War*, II, 239.
† George Locke, the son of Matthew Locke, of Rowan County, North Carolina.—Wheeler, *Historical Sketches of N.C.*, II, 384.

Davie's own justification of the defense seems to be a fitting one, marked by restraint in self-praise and by admiration for the militia:

"This action, altho' it carries a charge of temerity on the part of Col Davie and can only be excused by the event and that zeal which we are allways ready to applaud, furnishes a very striking instance of the bravery and importance of the American Militia; few examples can be shewn of any troops who in one action changed their position twice in good order although pressed by a much superior body of Infantry and charged three times by thrice their number of Cavalry, unsupported & in the presence of the enemys whole army and finally retreating in perfect order. The British chagrined to see their laurels snatched from their army by this detachment of Militia loudly charged the Legion with pusillanimity, while they excused themselves by saying that the confidence with which the Americans acted induced them to apprehend an ambuscade; surely no maneuvre of this kind could be seriously expected in an open village in open day."

This latter explanation of the British pusillanimity was taken from two British sources. Tarleton reported that the "conduct of the Americans created suspicion in the British: An ambuscade was apprehended by the light troops, who moved forwards for some time with great circumspection" until a charge of Major Hanger's cavalry "dissipated this ill-grounded jealousy, & totally dispersed the militia."[73] Taking exception to this statement, Roderick Mackenzie, lieutenant of the 71st Regiment, maintained that though Major Hanger was wounded "in attempting to lead the dragoons to this charge...no entreaties of his, no exertions of their officers, could, upon this occasion, induce the legion cavalry to approach the American militia" and that they "retreated without fulfilling the intention of the General." Whereupon, Cornwallis, "much dissatisfied, ordered the light and legion infantry to dislodge the enemy, which they immediately effected."[74]

There is also a division of opinion as to the pursuit by the British. Tarleton, stating that the pursuit "lasted some time," claimed that "about thirty of the enemy were killed and taken."[75] Graham was more specific, claiming that he, in command of the reserve, "covered the retreat of the Americans by molesting the advance of the whole British cavalry and a battalion of infantry for four miles, where, at Sassafras fields, with Davie out of supporting distance, a charge was made. As a result, Graham received nine wounds which compelled him to be hospitalized for two months." No part of the British army went more than two miles more on the Salisbury road.[76]

Graham, quite understandably, had no praise for Davie's action at Charlotte. He felt that it would have been "better policy," if, instead of attacking "a Regular army completely organized of ten times their number," these "three or four hundred mounted Militiamen, of whom not one-fourth were equipped as Cavalry," had kept fresh and "been in readiness to strike the foraging parties, which his new position would soon have compelled him to send out, and thus endeavored to take him by detail." He felt that the "small damage sustained in proportion to the risk, appeared providential."[77] Davidson, however, though mortified that the British had established their headquarters at Charlotte, did not fail to cite Colonel Davie, "our gallant partizan," for his defense of the village.[78]

Whether Davie is to be censured or applauded for this action, Stedman's conclusion cannot be denied that "The whole of the British army was actually kept at bay for some minutes by a few mounted Americans," which he said did not exceed twenty in number.[79]

That night Davie retired behind Rocky River, sixteen miles from Charlotte and four miles in front of General Davidson who was at Phifer's plantation.[80] Davidson wrote to Gates that night, reporting that "at 11 O'Clock the Enemy marched into Charlotte in force," where "Col. Davie Skirmished with them...and for several hours Since, retreating as pr Express." About two o'clock he had been reinforced by "about 300 Cavalry and infantry," but Davidson had not heard from him since. Sent by Davidson, they carried orders for Davie "to continue Skirmishing with them to cover our retreat." He further reported that the "inhabitants are flying before us in consternation, and except we are soon reinforced, the West side of Yadkin must inevitably fall a pray to the enemy" and that Rowan was able to give "very little assistance, on account of Col. Fergusons movements to the Westward."[81]

That same night, Lord Cornwallis was no doubt gratified by the situation in general. With Major Patrick Ferguson protecting his left and Major Archibald McArthur, commander of the 71st Regiment,[82] on his right, he expected to roll up North Carolina and be free to invade Virginia. His disillusionment was swift. "The spirit of this part of the country" and "the vigilance of Davidson and Davie" precluded him from learning "the force or the disposition of the troops collecting in his front." [83] Although the town of Charlotte itself, according to Tarleton, "afforded some conveniences," these were "blended with great disadvantages." In fact, the "aptness of its intermediate situation between Camden and Salisbury" and the number of mills in the neighborhood "did not counterbalance its defects," chief of which were that the town and environs "abounded with inveterate enemies," the neighboring plantations were "small and uncultivated," the roads were narrow, crossing in every direction, and "the whole face of the country covered with close and thick woods." Tarleton's next sentences are familiar to every student of North Carolina history: "In addition to these disadvantages, no estimation could be made of the sentiments of half the inhabitants of North Carolina, whilst the royal army remained at Charlotte town. It was evident, and it had been frequently mentioned to the King's officers, that the counties of Mecklenburg and Rohan [sic] were more hostile to England than any others in America." [84]

No doubt Tarleton had Davie and Davidson chiefly in mind when he wrote: "The vigilance and animosity of these surrounding districts checked the exertions of the well affected, and totally destroyed all communications between the King's troops and the loyalists in the other parts of the province. No British commander could obtain any information in that position, which would facilitate his designs, or guide his future conduct." [85]

On the morning of September 27, Davie made a hurried ride to Salisbury, where his corps was augmented by the regiment of Colonel John Taylor of Granville County. This reinforcement, according to General Sumner, amounted to "200 infantry and about 60 horse." [86] This gave him a command of "near three hundred mounted Infantry with a few dragoons." While Generals Sumner and Davidson continued their retreat beyond the Yadkin above Salisbury, Davie returned to the environs of Charlotte. Since his force was "insufficient to make any impression on the enemy" at Charlotte, all he could do was "to confine them if possible to the Town by attacking their foraging parties, and to distress them by cuting off their supplies." With this objective, Davie posted his men within fifteen and twenty miles of Charlotte and detached parties on all sides "to watch and harrass the enemy." Aware of Davie's dare-devil tactics, General Sumner had given him "express orders to remain always with the principal body in the direction between Salisbury & Charlotte, and by no means to risque being generally engaged." Though these orders limited his operations, Davie, never over-modest, wrote that "much was done by his perfect knowledge of the Country and the daring bravery of the militia under his command." As a result, "no party of the enemy ventured out without being attacked, and often retired with considerable loss." He did not fail, however, to give due credit to the inhabitants of the neighboring country who were "strongly attached to the American cause, and gave his Lordship no assistance." Under these circumstances "all information was cut off by the vigilance and activity of the militia cavalry," so that "His Lordship began to feel the greatest distress, under this species of blockade, for provisions forage and all the necessary supplies of any army."

Meanwhile the threatened rising of the Yadkin forced Sumner and Davidson to retire on the night of September 27 or 28 across the river above Salisbury. From this retreat, Sumner reported to John Penn that "the people of Mecklenburg County are very spirited, and a majority will be in the field in a day or two."[87] He also reported to General Gates on September 29, that on his retreat from Charlotte he had "endeavored to bring off all the public stores there, and effected it." He thoughtfully added that he had detached Colonel Davie and Colonel Taylor to remain in the vicinity "and prevent the enemy's plundering the inhabitants."[88]

Gates was none too pleased with Sumner's actions. After upbraiding him for not forwarding the express letter he had received from Davie, he proceeded to the more important point: "If you should have been obliged to cross the Yadkin—you must under no Account abandon the Defence of that Ford, nor withdraw your Guard from the West Side of that River, until you are by the near Approach of a superior Number of the Enemy obliged to do it." After informing Sumner that General Butler and "the Virginians near Guilford" had orders to join him, Gates resorted to sarcasm: "You seem to conceive the Importance of the Pass at the Yadkin—you must be answerable if that is too soon abandoned." To reinforce him, he was also sending General Smallwood and Colonel Daniel Morgan. Complaining that it had been "40 hours since the Arrival of your Letter Dated the

26th. Inst. from Phifers," he again upbraided him for not dispatching an express every six hours or oftener.[89]

The following day Gates had still not received "the smallest Intelligence" from Sumner, but had heard from a sergeant of the Maryland Troops that "Colonel Davie and all the Horse were at Salisbury." He reiterated that General Smallwood and Colonel Morgan would join Sumner as soon as they could march there, adding that he, Gates, would follow "if necessary." Until then, Smallwood was to assume top command over all. His parting injunction was for Sumner to make his camp "as strong as possible" and not to "abandon your Ground so long as you can maintain your Post."[90]

Davie, writing to Sumner on the same day from a "flying Camp" at Phifer's, reported that on the preceding night, Colonel Taylor, detached to reconnoiter the enemy, had reported that "a detachment of 2800 of the British marched that morning from Charlotte, partly foot, partly Horse, with two pieces of Artillery in the direction of the Catawba, near Tuckasegie Ford." Here a captain's command, dispatched by Davie, reported that the "Enemy are cajoling & flattering the People to take Paroles, & pursuing the same steps they did in South Carolina." This fact, continued Davie, coupled with "the Panic of the People, is an alarming circumstance." Since the British were reported as foraging "largely & carelessly below," Davie felt that "a few rifle light infantry companies might perhaps be of singular service," if Sumner deemed it "requisite and safe." In the event they were sent, Davie would "endeavor to support them." He was convinced that the British by "their paroling the People, bringing large quantities of liquors with them & provision," had serious intentions "to subjugate this State, but their halting & marching so slowly is unaccountable; but of a piece with their conduct in other places."[91]

The following day, on receipt of a letter from Sumner, dated "Camp on the Yadkin 29th ulto," Gates was in a more conciliatory mood and "entirely approved" of Sumner's proceedings, but he felt that a party of 250 infantry should have been detached to Davie, as "it would have been a good Support to ye Cavalry." He furthermore pledged Sumner every "Succour and Support in my power" and promised that he would "prepare the Moment it is necessary to join you with all the Continental Troops, collected and collecting, in Hillsborough."[92]

William R. Davie

On October 5, 1780, General Davidson, at the forward camp at Phifer's, planned to detach Colonel Davie the next evening "with 150 Foot and Horse... to show himself on the Enemy's Lines."[93] There is no record as to whether this plan was executed, but on that day Davie was able to report to Sumner that the enemy were said to be "reinforced Saturday or sunday last with the 2 Battalions of the 71st. & some Field pieces. They Forage, but in large parties of 2 or 300."[94]

The actual strength of Davie's corps at this time, according to Davidson, was four hundred, of which 183 were composed of "the Minute Horse." Some of these latter were "ingaged for no fixed term, & are chiefly on detached Commands near the lines."[95]

His forces in this period took "a good number of prisoners," of which "70 or 80 were brought to Hillsborough" around the first of October. Eighteen of them were British, the others Tories.[96] As to the disposition or treatment of these Tories, there was some doubt. Apparently in reply to a letter of inquiry from Sumner, Davie knew of "no particular crime" they had committed "but the general one of their being *King's Militia*." Though they considered themselves as His Majesty's subjects, Davie did not know "on what principle they ought to be treated—whether exchange or punishment,"[97] but he felt strongly that immediate notice should be taken of those "of our fellow citizens who have taken parole." He strongly condemned "so-bare-faced a strategem."[98]

Despite the evidences of Cornwallis's "serious intentions to subjugate this State," as reported by Davie on October 1, his plans were suddenly changed by news of the defeat and destruction of Major Ferguson's forces and of their commander's death at King's Mountain on October 7. Interestingly enough, there was found on Ferguson's body a letter which Cornwallis had written to him September 23, as his Lordship was about to move up from the Waxhaws to Charlotte. In this letter he informed Ferguson that he had "heard a report that a Major Davie, who commands a corps of about eighty horse militia, had marched against you."[99] Lyman C. Draper, it would seem, attributed unwarranted emphasis to the importance of this threat from Davie when he said that it was "possible... that Ferguson might have felt the necessity of feeling his way cautiously out of his difficulties; that while evading the mountaineers on the one hand, he should not run recklessly into other dangers," in the form of Davie's cavalry, "which Ferguson's apprehensions, and Tory fears, may have magnified into a much larger body than eighty dragoons." [100]

Though King's Mountain was undoubtedly the chief cause of Cornwallis's decision to evacuate Charlotte, due allowance should be made for the fact that "their situation at Charlotte hath been rendered very troublesome by the close Attention paid them by Davidson and Davie who, with Colonel Morgan are now hanging on and greatly distress them." [101]

The date of Cornwallis's departure has been given variously as October 9 [102] and October 14. [103] However, the true date of the departure of the main army was October 12, as seen by the correspondence of Davidson, Sumner, and Gates. On the night of the ninth, Davidson had "nothing new to communicate" to Sumner, except that his Lordship had, on the eighth drawn two days' provisions and had ordered all to be in readiness to march." This order, unknown to the Americans, was the result of Ferguson's express of October 5, which he received October 7, from Gilberttown (near the present town of Rutherfordton) announcing the approach of the over-mountain men. [104] Davidson also said that Davie was "very sick" and that he did not know what he would do "should he be rendered unfit for duty." [105]

Before seven o'clock on the morning of October 13, Davidson dispatched a report to Sumner that he had, the day before, "received Intelligence of a party of the Enemy's marching out of Charlotte towards Beger's Ferry on Catawba River consisting of 800 with on [one] Field piece." He had also had "a Report by a Man of Veracity just arrived from within 6 Miles that the Enemy have evacuated Charlotte, and that last Night at 10 o'Clock the Rear of the Army passed Barnett's Creek, five miles beyond Charlotte on the road to Beggar's Ferry"—a report that was confirmed at midnight by five Tories who had deserted in the evening. Apparently Davie had recovered from his illness because on the previous evening he had been "in the Neighbourhood of Charlotte, with a sufficient force to Gall the Enemy in the Rear." [106]

At seven o'clock in the morning Davidson was informed that the rear of the enemy had left Charlotte at four o'clock on the twelfth. His informer was William McCafferty, variously described as "a merchant, a Whig at heart, who had remained in Charlotte to save his property,"[107] an Irish merchant,[108] and as "a Presbyterian fanatick from Glasgow, the ambiguity of whose faith did not escape the discernment" of Cornwallis.[109] Nor was he trusted by Davidson. McCafferty had led the British to "Barnets Creek 5 Miles below Town, on the Road to Armours Ford."[110] Before reaching this place, according to Major Graham, McCafferty suggested that they were on the wrong road and that it was necessary for him to ride out to the left to find the right road. Just out of sight he wheeled about and rode nearly all night to reach General Davidson, to whom he communicated the retreat.*

Thanks to McCafferty's duplicity, the British army spent a wretched and terrified night. Not only was it dark and rainy but they were completely lost, stumbling through "thick woods, briars, deep ravines, marshes, and creeks scarcely fordable."[111] They became separated in the woods; by midnight they were three or four miles apart, panic-stricken lest the Americans should come upon them. Not until noon the next day were they able to reconcentrate seven miles below Charlotte, having left behind, according to Graham, "forty wagons and considerable booty" near Barnett's Mill.[112] Davie reported this as "twenty waggons containing a large part of the baggage of the 71st regiment & legion Infantry."

Immediately on learning from Davidson of the departure of the British, Sumner, stationed at the forks of the Yadkin, wrote Gates the night of the thirteenth that he would "recross the River Tomorrow, or early next Monday, with all the Troops at the place ... and march after the Enemy, so as to annoy as much as possible, preventing General Action."[113]

Davidson, meanwhile, had marched on the night of the thirteenth to Charlotte, where he found that the enemy were on the way to Old Nation Ford on the Catawba. They had, it appeared, left Charlotte in alarm "from what circumstances uncertain." Deserters had informed Davidson that they had received reports of General Clinton's defeat at West Point; other informers said that it was rumored the

---

* Hoyt (ed.), *Murphey Papers*, II, 252-53. Graham said that he rode to Davie's encampment, but this is obviously a mistake, as seen by Davidson's letter to Sumner, dated October 13, at 7 o'clock, and as will be seen by a later letter, Davidson to Sumner, October 14, 1780.

Americans had been reinforced with five thousand men. The inhabitants said the British "left their Kettles on the fire; & twenty Waggons which they left 5 miles from town, with a quantity of Valuable loading have fallen into our hands." Sumner had also found out that Colonel Davie, who was out with "140 Horse," had been "unfortunate enough not to hear of their movements till four o'clock last evening," but that he had at once set out in pursuit, "with all the Cavalry, except two Troops." An express from Davie had just informed him that "the enemy laid last night eleven miles from town, on the road to Nation-Ford."[114]

As soon as Davie heard of the retreat, he immediately marched on through Charlotte, whence he sent a reconnoitering party ahead, who came upon the British as they were reconcentrating after their night of frustration. Davie's spies, who kept up with them for three or four miles, reported that "their rear guard was composed of nearly half their Cavalry and marched in close order." Their march was "so condensed and in such perfect order, that, though Davie marched parallel to them, at a distance of three quarters of a mile, it was impossible to attack them without encountering at the same time, their whole army." That night Davie returned to Sugar Creek while the British proceeded southward by slow marches.[115]

Perhaps this excursion was the one to which Davie was referring when he wrote Sumner that he "hung on their flank till they arrived at the river," but that he "found no opportunity of skirmishing, as they marched in close order, with large flanking parties, and the old Indian fields gave them great advantage." His men had had no provisions for two days and the evening was rainy. They were therefore obliged to retreat.[116]

The following day, October 16, Davie reported to Sumner that the enemy's baggage had arrived at Old Nation Ford about three o'clock the previous day, after which Davie "was under the necessity of retreating and marching all night thro' the heaviest rain ever poor fellow lived through." As a result, "not a gun will fire in the corps, and the ammunition, for want of cartridge boxes, is principally lost." This meant it would be "three or four days" before he could move again. Tarleton, with two hundred dragoons and four hundred of the infantry mounted, had crossed the river two days before Cornwallis arrived at the ford and was being pursued by Sumter with

2,500 men. Cornwallis, moreover, had never been in "such a pound." The Catawba had risen too high to be fordable, with "Sugar Creek in the same condition to the Southward of him," and there was not "one mouthful of provisions or forage to be gotten within several miles." Davie felt that a "few troops would make him very uneasy."[117]

Sumner, too, wished that he and Davie "might by detachments annoy the enemy more effectually." He informed Davie that he was recrossing the Yadkin "with all possible diligence" and would march forward to join him without loss of time.[118]

After waiting impatiently two days to cross the Catawba at Old Nation Ford, Cornwallis's army, which was in "a miserable situation without supplies, surrounded by Militia Cavalry who prevented all foraging," marched precipitately down the east side of the Catawba. For want of provisions and ammunition Davie could not follow for several hours,[119] but soon caught up with them and "continued skirmishing with their rear" during the whole march. On the nineteenth they "completely evacuated the State," crossed the Catawba at Landsford, and continued on to Winnsborough, "which had the advantages of lying in the midst of spacious plantations between the Broad and Wateree Rivers and of being in the position to support the two important British posts of Camden and Ninety-Six." This evacuation of the state served as a stimulus to the spirits and enlistments of the patriots of North Carolina. There was, indeed, "an unusual alacrity in assembling,"[120] while at the same time the government of the state was given a respite in which to analyze the situation and gird itself for the impending danger. Aware of the appalling shortages of equipment, clothing, and ammunition and of the distressing lack of organization and leadership, the General Assembly, meeting at Hillsborough on August 23, had seen fit to try to remedy the situation. Because Governor Abner Nash had "so strongly represented his lack of authority without the Council, and complained so bitterly of his councilors' neglect of their duties," the Assembly conferred all the war powers of the governor and council upon a Board of War composed of Alexander Martin, John Penn, and Orondates Davis.[121] Yet this desperate step was unpopular with the army and, of course, with Governor Nash. Davie in particular was vehement in his denunciation. "Nothing could be more ridiculous," he said, "than the manner this Board was filled. Alexander the Little, being a Warrior of great fame, was placed at the head of the board—Penn who was only fit to amuse children, and O. Davis who knew nothing but the game of Whist composed the rest of the Board."

Yet two of these men—Alexander Martin and John Penn—were to receive two of the highest offices the state was able to confer. Martin was elected governor for six terms, twice exhausting the constitutional limit of three successive terms. He was also elected to the Continental Congress in 1786 and to the Federal Convention the following year.[122] Davie's animosity to him was perhaps based on his arrest for cowardice at the battle of Germantown, though he was acquitted by a court-martial. Or, more likely, it was based on Martin's break with the Federalists in 1790. Penn had not only been one of the state's three signers of the Declaration of Independence, but had continued to represent North Carolina in Philadelphia, 1777-1780.[123] Of Orondates, or Oroondates, Davis, little is known, except that he had been a lawyer in Halifax, the clerk of the Halifax Committee of Safety, 1774 and 1775, and senator from Halifax in the General Assembly, 1778-1781.[124]

This board, which so evoked the wrath of Davie, was given extra-constitutional powers for raising, organizing, and equipping the troops. Its most immediate task had been the selection of a competent commanding officer. With Gates's reputation "irrevokably lost," and Caswell's having "suffered only less than Gates," the Assembly settled on a Marylander as "the only general officer who survived the rout at Camden with an increased reputation for courage and military talent"—William Smallwood. Upon his appointment as major general, Caswell indignantly resigned and retired to his home at Kingston.[125]

As a result of this reorganization and the increased ardor occasioned by Cornwallis's retreat, North Carolina in October and part of November had about a thousand militia under the commands of Brigadier Generals Davidson and Sumner, nine hundred men under Allen Jones, about three hundred under Colonel Davie, in addition to approximately fourteen hundred troops of the mountaineer colonels, William Campbell, Isaac Shelby, John Sevier, Charles McDowell, and Benjamin Cleveland.[126]

Meanwhile Gates's shattered army had been reorganized at Hillsborough. The "broken lines" of the Maryland and Delaware troops were compressed into one regiment under Colonel Otho Williams of Maryland. Daniel Morgan, of Virginia, promoted to the rank of brigadier by brevet, was placed at the head of the recruits of the Virginia line who had just come down. The cavalry was reorganized under Colonel William Washington, also of Virginia. All told, Gates now had about fourteen hundred Continentals under his command. Morgan's corps and Washington's cavalry, dispatched westward, had reached Salisbury as Cornwallis retreated from Charlotte. After forming a juncture with Davidson they encamped on Six Mile Creek, about twelve miles south of Charlotte, where they remained some time.[127] General Gates, after making these dispositions, moved up to Charlotte. By these actions, he had, in the eyes of Lee, if not of Congress and the nation, presented "a strong contrast to his former conduct, and afforded a consoling presumption that he had discovered his past error, and had profitted by the correction of adversity."[128]

The forces of the three militia brigadiers, Davidson, Sumner, and Allen Jones, took post about twelve miles south of Charlotte, at Providence. Here, on October 22, Smallwood arrived to assume command, while Davie's cavalry advanced as far as Landsford on the Catawba. When Smallwood arrived, he found "the British had just crossed the Catawba at Lands Ford." Deeming it "ineligible" to follow with his "small Force, especially as we should have the River in our Rear, and no certainty of being supplied otherwise than from this side," he detached a "party of Colo. Davie's Horse... to watch their Motions." Davie returned with the intelligence that Cornwallis, with three hundred sick and non-effectives, "had taken rout down to the Ferry opposite Camden," while Tarleton's Legion, the light troops, and the Tories had taken the "rout of Fishing Creek, with a view, it is supposed, to proceed down the main Road to Charles Town, and to collect all the Provision on that rout."[129]

Though Tarleton's Legion did not proceed down the road to Charleston, but joined his Lordship at Winnsborough,[130] he was not remiss in collecting provisions. Davie wrote from the Waxhaws to Smallwood on November 7 that his detachment to Lynch's Creek had reported that "the British had all the beef cattle drove out of that country before the first of November, and that there is no wheat at their plantations." Another of Davie's parties, just returned from the neighborhood of Winnsborough, reported that they had left the enemy there the preceding morning, that the Legion had been to Camden for shirts and boots, but had returned, and that "the enemy had made no arrangement indicative of any *particular* movement, but were busy in bringing the provisions from Broad River and ordering in their militia." [131]

Tarleton, on Cornwallis's orders, was meanwhile engaged in a vain pursuit of the elusive "Swamp Fox," Francis Marion, who had been hovering in the recesses of the Pee Dee and Black rivers, darting out whenever an opportunity presented itself. At the same time, Cornwallis was being harassed on the east by the "Game Cock," Thomas Sumter. Both of these partisans had recently been elevated to brigadier generals by Governor John Rutledge.[132]

While Marion was eluding Tarleton, Sumter gave notice to the "remnant of the Whigs in the Upper part of So. Carolina" to rendezvous at Fishdam ford on the Broad River, only about twenty miles from Winnsborough. When Sumter had first tried to assemble the militia in this section he had, according to Davie, been surprised that "so large a number of the leading characters had fallen" and that it was "extremely difficult to collect the remaining Whigs," because they were "so dreadfully terrified by their past misfortunes." However, after the defeat of Ferguson, the retreat of Cornwallis, and the proximity of Smallwood, Morgan, and Davie, "their numbers became respectable." So public had been the orders for assembling that Cornwallis had immediate notice of it and at once dispatched Major James Wemyss, with the 63rd Regiment and about forty of the Legion cavalry, to disperse them.

The ensuing affair, reported by Gordon and Lee as a victory,[133] was erroneously represented, according to Davie in his "Sketches." The latter's version seems to be more nearly correct on the basis of a letter written by him to Smallwood on November 10, in which he said he had "just had the mortification to hear of General Sumter's army surprised on Wednesday night at Fish Dam Ford on Broad River. There are several of his men here, so there is no doubt of the fact." Though he was "just moving down to forage on the creeks below [the Waxhaws]," he had turned back upon this news.[134]

Davie's version of the fight was that Major Wemyss had approached the unsuspecting Americans about midnight and had fallen upon the pickets, who were routed and pursued into camp. The startled Americans had "instinctively seized their arms, and sought their individual safety as chance or recollection served them." As they retired, many of them fired on the enemy "who were engaged near the fires which gave light enough to make them a certain mark." The militia were dispersed in a few minutes, and Sumter escaped from his tent into the river just as the enemy entered it. Wemyss, wounded early in the action, was carried to a neighboring house and his troops, dispirited, "retreated so hastily that they did not carry off their wounded." The next morning about a hundred Americans, "finding every thing quiet ventured to reconoitre the camp... and, joined by those who were collecting under the orders of the General, took a more secure position by crossing Broad-river."

A sequel to this affair was told by Davie in his "Sketches," a more embellished version of which was later printed in the *Charleston Courier*, March 7, 1823. This latter version was submitted by Parson Mason L. Weems, on the basis of the story told to him by Davie.[135]

Davie's story forms one of the few light touches in a period of gloom and despair:

"Many of the Americans had brought with them into camp small contributions of spirits upon which they had made merry with their friends, among these was a Gentleman by the name of Crawford upwards of 60 years of life who had been always distingd. [for?] his patriotic zeal and that kind of enterprising spirit that courted every danger in the cause of Freedom. This veteran pleased with the prospect of seeing his country again in arms, had spent the eveng. jovially with his friends. About 11 O'clock he sunk into the arms of sleep overpowered by fatigue and copious libations of whisky. The surprise and dispersion of the camp had not disturbed his slumbers, towards day two wounded British soldiers crawled to the fire where he lay, and supposing Crawford to be dead, carelessly kicked him out of the way. This unceremonious treatment rousing the old man from his slumbers, he challenged them in an angry tone for their rudeness; the poor fellows declared they tho't he had been killed in the action, and being dead had no farther occasion for the fire, and concluded with emploring his forgiveness and protection. [He] shouldered a musket that lay by him, and immediately exclaimed 'By the God of battles I kin claim the ground and the victory for the Americans.' This patriotic veteran was found by his companions next morning walking as if on duty with the most soldierly composure near his prisoners."

The day after this last affair, November 11, Davie reported to Smallwood that he had "sent up twenty one wagons, loaded with corn," from the stores he had collected from the heads of the Waxhaw and Lenin creeks, the latter of which rises a few miles distant from the former. He had also examined the plantations on Berkleys and Gills creeks, about twelve miles from Waxhaw Creek, but could find no more than 140 bushels of corn there, all of which was "standing in the fields, detached at considerable distance from each other, through a wild and almost pathless country." The country between the Waxhaws, Camden, and Winnsborough had "been alternately in the possession of friends and enemies," and the corn and cattle were "not sufficient for the wants of the Refugee families." He closed by wishing he could finish his tour, but his orders had been "very extensive" and it would "require eight or nine days to forage the country on Lynche's creek." [136]

On the sixteenth of the month, Smallwood reported to Gates that Tarleton was "wasting and destroying the Country below Camden by fire and otherwise" and that Davie, with two hundred cavalry and as many infantry, had been detached "near a Month to scour the disaffected Settlements on Lynch's Creek and Waxhaw, from whence a Supply of provision and forage was obtained." However, there still remained "a Quantity on Lynch's Creek which could not be gathered and drawn in, as Colo. Tarleton with his Legion has latterly laid in Camden." [137]

During this tour Davie became increasingly worried by the loss of men who had served their term of enlistment. As early as November 10, he complained to Smallwood that "General Davidson's discharging some riflemen who were raised for two months, has put half my horse of opinion they ought to be discharged too—suggesting they were upon the same establishment." He thought that "This relieving men when on detachment is both dangerous and disagreeable; this morning the company of riflemen have gone in that very moment when I need them most," and the "troop of horse above mentioned have made application to Genl. Davidson." Davie hoped they would be "non-plused, as the command here will be quite reduced if they are discharged." [138]

William R. Davie

Five days later, Davie was even more perturbed. In another letter to Smallwood he said that the "torments of the *damned* are scarcely equal to the torture of my feelings these five or six days past, from the rage of the Militia for returning home," most of whom "deserted before the last evening," and "There remain no cavalry now but fifteen or twenty," whom he felt it would be better to discharge than "to keep to the 20th consuming forage."[139] With his reduced command, Davie retired to Smallwood's camp at Providence, whence he set out for Salisbury, arriving November 23.

By this time Davie, as a partisan leader, had succeeded in bringing himself to the attention of Cornwallis and, indirectly, to Sir Henry Clinton. Cornwallis's letter to Clinton, written from Winnsborough, December 3, 1780, is revealing:

"Smallwood has been encamped from the beginning of last month with about *thirteen* hundred Militia, a Corps of 250 Continentals under Morgan and 70 Dragoons Commanded by Washington, about 12 miles on this side of Charlotte Town, his front guarded by Davie and other irregular Corps, who have committed the most shocking cruelties and the most horrid Murders on those suspected of being our friends that I ever heard of...."[140]

And writing to the South Carolina Delegates at Continental Congress, Governor Rutledge revealed that "Colo. or Major Davy (of which gallant Officer witht. Doubt you have heard,) is just come up" and had reported, among other things, that Lord Cornwallis had moved "somewhat lower down the Country & so has Sumpter." The former was at Shiver's Ferry on the east side of the Broad; the latter, between the Broad and Saluda rivers. Here Davie hoped to collect a force and "give those who are desirous, an opportunity, to join him." Davie had also reported that Tarleton was still in "Quest of Marion, & doing much mischief in burning houses on Santee" and that "the Enemy mount many of their Infantry, in order to proceed rapidly, with their Cavalry," the latter of which consisted of at least 250 good men.[141]

On Davie's arrival in Salisbury, he was no doubt weary and downcast, after having served so long not only as the eyes and ears of the Southern army, but also, on occasion, as its fighting arm. His biographer, Hubbard, in fact, portrays him as expecting to leave the service altogether because he did not want to be placed at the head of a corps composed of new levies of militia, whose "habits and peculiar orgainization" did not suit him. However, General Smallwood was most eager to retain his services and promised that if he would remain and if a regiment of light horse could be raised, two hundred riflemen and three hundred light infantry would also be added to his command. This idea of being in command of "a kind of Legion" appealed to Davie, who, on the day he arrived in Salisbury, sent Captain James Cole Mountflorence, his brigade major, to confer on the subject with the Board of War then sitting at Halifax.[142]

The proposition was accordingly presented to the board, which in turn referred it to Governor Nash. The regiment of militia cavalry was "to be composed of 6 Troops only, which are intended to be incorporated with a Regiment of Light Infantry, forming thereby a kind of Legion." In its message to the Governor, the "Board," which apparently was then represented by only one man—probably Orondates Davis—observed that he and Smallwood were eager to retain Davie, because they had "a high Idea of his Military Merit." However, he feared that there were "obstacles unsurmountable against this scheme of Militia Cavalry." If they used small horses, they would "answer no purpose; and stout, strong Horses are not to be had but by impressment, and greater Evils would result therefrom than any probable Service could compensate for." Even if the length of service were shortened and each man required to furnish his own horse, "the arming and equipping them would be difficult."[143]

Davie's own version, written over a third of a century later, is somewhat different. He stated that after his own corps had been discharged about the last of November, he "was making arrangements to raise another body of Troops at the instance of General [Daniel] Morgan, who was to be charged with a seperate command to operate on the left of the Enemy." Thus "fired with the prospect of serving under this celebrated commander [he] was entirely absorbed with this favorite project when General Greene applied to him to accept the appointment of Commissary General."

In such a state of uncertainty were Davie's personal affairs when, on December 2, 1780, Nathanael Greene arrived in Charlotte to take over command of the Southern Army from Horatio Gates.

CHAPTER V

Subsisting an Army

"AN ARMY cannot subsist itself." This statement of General Nathanael Greene, though not the most original or profound ever enunciated, expressed succinctly one of the most urgent problems facing the new commander as he assumed command of the remnants of the Southern Army. Of course, the critical problem of subsisting the army was not peculiar to the South, but was one of the most harassing that had faced the embryonic nation. Under the colonial militia system, the colonists had a military organization designed primarily to protect it against attacks from the Indians on the frontier and the French and Spanish along the periphery of the English settlements. To supply an army for a protracted campaign, rather than for a brief expedition, was without precedent in their experience. Yet it became at once apparent, after the first exciting call to arms, that knapsack provisions—from inns, taverns, ordinaries, or hospitable and patriotic friends en route—were hopelessly inadequate. The Continental Congress and each state took steps to set up a regular, efficient commissary department. Uneven success was achieved. The evils of forestalling and monopolizing, the lack of co-operation between the commissariat and the quartermaster departments, the destruction wrought by the warring armies, the depreciation of the currency, the indifference of the states to congressional appeals—all seriously threatened the success of provisioning the armies.*

* For a detailed consideration of these factors and the entire problem of supply, see Victor Leroy Johnson, *The Administration of the American Com-*

Subsisting an Army

So important was the question of supply that less than a month after Washington had assumed command of the Continental forces, he recommended, July 10, 1775, the appointment of the first commissary general of the army of the United Colonies. His choice, in which the Continental Congress concurred three days later, was Joseph Trumbull, a Connecticut Yankee merchant-politico, the son of the intensely Whiggish colonial and Revolutionary governor of that state. The entire responsibility for the organization of the department fell upon his shoulders. For two years he operated without instructions from Congress. At first he served in the triple capacity of purchaser, issuer, and, to some extent, quartermaster general, even after the appointment on August 14, 1775, of Thomas Mifflin, a Philadelphia merchant and soldier, to the latter office. It is significant that in the fall of that year he was also assisted by Nathanael Greene as "a purchaser of salt." Greene was to cure the pork which was stored at Medford, Massachusetts.[1]

By the time that Greene appeared in Charlotte, three other commissary generals had succeeded Trumbull. A Baltimore merchant, William Buchanan, and another Connecticut Yankee, Jeremiah Wadsworth, had wrestled successively with the problems, until, exactly a year before Greene reached Charlotte, Congress appointed a Pennsylvania merchant, Ephraim Blaine, the grandfather of the "Plumed Knight" of the Gilded Age, James G. Blaine.

There had also been a number of changes in the organization of the department itself. After the two-year period of congressional inactivity under Trumbull's administration, Congress in June, 1777, had seen fit to set up an organization somewhat similar to that used in the British army. The resulting system was minutely detailed to the point of confusion, but its most salient features were that it divided the service into two departments, the purchasing and the issuing, with a commissary general of purchases and a commissary general of issues in charge. The department of purchases was to have four deputy commissaries; the latter department had three. All were appointed by Congress. These deputies could appoint as many assistant commissaries as they deemed necessary. The commissary general of each department assigned a definite district to each deputy.

---

missariat During the Revolutionary War (Philadelphia: University of Pennsylvania Press, 1941).

Within each district the purchasers procured the army provisions which they turned over to the deputy of the issuing department stationed therein. Thus, Congress had gone from a system in which the commissary general had been free to direct the smallest detail to a system so encompassed by regulations that the appointees were handicapped in the execution of their business.[2]

The following January Congress requested that the governors of North Carolina, Virginia, and Maryland co-operate with each other in forwarding five hundred barrels of meat weekly. Yet the more fruitful measure adopted was the appointment of state purchasing commissioners in each county. These agents, who spoke the language of the farmer, were temporarily able to achieve unexpected results.

By September, 1779, however, Congress, realizing its failure to provide adequately for the army, decided to turn over the responsibility to the states. The commissary general of purchases was to prepare an estimate of the provisions needed by the army and the fleet for the ensuing year. Congress, from this estimate, was to determine the amount each state should furnish and each state was to be exclusively responsible for its own collection of provisions. This system of specific supplies was adopted in February, 1780, shortly after Ephraim Blaine became commissary general.[3]

Up until the adoption of state responsibility, the area south of Virginia had not been considered an integral part of the commissarial system, but now that each state, with the exception of conquered Georgia, was called upon to furnish specific supplies, North and South Carolina were requisitioned in the same way as the other states.[4]

Moreover, North Carolina had, on September 14, 1780, made certain changes in its commissary organization to carry out more effectively the wishes of Congress. By act of Assembly, the sheriff of each county was instructed to call the justices of the peace together to elect a purchasing commissioner for their county. This commissioner was to purchase foodstuffs in accordance with the prices set out in the congressional resolution of February 25, 1780, which established the specific supply system. Moreover, provisions were to be impressed when deemed necessary. District superintendents were placed over them, charged with the duty of directing the storing of the provisions in accordance with directions from the commanding officer of the

Southern Army. At the top of the pyramid was the Board of War, to whom the superintendents were to make monthly returns.[5]

This system was none too successful. In fact, General Gates throughout the fall of 1780 had subsisted his army largely by impressment and purchases made by contractors appointed by Gates. To alleviate the situation the Board of War proposed to the governor the appointment of a state commissary general to have an over-all supervision of the collection and forwarding of provisions.[6] While they were deliberating over a person to whom the job could be safely entrusted, Ephraim Blaine, acting on a resolution of the Continental Congress, appointed on December 2—the same day Greene reached Charlotte—Robert Forsyth as a deputy commissary general of purchases for the Southern Army. Forsyth, armed with instructions to establish large magazines of provisions and to urge the state legislatures to comply with the requisitions of Congress, was to proceed southward with all possible dispatch to join General Greene at Charlotte.[7]

Such was the commissarial situation when Greene arrived in Charlotte. As to the status of the war and the supply situation in the Carolinas, a brief recapitulation is necessary. Lord Cornwallis was encamped at Winnsborough, South Carolina, about thirty-five miles below the advance posts of the Americans. In this strategic position he was able to support his other two important posts—Camden, which communicated with some smaller posts on the Pee Dee River, and Ninety-Six, which was able to keep open communications with Augusta, Georgia. By this chain, his Lordship was able to command the resources of the whole interior of South Carolina and to maintain his supply line to Charleston.[8]

The region extending for forty miles above Winnsborough had alternated between British and American possession since the fall of Charleston and "for a considerable part of that time had been charged with the support of the whole body of both Armies." The crops in this section had been neglected by the Whigs who had fled in June; the little that was harvested was consumed by the enemy. The Tories, of course, suffered in their turn when the Whigs held any of this intermediate country. Davie's censure of these practices was mitigated by his realism: "The troops of both armies took what they wanted without ceremony or accountability, and used it without measure or economy; an indifference common to all armies in similar situations, produced by the impression, that perhaps the next day these resources may be in the hands of the Enemy." [9]

The entire county of Mecklenburg had also been exhausted of provisions and forage. So destitute was it, according to Davie, that "the Militia in Providence under Genl. Smallwood and the regular force at Charlotte under Genl. Gates must have retrograded farther towards the interior had they not been supplied by Colo. Davie who commanded the principal advance post of the Army near Landsford on the Catawba river, and pushed his foraging parties down into the country towards Camden, occupied by people who were generally Loyalists, and who had been hitherto protected by the positions and advance of the British Army." Yet even this resource had failed and the post was abandoned when Davie's troops had been discharged some days before Greene arrived.[10]

A lesser man than Greene would not have been able to arise from the nadir of despair as he reviewed the army which he was to command. A call for exact returns as to his forces revealed that they numbered, according to Lee, "not more than two thousand of whom the major part was militia"; [11] a later and more detailed report showed that the whole army consisted of 2,307 men. Of these 1,482 were present and fit for duty; 547 were absent on command and 128 detached on extra service. The cavalry consisted of 90 and the artillery of 60. The Continentals numbered 949; all the rest was militia. Here was his Southern Army! In fact, by the end of the month Greene wrote LaFayette that his "whole force fit for duty that were properly clothed and properly equipt (did) not amount to 800 men." [12]

Despite the small size of his forces, their demand exceeded the supply immediately available. Lee reported that there were only three days' provisions on hand,[13] and Davie reported there was no regular commissariat, "or even the semblance of arangement for the support of the army, without any magazines on the line of expected operations or even at any point in his rear." The "total want of money, and the annihilation of public credit in consequence of the depreciation of the paper currency" increased the difficulties. This depreciation of Continental money had reached a hundred to one,[14] whereas the paper money of North Carolina had been made contemptible by "the public and careless manner in which it was given

SUBSISTING AN ARMY

away at the printing office." [15] Writing from Wilmington on Christmas day, 1780, John Bradley, an assistant issuing commissary, reported that if he had specie he "could purchase rice, flour, and liquor to a considerable amount." [16] In order to obtain the highly important article of salt, which merchants would not sell for paper money, Colonel Francis Locke felt he was making "an advantageous bargain when he agreed to allow the wagoners three bushels out of each wagon in part payment for their services." [17] The scarcity of specie was further apparent in a letter of a Major Burnet to Colonel Davie requesting the latter, "If it is in your power to advance the expresses money sufficient for their journey, I must beg you to do it, as it will be out of General Greene's power to supply them; but if not, we must do the best in our power." [18]

Writing to Colonel Thomas Polk a week after his arrival, Greene predicted that "if we are drove to the necessity, those in the neighborhood of camp will feel the disagreeable effects of the want of a regular supply"; that "if the troops are not subsisted one way they must be by the other." [19]

A week later Greene wrote that he "found the difficulties of subsisting an army far beyond all anticipation." Though the inhabitants were "generally well disposed," they would not "gather in their crops from the field, because depositing their grain in their barns exposes it to be seized by their friends, or burnt by their enemies." They were driven, therefore, to "collect subsistence by force, or disband." [20]

Greene, in a letter to LaFayette two weeks later, described their desperate plight: "Were you to arrive, you would find a few ragged, half-starved troops in the wilderness, destitute of every thing necessary for either the comfort or convenience of soldiers. Indeed... the department is in a most deplorable condition, nor have I a prospect of its mending. The country is almost laid waste, and the inhabitants plunder one another with little less than savage fury. We live from hand to mouth, and have nothing to subsist on but what we collect with armed parties." [21]

In an equally "deplorable" condition was the quartermaster department. As a result of Gates's defeat "all the public waggons and horses, with a great many which were private property fell into the hands of the Enemy," and "the transportation of the army depended principally upon the disagreeable and uncertain resource of impressment." No one knew better than Greene, who had served as quartermaster general under Washington, the importance of choosing an efficient and reliable man for this post. Fortunately, on his way down to Charlotte, he had met Lieutenant Colonel Edward Carrington of Virginia, who was then without command. At Greene's insistence he was induced to accept the onerous job. Described by Davie as "a man of considerable talents and the most persevering energy," he did not join Greene until February 7, 1781, at Guilford Court House.[22]

So discouraging was the condition of the commissariat that Greene spent his first night at Charlotte studying the resources of the country with Colonel Thomas Polk, who had acted as commissary general of provisions for North Carolina and as commissary of purchases for the Continental troops under Gates. Polk later reported to Elkanah Watson that Greene "better understood" the supply situation the next morning than Gates had done in the whole period of his command.[23]

Two days later Greene reported to Thomas Jefferson that the troops were in "a most wretched condition—destitute of every thing necessary either for the comfort or convenience of soldiers"; that they were "perishing with cold and hunger"; that Virginia's troops "may literally be said to be naked"; and that he was obliged to send the latter away. He implored Jefferson to do his utmost with the Virginia legislature, because North Carolina had "no magazines or provisions . . . , but depend upon daily collections for support; and this state has been so ravaged by the numerous militia . . . that it is a doubt . . . whether, with the great industry and best dispositions, any considerable magazines can be found."[24]

The commissariat had been rendered even more deplorable by the resignation of Colonel Thomas Polk. Because of responsibility to two masters, dependence upon county commissioners over whom he had no control, and other more serious factors, his usefulness had been so impaired that he had drawn expressions of lack of confidence from his superiors. General Smallwood had received serious complaints concerning Polk's failure to supply "Provisions even to the Continental Troops," and Gates had charged that "his conduct was deemed doubtful and suspicious." Polk felt that because "his Countrymen suspected his Fidelity, he would no longer act as Commissary, than until he had delivered Five Hundred Beeves, and One Thousand Bushels of Corn." He continued in office until after the arrival of Greene, who "could have wished the Col to have filled the place as he appears to be a man of some resource and influence at large." Polk's excuse, in a letter to Greene of December 10, 1780, was that he was "now too far advanced in years to undergo the task and fatigue of a commissary-general." In his stead, he recommended Davie. On the same day Greene wrote to Davie that Polk had found "the business of subsisting the army too laborious and difficult for him to continue," but that "the greatest difficulty with him, is, he cannot leave home, owing to the peculiar situation of his family." [25]

In this same letter to Davie, who was eager to be put in command of "a kind of Legion," Greene had pressed Davie to accept the vacancy of Polk:

Your character and standing in this country lead me to believe you are the most suitable person to succeed him. It is a place of great consequence to the army, and all our future operations depend upon it. As you are a single man, and have health, education, and activity to manage the business it is my wish you should accept the appointment, especially as you have an extensive influence among the inhabitants, and are upon a good footing, and much respected in the army.

I wish to see you upon this business as soon as possible, and beg you will be kind enough to come to Charlotte without loss of time, that I may have an opportunity to converse with you more fully on the subject.[26]

Four days later, in writing the North Carolina Board of War, Greene pointed out the "absolute necessity of appointing one person to have a general superintendance of all the commissioners in the different Districts." He proposed Colonel Davie for the office, and, should he refuse, he had spoken to "Major Read of this state" * for

* This was most probably Captain James Read of the First North Carolina Battalion, commanded by Colonel Thomas Clark. He was obviously one of Polk's assistants because on October 2, 1780, the Board of War wrote the North Carolina Delegates in Congress that "Captain Reed, of the first Regiment of the Continental Troops belonging to this State, purchased a considerable Quantity of Cloathing for our Troops, and that the Cloaths are now in Philadelphia."—S.R., XIV, 404-5; see also S.R., XV, 730; F. B. Heitman, *Historical Register of Officers of the Continental Army During the War of the Revolution, April, 1775, to December, 1783* (Washington: F. B. Heitman, 1893), p. 341.

the position. Greene, however, diplomatically meant "to suggest to the Board these characters; but not to solicit their appointments further than is perfectly correspondent with the views of the Board and the interest of the State." Yet as to the dire necessity of having someone in this position he was more insistent: "A man of resource activity and attention is necessary... without which the Army will want and the service suffer," it being "almost impossible to carry on any offensive operations even upon the partizan scale much less with the whole troops." [27]

A few days later, Greene again wrote the Board, urging the appointment of Davie. Between the lines of this letter there appears a revelation as to Davie's ambition and his resolution to settle for nothing less than plenary powers, if he was to accept the post:

He will not engage unless his powers are ample; for he is not willing to hazard his reputation without a fair prospect of succeeding. His ambition, popularity, good sense, and activity, give good reason to hope he will execute the business to our satisfaction, so far as the poverty of the public and the wretched state of our finances shall put it in our power. He must be authorized to remove all commissioners of districts or counties, who are negligent or remiss in their duty, and to impress provisions and supplies on emergencies. Nothing short of this will enable him to give such assurances to the commanding officer, as he can depend upon with safety to himself and security to the country.[28]

Davie, as might be expected, was none too eager to give up his hope of a regiment of his own and informed Greene that he "understood his plans had been approved by the general." The general admitted that he had given his approbation, but he urged that the supply situation was more crucial. He drew "a rapid but impressive view of the exhausted situation of the Country, and the distressed condition of the army," concluding that "if the army was not supplied it must retire to the interior towards Virginia or disperse, and the Enemy must be left in peaceable possession of the two Southern States." [29]

Still persistent, Davie observed that "being engaged principally in the field since he finished his collegiate studies in 76, although he knew something about the management of troops, he knew nothing about *money or accounts* that he must therefore be unfit for such an appointment, and was convinced he could render his country more Service by prosecuting his present plan."³⁰

Davie's report of Greene's reply shows the latter's insistence:

> The General replied that as to Money and *accounts* the Colonel would be troubled with neither, that there was not a single dollar in the military chest nor any prospect of obtaining any, that he must accept the appointment, and supply the army in the same manner that he had subsisted his own troops for the last six months; that he would render his country more useful service in this way than any other; that he might rely upon his support for the necessary detachments, and upon Colo. Carrington as far as practicable for the necessary transportation.³¹

The general's persistence finally prevailed. Davie, however, exacted "an express promise that it should be for as short a time as possible." *

In the absence of exact terminology, it may be assumed that Davie held an interim appointment as a temporary or acting deputy commissary general of the American army until the arrival of Robert Forsyth from Philadelphia. It is likely that Greene knew of Congress's intention to fill this position, but unlikely that he had received word of it at this time.

This decision on Davie's part was perhaps the most difficult and the most unselfish he ever made. Only twenty-five years old, he was to exchange the glamor and full-blooded activity of the field for a thankless and irksome job, beset with petty details and drudgery. Instead of indulging his own passion to lead a regiment of his own men, he resigned himself to the tedium of becoming "a purveyor of beef and bacon, an inspector of invoices, a contractor for salt and tobacco." In this new call to duty, however, he "speedily immersed himself in estimating the resources of counties, gathering herds of swine, and bargaining for barrels of rum"—a chore in which he showed himself "as punctual and diligent in the minute operations

---

* This interview between Greene and Davie was repeated *literatim* in George Washington Greene, *The Life of Nathanael Greene, Major-General in the Army of the Revolution* (New York: Hurd and Houghton, 1871), III, 76-77, along with a footnote to the effect that it was taken from "a very interesting narrative prepared by Colonel Davie a few years before his death, at the request of General Greene's youngest daughter; and of which extracts were published by Judge Johnson." The latter refers to William Johnson, *Sketches of the Life and Correspondence of Nathanael Greene,...* (Charleston: A. E. Miller, 1822).

of his new department, as he had been skilful in planning a surprise, and brave on the field of battle." [32]

He and Greene agreed that to insure "any regular supply" they would have to obtain the sanction and assistance of the North Carolina government.* The legislature not being in session, their appeal was made to the peripatetic and pusillanimous Board of War.

Davie accordingly set out to present Greene's letter of recommendation of December 14 to the Board. His quest was beset by difficulties. When he reached Hillsborough, he found that Orondates Davis was alone in Halifax and that "he did not consider himself authorized to transact Business *as a Board*." Davie therefore proceeded on to John Penn's plantation in Granville, to which Penn had retired "on *private* business." Penn, however, upon reading Greene's dispatches, wrote the other members of the Board "warmly recommending" Greene's proposed measures. Finally arriving in Halifax, Davie found Alexander Martin and Davis, who informed Davie that they were "embarrassed by the insufficiency of the late act of Assembly." Their hesitation was caused by "the novelty of the System, [and] Delicacy in *assuming* powers foreign from their Appointment." They assured Davie, however, that they would see to it that the matter would "be the first thing on the political Tapis" when the Assembly, which was then collecting, convened. Moreover, they would "use the most vigorous efforts...for the immediate regulation and supply of that Department" and would vest Davie "with all the powers they can for the present, which they hope will be arranged equal to your wishes as soon as the Assembly meets." [33]

As a temporary expedient, the Board appointed Davie, January 5, 1781, "to superintend Salisbury District, with powers to call on any Superintendant for supplies while the Army is in that district or in its

---

* Davie, in his "Sketches," was mistaken as to his movements at this time. He stated that, armed "with letters from the Commander in Chief demonstrating the necessity of vigorous and efficient measures to support the Army," he set out the next morning to gain the assistance of the legislature. The members of this body "were all animated with the most ardent patriotism, and arrangements were promptly made, by Appointing Colo. Davie Commissary General of the State, levying a specific Tax in grain and salted provisions to be deposited at the Court houses of the different counties or such places as the Commissary General might direct." After effecting these objects, Davie reported that he rejoined Greene upon his retreat to Guilford Court House, "where he entered upon the arduous duties of his appointment."

Vicinity."[34] Strangely enough, perhaps because of repeated pleas from Greene,[35] the Board on January 16, ten days before the Assembly convened, conferred on Davie the office of "Superintendent Commissary Genl. of provision Supplies for the State of No. Carolina." His powers were ample. He was "to superintend all the County Commissioners of provision Supplies in the State of North Carolina, and from them supply the different Posts of the Army in the said State or Vicinity thereof." He was also empowered to employ up to four assistants to carry out his orders in the different counties and a clerk to keep account "of all Provisions received and delivered to the use of the Army afsd."[36]

Such an appointment of course carried with it responsibilities of staggering proportions. An army had to be fed from the debilitated resources of a new state whose very existence was challenged by a hostile army on its borders. Large numbers of its own citizens had either openly resisted the Whig cause or feebly supported its efforts for independence. Added to these tribulations was the woeful condition of the state's finances and the complaints from the populace of being over-burdened with taxes. In addition to the regular taxes of a domestic nature, a special tax, levied to aid in the prosecution of the war, had grown in dimensions from year to year. In 1777 a tax of one half of a penny was levied "on each pound value of all the Lands, Lots, Houses, Slaves, Money, money at interest, Stock in trade, Horses and Cattle in this State." By 1781 it had been increased to "four shillings currency on every pound value of taxable property, and four pence in the pound on all monies within this State." Moreover, £850,000 had been issued in bills of credit in 1778, and £1,250,000 were emitted in 1780.[37] As a result, they sank to a "mere nominal value" and public credit was prostrate. By September, 1780, as has been noted, the Assembly, having exhausted all other means of providing for the exigencies of war, had resorted to the expedient of a specific provision tax.[38]

This tax specified that for every hundred pounds of taxable property there should be paid in to the county commissioners one peck of Indian corn, or an equivalent in other grains, and three pounds of good pork, or an equivalent in other meats. It authorized the collectors to distrain to double the amount, in case of a refusal or neglect to bring the specific articles to the appointed places. The commissioners were also empowered to impress one half of an estimated surplus above the current wants of a family in cases where they refused to sell the same to the state. This tax was re-enacted in June, 1781, and April, 1782, and the amount was increased to one bushel of corn and ten pounds of pork, or suitable equivalents.[39]

It was this system which Davie was to administer. Designed to relieve the state of a more oppressive form of exaction, the tax was paid, according to Hubbard, "with great reluctance." The actual collecting of the articles was a time-consuming ordeal, especially in the thinly populated districts. Even more difficult were the transportation of the heavy articles and the driving of the livestock to the peripatetic army of Greene. Though it was later described by Samuel Johnston as "the most oppressive and least productive tax ever known in the state," it was perhaps the best expedient that could have been evolved under the circumstances.[40]

In this capacity, Davie not only had to supervise the collection of specific supplies in every county, but he had to draw up a register of all the wagons and teams in each county so that the burdens of transportation might be distributed equally throughout. His plan was to collect a number of small magazines at various points in the rear of the army so that their size would not make them an object of attack by the enemy. These were located so as to serve best "the triple purpose of supplying the army, supporting the recruiting, and furnishing subsistence to the troops advancing from the north and west to his relief." In addition to these, "one extensive magazine" was established at Oliphant's Mill, high up on the Catawba River.[41] Moreover, it was found expedient to establish permanent magazines for larger quantities of stores in eastern North Carolina, where they would be beyond the reach of the enemy's probable maneuvers. Edenton and Tarborough were chosen, the latter being also the point of general rendezvous, until it was moved to Halifax, late in 1781. Here, in fact, Davie was to spend most of his time, after he left the service of Gates and while he was still commissary general of the state.[42]

In these activities, according to Judge William Johnson, who was not only a friend of Davie but who wrote during Davie's lifetime, Davie met with "the most prompt and liberal support from the state authorities." In concert with them he made arrangements "for collecting magazines at every court-house in the state, as well as officers appointed to register and report the produce and means of transportation in every county." However, "the want of zeal in the county deputies sadly baffled these judicious arrangements." [43]

Armed with his orders from the Board of War, Davie also received from Governor Abner Nash warrants on the state treasury for £100,000, in sums of £10,000 each. Instead of reporting to Greene at once, he was detained in Halifax in an effort to negotiate these warrants into money and in consulting with the legislature, which convened there on January 18. To them he submitted his plan, which they approved, for establishing magazines, determining the ratio of supplies, appointing his deputies, and the broad outlines of his department. He was particularly concerned with the appointments of county commissioners in the easternmost districts and with the removal of all provisions from the seaboard to places "higher up the Country." [44]

It was about this time also that Davie presented a memorial to the legislature, addressed to the Board of Auditors, in which he set forth that he had been "drawn early into the field with a seperate Command, & continuing in public Service all the past Summer made considerable expenditures, for which he thinks it reasonable to be repaid." Though he asserted that he had owed his services "as a Citizen and wishes no other reward but the Satisfaction of serving his Country," he hoped "your Honble Body will deem it equitable that his Expenses accrued as an Officer, amounting to Six or Seven thousand Pounds should be refunded." [45]

The Senate, in a patriotic mood and cognizant of Davie's outstanding services, saw fit on February 2 to allow him "ten thousand pounds as a compensation for his expenditures when in the service of this State during the late campaign," [46] but the House of Commons, in a more practical mood, appointed a committee to take the matter into consideration. The chairman, John Lutrell, did not report on it until the next session when he reported July 12 [47] that "the nature of the business will require mature Consideration and too much time to be taken up at this late Hour of the Session" and therefore recommended that it lie over until the next session.* Meanwhile, having set his

---

*Exhaustive research of all available records has failed to reveal whether Davie ever received this remuneration.

commissarial system in motion, Davie hastened to rejoin Greene at Guilford Court House early in February.[48]

During Davie's absence, Greene, reversing the plans of Gates to winter in Charlotte, decided that he could not reorganize an army when he was dependent upon daily collections for its daily food. Kosciusko, dispatched down the Pee Dee in search of greener pastures, chose a site in South Carolina on Hicks Creek, nearly opposite Cheraw Hill, on the east bank of the Pee Dee. Arriving there with his army the day after Christmas, Greene wrote Morgan that "It is no Egypt," but that food and forage were more available. Here he planned to put his army in shape.[49]

Meanwhile Cornwallis, reinforced at Winnsborough by Major General Alexander Leslie with fifteen hundred men, resolved to resume his long-cherished designs upon North Carolina. His army was put in motion December 27, while Tarleton was in pursuit of Morgan between the Catawba and Broad rivers. News of Morgan's victory at the Cowpens on January 17 did not reach Greene on the Pee Dee until a week later.[50] Yet Greene's exultation was tempered by grim reality: He could not follow up this victory "without men, without money, without clothing, and so scant even of provisions as to be obliged to gather the corn from the field, prepare it for the mill, and guard the mill during the process of converting it into meal."[51]

Accordingly, Greene began his strategic and brilliant retreat before Cornwallis across North Carolina and over the Dan River. Before setting out he sent word to Davie to remove all supplies from the seaboard and ordered the commissaries at Salisbury and Hillsborough to hold themselves in readiness to move both their supplies and prisoners towards the upper counties of Virginia. Carrington, his new quartermaster general, was charged with procuring boats to cross the Dan. Twenty-two days later, Greene had reached Guilford Court House, where he was joined by his newly-appointed commissary and by Carrington. Though he now had something of an organized force, it was "feeble, destitute and pennyless, and talents that merited a freer range of action, were wasted upon shifts and expedients." Without a dollar at their command and when they were "most in need of conciliating the favour of the people, they were compelled to disgust them, by supporting and transporting every thing by exaction."[52]

Greene was thus relieved of being his own commissary general in

SUBSISTING AN ARMY

his retreat across the Dan and his return to Guilford Court House. Nor were Davie's activities confined solely to those of procurement. In the memorable battle at Guilford on the Ides of March, Davie, along with the two North Carolina brigadiers, John Butler and Thomas Eaton, made "every effort" to stop the "unaccountable panic" of the North Carolina militia.[53]

The entire period from mid-February until the first week in May was described by Davie as "a continued display of military science in marches, countermarches, and positions, Lord Cornwallis exhausting all the strategems of war," while Greene, "greatly inferior in Strength and equipment... displayed the most consummate address in parrying and avoiding the blow." Such maneuvers necessitated his changing the position of the army "ever 24 or 48 hours." As usual, each new site was dictated by the old problem of supply, especially since the "well devised system of supply" made by the General Assembly of North Carolina was not yet in full operation. The situation was revealed by Davie:

"General Greene could make no movement until the important question was first decided whether one or two days subsistence could be procured at the point on which the General proposed to march; the subject continually presented the most distressing difficulties; Colo. Davie attended the General every night usually between 11 and 12 O'clock when every person being removed or asleep and the map spread, the expected movements of the Enemy, and the positions proposed to be taken by our own Army were discussed with a view to this interesting object, the direction of the supplies in motion from the interior were to be changed, new depots were to be formed at the mills and occupied by small detachments of troops, and our subsistence again put to painful hazard; the General tracing the direction on the map with his finger would observe if the Enemy move in this direction, I must take a position there, can subsistence be procured, the answer was not infrequently in the negative, 'the enemy has ravaged that quarter and we have already gleaned what they left, if the distance is not to exceed the distance you mention, subsistance can only be procured at such and such points, and not even then in time without the greatest exertions and the concurrence of some fortunate circumstances in the timely change of the direction of the supplies in motion on the place where we are now encamped.'"[54]

William R. Davie

But the problem of subsistence was by no means confined to the American army. When the royal army withdrew to Hillsborough in February, 1781, while Greene was across the Dan, Stedman had found it necessary to dispatch his cattle-drivers "a considerable distance" for cattle and even then they brought in "but a very scanty supply." The only reason Cornwallis was able to stay in Hillsborough as long as he did was that they had found "a quantity of salt beef, pork, & some hogs." Yet this windfall was inadequate to feed the men, and Stedman himself with "a file of men was obliged to go from house to house, throughout the town, to take provisions from the inhabitants, many of whom were greatly distressed by this measure, which could be justified only by extreme necessity."[55] Sergeant Lamb, of the Royal Welsh Fusileers, reported that provisions were so scarce while he was there that "it was found impossible to support the army in that place. They were even obliged to kill some of their best draft horses."[56]

Greene's biographer, Johnson, and Lee were in complete accord with Davie's description of the situation. The former pointed out the additional difficulty that they were afraid to collect magazines on their intended route, as this would have "unmasked" Greene's projected movements.[57] Lee reported that "the simple meal allowed us was always scanty, tho good in quality and very nutritious, being bacon and corn meal." These, he admitted, were procured day by day by Davie "with difficulty," so that Greene was forced "to extend or contract his march to correspond with the fluctuating supply of provisions."[58]

In his exhaustive search for these supplies, Davie was also forced to call upon Thomas Jefferson, then Governor of Virginia, from whom he made a requisition of livestock shortly before the battle of Guilford Court House.[59]

Davie was further hampered in his efforts by the militia who were "withholding their aid to the commissaries department in procuring provision." To remedy this, Greene, no doubt at Davie's instance, issued a special order on February 22 requiring "all the Militia Officers to furnish Col Davie Commissary General or his assistants ... with such men as the service may require," for which they would be paid a "reasonable compensation for their services." Greene exhorted "every good whig" to afford without delay "every assistance in their

SUBSISTING AN ARMY

power." Any officer who refused was to report to Greene at headquarters.[60]

After the battle of Guilford Court House, Cornwallis retreated to Ramsay's Mill on Deep River, March 19. Here he remained until March 28 when, at Greene's approach, he made a hasty passage of the river and marched towards Cross Creek, now Fayetteville, the center of the Highland Scots. When Greene's men came upon their camp at Ramsay's Mill, everything bore witness to the precipitation of the retreat. Unburied British dead lay around, and beef was still hanging in quarters in the slaughter pens. The hungry Americans devoured the meat at once and, still ravenous, seized upon the garbage which had been cast aside by the turkey buzzards.[61]

Their respite at Ramsay's Mill was a happy one, according to Lee, although supplies were lacking: "No magazines were opened for our accommodation" and "the exhilarating cordial" and "wholesome provision in abundance" were not available. Instead "the meagre beef of the pine barren, with corn-ash cake, was our food, and water our drink." [62]

So meager did Cornwallis find the supplies at Cross Creek, in spite of the efforts of the friendly Highlanders, that he was forced to proceed on to Wilmington, which was held by Major James H. Craig.[63]

When Greene realized that Cornwallis was retiring towards Wilmington, he reversed his pursuit and his entire plan of campaign. Though he wrote Governor Nash from Ramsay's Mill that he wished it were in his power to pursue Cornwallis, he was precluded from so doing by "want of provisions" and the fact that "a considerable part of the Virginia militia's time of service" had expired.[64] He then abandoned North Carolina and set out to crush Lord Rawdon's forces at Camden, South Carolina.

Yet this step was not taken without careful arrangements for provisions en route. Ever mindful of the necessity of providing a line of retreat and a supply of stores in the event he might again be forced to retreat up through North Carolina, he dispatched Davie to collect stores along the Catawba River, with special instructions to establish a considerable depot at Oliphant's Mill * on that river.[65]

* The exact location of this mill is subject to doubt. The local historian, Schenck (*N.C., 1780-1781*, p. 392), has the following note on it: "On Tarleton's Military Map, Oliphant's Mill is located in Iredell County, North Caro-

William R. Davie

In his march south Greene hoped to be joined by Thomas Polk, whom he had appointed brigadier of the Salisbury District, to succeed General William Lee Davidson, who had been killed at Cowan's Ford. This appointment had, however, "wounded" Colonel Locke, as well as two or three more "who so aspired with equal propriety to the Commissioners." [66] The General Assembly had also showed its disapproval by holding up the appointment and finally sending him one as "colonel commandant," which he returned. Yet Greene, on April 3, wrote Polk that he "had calculated largely upon his militia" and that Davie would make him "fully acquainted" with his intentions. Polk was apprised of Greene's intention of marching southward on the next day or the next and was ordered to join him on the west side of the Pee Dee near Colson's Ferry with "a considerable quantity of provision collected at or near Charlotte and another Magazine at Oliphants Mill or in that neighbourhood" and "at least ten days provision." [67]

While Davie was sent west to garner supplies, Greene's army set out about April 7 [68] for Camden. Davie's description of the privations experienced on the march down is the old familiar story. The route followed through the pine barrens of North Carolina was "extremely sterile" and the inhabitants "generally hostile to the American cause." In South Carolina, beyond the Pee Dee, the country had of course been "exhausted in the preceding summer and autumn by the contending armies."

By April 9 Davie had progressed as far as Salisbury, whence he was able to report to Greene that the Continental quotas were filling up "very rapidly" and should be ready to take the field by the twenty-fifth of the month. Not so encouraging was the supply situation. Davie found the country "almost entirely exhausted," not so much by "the two grand Armies," but by the "frequent Bodies of Militia collected so often in every part of the District and supported with

---

lina, where Buffalo Creek runs into the Catawba River on the present Western North Carolina Railroad; but the Hon. William M. Robbins, who has made some research, for the author, as to its location, can hear of no tradition of a mill of any kind at this point. But on the opposite side of the Catawba River, in Catawba County, on Ball's Creek, there was, many years ago, Iron Works, which continued to a recent period of time, and I am much inclined to the opinion that Oliphant's Mill was located at this Iron Works, which would be an appropriate place for the repair of arms and the storage of provisions."

so little economy." Even less encouraging was transportation, which was "a principal difficulty here; as it is in every place, and the want of a Quarter Master at this post embarrasses me exceedingly." But Davie's resolution did not flag: "Let the *Difficulties* be what they may, I was determined to meet with no impossibilities, and I therefore hope to have you 1400 bushels of Meal at the Pee Dee by the 16th with all the live-stock that can be collected." [69] He had also sent an order to Colonel Thomas Wade, of Anson County, who wrote Greene the next day that he had received an order from Colonel Davie "to provide 40 Thousand Rashens." Thus he had "some Meal and Cattle on the way up and have ordered the Mills to Grinding and Ordered up Corn but Waggons and teams are Scarse." If Greene could send some wagons it would be very "Sutable" and he would try to get the supplies down to him at Colson's Ferry, though "the cheaf of the Meal... is Damaged." Drovers had been sent down to collect cattle to be sent to such places as Greene directed. [70]

On the following day, Davie's tone was more optimistic. He wrote Greene that "the prospect of a supply from this place is tolerable, and I hope will meet you on the 17th. at furthest." He also reported that a refugee from Camden "says they were starving there; both the Families and Soldiers." [71]

Greene's reply, dated April 14, reported their prospects as "rather indifferent, not so much for want of provisions as the means of transportation." Davie was informed that they were marching that day for May's Mill and then to Lynch's Creek, along which route Davie was to direct his supplies as soon as possible. It would also be necessary for Davie to make some provision for the Virginia militia which Greene had ordered to collect at Salisbury. Greene added a strong hint: "NB If you can procure us some fresh butter it will be very acceptable." [72]

By April 23 Davie had reached Charlotte, where he relieved Greene's distresses "in some measure" by his shipments of twenty-eight wagons dispatched within the last ten days. Twelve hundred bushels more, he informed Greene, would be sent forward in a few days. These had "been borrowed with great difficulty, in small quantities thro' the Country." As soon as this shipment was fairly well under way, Davie planned to make proper arrangements for a regular supply from the back-country, because Mecklenburg and Rowan were "really exhausted." The chief problems, he warned Greene, were those of distance and transportation: "... The distance to Wilks and Surry counties lying under the Mountains so great, and transportation so difficult, our supplies, while you are at that point will ever be precarious, being in a country that affords nothing itself.

"Scarcity of Horses is always a natural consequence in any Country that has been the scene of war, This circumstance, with the busy season of the year, accounts for the difficulty of procuring transportation from these counties; a good Quarter Master is much wanted at this Post.

"The live-stock of this place is too poor for Service; I hope some may be procured in So. Carolina."[73]

Three days later, still at Charlotte, Davie informed Greene that he had sent forward that morning twelve wagons loaded with meal and flour and that he had "sent a Commissary to the Waxhaws, who has made a tolerable collection; but wants waggons." Also he felt that a considerable supply might be impressed in the neighborhood of Rocky Mount, on both sides of the Catawba. Again, there was the old complaint: "a Quarter Master is really much wanted at this Post," since "a number of public waggons and horses are scattered thro this Country and several waggons are lying in town unfit for service." He hoped to join Greene in a few days.[74]

By May Davie's department was beginning to show results, not only in the central and piedmont sections but in the eastern part of the state. The commissary of the Halifax District, Joshua Potts, had, "by order of Colo. Carrington, in Behalf of Colo Davie," sent to Hillsborough "upwards of three Thousand Wt. of Bacon, from Edgecombe" and had collected "twelve Thousand Weight from Warren County, three Thousand of which will be deposited in Hillsborough, & the other nine Thousand continued on to Salisbury," where the wagons would receive further directions on to headquarters. There were also stores of provisions already collected at Harrisburgh "and near it which may quickly be brought here." *

* Joshua Potts to Sumner.—Jethro Sumner Papers, S.H.C. Harrisburgh was in Granville County, on the main road from Hillsborough to Eaton's Ferry. See Henry Mouzon and Others, *An Accurate Map of North and South Carolina*... (London: Robert Sayer and J. Bennett, 1775).

Subsisting an Army

Meanwhile, by April 20, Greene's army had reached Logtown, six hundred yards north of Lord Rawdon's fort at Camden. Having satisfied himself that the fort was too strong to be taken by assault, Greene decided to fall back about a mile to Hobkirk's Hill and thereby so deprive the garrison of its usual supplies that the British would be forced to withdraw. Davie later described this new position, located on the road to the Waxhaws, as a "narrow sandy ridge...so close to Camden, that the village and the enemy's works were visible from our camp and the piquets were advanced to the edge of the common, within less than cannon shot of the works." [75] In this position, Lord Rawdon decided to attack them on April 25. Greene, however, had apparently sensed the attack as his orders of April 24 contained a welcome promise. "The troops are to be furnished with two days provisions, and a gill of spirits per man, as soon as the stores arrive." While the men were cooking these eagerly awaited rations, the first shots of the ensuing battle of Hobkirk's Hill were fired. [76]

Davie later wrote a critique of this victory of Rawdon, in which he attempted to correct the errors of both Gordon and Lee. [77] This critique was based on Davie's "frequent conversations with General Greene on the strange result of the battle," and his conversations with "almost every officer in the army respecting their posts in it." In fact, "it was the subject of constant discussion till we arrived before Ninety-Six, when we found other employment." [78] Davie rejoined Greene about the end of April and was with the army on its march to Ninety-Six.

Believing that Lord Rawdon would resume offensive operations upon being joined by Lieutenant Colonel John Watson, who had eluded Lee and Marion, Greene withdrew by stages from the vicinity of Camden. By May 9 he had reached a position on the west side of the Wateree, some miles above Colonel's Creek. On that night he sent for Davie earlier than usual. Davie, on entering, found the map spread out on the table and Greene in a most depressed state of mind. The General quickly came to the point:

You see that we must again resume the partizan war, Rawdon has now a decided superiority of force, he has pushed us to a sufficient distance to leave him free to act on any object within his reach, he will strike at Lee and Marion, reinforce himself by all the troops that can be spared from the several garrisons and push me back to the mountains; you acted in this quarter in the last campaign, and I wish you to point out the military positions on both sides of the river, ascending it to the mountains, and give me the necessary information as to the prospect of subsistence, you observe our dangerous and critical situation, the regular troops are now reduced to a handful, and I am now without militia sufficient to perform the convoy and detachment service, or any prospect of receiving any reinforcements of this description; Sumter refuses to obey my orders, and carries off with him *all the active force* of this unhappy State on rambling predatory expeditions unconnected with the operations of the army. North Carolina dispirited by the loss of her regular line in Charleston, stunned into a kind of stupor by the defeat of General Gates, and held in check by Major Cruger and the Loyalists makes no efforts of any kind; Congress seem to have lost sight of the Southern States, and to have abandoned them to their fate, so much so, that we are even as much distressed for ammunition as men. We must always calculate on the maxim that *Your Enemy will do, what he ought to do*—We will dispute every inch of ground in the best manner we can—but Rawdon will push me back to the mountains; Lord Cornwallis will establish a chain of posts along James River *and the Southern States, thus cut off, will die like the Tail of a Snake.*[79]

Such, according to Davie, were Greene's "very words," which "made a deep and melancholly impression, and I shall never forget them."

Greene then expressed his "anxious desire" to remain as near as possible to aid or cover the retreat of Lee from Fort Motte, just above the confluence of the Congaree and the Wateree rivers. With this in mind they recurred to the map. Davie reported the rest of the conference:

...I had it in my power from personal knowledge to assure him that the Country abounded in strong military positions, and as to subsistence, there would be no difficulty, as we should be falling back on our depots or Magazines in No. Carolina; that if he was obliged to retreat further, he must permit me to resume my original plan, as I was morally certain a respectable force could be raised in the Western Districts of that State.— The interview concluded by his informing me that he would dispatch an express to Philadelphia in the morning, and requesting me to write the members of Congress with whom I was acquainted, painting in the strongest colors our situation and gloom.

Subsisting an Army

This night marked the nadir of Greene's despondency. Davie, as a matter of fact, had "never observed his mind yield to despondency but at this gloomy moment, when he conceived himself not only abandoned by all the constituted authorities of the confederacy but even by that portion of the population of the Southern States who had every thing to hope from his success, and every thing to fear from his failure."

Davie employed the whole of this gloomy night writing letters to members of Congress. Wheedling, cajoling, imploring letters, no doubt, in which he invoked the aid and assistance of Congress in this, one of the darker moments of the Revolution. The first glimmer of dawn found him still with pen in hand. Yet the morning brought not only the dawn of a new day, but of a new hope and a new confidence in the future. At daybreak his labors were interrupted by a sergeant from Greene, who summoned him to headquarters. As Davie entered the General's tent, he "perceived some important change had taken place." One can well imagine the General's elation as he announced to his commissary: "I have sent for you, said he, with a countenance expressing the most likely pleasure, to inform you that Lord Rawdon has evacuated Camden—that place was the key of the Enemy's line of posts—they will now all fall or soon be evacuated—All will go well. —Burn your letters—I shall march immediately to the Congaree, arrange your convoys to follow us, and let me know what expresses and detachments you will want." *

Greene's grasp of the significance of this evacuation of Camden led Davie to make the following appraisal of this man with whom he had been so intimately associated since early December: "The Gen-

---

* Davie's "Sketches." It is perhaps of more than academic interest to note the controversy that ensued upon the publication of this interview between Greene and Davie, which first appeared in William Johnson, *Greene*, II, 116-18. Colonel Lee's son, Henry, two years later, in his *Campaigns of 1781 in the Carolinas* (pp. 349-63), doubted the accuracy of Davie's recollection as to the date, though he declared his veracity was beyond "imputation." Lee's chief evidence to refute the time of the interview was a letter of the same date as the alleged interview, May 9, from Greene to Colonel Henry Lee, in which Greene expressed great optimism. Later George Washington Greene also doubted the timing of this conversation (*Greene*, III, 266n.), while McCrady said that Greene's optimistic letter to Lee, followed later in the day by his conversation with Davie, was typical of Greene's "mutability of mind."—*S.C. in the Rev., 1780-1783*, pp. 216-24.

eral's mind was of that luminous cast which gives an extensive range to the mental view, and highly endowed with the powers of calculation and deduction he immediately fore-saw and predicted all the consequences of the mistaken movement of the British Commander and instantly changed his plan of operations and assumed the offensive."

From May 10 to May 15 the British posts of Camden, Orangeburgh, Fort Motte, and Granby fell. Greene, instead of advancing upon Lord Rawdon, turned aside to besiege Ninety-Six and Augusta. He reached Ninety-Six on May 22.[80]

During this period of the sieges of Camden and Ninety-Six, according to Davie, measures were adopted to draw subsistence from the depots in North Carolina, in spite of the distance and the "difficult and precarious" transportation. The arrival of supplies at headquarters was "irregular and uncertain." Yet the troops, "satisfied that every thing was done, that was practicable, appeared to be inspired with the zeal of the General who commanded them, and sustained their privations without a murmur."[81]

It was during this siege of Ninety-Six that Robert Forsyth, who had been appointed deputy commissary general of purchases for the Southern army, arrived and released Davie from "the arduous and disagreeable duties" of his department. Davie was accordingly dispatched as a confidential officer to the North Carolina General Assembly by Greene, who foresaw the difficulties to be faced in consequence of the arrival of three regiments of British infantry from Ireland. About the first of June, Davie set out to present to the North Carolina legislature Greene's situation and to urge upon them the necessity of adopting effective measures for the collection of magazines of provisions and the re-enforcement of Greene's army. Thus ended a half-year's close personal association between Davie and his commanding officer, whom he was never to see again. Yet, he was to continue as Greene's emissary and provisioner, for about a year.[82]

At least three and a half decades later, Davie wrote his final appraisal of Greene's heroic efforts in these trying times:

"The mind looks back with astonishment on the perseverance and success with which General Greene passed through this awful crisis on which depended the recovery of So. Carolina and Georgia and the Independence of the whole Southern Section of the Union. Many of the greatest Captains of every age have been obliged either to abandon their object, or sacrifice their Armies on the failure of Subsistence, even when they had all the advantage of previous arrangement, aided by despotic power. Frederic the Great has recorded with all the fidelity of History his numerous embarrassments and painful sacrifices in consequence of the failure of subsistence, and we have seen the most formidable army of modern times commanded by the late Emperor of France utterly destroyed from the same cause. The public Treasury sunk under the drain of millions expended in the support of the No. Western Army under General Harrison in the late war of 1812, and the embarrassment and sufferings of our Troops in every other quarter from the same source under all the advantages derived from an existing well organized government will never be forgotten."

Yet Davie, relinquishing the "arduous and disagreeable duties" of service as Greene's commissary general, was only to face similar burdens upon his return to North Carolina as commissary general of purchases for the state. When Davie took up his new task, Thomas Burke had succeeded Nash as governor and the Council Extraordinary, composed of Richard Caswell, Alexander Martin, and Allen Jones, had replaced the unpopular Board of War February 15, 1781.[83] The new governor wrote numerous detailed instructions to the commissary general. Davie was entreated to use "the utmost diligence in procuring Magazines to be laid up in such places as you deem best situated for supplying posts." Burke was "exceedingly sensible" of the sufferings of the inhabitants and was determined as soon as possible to "fall on the best measures in my power for procuring for them compensation for their past services and supplies, and for preventing the inequality of public burthens for the future." He hoped the people would "willingly assist" Davie with supplies and with the means of transporting them. In the event that the specific supplies of the previous year were insufficient, he hoped the people would supply Davie by contribution, "for which you may promise them credit on the next years specific tax, or certificates or payment in money or anything else as soon as the public funds will admit of it." As to transportation, he hoped that wagons could be hired from individuals "and that the people will cheerfully furnish them." If they did not, Davie would have to resort to the law for impressing them, but in such case Burke hoped that Davie would "take great care that it be done with as much equality and justice as possible, and that no Outrages insults or injuries be offered by any officers or other persons in the execution of their duty."[84]

The following day, July 2, Burke sent a message to the General Assembly in which he reiterated the need for ministering to the needs of "an unprovided army" in the Salisbury District, informed them that he had requested Davie to form magazines of provisions and forage in that district, and recommended that provision be made for compensation "to those who have already borne an overproduction of the public Burthens and for preventing such inequalities in the future."[85]

On this same day, Davie and Colonel Stephen Drayton of Charleston, South Carolina,[86] recommended to Burke that the counties in the present vicinity of the army and those through which the army might pass should be "laid under immediate contribution" and that the inhabitants be required "to carry their proportion of the above Aid, to the Mills pointed out by the Commissaries, as the Magazines of the Army."[87]

Davie's concern with the old problem of transportation impelled him to address a plea to the General Assembly on July 7. In this he cited the "want of water-transportation in the interior parts of this extensive country" and the failure of the legislature "to redress this evil by a land carriage." These factors had been "productive of many difficulties and abuses" in which a few counties of the Salisbury District had performed "the internal duty of the State, and a great part of the transportation of the Southern Army." Davie then pointed to the resources of the lower counties which were "equal perhaps to the ample supply of our troops, could they be put in motion," but which were then lost for want of transportation. The tragic upshot was that the army had been obliged "to subsist by odious impressments in its own vicinity." As a mode of "redressing this evil," he recommended either purchases "by contract, or a specific levy apportioned to the different counties."[88]

By the last of July, Davie was instructed by Burke to make proper arrangements for supplying the first division of the North Carolina troops which were to rendezvous at Harrisburgh, Tarborough, Kingston, and Duplin. However, no magazines could be formed with safety at Kingston and Duplin until a force could be advanced and posted between them and the 450 British regulars who were stationed at Wilmington under Major James H. Craig.

By this time, Davie, for several years a familiar figure throughout central and western North Carolina, was beginning to make an impression in the lower counties, where he was rapidly winning the esteem and admiration of the eastern leaders. In anticipation of a visit by him and Governor Burke to Edenton, Samuel Johnston's sister wrote on August 14 to her daughter: "Davie both your Uncle Sam & Uncle Iredell seem to have the highest opinion off both as an officer & Gentleman. Mr. Iredell says he is very handsome—that is he has a fine person tall & genteel his face not so good tho' handsome enough resembling a good deal Mr. A. Neilson whom you may remember." [89]

Even more complimentary was James Iredell, with whom Davie was later to join forces in fighting for the Constitution. Writing from Halifax to his wife he informed her that "you will probably receive this by the Governor and *Colo. Davie*. I wish you and your Sister would be as attentive as possible to them. The worth of the latter rises every day in my estimation. He appears to me to possess uncommon abilities, and much goodness as well as greatness of soul." [90]

Burke's advice against establishing magazines at Kingston and Duplin was sound. Two weeks later Davie wrote Burke that "the Enemy were on the 16th. on the Burn-Coat road * from Wilmington to Newbern" and that General Alexander Lillington with a small body of cavalry was following in their rear while General Richard Caswell was retiring before them. Consisting of four hundred regulars and as many Tories, they had already proceeded seventy miles

---

* This road probably derived its name from the creek of the same name which enters the northeast branch of the Cape Fear River about eleven miles above Kenansville and a few hundred yards from Kornegay Bridge, where the Kenansville-Kinston road bears to the right. The road from this point to Kinston was probably called the Burncoat road in Revolutionary days. This information was graciously furnished the writer in a letter of August 15, 1951, from Judge Henry A. Grady, of Newbern, an authority on local history. Burncoat Creek was the boundary line of the first land acquired by his ancestors in Duplin County.

towards Newbern. Davie felt that "a Body of 4 or 5 hundred Light Infantry and a few Cavalry might soon account for them." *

Still concerned with provisioning the posts on the line of communication between Virginia and Greene's army, Davie was eager to send up cattle and salted stores into the western districts. Burke's advice was sought on August 22 as to the disposition of the livestock which Davie had collected at New Currituck and which he thought should be stored in the upper country, "out of the circle of the Enemy's manoevre." As to the rum which had been impressed by the preceding governor, he felt that some of it should be retained for the use of the state, "for I believe that we have not a hogshead of State Property." [91]

The next day, August 23, Burke issued orders to Davie that "all live Stock, Salt, Spirits and provision of every kind taken from the Enemy" were to be delivered over to the commissary general. This included "all the provisions of every kind taken from the Enemy or Tories at any time or place" on order of Davie, who would give certificates of their valuation, "in order that clear accounts may be kept." [92]

As to the supply of that indispensable commodity—salt—Davie reported to Burke on August 30 that there was no salt nearer than Saura Town,† where there were originally 369 bushels, from which eighteen barrels were sent down to Oliphant's Mill and twenty-five barrels had been drawn the previous May by Davie as Greene's commissary. The hospital at Charlotte had also drawn and bartered for supplies "in considerable quantity." Burke was further informed that salt had been under the direction of the Board of War and that Davie "never received any Notice or Invoice of it; either as Agent for the State or Commissary to the So. Department." He supposed there were "about 200 bushels remaining, which should be removed into this State, and stored with a proper Quarter Master, who knew whose Order to honour." This was urgent as "Salt will be immediately

---

* Davie to Governor Burke, August 19, 1781.—Governor Burke's Letter Book, A.H. For a detailed account of this march of Major Craig to Newbern, based on "the concurred traditions" of the neighborhood, see A. O. Grady (Duplin County) to D. L. Swain, March 1, 1855.—David L. Swain Papers, S.H.C.

† This town, variously spelled Saura, Sarra, and Sawra, was in present Stokes County, North Carolina, near the intersection of Snow Creek with the Dan River. See Mouzon, *An Accurate Map of N. and S.C.*

[118]

wanted." Davie believed, moreover, that it would be proper to receive a draught from Burke upon the Board of Trade "With Instructions to procure the necessary supply—which will not be less than 2,000 bushels."[93]

Burke, on August 31, informed Davie that the Board of Trade was suspended by the legislature, and, as he was powerless to issue an order in regard to the salt, he thought that Davie should "take measures immediately for contracting for the quantity of Salt you may have occasion for, and include in your estimate what may be necessary for the whole Southern Army, because in no other State in the Southern Department probably can any be imported."[94]

Burke also was very solicitous in regard to the treatment of the merchants of the state. To them he gave assurances, which Davie must see were in no event violated, that their property would not be subject to impressments "whether it consists of produce for exportation or imported commodities." This, he felt, was necessary because their property "constitutes the only instruments of Commerce, and Commerce only can supply us with foreign necessaries." Burke did not think that such caution was necessary for Davie personally, but because he wanted the principles "to pervade your whole department." He ended by requesting Davie to make out an estimate of "the number of Beves that may be necessary to be stalled for supplying the force which will be on foot in this State and such as may be required from us for supplying the Southern Army and also the places where they may be most conveniently fed."[95]

On September 1 Burke again wrote Davie requesting him to furnish provisions for "considerable bodies of Militia of Virginia, of our own Militia and for the army under the command of the Marquis de la Fayette" who would "probably be operating on the rivers of Roanoke, Tar, and Neuse." In case the "ordinary means are insufficient," Davie was empowered to order the County Commissioners to levy them by contributions after he had submitted his estimates to the governor, who would furnish him with orders to the particular commissioners in question. Davie was requested in this levy "to take every precaution to prevent abuses and the people from being distressed."[96]

Numerous other orders were piling in on Davie in these weeks: orders to take measures "for securing some Cattle and Sheep which will be collected by Brigadier General Caswell for the use of the

WILLIAM R. DAVIE

State"; orders to supply "the whole force of Hertford and Bertie Counties" which was ready to march to Winton; orders to "take the necessary measures for supplying the prisoners and the Guard which conducts them with provisions from this place to Hillsboro'." [97]

By September 4 Davie was able to furnish Burke with an estimate of the rations needed for a force of three thousand men in the field for six months. In the light of modern dietary standards, one shudders at the dependence on spirits, meat, and starch:

16,875 Gallons of Spirits
2,400 Beves
600 Bushels of Salt
14,000 Bushels of Corn or Wheat

In field consumption, exclusive of the Forage which the Quarter Master General may estimate, about

500 Beves in Bar'l
500 as Live Stock

and 500 Bushels of Salt distributed to the different State posts, will be nearly adequate for the *State consumption* on the proposed scale.

Since the Edenton District abounded in corn and cattle, Davie proposed buying and stalling two thousand head of cattle there. For the remainder of the necessary supplies, they could depend on the lower counties in the Newbern District and on confiscated property. However, they would need some coffee, sugar, and wine for the hospital and headquarters.[98]

Burke was in total accord with Davie's estimates and recommended proceeding with the necessary purchases. The spirits would have to be purchased from importers and from "the people in the Country who distil." Payment to the importers would have to be on the principles laid out by Burke for the purchase of salt outlined in his letter of August 31. Payment to local distillers could be engaged in grain "which they can afterwards make use of for distillation." Davie's mode of "procuring the Beves is eligible," but Burke wanted Davie to include in his estimates what might be necessary "for the Federal Army and for our Allies." He approved, moreover, of the stalling of the "beves" as a "good mode of converting to good account the surplus Grain which the plenty of this year promises." [99]

These were the last instructions for some time from Thomas Burke,

SUBSISTING AN ARMY

who presently set out from Halifax for Hillsborough. En route he stopped at Williamsborough and there, on September 7, requested Davie to join him "as the greatest part of the business in your Department, will be in this part of the Country."[100]

There is no evidence that Davie joined the Governor at Williamsborough before His Excellency proceeded on up to Hillsborough, where, September 13, he was captured by the ruthless Tory, David Fanning.

Davie did not enjoy so close a co-operation and interest from Burke's temporary successor, whom Davie had satirically called "a "Warrior of great fame," Alexander Martin. Yet his duties and exasperations continued. From Kingston he had a report from one of his assistant commissaries, Captain James Winn, that their "prospects from that quarter are not equal to our first expectations." Nevertheless Davie charged Winn with the responsibility of supplying a detachment of Continentals and militia which marched from Tarborough to Cross Creek and Wilmington and all other troops ordered to that vicinity.[101]

As things turned out, Davie was entrusting to Winn the supply of a force of eleven hundred men under Generals Rutherford and Butler, who were sent to the Cape Fear by Governor Martin to relieve the countryside of the depredations of Major Craig. Davie, in the final analysis, was responsible for providing for this force which, by such skirmishes as those at Rockfish Creek, Moore's Plantation, North East Bridge (twelve miles above Wilmington), and Seven Creeks (below Wilmington), succeeded in clearing the Cape Fear section, except Wilmington itself, of the enemy.[102]

No doubt it was such strains as these which were responsible for Davie's being "very ill" some time during the latter part of September, though by the twenty-eighth he was able to plan a trip up to Nut-bush, in Granville County, to see the new governor and Council.[103]

By the time Davie was heard from again, Cornwallis had surrendered at Yorktown, but Greene was still struggling with the enemy in South Carolina, though after the battle of Eutaw Springs, September 8, there was no serious fighting in South Carolina or Georgia. Yet the Treaty of Paris and the evacuation of the British from Charleston December 14, 1782, were some time in the offing. Meanwhile Greene's army had to eke out a miserable existence, "naked, hungry and pennyless."[104] His correspondence with Davie reveals his destitution and the bungling policy of North Carolina.

Whatever hopes he had for assistance from North Carolina were dampened by Davie, who wrote him a lengthy letter on October 22. Davie's analysis of the situation in North Carolina and his criticism of the policies of Governors Martin and Nash are revealing:

> Should this letter pop in upon you planning some deadly manuvre, you can easily lay it aside, untill you have leisure to think on the old subject of *money* and *supplies*.
>
> You have felt, and without doubt must be convinced, that the resources of the State, either from a blunder in our policy or want of address in the Executive, are of no more service, than if they were really exhausted; and neither our money, nor our Credit are any longer a Midium.
>
> The ruinous policy of Governor Nash in impressing all imported Articles, on the moment of arrival, had discouraged trade so effectually, that we were left without fifty bushels of public salt in the State, and the inhabitants in the same situation. The Unfortunate Govr. Burke gave the merchants assurances of protection, which remedied part of the Evil, but the Government has made no provision for purchases.
>
> I am authorized to exchange the Articles of my own Depart., but Tobacco and *hard money* are principally wanting. Now Sir had I but a small, even a very limited Credit on the Continental Treasury or finance by applying this as specie in [payt.] of Contracts would enable me to supply you amply.
>
> This was suggested by a large quantity of Salt now lying at Edenton with some rum, the property of Morris and other Merchants in Philadelphia; for which it is not in my power to give them a proper consideration.
>
> I consulted Mr. Johnston one of our Delegates, who thought with me that an application through you, and Genl. Washington, if you thought it necessary would undoubtedly effect it.
>
> It answers little purpose to call upon this state for supplies she cannot procure, and, if you still rely on us, I must be furnished with other resources.[105]

By November 1, however, Davie was able to direct a little cheer to General Jethro Sumner's brigade of "Guilford runaways," who had been sentenced to twelve months' duty as Continentals and were then serving with Greene.[106] Davie had ordered some rum sent to them, which he had put in charge of one of Sumner's officers so that it would not "lose much on its journey," and may be "properly applied when it arrives." Sugar and coffee would also be forwarded soon.[107]

Davie, in acknowledging on November 12 a letter from Greene, assured him that "no man feels with more sensibility the wants and sufferings of your little army" and repeated that if it were "possible to obtain the *credit* I refer to, it would enable me to supply you amply; but at any rate, if you inform me of your wants as they occur, I shall endeavor to supply you, as far as I am permitted to use the resources of the State." However, Craig's presence at Wilmington, "the frequent insurections and the imbecillity of our Government have embarrassed all public business."[108]

Greene's reply to Davie's earlier letter of October 22 is significant as representing the one reprimand of Greene to his former assistant. Even here Greene seems to vent more of his scorn on the State of North Carolina than upon Davie himself, whom he charges with lack of patience and perseverance:

It is a great pity that such an extensive State as North Carolina naturally rich and powerful should be reduced to a degree of poverty and distress by impolicy so as to be unable to supply her own inhabitants with such necessaries as they want and the Army with such things as she is bound to provide. I hope more wisdom will appear in your future conduct and that all shall feel the happy effects of it. However if either you or Government wait until there appears a plenty of every thing to answer the public demands you will find the day distant. Many difficulties are over come by proper exertions and supplies are to be found by industry where there appears a scarcity. Let nothing discourage you therefore but press forward and repeat your demands again and again and persevere and persist in them until you tire out the Legislature with your applications and this and this only will rouse them to due attention to our wants and difficulties. You have abilities you have influence only add patience and perseverance and you will triumph in time; for I am persuaded the State can afford us great relief if they can but be brought to feel our difficulties. Wilmington being evacuated by the Enemy will enable them to do more and give you another opportunity to demand fresh supplies in consequence thereof.

The plan you propose of giving your bills is not in my power to comply with having drawn for more already than I fear I can justify. The Minister of Finance desires me to be very sparing on this subject.[109]

Davie, in his turn, on December 10, pleaded again "the weakness of our Government, the immediate presence of the Enemy and a blundering police [sic]" as an excuse for not sending supplies. More particularly, Davie pointed to the fact that the "specific levies of Government are quite inadequate" and that "our *money* and *promissory notes* are called *state tricks* and will be no longer receiv'd, so that I have been obliged to procure the necessary supplies by impressment and contribution." As a result he had "order'd a Beef supply to be immediately put in motion for your Army—and shall levy the remainder of your requisition as soon as possible risquing the sanction of Legislation." He had also delivered one hundred bushels of salt for Greene's army to Colonel Nicholas Long, the state quartermaster general. Davie hoped that "the General happy countenance of American affairs" and "the tranquillity we shall soon enjoy in this State" would "restore dignity and Energy once more to our Government, and enable us to give you the necessary assistance."[110]

Obviously Greene had not received Davie's letter of December 10 when seventeen days later he dispatched a letter to Davie by the hand of Lieutenant Colonel Walter Stewart, who was "delegated for the express purpose of laying several matters before your Assembly." A question of great urgency was that of beef. Without "great assistance in this article," Greene argued that it would be "utterly impossible to support ourselves." Therefore he begged Davie "by every public and private consideration to exert yourself to give us the assistance we want in the article of beef rum & salt." Since North Carolina was now "at liberty and free from the Enemy" she could give "very great support if proper assertions are made and a good disposition prevails." His urgency was pointed up by the fact that the "enemy are more than double our numbers and to have to contend with such superior numbers without provisions and without rum nothing but ruin can be expected." Though Greene would do all he could, he threatened that the "Enemy must prevail if you do not give us more effectual support."[111]

That Davie, in the face of feeble support from the state, was doing his utmost to meet these demands is revealed in a letter of November 15, in which he defended himself against a harsh insinuation from Brigadier General Rutherford:

Relative to the rum, sugar and coffee, which you suggest I have withheld from the militia, when you are informed that the supply I sent on was much larger than the Governor ordered, that I purchased the rum on my own credit, that I borrowed the sugar and coffee, and bound myself to replace it, a man of honor and sensibility would be sorry for the style and passion of your letter. At a time when the public have neither money nor credit, any thinking man would be at a loss to account for the lengths I have gone to serve them, but by my zeal for my country and natural attachment to the army.[112]

Others, too, were making demands on Davie. On November 28 General Arthur St. Clair, writing from Williamsborough on his way to join Greene, requested that Davie "direct provisions to be laid in for three thousand men, on the road from this place to Camden, by the High Rock Ford, Guilford, Salisbury and Charlotteburgh." He would need "provisions, bread especially, at as many places on our march, as it can be laid in with any convenience, as we have not the means to carry above one or two days' supply with us."[113]

General Sumner was also at this time pressing Davie for supplies. Of the articles Sumner requested, Robert Fenner, in charge of the "public & State store" at Halifax, reported on January 24 that none was on hand "except the spirrits and sugar, nor do I know of the smallest probability of receiving any more of them except some Coffee."[114]

Meanwhile some relief was forwarded to Sumner's brigade in January, 1782, when Governor Martin ordered "the greatest part of every kind of stores" on hand in the state storehouse at Halifax to be sent to them. This supply was obtained from the subscription collected by Davie and from the cargo of the *Industry*, which had been sent from Martinique by the Marquis of Bretigny, North Carolina's most successful purchasing agent. This cargo was to be paid for principally in old pork which Major Mountflorence was to collect from Kingston and other places in Newbern District and deliver over to the Newbern merchants, Van Schellebeck and Marshall, who were the factors of the Marquis of Bretigny. From this source Davie, rather than Colonel Long, was directed by the governor to furnish Sumner's officers with "as much Cloth as will make them a Suit of Clothes & a great Coat, as much Linen as will make them 2 Coarse Shirts and

2 fine, 2 Coarse pr. of Stockings." The remainder of the goods were to remain in Davie's custody in Halifax.[115]

Robert Fenner submitted the following return of the stores left on hand in the state storehouse at Halifax: [116]

	Rum & Brandy	700	Gallons
	Salt	88	bushels
	Sugar	173	lbs.
	Coffee	40	lbs.
5 pss.	coarse cloth contd	98½	yards
9 pss.	blue serge	199¾	do.
63 pss.	course French linnen	1,950	do.
6 pss.	linnen	148	do.
4 pss.	Britannias	28	do.
	Worsted stockings	40	pair
	Brown thread do	119	do.
	A considerable quantity of white and coloured threads.		

Governor Martin, despite Davie's accusations, attempted to satisfy General Greene's requisitions by directing Davie "to levy a Contribution of 1000 Head of Cattle on Edenton District, the like Number Cattle in Newbern and Wilmington Districts amounting to 3000, which the Comrs. are now collecting under the Aid of Generals Gregory, Caswell and Lillington, also 500 Barrels of pork, in Edenton District to make satisfaction to the Merchants for their supplies." In addition, since Colonel Stewart's arrival, Martin directed the Edenton quartermaster, Doctor Cooley, to deliver to Colonel Long for the use of Greene's army "100 Bushels of Salt, 1 Hoghd of Rum, 1 Hogshd. of French Brandy & 500 lb. of Sugar." [117]

But ten days later Martin informed Greene that his requisition would have to be deferred to the legislature which was to meet in April. Its complexion would be changed by the return of new members, who he felt would be more punctual in attending. This delay gave Martin "real uneasiness, which our civil Government cannot at present remedy," but he "flattered" himself that the conditions would be improved by the return of Governor Burke, who had broken his parole. The latter's exertions would "not be wanting to carry into Effect as far as in his power, every measure and everything

SUBSISTING AN ARMY

expected from this State for the General good." Martin, moreover, informed Greene that Colonel Davie and his assistants were endeavoring to have the cattle, levied by contributions, driven into South Carolina "to be fed in the Rice plantations, where they may be easier fatned than by being stall fed in this State." The Wilmington and Salisbury District had also sent almost their quota, which was one thousand cattle.[118]

By February 17 Davie was in Salisbury, trying to supply North Carolina's northern and southern neighbors. On that day he requested Virginia's Governor Benjamin Harrison to inform him when "a considerable body of Militia are to march soon from your State to the So. Army." This state being "drained and exhausted," it was necessary to know "what time they will be put in motion, what route they will march and their numbers, that proper provision may be made for them through the State."[119]

Davie was able, however, to inform Greene that they were "making every possible exertion" in favor of his requisitions, that Colonel Long had "much more Salt than he can forward at present," and that "the Beef supplies are collecting all over the state, but many of them are so wretched poor they cannot move on before the spring." Reiterating the old story in regard to the draining of the Salisbury District, he pointed out: "The Country here is really so drained & exhausted that it is with difficulty even a precarious Subsistence is procured."[120]

Greene's reply revealed that his little army was still in a most distressing situation: "The Difficulty of getting Things purchased for the Army is very great but to get them forward to the Army appears still greater; had I not procured a temporary Supply of Salt, we should have been without for Months together.... As for spirits we have had none for Months together nor can I see any Prospect of getting any: our Situation is truly deplorable."

Greene complained particularly of the "great want of Exertion among Men of influence in the District of Salisbury to aid the Army: the Delay the little Clothing has met with coming to us for want of means of Transportation has distressed us exceedingly: the Soldiers of your State for want of clothing excite pity from every beholder." Moreover, the want of supplies "even at the Posts of Charlotte & Salisbury are truly distressing and not a little alarming."

Greene also had a very serious complaint to make in regard to General Rutherford. He had been informed from different people that this recently-liberated officer "gives great obstructions to the Business of getting supplies," though Greene could hardly credit the rumor. However, he requested Davie to inform him if it were so and Greene would impeach Rutherford before the governor and his council. He thought it strange "that a Man who owes his Liberty to the Exertions of this Army, should take Measures to distress its operations."

Greene then posed to Davie a series of questions which reveal his helplessness and despair: "Will the States adopt the Plan recommended by Mr. Morris for supply [sic] the Army.* The ground work of it is a tax. Pray urge the Necessity, if the People will not pay a Tax to support Government it must fail, and then the Enemy will carry their Point after all the blood shed and Distress undergone for the support of the Cause, certainly they are not mad enough to neglect or rather desert the Cause from the Influence of Avarice. can you find any person to contract for Supplies? Will you undertake to supply the Posts of Communications by contract? or can you recommend any person that will? please to inform me as soon as possible, but at all Events I beg you to give such Directions in the Business as to have Posts of Communication properly provided for. how can you my dear Sir expect we can have success or even an existance when whole States desert us. & if not desert us their efforts are too feeble to assist us. Certainly no Army after the hardships it has endured was ever left in so deplorable a Condition as ours, and none but ours would keep together under such distress [sic] circumstances." [121]

Davie's reply to this, the last available letter from Greene, is unknown, though for at least two more months Davie was to exert his efforts in the commissary department, where he worked in unison with Governor Burke. The latter, more co-operative than Martin,

* The plan of Robert Morris referred to by Greene was one to abolish entirely the system of requisitioning supplies from the various states. Having had ample time in which to observe its weaknesses, Morris had suggested in a letter to the governors of the states, February 15, 1782, that the army should be provisioned by contract.—Johnson, *American Commissariat*, p. 217.

wrote Davie shortly after resuming the gubernatorial chair that he would do all he could to support his contracts "as long as I hold the administration, but that period, I hope, will not be long."[122]

Davie and many other leading citizens of North Carolina had been greatly concerned over Governor Burke's capture. Back in December, 1781, both he and his future father-in-law, General Allen Jones, had urged Greene to use his influence to effect Burke's "enlargement," either by exchange or on parole. Jones had been convinced that "the enlargement of that Gentleman would tend greatly to the advantage of the Southern States, as I know no one who can so well draw out the resources of the State or who has more Activity and Zeal."[123]

Davie was equally distressed by the situation in which Burke found himself after he broke his parole on James Island below Charleston. Though greatly censured for this act, Burke justified it on the grounds that his life was in danger. He thus maintained the confidence of such men as Samuel Johnston, William Hooper, James Iredell, the two Jones brothers, as well as Davie.[124] On February 23 Davie wrote the governor that Colonel Otho Williams, on his way from Greene's army to Maryland, informed him that "the propriety of your conduct in cancelling your parole has become a question of serious importance—that it was the opinion of the Court and General Greene that the Enemy have *legal* claims upon you as a *prisoner of war*, that your leaving Head Quarters before matters could be settled or adjusted, taking the Government under those circumstances is considered highly reprehensible in you, and dishonourable to the State." Davie, assuring him of his "Friendship and Attachment," wanted to know how he could serve him in this affair and urged him to "take some measures for your justification." Davie himself had already "been controverting some malicious attacks."[125]

Elucidating further on the matter, Colonel Williams wrote Davie the next day that, at Burke's request, a court of inquiry was held, presided over by Major General St. Clair. The latter's report "by no means justified the conduct of Governor Burk," and Williams was persuaded that Greene considered Burke a prisoner of war.[126]

In spite of the protests, Burke continued in business as usual and continued to work in conjunction with Davie. On February 26 he notified Davie of the immediate necessity of obtaining an account of "Specific articles delivered in the State ... in order that the Accounts thereof against the Continent be made up." For any commissioner who refused or delayed, Burke would use "every Endeavor to have them punished for Neglect of so Necessary a Service, in which the property of the people is so deeply concerned."[127]

In March Davie was also faced with the supply of the French army which marched through the state on its way to the southward. For this purpose he called for all the meat, both pork and beef, remaining in the Edenton district. He also ordered all the salt and other public provisions in that district to be forwarded to the state storehouse at Halifax.[128]

By April, 1782, the beeves ordered by Martin in November and collected by Davie had still not been sent to Greene's army. Davie wrote Governor Burke that they could not move until the grass was tall enough to support them en route and that they had no stalled cattle "but a few Weeks will now put them in good Order, and they shall be forwarded as soon as they are—in Condition for service and the Journey." Also the distance was "too great to drive Hoggs in the Summer Season and there is no Grain on the rout, for their support." There was also "very little rum in the State at present, but the first arrivals shall be purchased," and "Deliveries of Sugar and Coffee shall be immediately made in the Line you mention."

In the same letter Davie referred to his being favored with "the picture you refer to, it was just." No doubt Greene had again painted the pathetic plight of his army, because Davie continued: "This comes of the stupid policy of the Specific Act, making 'provisions for Bread alone.' The Flesh Contributions were too lean to be eaten, and the Qr. Masters Complain they cannot fatten them for want of assistance." Davie had ordered the quartermasters at Salisbury to send to the Narrows on the Yadkin "for Fish, where I was promised a few Waggon Loads—Beef they have on hand but it is too poor."

Finally, in anticipating the convening of the assembly, Davie informed Burke that he had sent for all his assistants to see him before he went up to the Assembly, so that he might furnish Burke with "an accurate State of the Department."[129]

Before going up to the Assembly, which convened April 13 at Hillsborough, Davie's time and interest were concerned with less irksome chores than getting an "accurate State" of the commissary department. Instead, he was interested in the state of matrimony. On

April 11 * he was married to Sarah Jones, the nineteen-year-old daughter of Brigadier General Allen Jones of Northampton County and niece of the more celebrated Willie Jones of Halifax, North Carolina. The only report, except her epitaph, of this marriage, is contained in a letter to Governor Burke, in which Davie wrote: "My happiness though very complete on Thursday last, would have been more so by the presence of some of my absent friends, I should have felt a singular satisfaction in seeing you unlaced from the cares of State.

" 'Mingling o'er the friendly bowl
The feast of *reason*, and the flow of *soul*.' " [130]

Unfortunately there is no record of Davie's appearance before the Assembly or of his report on the state of his department to the governor. The latter sent a message to the Assembly on April 22, in which he said he had taken measures to procure such a statement from the quartermaster and commissary departments, which he hoped would "produce some effect before the General Assembly adjourns from hence." [131] Davie had also written Burke that he expected to see him about the twenty-fifth.[132] This brief communication from Davie is the last available word from him on the subject of his duties as commissary general.

Meanwhile there was a growing discontent with the abuses practiced by the deputies in both the commissary and quartermaster departments. On May 5 a committee, headed by Thomas Person, of Granville County, presented to the House of Commons a report setting forth as a "grievance the establishment of a Commissary General in this State as now exercised by a numerous train of Deputies and Assistant Deputies." These deputies were depicted as "exercising the most unlimited powers in calling upon County Commissioners and receiving from them Public Stores of every denomination and making Grievances and unheard of impressments and requisitions on men of little or no property whereby the State or injured Citizens might be secured." These same abuses were found to prevail in "a very extensive latitude in the quartermaster department."

---

*Inscription on the tombstone of Sarah Jones Davie in the Colonial cemetery, Halifax, North Carolina. According to this, she was born September 23, 1762, and died at the age of forty, April 14, 1802.

William R. Davie

This committee therefore recommended that these two departments "ought to be annihilated."[133]

Within a fortnight, on the strength of these recommendations, the legislature saw fit on May 17 to abolish both the quartermaster and commissary departments and to restrain future impressments.[134]

It is therefore chiefly through the medium of the correspondence of the newly-elected governor, Alexander Martin, that information may be gleamed as to Davie's activities. On May 12 Martin wrote General Greene that Davie had informed him that his requisition of the long-awaited cattle made the preceding November was "near compleat, and will be ready to be driven as soon as they will be in order for that purpose." Martin did not know "whether any supplies of Spirits, Sugar and Coffee have reached you, which have been ordered both by water and land."[135]

Shortly thereafter, the governor instructed "Col. Davie, Late Commissary General, ... to finish the contributions, ordered by the late executive and deliver the live stock intended for the Southern army as soon as possible at head quarters" and that his "pay and expenses shall be allowed and accounted for in the same manner as before the passing of the Act."[136] Martin also felt remorseful at being constrained to dismiss Davie's assistants, but Davie put his qualms at ease on this score: "I am sorry your Excellency should feel a pang on that subject, as they have already dismissed themselves, and it was with the utmost difficulty I could prevail on them to collect the cattle of the contribution. No man could desire them to continue in a service, where they reap no recompense but reproach for their most active and zealous exertions."[137]

By August, 1782, ten months after Greene's requisition of the livestock in question, a new impasse prevented their being sent to him. This time, however, the blame could not be laid to the executive but to the legislature. On Martin's assumption of office he, on receipt of an urgent letter from Greene, had directed Davie before he closed his accounts to collect the remaining cattle and forward them on to Greene "as it became properly his duty." At this point, however, Governor Martin reported he had had the "Mortification to hear from Colonel Davie that my orders for this purpose to him, are generally disputed and opposed suggesting the mode of procuring this supply of provision illegal and oppressive to the people." He

Subsisting an Army

further reported that "As there is not any particular Act of Assembly to warrant it, some few Commissioners have complied and delivered what Cattle they had on hand (which I am told are gone on) others have not collected any, and what they collected have sent them back to the owners."

Martin was "sensible that the above objections at first sight had weight among the populace, and to make the measure palatable I required Colonel Davie in the first place, to appeal to the patriotism of the Inhabitants of those Districts to make voluntary contributions." He also appealed to General John Bryan, of Newbern, for one thousand head of cattle from Newbern District, deducting from that number whatever may have been received by Colonel Davie. He made a similar appeal to Edenton and Wilmington, but omitted Salisbury, Hillsborough, and Morgan districts, since they "were quite exhausted by the number of Troops marching and countermarching through that section of the State." Martin's final word was that "if Cattle cannot be procured by barter, purchase on Certificates, contributions or by private persons undertaking to supply the Army" Bryan would "be drove to the last odious and disagreeable measure of impressment which you will please to order agreeable to the Taxable property of the owners in the respective Counties."[138] Meanwhile, three hundred head had gone forward from Wilmington and as many more would soon start from Edenton and Newbern.[139]

Somehow Greene's little army survived the winter, though Christmas, even after the evacuation of Charleston by the British, was reported as "poor"—there was "no beef or rum for the men." April 16 brought news of peace, but the general illumination of Charleston and a *feu de joie* on James Island did not raise the army's spirit, dampened by having neither "bread nor rice." Gradually, however, the situation was eased for Greene by the return of the men to their homes.[140]

For his many arduous services as Greene's commissary general, Davie had great difficulty in trying to collect any payment. Unfortunately he was not in Halifax when General Greene passed through there August 31, 1783, on his way northward after the disbanding of his army. A letter from Davie to Greene, some months later, reveals that Greene wrote Davie of his regret at missing him and of the satisfaction he would have experienced at seeing him at "'the close of all our troubles' after the many anxious hours we have been together." Davie on his part regretted he had not had an opportunity "to assist in doing the Honors of my Country to the man, to whom of all others we are principally indebted."[141]

Yet Davie's chief purpose in writing to Greene was of a more practical nature. Recalling that he was from the first of January to the first of June, 1781, "in the employ of the Continent at your particular instance," Davie wrote that he had forgot, when he parted with Greene, to ask for a certificate of those services. However, he said it would "do as well now, and you can tell me How I shall get my money." Davie also wrote that he had "a few small credits to give the Continent, which, as I am an *Honest-Fellow*, I wish to know how to do." He concluded that he had already taken leave of Greene "as one of my friends I shall never see again, for public business will scarcely ever jostle us together hereafter; but I wish to know where you intend to live, that should I ever be in your neighbourhood, I may call upon you, and see what kind of quarters you keep in time of peace."[142]

In June, 1784, and December, 1785, Davie wrote Greene that he had still received no reply, though he had written Greene "in every quarter of the Continent, and indeed it seems more difficult to get a letter to you now; than when you were surrounded by your enemies." Davie again requested a certificate of his services, which he had not obtained on leaving Greene at Ninety-Six, because at that time "we thought of nothing but preserving our Country; our success has left us leisure to think of doing ourselves Justice."[143]

A few days later Davie reiterated his request, this time sending the letter by the hand of his old assistant, Major Mountflorence.[144] But there is no available record of his ever obtaining this certificate or of his receiving compensation for these services.

There is also a dearth of material on the final settlement of Davie's accounts as commissary general. There is no reason, however, to doubt the statement of Davie's son, forty years later, filial loyalty to the contrary notwithstanding, when he said that "the final settlement of these accounts in I believe 83 will shew what N Ca did then and for which she has never had due credit: you will see that we led our proud neighbors both North and South."[145]

The journals of the legislature, as a matter of fact, are very sketchy in regard to Davie's final payment. In May, 1783, Governor Alexander Martin reviewed the situation in a message to the legislature and asked their advice as to the settlement to be made to Davie and the other members of his department. Martin pointed out that the department had been abolished at the last Assembly without any allowance having been made to Davie or his five assistants and one clerk. He felt that "something is therefore due them for their trouble and the services they have rendered the public, which I am sensible were considerable, notwithstanding some abuses may have been committed in this business, as well as others of public nature, which time and circumstances could not obviate." He informed them further that the late Council Extraordinary, which had superseded the Board of War, had recommended to the governor that these officers, as well as those in the quartermaster department, should be granted payments from the state treasury equal to those of the same rank in the Continental line. Martin, however, had hesitated to carry out this measure until he "could take the sense of your Honourable body further on this subject." Meanwhile he had granted £200 specie to Colonel Davie and £100 each to his five assistants and £50 to his clerk.[146]

As might be expected, the settlement was long drawn out. It was not until over a year later that General John Butler, chairman of the joint Committee of Propositions and Grievances, to which Martin's message was referred, reported that this committee were of the opinion that the services of these men were "similar to those of officers of the same rank in the Continental Army" and recommended that Davie "be allowed the same pay per month, as fixed by a Deputy Commissary General of purchases for the Continental Army" and that the same should prevail for his assistants and for the members of the quartermaster department.[147]

It is most unlikely that either the governor or the General Assembly knew, at the time of their concurrence with this report, the complications to be faced in computing the salary allowed by the Continental Congress. By an act passed on January 1, 1780, by the Continental Congress the commissary general of purchases of the United States was to receive forty thousand dollars per year, plus six rations a day and forage for four horses. However, assistant commissaries were to be allowed "on all good merchantable articles which may be purchased by them, or under their direction, respectively, two per cent on twenty fold the prices they were sold at in the year 1774." Out of this sum they were to "pay all their agents, and defray the whole expence attending such purchases." Nor were assistant commissary generals or their agents to be entitled to rations or forage "except when called by the necessary business of their department to attend the army." [148]

The records are again silent as to the actual payment which Davie and his assistants received as a result of this act. It is known, however, that on May 17, 1782, John Johnston, chairman of the committee to examine the accounts of John Haywood, Secretary of the late Board of War, reported that his committee had found that there had been advanced to Davie, as commissary general, the sum of one hundred thousand pounds by Warrants on the Treasury from Governor Nash in February, 1781.[149] Furthermore, according to Hubbard, Davie began preparing his accounts after the spring session of the Assembly in 1782. "Exceedingly complex and numerous," they included almost every militia officer and merchant in the state. By August they were forwarded to the comptroller's office, at which time Davie invited the "severest legislative scrutiny." As a result of the comptroller's examination, his accounts were accepted and the settlements were closed "with honor to himself and satisfaction to the government." [150]

In any appraisal of Davie's efforts and contributions as commissary general it seems safe to hazard the statement that no man in the state, so hampered by the scarcity of provisions, the lack of transportation facilities, the inertia and at times antipathy of a divided people, and the governmental lethargy, could have better acquitted himself in handling so tedious and thankless a labor.

His success may perhaps best be measured by the respect and esteem with which he was viewed by the people of North Carolina. Nor should the fact be overlooked that, after all, the American states did win their fight for independence. This could not have been accomplished without the untiring efforts of the men who struggled to provide them with the sinews of war.

CHAPTER VI

A Conservative under the Constitution

PERHAPS as early as December, 1781, William R. Davie had selected Halifax, North Carolina, as his future home. No doubt his approaching marriage in the spring to Sarah Jones was foremost in his mind when, on December 8, he purchased, for two hundred pounds, lot number fifteen in that borough town. It was evidently in a pleasant and congenial neighborhood, for it had formerly been held by Colonel Joseph Montfort, whose daughter Mary married Willie Jones, Sarah Davie's uncle. Colonel Montfort had been appointed by the Duke of Beaufort in 1771 as the "Grand Master of Masons of and for America." As such he was the first, last, and only Grand Master of America. He had also served as the first clerk of the court of Halifax County, treasurer of the province, colonel of colonial troops, and a member of the provincial congress. Part of the land bordering on Davie's purchase was owned by Willie Jones and part had formerly been held by the affluent Tory, James Milner, who had owned the largest library of which there is any record in colonial North Carolina.[1]

In the absence of the plat of the town,* it was no doubt upon this lot that Davie built his home, "Loretta," which still stands two blocks directly behind the present courthouse in Halifax. This house, sturdily built and in good taste, has been in constant occupation since

---

* An extensive search for this plat has been made not only in Halifax and the Department of Archives and History, Raleigh, North Carolina, but also by the late Mr. Elliott Clark of Weldon, North Carolina, in the British Museum.

its construction.* Its exterior is of the pediment-roofed type first used in the Randolph-Semple House in Williamsburg, Virginia, and copied, with modifications, by "The Groves," Willie Jones's home, in Halifax, the Junius Tillery house, about ten miles away, in Tillery, and several others throughout this section. Less pretentious than these, and using only an ell on one side, instead of the two wings used by the others, it lacks their elegance and grace. Inside, its high ceilings, frescoes, interesting trim, wide floor boards, and mahogany balusters, however, all indicate a gracious way of life.†

Two years after purchasing his first lot, Davie also bought on May 4, 1783, for fifty pounds current money, five acres of land lying on the northwest of Halifax. This land was bounded by St. David's Street, extended, and the lands of Willie Jones and Cosimo de Medici,[2] scion of the great Florentine family, who gave his services to the Revolutionary efforts of North Carolina.

It was probably not until 1785, at least, that William Richardson and Sarah began building their home in Halifax. Like so many of the newly-married couples of that day and the present, they no doubt began their married life under the roof of the bride's father. General Allen Jones lived at that time in Occoneechee Neck on the Northampton side of the Roanoke River opposite Halifax at "The Castle." In 1774 the English visitor, Smyth, visited the seat of a "Mr. Jones," which was "in Occoneachy-neck, and extreme rich and valuable tract of land, about two miles from town, and is indeed an elegant seat." ‡

The assumption that Davie did not officially move to the town of Halifax until 1785 is based on the fact that he was elected to the House of Commons from Northampton County for the year 1784. If the Constitution of North Carolina was strictly adhered to, he

---

* At one time it was remodeled and altered, but its present owners, Mr. and Mrs. Turner Stephenson, have restored it as nearly as possible to its original plan.

† For a discussion of the influence of the Randolph-Semple House, see Frances Benjamin Johnston and Thomas Tileston Waterman, *The Early Architecture of North Carolina: A Pictorial Survey with An Architectural History* (Chapel Hill: The University of North Carolina Press, 1947), pp. 37, 38, 41, with illustrations on pages 91-95.

‡ John Ferdinand Dalziel Smyth, *A Tour in the United States of America* (Dublin: Printed by G. Perrin, for Messrs. Price, Moncrieffe, etc., 1784), I, 52.

A Conservative under the Constitution

would have had to have resided in the county which he represented for one year immediately preceding his election and should have been in possession of one hundred acres of land in that county in fee simple or for the term of his life for at least six months prior to his election. Yet there is no record in the office of the Register of Deeds, Jackson, Northampton County, of his ever having held any land in that county. Perhaps the local constituents and the House of Commons overlooked the technicality in the case of a military hero and the son-in-law of General Allen Jones. Another case of North Carolina's leniency is the fact that Judge William Gaston, eminent Catholic jurist of New Bern and friend of Davie, held office in North Carolina despite Article 32 of the Constitution which excluded all non-Protestants from office-holding. Also the avowed deist, Willie Jones, was never proscribed.

Inasmuch as the General Assembly sat from April 19 to June 3 and from October 22 to November 22 of that year, it is likely that Davie did not move across the river until sometime the following year. Here, in Halifax, he quite naturally took his place among the leaders of this, the political mecca of northeastern North Carolina, which vied with Edenton as a social center. A number of contemporary accounts attest to its importance. A glance at a few of them may serve to place Davie in his new milieu.

The town itself was older than the county. The colonial Assembly had granted a charter for the town's erection in 1757,[3] though the county itself was not formed from Edgecombe until the following year.[4] Named in honor of George Montagu Dunk, Earl of Halifax and a member of the Board of Trade, it was established on the lands of one James Leslie, on the south side of the Roanoke River, in the northern part of Edgecombe County. This land was described in 1757 as lying in "a healthy pleasant situation, well watered and commodious for commerce." The Assembly at that time appointed Thomas Barker, Alexander McCulloh, John Gibson, Robert Browning, and Sarah Davie's grandfather, Robert Jones, the younger, as trustees to supervise the buildings and the laying off of lots and to direct the affairs of the town until its completion.[5]

A market place of four acres was to be laid off in the center of the town; the remainder was to be cut up into at least 120 town lots, of half an acre each. Upon each lot, the purchaser was required to build, within three years, "one well framed house, sixteen feet square at the least, and ten feet pitch in the clear."[6] The town very soon attracted settlers and became the center of the commercial activities of the surrounding country.[7]

Located thus on the Roanoke River along whose borders—according to the peripatetic Elkanah Watson in 1778—lay "the wealthiest region of North Carolina," its soil was "rich and highly cultivated." The principal crops, he observed, were "corn pease, and tobacco, in immense quantities, and also some rice." He also saw "vast droves of hogs, ranging among these plantations."[8] George Washington, in his tour of the Southern states, said that "the lands are cultivated in Tobacco, Corn, Wheat and Oats, but Tobacco and the raising of Porke for market, seems to be the principal dependence of the inhabitants.... Cotton and Flax are also raised but not extensively." He continued by saying that to the town of Halifax, where he spent the nights of April 16th and 17th, 1791, "vessels by the aid of Oars and Setting poles are brought for the produce which comes to this place, and others along the River."[9]

While the President was there, Colonel John Baptiste Ashe, then congressman for the district, and "several other Gentlemen" called on him and invited him "to partake of a dinner which the Inhabitants were desirous to see me at and excepting it dined with them accordingly."[10] Whether Davie was among these "other Gentlemen" is unknown, but it appears that Samuel Johnston was, because he wrote James Iredell that Washington's reception "was not such as we could wish tho in every other part of the Country he was treated with proper attention."[11]

The English visitor, Smyth, in 1774, commented that Halifax was "a pretty town" to which "sloops, schooners, and flats, or lighters of great burden" came up the stream which was "deep and gentle." The town, he noted, enjoyed "a tolerable share of commerce in tobacco, pork, butter, flour, and some tar, turpentine, skins, furs, and cotton" and there were "many valuable fisheries at, or in the vicinity of Halifax."[12]

But with all its abundance of crops and the industry of its people, the town could not become a port for foreign trade. Its interior location and the frequent low water of the Roanoke caused it to depend mainly on Suffolk and Norfolk, Virginia, for import and export facilities. And the export of its products depended largely on the whim of the Virginia merchant, factor, or middleman. Virginia officials inspected their tobacco, selecting only the best and burning the rest. Virginia merchants paid for only the net meat of Carolina cattle driven up for slaughter, and appropriated the hide, tallow, livers, and remnants to their own use. Virginia merchants sold as Virginia pork the hogs from North Carolina, and slaughtered and salted them in Virginia. For all of these, the Virginia merchants paid their own prices.[13]

Regardless of this economic subservience to Virginia, Halifax had grown in population, commercial activity, and importance to a position where, on May 13, 1760, it obtained from the governor in council a charter of incorporation on the basis of the old Bath town sixty-family law of 1715. By this law, the town of Bath, and any other town which had at least sixty families, could elect a burgess to the Assembly.[14] In 1760 and 1761 it had sent Stephen Dewey as burgess to the House of Commons,[15] but when His Majesty's Commissioners for Trade and Plantations heard of it from Governor Arthur Dobbs, they declared June 2, 1762, that this admission of the burgess from Halifax to the Assembly was "unconstitutional and not warranted by any authority whatsoever." The sixty-family law did not apply to Halifax without a writ from His Majesty which first required "proper proof of such qualification."[16] In 1764, however, Governor Dobbs granted such a charter and from then until 1835, Halifax sent a burgess each year to the House of Commons.[17]

In 1758 the growth of Halifax was accelerated when the Assembly changed the place of holding the "Supreme Court of Justice, Oyer and Terminer, and General Gaol Delivery, for the District of Northampton, Edgecomb, and Granville" from Enfield to Halifax, because of the "Great Hardships and Inconveniences, for want of proper Accommodations and Entertainment" in the former place.[18] The same year it established public warehouses in Halifax,[19] and two years later it "enlarged the time for Inspection of Tobacco" at these warehouses.[20] In 1777 the General Assembly established biennial fairs to be held there in May and November, for "the sale of every kind of Horses and Black cattle, sheep, hogs, pork, and all kinds of provisions, tobacco and every other natural production of the

Country; and also for the sale of all and every sort of goods, wares and merchandise, whether foreign or manufactured in this State."[21]

The surrounding territory had become sufficiently populated and prosperous to petition the Assembly in 1758 for a separate county to be called Halifax. The resulting act, which became effective January, 1759, fixed the dividing line between the parish of Edgecombe, which became Halifax County, and the parish of St. Mary, which comprised the constricted Edgecombe County.[22] The new county was thus bounded by the present counties of Bertie, Martin, Edgecombe, Nash, Warren, and Northampton. Within three decades, about the time Davie settled there, it had become the most populous county in the state, with a population of 10,327—according to "an imperfect Census of the State... taken in the year 1786, by State Authority." It was also the only county which had more blacks than whites, the percentage being 50.7 blacks.[23]

The political importance of the town was soon manifest in its becoming the meeting place for the stirring third and fourth Provincial Congresses, in 1776, and of the General Assembly of 1780.

Its social importance is revealed in contemporary accounts. As early as 1767 Waightstill Avery, riding into Halifax in the company of Colonel Allen Jones, Dr. Cathcart and his daughters, one of whom married Samuel Johnston, "and 5 young Gent'n of Fortune," reported that he "was kindly rec'd by 3 Gent'n Merchts., and 6 Gent'n Att'ys. (viz.) Pendleton, Long, Brimage, Milner, Stokes & Coke." Here he received "a courteous invitation to a splendid Ball in the Evening, and was treated with great civility for 3 days."[24]

Seven years later, the observant Smyth, noting that Halifax was "a pretty town," said there were "many handsome buildings" in the town and its vicinity. These, however, were "almost all constructed of timber, and painted white." The particular homes he commented on, other than Allen Jones's country seat, were those of Joseph Montfort, Abner Nash, Nicholas Long, Thomas Eaton, and a Mr. Martin. Martin's home was originally built by Alexander Elmsley, former burgess in the House of Commons in 1762, a special agent of North Carolina in 1774,[25] and "an eminent practioner in the law." The house had been converted into an ordinary or inn and it was here, at "the best house of public entertainment in Halifax," that Smyth "put up." Mr. Long's home was about a mile out of Halifax "on the south side of a creek called Quankey (the Indian appellation for red paint, with which it abounds), with an exceeding lofty bridge over it, built of timber." [26]

About five or six miles beyond Mr. Long's house, in the same direction, there was "a considerable settlement, upon a pretty large watercourse, named the Marsh." Here Smyth was several times invited by Alexander McCulloh, "esq. a gentleman of considerable note, and Archibald Hamilton, esq.," the brother of the more famous Loyalist, John Hamilton. Archibald Hamilton was described as "a merchant of eminence, who carried on a very extensive and valuable commerce in Virginia, as well as in North Carolina." Both he and McCulloh entertained him with "great hospitality and politeness." He also "visited Willie Jones, esq. doctor Cathcart's, William Williams, esq., &c. among other gentlemen's seats, and met with a most courteous and friendly reception from all." *

The society in Halifax and vicinity was described in 1778 as "among the most polished and cultivated in the State," [27] and a Tory wrote James Iredell in 1785 that he had "received the most flattering marks of attention and hospitality from all the inhabitants of that polite and agreeable place," of which he had previously "formed a pleasing idea," but which exceeded his expectations. Particularly pleased was he to find in both Martin and Halifax counties "that the prejudices which unfortunately have been imbibed against me in this Country are confined to a very narrow circle." [28]

Numerous indeed were the visitors who commented on its grace, gaiety, and opulence. Thomas Iredell, on his arrival in Halifax in 1790, found the town "in the midst of gaity & Amusement, occasioned by the marriage of "the divine Miss Polly Long to a Virginia Beau of the Name of Stith, Six Bridesmen and Bridesmaids honord the Nuptials, a Rotation Dinner for Twenty two Families (& Dances at most of the Houses) with a General Ball, will settle them in domestic concerns." [29]

News of the Treaty of Peace, July 4th celebrations, Washington's visit in 1791, his birthday, weddings, court week—all were celebrated by "elegant dinners," "numerous toasts," discharges of cannons, and

---

* Smyth, *A Tour in the U. S.*, I, 56. Cathcart's seat was about twelve miles down the river in Northampton County; Williams' was in Halifax County near Brinkleyville. See Mouzon, *An Accurate Map of N. and S.C.*

"elegant balls." One such ball, celebrating Washington's birthday, was "graced by a very large and brilliant company of Ladies, who strove to do honour to the occasion by a display of uncommon elegance—several of their caps and sashes were ornamented with the initials of the President's name in golden embroidery." *

Fifteen years later, according to the Halifax *North-Carolina Journal*, a large tea party was "decorated with taste and elegance, adorned by beauty and wit, enlivened with vocal and instrumental music, and the evening gaily closed with the sprightly dance."[30]

Yet this "very gay and sociable place," which was "so remarkable for its sociability," did not seem to open its arms to young Will Blair, a cousin and assistant to James Iredell. He reported that he had been in town during court session for an entire week without an invitation except "a general invitation to Mr. [Willie] Jones'." Moreover, he had "been twice to Colo. Davie's Door but not yet in the House," though Davie had treated him "with great politeness & attention in Court."[31]

Even more disgruntled with Halifax was James Iredell himself, who wrote his wife, Hannah, that he would be "heartily glad when the Court is over, not only for my extreme impatience to get home, but to be clear of so disagreeable a place." Perhaps this aversion was fostered by a cold and the amount of business which prevented his going to a dance at Bond's the previous night. Or perhaps it was occasioned by the rowdiness which attended the great cock fight between North Carolina and Virginia, in which North Carolina was victorious by two battles.[32]

And perhaps such frivolities impelled Davie to spend Christmas at "Mount Gallant" † at his father-in-law's, to escape Christmas in Hali-

---

* Thomas Amis to Richard Bennehan, April 8, 1783.—Cameron Papers, S.H.C.; The Halifax *North-Carolina Journal*, Feb. 29, 1796; *ibid.*, July 9, 1794. This *Journal*, published weekly in Halifax by Abraham Hodge and Henry Wills, beginning July 18, 1792, and by Hodge alone, beginning with the February 6, 1793 issue, is an invaluable source of information on Davie, Halifax, and the state in general. Hodge died the year that Davie left North Carolina, 1805, but the paper was continued by several successive printers until 1814. See Clarence S. Brigham, *History and Bibliography of American Newspapers, 1690-1820* (Worcester, Massachusetts: American Antiquarian Society, 1947), II, 765-66. This paper will hereafter be referred to as *N.C.J.*

† The date of Allen Jones's move from "The Castle" to "Mount Gallant," about twenty miles up the Roanoke, is unknown. Mouzon's map, dated 1775,

fax, where "there has been much eating drinking and dancing." He observed that by December 29 they were "beginning to think of work again. This is the farce of human life." [33]

A rather startling assertion, unsupported by documentary evidence, in regard to the mores of the town was made in 1920 by the co-authors of the *History of Edgecombe County:* "Many [of the inhabitants] also became large land and slave owners, and operated large plantations near the town. Few of the men married, but lived a sedentary life of luxury and self-indulgence. Many free negroes and mulattoes intermarried with white women, while in the earliest period there was no recognized social restraint against exogamy to avoid incest." [34] It is regrettable that these authors did not document their interesting allegations!

Halifax was also the mecca of the neighboring counties in Virginia and North Carolina for the more masculine frivolities—horse races and cock fights. Before the Revolution an English traveler praised the excellence of the horses in southern Virginia and in North Carolina, where "they are much attracted to quarter-racing, which is always a match between two horses, to run one quarter of a mile straight out: being merely an exertion of speed; and they have a breed that perform it with astonishing velocity, beating each other, for that distance, with great ease; but they have no bottom. However, I am confident that there is not a horse in England, nor perhaps the whole world, that can excel them in rapid speed." [35]

Accustomed no doubt to the more politically-minded Edenton, Samuel Johnston observed that "Instead of Politics the general Topick of Conversation in this place [Halifax] is Horses, a Subject tho apparently perfectly understood and repeatedly talked over seems never to be exhausted." [36]

After the Revolution, indeed, the Roanoke Valley became, in the words of Davie's eldest son, Allen Jones Davie, "the race-horse region of America." This temporary supremacy, which passed from the Rappahannock to the southward, a later writer observed, was not based so much on the suitability of the region for breeding as it was

---

shows "Mount Gallant," while J. F. D. Smyth in 1774 mentioned his home as being in Occoneechee Neck. It appears that he maintained two homes at this time and probably used the older one when his attendance in Halifax was required.

a consequence of the depletion of the local bloodstock of Tidewater Virginia, New York, Pennsylvania, Maryland, and South Carolina—a depletion caused by British depredations and the necessity of supplying the American army. Left comparatively undisturbed in this section, the owners of horseflesh along the Roanoke were thus able to breed the old Virginia stock of Jolly Roger, Janus, Fearnaught, and Mark Anthony without interruption. Thus when English stock was imported from 1784-1805 it was to the Roanoke Valley that they had to be brought to cross with the blooded mares there.[37]

Beginning in 1793 there are frequent racing notices and racing advertisements in the *North-Carolina Journal*. These races, which seemed to take place semi-annually, in October and in April, usually consumed three days. On the first day four-mile heats were run, on the second, three-mile heats, and on the last, two-mile heats with a sweepstake as the grand finale.

Describing one such race, Allen Jones Davie wrote his fellow-student at the University of North Carolina, Thomas Bennehan of Hillsborough, that the plans for the races "were settled today and will commence on a splendid establishment and in high stile the 12th day of April, as the purses will be an object we shall have many horses and of course fine sport."[38]

Some of these races, perhaps all, were run on Willie Jones's private race track. He is said to have constructed the first bay-window in America in order to watch the races. Owning "one of the finest stables in the South," he no doubt was the leading spirit in fostering this form of sport in Halifax.[39]

Davie's interest in racing can only be inferred from a letter he wrote to his friend, John Steele, and from his owning at one time the celebrated race horse and foal-getter, Sir Archy. In the letter to Steele, in reply to an inquiry as to the pedigree of Steele's mare, Davie demonstrated his familiarity with the subject and agreed with Steele "that a man who breeds horses, should do it with a view to profit only." He furthermore disagreed with some plan of Steele's to improve his stock, maintaining that "the deficiencies of one stock should be remedied by the excellencies of another," that Steele's were "too small, they [are] all bone, an essential defect."[40]

Davie's stallion, Sir Archy, was variously described as "the best horse in America, of his day,"[41] "the most useful and celebrated horse ever owned in America," [42] "the sire of American thoroughbreds—the Godolphin of the American turf." [43] Davie was said to have been a fine judge of horseflesh and to have "readily paid" five thousand dollars for this horse as a colt, but parted with him later in deference to his friends who insisted that this price was too extravagant. Yet Davie's judgment in selling the horse was poor indeed, for it was later found that he had been worth eighty thousand dollars to the estate of his subsequent owner, William Amis, of "Mowfield" plantation in Northampton County.[44] As late as 1827 Sir Archy was still covering mares "at 75 dollars the season" at "Mowfield," where his "blood, great size, performance on the turf, and celebrity as a foal getter," were "sufficient recommendations" for such a price.[45]

Although Davie was a lover of horses, there is some question about his enthusiasm for the cockfights which were such a drawing card in Halifax. No extant letters or records reveal his interest or attendance at any of them. Yet it would be a great temptation not to have been at least an innocent spectator at one fight in particular between North Carolina and Virginia. This contest would show and fight a main of fifty-one cocks, which promised to furnish "much sport and diversion" to the local sportsmen and those of neighboring counties.[46]

On the other hand, Davie may have harbored the same sentiments regarding this fight as those of a young student of the University, George W. Long, who wrote a classmate that "they are fighting cocks ... with might and main ... in this thrice glorious splendid and immensurable city [Halifax]. This happy residence of cocks and men. This ever memorable Fabric whose blissful mansions are fill'd with beings of such refined Philanthropy and extreme christian Charity that the feeling cannot live among them." Nevertheless he intended to "go down into this great city before long if my passage is not impeded by too great exuberance, their christian charity and benevolence." [47]

Even before 1772 Halifax could boast of tavern facilities far above the average in the colony. Adjacent to the courthouse were three two-story buildings. One of these, forty-four feet long and twenty feet wide, had a large barroom at one end, a cellar beneath, a broad verandah running the length of the house, and three large lodging rooms upstairs. The second building, thirty-two feet long and sixteen feet wide, had three rooms below and two above, with a verandah on the front side. The third building was a "billiard-house," twenty-eight by eighteen feet, which contained a good billiard table and two lodging rooms above. All three were owned by one proprietor and were serviced by a kitchen sixteen feet square, a smokehouse, a stable, horse-lots, and a large garden. All the houses had "good brick Chimneys, and are well plaistered and whitewashed."[48] Later "houses of entertainment" in Halifax, such as the famous Eagle Tavern,* Benjamin Weaver's, and James Augustus Tabb's, addressed themselves to gentlemen attending courts, travellers, and others, and guaranteed "a good supply of the best liquors," "good Rum, Brandy and Wine," superior stables and lots, managers "under good character" and servants as good as any in the state.[49]

As to cultural and educational advantages, Halifax had little to offer of a civic nature. Culture seemed, indeed, to be confined to the living rooms and libraries of its more prominent citizens. An abortive attempt was made, presumably by Thomas Davis, publisher of the original *North-Carolina Gazette* and printer of the state laws at Halifax, to establish a weekly newspaper in 1784. On March 28 of that year James Iredell wrote his wife from Halifax: "They have begun to print a newspaper at Halifax, which is to be continued weekly."[50] No further information in regard to this paper is available.[51]

Eight years later, July 18, 1792, Abraham Hodge and Henry Wills founded the *North-Carolina Journal* at Halifax. Published weekly, it had the distinction of having the widest circulation of all the papers in the state in the eighteenth century.[52]

It seems rather surprising that Halifax should have turned a cold shoulder to the drama. Yet James Iredell, writing to his wife in 1787, reported that on the previous night "The Spanish Fryer was to be acted here, but there were not 5 Tickets sold at Sunset so that there was none acted. I am told the indelicacy of it was the cause, and if so I suppose it is very indelicate indeed."[53] However, by 1806, the year after Davie left the state, the *North-Carolina Journal* announced that a number of gentlemen had organized themselves into a company for the purpose of amusing the public with theatrical rep-

* Part of this tavern, moved from its original site, now forms the home of Miss Nannie Gary.

A Conservative under the Constitution

resentations and that they would perform the comedy of *Who Wants a Guinea?* by Coleman, the younger.[54]

Educational advantages for interested scholars could be enjoyed, beginning in 1795, at a Latin School near Halifax. Under the direction of "the Rev. Mr. Wilson," it advertised "genteel boarding" in the neighborhood "from ten to twelve pounds Virginia money per ann. for each student." Two years later the dominie had moved to the seat of Dr. Ponton, a short distance from Halifax. Now advertised as a Latin and English School, its tuition fee for Latin scholars was "five pounds Virginia currency per annum; for English, reading and writing, three pounds 12s 6 per ann. or twenty shillings per quarter; and for arithmetic, four pounds per annum, or twenty-four shillings per quarter." The Reverend Mr. Wilson apparently met with success, for the following year the school exercises were held "at the beautiful seat called Mount-Hope, near Halifax-Town." Board, washing, lodging, and tuition now came to twenty-five pounds, Virginia money.[55]

Though the microcosm that was Halifax was to be his official home for over two decades, Davie's political influence was to affect greatly the entire state of North Carolina, leave its mark on the national government, and impinge on international affairs. Thus his activities and his political ideas in general would have little meaning unless he is projected against the background of the state as a whole.

When Davie settled on the Roanoke River, the state of North Carolina, relieved from the hardships and the exhausting demands of war, was ready to enjoy the newly-won blessings of liberty and peace. Yet there was a definite cleavage in the ranks of its people as to how this liberty and this peace were to be enjoyed. Though there was no definite party organization in these years before the adoption of the Federal Constitution, the vocal elements of the state were definitely aligned into two factions, the Conservatives and the Radicals. This division, strikingly apparent at Halifax in the Provincial Congress which wrote the Constitution of 1776, became less and less fluid during the days of the Confederation and carried over into the struggle over the Federal Constitution. The chief differences were new appellations for old hats. The Conservatives were to assume the name "Federalists" and the Radicals that of "Anti-Federalists."[56]

That there was a definite continuity of alignment is seen most clearly in tracing the leaders of each division. With the notable exceptions of Willie Jones and Timothy Bloodworth, who sided with the Conservatives on the Loyalist issue, the outstanding leaders quite easily made the transition from Conservative to Federalist and from Radical to Anti-Federalist.

These two rival factions, since colonial days, had fought their battles against a backdrop of sectionalism. Davie, in moving from the Back Settlements to the Roanoke Valley, must have been acutely aware of the difference in the economic, social, and political climate. Though North Carolina was more democratic than either her northern or her southern neighbor, there was a very definite social and economic cleavage between the East and the West. In the East, the people were preponderantly of English extraction. Its dominant element had been closely associated with the Established Church and deeply imbued with English ideals of government and political theory. In the West, the inhabitants were predominantly Germans or Ulster Scots. The ruling element clung tenaciously to Presbyterianism, and the masses were led by Calvinist and, in some cases, Lutheran ministers, who held an almost theocratic sway over them. The East was characterized by the traditional large plantations, staple crops, and slave labor; the West by small farms, few slaves, and more democratic forms and ideals of society. There was a close economic, social, and intellectual tie between the East on the one hand and Virginia and the Mother Country on the other. In fact, a recent writer claims, not without reason, that the Roanoke-Albemarle region was but a continuation, "demographically, economically, politically, and culturally" of the Chesapeake-Tidewater section.[57] The West, on the other hand, was culturally allied largely with Philadelphia and Charleston. The Great Wagon Road to Philadelphia was too long for ordinary trading purposes, and Charleston, South Carolina, succeeded in luring the trade of lower Western North Carolina, while Petersburg, Virginia, claimed the upper half. Intercourse with Eastern North Carolina was impeded by a sparsely settled region of pine forests, the lack of good roads, and by the fact that the rivers of the West, especially the Yadkin and the Catawba, sought the Atlantic in South, rather than North, Carolina.[58]

The social, racial, and economic differences quite naturally led to

A Conservative under the Constitution

political divergencies which had already had serious repercussions in the Regulator troubles and in the debates over the Constitution of 1776. By this constitution, the East succeeded in maintaining its predominance in the General Assembly. Since the constitution apportioned representation equally, one senator and two representatives to a county, the East, with a larger number of counties, had a greater representation than its population justified. Beginning in 1787, there were repeated efforts to reapportion the representation by a revision of the constitution, but the East was able to block the movement until 1835.[59]

The Conservative, and later Federalist, leaders came primarily from three different areas of influence within the East. The Albemarle section, centering around Edenton, was led by an unusually strong and able clique. Universally recognized as the leader of these Conservatives was Samuel Johnston, an austere, aristocratic lawyer and statesman of unquestioned principles. Closely associated with him was his former law pupil and brother-in-law, James Iredell, an Englishman by birth, talented, ardent, and sincere. There was also the highly educated and capable former Presbyterian minister and doctor, Hugh Williamson. To this group might also be added Stephen Cabarrus, the genial, capable Frenchman who, as burgess from Edenton, made his political debut in the same year as Davie, 1784.[60] Cabarrus later identified himself with the Jeffersonians.

Allied to this group were the Cape Fear Conservatives, whose forces were marshalled by William Hooper and Archibald Maclaine. William Hooper, whose brother George was a Loyalist, was a Boston-bred lawyer and Master of Arts from Harvard. His letters to the provincial congress in 1776 had bitterly denounced democratic government, and his Loyalist proclivities were so pronounced that Thomas Jefferson, in 1819, in a letter to John Adams, declared that "we had not a greater Tory in Congress than Hooper." Closely connected with Hooper was Archibald Maclaine, whose daughter married George Hooper. A prominent lawyer and former merchant, he too was accused of Tory leanings. Farther up the Cape Fear River were John Hay and William Barry Grove, of Fayetteville. Hay was one of the most prominent lawyers of his day and was a member of the House of Commons from Sampson County in 1785 and from Cumberland in 1786 and 1805 and of the second ratification convention. His

[151]

wife was the daughter of Colonel Matthew Rowan, acting governor after Gabriel Johnston's death, and his daughter was the first wife of Judge William Gaston. Grove, described as a "warm Federalist," served in the House of Commons from 1787 to 1790 and at the two state ratifying conventions. From 1791 to 1803 he served continuously as a member of Congress.[61]

The third section in which there were a number of influential Federalists was the Roanoke Valley group, centered around Halifax. Davie may be said to have literally married into this group, the spearhead of which was Allen Jones. The son of Robert Jones, the younger, who had been agent for Lord Granville and for the Crown, Allen Jones had married the sister of Isaac Edwards, Governor Tryon's secretary. One daughter married Davie and the other John Sitgreaves, an important Federalist of Newbern, who served in the Continental Congress in 1784 and in the House of Commons from Newbern from 1786 to 1789, at which time he succeeded Judge John Stokes as United States District Judge of North Carolina. Jefferson reported Benjamin Hawkins as recommending him at this time "as a very clever gentleman, of good deportment, well skilled in the law for a man of his day."[62]

Allen Jones's half-sister, however, had, along with Willie, strayed from the family fold when she married Benjamin Williams, a Jeffersonian who represented Craven, Johnston, and Moore counties, successively, in the Assembly, served in Congress from 1793 to 1795, and was elected, ironically, to succeed Davie as governor in 1799. He served in this capacity from 1799 until 1802 and again in 1807.[63]

Another close connection was that Mrs. Willie Jones's sister, Elizabeth Montfort, married John Baptiste Ashe, the son of Governor Samuel Ashe. The owner of sixty-three slaves and twelve hundred acres in Halifax County in 1790, he represented Halifax County in the House of Commons from 1784 to 1787 and his district in Congress in 1787 and 1788 and from 1790 until 1793. Like Cabarrus, he joined the opposition soon after 1789.[64]

Aside from the Conservatives of these three sections, there were a number of other important Conservative leaders throughout the state. Especially influential were the three Blount brothers, William, John Gray, and Thomas, merchants, extensive landowners, and politicians, of Pitt, Washington, and Craven counties. These three "formed one of the most active and formidable groups in North Carolina." It should be noted, however, that by the late 1790's, John Gray Blount had become a Jeffersonian. From Newbern came Richard Dobbs Spaight, Glasgow-bred member of the Continental Congress, framer of the United States Constitution, and governor from 1792 to 1795. In Warren County there was Benjamin Hawkins, educated at Princeton, member of the Continental Congress 1782, 1783, and 1786. He served with Samuel Johnston as one of North Carolina's first two senators, after which he became Indian agent in the Southwestern District. Another Princeton graduate, Adlai Osborn, served as clerk of the court of Rowan County from colonial days to 1809. Also at Salisbury there was the prominent merchant, John Steele, close friend of Davie, member of Congress from 1790 to 1793, and comptroller of the United States Treasury from 1796 to 1802.[65]

Chiefly lawyers and merchants, with a sprinkling of planters, these North Carolina right-wingers differed from their brethren in Tidewater Virginia and the South Carolina Low Country, where a more stratified squirearchy or aristocracy, bottomed on large slave plantations, had been developed. Yet these North Carolina leaders, largely of upper middle class origin, had developed an aristocratic temper which shuddered at the leveling influences of the frontier and the masses in general.* Certainly each of these leaders had the prerequisites used to describe an aristocrat of that day: "a substratum of wealth, a sense of dignity, the habit of leadership and refined tastes."[66] As individuals it would be difficult to pinpoint their motivation. Certainly the Cape Fear group, particularly in their championship of the Loyalists, seem to have been impelled by mercenary motives. On the other hand, Davie, Allen Jones, and the Edenton group could hardly have accepted office for materialistic gain, but from a sense of public duty and service—*noblesse oblige*, if you will—and for a deep interest in the orderly reconstruction of the political and economic edifice.[67]

The leader of the Radicals, and later the Anti-Federalists, was indisputable—the enigmatic Willie Jones. Of distinguished lineage, educated at Eton, a former member of the royal governor's clique, this landed aristocrat lived sumptuously at "The Grove," the owner

---

*For a discussion of the Southern aristocrat in the last quarter of the eighteenth century, see Clement Eaton, *Freedom of Thought in the Old South* (Durham: Duke University Press, 1940), pp. 3-15.

of one hundred and twenty slaves in 1790. Yet when the Revolution came, he had not only taken the American side in the fight for home rule but had taken the side of the Radicals in the fight for rule at home. A consummate politician and an adroit strategist, he captivated his followers with a charm and insidiousness which made him the most powerful and influential politician in the state.[68]

Associated with him in his fight for the masses was a curious blend of intellectuals, religious leaders, self-appointed leaders of the masses, and Revolutionary veterans. Two of these Radical leaders were Princeton graduates, David Caldwell and Samuel Spencer. The versatile and erudite Caldwell, brother-in-law of William Richardson, no doubt influenced the political affairs of Guilford County and vicinity more than his political record, limited to the two ratification conventions, at Hillsborough and Fayetteville, would seem to indicate. Samuel Spencer, of Anson, able and active, had been a Superior Court judge since 1777 and was to play an important role in the coming fight over the Constitution. In line with these Western Presbyterians were several prominent Eastern Baptists, led by Lemuel Burkett, of Bertie County, a leader in the Kehukee Baptist Association, which flourished in Edgecombe, Halifax, Warren, Bertie, and Camden counties. In this same group were two members of this same association from Edgecombe—Elisha Battle, the well-to-do, Virginia-born planter, and William Fort.[69]

From Granville County came two of the most powerful and interesting political leaders, John Penn and Thomas Person. Penn, the father-in-law of the Virginian, John Taylor, of Caroline, read law under his relative Edmund Pendleton. A signer of the Declaration of Independence and a member of the Continental Congress, he had also served on the unpopular Board of War—provoking Davie's remark that he was "fit only to amuse children." He identified himself, like Person, with the Radicals, and no doubt would have been a more powerful figure had it not been for his untimely death in 1788, at the age of forty-seven. His neighbor, Thomas Person, had been a stormy petrel since the days of the Stamp Act and the Regulator troubles.*
A man of the people, he fought their cause, be it against British or

---

* Documentary evidence is lacking on his Regulator activities, but George Sim's pamphlet, *Address to the People of Granville County*, was dedicated to him.

local opposition, although at the time of his death he had amassed an estate of 67,437 acres and owned ninety-eight slaves in 1782.[70]

Particularly obnoxious to the Conservatives were two untutored leaders of the masses: Timothy Bloodworth, of Wilmington, and Griffith Rutherford, of Rowan County. Bloodworth, a child of poverty, had successively been a preacher, smith, farmer, doctor, watchmaker, wheelwright, and politician. In the last role he was described as "resolved almost to fierceness, and almost radical in his democracy." Yet he, like Willie Jones, was opposed to the Confiscation Act of 1779. Rutherford, a brigadier general, was an Irishman "uncultivated in mind or manners but brave, ardent and patriotic." Violently opposed to the Loyalists, whom he called "Imps of Hell," he was a colorful figure in the state Senate from 1777 to 1780, from 1783 to 1786, and at the Hillsborough convention.[71]

There were also several other Westerners, all Revolutionary officers, who were of note. William Lenoir, a self-made leader of Wilkes County, amassed, through Revolutionary grants and industry, 14,749 acres in Wilkes County, which he frequently represented in the Assembly from 1783 to 1795. An original trustee of the University, he became the first president of its Board of Trustees. Another influential mountaineer was Joseph McDowell, of Burke County, who served in the House of Commons from 1782 to 1788 and in the Senate from 1791 to 1795. In these bodies, as in the ratification conventions, he was described as "a man of action rather than words." In Mecklenburg County there were two other Revolutionary officers who sided with the radical majority: Joseph Graham, who aided Davie in the defense of Charlotte and who served as state senator seven times, and Caleb Phifer, who represented his county fourteen times in the House of Commons between 1778 and 1792. Finally, from Rowan County, there was Matthew Locke, ex-Regulator, Revolutionary brigadier general, member of the third, fourth, and fifth provincial congresses, state senator and member of the House of Commons, and United States senator from 1793 to 1799. He was classified as a warm "Republican."[72]

Three of North Carolina's most influential leaders at this time are perhaps best classified as moderates, who vacillated from one camp to the other—Richard Caswell, Alexander Martin, and Abner Nash. Caswell, who was described by Nathaniel Macon as "one of the most powerful men that ever lived in this or any other Country," had ridden with Tryon against the Regulators and was at first regarded as hostile to some of the Western leaders, but he gradually tended to the left. The first governor of the independent state, he was re-elected seven times to that office and also served fifteen times in the General Assembly.[73]

Alexander, or "Paddy," Martin, for whom Davie had had such scorn during the Revolution, was also a Princeton graduate. He served as state senator for a number of years, governor for six terms, and United States senator from 1793 to 1799. At the Federal Convention he was described as the "least strongly Federalistic and relatively inconspicuous member of the North Carolina delegation." By 1790 he made a clean break with the Federalist party. He and Davie met not only as politicians but as trustees of the University.[74]

Abner Nash, the speaker of the first House of Commons and the second governor of the independent state, and later a delegate to the Continental Congress from 1782 to 1786, was labeled a Radical at Halifax in 1776, but was later considered a Conservative by the members of the Assembly which had conferred his executive powers on the Board of War. Yet in 1784 he was vehement against the Loyalists.[75]

Before launching forth into the political arena, in which he was to be actively engaged for almost three decades, Davie participated in two trials which brought him dramatically before the public eye. During January, 1782, seven of the followers of the ruthless Tory, David Fanning, were seized and brought to Hillsborough for trial. It so happened that at this time Judge John Williams, of Granville County, the able Alfred Moore of Brunswick, and Davie were passing through town on their way to Salem, where Williams was to hold court. The judge was induced to stop over and hold a court for the immediate trial of these men. Court was accordingly held in what was then called Blackguard Hall. Davie, in a conversation with Judge Willie P. Mangum, thirty-seven years later, laconically reported the trial: "Moore prosecuted all, I defended all, and Williams convicted all." It is regrettable that there was no court reporter to enlarge on the argument of the defense, in this, his first case.[76]

Davie's second case was of a more dramatic nature. Dramatic not only for the fact that the fledgling lawyer was defending one of the

A Conservative under the Constitution

leading Tories of the state, but because that Tory was Colonel Samuel Bryan. It was his regiment which Davie's cavalry had almost annihilated at Hanging Rock, August 6, 1780. After the surrender of Cornwallis and the evacuation of Wilmington by Major Craig, Colonel Bryan, Lieutenant Colonel John Hampton, and Captain Nicholas White, all of the same Tory regiment, had returned to the forks of the Yadkin in the north end of Rowan County, where Bryan had originally embodied his Tories before the battle of Ramsour's Mill. Shortly thereafter the three of them were arrested for high treason. The ensuing trial at Salisbury in March, 1782, was presided over by Judges Samuel Spencer and John Williams. The prosecution was conducted by Alfred Moore, the Attorney General, and the defense by Richard Henderson, who had been a promoter of the Transylvania Company and a colonial judge of Granville County, John Penn, John Kinchen, of Orange, and William R. Davie.*

Public indignation ran high. There was little sympathy for these three prisoners, whose private lives had been exemplary, but whose political convictions had led them to remain loyal to their sovereign king. Colonel Bryan, especially, had been "esteemed a Man of Candor and Sincerity, remarkably honest in his dealing and very friendly in his disposition." †

At the trial, "scorning all concealment," he admitted "his uniform and active attachment to the interest of his Britanic Majesty, whom he considered his liege sovereign" and claimed that he never acknowledged any allegiance to the state of North Carolina. Hampton, a native of Granville, had removed to Rowan to 1774 and had "always maintained a fair character." Little is known of White, except that he did not have as kind a disposition as his two superior officers.[77]

Here was a case to test the legal and forensic ability of a neophyte

---

* John W. Moore, *The History of North Carolina;...* (Raleigh: Alfred Williams & Co., 1880), I, 348-49; Francis L. Hawks, David L. Swain and William A. Graham, *Revolutionary History of North Carolina in Three Lectures* (Raleigh: William D. Cooke, 1853), pp. 224-29. For a report of the case, *State v. Samuel Bryan*, see *ibid.*, pp. 229-33. Strangely enough, Hubbard claimed that Davie's participation in this case was "a pure fiction," since Bryan was never brought to trial.—Hubbard, *Davie*, p. 84.

† This description of his character was taken from the Petition for Clemency presented to Governor Burke, March 28, 1782.—Governor's Papers. Thomas Burke, A.H.

at the bar! And pitted against him was the able and brilliant Attorney General, later an Associate Justice of the Supreme Court of the United States. Yet it was said that as a result of his military fame, Davie was "the only advocate in attendance upon the court, who could have commanded a patient hearing in such a community, in reply to such an opponent, and in behalf of such clients." Comparing his defense of Colonel Bryan in his argument to the jury with his gallant defense of Charlotte against the entire army of Cornwallis, an ante-bellum historian maintained that this occasion was an exhibition "of equal courage and equal ability." From each encounter he had retired with an established reputation. This same historian stated that for years afterwards "his services were required in all capital cases" and "as a criminal lawyer he had no rival in the State." [78]

But Davie's brilliant defense could not save them—they were all sentenced to die. So aroused were the Rowanites that Governor Burke was forced to throw a military guard around the prisoners for protection.[79] Notwithstanding the prejudices and passions of the masses, the four members of the defense at once enclosed a copy of the case to the governor, advised him that a petition for clemency was being prepared, and stated that they were of the opinion that this execution would be a reflection on the state.[80]

This plea, accompanied by a petition for clemency, was no doubt the determining factor in inducing the governor to pardon them and exchange them for American officers of equal rank who were confined within the British lines.[81]

Davie's championship of the cause of the Tories in these trials was a fair indication of his future alignment with the Conservatives on the issues of the day. Parenthetically, it forms a striking parallel with Alexander Hamilton's championship of the Loyalists in the famous case of *Rutgers* v. *Waddington*.

The following September Davie revealed himself as definitely in their ranks on the momentous paper money question. In a letter to John Gray Blount, Davie, writing from Halifax, informed him that they were "devilishly frightened here at the prospect of the approaching assembly—Every body fancies they hear the press groaning under the iniquitous burden of a second emission. The poor Merchant already anticipates the honor of seeing his Cent per Cent van[ish] like *Majic* or a Jugler's ball—We must by [no] means emit more,

A Conservative under the Constitution

some measures should be taken to have it restruck on a good paper, such as the European Bank securities are impressed on." *

Yet, against Davie's opposition, William Blount, John Gray's brother, introduced the measure in the House of Commons that year and the emission of £100,000 was passed.[82]

Before Davie's election to the House of Commons, he had also bestirred himself in the interests of reform in the court system, the control of which had been a subject of controversy between the House of Commons and the Crown in colonial days. This controversy was resolved in favor of popular control when the Constitution of 1776 vested in the legislature the power of the election, salaries, and impeachment of the judges and the erection of courts. Implementing this mandate in 1777, a Court bill, drafted and presented by James Iredell, was enacted. It preserved the older judicial districts of Edenton, Newbern, Wilmington, Halifax, Hillsborough, and Salisbury (each a court town) and provided for the election of three Superior Court judges, who were elected December 20: Samuel Ashe, of New Hanover, James Iredell, of Chowan, and Samuel Spencer, of Anson County. These courts were to meet twice a year in each of the court towns, with one judge constituting a quorum "provided always, that demurrers, cases agreed, special verdicts, bills of exception to evidence and motions in arrest of judgment, should not be argued but before two or more Judges." [83]

Such a system necessarily had its defects. Distance to the six court towns, paucity of judges, and absence of any system of appeals all worked injustices on the people. To alleviate these ills, Davie in October, 1782, presented a set of proposals to John Gray Blount, at that time a member of the House of Commons from Beaufort County.[84] He pointed out that the people were "generally anxious for some change in our Judicial System" and he felt that this session was the proper moment for bringing up the question. His objects were "to increase the number of Judges, to lessen the expence both to the public and the suitor, and to finish the business of the Country in a

---

* September 1, 1782.—John Gray Blount Papers, A.H. Dr. Alice Barnwell Keith, editor of *The John Gray Blount Papers* (Raleigh: State Department of Archives and History, 1952), I, 30, has distorted the meaning of the letter by inserting the word "all" instead of the word "no" in the torn part of the letter.

reasonable time." The last two, he claimed, were objects "of real importance, and now subjects of *great complaint;* and no man will deny; but the first would be an advantage." He suggested two plans. The first would provide for a judge in each district who would hold court twice a year in his district and who would have the same common law jurisdiction which the Superior Court judges have, "as far as it relates to the trial of facts; as in the Courts of Nisi prius in England." These judges would compose a Court of Appeal and would be authorized to call Courts of Oyer and Terminer for the trial of criminals. A chancellor should be appointed to hold a Court of Equity at two places in the state "to seperate this business from the civil." The judges' salaries should be £1,000 a year "to be paid out of the public Treasury and an adequate Tax laid on suits to reimburse the Treasury of that sum."

His second plan was somewhat similar. The chief differences lay in the matter of appeal and in the provision that each district judge would have jurisdiction over law and equity, thereby eliminating a chancellor. The criminal procedure by which "public Justice would be executed with suddenness and certainty," would be the same in both plans.[85]

Characteristically, it was several years before any reform was made. In 1782 and 1787 court sessions were ordered for the Morgan and the Fayetteville districts, respectively. In 1790, 1798, and 1806, the number of judges was increased, one at a time. In 1790, the circuits were grouped into two ridings, eastern and western, and two judges were to hold court, but one in each riding was to exchange circuit with one of the other riding after each session. In 1806 the number of ridings was increased from two to six, and, even more in keeping with the democratic spirit, sessions of the superior court were to be held for each county twice a year. The greatest reform of all was the gradual creation of a Supreme Court of Conference. In 1805 the name was changed to Supreme Court.[86]

Thus the reforms suggested by Davie in 1782 were in large measure accomplished by 1805—the year of his retirement from North Carolina.

As one of the representatives from Northampton County in the House of Commons which convened in April, 1784, Davie began the

A Conservative under the Constitution

first of his nine terms of office in that body. He had already taken a decided stand on the question of strengthening the Federal Union. To his old commander, General Greene, he had written, in December, 1783: "We have nothing now to do, but to give strength and permanency to the *common union;* this will be a difficult task with our young republicks whose views are all local and limited, and whose councils cannot yet be illuminated with the *truest principles of policy.*" [87]

Davie appeared and took his seat in the House of Commons, April 26, 1784,[88] at Hillsborough.

The legislature was notable for the calibre of its members. Richard Caswell was chosen speaker of the Senate, and Thomas Benbury, of Edenton, speaker of the House. Prominent among those who had already rendered distinguished service were Samuel Johnston, William Hooper, Archibald Maclaine, William Blount, Nathaniel Macon, Charles Johnson, William Lenoir, and Thomas Person. In addition to Davie, there were three freshmen of note: John Baptiste Ashe, of Halifax, John Hay, of Sampson County, who moved the next year to Fayetteville, and Stephen Cabarrus, of Edenton.[89]

At few times in the history of the state have issues of such magnitude confronted an Assembly as those which confronted this, Davie's first. Regulation of the currency, compliance with the Treaty of Peace with Great Britain, and the state's relationship to the Confederation Congress all demanded deep and intelligent consideration. On each of these questions Davie took a decided though inconsistent stand.

The correspondence of the day seems to indicate that the problem of inflation was the one which caused the greatest cleavage between the Conservatives and the Radicals. Though the process of inflation in North Carolina was essentially the same as in the other American states, its misuse was particularly flagrant here. Beginning in 1775 with the emission of $125,000, this fiat money was struck off in ever-increasing amounts in an effort to finance the war and redeem the former bills. By 1781 it had reached the astronomical figure, for that day, of $26,250,000, making a grand total of $33,725,000. Quite naturally, hard money had soon begun to disappear and paper currency to depreciate. By 1782 the scale of depreciation had reached the ratio of eight hundred of currency to one of specie.[90]

In such a state of affairs, Davie at once introduced a bill in the House to amend the Act of 1783 for emitting £100,000 of paper money "for the redemption of the paper currency now in circulation, and advancing to the Continental Officers and Soldiers part of their pay and subsistence, and for laying a tax and appropriating the confiscated property for the redemption of the money now emitted" and also an act passed at Halifax in 1779 entitled "an act for punishing persons concerned in any of the several species of Counterfeiting in this State." This amendment passed three readings in the House, but it was obviously defeated on the third reading in the Senate, for it never became a law.* It is unfortunate that the specific provisions of this amendment are not known, but it is safe to venture the opinion that they were designed to curb the rampant inflation.

A year later, writing to Spruce Macay, in whose office he had read law, Davie expressed the prevailing sentiment of the Conservatives when he reported that there was "nothing new" to impart "except some disputes among our little politicians and candidates about emitting more paper money: the last mad thing I hope we shall do." [91]

Of scarcely less importance than the money question was that of the Treaty of Peace with Great Britain. On January 14, 1784, the United States in Congress assembled had ratified the definitive articles of the Treaty. On March 1, Governor Martin had proclaimed its ratification to all civil and military officers and other citizens of the state and on April 20, he presented it to the General Assembly with a recommendatory message.[92]

The previous year the Conservatives in the Assembly had made unsuccessful attempts to repeal all state laws contrary to the treaty.[93] Now they girded themselves for another fray.

Of chief concern to the people of the state were articles four, five, and six. Article four provided that creditors on each side of the Atlantic should meet with "no lawful impediment to the recovery of the full value in sterling money, of all *bona fide* debts heretofore contracted." Article five provided that Congress should "earnestly recommend" to the state legislatures to provide "for the restitution of

---

*S.R., XIX, 555, 566, 576, 602-3, 678. Unfortunately, the Senate journal for this session is missing.—Douglas C. McMurtrie, *Eighteenth Century North Carolina Imprints, 1749-1800* (Chapel Hill: The University of North Carolina Press, 1938), p. 15.

all estates, rights and properties" of "real British subjects" and of those who had not borne arms against the United States. Loyalists, who had borne arms, were to be free to go to any part of the United States and remain there for a year "unmolested in their endeavours" to obtain restitution of their interests. It was further recommended that these be restored to them on condition that they refund to the persons then in possession the bona fide price paid for the confiscated property. The sixth article provided that no future confiscations should be made, no future prosecutions commenced, and no future loss or damage suffered to the person, liberty, or property of any person by virtue of his part in the war. Those presently confined should be set at liberty and prosecutions against them discontinued.[94]

This problem of the Loyalists perhaps evoked more bitterness and strife in North Carolina than in any other state.[95] The explanation is simple. North Carolina probably contained more Loyalists in proportion to her population,[96] and her lands had been more ravaged by internecine warfare.

Beginning with the test act in 1776,[97] which presented the alternatives, allegiance to the state or banishment, the Assembly the next year adopted the first of a long series of confiscation acts. This act provided for the confiscation of the property of all persons who did not "appear and admit to the States, whether they shall be received as Citizens thereof."[98] In November, 1779, a more vigorous act was passed which not only confiscated the property of the Loyalists in general but also listed a large number of the more prominent Tories, such as William Tryon, Josiah Martin, Edmund Fanning, Sir Nathaniel Dukinfield, Henry Eustace McCulloh, Samuel Cornell, John and Archibald Hamilton, Samuel Bryan, and John Moore.[99] The severity of this act prompted fifteen members of the House of Commons, led by the usually radical Willie Jones, to enter a protest, declaring it involved "such a Complication of Blunders and betrays such ignorance in Legislation as would disgrace a Set of Drovers." They particularly protested against the repeal of the provisions made in the Confiscation Act of January, 1779, for "such unfortunate and Innocent Wives and Children resident in the State, who had been abandoned by their Fathers and Husbands, and also for aged parents in particular Cases."[100]

As a result of this act, the state not only had received large sums from the sale of this property, but had also guaranteed the title to the property thus sold to the many purchasers.[101]

A battle royal ensued when the Assembly took up debate on the restitution of this confiscated property to its original owners. Davie was allied with the Conservatives, Iredell, Hooper, Johnston, and Maclaine, and with his otherwise radical uncle-in-law, Willie Jones. These men, no doubt, were motivated by a number of forces: international honor, an abiding Anglo-Saxon respect for the sanctity of property, a certain sense of fair play and justice, and a genuine desire to bolster the common union. In their fight they "galantly attempted" to lift the new nation's banner "while yet unsullied by the infamy of a refusal to comply with the terms of its virgin treaty."[102]

These Conservatives devoutly hoped that the Treaty would be a means by which they could obtain justice for their friends and relatives. A surprising number of "political squibs" broke into print. Written by pamphleteers under such names as "The Citizen," "The True Citizen," "Atticus," "Sully," and "Cusatti," their identity is difficult to trace. Though Hooper wrote Iredell that Captain John Stokes, brother of Montfort Stokes, of Montgomery County,[103] thought "Sully" was Davie, he himself thought it must be Maclaine "from the fire of the composition." It was also reported, according to Hooper, that "Cusatti" was Alexander Martin, which he suspected, from the quaintness of the signature, which he observed was an ingenious transposition of the letters of the name "Atticus." He also had heard that "The Citizen" was "the production of a joint committee on Nutbush," which was Judge John Williams' home.[104]

Davie was a member of the grand committee to report on Governor Martin's message, which had urged the acceptance of the Treaty.[105] This committee recommended that it be concurred with *in toto*, and, after a debate, paragraph by paragraph, it was passed, except Article five, which recommended the return of confiscated property.[106]

On this issue the Radicals were in no conciliatory mood and there appeared "a settled resolution against the restoration of any part of the confiscated property." The illogical argument was advanced by Griffith Rutherford that Governor Tryon, Governor Martin, Henry McCulloh, and Sir Nathaniel Dukinfield were not British subjects and therefore did not come under the provisions of the Treaty. Leading the debate in the House was William Hooper, who supported Congress's recommendation "with the most masterly eloquence, though without support or success." Archibald Maclaine, the father-in-law of the Tory, George Hooper, would have assisted him if he had not been "laid up with the gout." In the Senate, the Loyalist cause was pled by the ironic alliance of Samuel Johnston and Willie Jones. Johnston later reported to Iredell that he "said everything that occurred" to him and that Jones "spoke very sensibly on the same side." Though there was "not a word of common sense spoken on the other side," this clause was rejected by a great majority.[107]

Davie's only official stand on this question was that he voted "yea" on the bill "to repeal such of the Laws of the State as are inconsistent with the Treaty of Peace." * Illogically, he voted "nay" on the bill "to amend and reduce to system the Confiscation Laws now in force in this State." The reason for his departure from his known convictions and from his Conservative friends, Benjamin McCulloh, William Hooper, David Stone, Archibald Maclaine, and Benjamin Hawkins, is unfathomable. The measure, which was rejected by a vote of 18 to 62, would have provided that all bona fide sales of the lands of the men mentioned in the confiscation acts held "good and valid in law." However, in line with the "peace and harmony" then existing between the United States and Great Britain, a spirit of conciliation prevailed in regard to the unsold land of these Loyalists. This property could be reclaimed by the original owner if he became a citizen of this or any other one of the United States or it could be sold to a citizen and resident of North Carolina within a certain period of time. Failure to adopt either of these two courses meant that the property would escheat to the state. A final provision excluded any claims of the late Lords Proprietors or their heirs or assigns.[108] It may well have been that Davie thought the provisions of the measure too stringent—especially in regard to the Granville claim. Yet in voting against the bill he chose strange bed-fellows: Timothy Bloodworth, William Lenoir, William Blount, Matthew Locke, Caleb Phifer, Jesse Franklin, and Henry Montfort.

Contrary to the recommendation of the Treaty, the Radicals passed a law for the sale of all confiscated property, real and personal, which

* The bill was rejected in the House by a vote of 32 to 37.—S.R., XIX, 674-75.

remained unsold.[109] Not content with this, the next year they sought further to protect the purchaser of confiscated property by putting through an act which provided that those who bought this property need not assume any suits brought against them by anyone named in the confiscation acts or by anyone representing them.[110]

Davie's reaction to this piece of legislation was probably similar to that of his father-in-law, who wrote William Bayard, Junior, of New York, in regard to it: "Thus you see all your hopes of justice destroyed by this tyrannical act of the assembly."[111]

This law involved the far-reaching issue of the relationship of the legislative branch to the judiciary as well as the future of Loyalist holdings in the state. The judiciary, in the case of *Bayard and wife* v. *Singleton*,[112] which was finally settled in November, 1787, in Newbern, seized their opportunity to apply the doctrine of judicial interpretation of acts of the legislature. The case was brought by the daughter of Samuel Cornell, a wealthy Tory merchant of Newbern. Her father had "taken shipping" in August, 1775, and gone to Great Britain where he stayed until the latter part of 1777, when he returned as a British citizen to Newbern, via New York, under the protection of a British flag. Not finding the new government "agreeable to his wishes," he decided to transport his family to reside under the British flag. Accordingly, he executed, on board the ship which brought him, a deed to his daughter for his "valuable house and lot, with a wharf, and other appurtenances" in Newbern. The daughter was now seeking to recover this property, sold under the confiscation laws to one Singleton.

The attorney general, Alfred Moore, and Abner Nash, counsel for the defendant, moved that the suit be dismissed on the basis of the law of 1785 which forbade the courts to hear such cases. The plaintiff had secured able counsel: Iredell, Johnston, and Davie. These three argued that the clause of the Constitution of 1776, guaranteeing trial by jury, took precedence over any legislative act. The court was in a dilemma and decided to defer judgment to see if the next legislature would repeal the statute.[113] In the November, 1786, session, charges were brought against the judges for their failure to dismiss the case and for a number of other reasons.[114] Judges Samuel Spencer and John Williams attended the hearings, but Judge Samuel Ashe absented himself on the grounds that the charges were malicious and groundless and that he was "righteous and therefore bold" in his judicial character.[115] The committee report, upholding the judges, was adopted January 1, 1787, and the doctrine of judicial review was thus sanctioned by the legislature itself.[116] This, of course, was seventeen years before Marshall's famous *obiter dictum* in *Marbury* v. *Madison* and only a few months after *Trevett* v. *Weeden* in Rhode Island, which set the precedent for this doctrine on the state level.

Before the final decision of the court in the November term, a pamphlet of unusual interest, dedicated to Davie, was launched on the troubled waters. Its imminent publication was announced in the Newbern *North-Carolina Gazette*, August 15, 1787:

> *Now in the press, and will be published next week*
> In a small PAMPHLET
> THE INDEPENDENT CITIZEN,
> or
> THE MAJESTY OF THE PEOPLE
> Asserted against the usurpations of the General Assembly of North-Carolina, in several Acts of Assembly passed in the years 1783, 1785, 1786, and 1787....

The imprint of this pamphlet shows no place, printer, or date, but some of the copies have a manuscript note on the title-page: "Printed by Mons. Martin, Newbern an apology for the Incorrectness of the Press." The author is unknown, but the name of Archibald Maclaine has been suggested.[117] This is not implausible because the author described himself as being "in a remote corner of the country," which could have been Wilmington, and because of the content itself.

The dedicatory page is interesting in the light of eighteenth-century eulogy and floridity:

> To the Honorable
> W. R. DAVIE, ESQ:
> Counsellor at Law, one of the
> members of the Federal Convention.

Sir,
IN a remote corner of the country, your name has reached me. The voice of Fame has informed me that, to the much honored character of

WILLIAM R. DAVIE

a Soldier, you have added the distinguished Statesman. If the ken of human foresight does not disappoint me, the same glow of patriotic spirit, which led you to the field, will be demanded from you, by your country, in the hour of peace.

HIDDEN enemies are dangerous; Treason in changing shapes stalks over our land; Men actuated by the Daemon of wickedness, folly and ignorance, listen with gasping mouths to her insinuating whispers.

IT is incident to humanity to remove the evil day far from us: while we think at a distance, we deem ourselves secure. Men wrap themselves up in the infatuated cloak of safety, until the storm bursts with dread thunder on their heads.

OUR COUNTRY IS IN DANGER, and with united voices we say: THOU ART THE MAN who can save us from destruction!

If the thoughts directed to the Printer of the State Gazette can claim your attention, for a moment, from the load of weightiest matters, you will oblige your country, and

AN INDEPENDENT CITIZEN

July 30, 1787.

The pamphlet's chief burden of complaint was the restrictions imposed upon the jury trials by the legislature of North Carolina. Particularly insistent was the author on the right of trial by jury "as the bulwark of liberty and the *fundamental right* of every freeman" —whose history he traced from Magna Carta through its various reconfirmations to the present. From the "most irreffragable evidence" he then attempted to prove "that great strides have been made most *ILLEGALLY* and *UNCONSTITUTIONALLY*, to overturn this Gothic structure." Especially flagrant was the law passed in 1785 "*ordering all suits then depending, or that afterwards might be commenced, relative to confiscated property*, instanter to be dismissed, on *affidavit!!!*" In answer to the question, "Cannot the Assembly do ANY thing?," he maintained, with reasons, that "this imaginery omnipotence of Assembly, that whatever is ordained must be law, without any exception of right or wrong, must be restrained within the bonds of *reason, justice, and natural equity*." This justice, he concluded, must be "properly administered" in a "public manner: not in a bush not in a drunken tavern, not in the private apartment, not in the retired corner, but in the forum of justice in the presence of the world."

The court, bolstered by legislative sanction, by the plea of Davie, and by such expressions as those voiced by "The Independent Cit-

A Conservative under the Constitution

izen," handed down its decision in the November term, 1787. It held unequivocally that the legislative act of 1785 was "unconstitutional and void." Whatever hopes Davie and his associates may have had were dashed by the decision that "Aliens cannot hold land, and if they purchase, the land is forfeited to the sovereign," and that the confiscation laws were "as effectual in vesting the property in the State, as any *office found* according to the practice in England." [118]

The decision was of such importance that twenty-seven similar cases, pending in the same court, were swept off the docket by nonsuits voluntarily suffered. Yet the ruling which allowed these cases to be brought before the court in the first place led in later years to frequent and prolonged litigation, the most notable being the Granville case in which the Earl of Granville's heirs attempted to repossess the Granville District.[119] Davie was the chief defendent.

Of equal magnitude with the problems of the currency and the Loyalists was that of the cession of Western lands. These lands consisted of the area beyond the Allegheny Mountains, the present state of Tennessee. The opening of county land offices in 1777, along with the issuance of paper money, had led to a frenzy of speculation in the transmontane country and land was rapidly entered. Moreover, in 1780 a military reservation was set aside south of the Virginia border and east of the Tennessee River, to be used as a bounty for enlistments in military service. In 1783 the remainder of the land, excepting Indian lands, was made security for the new state currency at the rate of £10 for each 100 acres.[120]

North Carolina, relying on these lands for bounty to soldiers and for the redemption of paper money, at first turned a deaf ear to the repeated urgings of Congress to cede them to the federal government. Yet by 1784 sentiment was changing. There was a movement on the part of the Confederation Congress to levy a continental land tax and to apportion requisitions according to population. It would therefore be advantageous to North Carolina to cede these lands, especially if they should be credited to the state's account with Congress.[121] Then, too, North Carolina would no longer be saddled with the duty of defending the inhabitants against the Indians.

Here again Davie took a decided stand and here again he stood with the Radicals. When the bill for the cession came before the legislature in April, 1784, for the third and last reading, Davie, suspecting that the bill would pass, proposed that it should be laid over until the next session. The motion failed by a vote of 47 to 46. The cession, with certain reservations, was approved by a vote of 52 to 43, with Davie voting in the negative. In so doing, he broke with his friends Hooper, Maclaine, Sitgreaves, Benjamin Hawkins, William and John Gray Blount, and Nicholas Long. Associated with Davie in his dissent were such Radicals as Thomas Person, Timothy Bloodworth,* William Lenoir, Joseph McDowell, Matthew Locke, and Caleb Phifer.[122] No doubt his possession of 5,800 acres of land in the transmontane country influenced his decision.[123]

The reasons for Davie's dissent were couched in a detailed protest, presented to the House of Commons by him and signed by thirty-six other dissenters, among whom were McDowell, Lenoir, Person, Locke, Phifer, and Henry Montfort. Their reasons were varied. They believed the cession to be "dangerous and impolitic" in view of the immense territory held by Virginia and Georgia and thought that North Carolina's retention of these lands "could never endanger the general Confederacy." They objected to the fact that "the whole expence of the Indian Expeditions and our Militia aids to Georgia and South Carolina" had not been credited to the state's quota "in the Continental expences in the Revolution." They maintained that this territory had been "justly considered by the people as a security to their claims against the public, and was solemnly pledged to them" and its surrender would be a *"breach of faith* to our own citizens." They argued that this measure destroyed the greatest resource for the reduction of the domestic debt; that it would thus necessitate more burdensome and oppressive taxes; that it would "prove ruinous to those *patriotick sufferers*" who had made "generous advances to the public in the hour of distress" during the Revolution; that a great body of deserving claim holders would be injured "to the aggrandizement of a few Land Jobbers who have preyed on the depreciated credit of their Country and the necessities of the unfortunate citizen."[124]

Dr. Hugh Williamson, delegate to Congress from North Carolina, wrote to Governor Martin, expressing many of these same sentiments and recommending that North Carolina reconsider the act of cession

---

*Bloodworth voted for postponing the vote, but sided with the Conservatives in voting for the cession. S.R., XIX, 643.

and hold the lands until matters were straightened out, especially in regard to getting proper credit for the state's aid to South Carolina and Virginia and for the Indian expeditions during the Revolution.[125]

When the legislature met in October of that year, the pendulum had swung again. The influence of Davie's protest no doubt accounted in no small measure for the repeal of the act, November 18, which passed the Commons 37 to 22 and the Senate 19 to 11.[126]

It was not until 1789–after the rise and fall of "The Lost State of Franklin"–that the land was finally ceded to the federal government and early in the following year the cession was accepted.[127]

Although Davie led the so-called Radical forces on this momentous question, a closer analysis of his reasons, cogently expressed in his protest of the cession, seems to reveal that his was, after all, the more conservative stand. From the standpoint of intra-state interests, he definitely sided with the creditor class who were interested in the preservation of state integrity in Confederation affairs and in upholding the bona fide claims of its citizens in regard to the Western lands. On the other hand, from the standpoint of inter-state affairs, he definitely took the anti-federalistic stand, being unwilling to surrender these lands to the Confederation. Therefore, his position at this time seems to have been at once conservative and anti-federalistic.

Unfortunately there is no record of Davie's vote on the other leading acts of the two sessions of 1784, but, judging by his action on the more important problems, his known proclivities, and his later political actions, there is little question but that he voted with a resounding "yea" on those acts which invested the continental government with certain powers over foreign trade and taxation.

That Davie was quite active in the Assembly of 1784 is shown by the number of important committees to which he was appointed and the number of bills and motions he presented. Among the committees to which he was appointed at the first session was the committee to report on the governor's message and other state papers; the committee to revise the laws; the committee to "prepare the necessary amendments to be made in the Bill vesting a power in the United States in Congress Assembled, to levy a duty on foreign merchandize"; the joint committee "to prepare and bring in a Bill for calling to account the several Commissioners of Confiscated Estates"; and the joint committee to bring in an estimate of supplies necessary for the Civil List and incidental and Continental charges of the current year.[128]

At the second session he was appointed to the committee to consider the Governor's message; the committee "to report what measures are to be adopted in aid of the public Taxes which shall make up the estimate for the year 1785"; the committee to consider "a Bill to improve the Inferior Courts of pleas and quarter sessions of the several Counties in this State, to order the laying out of public roads, and to establish and settle ferries and appoint where bridges shall be built, and to clear inland rivers and creeks"; and the joint committee to consider Governor Martin's message concerning "the claims and demands the Citizens of this State have for slaves taken, and damages sustained against persons acting under British authority in the late War, and the British Army while in the different districts of this State." [129]

The following year, 1785, Davie was not a member of the House of Commons. It is probable that his time was consumed in building his home in the town of Halifax. In December of that year, however, he was nominated for governor by the House of Commons. The Senate put in nomination Richard Caswell, John Williams, and Samuel Johnston. Caswell was elected.[130]

The following year Davie represented the borough of Halifax in the House of Commons.[131] That he was not at all happy over his colleagues is seen in a letter, February 9, 1786, in which Archibald Maclaine informed George Hooper that "Colonel Davie congratulates me on the rising of the most i-f-s assembly that ever disgraced a country." [132]

This characterization of the Assembly as infamous by Davie is surprising. Among the leading Conservatives elected were Maclaine, Hooper, Hay, Sitgreaves, Spaight, Stephen Cabarrus, John Gray Blount, Frederick Hargett (of Jones), and Allen Jones. These were not only friends of Davie, but they "formed a very formidable array, possessing talents, learning, and experience"—in the words of Iredell's Boswell, Griffith J. McRee.[133] Perhaps Davie's unjust accusation of the Assembly was caused by the election of Griffith Rutherford, Jesse Franklin, and John Baptiste Ashe. The last two of these, McRee "supposed" belonged to the opposition; the first was a "conspicuous leader" of the Radicals.[134] Yet Davie's first official act was the nomination of Ashe for speaker of the House, a nomination which was carried unanimously.[135]

Several months before the legislature convened in November, there had been great excitement over the alleged frauds committed by the military commissioners who had been entrusted with liquidating the accounts of the officers and soldiers of the Continental line. This commission, appointed in 1784,[136] originally consisted of Willie Jones, his brother-in-law Henry Montfort, and Benjamin McCulloh, the son of the former royal councillor, Alexander McCulloh, of Elk Marsh. Jones resigned and was succeeded by John Macon, of Warren County.[137]

Shortly afterwards, exaggerated rumors were noised about that two of the commissioners, as well as other persons, had been engaging in "many notorious, fraudulent, and indecent practices, to the public detriment, and to the injury of many of the citizens ... and had been guilty of pernicious and infamous corruptions, to the ruin of the public credit."[138] It was reported, specifically, that many certificates certifying the soldiers' claims had been either made out in blank, forged, or given to persons who had had no military service. These improper and fraudulent certificates, given by the various officers, had been passed on by the board, consisting of the three commissioners, and paid by the state treasurer.[139]

Public indignation led Governor Caswell on November 20, the second day of the session, to report the matter to the Assembly and request a "minute inquiry of the Conduct of their officers as well as the justice of the Claims."[140] The Assembly passed a resolution requiring the governor to issue warrants for the arrest of all the persons concerned, of whom twenty-eight were individually named.[141] A grand committee was promptly appointed and a special subcommittee to examine the prisoners and take depositions. Their findings were then referred to a joint committee consisting of Davie, Maclaine, Hay, Hooper, and Philemon Hawkins, who were "to state and arrange the Testimony contained in the Depositions." One of the commissioners, Henry Montfort, was expelled from the House of Commons after having been given two days in which to defend himself. The state treasurer, Memucan Hunt, also failed to satisfy the Assembly's investigations and was succeeded by John Haywood. Finally the accused were ordered to appear before a special Court of

WILLIAM R. DAVIE

Oyer and Terminer to be held in Warrenton the last Monday in January, 1787.[142]

At the trial, indictments were soon found against McCulloh and Montfort and "others of less note," while Macon was exonerated. Quite naturally, according to McRee, the "military and legislative services, the wealth, the social rank, the influential connections of the commissioners aroused public interest 'to the highest pitch.' Adding to the interest was "the array of attorneys, renowned for eloquence and learning."[143]

The prosecution was conducted by the attorney general, Alfred Moore; Davie and Iredell represented the defendants. Thus for a third time Davie was to take the unpopular side on a question of state-wide interest. McRee's appraisal of the trial is revealing: "The profound interest of the public in the success of the prosecution, and the heavy stakes of the defendants—their fortunes, and, more than all, their characters, stimulated the efforts of counsel to the greatest degree; and seldom in North Carolina has a more brilliant display of forensic power been witnessed."[144]

From Edenton, Hugh Williamson wrote John Gray Blount that he had "some Reason to believe the subsisting Tryals at Warrington may occasion a Small Revolution in the Sentiment of People respecting some of your very popular Members. It is said that Davie is the Professed Champion

> "Right against wrong in equal Scale he weighs
> And sollid Pudding against empty Praise." *

Davie's convictions were no doubt of the same complexion as those of Iredell, with whom he was "lodged very comfortably in a room." Iredell reported to his wife, January 31, that though the judges, Ashe, Spencer, and Williams, had arrived, the charges had not yet been brought. He, however, was "convinced the matter against B. McCulloch has been greatly exaggerated" and that the only charge

---

* Hugh Williamson to John Gray Blount, Feb. 16, 1787.—John Gray Blount Papers, A.H. This couplet is a corruption of Alexander Pope's lines in *The Dunciad*, Book I, line 52:

> Poetic Justice, with her lifted scale,
> Where in nice balance truth with gold she weighs,
> And solid pudding against empty praise.

which could justly be "pressed against him is, his undertaking to negotiate certificates for a certain proportion, but not with any view to pass any but such as were entitled to it." [145]

Iredell later wrote to his wife that Henry Montfort was acquitted, but "poor B. McCulloch" was convicted. Though he was tried "on much the same charge" as Montfort and "their case was nearly equal," he had to encounter "strong prejudices both of the People and Court." Iredell believed he was "convicted of more than he had done, or been capable of doing, which was, taking Accounts to *pass right or wrong*." He feared that the judgment would "not only be a large Fine but Imprisonment also." [146]

Iredell's fears were soon justified. McCulloh's sentence was a £4,000 fine and twelve months' imprisonment in Halifax gaol, which Iredell felt was "arduous and inhuman." He furthermore reported to his wife: "Through his whole Trial he met with the greatest tryanny & injustice from 2 of the Court" and was "charged I am sure beyond his real offence." The people in Warrenton, moreover, spoke "with the utmost horror & resentment of his Sentence." Davie no doubt felt the same dread as Iredell, who concluded his letter with the sentiment: "How can I bear to see his poor miserable Family!" [147]

Yet perhaps Davie on reflection would have agreed with McRee, who interpreted the trial in a broad light: "The moral result of the trial was most salutary, it vindicated the supremacy of the law, and the confinement of Mr. McCulloh in a rude and noisome cell, 'whose stench was intolerable,' proclaimed to the world, that in North Carolina neither wealth nor influence could shelter any man from the penalties of crime." [148]

This session of the Assembly was also notable for the eruption of a long-standing antagonism between the bench and the bar. One example of this breach was brought out in the proceedings growing out of the case of *Bayard* v. *Singleton*. The antagonism on the part of the bar seems to have sprung primarily from a feeling that the three members of the bench lacked the legal training and judicial wisdom and restraint necessary for their important posts. In 1784 John Hay and others had made a strenuous effort to drive Judge Samuel Ashe from the bench. In fact, as seen before, numerous squibs and pamphlets under assumed names issued from the press at that time. By 1786 matters had come to a head.[149]

The prime mover in the matter was Archibald Maclaine, who, as chairman of the committee to examine into the present mode of the administration of justice in the supreme courts of law and equity, preferred charges against the judges. Appearing with him on this committee were Davie, Hooper, Spaight, Sitgreaves, John Gray Blount, and John Stokes. The chief charges brought against the judges were that they had suspended the operation of an act of the Assembly when they illegally banished two Loyalists, Francis Brice and Daniel McNeill; that they had delayed procedure by "tedious disputes" on the bench; that they had been irregular in their court attendance; and that they had failed altogether to attend court in the Morgan District.[150]

The two houses, meeting in joint session, in the presence of Judges Spencer and Williams, heard the report of the allegations.[151] The judges were found not guilty of any malpractice in office, whereupon Davie required that the votes be taken. The resulting affirmation of 49 to 22 led Davie to enter a protest, which was also signed by Hooper, Spaight, Sitgreaves, Hay, and William Polk. Their reasons for refusing to concur in an "unlimited, unqualified approbation of the Conduct of the Judges" was that they felt that "banishment is a punishment unknown to our Laws, and that no Judicial power of this State have a right to adjudge the same against any of the free Citizens thereof."[152]

Yet the majority of the Assembly had upheld the bench and reflected the sentiment of the mass of the people. Thus the judges had been able to resist "the assaults of the best writers, the ablest advocates, and most erudite lawyers of the State."[153]

Davie was also active in other legislative affairs in the Assembly of 1786. He served as chairman of the all-important finance committee of the House of Commons, was a member of the committee of privileges and elections, introduced a measure, which was enacted into law, for the better regulation of the town of Halifax, voted "yea" on the bill to establish "a fund for the support of the Academy at Hillsborough, and providing funds for other Academies," and was appointed Lieutenant Colonel Commandant of the Halifax District.[154]

However, the most important occurrence at this Assembly, as far as Davie was concerned, was his selection as one of the delegates to the Federal Convention at Philadelphia.[155]

CHAPTER VII

A Federalist Star Rises

IN North Carolina, as in the twelve other states, there had been a growing dissatisfaction among the Conservatives with the weaknesses of the Articles of Confederation. These men, properly called "nationalists" at this time, envisaged a stronger national union as opposed to those "federalists," such as Willie Jones, Thomas Person, Timothy Bloodworth, Samuel Spencer, and David Caldwell, who preferred to live under the loosely-knit federation then in existence. While the "chaos and patriots to the rescue" interpretation of the Confederation period has been cast aside, the fact remains that such Conservatives as Davie, Johnston, Iredell, Williamson, and Maclaine welcomed the idea of strengthening the powers of the existing federal government.*

* During the last quarter of the eighteenth century, the nomenclature of the two opposing groups of men is somewhat confusing. From 1776 to 1786 the conservative group have been designated as "Conservatives" and the radical group, "Radicals." During most of the year 1787, while the new Constitution was aborning, the two forces have been designated as "nationalists" and "federalists." During the debates over the ratification of the Constitution, those in favor of it assumed the name "Federalists" and those opposed to it that of "Anti-Federalists." During the Federal period, the Federalists, adhering to Hamiltonian policies, retained their names, while the "Antis" became "Democratic Republicans," or plain "Republicans," under the leadership of Jefferson. For a discussion of the terms "nationalist" and "federalist" and for his conclusions in regard to the "critical period," see Merrill Jensen, *The New Nation: A History of the United States During the Confederation, 1781-1789* (New York: Alfred A. Knopf, 1950), pp. vii-ix, 422-28.

WILLIAM R. DAVIE

North Carolina had been tardy in answering the first bid in the general direction of a closer co-operation among the states. In July, 1786, Governor Caswell, with the advice of his council, appointed five representatives, Abner Nash, Alfred Moore, Hugh Williamson, John Gray Blount, and Philemon Hawkins, to represent the state at the trade convention to meet in Annapolis in September "to take into consideration the Trade of the United States, and to report to the several States such a draft of an act relative thereto, as will best promote the commercial interest of the United States."[1] Hugh Williamson, who arrived the day the convention adjourned, was the only one who made the effort to go.[2]

When the call came for the Federal Convention, the Assembly was so preoccupied with its investigation of the frauds in the army accounts, the trial of the judiciary, and the State of Franklin that it was not until January 6, 1787, the last day of the session, that the act was passed for appointing deputies to the Philadelphia Convention, which was called "for the Purpose of Revising the Federal Constitution."[3] It was primarily through the efforts of Iredell and his friends that the act was passed.[4] Nevertheless, of the five commissioners elected by the Assembly, three of the men were avowed particularists or "federalists"—Willie Jones, Alexander Martin, and Richard Caswell. Davie and Richard Dobbs Spaight represented the "nationalists."[5]

There was, according to what Williamson had gleaned in Edenton, "some maneuvering and jugling at the Assembly respecting the Choice of Deputies to attend at the Convention." Since Williamson had not met with any members of the Assembly with whom he "chose to converse very freely" he remained "perfectly in the Dark as to the mode of their playing the Game."[6]

Ironically perhaps, the complexion of the delegation was materially changed by the decision of two of its members not to accept the election. Willie Jones, unsympathetic to the movement, sent in his resignation to Caswell, with the excuse that he thought it would not be in his power "to attend there at the Time appointed," and requested Caswell to appoint a substitute "as a matter of so much importance must necessarily require the fullest Representation."[7]

Caswell, who did not receive this letter until March 1, wrote Davie that he was "exceedingly sorry for [Jones's refusal] not only on account of his Country's not having his able services but the difficulty I shall meet with in supplying his place." He inquired of Davie if he knew of any gentleman whom he could recommend who "would go willingly to supply Mr. Jones's appointment." He was anxious "to appoint one who would be agreeable to the Gentlemen who go on the service."[8] There is no record of Davie's reply to this inquiry, but Caswell could hardly have chosen one more to Davie's liking—Hugh Williamson.[9]

Caswell also informed Davie on March 1 that he was uncertain whether he would be able to go to Philadelphia, but he was "very glad that you accept the appointment of a deputy to the Convention. I am sensible you will thereby sacrifice Interest, but the public on some occasion require it and I think particularly in this Business."[10] Yet Caswell, apparently feeling that the interests of North Carolina exceeded those of the nation, also decided not to go. He appointed William Blount in his stead.[11] Thus only Alexander Martin was left to represent the particularistic or "federal" point of view.

Any doubt as to the political sentiments of William Blount, then a delegate to the Continental Congress, would have been dispelled by his letter of January 13, 1787, to John Gray Blount, in which he expressed sentiments which were shared by the Conservatives: "Must not every thinking Man," he wrote, "view our Republican Government as the most intolerable of all Tyranny? Can any Man be safe in his house while the Legislature are sitting? ... O Tempora! O Mores! O Time! O Manners! Blessed Fruits of Independence."[12]

Davie himself was informed of his selection by Governor Caswell, who wrote him January 7, 1787, advising that his allowance would be the same as granted to the delegates to Congress and would be paid "by the Governor's Warrant on the Collectors of Imports out of the monies now due for Goods Imported." This would amount to £64 per month.[13]

Three weeks later Caswell had not heard from Davie and again wrote him requesting that he be informed "as speedily as possible" whether he accepted so that he might "forward a warrant on the Collector of Port Roanoke for three Months allowance," which time Martin and Spaight felt would be necessary "for going to, attending the Convention and returning from thence."[14]

Three days later, Davie, then attending the Warrenton trials, wrote the governor that "The importance of the object to the public and the absolute necessity of the measure have induced me to accept the appointment, notwithstanding any inconvenience it may produce in my private affairs." He, too, felt that no more than three months would be consumed in the entire service.[15]

It appears that a great deal of Davie's animosity toward Caswell had been mollified in the preceding six years. In a letter of March 5, Davie apparently asked Caswell to make the trip up with him, to which Caswell replied that he "would be happy in travelling with you, but am not yet satisfied it will be prudent for me to leave the State."[16] So Davie made the trip alone—"a very fatiguing and rapid journey," arriving in Philadelphia on May 22, eight days after the Convention was supposed to have convened and three days before a sufficient quorum of seven states was attained to commence business.[17]

Davie reported to Iredell that on the twenty-fifth the New Jersey delegates, representing the seventh state, attended and that Washington was chosen president. He further reported that on the twenty-ninth, nine states were present "and the great business of the meeting was brought forward by Virginia, with whom the proposition for a Convention had originated." Iredell was not to look for any news for a while because "no progress can yet be expected in a business so weighty, and, at the same time, so complicated."[18]

Davie was already giving serious consideration to the fundamental issues presented in the Virginia, or Randolph, Plan as revealed in his request to Iredell:

"Be so good as to favor me, by the next post, with your opinion how far the introduction of judicial and executive powers, derived from Congress, would be politic or practicable in the States. And whether *absolute* or *limited* powers for the regulation of trade, both as to *exports*, and *imports*, etc.

"I shall trouble you frequently; and I shall expect your opinion without reserve, etc., etc."[19]

Unfortunately Davie did not trouble Iredell as often as he had threatened. There are only three surviving letters of his from Philadelphia to Iredell. Nor do contemporary records, other than the elliptical journals of the Convention, afford more light.

A Federalist Star Rises

An exception to this are the thumb-nail sketches of William Pierce, delegate from Georgia, who left the following characterizations of the North Carolina delegates:

"Mr. Blount is a character strongly marked for integrity and honor. He has been twice a Member of Congress, and in that office discharged his duty with ability and faithfulness. He is no Speaker, nor does he possess any of those talents that make Men shine;—he is plain, honest, and sincere. Mr. Blount is about 36 years of age.

"Mr. Spaight is a worthy Man, of some abilities, and fortune. Without possessing a Genius to render him brilliant, he is able to discharge any public trust that his Country may repose on him. He is about 31 years of age.

"Mr. Williamson is a Gentleman of education and talents. He enters freely into public debate from his close attention to most subjects, but he is no Orator. There is a great degree of good humour and pleasantry in his character; and in his manners there is a strong trait of the Gentleman. He is about 48 years of age.

"Mr. Davey is a Lawyer of some eminence in his State. He is said to have a good classical education, and is a Gentleman of considerable literary talents. He was silent in the Convention, but his opinion was always respected. Mr. Davey is about 30 years of age.

"Mr. Martin was lately Governor of North Carolina, which office he filled with credit. He is a Man of sense, and undoubtedly is a good politician, but he is not formed to shine in public debate, being no Speaker. Mr. Martin was once a Colonel in the American Army, but proved unfit for the field. He is about 40 years of age." [20]

If the North Carolina delegates were ranked according to their activity in the Convention, Davie would rank second only to Williamson. Blount, who spent most of his time in New York attending Congress, took no part in the recorded debates. Martin's only recorded activity was the seconding of three motions.[21] Spaight's part in the discussion was also a minor one, except that he dissented with his colleagues on two notable points. He failed to agree with them on approving the report of the grand committee, with its amendment which provided for equality of representation in the Senate, and he favored a majority vote, rather than a two-thirds vote, for the passage of navigation acts.[22]

Although Williamson played a more conspicuous part than did

Davie, the latter's role was far from insignificant. The empirical nature of their experiment was expressed in a letter of June 14, to Caswell, signed by all the delegates except Blount. Though they had been sitting "from day to day, Saturdays included," it was impossible for them to determine when the business would be finished. In fact, "a very large Field" presented itself to them "without a single Straight or eligible Road that has been trodden by the feet of Nations." They further pointed out that "An Union of Sovereign States, preserving their Civil Liberties and connected together by such Tyes as to Preserve permanent & effective Government is a system not described, it is a circumstance that has not occurred in the History of men; if we shall be so fortunate as to find this in descript our Time will have been well spent." There was a fair promise of "a Summer's Campaign," but those of them who could remain there "from the inevitable avocation of private business," were "resolved to Continue Whilst there is any Prospect of being able to serve the State & Union." Their patriotism did not reach such heights, however, that it kept them from pointing out that "the Money of our State is subject to Considerable Decrements when reduced to Current Coin," or from submitting to Caswell "the Propriety of furnishing us with an additional Draught for two months' Service." [23]

Four days later, Davie broached this same subject of warrants to Caswell "as the time of our Service here appeared every day less certain." He also informed him that "We move slowly in our business; it is indeed a work of great delicacy and difficulty, impeded at every step by jealousies and jarring interests." [24]

The injunction of secrecy and the system of voting by delegation leave some doubt as to Davie's reactions to a number of the more important issues facing the delegates. As a matter of fact, his recorded participation was small in quantity, but of great importance in quality.

On June 2 he seconded Williamson's motion to make the executive "removable on impeachment and conviction of mal-practice or neglect of duty." [25]

Davie and his colleagues did not take an important part in proposing the main features of the Constitution, but they did play a determining role in the compromises. In the most important compromise, Davie's vote was critical in saving the Constitution itself.

On June 30 Davie delivered his longest and most important speech

A Federalist Star Rises

in the Convention. The issue which provoked the speech dealt with the provision allowing the state legislatures to choose the members of the Senate on the basis of proportional representation, as set forth in the Virginia Plan. Oliver Ellsworth, of Connecticut, representing the smaller states, had offered an amendment to give the states an equal vote in the Senate.

Madison's report of Davie's speech is given in full:

Mr. Davy was much embarrassed and wished for explanations. The Report of the Committee allowing the Legislatures to choose the Senate, and establishing a proportional representation in it, seemed to be impracticable. There will according to this rule be ninety members in the outset, and the number will increase as new States are added. It was impossible that so numerous a body could possess the activity and other qualities required in it. Were he to vote on the comparative merits of the report as it stood, and the amendment, he should be constrained to prefer the latter. The appointment of the Senate by electors chosen by the people for that purpose was he conceived liable to an insuperable difficulty. The larger Counties or districts thrown into a general district, would certainly prevail over the smaller Counties or districts, and merit in the latter would be excluded altogether. The report therefore seemed to be right in referring the appointment to the Legislatures, whose agency in the general System did not appear to him objectionable as it did to some others. The fact was that the local prejudices & interests which could not be denied to exist, would find their way into the national Councils whether the Representatives should be chosen by the Legislatures or by the people themselves. On the other hand, if a Proportional representation was attended with insuperable difficulties, the making the Senate the Representative of the States, looked like bringing us back to Congs. again, and shutting out all the advantages expected from it. Under this view of the subject he could not vote for any plan for the Senate yet proposed. He thought that in general there were extremes on both sides. We were partly federal, partly national in our Union. And he did not see why the Govt. might not in some respects operate on the States, in others on the people.[26]

Yates's report of Davie's speech was briefer:

I have great objection to the Virginia plan as to the manner the second branch is to be formed. It is impracticable. The number may, in time, amount to two or three hundred. This body is too large for the purposes for which we intend to constitute it. I shall vote for the amendment.

[183]

WILLIAM R. DAVIE

Some intend a compromise.—This has been hinted by a member from Pennsylvania, but it still has its difficulties. The members will have their local prejudices. The preservation of the state societies must be the object of the general government. It has been asserted that we were *one* in war, and *one* in peace. Such we were as states; but every treaty must be the law of the land as it affects individuals. The formation of the second branch, as it is intended by the motion, is also objectionable. We are going the same round with the old confederation—No plan yet presents sufficient checks to a tumultuary assembly, and there is none therefore which yet satisfies me.[27]

The two different versions of this speech are given because of their importance to the very success of the Convention itself. Not only did this speech show Davie's willingness to compromise on the momentous question of the composition of the Senate, but it also was largely responsible for his appointment on the committee, consisting of one member from each state, "to devise and report some compromise."[28]

This committee was appointed as a result of a deadlock which threatened to break up the convention. When the vote was taken on Ellsworth's motion to give equal representation in the Senate, the states were evenly divided—North Carolina, ranking fourth in population, voted with the other large states, Massachusetts, Pennsylvania, Virginia, and South Carolina in opposing equality. The small states, Connecticut, New York, New Jersey, Delaware, and Maryland, favored it. The vote of Georgia, which had consistently voted with the large states, was split when Abraham Baldwin, a Yale graduate and a Connecticut native, voted for the motion, thereby prompting Pinckney to propose the calling of the grand committee which was responsible for what has been called the "Great" or "Connecticut compromise."* Another close call, which would have changed the situation by giving a narrow margin to the large states was the fact that Luther Martin alone cast Maryland's vote, because of the tardiness of Jenifer, which would have tied Maryland's vote.[29]

All states except New Jersey and Delaware voted for the selection

---

*Though Bancroft spoke of this arrangement of proportional representation in the House and equal representation in the Senate as the "Connecticut compromise," there have been objections to this appellation. However, the influence of Ellsworth and Sherman cannot be overlooked. See Andrew C. McLaughlin, *A Constitutional History of the United States* (New York: D. Appleton-Century Company, 1935), p. 173n.

A Federalist Star Rises

of the committee. The resulting eleven-man committee, chosen by ballot on July 2, consisted of Gerry of Massachusetts, Ellsworth of Connecticut, Yates of New York, Patterson of New Jersey, Franklin of Pennsylvania, Bedford of Delaware, Martin of Maryland, Mason of Virginia, Rutledge of South Carolina, Baldwin of Georgia, and Davie of North Carolina.[30]

The selection of Baldwin and Davie, both of whom were known to favor compromise, was of the utmost importance. It was now a foregone conclusion that such a committee would insure at least a partial victory for those who supported the compromise.[31]

Further support for this contention is that Yates in his "Notes" reported: "By the proceedings in the convention they were so equally divided on the important question of *representation in the two branches*, that the idea of a conciliatory adjustment must have been in contemplation of the house in the appointment of this committee." [32]

It is regrettable that the debates within the grand committee, of which Gerry was chosen chairman, remain in obscurity, except for the brief notes of Yates on the meeting of July 3. The committeemen were of course divided on how to effect "this salutory purpose" of a "conciliatory adjustment." Some favored "the indispensible necessity of a representation from the states *according to their numbers and wealth*"; others held out for such representation "*as was strictly federal*, or in other words, *equality of suffrage*." A "lengthy recapitulation" of the opposing arguments ensued, climaxed, if Yates did not exaggerate, by a speech of the hitherto-uncommitted Yates himself, who declared his "*attachment to the national government on federal principles*." This in turn prompted Dr. Franklin to introduce a motion "which after some modification was agreed to, and made the basis" of the committee report to the convention:

That in the first branch of the legislature, each of the states now in the union, be allowed one member for every 40,000 inhabitants ... —That each state, not containing that number, shall be allowed one member.

That all bills for raising or apportioning money, and for fixing salaries of the officers of government of the United States, shall originate in the first branch of the legislature, and shall not be altered or amended by the second branch; and that no money shall be drawn from the public treasury, but in pursuance of appropriations to be originated in the first branch.

William R. Davie

That in the second branch of the legislature, *each state shall have an equal vote.*[33]

By this compromise the committee sought to solve the riddle of a federated union. This report was submitted to the convention on July 5.[34] After eleven days of debate, its basic features, with minor amendments, but including the equality of votes in the second branch, were passed by a vote of five to four. The switch of North Carolina from her natural allies—Pennsylvania, Virginia, South Carolina, and Georgia, who voted against the report—to the side of the small states, Connecticut, New Jersey, Delaware, and Maryland, was the determining factor.*

Thus there was a concatenation of events, beginning with Davie's speech of June 30, through his selection to the grand committee, to North Carolina's willingness to join the ranks of the small states that made possible the great compromise over representation in the two houses.† Davie's vote in the grand committee was without doubt the most decisive single vote cast in the convention. Indeed, it was one of the most decisive votes ever cast in any constituent body. It made possible the success of the convention and the Constitution.[35]

While it is difficult to state categorically who was responsible for North Carolina's shift to the side of the small states in the final vote on the acceptance of the grand committee report, the available evidence points to Davie and, to a lesser extent, Williamson. The inarticulate Blount had been called back to the Continental Congress and did not attend from July 2 until August 7.[36] On July 9, three days after the final vote, he wrote John Gray Blount that he had left Williamson as head of the delegation. The aristocratic Spaight voted against the measure. Martin either sided with Davie and Williamson or abstained from voting. The latter possibility is doubtful on the basis of his later championship of the Constitution in the ratifying conventions. To Davie the greatest credit should be given on the

---

* Max Farrand (ed.), *The Records of the Federal Convention of 1787* (New Haven: Yale University Press, 1911), II, 15. The vote of Massachusetts was divided. It might also be repeated that Spaight voted in the negative.

† Attention should be called to the fact that this equal representation in the Senate, so feared by the extreme nationalists, neither injured the large states as such, nor destroyed the principle of nationalism, nor stood as a guardian of the weaker states. See McLaughlin, *Constitutional History of the U.S.*, p. 176.

A Federalist Star Rises

concrete evidence of his speech of June 30, when he said that if he were required "to vote on the comparative merits of the report as it stood, and the amendment," providing for equality in the senate, "he would feel constrained to prefer the latter." Undoubtedly his mind was already made up when he went into the grand committee.

Williamson wrote Governor Caswell August 20 that they would "on some future occasion be at liberty to explain to your Excellency how difficult a part has fallen to the share of our State in the course of this business and I flatter myself greatly if we have not sustained it with a Principle & firmness that will entitle us to what we will never ask for, the thanks of the public. It will be sufficient for us if we have the satisfaction of believing that we have contributed to the happiness of Millions."[37]

In the debate concerning the recommendation of the grand committee that each state be allowed one member for every forty thousand inhabitants, Davie spoke out in favor of committing the clause to a special committee of five. Madison reported that he "seemed to think that wealth or property ought to be represented in the 2d. branch; and numbers in the 1st. branch."[38]

The special committee, after reporting the apportionment of the fifty-six representatives for each state for the first meeting of Congress, recommended that Congress should be authorized to increase the number of representatives from time to time, on the basis of wealth and population as the states themselves changed in wealth and population.[39]

This report led Randolph to propose an amendment to the effect that a census should be taken periodically as a basis of reapportionment.[40] Despite Gouvernour Morris's objections to the census as "fettering the Legislature too much,"[41] Williamson offered as a substitute to Randolph's amendment a proposal that a census should be taken of "the free inhabitants of each State, and three fifths of the inhabitants of other description" and that "the Legislature shall alter or augment the representation accordingly."[42] In defending his amendment, Williamson reminded Gorham that "if the Southern States contended for the inferiority of blacks to whites when taxation was in view, the Eastern States on the same occasion contended for their equality." Concurring in neither extreme, he approved of the ratio of three-fifths as the equitable solution.[43]

WILLIAM R. DAVIE

When the debate on this question of the counting of slaves had occupied the floor for two days, Davie, the owner of thirty-six slaves in 1790,[44] felt "it was high time now to speak out." Realizing that "some gentlemen" sought to deprive the Southern states of "any share of Representation for their blacks," he felt "sure that N. Carola. would never confederate on any terms that did not rate them at least at 3/5. If the Eastern States mean therefore to exclude them altogether the business was at an end." [45]

On the final ballot on the compromise, North Carolina voted solidly in its favor. In the light of the insistence on the part of South Carolina and Georgia that the blacks be counted equal to whites in regard to representation, North Carolina's stand has been described as "magnanimous." [46]

Davie's only other officially recorded activity at the convention was his statements in regard to the executive. In this regard, he seconded the proposal that the executive should be "removable on impeachment and conviction of malpractice or neglect of duty." [47] Later, on the question of impeachment of the executive, he considered it "as an essential security for the good behaviour of the Executive," who would otherwise "spare no efforts or means whatever to get himself re-elected." [48] As for the executive's term of office, he proposed the period of eight years.[49] Later, he changed his mind and seconded Mason's motion "that the Executive be appointed for seven years, & be ineligible a 2d. time." [50]

Aside from the scant reports of the convention, little can be found about Davie's activities inside the convention hall or outside in Philadelphia. On June 19, he wrote Iredell again, but he had "nothing worth inclosing you, but a paper containing a list of members." Yet he did recommend to him a recent book of "particular merit, a performance of Mr. J. Adams, the American Minister at the British Court," entitled "a defence of the Constitution of the United States against the opinions of Mons. Turgot." Davie described it as "one continued encomium on the British Constitution, and that unequaled balance and security produced by the admirable mixture of democracy, aristocracy, and monarchy in the Government." [51]

By July 8, Davie was already thinking seriously of returning to North Carolina. On that date Williamson wrote Iredell that he "feared Davie will be obliged to leave us before our business is fin-

A Federalist Star Rises

ished, which will be a heavy stroke to the delegation. We have occasion for his judgment." Especially was this true because Williamson was "inclined to think that the great exertions of political wisdom in our late governor [Martin], while he sat at the helm of our State, have so exhausted his fund, that time will be required to enable him again to exert his abilities to the advantage of the nation." [52]

Nine days later, Davie himself wrote Iredell: "I shall not stay until the business is finished. I am sorry it will be out of my power. As soon as the general principles are established I shall set out." [53] Writing on the same day to Davie, Iredell "heartily wished" success to the "great business you are engaged in, and should not doubt it if less than an *entire unanimity* would do. But when that is the case it is difficult to carry any thing." [54]

Finally, on August 6, Davie again wrote Iredell that he was setting out for Halifax on the following Monday "as the great outlines are now marked, and have been detailed by a committee: the residue of the work will rather be tedious than difficult." [55] He finally left Philadelphia on August 13,[56] having served continuously since May 22.

Williamson wrote Caswell that he regretted Davie's departure "very much as his conduct here had induced me to think highly of his abilities and political principles." [57] Blount also reported to the Governor August 20 that Davie's "business at the approaching Superior Court called him so pressingly that he could not stay any longer," but that if "he could have complied with his own inclination, or those of the Delegation of the State he would have remained during the Session." [58]

Davie's own account of his departure and of the state of affairs in Philadelphia was reported to Caswell in a letter dated August 23, from Halifax: "I left Philadelphia on the 13th Ulto., before which date we had informed you of the progress of the business; it was not supposed the Convention would rise before the first of September, and all the general principles were already fixed and Considering the State and Nature of my business, I felt myself fully at liberty to return, especially as No. Carolina was so fully and respectably represented." [59]

By this time the acceptance or rejection of the Constitution had already become a political question of the first magnitude in North Carolina. The familiar Conservative-Radical pattern of political groupings now assumed a more closely knit formation, aligning itself into two rival parties, the "Federalists," first called "Federals," and the "Anti-Federalists," or "Republicans." The "Anties" feared a surrender of state sovereignty and of their power over paper money and the Loyalists. The Conservatives looked to the new Constitution to protect the sanctity of property, stabilize the currency, and promote the trade and general welfare of the state. The August elections for the 1787 Assembly were fought out along the lines of this cleavage. These elections were considered the preliminary skirmish in the approaching struggle over the Constitution.[60] Davie offered himself as a Federalist candidate for the town of Halifax.

The situation in North Carolina was reported to Davie by Iredell, July 19: "I have not a word about our election, so that I imagine there is some such manoeuvring going on as formerly. I flatter myself there will be no doubt of your being elected."[61]

The Federalists were the first in the field, mapping out their strategy before the final draft of the Constitution had been completed. Realizing the importance of the August elections to the Assembly, Williamson twice wrote to Iredell stressing the importance of electing "some men of understanding in the House who are capable of explaining and promoting such measures as may be recommended by the Convention." He also hoped that Samuel Johnston would be chosen governor and said that "there will be much need of abilities in the Senate as well as in the Commons."[62]

In the ensuing elections, Davie was returned to the House of Commons by Halifax. Despite the well-laid schemes of the Federalists, the "Anties" secured a majority in both houses. A number of the leading Federalists were defeated. Through mismanagement, the Federalist, Stephen Cabarrus, defeated Iredell, neither of whom wanted to run against the other.[63] Samuel Johnston did not stand for election, thinking that the opposition against him was too strong.[64] In Brunswick County, Benjamin Smith was defeated, and in Orange, William Hooper had a personal "engagement" with an Anti-Federalist, McCauley, as a result of which Hooper came off "second best with his eyes blacked."[65]

Yet when the Assembly met in Tarborough, November 19, 1787, there were a number of prominent Federalists in each house. Besides Davie, they could look to Spaight, John Sitgreaves, who was chosen speaker, Cabarrus, John Steele, and William Barry Grove. In the Senate there were Allen Jones, Isaac Gregory, of Camden, John Skinner, of Perquimans, and John Johnston of Bertie County—all of whom were to be active in upholding the Constitution. The Anti-Federalist leaders in the House were Timothy Bloodworth, William Goudy, of Guilford, Britain Sanders, of Wake, and Alexander Mebane, of Orange. In the Senate their forces were led by Thomas Person, Elisha Battle, James Kenan, of Duplin, and Joel Lane, of Wake County.[66]

When the houses were organized, one of those strange inconsistencies in political history occurred. Instead of choosing an Anti-Federalist for the gubernatorial post, partisanship was relaxed, and Samuel Johnston, the arch-conservative, was elected.[67] After the submission of the Constitution to the states, both parties had realized the importance of the issues involved and therefore now turned to their most respected, though not most loved, leader.[68]

Davie, attending court in Newbern, did not take his seat in the House until December 4.[69] While Davie was in Newbern, the Philadelphia merchant, William Attmore (who married Sallie, the daughter of Judge Sitgreaves), related that at a dinner party, Davie "produced a curious Tobacco Pouch, made of a young Mink Skin, the size of a little Cat, it was dress'd with the hair, Feet and Claws and Tail on, and when thrown on the Table with a bellyful of Tobacco look'd like a little dead black Cat." [70]

Though the issue of greatest importance in this Assembly, which met from November 19 to December 22, was the question of the Constitution and the calling of a state convention, there were a number of other public questions in which Davie took an active interest. He had hardly taken his seat when he was added to two important committees, the one on finance, of which he became chairman, and the one appointed "to report on such Bills of a Public nature as are necessary to be passed into Laws this session." [71]

As chairman of the committee to which were referred the governor's message and papers relating to pardons, after reviewing the cases of three state prisoners, Davie concluded that the governor's power of pardon "should be exercised with great discretion," because "pardons improperly and too frequently granted inspire Wicked Men with not only hope, but confidence of impunity, relax the Administration of the Laws and deprive the Citizen of that Security expected from Society and Government." The report was concurred in.[72] Davie was also on the committee to determine some measures "for quieting the tumults and disorders in the Western parts of this State."[73]

He presented a number of petitions, which attest to his power and influence. Included among these were the petitions of the state treasurer, John Haywood, of Nicholas Long, and of William Blount, the last of which set forth that "the sum reported against him by the Comptroller to be due the State, was Money received from Services actually performed & done." He also presented the memorial of Richard Dobbs Spaight in which it was contended that, while he was a minor, "part of the Ground on which the Palace and other public buildings in the Town of New Bern was built... was taken from him without his consent or that of his Guardian" and he was therefore "praying relief" for the consideration paid, as it was "far inadequate to the value of the ground so taken."* Of particular note is the fact that he presented the petition of "Sundry of the Inhabitants of the town of Halifax, praying against a further Emission of Paper Currency."[74]

A number of bills were presented by him, among which was a bill "to carry into further effect an Act entitled 'an Act for opening the land office, for the redemption of Specie and other Certificates, and discharging the arrears due to the Army,'" which was passed December 22, 1787. Indicating his fairness and liberalism was the bill he presented for erecting the counties of Davidson and Sumner in Tennessee into a new judicial and military district and for the appointment of an assistant judge and attorney general to meet the exigencies of the new district.[75]

Davie also served on the committee to consider the "sundry resolutions declaratory of the rights of the people of this State to the navigation of the Mississippi" and was chairman of the committee to consider the governor's message in regard to the disposition of the artillery of the state, which they decided should be divided as equally as possible among the several companies of the artillery regiment.[76]

---

* It was not until 1798 that this claim was finally settled. See Alonzo Thomas Dill, *Governor Tryon and His Palace* (Chapel Hill: The University of North Carolina Press, 1955), pp. 252-53, 257, 261.

WILLIAM RICHARDSON DAVIE

Photograph of a black and white preliminary study by John Vander-Lyn, used by him in executing his half-length portrait of Governor Davie, aged 44, in Paris, 1800. This study, now lost or destroyed, was in the possession of Alwyn G. Ball, of Charleston, S.C., a descendant maternally from Governor Davie. Photograph reproduced here was made from the original black and white study in 1882, Charleston.

WILLIAM RICHARDSON DAVIE

Miniature executed in Paris, 1800, by Eliza Mirbel, while Davie was representing the United States as Minister Plenipotentiary and Envoy Extraordinary to France. Original now in Independence Hall, Philadelphia, Pa. Bust-length miniature in octagonal enameled frame, showing him in the uniform of a Brigadier General, United States Army.

A Federalist Star Rises

His only recorded votes of any significance were two in the negative. Demonstrating his Eastern proclivities, he dissented in the appointment of a joint committee to consider "what alterations if any, be necessary to be made in the present Constitution of this State at the intended Convention." A vote of 43 to 39 defeated this proposal, and it would be forty-eight more years before the West triumphed. He also voted against Philemon Hawkins' resolution recommending to the people of the state that they "authorize and direct their representatives, to be elected for the purpose of deliberating on the Federal Constitution, to take into their serious consideration the second & third Articles of the Constitution of this State and so to alter them that the Legislature may be less expensive and its measures be more stable and uniform." This resolution was defeated by a vote of 39 to 44.[77]

But the chief concern of this Assembly was consideration of the Federal Constitution. In fact, the greater part of Governor Caswell's message dealt with the "Papers respecting the Federal Convention."[78] [78] Davie arrived in Tarborough the day before the date set for discussion of the document, December 5.[79] On that day the House sent a message to the Senate proposing a joint meeting in the Commons room.[80] Thomas Person attempted to block this proposal by speaking as often as the Senate rules permitted. Despite his opposition, the Senate agreed to the proposal and accordingly met in conference with the House. The joint houses formed themselves into a committee of the whole with Elisha Battle, of Edgecombe, as chairman.[81] On December 6 they adopted a series of resolutions, accepted by both houses,[82] providing that delegates should be chosen the last Friday and Saturday in March, 1788, for a state convention to consider the Constitution. Tax-paying freemen were qualified to vote, but only freeholders were eligible for election. A total of 296 delegates were to be chosen—five "Suitable Persons" from each of the fifty-eight counties and one from each of the six borough towns. The convention was to be held in Hillsborough on July 21, 1788. They ordered three hundred copies of the resolutions and fifteen hundred copies of the Constitution to be printed and circulated by the members of the Assembly among their constituents.

The ensuing campaign was vigorous and heated. North Carolina's convention was later than that of the other states and thereby provided an opportunity for detailed discussion and crystallization of public sentiment. All means of swaying their constituents were employed by the opponents—pamphlets, newspapers, private correspondence, mass meetings, discussions in private homes, at courts, militia musters, taverns, and churches.[83]

The Federalists, ably marshalled by Iredell, Johnston, Williamson, Maclaine, and Davie, were better organized in the presentation of their cause. Of these leaders, Iredell and Davie were especially active and lost no time in getting their case before the public. As early as November 8, 1787, Iredell had inaugurated what has been described as "the first public movement in the State, in favor of the Constitution."[84] The citizens of Chowan County convened on that day at Edenton, where they were presented with a preamble and a set of resolutions drawn up by Iredell. These resolutions, which met the approval of those present, instructed their representatives in the Assembly to use "their utmost efforts" for the calling of a convention "on as early a day as possible" and expressed "their hearty approbation of the new Constitution."[85] Not content with this, Iredell wrote an address to the court, which was presented by the grand jury for the Edenton District on November 12. Expressing sentiments similar to the foregoing resolutions, it pointed to the distressing situation under the existing government: "our public debts unpaid, the treaty of peace unfulfilled on both sides, our commerce at the very verge of ruin, and all private industry at a stand, for want of a united, vigorous government."[86]

Two months later, a pamphlet bearing the date January 8, 1788, was first printed serially in the Newbern *State Gazette* in fragments and then issued as a pamphlet, accompanied by an "Address," signed by "Publicola," who has been identified as Archibald Maclaine. The pamphlet, entitled "Answers to Mr. Mason's Objections to the New Constitution recommended by the late Convention at Philadelphia," was signed by "Marcus," who was immediately recognized "by his vigor" as Iredell. McRee made the valid claim that it was "greatly superior to any defence of the Constitution published in North Carolina anterior to its adoption" and that it "preceded all of the 'Federalist,' but the earliest numbers."[87] Iredell's answers to George Mason's eleven objections were cogently and effectively presented.

A Federalist Star Rises

A few days later, January 11, Davie wrote Iredell that he was "happy to find your election was secured at all events" and felt sure that there would be "no danger, either in the town or county for you." He also hoped that Samuel Johnston would not "think himself at liberty to refuse, should his country call upon him at this important crisis." [88]

Describing Willie Jones's activities, Davie reported that he "continues perfectly anti-federal; and is inducing the people here to doubt, very generally, of its adoption in the present form." Illustrative of the scurrility of the attacks in the newspapers and press is Davie's reaction to a piece signed "Freeman," which exceeded "in meanness" anything he ever saw, but he felt it was "a true picture of the person whose image it really bears." Davie's reaction was expressed in strong terms: "These fellows must be extinguished. I hope you will do your share of this business. You observe it is part of a fixed design to raise a general jealousy and distrust against every member of the profession."

Davie concluded his letter by reporting that he was very happy that Governor Johnston "was received in a proper manner" and that a number of men from the Assembly "were to meet him on his coming to town." Davie's cold animosity against Caswell, dating from Revolutionary days, was revived, as evidenced by his observation that *"Caswell must have felt some mortification at this attention to Mr. Johnston, as no notice had been taken of him.* I was happy in having the opportunity of showing *them* what homage freemen would bring to a *virtuous man* in office." [89]

Davie's letters to Iredell form one of the chief sources of information on the activities of the campaign, especially in Halifax, where the contest was unusually heated, being the home of the recognized leader of the "Anties," Willie Jones, and of the ardent Federalist, Davie. The latter wrote that all he had to report from that quarter was "the dissemination of anti-federal principles" and that "Mr. Jones continues to assail the constitution, and the Virginia communications have strengthened his party. You know his opinion has great weight here, and that it is much easier to alarm people than to inform them." Colonel John Geddy, "a late convert," had announced his candidacy and was "a most furious zealot for what he calls *W. Jones's system*, which is indeed all he knows about it; but he has raised the old cant

[195]

that 'the poor were to be ruined by taxes,' and no security for freedom of conscience, etc."[90]

The Federalists watched with great concern the action of the other states in regard to ratification. Davie's concern was expressed to Iredell after hearing that Delaware and Pennsylvania had ratified and before New Jersey's action was known. He thought that there was "little doubt" but that New Jersey would adopt the Constitution "as its consequences are so highly favorable to the non-importing States." His greatest anxiety, however, was over Virginia: "The great deference this State has been accustomed to pay to the political opinions of the Old Dominion, will, I believe, have a very bad effect on the determination of this great question: this circumstance, added to the opposition already formed, renders its adoption in this State extremely doubtful."[91]

Davie asked Iredell to forward him as many copies of "The Federalist" as he could "as we are in greater want of its assistance here than you are in Edenton." Governor Johnston had written Davie that twenty-five numbers had been printed.[92]

With the news of New Jersey's ratification, Davie thought "it is not improbable that nine States will receive it before the meeting of our Convention; should this not be the case, I believe the parties will be pretty equally balanced in this State—All the old Demagogues, the Friends of *paper money*, and the men who expect to prosper by public trouble and commotion will be certainly opposed to it, these added to the [illegible] proselytes of opinion will compose a formidable group."[93]

The Federalists had been restrained and scholarly in their appeal to the more conservative elements of the state, but the Anti-Federalists, led by the adroit and skillful Willie Jones, had made a direct appeal to the masses. With Halifax as his base of operations he directed the campaign in the northeastern part of the state. His henchmen were busy elsewhere: Lemuel Burkett in near-by Bertie, Timothy Bloodworth in the Wilmington district, Thomas Person in Granville, David Caldwell in Guilford, and Judge Samuel Spencer and Joseph McDowell in the western sector.[94]

Contrary to the predictions of Davie in regard to the March elections for the ratifying convention, the Federalists were far out-

A Federalist Star Rises

numbered when the returns came in. Though Davie was selected, Maclaine sadly recounted the list of prominent Federalists who were defeated: "It is ... no very good sign, that in some counties so many have been left out for their attachment to a form of government so well calculated to make the people happy. Gen. Jones, W. Blount, Mr. Hooper, Mr. Moore, Governor Martin, and even Judge Williams ... have been rejected." [95]

The Anti-Federalist victory seemed to accelerate the exertions of Davie. He and Iredell began to collaborate in the preparation of a pamphlet on the Federal Constitution. On May 1 Davie wrote Iredell that he had "today finished twenty-five pages of our little collection on the subject of the Federal Government." He was "sure what is done is extremely imperfect" because of constant interruptions by people on business the previous week. He felt that Iredell would "have much to add, if, on examination, you find room in the compass of such a pamphlet as we propose." Davie had struck out a part of what they had written on the subject of a religious test, but advised it could be reinstated if Iredell so desired. The subject of the judiciary was left to Iredell. Davie realized, he said, that "many of the popular objections" were still omitted and hoped they could be answered "without swelling the publication to too great a size." Iredell was given *carte blanche* to alter "the order and manner" of presentation, and he and Alfred Moore were requested to make the necessary corrections. Judge Sitgreaves, who was "extremely anxious for the success of our little publication," consented to assist "in attending and correcting the press." Sitgreaves and Hawkins* had already brought in subscriptions and the former had "promised to have it considerably enlarged, so that I am in hopes five or six reams may be printed." Davie felt that their pamphlet should be prefaced with a note to the effect that it "was not offered as an original production, but as a compilation from several fugitive pieces, etc., which will excuse us to the author of Marcus and others for the liberties we have taken with them." [96] Yet it may have furnished the basis for a pamphlet entitled *To the People of the State of North-Carolina*, by "A Citizen of North-Carolina." Reprinted in the Edenton *State Gazette of North-Carolina*, September 15, 1788, its authorship has been as-

---

* Probably Philemon Hawkins, Federalist of Warren County.

cribed to James Iredell.* It is regrettable that this is the only available information on the subject of this pamphlet and there is no evidence that it was ever printed.

The Federalists had been elated by the successive ratifications of the Constitution by Delaware, Pennsylvania, New Jersey, Georgia, Connecticut, and Massachusetts, all of which had occurred previous to the March elections. They had also noted the strategy employed by the Federalists in Massachusetts in agreeing to recommend amendments *after* unconditional ratification had been obtained. By the time of the July convention in North Carolina, four more states, Maryland, South Carolina, New Hampshire, and Virginia, had adopted the Constitution. One more than the requisite number of nine states had been obtained and the last three had followed Massachusetts' lead in recommending amendments.[97]

Less than two weeks before the Convention was to convene, Davie wrote another letter to Iredell in which he discussed among other things the effect of Virginia's ratification on Willie Jones's strategy: "The decision of Virginia has altered the tone of the Anties here very much. Mr. Jones says his object will now be to get the Constitution rejected in order to give weight to the proposed amendments, and talks in high commendation of those made by Virginia—they have reached you, no doubt, before this time. Those that were of any consequence by affecting the operation of the principles of the Constitution are, in my opinion, quite inadmissable, particularly the 3d, and the amendment to the Judiciary." [98]

In the same letter Davie reported that news had just arrived that New Hampshire had ratified the Constitution. Even more important was the information that General John Lamb, "chairman of a Committee in New York, which he styles the 'Federal Committee' has written to Mr. Jones, T. Person, and Tim Bloodworth, recommending them to be steadfast in opposition, and inclosing a large packet of anti-federal pamphlets to each of them. It is astonishing the pains these people have taken!" Davie added that "Wilie [*sic*] Jones felt some mortification in finding himself in the company of Bloodworth and Persons, etc., etc." [99]

*For a discussion of the pamphlet warfare at this time, see Hugh T. Lefler (ed.), *A Plea for Federal Union. A Reprint of Two Pamphlets* (Charlottesville: The Tracy W. McGregor Library, 1947).

A Federalist Star Rises

Davie and Iredell were active up to the last. On June 30 Davie received the debates of the Pennsylvania convention and "the second balance of the Federalist" from Iredell.[100]

There is also the implication that Davie and Willie Jones celebrated the Fourth of July together. After reporting the adoption of the Constitution by New Hampshire, Davie wrote: "We spent the 4th of July in good humor, notwithstanding our differences about the new Government." If this supposition is correct, it is another instance of the friendship of the two political opponents off the hustings.

When the long-awaited and much-discussed ratification convention convened at Hillsborough on July 21, 1788, only New York, Rhode Island, and North Carolina remained outside the new federal government and New York was to ratify within five days. North Carolina was thus faced with the alternative of becoming an independent nation, free to exercise its sovereignty as it saw fit, or of ratifying the Constitution and becoming an integral part of the new nation. The moment was decisive. The decision was momentous.

Of the 268 men who participated in the final vote,[101] the Federalists could claim only 31 per cent—a percentage which no doubt reflected faithfully the sentiments of the inhabitants of the state. The minority included many prominent lawyers, the landed gentry and large slaveholders, and the representatives of the towns.* With few exceptions this group was composed of the old Eastern Conservatives of Revolutionary days. The roll call of their leaders recalls most of the men with whom Davie had striven in his efforts to establish a stable, conservative government: Samuel Johnston, James Iredell, Archibald Maclaine, Richard Dobbs Spaight, John Gray Blount, John Sitgreaves, John Steele, Stephen Cabarrus, William Barry Grove, and Benjamin Smith. There were also lesser leaders of wealth and prominence in the Albemarle section, such as John Johnston, Isaac Gregory, Josiah Collins, Whitmel Hill, and from the West came Charles McDowell.†

---

* For a detailed discussion and intensive survey of the economic holdings of the entire membership of both ratifying conventions in North Carolina, see William C. Pool, "An Economic Interpretation of the Federal Constitution in North Carolina," *North Carolina Historical Review*, XXVII (Apr., July, Oct., 1950), 119-41, 289-313, 437-46.

† A list of the Federalists and Anti-Federalists is found in Jonathan Elliot (ed.), *The Debates of the Several State Conventions, on the Adoption of the Federal Constitution* (Washington: Printed for the Editor, 1836), IV, 250-51.

WILLIAM R. DAVIE

The great majority represented the more radical elements of the population, but their economic holdings were about equal to those of the Federalists. These men felt that the new Constitution would jeopardize the things they held most dear: local self-government, state rights, and the basic civil liberties. They believed that these rights should be safeguarded by amendments before they would ratify.[102]

The roll call of their leaders foreboded trouble for Davie and the Federalists. Led by Willie Jones, his most conspicuous followers were Samuel Spencer, David Caldwell, Thomas Person, Griffith Rutherford, Timothy Bloodworth, Joseph McDowell, Benjamin Williams, William Lenoir, Lemuel Burkett, and Elisha Battle. Other prominent ones were Thomas Wade, William Fort, William Goudy, John Macon, Henry Montfort, Alexander Mebane, Frederick Hargett, Caleb Phifer, James Kenan, Joel Lane, Matthew Locke, and James Galloway.

On the day that Davie took his seat, he was appointed to two committees. One was to prepare and draw up the rules of decorum, the other to be the committee on privileges and elections.[103] After the selection of Governor Johnston as president, the organization of the body, and the ousting of the two sets of returns from Dobbs County, the Convention settled down to business on July 23 with the reading of the Bill of Rights and Constitution of North Carolina and the various resolves of Congress and acts of the Assembly by virtue of which the Convention had been called. James Galloway, of Rockingham County, introduced the logical motion that the Constitution be discussed clause by clause.[104]

At this point Willie Jones, confident of the Anti-Federalist majority, astonished the Federalists by moving "that the question upon the Constitution should be immediately put." He justified his action on the grounds that "the Constitution had so long been the subject of deliberation of every man in this Country...that he believed every one of them was prepared to give his vote then upon the question." There was also the serious consideration of "the utmost economy and frugality" of the public money. Seconded by Person, the motion was promptly opposed by Iredell. After a brief discussion, Willie Jones, realizing perhaps that he had made a tactical error, yielded. The debate was on.[105]

A Federalist Star Rises

In the ensuing debate over whether the house should resolve itself into a committee of the whole, Davie spoke out in its favor, maintaining that it was the intention of the legislature, in voting so large a representation, "that their collective information should be more competent to a just decision." The convention accordingly resolved itself into a committee of the whole, with Elisha Battle in the chair.[106]

Defeated in their original plan as proposed by Willie Jones, the Anti-Federalists adopted the strategy of refusing to bring out and criticize all their objections to the Constitution. This led to a one-sided discussion, in which the Federalists were forced, by prolonged and patient explanations, to attempt to convince their opponents of the advisability and wisdom of first ratifying the Constitution and then recommending the desired amendments.[107]

The burden of these arguments fell principally on the shoulders of Iredell and Davie. Iredell must be credited with the ablest defense of the Constitution;[108] Davie was the second most frequent speaker and did a masterly job of upholding the Federalist cause. As one of the two delegates at this convention who attended the Philadelphia Convention, he frequently felt called upon to defend their actions.

The opening guns of the attack were fired by David Caldwell, who proposed that the convention formulate certain principles of government based on the compact theory and urged that the Constitution should be judged by these principles.[109]

Iredell, after repudiating the compact theory, was successful in his demand for consideration of the Constitution, clause by clause.[110]

Caldwell at once voiced the sentiments of the majority when he objected to the words "We the People" in the preamble. It was, he said, the representatives of the legislatures of the different states who had framed the Constitution. To this Davie replied with a long defense, in which he stressed the failures of the Confederation government and the general objects to be achieved by the Constitution. He conceived these to be protection against foreign invasion, defense against "internal commotions and insurrections," and the promotion of commerce, agriculture, and manufactures. To achieve these, he argued, it was "necessary that the foundations of this government should be laid on the broad basis of the people." Yet, he continued, "the state governments are the pillars upon which this government is extended over such an immense territory, and are essential to its existence." Therefore, the obvious solution was in a House of Representatives "immediately elected by the people" and a Senate which represented the sovereignty of the states. He emphasized, moreover, that "every member [of the Federal Convention] saw that the existing system would ever be ineffectual, unless its laws operated on individuals." [111]

That Davie could stoop to condescension and sarcasm is demonstrated in his reply to William Goudy, of Guilford, who objected "to be represented with negroes, especially if it increases my burdens."

"Mr. Chairman," he said, "I will endeavor to obviate what the gentleman last up said. I wonder to see gentlemen so precipitate and hasty on a subject of such awful importance. It ought to be considered, that some of us are slow of apprehension, or not having those quick conceptions, and luminous understandings, of which other gentlemen may be possessed. The gentleman 'does not wish to be represented with negroes?' This, sir, is an unhappy species of population; but we cannot at present alter their situation. The Eastern States had great jealousies on this subject. They insisted that their cows and horses were equally entitled to representation; that the one was property as well as the other. It became our duty, on the other hand, to acquire as much weight as possible in the legislation of the Union; and, as the Northern States were more populous in whites, this could only be done by insisting that a certain proportion of our slaves should make a part of the computed population.... It may wound the delicacy of the gentleman from Guilford, (Mr. Goudy,) but I hope he will endeavor to accommodate his feelings to the interest and circumstances of his country." [112]

In answer to Joseph McDowell's contention that the federal control over elections would lead "to the time when there will be no state legislatures—to the consolidation of all the states," Davie spoke at length, tracing how none of the departments of government could exist without the state governments, but said that "if there were any seeds in this Constitution which might, one day, produce a consolidation, it would ... with me, be an insuperable objection." [113]

On Saturday the twenty-sixth Davie, alarmed over the dearth of criticism by the Anti-Federalists, expressed his "astonishment at the precipitancy with which we go through this business." He felt it was "highly improper" to pass over in silence the section in regard to the

A Federalist Star Rises

executive, only to bring forth their objections later "at an unseasonable hour." He wanted to know the cause of "this silence and gloomy jealousy in gentlemen of the opposition," particularly in regard to this department which "has been universally objected to" and had been the target for "the most virulent invectives, the most opprobrious epithets, and the most indecent scurrility." Having been unable to draw forth criticism of the executive branch, he proceeded to explain the principle of the separation of powers and the reasons for a single executive, re-eligible for office.[114]

On Monday, the twenty-eighth, Davie defended the treaty-making power conferred on the executive "with the advice and consent of the Senate" against the objections of Judge Spencer and Joseph McDowell, who felt too much power was placed in too few hands. Davie pointed out the fact that this power has "in all countries and governments, been placed in the executive departments." The reasons were two-fold: "that degree of secrecy, design, and despatch, which is always necessary in negotiations between nations" and the desirability of preventing their "being impeded, or carried into effect, by the violence, animosity, and heat of parties, which too often infect numerous bodies." In fact, Davie would have preferred that this power should "be left to the President, who, being elected by the people of the United States at large, will have their general interest at heart." However, he continued, "that jealousy of executive power which has shown itself so strongly in all the American governments, would not admit this improvement." For this reason and because of the "extreme jealousy of the little states," it was necessary to grant this power to the Senate, thereby giving absolute equality in making treaties to the states. In refutation of Judge Spencer's further objection that such a blending of the different branches of government was dangerous, Davie showed a deep conversance with Montesquieu and his maxim in regard to the separation of powers. He argued that the American system came nearer meeting Montesquieu's principle than did the British government, on which the great political philosopher had "passed the highest eulogium."[115]

The following day, July 29, Davie again locked horns with Judge Spencer over the question of the federal judiciary. Spencer especially disliked the establishment of minor federal courts and the absence of a guarantee of jury trial in the federal courts. This in turn raised the serious objection of the absence of a Bill of Rights and a clause reserving all undelegated powers to the states. In reply Davie emphasized the necessity of a judicial power competent to decide "all questions arising out of the Constitution itself" and one which would be "coextensive with the legislative." In summary, he maintained that "It is necessary that the Constitution should be carried into effect, that the laws should be executed, justice equally done to all the community, and treaties observed. These ends can only be accomplished by a general, paramount judiciary." [116]

To the second clause of Article VI, making the Constitution and the laws of the United States and all treaties "the supreme law of the land," there was violent criticism by Timothy Bloodworth. He argued that it would "sweep off all the constitutions of the states," that it would be "a total repeal of every act and constitution of the states," and that it would "produce an abolition of the state government." After a defense by Iredell and Maclaine, Davie rose to make "a few observations." He stated that "Gentlemen should distinguish that it is not the supreme law in the exercise of a power not granted" and could "be supreme only in cases consistent with the powers specially granted, and not in usurpations." Quite logically, he upheld the supremacy of federal law in its proper domain: "To say that you have vested the federal government with power to legislate for the Union, and then deny the supremacy of the laws, is a solecism in terms." [117]

On July 30 the debate, clause by clause, was completed and Johnston moved that the committee of the whole "recommend that the Convention do ratify the Constitution, and at the same time propose amendments, to take place in one of the modes prescribed by the Constitution." [118] After considerable debate, Willie Jones, ominously silent up until then, moved that the previous question be put so that he might introduce, if it were carried, a resolution "stipulating for certain amendments to be made previous to the adoption by this state." [119]

Thus he brought forth the crux of the whole matter facing the convention. Should North Carolina ratify the Constitution before the desired amendments were adopted or should it first be assured of their incorporation? Willie Jones felt that North Carolina's refusal would give added weight to the general demand for amendments. In support

A Federalist Star Rises

of his contention he begged leave "to mention the authority of Mr. Jefferson, whose great abilities and respectability are well known." James Madison, he said, had received a letter from Jefferson while the Virginia convention was in progress. Jones continued: "... In that letter he [Jefferson] said he wished nine states would adopt it, not because it deserved ratification, but to preserve the Union. But he wished that the other four states would reject it, that there might be a certainty of obtaining amendments. Congress may go on, and take no notice of our amendments; but I am confident they will do nothing of importance till a convention be called. If I recollect rightly, amendments may be ratified either by conventions or the legislatures of the states. In either case, it may take up about eighteen months. For my part, I would rather be eighteen years out of the Union than adopt it in its present form." [120]

Judge Spencer immediately sided with Jones; Iredell again urged acceptance and *then* the proposal of amendments. He was followed by Davie, who contended that Jones's method of obtaining amendments, far from being "the most eligible" was "the reverse," and that Spencer's contention that it would be a "modest" stand was, on the contrary, "no less than an arrogant, dictatorial proposal of a constitution to the United States of America." He compared such a proposal to "a beggarly bankrupt addressing an opulent company of merchants, and arrogantly telling them, 'I wish to be in copartnership with you, but the terms must be such *as I* please.'" [121]

After more debate, Willie Jones's resolution, calling for certain amendments *before* ratification, was agreed to "by a great majority of the committee," despite Davie's hope that "they would not take up the whole collectively, but that the proposed amendments would be considered one by one." [122]

After the rising of the committee of the whole and the reading of the resolution passed by the Anti-Federalists, Iredell stated, on August 1, that he and "his friends are anxious that something may appear on the Journal to show our sentiments on the subject." He therefore introduced a resolution calling for the yeas and nays in order that "our constituents and the world may know what our opinions really were on this important occasion." [123] Joseph McDowell, Willie Jones, and Judge Spencer insisted that such a resolution was irregular, to which Davie heatedly replied that "he was sorry that gentlemen should not deal fairly and liberally with one another." Declaring it "perfectly parliamentary, and the usual practice in Congress," he stated "that nothing hurt his feeling so much as the blind tyranny of a dead majority."[124]

Nevertheless, Iredell was induced to withdraw his motion until after the resolution and proposed amendments were read.[125] The resolution took the form of a refusal to ratify, rather than a rejection of the Constitution. Specifically, it resolved that "a declaration of rights, asserting and securing from encroachment the great principles of civil and religious liberty, and the unalienable rights of the people, together with amendments to the most ambiguous and exceptionable parts of the said Constitution of government, ought to be laid before Congress ... [or another constitutional convention] previous to the ratification of the Constitution."[126]

The resolution was copied from the proposed Virginia resolution, which had been defeated by a close vote. The only difference was that the Virginia resolution would have referred its declaration of rights and amendments to the states rather than to Congress and to a general convention, if called. The bill of rights and the amendments also followed closely those of Virginia, with the notable addition of six amendments, which related to the special interests of North Carolina.[127]

After Judge Spencer, seconded by Joseph McDowell, moved that the above report be concurred in, Iredell proposed that its consideration be postponed in order to take into consideration an amendment calling for the ratification of the Constitution and the proposal of six amendments agreeable to the Federalists. This amendment was voted down, whereupon Iredell, seconded by Steele, moved that the yeas and nays be taken. Eighty-four revealed themselves as Federalists in the ensuing roll call, while the Anti-Federalists numbered one hundred and eighty-four.[128]

The following day, August 2, the report of the committee of the whole, which included Jones's resolution, was concurred with. Davie, seconded by Cabarrus, moved for the yeas and nays. The line held fast. Everyone who had voted for Iredell's amendment voted against concurring with the report of the committee of the whole, and everyone who had voted against Iredell's amendment voted for the committee report.[129]

A Federalist Star Rises

And so, despite the herculean efforts of Iredell, Davie, and other Federalists, the will of the majority, by a vote of 184 to 84, decreed that North Carolina should neither "reject nor ratify" the Constitution.

The main business of the convention having been settled, they turned to the business of selecting a location for the permanent seat of government. Davie voted against the bill which called for a ballot to be taken on the location of the capital,[130] probably because he realized that the Anti-Federalists would be able to carry their will in this instance too. Over the protest of 119 members to Willie Jones's proposal that a site within ten miles of the land of Isaac Hunter of Wake County should be chosen, the bill was carried, and the capital, which was to be called Raleigh, was in the course of time permanently located there.[131]

Willie Jones then presented a resolution recommending to the Assembly that "whenever Congress shall pass a law for collecting an impost" in the ten states which had ratified, North Carolina should "enact a law for collecting a similar impost on goods imported into this state, and appropriate the money arising therefrom to the use of Congress." The resolution was passed "by a large majority," Davie voting in the affirmative.[132]

Although defeated in the convention, the Federalists had a right to be proud of their part in the proceedings. Iredell and Davie in particular had done a statesman-like job in explaining, interpreting, and defending the Constitution. Moreover, Davie had twice displayed his moderating and restraining influence when the debates on the floor got out of hand. At one time he sought to cool the temper of the convention by disparaging "reflections of a personal nature." He stated that "we are all come hither to serve one common cause of one country. Let us go about it openly and amicably." Regretting "to see so much impatience so early in the business" he implored that they "examine the plan of government submitted to us thoroughly" and "deal with each other with candor," shunning "the employment of underhand means." At another time, he took issue with Thomas Person, who, he said, "had frequently used ungenerous insinuations, and had taken much pains out of doors to irritate the minds of his country men against the Constitution." Instead, he called on "gentlemen to act openly and above-board," adding that contrary conduct, on this occasion, was "extremely dispicable." He reiterated his former statement that he had come "for the common cause of his country, and he knew no party, but wished the business to be conducted with candor and moderation."[133]

After New York's ratification, only Rhode Island and North Carolina stood outside the pale. The undaunted Iredell and Davie set out at once to change the temper of the people of North Carolina. Fortunately a Mr. Robinson, or Robertson, had attended the Hillsborough convention as a stenographer. On the assumption that the dissemination of the debates "would produce a salutary change in the opinions of the people," the Federalists were eager that their commentaries and debates should be published. They therefore turned to Iredell and Davie, who "assumed the responsibility and care of the publication." These two secured the services of an Englishman in Edenton, Mr. Lorimer, who made "neat copies" from Robinson's notes. These in turn were submitted in all practicable cases to the various speakers for correction. One thousand copies were published in Edenton about the last of June by Hodge and Wills, the publishers of the Edenton *State Gazette of North-Carolina*.[134]

The extent of the labors of Iredell and Davie is revealed in their correspondence. In January, 1789, Iredell wrote Williamson: "Davie & myself are in a critical situation. We were engaged to get the Debates printed having no doubt we could sell the Copy, which we were empowered to do, upon condition to receive gratis about *100 Copies* for the Subscribers. We can't dispose of the Copy here or in Virginia, & I dare say he has not much more cash to advance than I have but the public [blot] so that we know not what to do, & a number of People who think everything can be done just as they wish it are very impatient about it."[135]

The following day, Davie wrote Iredell that he had received "the remaining copies of the debates, amounting to nineteen, nearly as rough as the former, accompanied by a long letter from Robertson, apologising for the delay and the imperfection of the copy." He further informed Iredell that he had received two letters from Williamson in New York, who wrote that he had obtained a printer, Hobson, to publish the Debates, but that he and Iredell would have to be "the guarantee" and that the debates would have to be printed "under his direction." These circumstances rendered it "still more

WILLIAM RICHARDSON DAVIE

Pastel portrait of subject, aged 43, by James Sharples (*circa* 1751-1811). Painted in America, 1799, before Davie embarked on his mission to France. Photograph from original now in Independence Hall, Philadelphia, Pa.

WILLIAM RICHARDSON DAVIE

Photograph of original "physionotrace" made in Paris, 1800, by Gilles Louis Chrétien (1754-1811). Now owned by the University of North Carolina, Chapel Hill. Chrétien invented the process of making profile silhouette portraits for which he coined the name "physionotrace." He instructed St. Memin in this art and the latter made similar portraits of a number of eminent Americans in the first half of the 19th century.

A Federalist Star Rises

necessary, that it shall be printed immediately." Davie could get a young man in Halifax "to copy it instantly for 20 s a day—but as Governor Johnston desires to correct his speeches, it will be impossible, and if done, you must have it done at Edenton, it would take too much time, trouble & expence, which I see must fall on you and myself to be sending them backwards and forwards, such a distance." [136]

On February 17 Iredell wrote John Steele that the "Manuscripts of our Debates" had just been received and that they had feared they would have to send them to Dr. Williamson in New York, "who engaged to see the work well done." They had just been able to induce Hodge and Wills to undertake the printing, and, "owing to circumstances that were unavoidable, I have made an agreement with them and hope the whole will be printed by the beginning of May." Hodge and Wills refused to purchase the copy, "but have agreed to give credit for the expence, and I think there can be no doubt but that will be reimbursed by the sale." Iredell proposed to have "1000 copies struck off, and you shall have a large share of them." [137]

An indication of the closely-knit political clique of the Federalists, as well as the strategy employed by Iredell and Davie, is revealed in a letter of Iredell's, dated July 1, 1789, and written to John Gray Blount probably. Iredell was forwarding one hundred copies of the *Debates* to him, with the following instructions: "Of these you will please to retain what you think proper for Washington and transmit the remainder when you can to Mr. Sitgreaves. He is entitled to ten more for the Newbern Subscribers, and Mr. Maclaine to fourteen more for those at Wilmington. The rest are for sale. Colo. Davie and myself proposed allowing a Commission for the trouble of selling &c. The Management of this at Washington I beg leave to submit to you, as you shall think proper. If any are sold at Washington, I will be much obliged to you if out of the sales you will give such a gratuity for the trouble of conveying them there as you shall think sufficient." *

The entire enterprise, no doubt, involved the outlay of a good deal

---

* Iredell to [John Gray Blount], July 1, 1789.—John Gray Blount Papers, A.H. Miss Keith, following S. A. Ashe, states erroneously that the copies referred to were the revised North Carolina laws, which were the work of Iredell. These were not published until two years later.—Keith (ed.), *The Blount Papers*, I, 490n.

of capital. McRee stated that "they suffered some pecuniary loss." Later he wrote David L. Swain, at that time President of the University of North Carolina, that "The Debates in Convention were prepared by Mr Lorimer in Mr Iredell's office—the expense fell chiefly on him & Davie." [138]

Regardless of the expense, Iredell and Davie performed a great service to the state in preserving these records which would probably have been lost otherwise, as were the debates of the Fayetteville Convention.*

Following close on the heels of the Hillsborough Convention were the annual August elections for the Assembly. There is no record of Davie's offering himself as a candidate. He probably declined for the same reason as Iredell, who felt it was necessary for him to attend the superior court which met at the same time.[139] The Federalists staged such an upswing in the election that it was doubtful which side was in the lead until the Assembly met in November.†

In the meantime, the Federalists, led by Iredell, Davie, and Maclaine, lost no time in circulating petitions requesting a second ratifying convention. Under a November 5 dateline, from Wilmington, the *State Gazette of South-Carolina* reported the circulation of such petitions in the Salisbury and Morgan districts "signed by all ranks of people with the greatest avidity." One correspondent reported that "almost every person seems more and more convinced of the bad policy of the decision of our convention." If they had adopted it, "we might have been represented in the first congress." The other consequences, it contended, were evident: "... this state must pay its proportion of the national debt—if we are not in union with the neighboring states, certainly our vessels will be considered as aliens, and laid under the same restrictions—perhaps prohibited from entering their ports. It is also evident that a great part of the produce of this state is exported and sold to the neighboring states, from whom we receive the greatest part of our specie." [140]

Davie wrote Iredell, September 8, that one of these petitions was "well received" in Halifax and that he would "disperse it all the way

---

* The debates of the first convention were later reprinted in Elliot's *Debates*.
† Newsome, "North Carolina's Ratification of the Federal Constitution," *N.C.H.R.*, XVII (Oct., 1940), 296. Dr. W. K. Boyd stated that the Anti-Federalists won the election.—*Hist. of N. C.*, II, 43.

A Federalist Star Rises

to Salisbury" and hoped it would "give a determination to the public mind, at present strangely unsettled and wavering." He thought that Governor Johnston was right "with respect to the *uniformity* of petitions," which he felt should be promoted. Davie asked Iredell to "correspond with the gentlemen at Newbern" on the subject, and he would "take care of this business to the westward," where he was going to attend court.[141]

Davie also reported that Thomas Person and Willie Jones "were both holding out the doctrine of opposition [to ratification] for five or six years at least." Davie, induced probably by the heat of the issues, then made the most serious indictment of his opponent that has been found: "Mr. Jones says we must have that time at least before their Judiciary are let in upon us; he is continually haranguing the people on the terrors of the Judicial power, and the certainty of their ruin if they are *obliged now* to pay their debts; we are almost led to believe there is something more than a mere mistake in point of principle in his conduct."[142]

The Federalists, still smarting over their defeat at the convention, vented their spleen on the opposing leaders. According to "a gentleman from Edenton" the "inhabitants of the sea-ports and all the lower counties" were "inexpressible chagrined" at their defeat, but were "striving hard to gain the assembling of another Convention." He described the "patriots of Tarborough" as having "strongly and openly discovered their abhorrence of the measures pursued by the anti-federal party, and have proceeded so far in their resentment, as to burn the effigies of a Spencer, a Jones, and a Parsons [Person] high anti-federal chiefs." He was "unable to determine whether a new convention would be called," but he could "venture to affirm, every man of sense and probity (except a few factious leaders) are warmly in favor of the measure."[143]

Not content with this, a pamphlet, signed "A Citizen and a Soldier" and published in August, 1788, was obviously directed at Willie Jones, though his name was not mentioned. The high point of its denunciation was reached when it stated that he would "execrate the Saviors of our Country, the Federal Convention, for a pack of Scoundrels, go to the Convention at Hillsboro full of d–mns & G–d d–mns, blow up an idle Fandango about Bills of Rights & Amendments, & what is still more infamous, throw us out of the Union.... Shall this man be allowed to brand the inimitable Washington with the Appellation of Scoundrel, when he is unworthy to clean his shoes?"[144]

Willie Jones immediately published a retort to this blasphemous attack in the Edenton *State Gazette of North-Carolina:*

> A SMALL pamphlet, signed "A CITIZEN and SOLDIER," addressed to the inhabitants of Edenton district, lately fell into my hands. I do not know who wrote it, nor where it was printed, but it was brought from Edenton to Halifax. The writer asserts, that I called the Members of the Grand Convention, generally, and General Washington and Colonel Davie, in particular, *scoundrels.* To this I answer that I never said so of the whole, or any one of these gentlemen. I know as little of many of the Members of that Convention, as this soldier (who perhaps never drew a sword in the service of his country) knows of me; therefore it would have been wrong for me to have called them scoundrels. As to General Washington, I have long tho't and still think him the first and best character in the world. As to Colonel Davie, I have a personal regard for him; I *think* him an honest man and a valuable member of the community, and I *know* him to be a man of genius, and knowledge in his profession. To make short of the matter, I swear that nothing can exceed the respect I bear for these two gentlemen, unless it be my scorn and contempt for the "CITIZEN and SOLDIER."[145]

When the Assembly met in Fayetteville on November 3, the great question was whether the Federalists could muster up enough votes for a new convention. Three days later one of the members, probably William Blount, doubted that it would be called, because Willie Jones in the upper house was "inflexible."[146] However, "No Party Spirit had yet appeared openly on any Subject." Two days later Governor Johnston felt that "a great number of our Friends were very warm for a New Convention and were very sanguine in their Expectations," but they had begun to "have apprehensions that they are too weak especially in the Senate many of the Members who are in favor of that measure being absent."[147]

By November 20, Johnston made an accurate prediction when he stated that there was "no possibility of a Convention till about the time of the meeting of the next Assembly in the Fall."[148] Despite the exertions of Willie Jones in the Senate and Thomas Person in the House, the call for a new convention was finally passed, but the

A Federalist Star Rises

"Anties" were sufficiently strong to postpone it until the third Monday in November, 1789, which coincided with the meeting of the General Assembly, thereby saving traveling expenses.[149]

Though the Federalists were thus forced to wait almost another year, the intervening months were marked by an appreciable defection in the ranks of the Anti-Federalists. The orderly and effective operation of the new Federal government, the returning economic prosperity, and the movement in Congress, led by James Madison, to amend the Constitution contributed largely to the undermining of Anti-Federalism.[150]

The effect of Madison's resolution is revealed by Davie in a letter to Iredell, June 4, 1789: "The Anties here were remarking with great triumph, the fulfillment of their prophecies with respect to Congress never taking up the question of amendments; when we, critically, received an account of Mr. Madison's notification that he would move this subject; nothing ever gave me so much pleasure, and this, coming from a Federalist, has confounded the Anties exceedingly." [151]

On June 10, Davie, jubilant over Madison's proposed amendments, wrote to him. Though he realized his "private acquaintance" with the Virginia statesman did not "warrant a correspondence of this kind," he felt that "the interest we have in your public character and exertions" was sufficient apology. Davie's appraisal of the situation in North Carolina is quoted in full:

You are well acquainted with the political situation of this State, its unhappy attachment to paper money, and that wild scepticism which has prevailed in it since the publication of the Constitution. It has been the uniform cant of the enemies of the Government, that Congress would exert all her influence to prevent the calling of a convention, and would never propose an amendment themselves, or consent to an alteration that would in any manner diminish their powers. The people whose fears had been already alarmed, have received this opinion as fact, and become confirmed in their opposition; your notification however of the 4th of May has diffused almost universal pleasure, we hold it up as a refutation of the gloomy prophecies of the leaders of the opposition, and the honest part of our Antifederalists have publicly expressed great satisfaction on this event. Our Convention meet again in November, with powers to adopt the Constitution and any amendments, that may be proposed; this renders it extremely important that the amendments, if any, should be proposed before that time—and although we may be nominally a foreign State, yet I hope the alterations will come officially addressed to the people of this Country, an attention however trifling in itself, that will be of importance in the present state of the public mind here.[152]

Davie continued on the subject of amendments, maintaining that "the farrago of amendments borrowed from Virginia is by no means to be considered as the sense of this Country," but were proposed "amidst the violence and confusion of party heat, at a critical moment in our convention, and adopted by the opposition without one moment's consideration." He reported that he had "collected with some attention the objections of the honest and serious." These objections were "but few & perhaps necessary alterations":

They require some explanation rather than alteration of the power of Congress over elections—an abridgement of the jurisdiction of the federal Court in a few instances, and some fixed regulations respecting appeals —they also insist on the trial by jury being expressly secured to them in all cases—and a constitutional guarantee for the free exercises of their religious rights and privileges—the rule of representation is thought to be too much in the power of Congress—and the Constitution is silent with respect to the existing paper money an important and interesting property. Instead of a Bill of rights attempting to enumerate the rights of the individual or the State Governments, they seem to prefer some general negative confining Congress to the exercise of the powers particularly granted, with some express negative restriction in some important cases.

Davie was "extremely anxious to know the progress of this delicate & interesting business" and felt that if Madison could give him some more information it "might perhaps be of some consequence to the Country, and would in my work be gratefully acknowledged." Unfortunately there is no record of Madison's answer to Davie.

In contrast to Davie's detailed and searching views on the political situation in the state, it is interesting to note the impressions of our "gentleman at Edenton." He wrote in September that the "people in the lower counties" were "all determined Federalists" and that he had gleaned from the back countries that there had been "an alteration in the sentiments of the people, who, it seems, from rank Anti's are now become perfect fed's; so fully are they convinced of the ill

A Federalist Star Rises

policy of separating themselves from the Union, and of the excellency of our Constitution." He also said that Willie Jones, the "celebrated leader of the anti-federal faction," appeared to be "convinced of his error," refused to attend the second convention, and had "been frequently heard to declare," that, after scrutinizing the Anti-Federalists, "he blushed to think that he was seconded by such a vile herd of infamous fellows."[153]

The elation of the Federalists at the second North Carolina ratifying convention can well be imagined. Meeting in Fayetteville from November 16 to November 23, 1789, they were easily able to re-elect Governor Johnston as president. Davie had been elected as a delegate to the Convention and to the Assembly—as had about half of the convention delegates. For this reason, the Assembly adjourned during most of the Convention.[154]

On his arrival at Convention Hall, Davie found a number of old Federalist friends, who had also served in the Hillsborough Convention: Samuel Johnston, John Gray Blount, Stephen Cabarrus, William Barry Grove, John Steele, Charles Johnson, Benjamin Smith, Charles McDowell, and Isaac Gregory. Prominent Federalists there who were not present at the previous convention were Hugh Williamson and William Blount, both of whom had served with Davie in Philadelphia. There were also David Stone, of Bertie, John Hay, of Cumberland, Thomas Blount, of Edgecombe, John Baptiste Ashe and Lunsford Long, of Halifax, Adlai Osborn, of Iredell, Benjamin and Philemon Hawkins, of Warren, and Davie's old comrade-in-arms, James Cole Mountflorence.[155]

The leading opponents of the first convention, except Willie Jones, were again on hand: Samuel Spencer, David Caldwell, Thomas Person, Timothy Bloodworth, William Lenoir, Joseph McDowell, James Kenan, Caleb Phifer, James Galloway, and Matthew Locke. Of the thirty-four new Anti-Federalists, none was worthy of particular note, except perhaps John Huske of New Hanover County, who was reported to have walked out of the convention with a discontented minority when the Constitution was finally ratified.[156]

The chief information concerning this convention consists of the brief journal of the proceedings, for there was no "Mr. Robinson" to take down the debates.

[215]

William R. Davie

On the first day of the sitting of the body, Davie was appointed to the committees on elections and on the rules of order and decorum to be observed during the convention. In an optimistic mood, he wrote Iredell that night that Johnston had been elected president of the convention, although the "Anties attempted to put Spencer upon us, but the business was better managed." Johnston had been "too unwell" to attend, but the Federalists had put Charles Johnson in as vice-president. Davie felt that "the calculations are greatly in favor of the Constitution: its friends say there is no doubt: of this, however, I am not so confident."[157]

The following day, after the reading of the Constitution, Williamson moved that the convention ratify. Objection to the motion led John Steele to move that Williamson's motion, along with the new plan of government, be referred to a committee of the whole. Though this was also objected to, it was finally carried on November 18. On Davie's motion, "all official papers relative to the Constitution or new plan of government" were also referred to this same committee.[158]

After the convention resolved itself into a committee of the whole, with John Baptiste Ashe in the chair, Davie, seconded by the Anti-Federalist, Bloodworth, resolved that the secretary contract with the local printers to strike off three hundred copies of the proposed amendments to the Constitution.[159]

After the committee of the whole had debated over the new Constitution and the proposed amendments from Wednesday until Friday, November 20, they submitted to the convention a report favoring the adoption of the Constitution. The following morning Davie moved, seconded by Mountflorence, that the convention take up the report of the committee. After it was read, Davie moved that the report be concurred in, to which the Anti-Federalist, James Galloway of Rockingham County, proposed that, previous to ratification, five amendments should first be laid before Congress.[160]

These amendments represented the demands of the Anti-Federalist minority. They provided that Congress should not "alter, modify or interfere in the times, places or manner of election" of members of Congress except when the state legislature failed to act; that any state legislature could raise its own quota of direct taxes or excises instead of having them collected by federal authority; that each state should have the exclusive right of making laws and regulations concerning

[216]

the redemption of paper money already emitted, or in liquidating and discharging the public securities of any of the states; that Congress should not introduce foreign troops into the United States without the consent of two-thirds of both houses; and finally that no treaties which were opposed to the laws of Congress or contradictory to the Constitution should be valid.[161]

Galloway's resolution, proposing these amendments, was defeated by a vote of 82 to 187, thus showing an overwhelming Federalist vote.[162] The convention again took up the report of the committee of the whole, which had resolved that the Constitution be ratified. Davie, seconded by Benjamin Smith, moved that this resolution be adopted. The resulting vote showed an even more overwhelming Federalist victory: 195 to 77.[163] The efforts of Davie, Iredell, Maclaine, and others had not been in vain.

Davie, again seconded by Mountflorence, moved that a copy of the ratification be sent to the President of the United States.

The Anti-Federalists had still not given up the idea of submitting to Congress the five amendments, proposed by Galloway. Again Galloway's motion for their adoption failed. Instead, a committee was appointed to prepare "such amendments to be made to the Constitution as they may deem necessary." Davie, Benjamin Smith, John Stokes, and John Hay represented the Federalists, while Galloway, Bloodworth, and Spencer represented the Anti-Federalists. Their resulting unanimous resolution, reported by Galloway, recommended eight amendments.[164]

These eight amendments included the first and third of those previously proposed, which restricted congressional control over elections, taxation, paper money, and state securities. In addition they proposed that members of both houses of Congress be ineligible to hold any other federal office during their term; that the proceedings of both houses should be published at least once a year; that "a regular statement and account of the receipts and expenditures of all public monies" should be published at least once a year; that all navigation laws should require a two-thirds vote of both houses; that no soldier should be enlisted for more than four years, except in case of war; and that "some tribunal, other than the Senate," should be provided for trying impeachments of Senators.

WILLIAM R. DAVIE

These amendments were carried and the convention, after passing an ordinance granting borough representation in the General Assemby to Fayetteville, adjourned, November 23, 1789.[165]

That night Charles Johnson wrote Iredell, who had worked so long with Davie for ratification: "I have the pleasure of informing you that on saturday the Constitution was finally adopted & ratified. On the Question the votes were 193 for it, 76 against it Majority 117. Permit me to congratulate you upon this glorious event, which I know will give you the most singular satisfaction, as I believe no body contributed more at heart than you; nor has any person contributed more to bring about the amazing change in the sentiments of the people, that is evident from the great majority in favr of the Constitution; even exceeding that at Hillsboro' against it.... Mr. Cabarrus who lives in the same room & Col. Davie in the next to us, are well— The Governor & Mr J. Johnston have been both very ill but are now perfectly recovered." *

Attention should be called to the fact that North Carolina ratified the Constitution and joined the Union before she knew that any state had ratified any of the twelve amendments which had passed Congress and been submitted to the states. Therefore, a tradition to the contrary notwithstanding, North Carolina was not exclusively or chiefly responsible for the Bill of Rights.[166]

Meanwhile the General Assembly had met in Fayetteville on November 2, and Davie had taken his seat as a member from the borough of Halifax four days later.[167] His friends were riding high on a wave of Federalism. Samuel Johnston was re-elected governor. Charles Johnson, after Caswell's death, and Stephen Cabarrus were elected speaker of the Senate and House respectively. Moreover, Johnston was soon selected, without opposition, as the first United States senator from North Carolina. The other seat in the Senate was hotly contested, but was finally won by Benjamin Hawkins. Alexander Martin succeeded to the governorship. On the third day of the session Richard Caswell, representing Dobbs County, was stricken with paralysis, while in his seat in the Senate. He died on November 10,

---

* Charles Johnson to Iredell, November 23, 1789.—Johnson Collection, A.H. A part of this letter is reprinted in McRee, *Iredell*, II, 273. Note should be taken of the difference in his report on the vote on the Constitution and the one recorded in the Journal.

[218]

A Federalist Star Rises

and Davie, among others, was on the committee to superintend his funeral.[168]

McRee states quite rightly that this Assembly seems "to have been actuated by a spirit of unusual liberality." His characterization was superficially based on the passage of three acts: the act for the establishment of the University, the act to encourage the manufacture of potash, and the act prohibiting the exportation of hides, skins, and furs, as a means of encouraging manufactures.[169] It is significant that Davie introduced the first two of these bills,[170] but they represent a small part of his accomplishments in this Assembly. On the basis of importance and quantity of legislation, Davie was the outstanding member of this legislature. He introduced thirteen bills or amendments, eleven of which were passed, presented eleven petitions, and served on twenty committees of consequence.

Among the important petitions and memorials which he presented, in addition to the purely personal, were those of the judges of the Superior Court on the subject of the depreciation of their salary, "sundry of the Inhabitants south of French Broad River," and the curiously-entitled petition of "the monthly meeting of the People called Quakers."[171]

Some of the more important committees on which he served were those "on Public Bills, on Finance, and the Committee appointed to take under consideration the necessary & most eligible plan for extinguishing the Certificate debt due by this State"; on Indian affairs; the joint committee to consider the partition of Hawkins County; the committee to consider Iredell's revisal of the laws of the state; the joint committee to equalize the Land Tax; the joint committee of which he was chairman "to prepare and introduce a Bill for ascertaining the manner, places and times of electing representatives of this State in the Congress of the United States"; the joint committee to consider the bill "to authorize the County Courts within this State annually, to elect a certain number of Justices in each County to attend the business thereof"; and the joint committee to consider the resolution for calling a Convention to revise the State Constitution.[172]

As to Davie's vote on important issues, the records reveal that he voted "yea" on the following bills: the bill for carrying into effect the act for the location of a permanent capital; the bill, previously referred to, to prevent the exportation of "Raw Hides, pieces of

Hides of neat Cattle and Calf Skins, Beaver, Rackoon and fox furs"; the bill to appoint commissioners to choose a suitable place for the location of the capital; the bill to allow the judges of the Superior Court "Five Pounds for every Court they shall attend in—1790, in addition to their present Salary"; and the important bill for ceding to the federal government "certain Western lands." His only recorded negative vote of any significance was on the bill to allow the judges an additional three pounds to their former salary.[173] Apparently he was holding out for the five pound increase.

Davie's most important contribution, however, was the introduction of a number of significant bills and amendments. Among these were an amendment to the act for "establishing Courts of Law, and for regulating the proceedings therein" and "an Act for giving an Equity jurisdiction to the Superior Court"; a bill providing "means for the payment of the public debt"; a bill "to alter the mode of trying Slaves accused of offences, the punishment of which shall extend to life or member"; the bill directing "the collectors of imposts and other duties to collect the same for the use of this State until the Congress of the United States shall make provision for that purpose," and the bill, previously mentioned, to encourage the manufacture of potash.[174]

It is significant that all of these bills introduced by Davie were enacted except his bill dealing with the trial of slaves and the bill to revise the court laws.[175]

Concerning the latter, Samuel Johnston wrote Iredell on December 1, 1789, that he had had a "considerable conversation yesterday evening with Col. Davie, who seems to think that, on account of some difficulties, no change will be made in the Court System this Session."

An interesting sidelight on the former Anti-Federalist, Judge Spencer, was also revealed by Johnston, who wrote that the judge was in Fayetteville at that time "soliciting some further consolation to himself and brethren for their faithful service, but is not likely to succeed." Spencer was "so dissatisfied with the conduct of the Assembly" that he was trying to get an appointment in the federal courts and had even condescended to ask Davie to recommend him to Oliver Ellsworth and Dr. William Samuel Johnson, signer of the

A Federalist Star Rises

Constitution and first president, from 1787 to 1800, of Columbia College.[176]

But among the many contributions of Davie in this Assembly, by far his most lasting, and the one for which he is best known, was his introduction and successful steerage through the Assembly of the bill to establish the University of North Carolina.

CHAPTER VIII

The Father of the University

ALTHOUGH there were several would-be fathers of the University of North Carolina, their attempts died aborning and to William Richard Davie must be given the credit for being its father and founder and chief supporter in its infancy. It seems entirely fitting that the first seeds of the state university should have been planted in Halifax at the provincial congress which met there in the fall of 1776. Fitting, because it was in Halifax that North Carolina was born into a new world of independent statehood, to join her twelve sister states in a concentrated effort to make good her new independence. Fitting, because here was the home of the father of the University from about 1785 to 1805.

In Davie there seemed to converge the two forces in the state which were striving to provide the means of education for its people—the Ulster Scot Presbyterians of the Mecklenburg and Rowan region and the landed gentry of the East, many of whom were imbued with the eighteenth-century concept of *noblesse oblige* and who saw the responsibilities which their newly-won independence had thrust upon them. These dual forces already had to their credit two tangible achievements, the founding of a college at Charlotte and the provision in the Revolutionary Constitution of 1776 for a state experiment in higher education.

It is significant that in the establishment of Queen's College, later called Queen's Museum and still later Liberty Hall, which Davie had probably attended, two of his closest associates and mentors were trustees: his uncle, William Richardson, and his uncle's colleague, Henry Pattillo,[1] who in 1795 was to dedicate his curious and interesting *Geographical Catechism* to Davie.[2] The influence of these two forces must have been profound.

It is equally significant that among the eighteen members of the committee who were appointed to write the Constitution of 1776 were Davie's father-in-law, Allen Jones, and the latter's brother Willie,[3] both of whom had attended Eton.* This committee, composed of fifteen Easterners, had been charged "to form, and lay before this House, a Bill of Rights, and Form a Constitution for the Government of this State."[4] Realizing its great responsibility to unborn generations, the committee accordingly saw fit to lay the basis for state patronage of education by incorporating into that instrument Section 41. This section, a literal analogue of Section 45 of the Pennsylvania Constitution of 1776,[5] provided "that a School or Schools shall be established † by the Legislature for the convenient Instruction of Youth, with such Salaries to the Masters paid by the Public, as may enable them to instruct at low Prices; and all useful Learning shall be duly encouraged and promoted in one or more Universities."[6]

Immediate compliance with this mandate was of course impossible. Even after the surrender of Cornwallis, the resources and energies of the state were so nearly exhausted that it was not until 1784 that an abortive attempt was made to implement this mandate. The cue was given by Governor Alexander Martin in his opening address to the Assembly, October 26, 1784, when he exhorted: "Your schools of learning ... are great objects of Legislative attention which cannot be too often repeated and held up to your view, that the mists of Ignorance be dissipated and good morals cultivated."[7] Shortly thereafter, on November 8, William Sharpe, of Rowan County, presented to

---

* In 1922 the late Colonel Fred A. Olds of Raleigh carried on a correspondence with the historian of Eton, Mr. Austin-Leigh, in regard to the Jones brothers' stay at Eton, but could only find the dates of their departure, and not of their entrance, because the records of the college from 1748 until 1753 had been destroyed.—Fred A. Olds, "Sketch of Willie Jones," *The Orphan's Friend and Masonic Journal* (Oxford, N.C.), Feb. 15, 1924.

† Here the North Carolina section left out the words "in each county" —the only variance with the former constitution.—Francis Newton Thorpe (ed.), *The Federal and State Constitutions, Colonial Charters, and Other Organic Laws*... (Washington: Government Printing Office, 1909), V, 3091.

the House of Commons the first bill for establishing a state university in North Carolina.[8] Drafted by a former trustee of the college at Charlotte, Dr. Samuel Eusebius McCorkle, it was intended to be presented, along with a bill to incorporate the Salisbury Academy, by Judge Spruce Macay, who, however, was riding the circuit of the recently-established Morgan District, which stretched from Salisbury to what is now Jonesboro, Tennessee.[9]

The Salisbury Academy bill was readily passed November 23, 1784,[10] but the University bill had short shrift in the Assembly. This might be attributed to the fact that the conscientious Presbyterian divine, eschewing such mundane devices as a tax on spirituous liquors employed by Queen's College and the New Bern Academy as a basis of revenue, had devised a scheme by which a poll tax was to be levied upon professional men, merchants, and county officials, and upon salaries.*

On November 11, having been "read the first time and passed,"[11] the bill was sent to the Senate, where it was taken up on the following day, and, without record of discussion, was ordered "to lie over until the next Session of Assembly."[12]

Its defeat may also be attributed to the financial stringency and general confusion of the times, the woeful scarcity of hard money, and the fear, on the part of the more radical republicans who were in the ascendancy, that this proposed university might be used as "an engine of political propaganda and as a bulwark of aristocratic privilege."[13]

Yet the aristocratic forces in the East, led by Davie, had succeeded in the year 1786 in securing from the General Assembly the passage of "An Act for Erecting an Academy in the Town of Warrenton in the District of Halifax." Recognizing that it was "necessary, especially in republican governments, to hold forth every possible opportunity and encouragement to liberal education," they had provided for the establishment of an academy "for the education of youth, under the name, stile and title of the Warrenton Academy." It is not

---

* This bill, an unpublished document consisting of eight large sheets of thick parchment stationery, was curiously entitled: "A Bill for establishing a University in this State to be distinguished by the title of the President and Trustees of the North Carolina University."—Legislative Papers, House of Commons, 1784. A.H.

The Father of the University

without interest that Davie placed at the head of the list of the original trustees the Reverend Henry Pattillo and himself, followed by six of the twenty who were likewise to be original trustees of the University of North Carolina: Benjamin Williams, of Moore County, later governor; John Williams, of Granville; Thomas Person, of Granville; Benjamin Hawkins, of Warren, later United States senator; John Macon, of Warren; and Willie Jones.[14]

The succeeding years, in which the forces of conservatism were gaining strength, saw an accompanying increase of popular interest in both secondary and higher education. This interest was fanned and inflamed in Western North Carolina by such leaders as Joseph Alexander, Thomas Polk, Waightstill Avery, Ephraim Brevard, Alexander Martin, Samuel Eusebius McCorkle, James Hall, and David Caldwell. The eastern and central portions were represented by such men as Hugh Williamson, a graduate of the College of Philadelphia, student of science and medicine at Edinburgh, London, and Utrecht; William Hooper, a Harvard graduate and founder of Science Hall at Hillsborough in 1785; the two Etonian Jones brothers of Halifax and Northampton; James Iredell; and, of course, the conservative triumvirate, Davie, Alfred Moore (then attorney general), and Governor Samuel Johnston.[15]

Contemporary evidence is scant as to the persuasive campaign waged by Davie in behalf of securing a charter for the University. It will be remembered that at this time Davie and Iredell were also using their powerful influence to obtain the ratification of the Federal Constitution. In fact, the Constitution was ratified by the people in convention at Fayetteville on November 21, 1789,[16] and twenty days later, December 11, the General Assembly, composed of a great many of the same men, passed the act to establish the University. Davie introduced both measures.

In the campaign for the passage of the University bill, it is known that Davie was aided by Governor Johnston through the "exterior influence of the executive," and it may be assumed that he was assisted by James Iredell, for he put Johnston and Iredell at the head of the list of trustees.[17]

That Alfred Moore lent his powerful influence is attested to by Archibald DeBow Murphey, the early promoter of a state public school system and internal improvements. In an oration delivered in

WILLIAM R. DAVIE

1827 in the old chapel, now Person Hall, at Chapel Hill, he analyzed two of his youthful inspirations:

"Two individuals, who received their education during the war, were destined to keep alive the remnant of our literature, and prepare the public mind for the establishment of this University. These two were William R. Davie and Alfred Moore. Each of them had endeared himself to his country by taking an active part in the later scene of the war; and when public order was restored and the courts of justice were opened, they appeared at the bar, where they quickly rose to eminence, and for many years shone like meteors in North-Carolina. They adorned the courts in which they practiced, gave energy to the laws and dignity to the administration of justice. Their genius was different, and so was their eloquence. Davie took Lord Bolingbroke for his model, and Moore, Dean Swift; and each applied himself with so much diligence to the study of his model, that literary men could easily recognize in the eloquence of Davie, the lofty, flowing style of Bolingbroke; and in that of Moore, the plainness and precision of Swift—they roused the ambition of parents and their sons; they excited emulation among ingenuous youth; they depicted in glowing colours the necessity of establishing a public school or university, in which the young men of the State could be educated." [18]

Instructed in his youth by his Glasgow-bred uncle, educated probably at Queen's Museum, and a graduate of Princeton, influenced by his father-in-law and his aristocratic associates in Halifax and elsewhere, it is only natural that Davie should have been the one to carry the torch which had been lit in his adopted Halifax thirteen years before. Surely, moreover, he possessed the physical attributes which made his cause more appealing. To Archibald D. Murphey, writing almost three decades later, we are again indebted for an illuminating description:

"Davie was a tall, elegant man in his person, graceful and commanding in his manners; his voice was mellow and adapted to the expression of every passion; his mind comprehensive, yet slow in its operations, when compared with his great rival [Moore]. His style was magnificent and flowing; and he had a greatness of manner in public speaking, which suited his style, and gave to his speeches an imposing effect. He was a laborious student, arranged his discourses with care, and where the subject suited his genius, poured forth a torrent of eloquence that astonished and enraptured his audience. They looked upon him with delight, listened to his long, harmonious periods, caught his emotions, and indulged that ecstacy of feeling, which fine speaking and powerful eloquence alone can produce. He is certainly to be ranked among the first orators, and his rival Moore, among the first advocates, which the American nation has produced." [19]

The Assembly to which Davie presented his bill to establish a university was strongly Federalist in complexion, and it was undoubtedly with a sanguine confidence that, on November 12, 1789, he introduced a measure so close to his heart.[20] Four days later, his optimism is reflected in a letter to Iredell in which he states: "The University Bill will certainly pass." [21]

In the preamble he set forth in Beccarian phraseology and sentiment the premise that "in all well regulated governments it is the indispensable duty of every Legislature to consult the happiness of a rising generation, and endeavour to fit them for an honourable discharge of the social duties of life, by paying the strictest attention to their education." It followed that "an University supported by permanent funds and well endowed, would have the most direct tendency" to answer this purpose. A co-optative board of the most prominent men in the state was therefore declared to be a body politic and corporate. These trustees, in order to carry the bill into effect, were to meet at Fayetteville during the session of the next General Assembly. Cognizant that it should be supported by "permanent funds" and "well endowed," Davie's bill sought to encourage gifts and subscriptions by provision to the effect that anyone subscribing, within the next five years, ten pounds, at five equal annual payments should be entitled to have one student educated at the University free from any expense of tuition. Article X, moreover, provided that "the public hall of the library and four of the colleges shall be called severally by the names of one or another of the six persons who shall within four years contribute the largest Sums towards the funds of the University, the highest subscriber or donor having choice in the order of their respective donations." [22]

Contemporary evidence is unfortunately lacking concerning the debates which ensued upon the bill. Davie's ante-bellum biographer asserted that they encountered "much resistance," because "men of liberal culture were many indeed, but not common." Thus a large portion of those "who would be called on to vote, indirectly at least, upon the project, had never enjoyed the benefits of learning, and could not easily appreciate them." Many ignorant men saw the plan as "one step towards a permanent aristocracy"; others, "who had felt the hard pressure of the public burdens, might find the expense a sufficient objection." Finally, the question "mingled itself also, to some extent, with party politics." Therefore, to disarm the cries of the opposition for "economy" and "a peculiar regard for the poor" was a task of no mean proportions.[23]

Davie met his strongest opposition in the legislature, where "the dread of forfeiting public favor gave greater force to objections which the people, out of doors, had entertained." In fact, it took a combination of "tact, logic, satire, eloquence" to carry the measure.[24]

An examination of the University Act, passed December 11, 1789, reveals that there was no appropriation of money for the newly-founded institution. Four days later a bill, probably drafted by Davie, was introduced to meet this deficiency by providing for a building fund and for the support of the University. Chief opposition to this bill was encountered in the House of Commons, where Thomas Tyson, of Moore County, entered his protests against its passage. His opposition was based on the fact that he believed the bill "to be repugnant to the Constitution of this State to grant any exclusive emoluments to any man or set of men except for services rendered." Secondly, he believed that "applying part of the public revenue to the above mentioned purpose must augment the Tax on the Citizens who can by no means be in any measure benefitted thereby." But Tyson's protest was not of sufficient weight to prevent the passage of the bill.[25]

The Act, as passed, vested in the Board of Trustees "all monies due and owing to the public of North Carolina, either for arrearages under the former or present government" up to January 1, 1783, "except monies or certificates due for the purchase of confiscated property." It also vested in the Trustees "all the property that has heretofore or shall hereafter escheat to the state." Finally, it provided that all property, of whatsoever kind, belonging to the University should be "exempt from all kind of public taxation."[26]

According to the late R. D. W. Connor, these "liberal provisions" made the University of North Carolina "potentially one of the most richly endowed institutions of learning in the American Union but

The Father of the University

many years were to pass before the Trustees were able to turn these resources into ready cash."[27]

The arrearages referred to were those due from sheriffs and other officers prior to January 1, 1783; none of them was less than six years old and some far more. The gift of the proceeds from the sales of confiscated property was withheld, because, according to Dr. Kemp Plummer Battle, the University's historian, the legislature deemed them easily collectible. Dr. Battle further describes the grant of escheats to the University as a right which was "shadowy, uncertain, well nigh *in nubibus*, but which in the course of time by skillful management brought considerable money into the treasury." Thanks to the "energy and good management of the Trustees, this grant became the "source of the endowment of the University" up to the Civil War.[28]

Three days after the passage of the Escheats Act, the first meeting of the new Board was held at Fayetteville. The chairman, Charles Johnson, of Chowan County, was also speaker of the Senate. Other trustees who attended this first meeting were Stephen Cabarrus, of Chowan (speaker of the House), Benjamin Smith, of Brunswick, Hugh Williamson, of Edenton, Thomas Person, of Granville, William Lenoir, of Wilkes, Robert Dixon, of Duplin, John Hamilton, of Guilford, Frederick Hargett, of Jones, James Holland, of Rutherford, John Stokes, of Surry, William Blount, of Tennessee, William Porter, of Rutherford, Joseph Dixon, of Lincoln, Alexander Mebane, of Orange, William R. Davie, of Halifax, and James Hogg, of Orange.[29]

To Davie the battle had just begun. Not content to rest on his brilliant achievement in securing the charter for the University, the realist Davie was aware that without the untiring efforts of himself and his fellow trustees, the successful founding of the University would be problematical. It was meet and right that Davie and James Hogg were assigned the first labor in its founding: they were charged with getting "a sufficient number of Copies printed" of the two subscriptions which were to be opened. One was to be conducted in the manner specifically directed by the act of Assembly; the other "on the principle of a mere donation."[30]

It was also Davie who announced to the trustees "the donation of twenty thousand Acres of land" by Colonel Benjamin Smith, of Brunswick County. These 20,000 acres of land warrants, representing

Colonel Smith's reward for his services in the Revolution, were located in Western North Carolina, later to become Obion County, in the extreme northwest part of Tennessee.*

Unable to attend the next meeting of the Board, which met in November, 1790, in Fayetteville, Davie wrote Governor Alexander Martin, November 1, that he was certain that the latter would "give the University every assistance in your power, as a man who knows the importance of education in a country just forming its manners and government." [31]

At the fourth meeting, which took place at Newbern, December 19, 1791, he directed his attention to the finances of the institution and was appointed, along with Judge John Williams, of Granville, Judge Samuel Ashe, of New Brunswick, Judge John Sitgreaves, of Craven, and Richard Dobbs Spaight, of Craven, "to take into consideration the communications made to the board of the Escheated property, and that they make report of the necessary measures to be adopted." [32]

This same group of men were likewise appointed to the all-important committee "to prepare an address to the Genl. Assembly Soliciting the Loan of £ [blank in MS] to enable the Trustees to errect the Building of, or other ways, advance the said University." Three days later, December 23, they decided on the sum of *"Five thousand pounds* or such sum and for such length of time as to them shall seem proper and adequate." [33]

In presenting the memorial to the Assembly, Davie's appeal was magnificent. Describing the power of his oratory, Archibald DeBow Murphey later wrote: "I was present in the House of Commons, when Davie addressed that body upon the bill granting a loan of money to the trustees for erecting the buildings of this university; and although more than thirty years have since elapsed, I have the most vivid recollections of the greatness of his manner and the powers of his eloquence

---

* University of North Carolina, Trustee Minutes, 1789-1791, p. i. Bound manuscript volume in the Carolina Room of the Louis Round Wilson Library, U. N. C. (hereafter cited as T. M.). It was not until twenty-five years later that a sale of these lands was effected, by which the University realized $14,000. Smith Hall, the old library, later the law school, and today the Playmakers' Theater, commemorates the munificence of Colonel Smith.—Collier Cobb, "Governor Benjamin Smith," *North Carolina Booklet*, XI (Jan., 1912), No. 3, p. 161.

upon that occasion. In the House of Commons he had no rival, and upon all great questions which came before that body, his eloquence was irresistable."[34]

The loan was not secured without a hard-fought struggle. Again Davie had to overcome the same prejudices which characterized the opposition to the charter. The Jeffersonian philosophy—"that government is best which governs least"—had many adherents in North Carolina. Yet the champions of the University were able to carry the loan December 29, 1791, by a vote of 57 to 53 in the Commons and 28 to 21 in the Senate.[35]

No further action was taken towards implementing the progress of the University until the next session of the Board at Hillsborough in August, 1792, when twenty-five out of forty trustees answered the roll call—a demonstration of their interest in the problem of locating the University. As a solution, Willie Jones offered a motion, which was adopted, that "the board will not determine on any given place; but the ballots shall be taken for a given point, with a latitude of erecting the buildings within fifteen miles of said point." In accordance with this, Davie secured the passage of a motion to the effect that the balloting should take place the next day, "whereupon the following places were nominated, the Seat of Government [just established at Raleigh], Pittsborough in Chatham County, Williams-Borough, Hillsborough, Charlotte, Goshen, Smithfield, and Cipritz Bridge on New Hope."[36]

The following day, August 3, pursuant to this resolution, Cipritz Bridge on New Hope Creek in Chatham County was chosen as the geographical center, within fifteen miles of which the University was to be located. This bridge, later Prince's Bridge, the remains of which are still discernible, was on the old great road from Newbern, by Raleigh, to Pittsborough. This choice represented the desire to place the University as near the center of the state as practical—as was also true of the location of the capital.[37]

The more tedious business of preparing an ordinance fixing the seat of the University was left up to Davie, Willie Jones, and Alfred Moore. On August 4 it was unanimously passed. One person from each district was to be elected by ballot from the trustees and those so elected were "to view the Country within the limits aforesaid, and determine on the spot or place most proper ... and to contract with, and purchase from the owner or owners the place they shall so fix or determine on, together with not less than six hundred and forty acres of land thereto adjoining." They were also empowered to purchase "one thousand four hundred acres so conveniently situated in the neighborhood thereof as to answer the purposes of a farm and a sufficient supply of firewood and timber for the University." [38]

Six of the eight commissioners met in Pittsborough on November 1, 1792, prepared to visit all places deemed eligible. "An excellent committee," according to Dr. Kemp P. Battle, the University's historian, it was composed of Frederick Hargett, of Jones, Alexander Mebane, of Orange, James Hogg, of Cumberland, William H. Hill, of New Hanover, David Stone, of Bertie, and Willie Jones, of Halifax.[39]

These commissioners viewed several places within the fifteen mile radius of Cipritz Bridge and received several offers of donations if the University were fixed at those places—several places near Pittsborough, the confluence of the Haw and Deep rivers, Tignal Jones's place, and Nathaniel Jones's place (the latter being at the cross-roads in Wake County). On November 5 they "proceeded to view New Hope Chapel Hill, in Orange County." Here they received offers of donations of land amounting to 1,390 acres, on and adjoining Chapel Hill, and subscriptions for donations in money amounting to £798 or thereabouts—all conditioned upon the seating of the University there.[40]

There is an apocryphal story which will not down to the effect that it was Davie who led this group of trustees in their quest for a suitable location for the University. The legend conjured up a hot summer day on which these men relaxed in a cool, grassy spot beneath a giant poplar. Having regaled themselves with mint juleps, or other "exhilarating beverages," and gorged themselves with a picnic lunch, they were easily persuaded by Davie to settle on this spot as the object of their search. To commemorate this story, Mrs. Cornelia Phillips Spencer allegedly gave it the name, the "Davie Poplar." Its antiquity is attested by Governor William D. Moseley's reference to it as "the Old Poplar" in a reminiscence of his days at the University in 1818.*

---

* See Archibald Henderson, *The Campus of the First State University* (Chapel Hill: The University of North Carolina Press, 1949), p. 10; Battle, *University*, I, 273.

The Father of the University

The fact that the great roads or highways from Petersburg to Pittsborough and the country beyond, and from Newbern towards Greensborough and Salisbury, crossed at this point was also a deciding factor. At the northeast corner of the crossing there was a chapel of the Church of England, hence the name "New Hope Chapel Hill or the Hill of New Hope Chapel." [41]

While these purely mercenary considerations had great weight with the selecting fathers, another factor surely had its effect—the idealness and enchantment of the "Hill" itself. Davie, in a graphic description, written the following September, in announcing the sale of lots, seems to have felt this charm:

"The seat of the University is on the summit of a very high ridge —there is a gentle declivity of three hundred yards to the village; which is situated on a handsome plain, considerably lower than the site of the public buildings, but so greatly elevated above the neighbouring country, as to furnish an extensive and beautiful landscape, composed of the heights in the vicinity of Eno, Little and Flat Rivers.

"The ridge appears to commence about half a mile directly east of the buildings, where it arises abruptly several hundred feet: the peak is called Point-Prospect; the flat country spreads off below like the ocean, giving an immense hemisphere, in which the eye seems to be lost in the extent of space.*

"There is nothing more remarkable in this extraordinary place, than the abundance of springs of purest and finest water; which burst from the side of the ridge, and which have been the subject of admiration both to hunters and travellers ever since the discovery and settlement of that part of the country—several of the lots on the north side of the town have the advantage of including a spring.

"The University is situated about 25 miles from the city of Raleigh, and 12 from the town of Hillsborough; and is said to be the best direction for the road—the great road from Chatham, and the country in the neighbourhood of that county, to Petersburg, passes at present directly through this place, being the nearest and best direction.

---

* The peak here referred to is the site of Gimghoul Castle and the summit of the plateau upon which the University is located. The plateau was presumably caused by a volcanic eruption and its peak overlooks a great depression to the East, described as the bed of a "Triassic sea"—a primeval arm of the ocean some sixteen miles wide. See Henderson, *The Campus*, pp. 24-25.

WILLIAM R. DAVIE

"This town being the only seat of learning immediately under the patronage of the public, possessing the advantages of a central situation, on some of the most public roads in the state, in a plentiful country, and excelled by few places in the world either for beauty of situation or salubrity of air, promises with all moral certainty, to be a place of growing and permanent importance."[42]

Prophetic and visionary, practical and efficient though Davie was, little could he have dreamed of the magnitude of the institution that was being created.

Davie was a member of the committee which was to carry into effect the report of the commissioners for "fixing on the spot for the public buildings" and, as a result of their report, on the following day, December 5, it was ordained that "the said Newhope Chappell Hill" was declared to be the seat of the University.[43]

Davie was also responsible for the ordinance "for appointing Commissioners to erect the buildings of the University and lay off a Town adjacent thereto." The commissioners chosen were Davie, Alfred Moore, Frederick Hargett, Thomas Blount, Alexander Mebane, John Williams, and John Haywood.[44]

These seven commissioners were charged with the responsibility of allotting and laying off "in the most pleasant and commodious part of the Tract... a proper quantity of Land to erect the buildings of the said University upon... and to lay off and survey adjacent thereto a town containing twenty four lots of two acres each and six lots of four acres each," which lots were to be sold at public vendue on twelve months' credit. Furthermore, they were empowered "to cause to be built... a House or Houses sufficient if practicable from the sum appropriated for that purpose to accomodate fifty students," the "indispensibly necessary" expense to be met by drawing on the Treasurer of the University for any sum or sums not exceeding in the whole the sum of five thousand pounds.[45]

Four of the commissioners, Davie, Moore, Mebane, and Hargett, met after the Board adjourned "in Order to find out the most practicable and expeditious way to procure Lime or shell" for the construction of the buildings and concluded that the best way was to get it "Carried up to Fayette or Averysboroh. this Season in Boats." The services of James Hogg, a trustee and merchant of Wilmington, were implored to attend to this.[46]

The Father of the University

So eager were they to do "everything Necessary to forward the work by the spring of the year" that the commissioners were to meet at Hillsborough three days before the next Superior Court rose to make plans for fixing the spot and laying off the village.[47]

In the meanwhile, Davie and other champions of the University turned their attention to the laborious and seemingly thankless job of gaining subscriptions for the University. Not content with a personal subscription of $100, which was exceeded by only two others who contributed $200 each,[48] Davie and Willie Jones on January 9, 1793, issued a joint appeal in the Halifax *North-Carolina Journal*. Adhering to diverse political tenets, these two men, fellow-townsmen and kindred-in-law, were of the calibre to rise above political grudges off the hustings and to stand united in their fight for the University. In this appeal, they "flattered" themselves "that the Gentlemen of Halifax county, will not, on this occasion, so interesting to the rising generation, suffer any county in the State to exceed it in making efforts to promote an institution of such vast and general utility." They held up the example of Orange, which had subscribed "near *one thousand pounds* towards the endowment of this important institution." [49]

This appeal, however, did not fall on ears completely receptive. Indeed, one critic, ironically signing himself "Ignoramus," attacked these two Halifax gentlemen:

"—— I was surprised to see such respectable names as Willie Jones and Wm. R. Davie—expressing approbation of the sentiments contained in that piece...[50] On the joint or several opinions of those gentlemen, I have almost implicitly relied, but in the present instance cannot forego my own on a principle of a confidence in their judgement; yet shall remain open to conviction, and be happy if either of them will devote a leisure hour to this subject, on which there is so great a diversity of opinions—I shall be uneasy till relieved from the disagreeable situation of differing in opinion with two men who I look upon as the greatest characters in this State." [51]

A reiteration of this appeal, February 6 and February 20, did not bring forth a reply from "the greatest characters in this State." However, a reply was forthcoming from a temporary protégé of Davie, William Hill Brown, the "first American novelist." The Boston-bred author of *The Power of Sympathy*, who had been visiting relatives in Murfreesborough since the preceding summer, took up a course of legal instruction in Davie's office in the early months of 1793. Here, his association with Davie undoubtedly induced him to defend such attacks on the University.[52]

Writing under the pen name, "Columbus," he submitted the following letter to the Halifax *North-Carolina Journal*, July 10, 1793:

> Mr. Hodge
>
> That the proposed University of North-Carolina would operate [to] the happiness of the State, has been doubted, and the idea of its utility to the people at large has been combatted in your paper. It may appear extraordinary that the progress of learning should be opposed in a young Republican Country, since the *experience* of mankind, from the infancy of government to the present day, exhibits a clean illustration of this truth, THAT KNOWLEDGE MUST BE THE GUARDIAN OF LIBERTY. Whatever strengthens this sentiment, is important at this juncture, when subscriptions are circulating in various counties for the establishment of a fund for the promised seminary of learning. I, therefore, send you the enclosed manuscript containing observations on Education, &c. written a year or two since—and though originally thrown together for a different purpose—for shewing the *means of Preventing Crimes*—they are nevertheless applicable to the present period and subject....[53]

But in spite of opposition, by July 10 Davie and Willie Jones were able to announce that it gave them "pleasure to see that the county of Halifax, now, as heretofore, stands among the foremost in liberal, disinterested and patriotic exertions for the happiness and welfare of the state." They reported a list of the donations by which Orange County had contributed £909 s4 and Halifax £804—a commendable record considering the distance. They announced that further donations would be thankfully received.[54]

The building commissioners had first met in Hillsborough in April and had "contracted with Mr. George Daniel of the County of Orange for the making and delivering three hundred and fifty thousand Bricks at the rate of forty shillings pr. thousand." On July 19 they contracted with an "undertaker," James Patterson of Chatham County, to "undertake" the construction of "a house of ninty six feet seven inches long and forty feet one Inch & a half wide" for two thousand five hundred pounds. This represents the beginning of Old

The Father of the University

East Building—the first building to be erected on the campus of any state university in the United States.[55]

By July 22, 1793, Commissioners Davie, Moore, Mebane, and Thomas Blount were able to announce that the lots laid off would be sold on the premises on Saturday, the twelfth of October, and that "considerable time will be allowed for payment, the purchasers giving bond with approved security."[56] On August 10 they met again and "proceeded to lay off... a proper quantity of Ground to erect the buildings on; the perticular sites of which were fixed and accurately marked off, together with the necessary quantity of Land for offices, Avenues, and ornamental grounds." They were pleased to report that "much might justly be said of the beauty and natural advantages of the grounds laid off for the public buildings and for the Village."[57]

Despite his strenuous activities in laying and perfecting plans for the actual physical construction of the University, Davie was not too busy to invite his old friend and law teacher, Judge Spruce Macay, of Salisbury, to attend the laying of the cornerstone, or to give due credit to the inspiration of Dr. Samuel Eusebius McCorkle. As showing Davie's magnanimity to his old friends, this letter is of peculiar interest:

...As one who sat at the feet of Gamaliel in the intermissions between tours in the field, I write to press for your attendance at Chapel Hill in Orange on October 10 [though this is legibly "10," according to Dr. Archibald Henderson, who found the original, it of course should have been "12."]—laying of a corner stone, great doings of the Masonic brethren, with your correspondent wielding a silver trowel and setting a stone in mortar. All are expecting our worthy and learned friend Dr. McCorkle, *pater benignus,* who got up the first University bill. It is right and proper that he should now stand atop the Mount of Fulfillment and solemnly invoke blessings upon this embryo college. Rumor hath it that you shaped to final form that ill-starred bill which was dismissed to a subsequent session by harried representatives confronted with a multitude of claims and an empty till—Our ambitious friend, Billy Sharpe, who was charged with the handling of that delicate matter, should be present; but I hear that his ailments will probably forbid. He was ever eager to serve, but being no Verulam, seems better suited to a treaty with the savages in the Western Woods than to set afoot a seminary of learning....

W. R. Davie [58]

WILLIAM R. DAVIE

Still zealous for the weal of the University, Davie assured the public on September 25 that "the cornerstone of the building of the University, undertaken by Mr. Patterson, will be laid on the 12th of October next; when the Commissioners and a number of gentlemen will attend to assist at the ceremony." Announcing again the sale of the lots on the same day, he described the town as consisting "of one principal street, laid off in lots of two acres each, parallel with the north front of the buildings" and that there were also "six lots of four acres each, located on the most elegant situations contiguous to the University." [59]

At long last the auspicious day—October the twelfth—arrived. The only extant contemporary account of the proceedings, appearing first in the *North-Carolina Journal*, was presumably written by Davie: [60]

"On the 12th inst. the Commissioners appointed by the Board of Trustees of the University of this State, met at Chappel-Hill for the purpose of laying the cornerstone of the present building, and disposing of the lots in the village. A large number of the brethren of the Masonic order from Hillsborough, Chatham, Granville and Warren, attended to assist at the ceremony of placing the corner-stone; and the procession for this purpose moved from Mr. Patterson's at 12 O'clock, in the following order: the Masonic Brethren in their usual order of procession, the Commissioners, the Trustees not Commissioners, the Hon. Judge Macay and other public officers, then followed the gentlemen of the vicinity. On approaching the south end of the building, the Masons opened to the right and left, and the Commissioners, etc., passed through and took their place. The Masonic procession then moved on round the foundation of the building, and halted with their usual ceremonies opposite to the southeast corner, where WILLIAM RICHARDSON DAVIE, Grand Master of the fraternity, etc., in this state, assisted by two Masters of lodges and four other officers, laid the corner-stone enclosing a plate to commemorate the transaction.*

* On this plate were the following inscriptions, the face engraved in English, the reverse in Latin:

The Father of the University

The
Right Worshipful
William Richardson Davie, GRAND MASTER
of
The most Ancient and Honorable Fraternity
Of FREE MASONS, in the State of North Carolina
One of the TRUSTEES of the UNIVERSITY
of the Said STATE,
And a Commissioner of the same
Assisted By
The other Commissioners, and the Brethren
Of the EAGLE AND INDEPENDENCE LODGES
on the 12th day of October
IN THE YEAR OF MASONRY 5793,
and in the 18th Year of American INDEPENDENCE
LAID THE CORNER STONE
of this EDIFICE.
R. Huntington, Sculp.

HUNC LAPIDEM.
Honorariis Curatoribus hujus Academiae
nec non
FRATRIBUS MASONICIS HILLSBORIA aliundeque
RITE presentibus
GULIELMUS R DAVIE, equestris praefectus
Carolinaque Septentrionalis ARCHE-ARCHITICUS.
Anno Lucis 5793°. Salutis 1793°
AMERICANAE LIBERTATIS 18.
& 12mo die Octobris
MULTO CUM ORDINE
LOCAVIT
SIT AERE PRENNIUS

See "The Presentation of the Plate," *University of North Carolina Alumni Review*, V (Nov., 1916), 38-41, for the story of the recovery of this plate, which was taken from the cornerstone of Old East presumably between the years 1865 and 1875. Its whereabouts remained unknown until discovered in late September, 1916, by Thomas B. Foust, proprietor of the Clarksville Foundry and Machine Works, Clarksville, Tennessee. The plate is bronze, one-eighth of an inch in thickness, five and a quarter inches wide and seven and a half inches long. Rescued from a junk pile of scrap brass and destined for melting into various brass castings, it was discovered by a workman attracted by its strange lettering. An alumnus (1903) of the University of North Carolina, Mr. Foust observed the name "William Richardson Davie" inscribed on the plate and had it cleaned. Through the offices of Mr. A. B. Andrews, Jr., of Raleigh, who read an article in regard to it in the Charlotte *Observer*, it was returned to its rightful place.

William R. Davie

"The Rev. Dr. McCorkle then addressed the Trustees and spectators in an excellent discourse suited to the occasion....

"This discourse was followed by a short but animated prayer, closed with the united AMEN of an immense concourse of people.

"The Commissioners then proceeded to sell the lots in the village, and we have the pleasure to assure the public, that although there were but twenty-nine lots, they sold for upwards of one thousand five hundred pounds, which shews the high idea the public entertain of this agreeable and healthful situation." [61]

This was indeed a prosaic account of a proceeding so important in the annals of the history of North Carolina. Surely a more glowing picture of this day could have been painted. Anyone who has known Chapel Hill in the fall could well imagine the beauties of the natural setting, which formed a fitting background for the procession of earnest men who marched with stately tread along the narrow road. At the head of this procession was the commanding, almost marmoreal, figure of Davie, resplendent in his Grand Master's regalia. One can imagine his mixed emotions—honest and deserved pride in the success of his achievements thus far so nobly advanced, weighed against deep humility in the face of the herculean task yet ahead.

Next to Davie was his great rival, Alfred Moore, described by Murphey as "a small man, neat in his dress, and graceful in his manners." Murphey continued: "His voice was clear and sonorous, his perceptions quick, and judgment almost intuitive; his style was chaste and manner of speaking animated. Having adopted Swift for his model, his language was always plain. The clearness and energy of his mind enabled him almost without an effort to disentangle the most intricate subject, and expose it in all its parts to the simplest understanding. He spoke with ease and with force, enlivened his discourse with flashes of wit, and where the subject required it, with all the bitterness of sarcasm. His speeches were short and impressive: when he sat down, every one thought he had said every thing he ought to have said." [62] These qualities were later recognized in his appointment to the Supreme Court of the United States.

Next came William H. Hill, a descendant of Governor John Yeamans, an able lawyer of Wilmington, and later state senator and member of Congress. [63]

Conspicuous in the group also was John Haywood—for forty years

The Father of the University

treasurer of the state (1787 to 1827). Described by Battle as "the most popular man in North Carolina" for many years, renowned for his hospitality, kindness, and charity dispensed from his Raleigh seat, he served the University faithfully and well for almost thirty years.[64]

By his side was General Alexander Mebane. Of Ulster Scot descent, he had been a member of the provincial congress at Halifax, 1776, an able officer in the Revolution, and a member of the state legislature. He was to be elected to Congress the following year.

Judge John Williams was next—founder of Williamsborough, in Granville County, judge of the first court under the Constitution of 1776, and a member of the Confederation Congress. Thomas Blount and Frederick Hargett completed the line of the commissioners. The former, a member of the state legislature from Edgecombe, was soon to enter Congress. The latter, a senator from Jones County, was "plain, solid, but eminently trustworthy."

Next in the procession came the other trustees, not commissioners, followed by the state officers, not trustees (among whom was Spruce Macay), officers of the county and gentlemen of the vicinity. Truly this was an imposing array of North Carolina's great.[65]

Dr. McCorkle's address was worthy of the occasion. Following the philosophical creed of Beccaria and Jeremy Bentham, he laid down the proposition that "Happiness is the center to which all the duties of man and people tend" and "To diffuse the greatest possible degree of happiness in a given territory is the aim of good government and religion." This happiness of a nation, he reasoned, "depends on national wealth and national glory"; they in turn depend on "liberty and good laws," which in like manner call for "general knowledge in the people and extensive knowledge in the ministers of the state, and these in fine demand public places of education."[66] Prophetic and optimistic was his peroration:

"The seat of the University was next sought for, and the public eye selected Chapel Hill—a lovely situation in the centre of the State, at a convenient distance from the capital, in a healthy and fertile neighborhood. May this hill be for religion as the ancient hill of Zion; and for literature and the muses, may it surpass the ancient Parnassus! We this day enjoy the pleasure of seeing the cornerstone of the University, its material and the architect for the building, and we hope ere long to see its stately walls and spire ascending to their

Summit. Ere long we hope to see it adorned with an elegant village, accommodated with all the necessaries and conveniences of civilized society." [67]

After the "short but animated prayer," the sale of lots ensued. Undoubtedly the impassioned plea of McCorkle had its effect upon the auction. Later, in a report to the Board of Trustees, it was announced that all the lots were sold with the exception of one, which was reserved for the president's house. The commissioners observed "with pleasure" that "although many were present from different parts of the State... all appeared satisfyed and content." [68]

The trustees met next in December, 1793, in Fayetteville, where they turned to such serious matters as investing their surplus money in the "6 per C funds of the United States," the appointment of attorneys in the different districts, and "the propriety of employing Teachers, what number, what subjects or Sciences they shall respectively teach, and their opinion as to a proper salary and the price of tuition." [69]

A committee, composed of Davie, Haywood, John Louis Taylor, of Fayetteville (later the first Chief Justice of the Supreme Court of North Carolina), James Hogg, Adlai Osborn, and William Polk, brought in a comprehensive and detailed report which provided for a plethora of details: "The exercises of the University" were to begin "on the 15th Day of January which shall be in the Year 1795"; the time for the visitation of the trustees for the public examinations, which would "occasion a time of recreation or Holliday of one week only"; the time for the "Yearly Vacation" from December 15, 1795 to January 15, 1796; and a steward's house, containing a large dining room, kitchen and such other rooms as were deemed necessary. Prices for tuition were to depend on the subject matter: "reading, writing, arithmetic and bookkeeping for all or any of them eight Dollars pr annum"; the "Latin, Greek, and French languages, the English grammar, Geography, History and the Belles Letters, for any or all of them twelve and a half Dollars"; "Geometry with its practical branches Astronomy natural, natural and moral Philosophy, Chemistry, and the principles of agriculture for all or any of them fifteen Dollars." For the first year the committee recommended "that one person be employed in whose charge, and under whose direction

& government the University shall particularly be." He was to have the temporary use of the president's house, be "styled the Professor of Humanity, receive a salary of three hundred Dollars" plus "two thirds of all tuition monies." One other person was to be employed "in character of Assistant or Tutor...whose salary shall be two hundred Dollars... [and who] shall have a room in the University, shall live at Commons free of expence, and be entitled to the remaining one third of the tuition money." [70]

This report having been concurred in, they proceeded on January 10, 1794, to cast ballots for the Professor of Humanity, or "Presiding Professor." Though Davie was not present at this meeting, it may be assumed that his preferences and prejudicies were well known to the other members. Of the seven nominees brought forward, it was taken for granted by many that Dr. McCorkle would be chosen. Yet Davie, who respected his erudition, distrusted his executive ability—perhaps with just cause. There was, for example, a story about his farming. The worthy divine was in the habit of carrying into the field theological books to read in intervals of manual labor. A man on business once found him stretched out, deep in his tomes, while the negro plowman was asleep under a tree and the mule was cropping the corn-tops.[71]

The records are silent as to the discussions concerning the nominees, stating merely that the Reverend David Ker was elected. An Ulster Scot, educated at Trinity College, Dublin, and later a Presbyterian minister in Fayetteville, he was described as "very capable," but he soon "imbibed infidel notions" and lost his place.[72]

Perhaps this is why Davie, writing in November, 1794, to his friend, John Haywood, had said that *"entre nous,* the institution should be committed to other Hands than our present professor of Humanity." [73]

Meanwhile Davie and Judge Williams were very much concerned with the plans for "the principal building" (later South Building) which Davie feared would cost a larger sum than they could spare. Their plans called for a building "116 feet by 50 or 54—to contain 24 lodging rooms—a Hall 30 by 36—a library room 10 by 36—2 rooms for Philosophical apparatus 16 by 12—2 recitation rooms—2 rooms 16 by 10 for lodging rooms or any other purpose." The structure was to

WILLIAM R. DAVIE

be three stories high and was not to be "much larger than the other" —Old East.[74]

At the next meeting of the Board, at the new seat of government in Raleigh, Davie, now a major general, presented a letter from McCorkle in which he had drawn up the by-laws of the University. A rigorous and Spartan set of laws it was, but in complete harmony with the diet prescribed by the trustees.[75]

To Davie was also entrusted the responsibility of contracting with some person "to engrave a plate to be used in striking off [blank] to be placed within the covers of such books, as may hereafter be presented to the University."[76]

These books comprised the last public library to be organized in North Carolina in the eighteenth century. Although little is known of the facilities and number of books, it is known that the sum of two hundred dollars was placed in the hands of Hugh Williamson to purchase "such Grammar, Classical and other books as in his opinion will be first needed." These, however, were to be sold to the students at cost. Also, various University supporters, mostly trustees, donated a number of books. Stephen B. Weeks credits Davie with presenting fourteen volumes in 1795, to which he subsequently added twenty-five. The University Letters, however, credit Davie with only six books in 1795, viz:

Account of the Pelew Islands		8 octs.
Sheridans Art of Reading		"
"	Lectures on Elocution	"
"	British Education	"
"	Plan of Education	"
Debates of the Convention of N. Carolina.		

In 1799 this same source reported him as having donated the sixteen volumes of Hume's *History of England* and twelve volumes of Gibbon's *Decline and Fall of the Roman Empire*.[77] A composite list, however, appeared in the Raleigh *Register*, November 23, 1802, and in the *N. C. Minerva*, December 7, 1802:

Donations by Gen. W. R. Davie

Hume's History of England, 8 vols.
Smollett's Continuation of do, 5 v.
Gibbon's Decline of the Roman Empire, 12 v.

The Father of the University

Rollin's Ancient History, 10 v.
Travels of Anacharsis, with Maps, 8 v.
Robertson's Charles V. 3 v.
Sheridan's Lectures, 3 v.
Ramsay's Revolution of South Carolina, 2 v.
Instructions for Cavalry.
Reverie, 2 v.
Account of the Pelew Islands.

There also appeared in these same two papers, same dates, the following rather curious donations by Davie. Most of them were presumably brought back from his mission to France.

THE MUSEUM
Donations by Gen. W. R. Davie

Two Medals of Bonaparte, in Bronze, representing him at the Battle of Marengo.
The tooth of a Mammoth.
A number of Specimens of Paper Money, emitted by the Continental Congress and by the State of North Carolina.
One Specimen of Spanish copper coin, three of English copper coin, and three of French copper coin.
A Piece of Iron Chain, such as is said to be best for applying to the circumference of Wheels in Machinery, brought from France.
Several Pieces of stained Glass, such as was formerly made for churches and cathedrals in Europe, the art of making it being now lost. Procured at Leon in Old Spain.
Indian Ornaments of Copper, dug up with the bones of an Indian on Mush Island, near Halifax.
Two Indian Pipes of curious workmanship.

It was also at this meeting that Walter Alves [78] was nominated by Davie and unanimously elected as treasurer of the Board of Trustees.

Davie must have felt a sense of infinite relief when he reported to his friend Richard Bennehan, of Hillsborough, that the General Assembly had vested all confiscated property in the trustees; this meant, according to him, that the institution was "permanently established." [79]

At the next meeting of the trustees, July 13 and 14, called ostensibly

[245]

for the first examination of the students, Davie complained strongly of the charges of James Patterson, the "undertaker" of the first University building (later called Old East) and the president's house. Patterson was "extremely clamorous to be paid for this extra work," which charges were "so excessively exhorbitant, and his work so infamously done," that the matter was referred to the commissioners. Davie further complained that he had "charged six or seven prices for the painting" and "that the rest of the work was on the same ratio." To his astonishment, Samuel Hopkins, the superintendent of the construction of the chapel, later called Person Hall, submitted a bill "almost as bad." Nevertheless Davie was "very desirous that we should close our accounts before the meeting of the next board, at least so far as regards the principal building, the Presidents House, and the Stewards."[80]

The undertaker, Patterson, presented a very different side of the picture. Aware of the "Laudable Exersions of the Gentlemen Commissioners to Promote the University for the Benefit of their Constituants," he felt that they must by this time be aware that he had been "a Very Considerable Sufferer by the Contract having Not only Sunk Several hundreds of Pounds. but also Nearly two years Hard Service without benefiting one farthing by it." Pleading that his case be weighed "in the Scale of Equity" he made "No Dout" he would be allowed the full amount of his account which he claimed to have fully satisfied.[81]

Davie was further worried by the "serious" and "well-grounded complaints" against the conduct of the steward, John Taylor, called "Buck T.," who was a Revolutionary veteran and a plain farmer. So perturbed was Davie that he wrote "fully" on the subject to Ker and Harris, who had promised the students that they would mention it before this meeting of the board, but had failed to do it.[82]

Granted that the culinary delights prepared by "Buck T." were not succulent enough to set before a king, Davie's reaction was no doubt colored largely by the fastidious tastes of his two elder sons, Allen Jones and Hyder Ali, both students at the University at the time.[83] Relief, however, was found in the room situation for the students, who, Davie predicted, would "soon suffer very much for want of rooms." An expedient was adopted to give "temporary relief from this mischief" by "building a House for a grammar school with three or four lodging rooms." *

Davie was able to report that the students, "everything considered, acquitted themselves well," in their examinations but the "next examination will be a better test of the capacity and the attention of the professors." [84]

At the fall meeting of the Board, Davie, on December 1, 1795, presented his "plan of education." [85] For over a year at least, he had been working on it and had hoped to present it at the meeting the previous January.[86] The resulting plan was characterized by liberalism and progressivism. The earlier curriculum, planned by Dr. McCorkle, and presented by Davie to the Board back on January 10, 1795, had followed classical traditions, with a grudging concession to progressivism by admitting weekly lectures on "the Principles of Agriculture, Botany, Zoology, Mineralogy, Architecture and Commerce." [87]

Undoubtedly realizing the deficiency of this curriculum and the great need for an adequate preparatory department, Davie presented a new plan, the keynote of which was "utility" rather than culture. He most probably discussed this projected idea with a recent Princeton graduate, Charles W. Harris, the University's first tutor in mathematics, who wrote in 1795, after deploring his alma mater's deficiency in the sciences:

The constitution of this college is on a more liberal plan than any in America, & *by the amendments which I think it will receive at the next meeting of the trustees*, its usefulness will probably be much promoted. The notion that true learning consists rather in exercising the reasoning faculties, & laying up a store of useful knowledge, than in overloading the memory with words of a dead language, is becoming daily more prevalent. It appears hard to deny a young Gentleman the honour of a College, after he has with much labour & painful attention acquired a competent knowledge of the Sciences; or composing & speaking with propriety in his own language, & has conned the first principles of what-

---

* Davie to John Haywood, July 22, 1795. Univ. Letters, 1796-1835. This grammar school was located in what were then woods, to the north of the University, somewhere between the present Presbyterian Church and the southeast corner of the intersection of Rosemary and Henderson Streets. According to Battle, the school was well patronized by some of the most important men of the state.—Hamilton, "W. R. D.," p. 6n.; Henderson, *The Campus*, p. 42.

ever might render him useful or creditable in the world, merely because he could not read a language 2000 years old. Tho' the laws at present require that the Latin & Greek be understood by a graduate, they will in all probability be mitigated in this respect.... That there is much wrong in the old manner of educating is plain & whatever alteration will be made in our University will be made by those who can be actuated by no other principle than general utility.[88]

The new Davie plan, presented to the trustees, December 1, 1795, and referred to a committee consisting of John Williams, James Hogg, John Haywood, Adlai Osborn, and Davie, was adopted by the trustees seven days later.[89]

Far more than mere "amendments" or "alterations," the new curriculum set forth a complete and detailed plan of studies which included curricula and regulations for both a preparatory department and the University proper. Too much of a pragmatist to throw out cultural studies, Davie solved the problem by placing the "bourgeois" sciences on an equal plane with the "aristocratic" classics.[90]

The new plan was bottomed on the premise of education for leadership and, according to the preamble, was based on the proposition: "That in every free government the law emanates from the people... that the people should receive an education to enable them to direct the laws, and the political part of this education should be consonant to the constitutions under which they live." Its more specific aims, predicated on this principle, were "designed to form useful and respectable members of society—citizens capable of comprehending, improving, and defending the principles of government, citizens, who from the highest possible impulse, a just sense of their own and the general happiness, would be induced to practice the duties of social morality." Feeling that it was "degrading to be tributaries to other States or countries for our literary and public characters," the author pointed to an awakened "general and strong desire to promote education and improve our national character... from which the most happy effects may be expected." [91]

Described by Battle as "far ahead of the times," it "anticipates in some respects the work of Jefferson with the University of Virginia." * In regard to the principles underlying this plan of education, Davie wrote at length to Caldwell:

* See Appendix C for a reprint of the entire plan.

The Father of the University

"The subject of conferring degrees has been attended with some difficulty, ... and this difficulty has been occasioned principally by the variation of our plan of education from that of other colleges or Universities. A Bachelors degree generally imports a knowledge of the learned languages as well as the sciences. To confer such a degree upon a person who understood neither Latin nor Greek does not appear to be proper. The ruling or leading principle in our plan of education is, that the student may apply himself to those branches of learning and science alone which are absolutely necessary to fit him for his destined profession or occupation in life, that as you observe 'one study does not imply the necessity of any other, unless of one which is necessary to make it intelligible:' but I am well convinced of the utility and policy of conferring degrees, and granting special certificates as soon as a general plan can be adopted...."

Maintaining that his "own mind has not been perfectly made up on this subject," he requested Caldwell to advise him as to his opinion on the following plan:

"That every student who should stand an approved examination upon the English language, and such of the Latin *or* Greek classics as are directed to be studied, and the sciences shall receive a Bachelors degree in the usual form conferred by a diploma in the Latin language, making a knowledge of one of the dead languages necessary.

"That the student who should pass an approved Examination upon the English language, and the sciences as taught at the University should receive a diploma in English certifying his knowledge and progress of the arts and sciences.

"That these diplomas should be signed by the President and some members of the Trustees, *as well as the certificate of Masters degree* [italics mine], and distinguished as Diplomas; that in all other cases certificates should be granted by the Principal of the University, especially stating the progress of the student on application made." [92]

There is a decided hint, in the paragraph above, that there was also a plan for graduate study, and a guess might be hazarded that Davie was also the architect of this plan, though exhaustive research has been to no avail on this point.

Caldwell's reply to this advanced and liberal order must have been in the negative. In fact, soon after Caldwell was elected the first president in 1804 and after Davie left the state in 1805, Caldwell's

[249]

predilection for his alma mater, Princeton, led him to pattern the new University more closely after that institution. Consequently only one degree was granted, that of Bachelor of Arts, for the achievement of which both Latin and Greek were prerequisites.[93]

Yet Davie's foresightedness and struggle were not entirely fruitless. In 1875, after the reorganization of the University, a modification of his plan was reintroduced. Although both classical languages were required for a Bachelor of Arts degree, only one was required for "the new degree of equal dignity," Bachelor of Philosophy, and neither language was required for the degree of Bachelor of Science.[94] The present system of electives, of substitutions for the classics, of elevating chemistry, agriculture, and mechanical arts to separate schools, are further manifestation of the modernity of Davie's plan.

This plan, after having been referred to a committee, was approved by the Board of Trustees, December 7, 1795.[95] Davie considered it "a matter of some importance," that the plan "should be published as soon as possible together with the present establishment of the University." The publication of these two "would have a considerable influence upon the number of students, and tend to do away some prejudices which have gone abroad respecting the Government and character of the late Faculty." In spite of the difficulty "of procuring a person capable of copying even for money," Davie entreated Haywood to have all the ordinances and resolutions of the late Board copied "let them cost what they may." Particularly eager was he that David Ker, the "presiding professor," be furnished with copies, in order that he might not have "an excuse for some degree of confusion and derangement." How lamentable never to have "a President who attends a moment to his duty except when draged to it by some of the members."[96]

Davie himself must have realized that his plan for five professors and a president was more of a desideratum or blueprint for the future than one which could be put into full operation at the outset. Lack of funds and the difficulty of procuring a man with the prerequisites desired for a president were the delaying factors. It was upon Davie's initiative, in fact, that the Board proceeded to ballot for the faculty. Unanimously elected were Samuel E. McCorkle as professor of moral and political philosophy and history; Charles W. Harris as professor

The Father of the University

of mathematics; and the Reverend David Ker as professor of languages.[97] To Davie, Willie Jones, the president of the Board (Governor Samuel Ashe), James Hogg, and David Stone was also entrusted the responsibility "to correspond and make enquiry for some proper person to fill the place of President of the University." At the same meeting, Davie, Willie Jones, and Thomas Blount were appointed a library committee for the year 1796.[98] The same members were appointed for the year 1797; for 1799 the committee consisted of Davie, Willie Jones, and David Stone.[99]

Of the three professors chosen, it was intended that Dr. McCorkle should replace Dr. Ker as presiding professor, because Ker was developing into a "furious Republican" and an "outspoken infidel."[100] Yet this decision produced repercussions: First, Ker submitted his resignation, which was accepted, despite his defying an ordinance of the trustees requiring six months' notice. Secondly, McCorkle, foreseeing he would lose the president's house when a president was chosen, signified to the Board that he would accept the professorial appointment and take charge of the University provided it was agreed that when he was deprived of the use of the house, the Board would give him an additional allowance, equal in value to the use of the house. Yet, strangely enough, he would accept the appointment without this additional allowance. The Board were of the opinion that McCorkle's terms were inadmissible and therefore appointed the professor of mathematics, Charles W. Harris, July 13, 1796, to take charge of the University until the next Board meeting.[101]

Though Willie Jones was the chairman of the committee responsible for the above actions, Davie got most credit for the ousting of McCorkle. In fact, his stand on the issue caused a four-year cleavage between him and his friend and co-Federalist, General John Steele, Comptroller General of the Treasury. The latter, the uncle of McCorkle's wife, wrote Davie so severe a letter that it was not until the late summer of 1799 that Davie, preparing to leave on his French mission, offered to renew their old friendship. General Steele's reply, beginning with a dry "Sir," was restrained and formal. Referring to his earlier letter, Steele said it "was the dictate of what I considered at the time, and still think, a just indignation for the ill treatment which Doctor McCorkle received." He continued by saying that he himself had no sons to educate and that his nephew, McCorkle's son, was "relieved of the humiliation of acquiring his education at an institution whose outset was characterized by acts of ingratitude and insult towards his father." [102]

Of a slightly more conciliatory nature was Steele's report of the rapprochement to their mutual friend and correspondent, John Haywood. After informing Haywood of Davie's letter proposing "the renewal of those offices which once marked our friendship and confidence," he presumed that their meeting at Trenton, New Jersey, would be "respectful; circumstances may perhaps make it friendly." He further reported that he had written Davie that *"the causes which contributed to the suspension of our former intercourse need not be retraced; they are in Oblivion but I must be permitted still to think that Dr. McCorkle had been ill-treated. As long however, as he [McCorkle] had thought fit to overlook that ill treatment I—as one of his friends could have no further inducement to resent it."*

Accordingly, Steele meant to wait upon Davie as soon as he arrived in Trenton and would never again mention the subject of their disagreement unless Davie introduced it. Political reasons and a certain state loyalty were further justifications for his relaxing his formality —his feeling that "our own characters (I mean as public men) and that of the state we belong to, are concerned in keeping up appearances, at least so far as to shew no disagreement, or coldness here." *

It was most probably Davie who, ever zealous to forward the interests of the University and augment the student body, submitted a "public testimonial" in the Halifax *North-Carolina Journal*, that he hoped would "prove a stimulus to still greater exertions" at the University: The trustees who had attended the examination of the students after the first year's term, were "happy to inform the public ... that their expectations were agreeably answered in respect to the

---

* September 19, 1799. Ernest Haywood Collection, S.H.C. The only extant evidence of their meeting is a letter from Steele to Mrs. Davie stating that Davie, before his departure for France, had placed in his hands his will, addressed to his father-in-law, General Allen Jones, and $102.67 with which Steele had, at Davie's request, purchased a quantity of "sattin," lutestring, muslin, and "a new hair trunk & cord" for Mrs. Davie. The silks, he stated, were "of the best quality to be procured here at the present time goods of that kind being scarce," but he flattered himself that "the colours will be agreeable to your taste." December 14, 1799.—John Steele Papers, S.H.C.

improvement of the students, since the semi-annual examination in July; and that the promptitude with which they acquitted themselves ... did honour ... both to themselves and to their teachers." [103]

Thus the first year of the founding of the University drew to a close. A contemporary account appeared in Henry Pattillo's *Geographical Cathecism*, whose dedicatory page, previously mentioned, was inscribed to Davie. The book has been described as "the most curious and interesting of these early books, perhaps, as well as the most valuable," published in eighteenth-century North Carolina: [104]

"A University is established by act of Assembly, in Orange county, with liberal appointments by the state, and numerous benefactions. It is yet in its infancy, has about sixty students, and if under the government of good and learned men, must prove an extensive blessing, as well as an honour to the state. What can more loudly call for the prayers of all good people, than that GOD's blessing may reside on our principal seat of learning, from which fountain are to flow those streams that must poison, or purify, and nourish our country. Its short progress has been rapid; may its success be glorious!" [105]

Meanwhile, Davie was playing a leading part in the physical construction of the buildings and the selection and replacements of the faculty. He and the other building commissioners were having great trouble trying to induce an "undertaker" for the construction of the "principal building"—later called "Main" and now "South." Advertisements were sent to the *Aurora* at Philadelphia and to the *North-Carolina Journal*, but Davie reported to John Haywood that he was informed by Thomas Blount that "there is little hope of inducing an Undertaker from that part of the Country to come forward, the spirit and rage of building is such in New York, Philadelphia and the Federal city, that every man of any talents in that way is already advantageously engaged, and the wages of Carpenters bricklayers &c enormously high, far beyond anything given in this Country." Davie, moreover, was acquainted with "no person who would probably offer to whom I would willingly give the contract; unless we can get some man of character, and a professed workman, we shall experience the endless vexation, we have already undergone in that sort of business with Mr. Patterson and where the man can be found on whom we could rely for the literal fulfillment of his contract in the absence of the Trustees, I do not know." Also of great concern to Davie were the ways and means of constructing the building since it could not be built for "much less than £10,000."[106]

The same problems of finance and procurement of desirable undertakers and workmen delayed the work on the chapel. Davie and Judge Alfred Moore accordingly turned to General Thomas Person, of Granville, a charter trustee, and prevailed upon him to make a cash donation to be applied towards finishing the chapel. The resulting gift of 1,040 silver dollars, however, was not forthcoming without the promise on the part of the solicitors that they would use their endeavors "to have his munificence properly commemorated." No such vague promise appeased the General, who wanted to ascertain *"the manner"* in which they proposed to commemorate it. Whereupon Davie and Moore suggested "that the Trustees would after his death erect in the chapel some monument of marble to his memory." Recalling the incident a decade and a half later, Davie reported to the Board of Trustees that upon General Person's inquiry as to the cost of such a memorial, he remembered telling him "that a neat marble slab set into the wall and surmounted by an urn or some ornament of that kind would not cost more than £40 or £50." This sum he thought had been added to the donation.*

It is a sad commentary that the resolution of the trustees to place this marble slab, bearing a suitable inscription, upon the front of the Old Chapel, was never carried out.[107]

Soon after this bequest of General Person, Davie was tormented

---

* A fragment of a letter from William R. Davie to John Haywood, Ernest Haywood Collection, S.H.C. The date does not appear on this letter, but it is unquestionably the one referred to in the following extract from the T. M., 1801-1810, pp. 220-21, dated December 12, 1810:

"A letter of the 1st of February last from the Honorable Major General William R Davie of South Carolina formerly of this State and one of the Trustees of our University and in fact *the founder* [italics mine]; making known to the Board certain circumstances relative to these donations of Brigadier General Thomas Person late of Warren County but now deceased which enabled the Trustees to erect a Chapel at the seat of the said University, was read: whereupon

"Resolved that the Reverend Joseph Caldwell and Duncan Cameron be and they are hereby authorized & requested to draw on the Treasury of the University for such sum of money not exceeding fifty pounds as shall enable them to procure and have fixed in the inner walls or otherwise of the Chapel, a marble slab or other monument suitably calculated in their opinion respectfully to commemorate the magnificence above mentioned."

again by the enemies of the new University: There was a report circulating to the effect that General Person had been defeated for the state legislature because of his donation to the University. If this were really true, Davie "should be very sorry," but he had been informed on the other hand that Person's opponents had succeeded against him on the charge of non-residence, which fact, Davie maintained, was true since his residence in Granville was merely nominal.[108]

In a more optimistic mood, Davie wrote his friend, James Hogg, that he was "very happy that everything goes on well at the University for a thousand reasons, and that certain croakers may be disappointed."[109]

Equally optimistic was Davie's communication to Thomas Bennehan, a student at the University and a native of Hillsborough, that all his letters from Chapel Hill announced "an uncommon spirit of industry and emulation among the Students, while the utmost harmony prevails in the several departments of business."[110]

Progress on the construction of the chapel was at a standstill. Governor Richard Dobbs Spaight, on the opening day of the University, January 15, 1795, saw only "a pile of yellowish red clay, dug out for the foundation of the Chapel." Joseph Caldwell, arriving from Princeton in November of 1796, saw only the "foundation of a Chapel ... but the completion is uncertain, as the mason and his negroes have spent the favorable fall in raising the foundation to the surface of the ground"—although the Person bequest had been made six months earlier.[111]

Davie's continued interest in the chapel, despite allegations of his deism, was unflagging. In December, 1796, he reported to John Haywood "the insufficiency of the work which had been done" by Philemon Hodge, the contractor, and entreated Haywood "to take the necessary measures with regard to Hodge before he proceeds further with the building that he may have no reason to complain of us." Being "fully convinced that man has no intention of compleating his contract without a Law-suit," Davie thought they should be "circumspect, and continually press him without relaxation to do his duty."[112]

Though the chapel was scheduled to be finished by July 1, 1797,[113] much remained to be done. Davie told Haywood, August 20, he thought the walls should be raised, it being "essential both to its

[255]

appearance and convenience." Davie, ever the canny Scot, was dubious about accepting Hopkins' proposal to make the bricks himself at forty shillings per thousand, because "of his being the man to make them, judge of their quality, and report or charge their quantity." Yet, since it was "of great importance that the principal part of them should be made this season," he felt they had better accede to his offer.[114]

The date of completion of this—the second permanent building to be erected upon any state university campus in the country—is unknown, but it is probable that it was used as the scene of the University's first graduation exercise in July, 1798. Commencements were held here until 1837, when they were shifted to Gerrard Hall, but the diplomas continued to bear the inscription *In Aula Personica* for thirty years, thus attesting to its place in the affections of the administration.[115]

"Main Building," later South, not only received Davie's attention but also was the *raison d'être* for a philippic against him. In February, 1797, Davie inquired of John Haywood as to "the progress of the main building" and as to "whether anything has been done to forward the contract with Hopkins."[116] At least by April 14 of the following year, the building had progressed enough for the laying of the cornerstone, the dedication being performed by "the Most Worshipful Gen. Davie, Grand Master, assisted by a respectable number of the Craft." Also present were "several Members of the Council of State... the Judge, the Bar and the Grand Jury of the superior court of the district of Hillsborough, and a number of gentlemen from the vicinity." There were also one hundred and sixteen students —a commendable number for an institution scarcely three years old.[117]

A year later Davie lamented to Haywood that "we cannot progress faster... but the want of funds is not our fault and cannot be immediately remedied." A ray of encouragement was that "some lands have been recovered in Edenton District as esceated property; so providence does not forget us nor with hold its assistance."[118]

Yet from Davie's standpoint, upon his return from France in December, 1800, providence had surely deserted the University, the State of North Carolina, and the nation as a whole. The Jeffersonian "Revolution of 1800" had had serious repercussions at the University

The Father of the University

in the form of the repeal of the act of 1794, giving all unsold confiscated land to the University, and the repeal of the Escheats Act of 1789.* Davie, undaunted, was not disposed to let the University or its buildings disintegrate. Nine days after the inauguration of Jefferson, he made arrangements to meet John Haywood in Chapel Hill to consider "the business of the University." While he did not know "the state of the finances of the University," he supposed "the buildings must stop, and... all that can be done now is to take measures for their preservation." He felt that "this valuable institution must not be immolated at the shrine of vandalism in the 19th. century." [119]

The following June, in the face of curtailed finances, the Building Commissioners, composed of Judge Alfred Moore, Walter Alves, and Davie, with an admirable bravado bordering on temerity, gave orders for the continuation of work on the "Main Building." They resolved unanimously that "the workmen proceed to carry up the Walls... to the top of the first Story." [120]

It was about this time that a man, writing under the pseudonym, "Citizen," published a vitriolic attack against the University as a bulwark of aristocratic Federalism, against the construction of South Building as a useless extravagance, and against Davie as the symbol of this seat of privilege. This Jacobin Republican charged that "every effort is made to give direction to the minds of the students on political subjects, favorable to a high-toned aristocratic government," as a result of which the "country will be imbued with aristocratic principles because an aristocrat is at the head of it." [121]

That Davie was the object of this attack—rather than Caldwell who did not become president until 1804—seems indisputable. Not only was Davie recognized as the virtual head of the University, but also he was singled out by name in an ensuing paragraph, in which "Citizen" denounced "the palace-like erection, which is much too large for usefulness, and might be aptly termed the 'Temple of Folly, planned by the Demi-God Davie.'" [122]

---

* The repeal of the grant of confiscated property was not too grave as it was to expire in 1804, but the deprivation of escheats, had they not been restored in 1805, would have been fatal to the University, because they furnished 69 per cent of the total revenue of the University in its first fifty years. —Blackwell P. Robinson, *The History of Escheats* (Chapel Hill: The University of North Carolina, 1955), p. 20.

WILLIAM R. DAVIE

It is contended by two authorities on the University that it was not Davie, but Richard Dobbs Spaight, who designed the building in question. The earlier authority gives no proof for this assertion, and the latter cites the former, and adds that Spaight was appointed as a commissioner on buildings on December 13, 1796. Actually, this appointment was made December 17 and this sole fact seems flimsy evidence for such a statement. Furthermore, Davie, on December 1, 1795, "in the name of Mr. J. Williams and himself laid before the Board a proposed plan for the principal Buildings of the University."[123]

It might be added that after a great many vicissitudes, the building was finally completed in 1814, its completion celebrated by the firing of a cannon for the only time in the history of Chapel Hill.[124] But Davie had retired nine years earlier to his South Carolina plantation.

In addition to performing meritorious service in promoting the construction of the buildings, Davie continued to give himself untiringly to the task of maintaining the staff of the University. Particularly difficult was the search for a successor to fill the vacancy of Charles W. Harris, who announced he would retire in December, 1796, as presiding professor and professor of mathematics. Harris himself was the one who nominated his successor as professor of mathematics, Joseph Caldwell, whose character and ability he had observed at Princeton. Only twenty-three years old, Caldwell had graduated, with highest honors, a year ahead of Harris. Since graduation he had taught mathematics there. Harris's nomination, according to Battle, was unanimously accepted by the trustees despite his youth. Their ready acceptance can be attributed no doubt to a letter from Hugh Williamson, then in New York, who had been commissioned to inquire for a competent person. His discouraging letter revealed that the salary of $600 was "so small as to preclude any respectable man of learning to remove to a Southern State, where, as they all believe, the chances of health are greatly diminished." His further commentary has a familiar refrain: "men of moderate ability expect to make more money in other business than teaching, hence capable teachers are only among the clergy."[125] Davie himself considered it "absolutely necessary that we should enlarge the establishment of the University; for this purpose it appears to be necessary to extend the loan from 10 to 30 years, for that is the present fund out of which

The Father of the University

the professorships must be endowed; and few men would choose to leave any tolerable prospects for an establishment upon funds which might fail in ten years."[126]

Harris was instructed by Davie to apprise Caldwell of his election. Prompt acceptance was forthcoming, based on the fact that the situation they described at the University enabled him to compare it "without difficulty" with his present situation. His acceptance letter also revealed that the situation at Chapel Hill appeared so attractive and the situation at Princeton so unattractive, that Dr. John McLean, the professor of chemistry, from Glasgow, and even Samuel Stanhope Smith, D.D., the president of Princeton, were both eager to entertain proposals from the Board of Trustees. The new University was thus offered an opportunity of transferring the reputation of Princeton, "as far as the reputation of this college depends upon its [im]mediate professors" to Chapel Hill.[127] But such an opportunity was naturally beyond the immediate pecuniary grasp of the founding fathers.

Caldwell further reported to Davie that he thought four weeks would be sufficient time for the journey to Chapel Hill and he hoped to arrive sometime between the end of October and the middle of November.[128]

At the July and December, 1796, meetings of the Board, Davie also was entrusted with a number of details, such as having the "Avenue at the Seat of the University cleared, grubbed & put in such order as he may judge proper" and having "the Spring enclosed." He was added to the committee on escheated and confiscated lands and was paid "the sum of Eleven pounds three shillings & four pence, for Medicine furnished the students by him and Mr. Willie Jones."[129]

Caldwell arrived at the "seat of the University" on October 31 and soon thereafter made a trip to Raleigh, where he reported that the "Legislature in numbers appeared respectable" and that "General Davie stands foremost and an almost unrivaled leader in every capital enterprise." His further appraisal—particularly in the light of present-day enonomic determinism—is worthy of note: "In the Legislature he seems like a parent struggling for the happiness and welfare of his children. No doubt he frequently finds them refractory." After spending the greater part of two evenings with Davie, he pronounced him "a man of good abilities and active in every measure for promoting the honor and interest of the State."[130]

WILLIAM R. DAVIE

It is also through the medium of Caldwell's correspondence that the religious situation in North Carolina and an intimation of Davie's deistic tendencies are revealed.* "The State," he wrote, "appears to be swarming with lawyers. It is almost the only profession for which parents educate their children. Religion is so little in vogue, that it affords no temptation to undertake its cause. In New Jersey it had a public respect and support. In North Carolina, *and particularly in the part east of Chapel Hill* [italics mine], every one believes that the way of rising to respectability is to disavow as often and as publicly as possible the leading doctrines of the Scriptures. They are bugbears, very well fitted to scare the ignorant and weak into obedience to the laws; but the laws of morality and honor are sufficient to regulate the conduct of men of letters and cultivated reasons. One reason, why religion is so scouted from the most influential part of society, is that it is taught only by ranters, with whom it seems to consist only in the powers of their throats and the wildness and madness of their gesticulations and distortions. If it were taught by men of prudence, real piety and improved talents it would claim the support of the people." [131]

Caldwell also had a private conversation with Davie on the "Evidences of Christianity." Though Caldwell failed to report the effect of his arguments on Davie, he gave a summary of his own, which were "pronounced, judicious, and forcible." †

Others [132] have read pronounced free-thinking proclivities into Davie's letter of condolence to John Haywood, upon the death of the latter's wife, in which he wrote, "I regret the various causes which produced your absence from the board. However, as the Arabs say 'God would have it so, and man must submit,' under misfortunes like yours there is no comfort, because nothing can be substituted, the only recourse for the Human mind in such cases is

---

* Note should be taken of the fact, however, that these observations were made, after only a few days in the state, by a youth of twenty-three, whose pious mother was the daughter of a Presbyterian clergyman and a Huguenot refugee's daughter.—Battle, *University*, I, 110.

† *Ibid.*, p. 115. Battle followed this quotation with an appraisal of Caldwell, which he erroneously attributed to Davie. However, this letter, quoting this estimate of Caldwell, was from James Hogg to Davie and not *from* the latter. See Hogg to Davie, June [?] 1797.—Univ. Letters, 1791-1867, pp. 10-12. This is a manuscript copy in President David L. Swain's handwriting.

in a kind of philosophical fortitude, the calm result of time, reason and reflection." [133]

More indicative of Davie's religious sentiments were his sarcastic observations in referring to certain criticisms of the University: "Bishop Pettigrew has said it is a very dissipated and debauched place. Some priests have also been doing us the same good office to the westward. Nothing, it seems, goes well that these *men of God* have not had some hand in." [134]

The above statements, though meager, constitute the sole contemporary evidence available as to Davie's religious convictions.

Caldwell assumed his duties as professor November 2, 1796, but was soon induced to take over as presiding professor after the resignation of Charles W. Harris. The latter, in the spring of 1797, settled in Halifax, where he entered the law offices of General Davie. Here he reported that he was "pretty well fixed for study," but was "surrounded on all sides with a great variety of amusements" which were "in every respect calculated to engage the attention of one in the vigour of youth." Having entered at once "into the drudgery of Gen. Davie's office," he was relieved that court had risen the day before. He further reported that everyone in Halifax was "much agitated by the near approach of a *cock fight*," which had been preceded by several "hack-fights." In these contests, the "gentlemen in town fight against those of the country, otherwise it is the Longs against the Alstons." *

It was about this time that Davie reverted to his Calvinistic background by vetoing the production of full-length plays at the University. The occasions evoking his disapproval were, supposedly, the presentation of two plays during the commencement exercises, July

* Charles W. Harris to Dr. Charles Harris, May 8, 1797.—Charles W. Harris Papers, S.H.C. After reading law in Davie's office and assisting him in the office, Harris procured his license to practice in 1798 and no doubt stepped into a very lucrative practice when Davie was elected governor of the state in September of that year and left as minister plenipotentiary to France the following year. Harris was, in fact, intrusted with the bulk of Davie's practice. This practice, as well as a budding political career, was cut short by tuberculosis. A trip to the West Indies in 1803 brought no relief and he died January 15, 1804, in Anson County at his brother's home. See Henry McGilbert Wagstaff [ed.], "The Harris Letters," *James Sprunt Historical Publications*, Vol. XIV, No. 1 (1916), 49n.; also Battle, *University*, I, 115-16.

11 to 15 inclusive, 1796, by the Dialectic and Philanthropic Societies. They were produced under the direction of William Augustus Richards, a young London adventurer, who had deserted ship at Norfolk, joined a traveling theatrical company which folded up at Warrenton, North Carolina, taught several years in the Reverend Marcus George's Warrenton Academy, and finally became a teacher in the preparatory school at the University. The two dramatic performances were the first ever given at any state university in America and were followed the ensuing year by two other performances. This precedent, however, was nipped in the bud by Davie, who perhaps was most responsible for delaying the encouragement of full-scale dramatics at Chapel Hill for a century and a quarter.[135] Ironically enough, the University is now a nation-wide mecca for dramatics.

Davie's objections were incorporated in a letter, August 3, 1797, to James Hogg: "As to acting plays at the university, I think they are by no means as well calculated for improvement in elocution as single speeches, and I believe this will be found to be the result of the experience of every college either in Europe or on the Continent, in which they have been generally laid aside; single scenes from most of the best plays might still be acted to advantage; but acting a whole play is absurd and unprofitable from every point of view. If the faculty insist upon this kind of exhibition, the trustees must interfere. Our object is to make the students men, not players."[136]

Their object also was to allay criticism of the University, which was emanating from various quarters. Davie, with this in mind, observed that "Human malevolence in some, interested views in others, the ignorance and caprice of parents, will Continue to injure our institution, until it has acquired some stability, some fixed character, and this process will require some years."[137] It was probably for this same reason that he had introduced a bill in the House of Commons to prevent "gaming tables in the neighbourhood of the University of North-Carolina."[138]

Despite his thumbs-down to the youthful Thespians, Davie sought to encourage Terpsichore. Being "very desirous" that his sons, Allen Jones and Hyder Ali, then at the University, should be taught to dance well, he wrote that there were some "French Gentlemen at Newbern who teach dancing in the most elegant stile" and that they were "really Gentlemen and unfortunate refugees from St. Domingo."[139]

It was evidently one of these gentlemen, Mr. Perrin, whom Davie induced to come to Chapel Hill to teach "the young gentlemen to dance." Although Mr. Perrin, then at Newbern, would not undertake to teach the English dances, he would teach "the minuet, & french dances such as Cotillions, Congas &c, &c" for which he would charge two dollars per month for three afternoons per week. Davie supposed that he might get "between fifty & sixty scholars at the University" and Judge Sitgreaves thought it probable that he might have a "tollerable good school at Hillsborough" which he could attend for the other three days.[140]

Not only was Davie concerned with the more esthetic and polished sides of his sons' education, but also he was eager to see that they should have a room "with a good companion" and meticulous care in their rudimentary education. In reply to a request from Davie, Caldwell wrote that they would live in a room opposite to his and would thus be "near at hand should any improper proceeding be taking place." He further reported that Allen was studying Sallust, French, "arithmetic reading writing and spelling" and would be ready two years hence "to stand a good examination in the studies of the preparatory school." Hyder was reported as reading "latin grammar from which he wants to go into Corderie" and he also "reads writes and spells in english."[141]

Serious problems were laid before Davie in June, 1797, when James Hogg reported his findings at a meeting of the Board of Trustees in Chapel Hill. On the bright side he was able to acquaint Davie with the facts "that all the classes under Mr. Caldwell and Mr. Holmes [Samuel A., first a tutor and then a professor of ancient languages, 1796-1798] had acquitted themselves well;" that "Mr. Delvaux's classes on Sallust, Caesar, Cor-Nepos, Eutropius, and 2 classes on Corderius, seemed to me to be taught with accuracy"; that the latter's "students in the French Grammar gave satisfaction"; that "Mr. Richard's classes on Telemachus and Gil Blas French Exercises and Fables and in French Grammar made a satisfactory examination"; and that Willie Jones "was much pleased with our examination and in a short but comprehensive speech, highly complimented the Teachers and Students."

WILLIAM R. DAVIE

On the dark side, Hogg reported first that he had "been long apprehensive that Reading, spelling and writing have not been attended to with such care as to give general satisfaction" and that there was a serious misunderstanding between Delvaux and Richards which prompted the Board to authorize an assistant to them. Of more gravity was his announcement that Caldwell had "notified his determination to leave us," because he felt "his constitution is too weak, to undergo the anxiety and fatigue of the President's place." As though this were not trouble enough, he stated that Willie Jones had told him that Josiah Collins, a wealthy citizen of Edenton and a trustee, had told *him* that "our seminary was under disrepute there" and Henry Watters, a Hillsborough lawyer and an attorney of the University, said the same opinion prevailed in the "North East" and that "it was mere necessity, made them send their children from that place," because "they think meanly of all our teachers." [142]

Davie's meticulous concern was shown in his letter of July 19, 1797, to Caldwell, in which he tried to resolve some of the difficulties facing the struggling institution. The letter has a definite paternal note and his opinions have a certain *ex cathedra* ring. He sincerely regretted Caldwell's resolution to resign and hoped his situation would become "as agreeable to you as it was important to the State." Yet he philosophically observed, "We are all however in pursuit of happiness, and it is not for me either to judge for you, or call upon you to make sacrifices which perhaps nothing could compensate."

Davie was "very sorry that a proper spirit of accommodation" did not exist between Richards and Delvaux, and, respecting the manner of conferring degrees, he "was in great hopes that the board would have met on the 14th. of July so that an ordinance could have passed." [143]

The following month, Davie was still harassed over a successor to Caldwell, who had agreed, however, to stay on until the next July. It would have given Davie "great pleasure if he could be retained for some years; but it will be our duty to find him a successor in January next if possible; because every man worth employing is so important a trust [that he] will be some way or other engaged for the year." Davie therefore wrote to James Smiley Gillaspie, as a successor, of whose "learning and good sense" James Hogg "and all the Literary men I have seen, who are acquainted with Mr. Gillespie [sic] speak highly." Davie had been informed that he was "attached to a studious academic life, and would probably remain long with us: this is a great object," for it was a "melancholly thing to have these difficulties returning upon us every year." He was, moreover, at a loss to find a successor to Delvaux, but saw "no impropriety in advertising such a vacancy." [144]

The trustees, by securing Gillaspie as professor of natural philosophy and as presiding professor, were successful in inducing Caldwell to remain as professor of mathematics.[145]

Other vacancies also plagued Davie about this time. In November and December, 1798, he and Willie Jones advertised in the *North-Carolina Journal* for a teacher in the Preparatory School to teach the English and French languages and reading, writing, and arithmetic to replace William Richards.[146] In November Davie advertised in the same paper for a steward of the University.[147] The following October he and John Haywood were still advertising for such a person.[148]

Six days after Davie was elected governor of the state, he was unanimously chosen as president of the Board of Trustees. This practice of electing the governor as the head of the trustees was evolving—so far as can be determined from the records—into an unwritten precedent. Though the first president of the Board, William Lenoir, was not governor, the next three presidents, who preceded Davie, were all governors: Alexander Martin, Richard Dobbs Spaight, and Samuel Ashe.[149] In 1805 the governors were made presidents of the Board *ex officio*, but could, if they wished, appoint a substitute.[150]

It was unfortunate for Davie that the new "Principal of the University" (as his title now read), Gillaspie, was at the helm. His first term was described by Battle as "fairly successful," but the term preceding the commencement of 1799 was "especially stormy." This was indeed a mild characterization of the rebellion which broke out among the students against the laws and the faculty. This revolt, which lasted for a week, was motivated primarily by their antipathy to Gillaspie, who had become "personally obnoxious" to them. Not only did they beat him personally, but they waylaid, stoned, accosted, or threatened the other members of the faculty and proposed that Caldwell should assume complete authority.[151]

WILLIAM R. DAVIE

The "Anarchy & Confusion which prevailed there" led Willie Jones to report the drastic diminution in the number of students: from 115 "some time past" to only "seventy odd" and many of these "declared that they will not return to the University." Jones further reported that the "University totters, the Reputation of it is gone: But it may be recovered & made to shine with brighter Lustre than it has hitherto done." His panacea went to the root of the evil. "Instead of building useless Palaces, for there is now Room at the Village for 150 Students, apply the Funds to the purpose of Tuition." All the trustees at the last meeting, he continued, agreed with him that "it was absolutely necessary to have a President, a Man skilled in the Sciences, of polished manners, with dignity in his Appearance, & an established Character,—and also able professors." [152]

In an effort to do his utmost "to promote the Interest of the Institution," Jones immediately wrote to Davie, who had just resigned as governor and as president of the Board of Trustees, to become minister plenipotentiary to France. Jones apprised him of the state of affairs and gave him the names of three gentlemen who, he supposed, "were qualified to fill the Chair of the president,—Doctr. Ashbel Green of Philadelphia,* Doctr. Smith of Princeton, & Doctr. Linn of New York." Davie, who had left Halifax September 22 or 23, was asked to interview these men on his trip up to Trenton, New Jersey, the port of embarkation, but Jones's request was apparently too late, because none had been heard from.

None other than George Washington had also informed Willie Jones, the latter reported, that "there was a Gentleman in Virginia, out of Employment, who had been highly recommended to him as a man of Science; but unfortunately he had forgot his Name." However, at Washington's instance, he had written to a "Doctr. David Stewart, who lived in Prince William or Loudon County," Virginia, who knew him, but Jones had heard from neither.

Not content with these exertions, Willie Jones had also "addressed" himself to Marcus George, of the Warrenton Academy; had talked with Colonel William Polk, who knew a "respectable Character in

---

* Green was to be the second recipient of the degree of Doctor of Laws, conferred by the University. This was conferred in 1812, the year after Davie's, which was the first. See Hamilton, "W. R. D.," pp. 65-66.

[266]

the Neighborhood of Charlotte"; and had received an application for a professorship from "Mr. Archibald, who conducts the Seminary at Williamsborough," which application he enclosed to the Board.

This report is further significant in that it marks the final exertions and retirement from active interest in the University of one who, from the beginning in 1776 had given almost a quarter-century of loving and devoted attention to the cause of higher education in North Carolina—Willie Jones. And in the last ten years he and Davie, leaders of opposing political parties, had stood shoulder to shoulder in founding and upholding the University. Debilitated by gout, Jones now realized that his days of usefulness were over. His last words to the Board of which he was a charter member were typical in their mixture of genuine love and practicality: "My Heart is warm in its Interest, and I know that active and intelligent, & not honorary members are necessary."

It is fitting that his son, Willie William Jones, also a first cousin of Mrs. Davie, should have succeeded Davie, upon his retirement in 1807, as a member of the Board of Trustees.[153]

It was perhaps this report of Willie Jones that induced a committee of the trustees, after the resignation of the entire faculty, to advertise for a "Professor of Natural, Moral and Political Philosophy, of the Languages and Belles Lettres, and of Mathematics," with salaries and emoluments that had been "upwards of 500 dollars per annum, exclusive of board at Commons." As a result, Caldwell was re-elected to the chair of mathematics and also to succeed Gillaspie as presiding professor.[154]

Shortly before Davie was elected president of the Board, Major Charles Gerrard, a native of Carteret County, but a resident of Edgecombe at his death, left a grant of over 14,000 acres of land, 2,560 of which were land warrants which he received by virtue of having been a lieutenant in the Revolution. They were located at the junction of Yellow Creek and the Cumberland River, not far below Nashville, Tennessee.[155]

The same day that Davie was chosen president of the Board, he, John Haywood, Thomas Blount, and Willie Jones were appointed a committee to collect "the evidences of Title to the Lands devised to the Board by Maj. Gerard" and were authorized to employ an agent

William R. Davie

in Tennessee for that purpose.[156] No doubt on the basis of information furnished to Davie by Howell Tatum, who had looked briefly into the status of the grant on Davie's request,[157] the committee appointed Tatum their agent and granted him a power of attorney.[158] This bequest later made possible the completion of the new chapel, which was, in commemoration, named Gerrard Hall.[159]

Scarcely two months after Davie's departure for France, there was some criticism of his charging the University an excessive fee in his suits against the McCulloh heirs. These suits were brought in consequence of the act of the General Assembly of December, 1794, which gave the University all unsold confiscated land, including the forfeited rights of Henry Eustace McCulloh, a British subject. To realize funds under this act, the trustees employed able lawyers, among whom was Davie.[160] A letter from John Whitaker, a trustee from Halifax County, to Gaven Alves is the only available evidence of the dissatisfaction of the committee to settle accounts with Davie's charge. Whitaker was distressed to hear of this dissatisfaction, which was occasioned by his paying Davie the amount he had charged—which, according to Whitaker, Davie said "was Only half fees What he Should have charged an Individual for the same Services." Whereupon, Whitaker had paid him "with cheerfulness, knowing he was at some pains to secure the property for the benefit of the University." Apparently, there was also some suspicion that Davie received a fee from the defendant. Whitaker continued: "Whether he did receive any fees from the defendant or not cant Say. With certainty. incline to think not." Whitaker's feeling was that he did "not believe the compensation to great When compared With fees in Similar cases charged by attorneys."[161] The accusation of taking fees from the defendants was indeed a serious one, but perhaps little credence should be accorded to it in the light of the political animosities of 1800 and in the light of Davie's entire life of political impeccability.

Upon Davie's return from France, he resumed his activities in behalf of the University. He was very much afraid that he would miss the next meeting of the Board, because of "a fever which has increased upon me very much for two days," but he assured John Haywood that "nothing however but ill health will prevent my attendance."[162] His fever apparently abated, for he was present at

THE FATHER OF THE UNIVERSITY

the next meeting in Chapel Hill on June 25 and 26, where he took his usual active part and was primarily interested in the progress of the work on the main building.[163]

Yet his blood-pressure, if not his fever, no doubt went up over the legislature's failure, in December, 1801, to repeal what Davie referred to as "the Gothic law of the preceding session"—the bill which disallowed the collection of escheats by the trustees of the University. Though he had not been "sanguine as to the passage of the bill," he "considered the support it received as a proof of the reaction of the public mind, and the progress of reason." His succeeding statements reflect his disillusionment and increasingly caustic sentiments: "... a sort of Gothic ignorance and political fanaticism are the fashionable order of the day; these infectious moral evils like the yellow fever and the plague have their limits, some invisible power has always said, 'So far shalt thou go and no farther'—They intercept for a time the progress of nature or Society, after which they again resume their march, and become progressive; Every man really attached to the liberties of his Country, every genuine republican must sincerely lament this sort of suicide committed by the Legislature, ignorance and despotism, are as certain cotemporaries and relations as light and Liberty." [164]

The next trustee meeting which Davie attended was in December, 1802, where he presented the report of the committee of the faculty which recommended a series of ordinances. The first of these called for the expulsion of three students, Samuel G. Hopkins, John W. Hawkins, and Hugh Nunn. The first two had engaged in a duel, while the last-named had been "guilty of misbehavior and gross violence to his Teacher in the preparatory school."

Of especial interest was Ordinance B, which was drawn up in the opinion that "it would contribute greatly to reclaim dissipation among the Students, and ... remove certain prejudices entertained in several parts of the State, against the collegiate and moral obligations of the Institution." This ordinance directed that a circular letter be addressed to the parent or guardian of each student. In the interests of frugality, these letters contained the following list of the established and ordinary expenses of the University, in the hope "that the indulgence of the Parents would not exceed those limits so far as to furnish

WILLIAM R. DAVIE

a temptation to dissipation, misapplication of time and a relaxation of morals":

Expenses of 1st. Session		Expenses of 2nd. Session	
Board	$34	Board	$24.00
Tuition	12	Tuition	8
Room Rent	1	Room rent	1
Library	.50	Library	.50
Servant hire	.50	Servant hire	.50
Washing & mending	5.00	Washing & mending	4.00
Wood & Candles	2.	Wood & Candles	1.
Bed hire	3.	Bed hire	3.
	$58.00		$42 [165]

In their desire to maintain "correct principles, pure morals and a proper reverence for religion," the committee inclosed also an abstract of the laws respecting "some of the Collegiate duties, and the moral and religious conduct of the Students."

A few excerpts from these will suggest some of the spartan strictures, as well as the more colorful aspects of student life in the early days:

Every Student, whether in the College or in the village, shall attend public prayers morning and evening in the Chapel, and during the worship, shall refrain from any noise, conducting himself with such decorum and reverence as is suited to these solemn services. On Sunday it shall be the duty of every Student to be present at the reading or delivery of a sermon in the Chapel, at the hour appointed by the Faculty for that purpose. No whispering, talking, laughing, or indecent behavior of any kind shall be manifested on such occasions.

A Student shall not make horse races, nor bet thereon, nor shall they keep cocks or fowls of any kind, or for any purpose—

No Student shall raffle, play at cards or dice, or bet at any game, without being punished by the Faculty according to the aggravation of the offence.

No Student shall keep a dog or fire arms; nor shall he use fire arms without permission from some one of the Faculty—

No Student shall have spirituous liquors in his room without particular permission from the President or from some member of the Faculty.

Every Student who shall be guilty of intoxication, shall receive an admonition before the Faculty for the first offence, and on repetition of

The Father of the University

the crime, shall be publicly admonished or suspended, according to the nature and aggravation of his conduct.

All swearing and profane, blasphemous or impious language shall be utterly excluded from the University.

The Students shall keep their rooms clean, and shall not put or procure to be introduced into the College filth of any kind—

It is recommended to the students to be plain in their dress; but it is required of them always to appear neat and cleanly: and if any student shall be grossly negligent in this respect, it shall be the duty of the College officers to admonish him for it, and see that he preserve a decent appearance.

The above report of the committee of the faculty, presented by Davie, was concurred in by the Board, with the exception of the expulsion of the three students.[166]

As an active member of the Board of Trustees, this represents his last important contribution to the University, save one: when he was summoned to an extraordinary meeting of the trustees May 18 and May 19, 1803, called for the purpose of handling a serious situation which had developed at the University. Sometime in the spring of 1803, despite the case of Hopkins and Hawkins in the preceding December, the entire student body was in a turmoil because of a number of bitter quarrels among the students. There was, in fact, a serious threat of four or five duels.[167] So serious did it become that Caldwell "immediately dispatched Messengers after the Trustees." The Board which met consisted of Colonel William Polk, John Haywood, Judge Potter, Walter Alves, and General Davie, "who happened to be in the Neighbourhood." As a result, three of the principals were expelled, two of the seconds suspended, and the informant, originally a principal, received the thanks of the Board.* The Board then adopted a stringent ordinance commanding the faculty to expel all students engaged in duels either as principals or as aiders and abetters, to be turned over to the civil authorities.[168]

Commenting on this "melancholly occurrence," Davie, writing to Richard Bennehan, was sure it had "given you as well as all the friends

---

* [Duncan Cameron] to [his brother-in-law], May 22, 1803.—Cameron Papers, S.H.C. For a different version of what occurred, see Battle, *University*, I, 198-99. This author has confused the dueling incidents of December, 1802, and those of May, 1803.

of Literature much pain." He thought that "there would be no end to the vexation that arises out of the management of that Institution: the ordinance was to be sure objectionable, but the conduct of these men will be come a most dangerous precedent." [169]

It is most fitting, however, that at his last official visitation at the University, he and the other members of the committee were able to look into the future with sanguinity and confidence. This committee, composed of William Polk (the president of the Board), Walter Alves, and Calvin Jones (a prominent physician of Raleigh), felt "happy to have it in their power to inform the public of the flattering prospects which the University at this time offers to the friends of humanity." It further reported that "under all its embarrassments it has continued to flourish; the number of Students has increased; the plan of education has been extended, and the discipline of the Laws improved." Prophetic of the future were its final remarks: "... A new spirit and activity has been given to the business of the institution. Its friends have shewn new zeal for its prosperity, and the Trustees entertain the fondest hope that this national institution will ultimately and quickly triumph over every difficulty, and by diffusing useful knowledge, and affording to our young men the easy means of liberal education, will shortly raise North Carolina to that rank in the Union to which she is entitled by the number of her inhabitants, the genius of her citizens and the extent of her resources." [170]

Just before Davie's retirement to his South Carolina plantation, "Tivoli," another serious upheaval occurred at the University. Described by Battle as "the great rebellion" and "the great secession," the student revolt was precipitated by the adoption by the Board of Trustees of "laws of such inquisitorial severity as outraged the sense of justice among the students." These laws required the president and faculty to take an oath before a justice of the peace or judge to execute the laws of the institution. A more stringent ordinance was passed which required two monitors to be appointed by lot from the twelve senior students of each class to serve a month. These monitors were to take an oath to execute faithfully their duties and to make weekly written reports, minutely stating all breaches of the laws, all immoralities, irregularities, or instances of indecent behavior by any student. Forty-five students, a majority of all the students in attendance, and "a very large majority of the ablest and most mature,"

THE FATHER OF THE UNIVERSITY

presented a remonstrance to the faculty and trustees and bound themselves to leave if one of them should be punished. The substitution of a "pledge of honor" in lieu of the oath was unanimously rejected by the recalcitrants and forty-one of the forty-five signers "seceded" and went home.*

Davie, in a letter to John Haywood, wrote that "the situation at the University is a distressing one, and the more so, as it is not likely to be soon capable of any Remedy, being the necessary consequence of Legislative hostility to the Institution." [171]

His contrast of the situations in North and South Carolina and his indictment of the North Carolina legislature, on the eve of his moving to the latter state, is revealing:

"... the friends of science in other states regard the people of North Carolina as a sort of Semi-Barbarians, among whom neither learning, virtue nor men of Science possess any Estimation. The conduct of the Legislature for several years past has stamped this character on the State and it will take a long course of Time, and contrary conduct and policy to efface the impression.

"In South Carolina a Professorship is more eagerly canvassed for than a Secretaryship in the Government of the U. S., the consequence of that liberal spirit which has been displayed by their Assembly; after a handsome and permanent endowment of the offices of the Institution, they voted $10,000., to purchase a Library and Philosophical apparatus—What a contrast!! Poor No. Carolina!" [172]

In this same letter Davie informed Haywood of his intention "to set out for South Carolina with a View to reside permanently on my Estate there." On his way he had hoped to be at the University at commencement, but he had to take his daughter, Sarah, to Salem College, the Moravian school in Salem, North Carolina, about July 25. He would not be able to make the second trip, because his constitution could not "now bear that degree of suffering, privation and incessant Toil, which when I enjoyed youth and health only gave me spirits and pleasure."

Before leaving North Carolina permanently, Davie wrote his last words of advice in regard to the University and particularly in

---

* See Battle, *University*, I, 200-14, for a lengthy discussion of the causes, the ordinances, and the list of seceders.

regard to the recent revolt. The letter is dated September 22, 1805. In it Davie says:

"I have reflected much and seriously since this event on the causes of the spirit of insubordination and the means of preventing it—It has always existed in a considerable degree, the ordinance may be considered as only an accidental cause; I think the real causes may be found in the defects of domestic education in the So. States, the weakness of parental authority, the spirit of the Times, the arrangement as to vacation, and some errors of the Board which I will notice hereafter.

"Every man of discernment, who has lived 40 or 50 years must have observed and lamented the general decay of parental authority, and the consequent presumption and loose manners of our young men; Boys of 16 or 17 years, without judgment without experience or almost any knowledge of any kind arrogantly affect to judge for themselves, their teachers and even their parents in matters of morality, of Government, of Education, in fact in every thing. The effect of the other general cause is visible throughout the whole of their remonstrance—Nothing can be more ridiculous than *Boys at school* talking of 'a sacred regard to their rights' 'the high and imposing duty of resistance,' and of 'denouncing laws' etc etc, the general Slang of the times culled from the columns of Newspapers; yet these very sounds are attended with the most mischievous consequences. Over all these causes however the Board of Trustees have no power or influence, but they must be considered to be counteracted as far as possible. . . .

"The Difficulty we have continually experienced in the management of youth at this Institution has often obliged me to reflect on the means we have used, and the nature of the Government of such Institutions—. I am now perfectly convinced the best governed Colleges are those which have the most respectable Faculties, and the fewest *written* Laws, and that we have committed a serious error in making an ordinance for *every thing,* or in other words legislating too much.—It is now my opinion, that after describing the kind of punishment to be used on the Establishment, and reserving in all cases the punishment of *Expulsion* to be confirmed by the Board, all the rest should be left to the *discretion* of the Faculty. It may perhaps require some reflection to see the justness of this remark, owen to

The Father of the University

certain habits among us of writing & thinking, and I will only add, that the principles of the parental Government are the true model for that of literary Institutions for youth of all kinds from the University down to the common school: The parental Government has no written laws, and I would observe, that no mortal man could govern his family if he adopted that mode—If he did, his whole Household would become, like these students, lawyers and legislators, discussing his ordinances, chattering about 'their rights' 'despotism' 'duty of resistance,' etc. etc. They would form themselves into revolutionary committees, and be always deliberating, remonstrating, and revolting...."[173]

After his retirement Davie was not forgotten by a grateful University. Recognition of his part in its creation was acknowledged on two occasions in the next thirteen years of his life. The trustees, December 12, 1810, referred to him as "the founder."[174] In the following year they saw fit to confer on him the first degree of Doctor of Laws awarded by the University. The rough draft of the letter announcing this action to Davie is interesting:

Chapel Hill Novemr 16th 1811.

Honourable Sir

The President, Faculty & Trustees of the University of North Carolina at the late anniversary of their annual examination have conferred on you the degree of Doctor of Laws.

This is presented to you as evidence of the high degree in which your virtue, talents and learning are estimated

R Wms., Secretary

As soon as a diploma can be   )
made ready it will be forwarded to you)

Genl Wm R. Davie

This is the first degree of Doctor of Laws conferred by this University, and which is sent to you particularly as the Founder of our Institution, and principal supporter, when in its infant state.

This resolution of the Faculty was expressed was [sic] nearly as follows.
The Honourable William Richardson Davie formerly Governour of N. Carolina, late envoy extraordinary and minister pleny to the French government, who received the degree of Master of Arts in Nassau Hall, is now admitted to the degree of Doctor of Laws in this University.[175]

WILLIAM R. DAVIE

His name also headed the list of graduates in 1811. Among the University Papers there is a catalogue, in Latin, of the University, published in Raleigh, 1817, by E. Tysis and J. Gales. Its entry in regard to Davie reads:

> Gulielmus R. Davie, Arm. Caro. Septen.
> Gub. E. Cong. Sen. et apud, Gal.
> Rem. Legat. Rerump. L. L. D.[176]

The citation of his degree was as follows:

> The Honourable William Richardson Davie formerly Governour of North Carolina, and late envoy extraordinary and Minister Plenipotentiary from the United States at the French Court, who has received the degree of Master of Arts at Nassau Hall Princeton, is admitted to the degree of Doctor of Laws in this University.[177]

A grateful Davie wrote his letter of acceptance to Robert Williams, Secretary of the Board:

> Landsford, Catawba.
> Jany. 10th. 1812
>
> Dear Sir
>
> I have the pleasure to acknowledge your letter of the 25th. of November, and beg you to present my thanks to the President, Faculty and Trustees of the University of North Carolina for this mark of their polite attention, and to assure them of the high sense I entertain of the honor they have been pleased to confer upon me, with my warmest wishes for the success of the institution.
>
> I pray you Sir, also to accept my thanks for the polite manner in which you have been pleased to communicate this act of the Board.
>
> I am very respectfully
> Sir
> Your Mo Obt.
> W. R. DAVIE.[178]

This recognition on the part of the Board of Trustees was an appropriate finale for his twenty-three years of unceasing efforts as father and founder of the University and as its chief supporter in its early years. Had this been his sole achievement, he would have deserved the undying gratitude of his adopted state. Yet in the years 1790 to 1800 his star continued to rise, culminating in his election as governor and as minister plenipotentiary to France in 1800.

CHAPTER IX

A Federalist Star at its Zenith

NORTH CAROLINA had ratified the Federal Constitution and had thereby established, for better, for worse—and, as it happened, irrevocably—its relationship with the Union. North Carolina had chartered a state university and had thereby assumed a responsibility to her promising youth—a responsibility that was finally to include every six-year-old in the state.

William Richardson Davie, by introducing both bills, had played an integral part in these two developments. And he and his associates were apparently riding high on the surface wave of Federalism, though underneath there was a strong radical undercurrent. His Federalist friends, Samuel Johnston and Benjamin Hawkins, were chosen by the legislature for the United States Senate. In the House of Representatives were Federalists Hugh Williamson, John Steele, and John Sevier, leaving only John B. Ashe and Timothy Bloodworth to represent the left-wing, particularistic party in Congress. Then, too, James Iredell, Davie's closest political friend, was appointed by Washington in February, 1790, as an Associate Justice of the Supreme Court of the United States.

By the time North Carolina joined the Union, the country was struggling in the maelstrom precipitated by the efforts of Alexander Hamilton to establish the credit of the United States at home and abroad, to build up its prestige among the chancelleries and counting houses of Europe, and to make even the backwoodsman of Pennsylvania and Carolina aware of the strong arm of the federal government.

William R. Davie

The resulting Funding and Assumption Acts, the Excise Tax, and the Bank of the United States became burning issues throughout the new nation. In North Carolina the political alignment was fluid enough for the Federalists to approve some of these measures.

North Carolina's representatives did not reach the seat of government, New York, until after the funding of the $12,000,000 national debt owed to French, Spanish, and Dutch bankers for their aid in financing the American Revolution, and the $42,444,185 domestic debt. But on the question of the assumption of the $25,000,000 state debt by the federal government, they at once took their place among its opponents. After all, North Carolina had already levied taxes on its specie-scarce populace to meet its Revolutionary debts and was in no mood for a new assessment to aid more delinquent states. Their own legislature condemned the bill by declaring that assumption of state debts without the state's consent "would be an infringement of the sovereignty of this state, and prove eventually injurious and oppressive to the same, dangerous to its interests." [1] Accordingly it instructed its representatives to vote against such a measure. Her congressmen complied; her senators defied their instructions.

Even the nationalistic Davie wrote James Iredell in April, 1790, in regard to the Assumption Act, that inasmuch as he was "tremblingly alive to everything that may threaten the prosperity of the government," he feared that "such bold policies are rather unfitted to its infant resources." [2] Yet this "bold policy" was agreed upon by Southerners in exchange for the Federalist vote to locate the capitol on the banks of the Potomac River—the first piece of log-rolling in the national political arena.

Davie's stand on Hamilton's Excise Tax on spirituous liquors can be read between the lines in a letter to Hamilton himself, with whom he had had "a slight acquaintance" during his service at the Constitutional Convention in Philadelphia. Davie's objection to the excise was the requirement that it be paid in specie. To alleviate this injustice he sought Hamilton's advice on addressing Congress on the possibility of reissuing the state's paper money in the revenue of the United States collected in the state. This paper money, he wrote, had first been emitted "for the express purpose of paying the Continental line; the second to purchase Tobacco to pay the interest of the Federal debt." Both emissions, amounting to two hundred thousand pounds,

A Federalist Star at its Zenith

were made a tender in discharge of private contracts and had been so received. Therefore, a reissuance of this money would "be highly beneficial" to the state and "not injurious" to the federal government: "the paper money which is now generally at ten shillings to the dollar would rise instantly to *par*, a benefit the people would attribute to its proper cause; the commercial part of the State would be relieved from great and very distressing difficulties, and the demand for *specie* created by the duties would no longer operate injuriously on the value of our paper money; it would effectually remove the only rational ground of complaint made against the excise in the interior and western parts of the State, that is the difficulty or as they say impossibility, of procuring specie sufficient to pay that Tax: And would also prevent a very delicate and perhaps dangerous question that must otherwise soon arise on execution issuing from the Federal Const." [3]

There is no available evidence as to Davie's stand on the first United States Bank, but it may safely be assumed that he followed the Federalist line, agreeing with the two North Carolina senators.

It was the national judiciary system, as set up by the Judiciary Act of 1789, which was Davie's chief object of attack on the national level. This act, implementing the judicial powers outlined in Article III of the Constitution, set up a Supreme Court consisting of a chief justice and five associate justices and created three circuit courts and thirteen district courts. The greatest objection to the act was the provision by which, in a number of cases, the decisions of state courts might be taken on a writ of error to the United States Supreme Court for final settlement. State-rightsmen throughout the country deplored this usurpation of power. Many Federalists joined in the storm of protest. Davie himself complained that the act was "so defective in point of arrangement, and so obscurely drawn or expressed, that, in my opinion, it would disgrace the composition of the meanest legislature of the States." [4]

It is not surprising, therefore, that Davie declined an appointment as judge of the Federal Court for the District of North Carolina in the late spring of 1790.[5] Commenting on the appointment, Davie wrote Iredell that though he was "anxious to escape from 'our d—d Judges,' the salary was so paltry that he was constrained to decline." [6] Instead, he recommended his brother-in-law, John Sitgreaves, whose "situation and prospects would both be accomodated." In Davie's view, "his character as a Gentleman—as a public man in the offices he has filled is respectable, and I cannot help hoping that he will meet the approbation of the President." [7] Colonel John Stokes received the appointment, but he died in October, 1790, and Sitgreaves was appointed in his stead.

As might also be expected, Davie sided with the Hamiltonian Anglophiles in regard to the approaching titanic struggle between aristocratic Britain and republican France. Notwithstanding the recent mortal battle with the Mistress of the Seas, Davie did not hesitate to endorse the writings and speeches of Edmund Burke, late champion of American liberty, when he took issue with the excesses of the French Revolution. Davie thought that Burke's "enlightened mind and superior talents have reflected honor upon human nature," but he did feel that "Mr. Burke may have carried his veneration for old establishments too far, and may not have made sufficient allowance for the imperfections of human nature in the conduct of the French Revolution." [8]

In the field of state politics, Davie abstained from running for the state legislature in 1790; but he did not hesitate to voice his opinion on all issues to Governor Alexander Martin and other leaders. His chief objectives at this time were the funding of the state debt, the calling in of all paper money emitted by the state, and the improvement of the state court system; the last-named he deemed "indispensably necessary." [9]

Indeed, he was "extremely chagrined at the want of decision and firmness in the legislature with respect to our State debt" and "had it exceedingly at Heart that they should fund every farthing we could raise," inasmuch as "we had no other means left to secure ourselves justice from the Hands of the U. States, and avoid the evils of the assumption." [10]

He was "exceedingly desirous too that something should be done with our paper money." The reasons for this he deemed so important that it was "ever an unpleasant thing to indulge in plain reflection on the *motives* of the Assembly for passing by this object," because it had "so much the aspect of *Knavery* or *Folly* that it might be easily mistaken for either." [11]

A Federalist Star at its Zenith

The question of reform of the court system had been a trying one since the law of 1777, implementing the brief mandate of the Constitution of 1776. This law had provided for three superior court judges and had created six judicial districts, each with a court town where a superior court should be held twice a year. Morganton and Fayetteville, in 1782 and 1787, had been added as court towns for two additional circuits. To alleviate the hardships of this set-up, the General Assembly in 1790 provided for east and west ridings of four districts and two judges each.[12]

Yet this reform, Davie wrote Haywood, "cannot stand as it is—a mere piece of disjointed ground-work"—far from what he had wished —but he did hope it would "lay the foundation of that fabric which I have long and anxiously been desiring to see raised."[13]

In an effort to correct some of these abuses, Davie, despite his crowded law practice, decided to run for the next General Assembly, especially in order to put the court system "on a better footing."[14] Rated by James Iredell as one of "the two best lawyers in the state" (along with Alfred Moore), Davie was in a superior position to recognize and correct its defects.[15] Moreover, he had been recognized as the person of most "consequence" in the preceding Assembly of 1789.[16]

Davie's candidacy was tantamount to election. He accordingly took his seat as a member from the borough of Halifax, December 9, 1791.[17] A member of most of the important routine and non-routine committees, he was one of the most active members of the Assembly, but his influence was decidedly less than it had been in 1789. James Iredell received word, in fact, that Davie "became very unpopular" during this session and came within an ace of being embroiled in a duel. He and John Hamilton, of Edenton, "had high words in the House" over an unrevealed question, and Davie observed "that some personal reflections had been made" by Hamilton and he was going to procure "private satisfaction." Hamilton at once replied across the house, "any time & place" Davie thought proper, but, "to every person's astonishment," nothing further happened.[18]

It is clear that a number of stands taken by Davie alienated him from the more liberal elements in the Assembly. For one, there was the old question of the return of Loyalist property. Davie himself presented the petitions of John Hamilton, his Britannic Majesty's Consul for

WILLIAM R. DAVIE

Virginia, and of Archibald Hamilton and Co., "late merchants of Halifax." Davie sought the repeal of the confiscation laws under which their property had been seized and for the refund of over £73,000 allegedly due them. The petition was referred to the committee on public bills and sent to the Senate, where it was killed.[19]

Anathema to the Western forces also was his bill to bolster the obligation of contract [20] and his votes to block the formation of more counties in the West in order to give more equitable representation in the Assembly to that section. He accordingly voted against the division of Wilkes County in the West, but favored dividing the Eastern county of Dobbs and the piedmont county of Caswell, whose inhabitants were more Eastern-minded.[21] Nor did he approve of raising the salary of members of the Commons to twenty-five shillings per day. Also in line with the sentiments of the Eastern aristocrats was his resolution to the effect that United States senators should be bound by the instructions of the legislature,[22] which of course was dominated by the Easterners. But, interestingly enough, he did an about-face on this question when he ran for Congress in 1803.

Davie favored the participation of the state government in internal improvements and voted to cut a canal joining the Pasquotank River in this state and the Elizabeth in Virginia, a proposal rejected by a vote of 39 to 46.[23] Also of a constructive nature was his bill "to advance the administration of justice by erecting courts of chancery," which was passed and sent to the Senate, but was killed there.[24]

Realizing the great difficulties of a peripatetic capital, Davie introduced a bill to implement the ordinance passed by the Hillsborough convention in July, 1788, to establish a permanent capital for the meetings of the Assembly and the official residence of the chief officials of the state. This act barely slipped through, by a vote of 59 to 57 in the House.[25] Not content to rest on these laurels, Davie nominated his old friend, Richard Bennehan, as one of the commissioners of the public buildings and advised the other members who were present at Newbern to advertise "as early as possible in the Richmond and Philadelphia papers" for an "undertaker" of these buildings. He hoped they could secure one from New York or Philadelphia, because "the work would not only be executed better, but with more certainty" and they would also bring workmen "sufficient to despatch it at once."[26]

A Federalist Star at its Zenith

The commission, on April 2, 1792, purchased the Joel Lane plantation of a thousand acres near the Wake County Courthouse and on this site laid off the new capital city of Raleigh. The cornerstone of the capitol building was laid in the fall of that year. Two years later Richard Dobbs Spaight was able to set up his executive offices in the new structure, and on December 30 the legislature met there for the first time.

A review of these accomplishments indicates that Davie could not have been very unpopular in this session, which he described as "tedious and irksome."[27] After all, he was able, by the sheer force of his persuasive powers and personal magnetism, to wangle a loan of $10,000 from an impecunious and tight-pursed Assembly. No mean accomplishment in itself.[28]

Perhaps disgusted with the proceedings of the "tedious and irksome" sessions of the Assembly, Davie spent the following year attending to his plantation, enjoying his growing family, of two sons and a daughter, and continuing an active practice of the law.

In August of 1792 Colonel Davie and Willie Jones, their wives and children "and other ladies" all paid a visit to Salem, the Moravian center. Probably they were on their way to or from the famous mountain summer resort then called Warm Springs (now Hot Springs) which Davie was later to visit for the curative properties of its waters. In honor of the distinguished visitors—Davie was singled out as "a good friend of the Brethren"—a "public singstunde," or song fest, was held in English "in which the hymns were sung alternately by the choir and the congregation." The following day the Moravian schoolboys held a "lovefeast," attended by the visitors, who "spoke enthusiastically of the pleasure they had in seeing so many children and hearing them sing so nicely."[29]

That winter state politics engaged the interest if not the active participation of Davie, who journeyed down to Newbern in November to attend a Federal Court, which, to his disgust, did not meet. But at least he was able to get the inside story on the political machinations of the Democratic-Republican legislature. The Federalists were successful in supplanting Governor Alexander Martin, whose constitutional term had expired, by the victory of Richard Dobbs Spaight over William Lenoir. Spaight thus became the first native-born governor of the state, though he was Glasgow-trained. The real struggle, however, came over the post of United States senator, vacated by the venerable Federalist, Samuel Johnston, the state's first senator. John Leigh and Thomas Blount, members of the Commons from Edgecombe County, Federalist John Steele, of Salisbury, and the recent governor, Alexander Martin, composed the list of candidates for the post. There resulted, according to Davie, "a strange coalition" between the friends of Lenoir and Leigh, with "the heterogeneous mixture" of Martin's friends, to defeat John Steele.[30]

The contest was heated. On the first ballot, described as "a mere *essay*," the two Cape Fear districts refrained from voting. On the second and third, they generally, along with Halifax District and "a few friends" from Salisbury, voted for Steele. At this point, Leigh withdrew his name and Blount engrossed his votes, carrying the latter with 63 votes, a little ahead of Steele, who had 52.[31]

The next move aroused the scorn of Davie, who wrote that "nothing could equal the activity and scandalous behavior of several of Martin's friends," who, "not willing to step forward openly themselves... found a proper tool" in Montford Stokes, whose talents and principles Davie deplored. Stokes's attack on Steele was vitriolic. He charged Steele "with *deception* and *duplicity*" in his public character. This charge he based on Steele's writing of "two letters to two different men, containing different principles and *contradictory* assertions." Martin also accused Steele of political views and principles that were "all aristocratical, xc., nay that you were the devoted ———..——— of Mr. Hamilton." Later, such epithets as "vain, pompous, arrogant" were hurled at him. As a result, "so completely had that wretch [Martin] poisoned the minds of the Edenton members" that they would not even examine the reports. The Cape Fear men and the Westerners were also influenced, and Martin was chosen. The efforts of David Caldwell, of Iredell, Major Joseph Dixon, of Lincoln, and Lewis Beard, of Salisbury, in behalf of Steele were in vain.[32]

Davie was "damnably mortified" to see "that despicable creature" prevail over Steele and "felt for the disgrace and degradation" of his country. But resignedly he realized that "every thing is not possible at all times in politicks; I am strongly inclined to fatalism of late, and have believed for some time that God almighty made *that man* on purpose to disgrace this country." In somewhat the same vein was Davie's condemnation of the Senate whose actions "would make men

A Federalist Star at its Zenith

suspect the Messiah, they will never trust any man there twice if they can help it."[33]

At any rate the erstwhile opponent of the Constitution won over John Steele, one of its ardent supporters. But Steele was soon rewarded by George Washington in his appointment as Comptroller General of the Treasury.

While Davie was sojourning in Newbern, a signal honor was conferred on him when the Grand Lodge of North Carolina, meeting in Newbern, elected him Grand Master of the Grand Lodge of North Carolina and Tennessee on December 14, 1792, and he was duly installed by proxy on December 30 of that year. In the ensuing years he played an active role and was annually re-elected Grand Master for eight terms.[34] No doubt he was present at the celebration of the anniversary of St. John in Halifax, in December, 1796. In the evening, it was reported, "a brilliant assemblage of Ladies and Gentlemen convened at the Ball Room" of the Royal White Hart Lodge and "after having spent some time in festive mirth and social glee, partook of an elegant repast provided for the occasion."[35]

When Davie finally retired he received "an unanimous vote of thanks while at the head of the Craft" and a certificate "as a testimony of the high estimation in which his talents and virtues are by us held, as a man and a Mason."[36]

Though Davie and his friends were unable to get Steele elected, Davie was able, by posting himself at the door of the court house during both days of the election, to bring about the re-election of his friend, John Baptiste Ashe, as United States congressman.[37]

The most important constitutional case in the pre-Marshall days of the Supreme Court of the United States—and the one which led to the adoption of the Eleventh Amendment—evoked great ridicule from Davie. The facts in this case, *Chisholm* v. *Georgia*, were that the heirs of Alexander Chisholm, a citizen of Georgia, had brought suit against the state of Georgia for payment of a private claim. The majority of the United States Supreme Court, led by Chief Justice John Jay and James Wilson, upheld the right of the court to hear suits by citizens of one state against another state. Justice James Iredell, however, wrote a vigorous and brilliant defense, in which he upheld the doctrine of state rights.[38]

William R. Davie

In his dissenting opinion, Iredell introduced the doctrine of divided sovereignty, that the states were sovereign as to all powers not expressly delegated to the federal government by the Constitution. The Supreme Court in 1890 declared Iredell's opinion to be the correct interpretation.[39]

This dissent was popular in North Carolina and in the nation, and, as the first significant state rights opinion of the Supreme Court, it became the judicial basis of state rights policy and the cue to the most powerful political principle of the Democratic-Republicans.[40]

Davie alone, of all the Federalists, upheld Iredell and in writing to him sprinkled his judicial opinion with barbs of sarcastic wit so characteristic of his writing from this period to his death.

"I confess," he wrote, "I read some of these arguments and particularly that by Mr. Wilson with astonishment: however, the scope and propriety of this elaborate production called an argument, were expressly reserved for the contemplation of 'a *few*, a *very few*, comprehensive minds;' and, perhaps, notwithstanding the tawdry ornament and poetical imagery with which it is loaded and bedizened, it may still be very 'profound.' On this I shall give no opinion; but as a law argument it has certainly the merit of being truly '*original*.' His definition of the American States as sovereignties is more like an epic poem than a Judge's argument, and we look in vain for legal principles or logical conclusions.

"The illustration which he has drawn from the relation of the word subject to the word sovereign, as contradistinguished from the appelation of *citizen*, as a correlative of the American Government, is no better than a contemptible play upon words, like his 'collection of original sovereigns:' indeed, speaking professionally, or as he says '*politically* and *classically*,' this whole argument of his seems to be the rhapsody of some visionary theorist, and entirely unworthy of my former idea of that man.

"Mr. Jay, whose talents appear to be of a superior genious, appears to be also taken by the novelty of this idea, and gravely gives his sanction to the solecism of 'sovereigns without subjects'—that is, without sovereignty. To use the style of Mr. Wilson, 'this trancendentally sublime' antithesis seems to be transplanted from some speech in the Jacobin Club, or the satire of Peter Pindar, and looks quite like an exotic in his Honor's argument.

A Federalist Star at its Zenith

"The supposed spirit or design of the Constitution is a dangerous guide in a case of this sort, where mere general principles or objects are expressed in general terms: there is no doubt but it does not follow, that although it would be *'honest'* to comply voluntarily with such contract, that it would be *wise* or *useful* for the Federal Government to enforce it. The policy of no nation has gone so far as to enforce every *moral* obligation; and the instances where matters of mere *moral right* have submitted to the policy of institutions, or the general interests of the community, are numerous even in the municipal laws of our own country; and with respect to maintaining suits of this kind against a State, I am not only clear there is no authority beyond the opinion of the Court for such a doctrine, but that it is neither warranted by necessity nor policy." [41]

Four days after this, Davie was in Fayetteville, presumably attending court. From here he wrote the only extant letter to his wife. It reveals something of the heartache of long days and months of separation:

"Fayetteville June 16th '93

"My Dear girl I thought to have been on my way by this time, but in spite of all I could do the business is not yet finished but promises to close in a day or two more—and you know my reasons why I cannot leave them—

"I received your letter by the last post, and flatter myself I shall receive another in an hour or two, nothing could support my situation but the assurance of that lively attachment which time cannot diminish. I have sworn an hundred times that I would never be a member again, nothing but absolute necessity shall ever oblige me to make so great a sacrifice—This [ends?] the case now I hope it will not be so again.

"No man ever suffered more than I do on being separated from my family, no man has been more unfortunate in this respect, there is nothing I long so much for, as the uninterrupted enjoyment of family life, it has more charm for me, than all that acclaim or ambition can suggest.

"My Health has never been [settled?] since I have been here but I have been careful and have not reason [torn] complain more than others.

WILLIAM R. DAVIE

"I hope you and my childr [torn] continue well—Don't send [torn] away till I get home.

"Farewell my dear [torn] I shall not [illegible]—
"Your Husband
"W R DAVIE" [42]

But these endearing sentiments did not prevent Davie's again representing the borough of Halifax in the House of Commons in December, 1793, which met for the last time in Fayetteville. During this session, he was placed on the important committees of finance, public bills, and the first subcommittee on finance, as well as on a number of joint committees, the most interesting of which was a committee which drew up a law, which was enacted, "to extend the right of trial by jury to slaves, and to make provisions for the payment of outlawed and executed slaves." [43]

Among the important bills he introduced in this session, other than those pertaining to the University, were those to direct "the mode of proceeding upon impeachments" and to establish courts of chancery. Ever a friend of the Moravians, he voted against levying a tax of one shilling on "all Moravians, Quakers, Dunkards, and Menonites ... between the age of eighteen and forty-five" who had been exempted from military duty. He naturally voted "yea" on the successful resolution that the next legislature should convene at Raleigh, the new seat of government, on December 1, 1794. He also cast an affirmative vote for an act to establish a militia in the state—an act occasioned by the depredations on our commerce by Great Britain in its struggle with the new French Republic.[44]

The imminence of a declared war against Great Britain induced the legislature to pass an act for the establishment of a militia in the state. Colonel Davie * of course favored such a move and was commissioned by Governor Spaight, January 8, 1794, as a major general to command the third, or Halifax, division of the state militia. The other three divisions were commanded by Thomas Brown, John Steele, and Frederick Hargett.[45]

As the commanding officer of the Halifax division, Davie obtained

---

* He had been commissioned as Lieutenant Colonel Commandant of the Militia Regiment of Cavalry in the District of Halifax by Richard Caswell on January 6, 1787.—Original in the W. L. Saunders Papers, S.H.C.

A Federalist Star at its Zenith

Governor Spaight's permission "under the present prospects of an immediate war" to have returns made in each district of the men and the available arms, muskets, bayonets, cartouch boxes and cannon. Spaight feared that few would be left from the Revolution and lamented that the militia had been "so little attended to since the peace, that they have become merely a name." It would therefore "require considerable exertions of the officers... to make them provide themselves with arms xc and attend more strictly to their musters and discipline." Davie accordingly issued orders for raising, organizing, and equipping his division, although the *North-Carolina Journal* was of the opinion that "there is every reason to believe that there will be little occasion for the service of this detachment, as our differences between the United States and Great-Britain will probably be speedily and honourably accommodated." [46]

So threatening did the situation become that Governor Spaight called a special session of the Assembly to meet in Newbern in July, 1794, at Tryon's Palace—the last Assembly held in that historic building. At this session, which Davie did not attend, the governor reported on "the piratical depredations committed on the commerce of the United States by the British," which had "increased to so great a degree as to occasion a very serious alarm throughout the Union." To meet the threat of war, Congress passed an act to detach 80,000 men from the militia. North Carolina's quota was to be 7,331. The Francophile, anti-British legislature promptly acceded to the request.[47]

In December of 1794, Davie, representing the town of Halifax, again made his way to the General Assembly, which met on the thirtieth in the new "seat of government"—Raleigh. Having been accustomed to the polite society and reasonably good accommodations in Newbern and Fayetteville, the assemblymen had a trying time in their new capital, with only a hastily thrown-up tavern or two for lodging. But at least the new State House, designed by Rhody Atkins, was permanent.[48] Davie, aside from serving on the usual routine committees such as those on privileges and elections and on finance, made his influence felt as chairman of two important special committees. One of these considered a bill "to increase the staple produce of this state, and to provide for the public safety by granting encouragement to certain manufactures." Davie, as chairman, reported out a resolution, adopted by the House, recommending the encouragement of these measures, because it was "unquestionably the duty of the legislature of an enlightened republic, by all reasonable and practicable means to animate the industry of the people, and by bounties to give their efforts a proper direction." The House also concurred with Chairman Davie's resolution to appropriate 416 £ 1s 4d for additional improvements in the new state house.[49]

During this session, Davie was responsible for the introduction of an important act dealing with slavery, entitled an act "to prevent the owners of slaves from hiring to them their time, to make compensation to patrols, and to restrain the abuses committed by free negroes and mulattoes." He also voted to prevent the further importation of slaves and "indented servants of colour" into the state—almost a decade and a half before the Federal bar on importation of slaves.[50]

Again, he introduced a bill to establish courts of chancery (which was successful) and such bills as one "prescribing the residence of the Governor," one for the regulation of the city of Raleigh, and one "to prevent gaming tables in the neighbourhood" of the University. He also introduced the resolution for the adoption of the Eleventh Amendment to the Constitution, a position in accord with his sentiments in regard to the *Chisholm* v. *Georgia* decision. As a result, the judicial power of the United States would be not "construed to extend to any suit commenced against a state by citizens of another state."[51]

At this session, Davie "felt considerable anxiety" over the choice of a United States senator to succeed Benjamin Hawkins. Timothy Bloodworth, "the positive Republican," "the blacksmith politician," was chosen by a single vote over the more astute and accomplished Alfred Moore. Davie, who had the state's "reputation at heart," confided to James Iredell that he had already suffered great "mortification" on this account. No doubt he meant Bloodworth when he stated that the "gentleman you mention has good dispositions; and I believe is strongly attached to the interests of his country; and is not deficient in integrity and independence." These qualities, according to Davie, "may render a man harmless, but with these qualifications alone he would be useless." In fact, he concluded, "our whole representation is but a type of Shakespeare's old man—'sans teeth, sans eyes, sans everything.'"[52]

In a more optimistic mood was Davie in February, 1795, although he had been confined since his return from Raleigh with "a kind of pleurecy." Writing to his friend, Richard Bennehan, with whom his son, Hyder Ali, was spending the winter, Davie congratulated his correspondent "on the prospects of a lasting good understanding being likely to be established between this country and Great Britain" as a result of the Jay Treaty. He reported that the terms were said to be "liberal and particularly advantageous to the U. States."[53]

By September, however, his tone had become more somber and foreboding—a change partially induced by his personal misfortune. His family had been "more sickly than usual" and his youngest son had been "the first victim of the season in this part of the Country." This represented to him "one of those dreadful strokes in human life," one which he sincerely hoped Judge Iredell would never feel.[54]

Meanwhile, the exact terms of the Jay Treaty had been revealed to the American populace, and the Jeffersonian Republicans lost no time in vicious attacks on the Federalists and the Washington administration, which, in their view, had stopped far short of their hopes, even though it delayed war for another eighteen years. North Carolina strenuously objected to its unfavorable commercial clauses, to the provisions for the liquidation of British debts, to the failure to provide for slaves seized by the British during the Revolution, and to the clause which permitted aliens to hold lands in the United States. The last-named might jeopardize titles to property confiscated in the Granville District.[55]

To Davie the crisis over the American reception of the treaty seemed "the most delicate and important since the organization of our government." He reported that "the antifederalists and the personal enemies of Administration have rallied with astonishing activity," and he feared that they would "make their last effort to shake the Government." The treatment of John Jay he considered "a satire upon humanity; no calculation on the baseness of Human Nature would have produced so shameless a degree of ingratitude."[56]

But Davie took a solitary stand in the state—with the exception of William Barry Grove, who voted in the House of Representatives for the appropriation necessary to carry the treaty into effect. Even Samuel Johnston denounced the treaty as "a hasty performance," which reflected no credit on "Mr. Jay's abilities as a negotiator."[57]

The treaty, however, was finally ratified by the Senate June 24, 1795. Davie was elated over "the triumph of reason and principle" and the fact that "the leaders of anarchy and faction in both Houses have been disappointed." He hoped that "our growing prosperity will continue to give these croaking prophets the lie."[58] Yet the Federalist party suffered a serious blow in the state. Ten Republican congressmen were elected in 1795, and the Republican legislature elected Bloodworth over Alfred Moore and the Republican Samuel Ashe as governor.[59] By the following spring Jefferson's adherents had real ammunition for the coming presidential election. Davie wrote satirically to John Haywood that he was "in hourly expectation of hearing the dreadful explosion of the political Vesuvius in Philadelphia," where "they have been assiduously collecting combustibles of all sorts for three months past," and, if he was not "greatly mistaken... the phlogistic patriotism of our new-fangled republicans will not be much longer repressed." His conclusion was typical: "What a ridiculous farce is 'this world's mad business.'"[60]

With the growing opposition to the Federalist administration, it surprised no one that in the ensuing presidential election, the state gave eleven electoral votes to Thomas Jefferson, with only one (from the Cape Fear District), going to John Adams.[61]

Writing to Iredell on November 11, 1796, while the outcome of the election was still in doubt, Davie reported that "uncommon pains have indeed been taken by the Jacobin party to insure the election of Jefferson, particularly in the Southern States, and considerable hopes are entertained by them of Pennsylvania, where neither activity nor expense have been spared, etc. etc."[62]

On the state level, Willie Jones came out of political seclusion, and the three Blount brothers and Richard Dobbs Spaight, though staunch supporters of Washington, switched their political allegiance to Jefferson at this time. Davie believed that "with these men something ... may be done," and as he owed "nothing to any man or party in or belonging to the Federal Government," he felt himself "entirely at liberty to act without reserve in any direction the public good may require," and "any little good" he had would be exerted.[63]

This influence Davie attempted to exert in the Republican House of Commons, which met in November, 1796, in Raleigh. He was forthwith proposed for speaker, but was defeated by John Leigh, of Edgecombe. Few sessions accomplished less. Davie again served on such committees as the one on finance, one to consider Governor

A Federalist Star at its Zenith

Ashe's message, one to "view the several acts of Assembly for the regulation of ordinancies," *et cetera*. Two of these committees do deserve passing attention. A joint committee, of which Davie was a member, prepared a "warm address" of appreciation to George Washington upon his retirement. This address, unanimously passed, was regarded by the Federalists as a rebuke to Nathaniel Macon, the torchbearer of Jefferson, and Willie Jones, who had voted against a similar address in Congress. Davie felt it had been "very indifferently written," but at least it was "warm, affectionate and respectful; and will surely contradict in plain and strong terms the ... conduct of some of our members of Congress; and let *Posterity* (for whose good opinion these gentlemen appear to be anxious) see that they were actuated by their own factious views, not the sense or feelings of their constituents." Davie further vented his spleen by saying it was now clear "that this unprincipled faction are determined to embitter even the *last drop* of the Presidential cup; and although their public conduct appears to receive its direction from personal animosity, I think it is not to be expected that their political principles or dispositions will be meliorated by their late disappointment." [64]

Another joint committee in which he was vitally interested was "to report a plan for the improvement of the inland navigation of the state." To implement this, Davie presented the report of Thomas Amis, Eaton Pugh, and Willis Alston, commissioners appointed by the previous Assembly to report on the practicality of improving the inland navigation of the Roanoke River. This report was referred to the former committee and sent to the Senate. Davie also presented a bill to improve the navigation of the river "from the great or main falls [at the present site of Roanoke Rapids] to the Virginia line." [65]

The preceding year, Davie had joined "a number of Gentlemen who were desirous of promoting the navigation of Roanoke River." They had employed two men to make a survey of the Falls and to estimate "the expence that would be incurred in making an easy, safe, and compleat passage for batteaux, or ordinary river burthen." As a result of this survey, Davie, Willie and Allen Jones, Nicholas Long, and John Sitgreaves proposed that "the several neighbourhoods or counties interested in the navigation of the Roanoke, should send Commissioners as Representatives to the town of Halifax on the 29th day of

October" to adopt proper measures therefor before the meeting of the legislature.[66]

The legislature granted Davie's charter, and in February, 1797, the newly-created Roanoke Navigation Company opened its books of subscription. At a general meeting of the subscribers on October 23, 1797, Willie Jones was chosen president. Among the directors were Davie, Samuel Johnston, and Allen Jones. It was reported that 256 shares had been subscribed at one hundred dollars a share, and the Board therefore agreed to proceed in person to survey the falls and make recommendations. The resulting improvements constituted the chief transportation facility of the Roanoke Valley until the coming of the Wilmington and Weldon Railroad in 1840.[67]

In the Assembly of 1796, Davie cast several votes of interest. He voted in favor of establishing "a court of errors and appeals" (one of his pet objectives), which was again rejected, and also he favored making "further provision for the widows of intestates." But his vote was in the negative on a bill "to authorize and empower any person or persons to emancipate and set free such people of colour as they hold in slavery"—a bill that was rejected 41 to 63.[68]

Finally, as chairman of a committee to consider "the petition of sundry persons," who were owners of Tennessee lands which had been since ceded to the Indians by the United States, he won the concurrence of the House in his recommendation that Congress was "bound by every principle of justice and equity to grant compleat and ample redress" to these petitioners. The state's representatives in Congress were also requested to use "their utmost endeavours" in their behalf.[69]

But affairs of more moment were in the air. The United States had temporarily staved off war with Great Britain, but her relations with Republican and Directory France had worsened since 1793. By February, 1797, Davie confessed to "some uneasiness respecting the present aspect of our affairs with the French: these madmen possess nothing upon which you can certainly calculate, no moral principle, no fixed political data: they seem to have no system but anarchy, no plan but plunder and military tyranny."[70]

As a result of the "X.Y.Z." affair of that year, the seizure of American ships, and the unfriendly actions by the French, an undeclared naval war was in full swing by 1798. Congress and President

A Federalist Star at its Zenith

John Adams immediately took action. Among other defense measures, the Navy Department was created and Washington was called from retirement to command the new provisional army. In North Carolina, Governor Ashe, acting on the order of Congress of June 24, 1797, called for a detachment of 7,268 men (the state's quota) to be commanded by Major General William R. Davie and to be divided into two brigades, to be commanded by Brigadier Generals Martin Armstrong and Stephen Moore.[71]

As commander of this division, Major General Davie issued, June 25, 1798, a stirring order to the officers of his two brigades. In it he referred to the "continued system of tyranny, injustice, and depredation" by the French, in spite of the efforts of the President to preserve peace. The French had replied with arrogance, insolence, and outrage. Therefore, he stated, it behooved his officers to rise up with alacrity and zeal, fully aware of their "sacred trust of avenging the injuries and defending the honour of their country." In his peroration he relied "with confidence upon that ardent and enlightened patriotism, which I often witnessed during the late war, to evince to the world that the exertions of the militia will always be commensurate with the exigencies of their country, and that the spirit which established our *national independence*, will be adequate to the protection of our *national rights*."[72]

At least one company—the Scotland-Neck Volunteer Company of Infantry—expressed in the *North-Carolina Journal* "their warmest approbation" of the sentiments expressed by Davie, to which Davie replied very graciously the following week in the same paper.[73]

Meanwhile Secretary of War James McHenry wrote Davie on July 18 that President Adams had that day appointed him a brigadier general of the provisional army. This, as McHenry realized, put Davie in a "delicate situation," because he could not hold an office under both governments, but, in consideration of "the general interest, and the effect it may have on the public spirit," McHenry had no doubt of his "determination conforming with the true interest of the Country."[74]

Davie found himself embarrassed by his appointment. After all, he had just been elected to the House of Commons for that year, he was a major general of the state militia, and he was being "warmly solicited by the Friends of Government to allow himself to be appointed Governor." His friend, Federalist Congressman William Barry Grove, of Fayetteville, agreed with Davie that he could "serve the country more effectually in times like the present" by remaining in the state's service, especially because it seemed unlikely that the Provisional Army would be called. But General Davie assured Grove that "he would prefer the service of the United States—when it is certain *active and real service will be required.*" When that day came, Grove wrote McHenry, he was sure Davie would be found "an excellent officer and that he will be ready at all times to serve his country in such a manner as is most likely to conduce to the public interest." Grove also assured the Secretary that Davie, who had useful and reliable "knowledge of men & characters in this state," would be glad to make recommendations for military appointments.[75]

Davie was assured by McHenry of Adams' "full approbation and acquiesence" to hold the federal appointment in abeyance until his services in the field became "indispensible to our country." Meanwhile he requested Davie to forward him at once the names of "ten or twelve Gentlemen...best qualified for Captains" and twenty-four each for lieutenants and ensigns, "whose local situation, and popularity, would enable them, to raise companies, and whose attachment to the Government is unequivocal." McHenry also requested the names of deserving Revolutionary officers who had "never shewn a decided inclination, towards France, or French principles."[76]

In accordance with this request, Davie sent out letters to responsible officers throughout the state asking for recommendations for these posts. His criteria were that they should be "warm and attached friends to their country, & untainted in any manner by French politics or principles," and he preferred that they be "single men of personal popularity & connections," with "some education, a high sense of Honor, and genteel habits connected with native energy and a robust temperament."[77]

George Washington himself was deeply concerned over the selection of officers in the South. He felt confident that Generals Charles Cotesworth Pinckney and Bushrod Washington would be careful in their choices in South Carolina and Georgia and, "from the character of General Davie, I should hope he would not be less attentive to those to be taken from No. Carolina." He was dubious, however, of the situation in Tennessee, and as to Kentucky he was "more at a loss to

A Federalist Star at its Zenith

express any opinion." A week later Washington asked McHenry to request General Pinckney to call on "Brigr.-General Davie on his route to Charleston, and, after a full & free conversation with him on fit characters to officer the quota of Troops from the States of No. Carolina (and Tennessee, if he can aid in it) to inform you of the result *without delay*." Washington throughout was afraid that "most of the candidates brought forward by the opposition members possess sentiments similar to their own, and might poison the army by disseminating them." [78]

A fortnight later, Washington wrote Davie (or took "the liberty to address him," as he phrased it) that he was calling upon the General Officers in each state for their aid in this selection, "the presumption being, that the Reputation of the Army, in which they may have to act a conspicuous part, and their own honor and responsibility will put them above local attachments, and self-interested views, and, consequently, produce more circumspection in the selection of fit and proper Characters for Officers than is likely to be obtained by any other means." To assist Davie, he enclosed "a list of all the field Officers of the No. Carolina line, who served to the close of the Revolutionary war;—and a list of the present applicants for Commissioners." Washington advised that "where Officers of *celebrity* in the Revolutionary Army can be obtained; who are yet in the prime of life,—habituated to no bad causes—and well disposed, that a preferance ought to be given to them." Next to these should be chosen "gentlemen of Character, liberal Education,—and, as far as the fact can be ascertained from experience, men who will face danger in any shape it can appear;—for if we have a land war, it will be sharp and severe." He also added that "all violent opposers of the Government, and French Partisans should be avoided; or they will disseminate the poison of their principles in the Army, and split, what ought to be a band of brothers, into Parties." [79]

Davie replied by the earliest post that he would take the necessary measures to comply with the request, but meanwhile he wanted Washington to clarify whether these officers would be in the provisional army or "on the establishment," because some of the former officers declared "they had no intention of going into service unless the provisional army was raised, when they would consider it their duty to offer their services." [80]

WILLIAM R. DAVIE

Washington replied that he had consulted with Major General Alexander Hamilton and C. C. Pinckney in Philadelphia and they thought best, "from the want of knowledge of proper characters in the three Southern States," to postpone a selection there until General Pinckney, who delivered this letter in person, came down and consulted with Davie and Brigadier General Bushrod Washington.[81]

According to his many letters, Davie worked earnestly and assiduously at his assignment, sparing "no trouble or pains" to obtain the best qualified officers. His recommendations, approved by Pinckney when he came by to see him, were sent to Washington January 7, 1799.[82]

Davie was also concerned with the naval defense of the state. As a result of a letter from General Pinckney, requesting his "sentiments on the most advantageous mode" of protecting the Carolina coast, Davie wrote the merchant prince, John Gray Blount, to glean his opinion on the subject.[83]

With his many other occupations at this time, Davie also blossomed forth as an author in 1798. And, with the imminence of war with France, the publication came at a propitious time. Printed by Abraham Hodge of Halifax, the 180-page work was entitled *Instructions to be Observed for the Formation and Movements of the Cavalry*, but was generally referred to as Davie's *Instructions to the Cavalry*. No extant copies of the 1798 edition have been found.*

Originally designed, according to Davie's preface, for the use of his own regiment, the book was reprinted the following year on authority of the legislature, which authorized the governor to contract with the printer for 150 copies and to have them distributed in "equal proportion among the several officers commanding the different regiments of cavalry in the state, in such manner as he shall judge most convenient."[84]

Davie's preface set forth his purpose:

The importance of Cavalry in the southern states, was sufficiently evinced during the revolutionary war; and officers will observe with pleasure, that the late improvements have given this important branch

---

* A letter written from Raleigh, February 24, 1806, establishes the fact that there was an earlier edition. Further proof also appears in Davie's preface to the 1799 edition. See Stephen Beauregard Weeks, *The Press of North Carolina* (Brooklyn: Historical Printing Club, 1891), pp. 77-78.

A Federalist Star at its Zenith

of tactical knowledge the perfection of a regular system, in which the rules are few, plain, and simple, and adapted to the comprehension of every individual.

The instructions are carefully compiled from the latest European publications, and contain the most important of the modern improvements.

The advance notice of the publication, appearing in the *North-Carolina Journal*, May 13, 1799, reprinted the preface and proclaimed it "the most ample and complete system of cavalry tactics ever published in the United States." It "supposed" that the 150 copies would be "scarcely sufficient to supply the whole of the commissioned officers, and that these Instructions would be a desirable acquisition at the present crisis to private gentlemen." Therefore an extra number was being printed. It would be printed "on a good Paper, in a distinct and legible manner," would be "bound in boards," and sold in the principal towns of the state for one dollar to subscribers and $1.25 to non-subscribers. Later, several state weekly papers advertised it for sale. Davie also sent a copy to George Washington, who asked McHenry to "mention" his receiving it to Davie.*

By the summer of 1798, the Federalists—and many Republicans—had rallied behind the temporarily popular John Adams and were demanding redress for the insults and abuses of Republican France. Throughout the nation, the war fever was at its height. And, in line with these sentiments, the political pendulum in North Carolina swung over to the Federalist side.

By July 22, 1798, Davie could report to Iredell that the elections were going on "tolerably well" and predicted "an important change in favor of Government." He hoped, too, that "the Assembly will see the importance of appointing a man of business and energy Governor: in time of war it is the most important office in the State: in time of peace its duties may be performed by any body, even A. M. [Alexander Martin]."[85]

Davie did not rest idle, awaiting the results. Instead, he busied himself with disseminating to strategic men throughout the state the famous "X.Y.Z." papers comprising the dispatches from the Ameri-

---

* The Library of the City of New York, Reserved Books, has a copy bearing Washington's autograph. Also see Steiner, *James McHenry*, p. 411; Fitzpatrick (ed.), *Writings of George Washington*, XXXVII, 352.

can envoys in their humiliating encounter with the French Directory. He hoped they would serve as campaign ammunition by which to offset the false impressions conveyed by the North Carolina congressmen. In fact, he reported to Thomas Pickering, Secretary of State, that "the partisans of the French faction have been lately making extraordinary exertions in the Southern States, whether the elections are the sole object of these movements, I have not been able to learn, they certainly however deserve the attention of Government."[86]

By August 20 William Barry Grove gleefully reported that the elections were closed and that the changes were greater than he had expected—"and in every change of men there is a complete change in their political tenets, and in general a *vast increase* of weight of character & respectability of talents."[87]

When the votes were finally counted, the Federalists could claim a majority in the state Senate, a considerable increase (though not a majority) in the House of Commons, and the capture of six seats in Congress. Four of these, William Barry Grove (the incumbent), Joseph Dixon, William H. Hill, and Archibald Henderson, remained true to their party, but the other two, Richard Dobbs Spaight and David Stone, were to apostatize to the Republicans in their support of the repeal of the unpopular Alien and Sedition Acts.[88]

Mr. Secretary McHenry elatedly wrote Davie that he was "truly happy to learn the progress that has been made in N. Carolina in the developments of the principles which have actuated the French towards us, and the effects which it is likely to produce. A State so important as N. Carolina is, ought not to suffer its weight to be lost, or its consequences to be thought lightly of by the conduct of a few of its citizens."[89]

In the Assembly which met in November, 1798, in Raleigh, Samuel Johnston was expected to direct Federalist policy in the Senate; Davie, representing the borough of Halifax, was to uphold it in the House. Samuel Johnston, especially jubilant over the triumph of his party, wrote Iredell that "all the members with whom I have conversed are wonderfully federal, I say wonderful because I never conceived it possible there could be so universal a conversion in so short a space."[90]

Both houses formed the first day, November 19, and chose the two former speakers, Benjamin Smith and Mussendine Matthews, of the Senate and House respectively, without opposition. Johnston reported

A Federalist Star at its Zenith

that Senator Alexander Martin had appeared and was *"wonderfully federal"*; that Alfred Moore, a candidate for Martin's seat in the Senate, was "much less popular than I had reason to expect, tho I believe he may be appointed a Judge, which his friends say he will accept"; and that "Davie is talked of for Governor and will meet with no opposition if he inclines to accept it." [91]

In a later letter Johnston wrote that Davie arrived in Raleigh November 27, but had been engaged all the following day—in company with General Pinckney—in reviewing the local militia. He reiterated that Davie was "spoken of for Governor, but I have not heard with certainty whether he means to accept it," but he did "heartily wish he may." [92]

On November 29 Davie finally took his seat and on December 3 was nominated, together with Benjamin Williams, for the governorship. The following day, as a result of a joint ballot of the two houses, Davie was elected "by a majority of votes." [93]

Davie accepted "this honorable testimony" with "great sensibility ... of the public confidence in the present situation of our country; and in accepting this appointment, of so much responsibility at the present crisis, it gives me particular consolation, that in the principal difficulties which may be anticipated in my administration, I may assure myself of the firm support of the Legislature and my fellow citizens." [94]

On December 7, Davie, "attended by several officers of the state, waited on the two Houses," which had convened at noon in the Commons Hall and took the oath of office as chief magistrate of North Carolina. The following day, upon the resignation of Davie as Major-General of the Third Division, the House nominated Stephen W. Carney of Halifax to fill his place, to which were later added William Brickell, of Louisburg, and Samuel Benton, of Granville County. Carney won the election by a majority of votes.[95]

CHAPTER X

His Excellency the Governor

WHEN he assumed the governorship, Davie had certain personal problems to work out. He had to find someone to take over his legal practice, a builder to construct a house for him in Raleigh, and someone to superintend the management of his plantations in Halifax. He managed to get Duncan Cameron to attend to his cases in the Hillsborough court. Judging by the announcement of his frequent visits to Halifax—which lasted for several weeks at a time—he personally superintended his business there. As builder of his Raleigh residence, he employed Rhody Atkins, architect of the first State House, who was also engaged in building the finest mansion in Raleigh, Haywood Hall, for Davie's intimate friend, Treasurer John Haywood. This choice proved to be a mistake, because of the inebriety of Atkins—"everything is generally lost upon a drunkard, even the liquor he drinks," wrote Davie to Haywood. The house was not completed until at least the latter part of July.[1]

Although the Federalists had made signal triumphs, the Republicans were able to secure their choice as United States senator. The race boiled down to Alfred Moore, of Wilmington (late Attorney General), Alexander Martin (the incumbent), and the strong Republican, Jesse Franklin, of Surry County (a former congressman). Information is obscure as to why Moore was suddenly dropped. Samuel Johnston said that he preferred being Judge of the Superior Court—to which position he was promptly elevated after the Senate race.* Congressman Richard Dobbs Spaight, however, was dubious and wrote John Haywood that he could not "see through the politics that made Moore a judge instead of sending him to the Senate of the United States, for which post he is certainly better qualified than Franklin." He continued:

"There certainly must have been some jugling in it. Was Davie afraid of Martin and kept Moore out of sight as Senator, least M. should oppose him as Governor? What other reason could induce him to drop Moore for the Senate after so hard a struggle was made for him as a senator four years ago, and the Idea of his offering again has been uniformly kept up?" [2]

The Federalists, at any rate, backed the "wonderfully Federal" Alexander Martin. The Republicans, irate over his voting for the Alien and Sedition Acts, ditched him and succeeded in electing Jesse Franklin, who was later described as "not so scholarly as Martin, nor so eloquent as many others, but of solid worth, typifying the best North Carolina characteristics—integrity and honesty of purpose, united with intelligence, broad views and patriotism." [3]

Meanwhile, the reaction of the legislature in regard to the Alien and Sedition Acts of the Adams administration made itself known. War hysteria had more or less precluded any resentment against them, until Jefferson and Madison began their famous attack through the Virginia and Kentucky Resolutions. The Kentucky Resolutions, with their state-rights doctrine of interposition, were laid before the North Carolina legislature by Davie on December 21. Johnston described the events: "Two or three days ago the Governor laid before the House of Commons a string of resolves from Kentucky, prefaced with a most indecent and violent Phillippic on the measures of the General Government. The Commons sent them up to the Senate who after, *with great impatience*, hearing them read ordered them to lie on the Table and I believe in the temper they were in, might easily have been prevailed on to have thrown them into the fire, which was proposed in whispers by several near me." [4]

Meanwhile the House sent up to the Senate a resolve proposing to instruct its senators and representatives in Congress "to use their influence to procure the repeal of the Alien and Sedition Acts," but

*Later, upon the death of James Iredell, Moore was appointed an Associate Justice of the Supreme Court by President Adams.

[303]

the Senate rejected it by the overwhelming vote of 31 to 8.[5] The more democratic House, however, disregarding the Senate, adopted strong resolutions against the two acts and ordered them forwarded to its senators and representatives in Congress, with the implication that they were to vote for their repeal.[6]

In spite of such independence of action, Davie was able to get the co-operation of both houses in drafting an address to John Adams, endorsing his actions. Even before Davie's arrival in Raleigh, Johnston had proposed such an address to some of the members and had found it "pretty generally approved." Johnston waited, however, until the arrival of Davie before introducing the matter in order that he might avail himself of Davie's influence in the House of Commons, "in hopes of getting an unanimous vote for it."[7]

Johnston was too optimistic. The address to the President, as he reported on December 23, had "been for some days before the House of Commons without being acted on, and I fear will come to nothing, though I believe it would pass the Senate without opposition."[8]

The following day, the House finally, with a respectable majority, did adopt an Address to the President which the Senate passed unanimously, though it was not so high in praise of Adams' "great abilities and integrity" as Johnston wished.[9] Davie passed it on to the President with assurances that it contained "a deliberate and explicit declaration of their sentiments upon the measures which have been taken by the Federal Government with respect to our foreign relations, and particularly the Government of France."[10]

Davie's further comments reflect his interpretation of the Federalist temper of the people of North Carolina:

"As long as the French nation appeared to have for their object the improvement of their own political Situation, and the establishment of a Government on the principles of rational liberty, the Citizens of North Carolina beheld their struggles and exertions with the most anxious solicitude—They were every where disposed, to draw a veil over excesses which had stained the character of the Nation, and to forget the criminal conduct and dangerous intrigues, of their Ministers in the United States and would even have sacrificed important interests to the Support of a cause, which to them in its commencement, appeared to be the cause of virtue and humanity—and it was not untill the French Government had added insult and Systematical indignity

His Excellency the Governor

to years of hostile depredation, that these friendly dispositions were changed; they now see that their motives for forbearance have been mistaken, and that their Country has been degraded by her patience and suffering, and are also convinced that no people possess any National rights in the eyes of this new Military Republic, but those who have the power and the Spirit to protect them." [11]

Davie added his personal sentiment that "we are greatly indebted to the firm and explicit manner in which the Chief Magistrate of the United States has upon all Occasions developed the policy and declared his opinions on the conduct of France towards this Country." [12]

Adams was grateful for "the very polite and pleasing manner" in which Davie communicated to him "the important expression of the Sense and the pleasure of a State of so much weight in the Union." [13]

Having succeeded in this effort, the Federalists devoted their energies to obtaining another political advantage. At that time, North Carolina was one of the three states in the Union which chose their presidential electors by the district system. The Federalists, therefore, with the approaching presidential election of 1800 in mind, attempted to transfer the choice of electors from the people to the legislature, in the hopes that they could secure the election for the Federalist candidate. According to Dr. Wagstaff, "the party whip was vigorously used and all the influence of Samuel Johnston and Governor Davie was exerted without avail," because the lower house "balked the plan and would have none of it." [14]

Aside from these purely political issues, Davie addressed himself to the regular duties of his office "with vigor and intelligence." [15] The principal issues to which he devoted his attention were the military preparedness of the state, a serious exposé of frauds in the land office, and the running of the Tennessee and the South Carolina dividing lines.

First on Davie's agenda was the organizing of the state's military might and the construction of its defenses against threatened French invasion. In the first few months of his administration a great amount of his official correspondence testifies to his exertions in filling the "United State establishment"—a task to which he had already devoted much time and effort.

Ten days after his inauguration he sent a message to the General Assembly on the alarming condition of the coastal defenses of the state. He reported that "very little progress had been made in erecting the forts intended for the defense of Cape-Fear river and Occacock Inlet" which had been undertaken in 1794 by the federal government. In emphasizing the urgency of their completion, he maintained that the state was "almost exclusively interested in establishing and completing those works, intended for the protection of her commerce and her sea coast." His message was referred to a joint committee, which acted favorably upon his request.[16]

And yet by May little progress had been made. So concerned was Davie over the "exposed situation" of Wilmington, that he wrote to Major General Thomas Brown and to Colonel Griffith J. McRee, requesting them as "professional" men to "inspect and examine the true situation of the Works at the mouth of the [Cape Fear] River and report" to him as soon as possible. Brown reported that in 1798 a Mr. Martignor, sent down by the federal government, had demolished old Fort Johnston and had replaced it by a heavy sand battery. Recommendations for a new plan of defense were also to be forwarded to Davie. A similar report on the status of the fort at Ocracoke was requested by Davie from Josiah Collins, Edenton merchant and planter.[17]

At this time, Davie's office was flooded with requests for military appointments, one man even seeking the office of health officer or port physician for the town of Washington.[18]

Davie also dispatched letters to John Gray Blount, of Washington, Richard Dobbs Spaight, of Newbern, and Josiah Collins, of Edenton, regarding the "most advantageous mode of employing the gallies to protect the coasts and inlets of the Southern states." A system was worked out, according to Davie's report to General Pinckney, whereby the state's two galleys would make a constant patrol of the three ports of the state, Cape Fear, Beaufort, and Ocracoke Inlet. One would regularly leave Cape Fear headed north at the same time that one left Ocracoke headed south, with the idea that they would meet each other "about the proper point." [19]

By mid-July Davie, far from happy over the defense picture in the state, wrote General Pinckney that "the want of arms and amunition in the Southern States, is a subject of serious uneasiness to me." He enclosed a report of the number and quantity of these arms which amounted "to nothing." In case of invasion, he felt that "the Mili-

His Excellency the Governor

tary must by substituted for the Civil patrol in every part of this State, otherwise it is believed that no part would be secure a moment against the insurrection of that unhappy species of our population who have no interest in the preservation of our country." [20]

While these military affairs were in progress, Davie did not neglect civil affairs. The biggest headache which he had inherited as governor was the problem of land frauds in the state of Tennessee, involving lands set aside as part of the military district reserved by the legislatures of 1782 and 1783 for payment of Revolutionary officers and soldiers. These grants could be obtained by applying to the secretary of state for a warrant directed to an official surveyor at Nashville, Tennessee, upon whose survey a grant was to be issued by the governor. Also in 1783, to redeem the state's Revolutionary paper money, a land office was opened at Hillsborough, usually called "John Armstrong's office," where any citizen might enter a claim for not more than 5,000 acres of vacant and unappropriated Western lands by paying £10 in specie, or in paper money at a depreciated value, for every 100 acres.

It happened that in 1796 Andrew Jackson, then a congressman, had by chance discovered some wholesale frauds in the land office, involving Martin Armstrong, Surveyor General of the land grant office in Nashville, and James Glasgow, Secretary of State of North Carolina and business partner of Senator William Blount. To make matters worse, Governor John Sevier of Tennessee was deeply implicated in the irregular proceedings. Jackson, undeterred, laid the matter before Governor Samuel Ashe, Davie's predecessor. Ashe immediately requested Sevier to forward the records of Armstrong's office to him at Raleigh for investigation, but Sevier refused. While a legislative committee was undertaking to investigate the matter, the Glasgow books and papers were stored in the comptroller's office for the committee's use. The office was surreptitiously broken into and a large chest and trunk containing the incriminating evidence were stolen. The robbery, however, was waylaid and most of the papers recovered, but all the robbers, except an uncommunicative slave, escaped.[21]

Meanwhile, back in Nashville, a group of deeply involved land speculators met in the home of William Blount to review plans to prevent exposures which would involve Governor Sevier, the three

Blount brothers, Stockley Donelson, and William Tyrrell. After consultation, Tyrrell, an accomplice of Donelson's in several frauds, was dispatched to Raleigh to attempt another theft of the incriminating papers, and in case of failure, to burn the State House in which they were deposited. This nefarious plot was betrayed, however, by a frightened associate, to Judges John McNairy and Howell Tatum, of Tennessee, who informed Governor Ashe by an express rider. Ashe foiled the plot by doubling the guards in the comptroller's office, and the investigating committee was able to reveal "one of the most comprehensive records of fraud and land thievery in the history of public lands."[22]

And so matters stood when it devolved upon Davie to see that justice was carried out. Davie entered into the prosecution with his usual vigor by appointing two commissioners, Basil Gaither and Elija Lam, to investigate the matter even further.[23] He also requested that Martin Armstrong submit to him "a full report of the State and condition" of his office at the time it was suspended by act of the assembly—or that he "cease to do any business as Surveyor General in the office."[24]

Acting on the resolution of the Assembly, Davie commissioned General John Willis, of Robeson County, and Francis Locke, of Salisbury, to go to Tennessee in person and obtain from Governor Sevier the books and papers of Armstrong's office. In the event Sevier refused to relinquish them, they were to make exact copies, "carefully transcribing them from their face Original enteries, interlineations, erasures by blotting or strokes of the pen." The originals or the copies were to be brought to Raleigh and lodged in the office of the secretary of state. Davie included in their letter of instructions one to Governor Sevier, urgently requesting the delivery of these papers in order that the State of North Carolina might fulfill its "sincere desire to discharge a duty she conceives she owes her own Citizens as well as the Citizens of Tennessee who may have claim to lands under Warrants entered in her Office lately held at Nashville."[25]

Willis and Locke finally reached Knoxville April 20 and immediately "waited upon" His Excellency, John Sevier, who "appeared to be quite unprepared for the application of the books & papers in Martin Armstrong's office, tho' well aware of the Necessity of their being placed in other hands...." The North Carolina commissioners "strongly & properly urged" "*the Right of the State*," but Sevier, deeply involved as we have seen, replied that "it was not in his power, nor was he at liberty to Comply," but at their request he would ascertain the opinion of the attorney general. The following day Sevier announced he would delay the proceedings until the meeting of the Tennessee legislature. Realizing the hopelessness of securing the originals, Willis and Locke proposed that he allow them to transcribe them, to which Sevier "readily agreed" and "appeared quite disposed to render us every assistance in his power."[26]

Locke and Willis were not prepared for what they saw. They found it "not in the power of Language" "to convey... an Idia of the Situation in which they found these books...." The books had not only been "abused and worn by time and use, so as to be in many parts obliterated and unintelligible," but there were "the Most Atrocious frauds." In the first book of Locations, which was "in a Mangled State Sewed Together," many names had been entirely erased and others inserted in their place. They also discovered that persons had been allowed to file a number of locations, without names, with a blank left to be filled in later. Another method "of a most scandalous nature" was the removal of about 150 pages involving about 500 false claims of the first book and beginning a new book, "leaving out such parts of the old one, as best suited the parties concerned."[27]

The examiners greatly lamented that "this business has been placed in hands so unworthy of public trust." Also lamentable was the fact that the North Carolina legislature had paid so little attention to the subject and that "Supiness prevailed while a Combination of men Capable as designing, laid and executed their plans, while the Right of the State & property of individuals were Swallowed in the Vortex."[28]

The arduous task of transcription, with the aid of three young men, was finally completed July 13 and deposited by General Willis in the office of the Secretary of State in Raleigh August 2, 1799. Great care had been taken, according to the agents, in reproducing the original "erazures, alterations, interlineations or blotches." The task of identifying every fraudulent entry being an insuperable task, the agents merely pointed out, under distinct heads, the "most general and prevalent methods by which frauds have been effected." On the basis of these six categories of fraudulent practices, the agents concluded, in a report to Governor Davie, that they conceived "it may be important for your Excellency to endevour to have a fair and full settlement with the said Armstrong, effected by such measures as your Excellency may think proper to recommend to the next Legislature." They concluded that "much injury had been suffered & done in the Office at Nashville by neglect and want of Judgement in those who superintend'd it, as by frauds & design; that many individuals have and will be injured and deprived of their rights by the irregularity of these books." Finally they submitted the books themselves as sufficient evidence for prosecution.[29]

Upon receipt of this detailed report, Davie requested William White, the Secretary of State who succeeded Glasgow, to prepare "such a Statement of their respective claims as will enable the Legislature to act on that subject with the necessary information."[30]

Probably on the basis of White's statement, Davie, on September 10, 1799, prepared a strong message which he left, upon his departure to France, to be presented to the approaching legislature. In this message, presented November 21, he enclosed all pertinent papers and reviewed briefly the recent transactions and reports. He concluded by strongly recommending that "legislative provision is necessary to prescribe the mode of adjusting and finally settling the claims and accounts of Martin Armstrong, and all his deputies." He felt that it was "an object worthy of legislative attention, to place this office on a footing that the whole of the business dependent upon it might be closed in the course of one or two years, by placing it under the direction of a man of business, worthy of the public confidence, and under the regulations, precluding, as far as possible, future frauds and impositions."[31]

As though the Tennessee side of this fraud link were not headache enough to Davie, there was the distressing situation in the office of the former Secretary of State, James Glasgow, and that in "the office usually called John Armstrong's" in Hillsborough. Here again Davie took a strong hand. The previous December the General Assembly had authorized him to call a Court of Oyer and Terminer and General Gaol Delivery to prosecute the persons found principally chargeable with the land frauds on the basis of the findings of the two commissioners appointed to investigate the case. Even before the report of the two active commissioners, Basil Gaither and Samuel D. Purviance, Davie wrote the Attorney General, Blake Baker, and the Solicitor General, Edward Jones, to ask them to give an official opinion as to the advisability of appointing such a court and, incidentally, to request that they take "the most decided and effectual measures for supporting those prosecutions and bringing the offenders to justice." [32]

After a preliminary "rude sketch" of their proceedings, handed to Davie on June 6, 1799,[33] the fraud commissioners, after having sat for sixty-three days, turned in their official report on June 28. The findings in each office were appalling. Eleven serious types of fraudulent practices were uncovered in James Glasgow's office, as a result of which between six and seven hundred thousand acres of land had been granted to persons, military warrants, "whose titles, in the opinion of the Commissioners, have not been fairly derived." Among other "irregularities" they found that Glasgow had issued grants to himself and others, on forms of warrants without any signature, that he had issued grants to himself on such unsigned warrants, as the assignee of the soldier, and also that he had issued grants without any warrant whatever. However, according to the commissioners, "the most flagrant, and perhaps the most numerous branch of these frauds, has been the forging of assignments from the soldiers to some other person, to whom, or to the assignees of whom, grants have accordingly issued." [34]

As to John Armstrong's office, the situation was equally scandalous. Here there were fourteen categories of fraudulent practices, including frauds committed in issuing warrants, forged assignments, grants without warrants, *et cetera*.[35]

The fraud commissioners, in a separate report, set out into distinct classes the duplicate warrants issued from Armstrong's office in which John Gray and Thomas Blount "had a concern." These included duplicate warrants drawn by the Blounts (1) "where they have made no assignment either of the original or duplicate, but where they had obtained grants on the one, and Donelson and Tyrrell on the other"; (2) cases "where they assigned the original to James King, and obtained grants for themselves on the duplicate"; and

(3) cases "where they have obtained grants on the duplicate and assigned the duplicate to Donelson and Tyrrell."[36]

Meanwhile, a Court of Patents had been set up to annul the fraudulent grants and to "take the necessary measure to bring the principal Offenders to Justice." Davie also appointed Purviance to assist the attorney general and the solicitor general in its prosecution. This court, scheduled to meet the first part of August, for some mysterious reason did not meet.[37]

Perhaps it was chiefly for this reason that Davie, intent on expediting the prosecution, called a meeting of his Council of State to seek their advice. The Council, consisting of General Thomas Brown (who was elected president), Ransom Sutherland, Elijah Mitchell, Nathaniel Jones, and Henry Watters, met in Raleigh from August 12 to August 16, 1799. Chief among the problems presented to them was the question of whether or not to call a special court to prosecute those guilty of land frauds. Following, no doubt, the official opinions handed down by the attorney general and the solicitor general, the Council unanimously decided against the calling of this court. The principal reason for this action was the lack of jurisdiction—without special legislative authority—over the trials which would have to take place in different districts. Therefore the only alternative was to await the fall session of the legislature. The Council, moreover, recommended that Davie impress that body with "the expediency of making full and ample provision for the detection and punishment of the numerous and black crimes, which have been committed...."[38]

Accordingly, when the legislature convened in November, 1799, Davie, who had left for France, had John R. Eaton, his private secretary, present his message, laying before the Assembly the report of the fraud commissioners, which, according to Davie, had been drawn up in "a brief but perspicuous and masterly fashion." Davie observed further that "while the citizen may lament that crimes so dishonourable to the reputation of his country have been committed within it, he may cherish some hope that the character of the State will be vindicated by the energy of the laws." Along the same line he recommended the calling of a Court of Oyer and Terminer "expressly constituted by law, with jurisdiction commensurate with the various frauds which have been committed in the various offices."[39]

His Excellency the Governor

Because so many people were implicated in the reports, investigation of the matter was referred to a joint confidential committee. A public reading might "be a means of conveying information to some of the guilty, who might escape from justice." [40]

As for the outcome of the ensuing trial, conducted in June by the newly-created Court of Conference while Davie was in Paris, suffice it to say that it was the cynosure of the state's attention. Not only was the long-time Secretary of State, Glasgow, involved, but also the great criminal lawyer and jurist, John Haywood, cousin of Treasurer John Haywood. Judge Haywood sealed his political future in the state by resigning from the Superior Court bench to undertake Glasgow's defense for a fee of $1,000. The late Colonel Ashe described the situation:

"Seldom has a trial so greatly shocked public attention—the chief defendant was a public character whose long career had until this period been marked with particular excellence and now, singularly enough, defended by one who had with unusual luster worn the judicial ermine, while the issues were of the highest concern to the people of the State." [41]

Despite Haywood's able defense, Glasgow was convicted and fined £2,000; the Negro who attempted to burn the Capitol was executed; and all others implicated in the frauds managed to escape punishment.[42]

The relatively mild judgment against Glasgow, with the failure to mete out just punishments to the other fraudulent offenders, remains perhaps the blackest spot on the escutcheon of the Old North State. Had Davie remained as governor, there is good reason to surmise that he would not have hesitated to continue the attack on the citadels of privilege and plutocracy, behind whose walls such perfidies had been perpetrated.

The running and completion of the state's boundaries on the west and south also faced Governor Davie during his administration. Here again he proceeded with vigor. As to the Tennessee boundary line, the act of cession of 1789 by which Tennessee was finally ceded to the United States provided that the line dividing the two should follow the high mountain ranges between Stone Mountain on the Virginia border and the Georgia line.[43]

William R. Davie

The first action on this had been taken during Governor Ashe's administration when the North Carolina legislature appointed a commission consisting of Mussendine Matthews, Joseph McDowell, and Colonel David Vance to complete the running of the line. Governor Ashe, in accordance with legislative instruction, on July 21, 1797, had sent a copy of the act to Governor Sevier of Tennessee requesting that he take the necessary measures to co-operate with the North Carolina commissioners. When Davie assumed office, nothing further had been done. Davie therefore wrote Governor Sevier another letter apprising him of the intentions of the North Carolina commissioners to begin the actual survey in April or May in order that there should be "no difficulty or delay" in consequence "of a want of proper concern" on Sevier's part. Privately Davie wrote the three commissioners that he had "some reason to believe that every means will be used to effect delays and to create obstructions" on the part of Tennessee, but he trusted that they would "carry the intention of the Legislature as soon as possible into execution."[44]

It was not until May 23, 1799, that the commissioners began the actual running. At that time they located the Virginia line on the extreme summit of Stone Mountain, and after three days they reported the great hardships of their undertaking. Not only was the ground "very uneaven and Stoney," but "Climbing the hills causes such an Exertion of the knees, that it makes the Warm Water run out of both Back and forehead." Also they had to be on constant guard against numerous "enemies, having already killed four large Rattle-Snakes." They foresaw a "tedious, Difficult, uncomfortable tour of it." Because they were so far from any inhabitants, it required four pack-horses to supply them and three attendants, one to contract for and collect provisions and two as pack drivers. They predicted that, even if they could procure good pilots, they could progress only from three to five miles a day. Finally they reported that no Tennessee commissioners had appeared and they had "no reason to believe they will," all their letters to Sevier having been ignored.[45]

After great vicissitudes, the North Carolina commissioners, unassisted throughout by their Tennessee counterparts, finally reached the Painted Rock on the French Broad River on June 28. Here they were forced, because of "excessive rains, extream fatague, an absolute necessity both for men & horses," to stop and refit. Their chief concern was over the wisdom of extending the line further than the boundary of the Cherokee Reservation. On this last point, they sought the advice of Governor Davie, who in turn sought the advice of his Council of State, suggesting to them that it would be "extremely impolitic to carry the line within the boundary... untill the consent of the interested Tribes was obtained." Instead, he suggested that the difficulties might be avoided "by availing ourselves of the friendly Agency of the General Government," inasmuch as the federal government had now taken over the conduct of Indian affairs. The Council was of the unanimous opinion that the line should not be extended further without the approbation of the Indian tribes themselves. Finally, upon Davie's departure for France, he wisely left the matter up to the legislature. Two decades of negotiation were to pass before the completion of the line.[46]

An even more annoying problem was that of the extension of North Carolina's southern line, which bordered both South Carolina and Georgia. Here the problem was one of extension of the line which, through surveys of 1735, 1737, 1764, and 1772, had been run for a distance of approximately 215 miles up to the Cherokee Mountains. But the line had not kept pace with the rapid western movement. The frontiersmen of this region had been faced with the usual evils attendant upon the uncertainty of a dividing line: tax collection, land grants, judicial jurisdiction, militia service, Indian relations, imperial relations, and the every-day functions involving the relations of men and governments.[47]

By the final survey of 1772, the commissioners had begun at the Salisbury Road, skirted the Catawba Lands to the forks of the Catawba River, and then proceeded due westward (supposedly) along the 35th parallel to the Cherokee Mountains. As a result of an error of computation, however, South Carolina gained the district between the 35th parallel and the line from the forks of the Catawba to the Cherokee boundary, and from the Catawba River and Catawba Lands to the Cherokee line—a fertile region inhabited by more than 5,000 whites and originally called the "New Acquisition." Later it was organized into York and Spartanburg counties in 1785. This error, according to the South Carolinians, compensated for errors in the previous surveys of 1735 and 1737, by which South Carolina had lost territory, but North Carolina refused for years to recognize this latest survey.[48]

So intent was North Carolina on securing her rights that she described the boundary line in the Bill of Rights of the Constitution of 1776. In Section XXV she ignored all previous surveys of the line, except that which extended from the seacoast up to the 35th parallel and insisted on the original agreement entered into between the colonies in 1735. She agreed to correct the error of 1737 and return to South Carolina the strip between 35° and 34° 49'; but she demanded unconditionally her ancient charter right (granted by Charles II) of extending the 35th parallel to the Mississippi. Thereby she would gain the northern corner of the Catawba Lands and the "New Acquisition."[49]

All legislative bills to implement this ordinance failed until in 1792 a bill was passed for the appointment of commissioners to "extend" the line. The commissioners chosen were the Reverend James Hall, Alfred Moore, Joseph McDowell, Jr., and Davie. The choice of Davie was a happy one, because of his South Carolina lands along the Catawba and of his first-hand knowledge of the territory involved. The commissioners were empowered to "settle and compromise" all differences in the boundary dispute and "to fix and establish permanently" the line as far as the eastern boundary of Tennessee, which had been ceded to the United States in 1789. The act further provided that North Carolina would "ratify and confirm" whatever the commissioners should do, with the proviso that Section XXV of the Bill of Rights should not be violated.[50]

South Carolina, however, taking issue with this proviso, refused to appoint commissioners until North Carolina granted its commissioners "full powers" to negotiate. North Carolina refused. Here the case rested, except for a few feelers on the part of Governors Moultrie and Spaight, until 1796, when the North Carolina legislature passed an act appointing Davie, Moore, and Jonathan Price as commissioners to co-operate with South Carolina in establishing the line "permanently." Now South Carolina refused to co-operate. And here the case stood when Davie became governor in December, 1798.[51]

Now in the dual capacity of chief executive and a commissioner, Davie attempted to resolve the problem by proposing to the legislature that he "enter into a friendly discussion of our rights" with the

His Excellency the Governor

Governor of South Carolina and submit the outcome to the next legislature. In accordance with legislative authority he therefore wrote a firm, yet conciliatory, letter to the Governor of South Carolina on March 12, 1799. After a review of past difficulties, he stated that since a large part of the line had been admitted to be "inaccurate and erroneous by both parties," and since a large part of the line had never been extended, he felt there was a real necessity of settling "so old a dispute" and he would be "extremely happy, to contribute in any manner in my power to effect an object, of so much importance to both States." Concretely, as a means of putting "the business into a train of amicable adjustment," he proposed that the North Carolina commissioners proceed "to ascertain the latitude of the lines now claimed by your State, as the present boundary, and to fix the true Latitude agreeably to the Charter of Charles the 2d and the Constitution of this State." In this way "the nature and extent of the claims of the two States will be perfectly understood, after which I suppose, little difficulty would arise." He furthermore proposed that a provisional line be established which could later be ratified by each state. Finally he signified his determination to proceed with the line by stating that when the North Carolina commissioners had set a time and place for meeting he would notify the Governor of South Carolina in order that he might appoint commissioners to represent South Carolina.[52]

After awaiting a reply for five months, Davie reported to his Council of State that, despite his efforts, South Carolina had "continually evaded the measure in some pretence or other." The commissioners, therefore, felt it their duty to proceed in September or October to ascertain the true latitude "so that the rights and claims of the State may be perfectly understood." Such action would also be a "means of enabling the Commissioners, should they take the measures contemplated by the Act, to State our claims before a proper Tribunal." —a veiled threat to refer the dispute to the Supreme Court of the United States. He also requested the Council's advice on the expediency of appointing a commissioner to serve in his stead. The Council recommended such an appointment, though Davie did not fill the vacancy. However, he did, on August 27, 1799, appoint Wallace Alexander, of Lincoln County, to take the place of Alfred Moore, who resigned. And so matters rested when Davie resigned as governor and departed for France.[53]

Appraisal of Davie's brief administration must necessarily be limited. Yet it may be safely stated that, in the matters of military preparedness, prosecution of the land frauds, and the running of the southern and western lines, Davie vigorously pushed ahead and—to use his phraseology—put them in a train of "forwardness" which would eventually lead to a successful conclusion.

Or maybe a toast drunk to Governor Davie on July 4, 1799, gives the appropriate flavor to his administration. On that day the Wake County Troop of Cavalry, commanded by Captain Theophilus Hunter, staged a review in Raleigh for interested spectators. After "going through the manoevres and evolutions of the new system of cavalry tactics, instructed by his Excellency the Governor," they sat down to a public dinner after which a number of toasts were drunk. Among them was one to His Excellency William R. Davie: "May the manly and dignified measures of his administration, prove to the most distant corner of the globe, that we are part of a Great, Free, Powerful, and Independent Nation."[54]

CHAPTER XI

The French Mission

DURING Davie's incumbency as Governor of North Carolina, the French imbroglio became increasingly serious. French indignation at the Jay Treaty and the resulting "X.Y.Z." affair had led to an undeclared or quasi naval war which raged on the high seas. By 1800, no less than 1,853 authentic cases of spoliations had been committed by French warships, with a total damage later reckoned at $7,149,306.10. To this class of recognized damages were added those involving other claims eventually adjudicated, such as claims for embargoes, seizures of cargoes in French ports, and arbitrary purchases. The entire amount totalled $12,149,306.10.[1]

During this period, President John Adams enjoyed—if he were capable of such human instincts—a brief period of popularity on the part of an aroused American populace. Federalist policy triumphed and from May 28 to July 10, 1798, a series of laws placed the country on a war footing. American armed ships could capture French armed ships and bring them into a prize court. All commercial intercourse between the United States and France or French possessions was suspended. The American Merchant Marine was allowed to arm defensively and to take as prizes French armed vessels which attacked them. All treaties with France, including the famous French Alliance of 1778, were unilaterally abrogated. Provision for internment of enemy aliens, stricter naturalization laws, and an enlarged army were passed. And finally, on March 2, 1799, the Navy Department was created.[2]

WILLIAM R. DAVIE

These retaliatory measures came as a surprise to the French Directory and constituted one of the reasons for France's reversal of her high-handed policy against the young Western republic. The new American warships spiritedly attacked and worsted French public vessels of their own calibre, thus exhilarating and unifying American public opinion and showing France and the world that America would strike back.[3]

There were other factors responsible for a change in French sentiment. Pro-French Americans in Paris convinced the wily Talleyrand, Secretary of Foreign Affairs, that its policy was alienating Francophiles in the United States; Frenchmen who had served in subordinate diplomatic posts in America reiterated this sentiment. By a reversal of policy there was also a chance that Jefferson and his Democratic Republicans would win the election of 1800. But perhaps the most compelling reason of all was the fear on the part of the imperialistic Talleyrand, who was even then envisaging a great French colonial empire in the Mississippi Valley, that, in case of war, the United States would seize Louisiana before France could wrest or wrangle it from decadescent Spain.[4]

Abruptly Talleyrand and company reversed themselves. Forthwith the Foreign Minister dispatched a letter to M. Pichon, the French *chargé d'affaires* at The Hague, to be shown to the American minister there, William Vans Murray, a Federalist from Maryland. The letter stated that if the United States sent an envoy to France he would be "undoubtedly received with the respect due to the representative of a free, independent and powerful nation." President Adams, sensing the diplomatic situation, sent to the Senate, February 18, a copy of Talleyrand's message, together with the nomination of Vans Murray as the new minister to France. A thunderbolt would have been less surprising. The Federalist leaders, shaken out of their complacency, feared that a successful settlement with France would endanger their current popularity.[5]

The Senate committee, to whom the appointment was referred, took the unprecedented step of calling upon Adams in person to express their dissatisfaction with Murray's appointment. Finding the President adamant, they let it be known that a commission, rather than a single individual, would be more acceptable to the Senate and to the public. Adams accordingly assented and the following morning,

The French Mission

February 25, 1799, sent a message to the Senate in which he added to Murray's name those of Oliver Ellsworth, Chief Justice of the United States, and Patrick Henry, late governor of Virginia, as envoys extraordinary and ministers plenipotentiary to the French Republic. "Full powers were granted to discuss and settle by treaty, all controversies between the two countries." [6]

Senate consent was forthcoming and the commissions were duly prepared. However, Patrick Henry declined to serve, on account of his "advanced age and increasing debility." Whereupon Adams went one state lower and chose the governor of North Carolina, William R. Davie.[7]

"Such," according to John Adams' grandson and biographer, Charles Francis Adams, "is the history of this, the most noted event of Mr. Adams's administration." Its publication provoked varied sentiments throughout the land. Francophiles, led by Jefferson, rejoiced, believing that "the nomination silenced all arguments against the sincerity of France, and rendered desperate every further effort toward war." Others rejoiced because they thought it would increase the strength of the Republicans. Anglophiles, led by Hamilton, mourned, viewing the nomination as "a fatal and dishonest desertion of a settled policy, which required war at least until the time when the French should publicly sue for peace." Others rejoiced, because they thought that it seriously split the Federalists. Yet John Adams' grandson perhaps was not too eulogistic when he said that Adams was "ready for war, if France continued faithless," but he was "not less ready for peace the moment she showed signs of returning reason." [8]

Davie, lately immersed in war preparations against France, was probably as thunderstruck at his appointment for such a mission as had been the Philadelphia politicos. His own picture of the French situation had been colored by his old friend, General Pinckney, who dropped by Halifax to visit Davie in the latter part of January, 1799. He reported that the French Directory was engaging in "arbitrary proceedings," that "spies were regularly set to watch those who might have any intercourse with the Envoys," and that "each of the Directory had their particular & favorite General." In short, the French government was "in the most deplorable oppressive State we can form any Idea of." [9]

The appointment of Davie seems first to have been suggested by

[321]

WILLIAM R. DAVIE

Oliver Ellsworth, who spent a day with Davie in Halifax in March, 1799. Expecting Patrick Henry's refusal, he wrote the Secretary of State from Halifax on March 25, recommending his host for the appointment, citing "his dignified manners, extent of political information, and correctness of opinions." [10]

Upon notice of Henry's refusal, Adams notified Pickering to make out Davie's commission for the important appointment. Pickering, although favoring Davie's appointment, strongly urged discretion. He felt that "for the very reason that he is Governor of North Carolina" it was "important to the state and to the Union, that such a man should hold the reins of government there." He therefore suggested the "expediency" of not requiring his immediate acceptance, especially because it "remained uncertain whether he would ever be called upon to proceed on his mission to France." As a result, Pickering advised "perfect silence" on the subject and the suspension of the publication of Henry's resignation. This was particularly advisable until Talleyrand's reply to Murray's overtures should be known. In case of a favorable reply, Davie's appointment could become operative and "he would not be ousted of one important office, until he could assume the *exercise* and receive the *compensation* of another." [11]

In accord with these sentiments, Adams authorized Pickering to send the conditional appointment of Davie, which he did on June 1. As an "Envoy Extraordinary and Minister Plenipotentiary to the French Republic," Davie, Ellsworth, and Murray were authorized "to discuss and settle all controversies between the United States and France." Pickering requested, on Adams' authority, not Davie's "*immediate* acceptance," but only Davie's answer "whether, if it should become necessary, your acceptance of it *may be expected*." Davie's reply would be confidential.[12]

Davie's letter of acceptance was brief. He stated that the appointment was "consistent with my duty to the State; and as my present situation would oblige me to state the fact upon enquiry, I have no desire that it should be considered in any other light than answers in such cases usually are." [13]

Meanwhile conciliatory events were progressing on the Continent. On May 5 Murray advised Talleyrand of the three-man appointment to France, but stated that they would not embark for Europe until they had received from the Executive Directory "direct and un-

The French Mission

equivocal assurances" that they would be properly received and would "enjoy all the prerogatives" attached to their positions. Talleyrand replied posthaste that the appointed ministers would be received in their official character and that they would "enjoy all the prerogatives attached to it by the law of nations." [14]

When this assuring reply reached Adams, many thought that the United States ought to accept in good faith the peace offer of the French Republic. Yet there were still Federalists such as the senator from Connecticut, Uriah Tracy, who had decided misgivings. Writing to James McHenry, Secretary of War, he inquired if it was true that Davie had been appointed in lieu of Henry and if he and Justice Ellsworth were going to Europe and added, "I am mortified & discouraged for fear this is all true." He declared that he had sacrificed "as much as most men or at least as much as any individual to support his Govt. and root out Democracy, & French principles, but really, Sir, I feel it to be lost and worse." In fact, he threatened to resign "if all must be given up to France & our Democrats." [15]

John Steele, Comptroller General of the Currency, and Davie's erstwhile friend,* was also skeptical of the whole thing. From Philadelphia he wrote Justice Iredell of Davie's appointment to succeed Henry "in the Embassy to the Great Nation," informing him that the French assurance of a favorable reception was "in the old style, and though far from being what it ought to be is nevertheless such as I suppose the President will consider himself bound to admit." Steele did not "forbode any good" from the mission and lamented "our passion for humility and submission." In fact, he said it was "impossible to think that as a Nation our honor can be preserved, or our interests promoted by such condescensions." [16]

Upon receipt of Talleyrand's assurances, sent through Murray, the Secretary of State, Pickering, wrote Davie, relaying President Adams' request that he make "immediate preparations for embarking." Pickering also thought it would be "useful as well as desirable" that Davie and Ellsworth take passage on the same vessel. He therefore informed

---

* Perhaps Steele's reaction was somewhat colored by the grudge which he harbored against Davie in regard to Davie's disapproval of Samuel Eusebius McCorkle as President of the University. However, just before Davie departed for Trenton, New Jersey, to embark for France, there was a rapprochement between Davie and Steele (see *supra* pp. 251-52).

Davie that he expected him to proceed to Philadelphia, where he would be met by the Chief Justice and where a frigate would probably be ordered to take them to France.[17]

On the following day, Ellsworth wrote Davie, hoping that he could leave "so early as that we may have a favourable season for our passage" and that as they were to choose their own secretaries, he hoped that Davie's secretary as well as Davie himself, would understand the French language of which he had "the misfortune to be ignorant." This latter request was reiterated by Pickering.[18]

A later letter from Pickering advised Davie that Ellsworth was eager to embark in the beginning of October, "for the chance of better weather than a later passage may afford; for at best he expects to be sick the whole voyage." [19]

Urged on by these communications, Davie, on September 10, officially informed the General Assembly of his appointment. Aware of the honor bestowed upon him by that body in electing him to the chief magistry of the state, he said that "every consideration led me to believe, that I could not promote their views more essentially, or render my country a more important or agreeable service, than by utilizing my efforts to a Mission, which had for its object the prevention of war, and an amicable adjustment of all differences between the U. States and the Republic of France." [20]

After leaving behind his report on the state of the affairs of the commonwealth, with suggested recommendations, Davie made ready for his journey. The day before his departure the citizens of Raleigh met and presented him with a glowing address. Although they were "well pleased and gratified" at this "distinguished mark of the high trust & confidence" reposed in Davie by his country, they could not view his departure without expressions of regret and of their "affectionate and respectful sentiments" concerning his mission. They profusely offered "their sincere and best wishes" for his personal safety, health and prosperity.[21]

Davie thanked them effusively for their "polite and friendly address" and expressed "sincere regret" at leaving the city of Raleigh, "where every moment has been marked with the most respectful attention." [22]

On the following day, the officers of the cavalry, a number of their troops, and a group of Raleigh inhabitants waited on the Governor as he set out for Halifax, his first stop. They escorted him for four miles on his journey, and then "alighted and bid him an affectionate adieu." [23]

Yet as Davie pursued his journey towards Halifax, his emotions were troubled by the "unknown and ever-varying situation" of the French government and "its strange, unparalleled character, and unsettled policy." [24] Such thoughts, however, were perhaps driven from his mind as he rejoined his family and friends in Halifax. The day after his arrival, the gentlemen of the town entertained him at Hannon's Tavern, where "a number of patriotic toasts were drank, accompanied with convivial songs, and the greatest mirth and harmony prevailed." [25]

A week was consumed in attending to his plantation affairs at Halifax, in leaving directions in regard to his estate in South Carolina, and in instructing Charles W. Harris, whom he left in charge of his law office at Halifax. All these affairs he "predicated upon a six months absence." [26]

Finally on September 22, after an emotional farewell to his wife and family, Davie set out, accompanied by Joseph B. Littlejohn as his secretary. A former University of North Carolina student, Littlejohn had been chosen by Davie on account of "his prudence, his education, and skill in the French language." [27]

On September 24 Davie reached Petersburg, Virginia, and from there he wrote Iredell of his choice of Littlejohn, in whom he had "a perfect confidence" as a man of "virtue, prudence, and principles." It also gave Davie satisfaction to bring forward a young man of his own party, especially in view of the fact that "Our Jacobins render by their exertions every attention of this kind to the youth of our Country necessary." [28]

Three days later, September 27, Governor Davie reached Mount Vernon. Washington laconically reported that he "called, dined, and proceeded on." [29] Probably here Davie learned that yellow fever had driven the governmental officers from Philadelphia to the haven of Trenton, New Jersey. When he reached there on October 6,[30] he discovered some of the events which had taken place in the meantime.

Before John Adams had removed his family from yellow-fever-infested Philadelphia to the security of Quincy, Massachusetts, and before the cabinet and government had refugeed to Trenton, Adams had called together his cabinet to consult on the instructions to be given the envoys. According to Adams, they had "entered into a very serious and deliberate discussion of every article that was to be demanded and insisted on the proposed treaty." All the articles were "unanimous agreed upon" to Adams' satisfaction.[31]

At Quincy, Adams anxiously awaited the draft of the instructions which he had requested of Pickering. Meanwhile the revolution of 30th Prairial had occurred in France, by which the entire Directory, with the exception of Barras, was changed. Skeptical of the permanency of this government and of their reception of the American envoys, the majority of Adams' cabinet recommended suspending the mission. Therefore, instead of receiving the draft of the instructions, Adams received a letter from Pickering "earnestly entreating" him "to suspend the mission!" To make matters worse, this letter had been approved by Oliver Wolcott, Secretary of the Treasury, and James McHenry, Secretary of War, and concurred in by Ben Stoddert, Secretary of War. Only Arthur Lee, the Attorney General, did not agree with the sentiments of the letter.[32]

Adams had been "astonished at this unexpected, this obstinate and persevering opposition to a measure that appeared so clearly" to him "to be so essential to the peace and prosperity of the nation, and the honor of the government, at home and abroad." The letter, followed by one expressing the same sentiments from Stoddert, prompted Adams to set out for Trenton to "meet the gentlemen face to face, to confer with them coolly on the subject, and convince them, or be convinced by them if I could."[33]

Unknown to Adams, Pickering had also written, on September 13, a letter to his friend George Cabot, expressing his adverse sentiments. He reported that Ellsworth while in Trenton in August had seen no alternative "*but that he must go.*" But Pickering felt that "subsequent changes in Europe, and especially in France" would change his ideas. He asked Cabot to write Ellsworth and propose that he "dissuade the President from the pursuit." This should not be too difficult, because there was "nothing in politics he [Ellsworth] more detests than this mission, and nothing he more dreads than the voyage across the wide Atlantic." On the other hand, he reported that "Governor Davie is evidently pleased with the business; but his letter to me was prior to the late arrivals from Europe."[34]

The French Mission

Not content with these efforts, Pickering addressed another letter, September 24, to John Adams, in which he reported that he had consulted with his colleagues, who thought that Adams' coming to Trenton would be "an eligible step." He further stated that "Governor Davie, having relinquished his government and made arrangements for the voyage to Europe, will probably be better satisfied, after making the long journey from North Carolina, to return home again, if the further suspension of the mission take place, after a personal interview with you and his colleague." [35]

On his way to Trenton, Adams called upon Ellsworth at his home in Windsor, Connecticut, on October 3. The latter, Adams reported, was "perfectly candid" and was agreeable to any decision Adams made. When Adams arrived in Trenton, he found Davie, Alexander Hamilton, and four cabinet members waiting. [36]

On October 5 Ellsworth wrote Adams of his decision to meet Davie at Trenton where they could pay their "joint respects" to Adams and receive "any communication of your views as you may wish to make." Ellsworth arrived accordingly on October 10. [37]

The press, announcing the various arrivals in Trenton, reported that "matters of great pith and moment are shortly to engage the heads of the nation now in Trenton; the most important of which are, probably, the question respecting the sailing of the Ministers to the French Republic, and the spoilations by British cruisers on the American commerce, which, we are creditably informed, have strongly excited the sensibility of administration." [38]

Numerous were the conflicting reports emanating from the press along the Atlantic seaboard as to the fate of the mission. These reports, reprinted in the *North-Carolina Minerva and Raleigh Advertiser*, must have had a confusing effect upon the public mind. On October 15, 1799, the report was published that the envoys had received their orders and were "preparing immediately to embark for Europe;—any thing in the Salem Gazette, of yesterday to the contrary." Two weeks later, the Raleigh paper announced that the mission had been suspended and that "the cause of the suspension originates in certain advices which the President has recently received from high authority in Europe, that propositions have been made by the combined powers, to admit of *no neutralities*, and to treat all nations as *enemies*, who were not *decidedly* in their interest."

WILLIAM R. DAVIE

The Federalist editor, William Boylan, attributed this suspension to the "change of men and of measures in France" and was sure that the decision was "dictated by the *wisdom, patriotism*, and *experience* of administration." He also tossed out the query: "May it not have happened that the President has received intimation from the coalesced powers, that WHOEVER IS NOT THEIR FRIEND, IS THEIR FOE?" He urged that, though our embarrassment over such a dilemma was great, "our FIRMNESS must be greater" and that we must be "united in support of our administration."

On the same day, the *Raleigh Register*, the Democratic-Republican organ of Joseph Gales, likewise reported the suspension of the mission for the same two reasons, but added simply, "Whether either of these be the true ground, upon which our Executive has acted, time will discover."

And from Davie himself came uncertain reports. Charles W. Harris wrote his brother on October 19 that "Letters from Gen Davie by yesterday's post inform us that he is at Trenton waiting the arrival of the President and J. Ellsworth" and that "many have ventured to assert that these envoys will not sail shortly for France, alleging that the President has not yet received the assurances expected from the French government." However, Harris was of the opinion—which may have been a reflection of Davie's—that the envoys would be sent "even without these much spoken of Assurances, as there is great reason to expect at the close of this campaign a general convention of all the powers at war for the object of settling all their differences. America should be represented in such a conference."[39]

Finally on November 5 the *North-Carolina Minerva* published an extract from the *New-York Gazette* which announced that it had learned "from undoubted authority, that the envoys to France are to sail on the 5th of November, in the frigate United States, which now lies at Newport, ready to receive them."

No less in a fever pitch were the inhabitants of Trenton. For six days, from October 10 to October 15, Adams held conferences with all his cabinet heads except Charles Lee, who was in Virginia. The chief tenor of their arguments—and the chief opinion of the inhabitants of Trenton—was that the next packet from Europe would bring "the glorious news that Louis the XVIII. was restored to the throne of France, and reigning triumphantly at Versailles."[40]

The French Mission

According to their version, General Suwarrow,* leading a victorious Russian army, and Prince Charles, leading a victorious Austrian army, were to converge miraculously upon Paris and march together to meet Louis XVIII, who was to be brought over by the British fleet and escorted to Versailles. Upon hearing this report the realistic Adams reported: "I could scarcely believe my own senses when I heard such reveries." In vain he urged "the immense distances the two imperial armies had to march, the great number of towns and cities in the route of both, in positions chosen with great skill, fortified with exquisite art, defended by vast trains of heavy ordnance, garrisoned by numerous troops of soldiers perfectly disciplined, and animated with all the obstinacy and ardor of the revolutionary spirit." Other arguments propounded were equally futile. Finally, in desperation, Adams asked the question: Suppose Louis XVIII should be ensconced on the French throne when the envoys arrived, "what harm will there be?" Certainly they would be graciously received until they could get fresh commissions from home.[41]

Finding his cabinet heads obdurate, Adams invited Ellsworth and Davie to dine with him alone that they might "converse with entire freedom." Adams' account of the conversation follows:

"... At table, Mr. Ellsworth expressed an opinion somewhat similar to that of the heads of departments and the public opinion at Trenton. 'Is it possible, Chief Justice,' said I, 'that you can seriously believe that the Bourbons are, or will be soon, restored to the throne of France.' 'Why,' said Mr. Ellsworth, smiling, *it looks a good deal so.*' 'I should not be afraid to stake my life upon it, that they will not be restored in seven years, if they ever are,' was my reply. And then I entered into a long detail of my reasons for this opinion....

"The result of the conversation was, that Mr. Davie was decidedly for embarking immediately, as he always had been from his arrival, and Mr. Ellsworth declared himself satisfied, and willing to embark as soon as I pleased."[42]

Thus Davie stood out alone as the single advocate and supporter of Adams' determination to dispatch the mission. Unfortunately the records are silent as to his reasons for his stand, but it may be surmised that he too realized how well-nigh impossible was a Bourbon restora-

* Undoubtedly the Russian Field Marshal Alexander Vasilyevich Suvarov.

tion at this time. And even the astute Adams had underestimated by one hundred per cent the time it would require for a coalition of European powers to restore the Bourbons to the throne of France.

But before Adams made public his decision there was yet another vigorous opponent to be encountered—Alexander Hamilton, who also had been misled into predicting the immediate success of the Russian and Austrian armies, in concert with Great Britain, in the Bourbon restoration. Especially, Hamilton pointed out, would this be accomplished by the influence of William Pitt, who was determined to restore the Bourbons. Adams differed with Hamilton on every point and predicted, rightly, that Britain would soon make peace.[43]

Finally, October 15, with the moral support of Davie alone among his advisers present, Adams directed that the instructions for departure be prepared. He assembled his cabinet for a meeting at which the instructions were "deliberately considered, paragraph by paragraph, and unanimously approved by me and by them." He averred, moreover, that "there had never been any difference of opinion among us on any article of the instructions."[44]

The following day Adams wrote Pickering requesting him to send copies of the instructions, "as corrected last evening," to the envoys and to write them a letter expressing the President's desire "that they would take their passage for France on board the frigate the United States, Captain Barry, now lying at Rhode Island, by the 1st of November, or sooner, if consistent with their conveniences." Captain John Barry, second only to John Paul Jones as a Revolutionary naval hero, had orders "to land them in any port of France which they may prefer, and to touch at any other ports which they may desire." Adams sent his "best wishes for their health and happiness, as well as for an honorable termination of their mission" and pointed out that "As their visit to France is at one of the most critical, important, and interesting moments that ever have occurred, it cannot fail to be highly entertaining and instructive to them, and useful to their country, whether it terminates in peace and reconciliation, or not."[45]

Davie had accepted the delay with good grace, recognizing that the "great changes which have lately taken place in Europe naturally demanded the attention of our Government." He reported on October 21 to John Haywood that he had been "very politely received by the Gentlemen of the Government," and was "greatly indebted to our

THE FRENCH MISSION

friend Mr. Steele for his polite and unremited attention," adding that the latter was "one of the best informed men" in the administration.[46]

Davie also made several acute observations in regard to the internal affairs of France: that this "submission, and the presence of common danger has restored a moment of harmony between the constituted authorities." In fact, "this change produced some confidence and energy, the clubs have been suppressed, the insurrections generally quelled, and the new levies of conscripts have been embodied and marched to the Armies with more care and despatch than was expected by the Coalition Powers."[47]

Meanwhile preparations were amaking for their departure. Secretary Pickering instructed the cashier of the Bank of Discount and Deposit in New York to supply the envoys with gold "to the amount of five thousand dollars, for which Governor Davie will send you my check on the bank of the U. States." The gold, he instructed, should be in French, Spanish, and Portuguese coins.[48]

On the same day Pickering sent Davie and Ellsworth a list of the names and residences of several United States consuls and agents in Portugal, Spain, and France, because it was "uncertain what ports you may touch at in Europe before you proceed to Paris." They were also assured that adequate funds would be lodged in Amsterdam for their use.[49] Also on the same day, Adams drew up letters of credence, addressed to the Executive Directory of the French Republic, informing them officially of the appointment of the envoys and of the desire of the United States to terminate "all differences" between the two countries and to form "arrangements for a commercial and friendly intercourse, which may be mutually beneficial."[50]

The following day Oliver Wolcott, Secretary of the Treasury, dispatched a letter to Davie and Ellsworth enclosing several confidential statements conveying "satisfactory information respecting the commerce navigation, and revenue of the United States." The reports added up to the fact, according to Wolcott, that "what is called the *general balance of trade* will appear greatly against the United States; this arises from the capitals which are continually brought to, and permanently invested in the United States, for which no remittances are to be made." He concluded that this balance "may be considered as one proof of the increasing resources of our country."[51]

Final instructions to the envoys were also sent by Benjamin Stoddert, Secretary of the Navy, who advised that Captain Barry had the frigate *United States* "in perfect readiness to proceed with you" and recommended that L'Orient, France, would be the most convenient port of debarkation "as the distance to Paris is not greater than from Brest, where the French Ships of War rendezvous; and at Havre de Grace there is not water enough for the Frigate." Since the envoys had determined not to touch at an English port, the Secretary believed Lisbon would be the best place to pay a port of call for latest information before proceeding to France. Captain Barry had been instructed to wait at the port of debarkation for their dispatches from Paris—if the envoys determined not to return with him. Meanwhile the *George Washington*, of 32 guns, would be dispatched from America to arrive at L'Orient around the 15th of March, there to await the convenience of the ministers.[52]

Everything seemed finally to be in order for the departure. Just before leaving Trenton, Davie, as previously stated, left with John Steele a "memorandum" to be sent to his wife, along with "a sealed letter containing his will addressed to Genl Jones," his father-in-law, and the sum of $102.67. With the money Steele purchased "sattin," lutestring, muslin, and a "new hair trunk & cord." In forwarding these articles to Mrs. Davie, Steele stated that the "silks are of the best quality to be procured here [Philadelphia] at the present time goods of that kind being scarce and I flatter myself the colours will be agreeable to your taste."[53]

On October 23 Davie proceeded to New York,[54] where he presumably picked up the $5,000 in gold authorized by Wolcott.

A final word of advice was sent to them on October 26 by Pickering. If passports should not be awaiting them at the first French port it would be judicious to wait for them on the spot "before you venture to set out for Paris."[55]

Davie and Ellsworth arrived in Newport on November 1 and made their preparations to leave on the third. They informed Pickering that they had "found the most ample and satisfactory preparations for our accommodations on board The United States, and feel ourselves particularly indebted to the Secretary of the Navy for his polite attention to the subject." Stoddert also received a substantially similar letter.

The great day of departure, Saturday, November 3, finally ar-

THE FRENCH MISSION

rived.[56] No doubt the local inhabitants were not too blasé to come down to see so important a mission sail and to wish them *bon voyage*. Certainly Davie went with the blessings of the Federalist organ in North Carolina, *The North-Carolina Minerva*, which hoped *"that pleasant and prosperous gales may waft him to the destined port, that success may attend his mission, and that he may speedily return to the bosom of his country, and be received with the united plaudits of all real Americans, of 'well done thou good and faithful servant.'"* [57]

The next word in regard to their voyage is the simple announcement of the *New-York Merchant Advertiser* that their ship "was spoken the 24th of November within two days sail of Cadiz—all well." [58] Three days later they reached Lisbon—twenty-four days having been spent at sea.[59]

Even before they regained their land legs they doubtless inquired into the situation in France. Again the ephemeral political picture had changed. The Revolution had gone through all its phases but one. The Revolution of the 18th Brumaire (November) had been accomplished, the constitution thrown out the window, the Directory dissolved, Napoleon Bonaparte installed as First Consul, and Talleyrand (temporarily deposed) back again as Secretary for Foreign Affairs.

It is only natural that the envoys should have been gravely concerned. Had they but known, these changes were advantageous to the young Republic of the West. Among Bonaparte's vast dreams was the formation of a maritime league against Britain. And the United States would be a valuable ally in this scheme.

Desirous of obtaining "a more accurate knowledge of the features and effects of this Revolution" before they entered France, they proposed to Captain Barry that he land them in Holland where they could join William Vans Murray, but Barry was apprehensive that such a voyage "would hazard the frigate" at such a season. They therefore proposed to sail immediately for L'Orient.[60]

Again their plans were foiled by the weather. They were detained in the Tagus River by contrary winds and could not set out for L'Orient (which they had expected to reach in seven or eight days) until December 21. By the twenty-fourth, according to their letter to Pickering, they "encountered a severe gale, which blew, with little intermission, until the 2d of January, at which time it was ascertained that we had drifted as far as Latitude 50, and to the West of

Cape Clear." At this point they realized that Captain Barry "was extremely apprehensive of approaching any port of the French coast, on the bay of Biscay in bad weather, and as so much time had been already lost," they directed him to land them "in any port of France or Spain that he could make with safety and convenience." Accordingly, Captain Barry "thought proper to choose the port of Corunna, and anchored in the bay of Ares, a few leagues from that place on the 11th. of January." [61]

Davie and Ellsworth were "anxious to make the necessary preparations for our journey to Paris, and the winds continuing unfavorable for the sailing of the Frigate to Corunna, we landed at the village of Puente d'Eume," * and immediately set out for Corunna, where they arrived January 16, 1800.[62]

The following day they dispatched a letter to Talleyrand telling him of their arrival at Corunna after a ten weeks' voyage. What concerned them was that their letters of credence had been addressed to "the Executive Directory of the French republic," instead of to the Consulate. Regardless of this irregularity, they requested that passports be granted for them and their suite and that they be forwarded to them and to Murray by courier.

Meanwhile the envoys proceeded on to Burgos, arriving January 24, where they were met by the returning courier who bore the necessary passports and a letter from Talleyrand. The latter assured them they were "expected with impatience" and would "be received with warmth" and that the form of their letters of credence would "occasion no obstacle to the opening of a negotiation," from which he dared "anticipate the happiest results." [63]

Writing to Pickering from Burgos on February 10, the envoys regretted "exceedingly the time that must be consumed in a long and tedious journey by land, in the most rigorous and unfavorable season of the year." They felt, however, "after the ineffectual attempt to go to L'Orient by water, this measure appeared indispensable, notwithstanding any difficulties with which it might be connected." They planned to set out for Paris the following day, hoping to arrive "about the first of March." [64]

On the sixteenth, they were still in Burgos, from which Davie wrote

---

* The present Puentedeume, population 7,775.

The French Mission

John Haywood of some of their vicissitudes: It was nine hundred miles from Corunna to Paris and "the road difficult and mountainous." It was "the depth of winter" and they had travelled only three hundred miles so far. On the other hand, they had received their passports from Paris along with "every proper assurance respecting the object of the mission." Moreover, reports were that "all is tranquil in France and actual preparations making for the next campaign." [65]

Judge John Sitgreaves later reported that letters had been received from Davie from "a small town in Spain." Davie had stated that his health was "a good deal impaired by the passage at sea," by "their tedious mode of traveling over very rough roads," and by "wretched accomodations on them." [66]

While in Burgos the envoys wrote a letter, February 10, to the Secretary of the Navy thanking him for his "kind and particular attention to our accommodation on board the Frigate," which they found "in all respects, ample and comfortable." They had been "duly impressed with the civilities we received from the Commodore, and the Officers of the Frigate" and felt it "a pleasure" in having it in their power "to recommend to your attention Capt. James Barron, now second in command on board the United States, as an officer well calculated to serve his country with advantage and reputation."

From Burgos, a third of their overland journey behind them, they proceeded on to Bordeaux, where it was reported that "they were every where received in France with the highest demonstrations of respect—and that the French government was making splendid preparations to receive them." [67]

A conflicting account reported that they traveled through the French territory incognito "but wherever they were discovered, were received and entertained with the most enthusiastic respect and hospitality." The same account stated that they arrived in Paris a few days before a national fete was to be performed in honor of George Washington, who had died December 14, 1799. On this occasion, a bust of Washington was placed in the gallery of the Tuileries in the presence of the consuls and chief officers of the French nation. A particular seat, according to this account, was assigned to our envoys, but they "declined the intended honor, and mixed among the crowd of the populace." [68]

Be that as it may, the travel-weary envoys reached Paris March 2 after a four months' ordeal. Great must have been their relief to have reached their geographic goal at least and to find that William Vans Murray had arrived the previous day. But great must have been their anxiety in regard to their diplomatic goal—especially when they were to confront the most powerful ruler and the craftiest diplomat in Europe.

Was the omen propitious or not that upon the arrival all the standards of the French Republic were hung with a piece of black crepe in honor of the memory of George Washington—by order of Bonaparte himself?[69]

Indicative of the change in French sentiment were the French newspapers which were "honied o'er" in their praise of the American ministers. Particularly fulsome was the Paris *Publicisse* of February 8,[70] which described Oliver Ellsworth as "chief of the five great Judges" of the United States Supreme Court, whose life had been "wholly devoted to public life." A member of the Continental Congress and the Federal Convention and a United States senator, he was described as "a man of acknowledged virtue, of rigid probity, and strict morals."

Murray was described as "a landholder of Maryland," a Revolutionary soldier, and a member of Congress, "which found him one of its most able and zealous supporters," one of "the best orators in Congress," and one of "the most esteemed and noticed by that Great Man [Washington] upon whose tomb the whole U. States, with every demonstration, and with entire unanimity, and this moment are pouring the tears of gratitude and sorrow."

Davie was described as a landholder of North Carolina, who "partook largely of the glory of the war of Independence." Also he had been a member of the Federal Convention and the governor of North Carolina, in which capacity he had united "the esteem & approbation of his fellow citizens."

The very day after the meeting of the three envoys, they dispatched a letter to Talleyrand, requesting to be received by him and requesting "cards of surety" for the three envoys and their secretaries and servants: "Mr. Swift, secy. of Mr. Ellsworth, Mr. Mc.Henry, Secy. of Mr. Murray; Mr. Littlejohn, Secy of Mr. Davis [sic]; Oliver Ellsworth Junr. attached to the Legation—Charles Cambourg, servant to Mr. Ellsworth: Robt. McKee, servant to Mr. Davie: William

Loretta

Halifax residence of William Richardson Davie from *circa* 1785 until his retirement in 1805 to his plantation, "Tivoli," in the Garden of the Waxhaws. Owned and redecorated by Mr. and Mrs. Turner Stephenson.

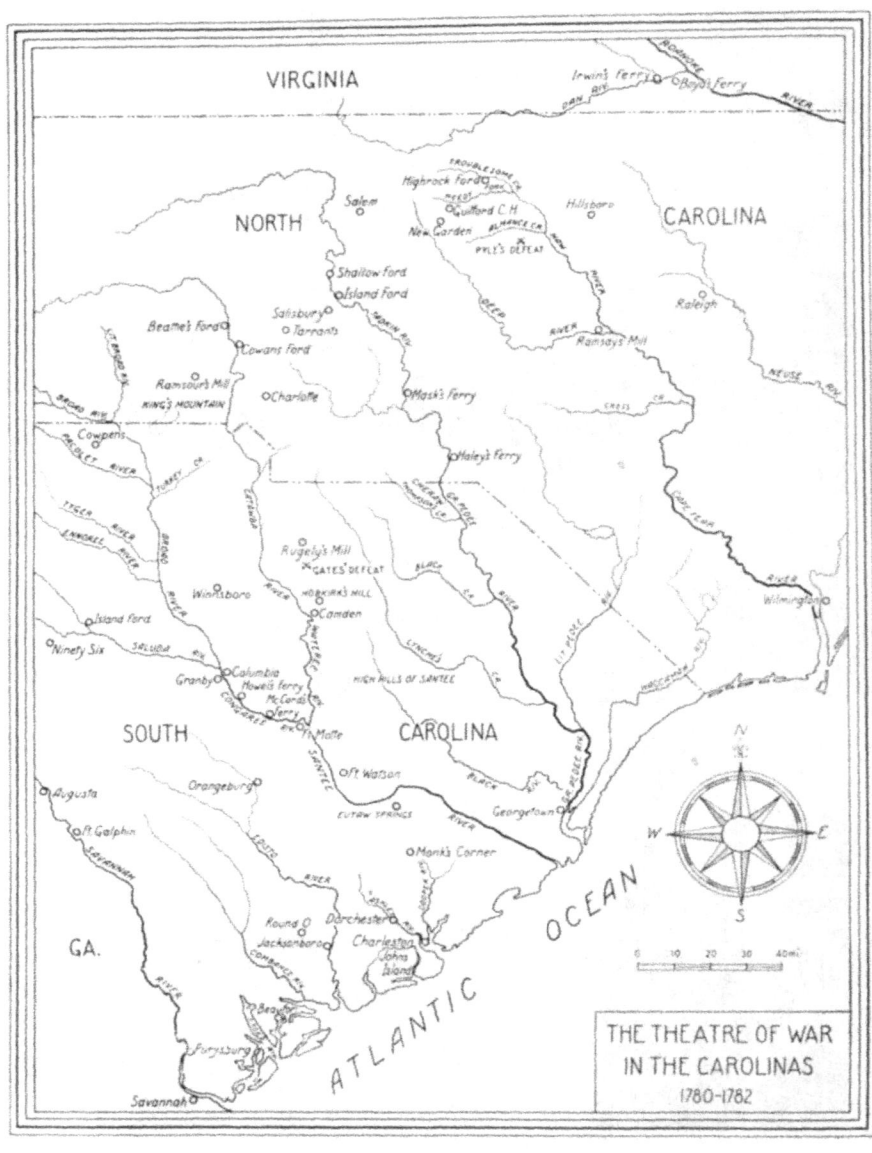

Permission for reproduction of map granted by the Historical Society of Delaware.

The French Mission

Gansby, (a black) servant to Mr. Murray." Davie and Ellsworth were staying with their suites at the Hôtel des Oiseaux, Rue de Sevres; Ellsworth, with his family and suite were at the Hôtel Casa Nova.[71]

Talleyrand, in contrast to the reception of the American ministers in the "X.Y.Z." affair, replied on the same day that if they would "take the trouble to call" upon him at 12:30 the following day he would "be exceedingly gratified at having the honor" of receiving them. He also informed them that Bonaparte, the First Consul, would give them an audience on the eighth at the Tuileries, in the hall of the ambassadors "a little before one o'clock."

On the appointed day the three envoys were properly received by Bonaparte at the Tuileries Palace, where it was announced to them that four days previously the First Consul had appointed French ministers plenipotentiary to negotiate with the Americans. Heading the commission was no less a person than Napoleon's brother, Citizen Joseph Bonaparte, "ex-ambassador at Rome," and soon to add to his laurels the negotiation of the Treaty of Lunéville with Austria and the Treaty of Amiens with England. The other two were Citizens Charles Pierre Claret Fleurieu, "late Minister of Marine," and Pierre Louis Roederer, "counsellor of state." Fleurieu, after a fourteen months' imprisonment during the Terror, had recently been rewarded by Bonaparte by appointments to the Council of State, as a grand officer of the Legion of Honor, and as a senator in 1805. Roederer had represented the Third Estate in the National Assembly and he, too, on December 25, 1799, was appointed to the Council of State by Bonaparte. They were, according to Talleyrand, to treat with the American envoys "concerning the differences existing between the two nations, to effect the accommodation which they mutually desire, and to fulfil the wish, expressed by the two Governments, to remove a misunderstanding which comports, as little, with their interests as with their sentiments." All augured well for a favorable agreement.*

Privately, Talleyrand instructed the ministers to consider the negotiations from the standpoint of the past (in which America

---

* Twenty-one years later Colonel Ransom Sutherland, writing to Judge Archibald D. Murphey, reported: "It is said Bonaparte took an uncommon notice of Davie, more than of any other ambassador at his court, and thought him a great man."—*N.C. University Magazine*, III (Sept., 1854), 324.

should be recalled to her obligations to France), and of the present (in which the commercial relations and bad feelings were to be corrected), but principally they should be concerned with the future. As in the French treaty of 1778, France should separate America from England, strip England of influence in America, provide for the security of the French and Spanish colonies, open commerce between America and all nations (especially France and her colonies), and attach the United States politically to France in order to secure the advantage of American neutrality and sympathy in future wars.

Specifically the French ministers were instructed to follow three principles: (1) re-establish the treaties and conventions as before the present hostilities; (2) reclaim the jurisdiction of French consuls in the United States, and (3) demand a revision of the treaties in order that France would enjoy the same privileges accorded England by Jay's treaty. After these accomplishments, there would remain only the question of damages, which Talleyrand admitted would be on the side of the Americans.[72]

On March 9 Ellsworth, Davie, and Murray communicated to Talleyrand that they were ready to enter into negotiation as soon as the French ministers were so disposed. They waited impatiently until March 15 "for some intimation" from them on the subject and finally addressed a note directly to the French ministers reiterating their desire to begin.

The days of procrastination began. They were informed verbally that "the delay was much regretted by the French government and the ministers, and that it was occasioned by the indisposition of Mr. Joseph Bonaparte, president of the French commission." The latter also wrote a note, March 25, thanking Ellsworth and Davie for their concern over his indisposition and communicating to them his regrets over the delay.[73] Ellsworth and Davie replied the same day, expressing their hope that "Mr. Bonaparte will soon be sufficiently recovered to permit him, without danger of compromising his health," to enter upon the important business at hand.

After another exchange of notes between the two sets of ministers, the French ministers finally invited the Americans to meet on April 2 at the house of Citizen Bonaparte. The ministers convened at the appointed hour, and their respective powers were exchanged and the mode of conducting the negotiation adjusted. Because of the lan-

The French Mission

guage difficulty, they decided to treat most matters in writing. The arduous task of handling the correspondence was entrusted to Louis-André Pichon, who had been Talleyrand's agent in the conversations with Murray at the Hague. Pichon, who had been appointed secretary to the French commission by Bonaparte, had served in the United States in 1794-95 as secretary to Fauchet, the French minister.[74]

Quibbling began at once. The following day the Americans sent a note to the French in which they questioned whether the latter had powers "sufficiently full and explicit," because they were empowered only to *"negotiate respecting the existing differences,"* and "not to settle them also by treaty."

Perhaps this was a petty insistence on the part of the American ministers, but a chip-on-the-shoulder attitude could easily be understood. At least it was not deemed too inconsequential for the French ministers to consult Talleyrand, who in turn consulted Bonaparte himself. On April 7 a reply came from the French ministers, enclosing an assuring letter from Talleyrand and the decree of Bonaparte which empowered his ministers "to negotiate ... as well as to sign and conclude, in the name of the republic, whatever shall to them appear necessary to effect a perfect re-establishment of good harmony" between the two nations.

Now at last the time seemed ripe to get down to business. The Americans, upon the receipt of these communications, sent a note to the French ministers informing them that they were ready to "enter directly on the great object of their mission, an object which they believe may be best obtained by avoiding to trace too minutely the too well known and too painful incidents which have rendered a negotiation necessary." Instead, they proposed an arrangement "to ascertain and discharge the equitable claims of the citizens of either nation upon the other, whether founded on contract, treaty, or the law of nations." Their "general view" was that "reciprocity and freedom of commercial intercourse" should be established between the two nations.

The French replied on April 9 that they felt there were two primary objects to be accomplished in the negotiations: The first ought to be the determination of the rules and steps to be pursued for the indemnification of damages of each nation and of its citizens. Secondly, they should assure the execution of treaties of amity and

[339]

commerce already existing between the two nations along reciprocal lines.

By this time the envoys, it may be assumed, had thoroughly digested the specific instructions drawn up by John Adams and his cabinet and submitted to the American envoys before their departure for France. The instructions themselves were prefaced by an explanation or justification for sending such a mission. Attention was called to the "unexampled aggressions, depredations, and hostilities" perpetrated by the French republic against the commerce and citizens of the United States. These in turn had forced the United States to adopt measures to put a stop to them, but these new measures had only been followed by new aggressions and depredations against American commerce. Moreover, there had been the humiliating "X.Y.Z." affair. The upshot of the matter was that the United States would have been justified in declaring war, but in the interests of peace they had contented themselves with preparations for war and measures calculated to protect their commerce. Meanwhile there had come the about-face of Talleyrand and the assurance that a new minister would be properly received.

The instructions then proceeded to admonish the envoys that they were to brook no indignity or insult in the form of procrastination from the French, but should terminate their mission at once in such an event. They were also advised that an agreement should be reached by April 1 at the latest so that the present session of Congress could take any necessary action.

The ensuing instructions—thirty of them—were explicit and detailed. The first article, set forth as "an indispensable condition of the treaty," was a stipulation that France would be expected to make to the citizens of the United States "full compensation for all losses and damages" which they had sustained "by reason of irregular or illegal captures or condemnation of their vessels and other property." These were to be deemed "irregular or illegal" when they were "contrary to the law of nations ... and to the stipulations in the treaty of amity and commerce of the 6th of February 1778." This instruction was further amplified by five detailed rules for the adjudication of these illegal seizures.

Article II provided that, if the above were agreed to, a Board of Commission of five men should be appointed to examine and adjust

The French Mission

all the claims of the citizens of the two countries. Specific instructions were given as to the composition, duties, and jurisdiction of this board. The claims of the United States and the French government, as distinguished from those of their citizens, should also be submitted to this board, but authority was given the envoys to waive this claim if the French government waived its claim.

If these first two instructions were agreed upon, the envoys were then to proceed "to the regulation of navigation and commerce... between the two nations." They were accordingly empowered to stipulate that "there shall be a reciprocal and entirely perfect liberty of commerce and navigation between France and the United States, and their territories and dominions, in every part of the world." The framers were aware that this opening of a colonial trade was not the "usual policy of European nations," but they pleaded the "singular injuries" our commerce had sustained from France as a justification. They also very astutely pointed to "the inability of France immediately to furnish the requisite navigation and supplies for the commerce of her distant possessions." However, if France refused to acquiesce, the envoys should "remain silent on the subject."

Another important feature of the instructions was a reciprocal most-favored-nations clause, although it was not so called. Also reciprocal citizenship and property rights between citizens of the two countries should be agreed upon. And such things as "the free exercise of religion, at least in their own houses" should be accorded to each country's citizens.

As to rights upon the high seas, they insisted that ships of war and other public vessels as well as private ships of each country "should at all times be hospitably received in the ports of the other." Other instructions provided for the jurisdiction of consuls, the operation of prize courts, and the exact interpretation of what was to be deemed contraband of war.

Article XXX provided that "the articles of the treaty which you may conclude, as far as they respect compensation and payment for past injuries and contracts, should be permanent, until the objects thereof be fulfilled."

Finally they instructed—in archaic terminology—that certain other points were "to be considered as ultimated." Particularly important was the fact that the French Treaty of 1778, "no longer obligatory by act of Congress," should not be "in whole or in part revived by the new treaty; but that all the engagements, to which the United States are to become parties, be specificied in the new treaty." Also there was to be no guaranty or engagement "in the nature of an alliance." Finally, the duration of the treaty was to be limited to twelve years "at furthest."

Armed with such optimistic, exact, and exacting instructions, the American envoys must have taken up the tug of war with a good deal of misgivings.

The Americans acquiesced in the French proposal of April 9 to include such claims as either nation might have against the other. Their only object in omitting it in their preliminary proposal, they averred, was "not from the apprehension of an unfavorable balance, but ... because their discussion might be unpleasant and dilatory, and because also, to insist on pecuniary compensation for themselves, would be incompatible with that magnanimity which it was presumed both nations would prefer in an act of accomodation, so auspicious to their future prosperity."

The Americans also made it clear they did not expect to renew or amend the former treaty of commerce, but to pose a new one. With these considerations firmly in mind, the Americans announced they would soon be ready to offer the details of their proposals.

The French in turn demanded, as a condition precedent to further negotiations, that the American envoys should give an assurance that their government would "terminate, without delay," the hostile measures adopted against the French republic. The American reply declared that they had no such authority, but had assumed that these would be incorporated in the treaty. However, if they received notification of any such repeals, it "would be as well their pleasure as their duty" to transmit them to the French ministers.

Assuming that this arrangement would be amenable to the French, the Americans, on April 18, presented for consideration "some details respecting the claims of individuals," which they "preferred to offer ... at once in the form of articles of the treaty, as containing a full and frank expression of their views." These six articles were designed to establish "a firm, inviolable, and universal peace, and a true and sincere friendship" between the two nations. Most important among them were the agreements that there should be "full and complete

The French Mission

compensation" by the two governments of the claims of the citizens of each country as a result of the individual losses and damage, as a result of "irregular or illegal captures or condemnations" or by "irregular or illegal seizures or detentions" of their vessels and other property.

In order to ascertain the amount of any such losses and damage, they provided that the five commissioners should be appointed and authorized to assess the damage. The composition of this board, its powers, duties, and restrictions, were set out at length.

It was not until May 6 that the French ministers sent their measured reply. Stripped of its verbosity, it acknowledged the expediency of providing a suitable indemnity, *but* they maintained that the original treaties of 1778 would have to be "the sole basis of their negotiations." In conclusion they reiterated their stand:

"In hastening to recognize the principle of compensation, it was the intention of the undersigned to exhibit an unequivocal proof of the fidelity of France to her ancient engagements; *all pecuniary stipulations appearing to her proper as results from ancient treaties, not as preliminaries to a new one* [italics mine]."

Upon receipt of this letter, Messrs Davie, Ellsworth, and Murray held a prolonged conference during which they prepared their reply. The envoys abruptly decided that they "would facilitate the arrangements as to the preliminary object, and avoid the waste of time, in the discussion of abstract principles, by sending the entire project of a treaty which they had then prepared."

Therefore, on the following day, May 8, they forwarded to the French ministers the remaining part of their projected treaty, from Article VII to Article XXX inclusive, which was, almost article for article, a recapitulation of their original instructions. Accompanying this draft was a letter in which they sought to justify their position of employing the treaties of 1778 up to July 7, 1798 only (the date of their unilateral abrogation by the United States Senate) and "leaving their subsequent causes of complaint to rest upon the law of nations."

They restated the American position that it was not until after the treaties had "been violated to a great extent on the part of the French republic, nor till after explanations and an amicable adjustment, sought by the United States, had been refused, that they did, on the 7th day of July, 1798, by a solemn act, declare that they were freed and

WILLIAM R. DAVIE

exonerated from the treaties...." They stated emphatically, therefore, that "that declaration cannot be recalled." Instead they posed two questions, with the accompanying answers, on which their negotiations should be based—the political and the commercial relations between the two nations.

As to the political relations, they reiterated the sentiments of the late George Washington in his Proclamation of Neutrality, which were later to be embodied as an integral part of the Monroe Doctrine. They stated that "the interest of the United States, while it prompts them strongly to cultivate a good understanding with France, forbids them to wish such relations to any Power as might involve them in the contests with which Europe is so often scourged."

As for the commercial relations between the two nations, they called for a most-favored-nation clause, and an "unembarrassed intercourse between the United States and the French West Indian island."

While awaiting a reply, Davie and his associates, on May 17, addressed a long letter to Pickering, to explain the delays. Talleyrand, to whom all important points were referred by the French, had "been confined by a severe illness from about the 15th of April to the 14th or 15th of this month." Also, the "situation of the army of Italy, commanded by General Massena, has been extremely critical, and has attracted the particular attention of the Premier Consul." A reserve army of 60,000 men had been sent to its relief. But the French, they reported, were "very successful in the Rhine, and the Government is as yet unshaken; it professes justice and moderation, and appears to be desirous of peace, which, there is some reason to believe, may be the result of the present campaign."

As for their own success, the ministers were "doubtful," because the French thought it "hard to indemnify for violating engagements, unless they can thereby be restored to the benefits of them." They furthermore reported that "very few American vessels have been brought into European ports since our arrival at Paris, and, for some time past, we have heard of none." They did not know, however, of any orders of the French government "for the restraining of captures," but American prisoners had been "generally released, on a receipt being given by the American agents, promising the discharge of as many French seamen from confinement in the United States."

By May 22 there was still no reply to the American proposals. The

The French Mission

Americans, in their journal, attributed the delay to "the insuperable repugnance" of the French government "to yield its claim to the anteriority assumed to it in the treaty of amity and commerce of 1778." Moreover, the French "strenuously" denied "the power of the American Government to annul the treaties by a simple legislative act and always concluding that it was perfectly incompatible with the honor and dignity of France to assent to the extinction of a right in favor of an enemy, and much more so to appear to acquiesce in the establishment of that right in favor of Great Britain."

On the following day at a joint interview the American envoys were "officially informed that the negotiation was at a stand on the part of France" and that "no further progress would be made until other powers were procured from the Premier Consul, as the tenor of their instructions made the acknowledgment of former treaties the basis of negotiation and the condition of compensation." The French commissioners further advised that they were working on a report which would be delivered in a day or two to Talleyrand and forwarded immediately by a courier to Bonaparte, who "had left Paris the 6th of May, and was supposed to be at this time in Switzerland or Italy."

And so the negotiations were brought to an abrupt standstill at this critical juncture. The frustrated Americans, thinking that the judgment of Bonaparte "would probably be formed upon the impressions made by the report" and that his instructions might be conclusive, deemed it expedient to send another note "containing an intermediate ground, conciliatory to the pride of the French Government, without sacrificing the honor or interest of the United States." They therefore proposed to add to Article XXXII the following clause:

"Nor will either of the said parties, while they continue in amity, make a treaty with any foreign Sovereign or state, stipulating for the privateers and prizes of such Sovereign or state an asylum in the ports of either, unless they shall have assured to each other such right of asylum for the privateers and prizes of each in the ports of the other."

While the Americans were cooling their heels, they received a dispatch dated April 9 from Pickering, acknowledging their letter of February 10 from Burgos, and informing them that Captain McNeill, aboard the *Portsmouth*, was conveying this letter to Havre de Grace, whence he would send one of his officers to Paris to receive their orders. The President assumed—erroneously—that by then their negotiations would be concluded.

Meanwhile, June 1 arrived. Still no answer from the French. Finally, on June 5 Messrs. Joseph Bonaparte, Fleurieu, and Roederer wrote the Americans that they had considered the American propositions so seriously that they had submitted them to Talleyrand, "by whom they are informed that he has himself deemed it necessary to take the direction of the First Consul," upon whose decision they were waiting. They were also confidentially informed that "the whole business was referred to the decision of the Premier Consul, who was then in Italy" and that Joseph Bonaparte had set out to join his more illustrious brother. The journal of the Americans stated simply that the "object of his journey to the Premier was not publicly known, nor was his departure announced to the American ministers." It continued by recording that the important battle of Marengo took place on June 14, and that Napoleon Bonaparte returned to Paris July 3, followed by his brother a few days later.

The Americans anxiously waited until July 6 before addressing one of their many requests to the French in an effort to expedite the tedious and harassing business. The following day they received an invitation to dine with Joseph Bonaparte on the eleventh—at which time they anticipated the long-awaited conference.

Again they were disappointed. After arrival at the *hôtel* of the president of the French commission, they were informed, before dinner, that the whole business was still in the hands of the Premier Consul, but that his decisions and instructions were expected "in the course of a few days." Whereupon, the Americans "repeated their regret at the long delay" and asked for a conference that evening. The French ministers "readily consented."

At this conference Joseph Bonaparte reiterated, in strong language, the French position and the fact that it was, confidentially, "the decided opinion of the First Consul that the ancient treaties ought to be the basis of the negotiation; that compensation could only be a consequence of the existence of the treaties, and the re-establishment under them of the former privileges and relations; and that he would never consent to make a treaty which would surrender the exclusive rights of France, in effect in favor of any enemy; or in any event, make a treaty with the United States, which would not place France on a

THE FRENCH MISSION

footing of equality at least with Great Britain." His brother also thought that "it would be derogatory to the present Government to make a treaty, less advantageous and less honorable than that made by the royal Government." The conference closed, of course, on a continued note of suspense.

After prolonged deliberations, the Americans requested another interview, at which they determined to make a proposal to the effect that the indemnities should not be paid until the United States government should have offered to France "an article, re-establishing her in the exclusive privileges, she claimed, under the treaty of 1778." They were well aware that the American government "might or might not perform this condition," but they were also aware that "unless the indemnities were secured by some means under the present negotiation, they would be forever lost."

Accordingly, at a conference on July 15, they proposed that the indemnities which might be awarded the United States should not be paid "until the United States shall have offered to France an article, stipulating free admission into the ports of each for the privateers and prizes of the other, and the exclusion of those of their enemies; nor unless the article be offered within seven years." Needless to say, this concession "was not perfectly satisfactory to the French ministers."

The concession on the part of the Americans, it may be surmised, was the result of events which had recently occurred in the United States. The full import of these changes was certainly not lost on Talleyrand, who reported to Bonaparte early in July that Secretary of State Pickering had been replaced by John Marshall, one of the American ministers in the "X.Y.Z." affair, and even more important, that the Democratic-Republicans had been so successful in state elections that it seemed highly probable that the Francophile Thomas Jefferson would be elected President in November.[75] Again reporting to Bonaparte, July 13, he stated that the attitude of the American ministers had changed, that they showed "with appearance of conviction, a desire to terminate their mission in a manner equally agreeable to the two peoples."[76]

Another meeting was held July 20, this time at M. Roederer's, where after dinner an interview took place. Again, no progress, except that Joseph Bonaparte said he had conferred with Talleyrand that morning and had been assured that they would receive an official answer "in a few days."

The conference was followed by another exchange of notes between the commissioners, in which each tried, on the bases of national honor and the writings of Vattel, to justify their respective positions. There was nothing accomplished. There was nothing to do but wait, wait, wait.

At last, on August 11, the French commissioners informed the Americans, by a diplomatic note, that they had received their new instructions and were therewith presenting "the reflections and overtures which the actual state of the negotiations appears to demand." They insisted adamantly on two principles. The first was a strong reiteration of their historic stand: "to stipulate a full and entire recognition of the treaties, and a reciprocal promise of indemnities for the damages resulting, on the part of either, from their infraction."

The second proposition, in case the first should not be accepted, was the abrogation of the former treaties, conditioned upon the formation of a new treaty, "in which the French nation, abandoning a privilege inconvenient to the United States, shall be placed, in her political and commercial relations, on an equal footing with the most favored nations: and an entire silence on the subject of indemnities."

Thus presented with these double overtures or dual ultimata, the American ministers, on August 15, reported their dilemma to the Secretary of State. After a detailed recital of the proceedings, they concluded that "the negotiation must be abandoned, or our instructions deviated from." They said further that if "the latter be ventured upon, which, from present appearance is not improbable, the deviation will not be greater than a change of circumstances may be presumed to justify."

Shortly thereafter a conference was held with the French ministers to ascertain more precisely their views on certain points in their recent note. As might be expected, the results were "little satisfactory," the French ministers being "extremely reserved, answering with great caution to every inquiry in the general terms of their note."

A deadlock had been reached and it therefore became necessary for the Americans to decide "whether the negotiations should be broken off, or the instructions departed from; whether the treaties should be revived, or the indemnities sacrificed." And for the first time, heated words passed between the French and the Americans. Joseph Bonaparte stated he would resign rather than sign a treaty modifying the treaties of 1778 and yet providing indemnities to American citizens.

The Americans resorted to various stratagems, modifications, and overtures, through conferences and notes. All proved unavailing. All was discouraging. And August had given way to September. And it had been an entire year since Davie, with high hopes, had left Raleigh.

By September 13 the American ministers were "now convinced that the door was perfectly closed against all hope of obtaining indemnities, with any modification of the treaties." It therefore "only remained to be determined whether, under all circumstances, it would not be expedient to attempt a temporary arrangement which would extricate the United States from war, or that peculiar state of hostility in which they are at present involved, save the immense property of our citizens now depending before the council of prizes, and secure, as far as possible, our commerce against the abuses of captures during the present war."

Having arrived at this conclusion, they dispatched a note that day to the French ministers, reiterating these sentiments and stating that nothing remained but "to consider the expediency of a temporary arrangement." With this in mind, they offered the following overtures:

"1. The ministers plenipotentiary of the respective parties, not being able at present to agree respecting the former treaties and indemnities, the parties will in due and convenient time further treat on those subjects; and, until they shall have agreed respecting the same, the said treaties shall have no operation. In the meantime,

"2. The parties shall abstain from all unfriendly acts; their commercial intercourse shall be free, and debts shall be recoverable in the same manner as if no misunderstanding had intervened.

"3. Property captured and not yet definitely condemned, or which may be captured before the exchange of ratifications, shall be mutually restored. Proofs of ownership to be specified in the convention.

"4. Some provisional regulations shall be made to prevent abuses and disputes that may arise out of future cases of capture."

By September 19 the two commissions had tentatively agreed on the above articles, plus a mutual most-favored-nation clause. Having for the first time achieved something approaching a meeting of the minds, they further agreed to meet from day to day until the business was finished. As a result, the ministers moved rapidly to a settlement of the issues between the two nations.

The resulting draft, ready for signatures September 30, was composed of twenty-seven articles and provided for a settlement somewhat more comprehensive than the American ministers originally intended. Recognizing "a firm, inviolable, and universal peace, and a true and sincere friendship" between the two countries, the instrument was based on two already-agreed-upon premises: the former treaties were to have "no effect" and the two countries would "negotiate ulteriorly" on the subject of indemnities. The ensuing provisions provided for restoration of naval vessels by each country; the restoration of property captured but not yet definitely condemned; the resumption of free commerce on a most-favored-nation footing in regard to privateers, prizes, commercial privileges, and tariffs; a liberal definition of contraband of war; a recognition of the principle of "**free ships, free goods**"; measures for the payment of debts due each country; and an agreement by the French not to require American ships to carry any papers other than those customary in the United States.

Two additional hurdles remained: the title of the instrument and the language to be used. The French wanted to make it more than a temporary agreement and to call it "a treaty of amity and commerce." The Americans insisted that they had consented to negotiate only on the basis of a "convention." The French accused the Americans of treating in a spirit of enmity and ill will; whereupon the Americans withdrew to confer. The French confessed in a letter that day to Talleyrand that they were amazed when they realized how heatedly they themselves had spoken. The Americans returned with the announcement that they were willing to discuss the *substance* of a treaty and to call it "a provisional treaty." The French, realizing the serious threat to the entire negotiation, consented.[77]

The French also insisted that the instrument should be signed in French, after the manner of the treaty of 1778; the Americans refused to recognize this precedent. A sharp debate ensued, followed by an insistent letter from Messrs. Fleurieu and Roederer. Finally, the Americans, "with great reluctance," agreed to the signing in the form of the treaty of 1778, which was signed in both languages, but was declared to have been prepared in French.

The French Mission

The draft of the provisional treaty was accordingly signed at the Hôtel des Oiseaux at 2:00 A.M., October 1. The original date, September 30, was allowed to remain.[78]

But all difficulties were not yet adjusted. On the morning of October 2, the French ministers called again at the abode of the Americans, proposing two alterations requested by Bonaparte. Instead of being drawn up in the name of the French republic it should read in the name of the First Consul—a concession the Americans willingly granted. The other requested that the word "provisional" in the name of the treaty be stricken out. The Americans, however, seized this opportunity to resume their opposition to the admission in favor of the French language. They agreed to change the term "provisional treaty" for that of a "convention," on condition that that part of the treaty which respected the French language be stricken out. The French agreed. It was then decided that the revised convention needed new signatures. The final ceremony took place on October 3 at 6:00 P.M. at the chateau of Joseph Bonaparte—Mortfontaine, eighteen miles north of Paris. The convention is therefore often referred to as the "Treaty of Mortfontaine." Six copies were signed and sealed under the former date of September 30. Two copies were kept by the French commissioners, two by Murray, and two were taken by Davie and Ellsworth.

In conjunction with the signing, a splendid fête was held to celebrate the Franco-American reconciliation. The affair, staged by Joseph Bonaparte, was intended, according to a Paris newspaper, "to give to the American ministers a testimony of the disposition of the government towards the United States, and of the general satisfaction produced by the rapprochement."[79]

The American envoys and their suites arrived about 2:00 P.M. Also in attendance were the two consuls, all the French ministers, the members of the diplomatic corps, several counsellors of state, the presidents of the Senate, of the legislative body, and of the tribunate, and "various people with various titles," including General Lafayette. An hour or so later Napoleon Bonaparte and his family were announced by the firing of cannon and the playing of bands.

Throughout the afternoon the guests "amused themselves by walking in the park, or gardens attached to the Chateau, which are laid out in English style, affording picturesque views." A canal flowed behind the chateau, and in front, "at a small distance, is a park with rocky, barren hills, topped by an ancient tower on one side, & a large, natural pond with Islands interspersed, and fine cultivated hills here and there on the other."

At six o'clock Talleyrand delivered the convention to the First Consul, who told the Americans he approved of it. Cannon were fired to announce the final signature and the ratification by Napoleon.

Afterwards dinner was served on three tables with 180 place settings in three adjoining halls. The first, called the "Hall of the Union," was "superbly decorated and illuminated, hung with verdant wreaths and numerous inscriptions commemorating the 4th of July 1776 and other periods and places celebrated by important actions in America during the struggle for Independence." The second and third halls, called the "Hall of Washington" and the "Hall of Franklin," were adorned respectively with the bust of the man commemorated and other elaborate decorations.

The toasts proposed carried out the spirit of American Independence and French liberty. Napoleon's was "To the memory of the French and Americans who died on the field of battle for the independence of the new world." He was seconded by the Second Consul, Cambacérès: "To the successor of Washington."

After dinner, on the terrace, there was "a splendid and ingenious display of Fireworks" depicting the union of France and the United States. Afterwards a concert was "presented by the most distinguished artists of the capital." And after this—about twelve o'clock—there were "two short but interesting Comedies," which were performed in the private theatre within the chateau by "the most distinguished artists that Paris could afford," with "a perfection and harmony beyond all expression." About two o'clock some of the company "took to their beds, some took a second supper, and some their exit for Paris at 3 o'clock."

It was at this same affair that an interesting episode occurred between Napoleon Bonaparte and Davie. It seems that one Citizen Cambry, prefect of the department of Oise, presented to Bonaparte several gold coins of the period of the Roman republic and empire, which had been found in a large earthen vessel in his department. The prefect observed that they were difficult to procure because the people were afraid they would be taken from them, according to an

ROBERT JONES, JR. (1718-1766)

Of "The Castle," co. Northampton, province of North Carolina. Attorney General for Lord Granville and for the Crown, province of North Carolina, member of the General Assembly (1754-1761), and father of Willie Jones of "The Grove," co. Halifax, and Brigadier General Allen Jones of "Mount Gallant," co. Northampton. Oil portrait, by an unknown artist, now in possession of Colonel Preston Davie, New York City.

BRIGADIER GENERAL ALLEN JONES (1743-1808)

Of "Mount Gallant," co. Northampton, North Carolina. Father of Sarah (1762-1802), wife of William Richardson Davie. Miniature by an unknown artist, now owned by Colonel Preston Davie, New York City.

BOOKPLATE of William Richardson Davie, displaying Davie heraldic Arms. (*left*)

HATCHMENT displaying Davie heraldic Arms used at funeral ceremony of Mary Richardson (1723-1767), wife of Archibald Davie (1724-1800) and mother of William Richardson Davie. Replica of this hatchment is in the Old Waxhaw Presbyterian Church, near Lancaster, S.C. (*right*)

TOMB OF GOVERNOR WILLIAM RICHARDSON DAVIE (1756-1820)
In Davie Family burial enclosure, Waxhaw Church, Lancaster County, S.C.

ancient French law that all such treasures belong to the government. Bonaparte replied that this was no longer true and instructed the prefect to buy up as many as possible lest they be melted down into bullion. After this exchange, the First Consul advanced toward Davie and said to him: "These Roman medals, Sir, have just been found in France. Accept and carry them with you to America, so that monuments of the Roman Republic may become pledges of amity and union between the republics of France and the United States." *

After such a gala and festive affair the Americans took their official leave of the First Consul, to whom they were presented by Talleyrand. Ellsworth, speaking for his colleagues, said that "he hoped the convention ... would be the basis of a lasting friendship between France and America." Murray added "that the American ministers would omit nothing to accomplish this end." Bonaparte replied that "the differences which had existed being terminated, there should only remain a trace of the family quarrel; that the liberal principles consecrated in the convention of the 9th Vendemaire in regard to navigation should be the basis of the rapprochement between the two nations, as they were of their interests; and that it became more important than ever, in the present circumstances, for the two nations to adhere to it always."

Davie and Ellsworth and their suites took their leave from Mortfontaine on October 4 for Havre de Grace, but Murray remained in Paris with his wife. That afternoon the homeward-bound envoys had only reached St. Denis, where they were forced to send back to Paris for stronger carriages. Again fate was against them. They did not reach the port until the evening of the sixth "too late to take passage in the *Portsmouth* which might have sailed that morning but as the tide would not allow her to go to sea but one in 8 or 10 days she could not sail till after the middle of the month." This delay caused Ellsworth, whose health had been broken by "frequent attacks of the gravel" during the summer in Paris, to eschew a late fall voyage. Instead, when the *Portsmouth* sailed after October 15, Ellsworth

---

* *Raleigh Register*, December 30, 1800. The whereabouts of these coins is unknown today, although a number of interesting mementos and curios from his French mission have recently been presented to the Louis Round Wilson Library, Chapel Hill, by the children of the late Dr. William Richardson Davie Crockett of Austin, Texas.

debarked in England "to try the efficacy of the mineral waters of Bath." His resignation as chief justice was sent to the President by his secretary.[80]

There is little available information on Davie's private affairs while in Paris. His sojourn there was no doubt made more comfortable and enjoyable by the presence of Gaven C. Mountflorence, who was in charge of the "Ex Consulate General of the United States at Paris." Judging from a number of letters from Mountflorence to Davie, Mountflorence also served as a "leg man" for Davie; he looked up various points of international law in the public library and kept Davie and his colleagues informed of the latest occurrences, seizures and prize cases in France.[81] These letters also reveal that Davie took advantage of the Paris opera and concerts. On one occasion at least he was invited to accompany Mrs. Mountflorence to a concert.[82]

Mountflorence also served as Davie's purchasing agent. At the time of Davie's departure, he submitted a final account of his disbursements, which included "the last Purchase of Wine, fruits & liquors amg to £1708 10s," and an account against the United States for house rent for eighteen months for $210.[83]

The only other evidence concerning Davie's personal and social life in Paris is that he was "exceedingly healthy" while there[84] and that he was recognized and called upon by the diplomatic corps in Paris. A number of visiting cards now in the Davie Collection at the University of North Carolina reveal such names as the Spanish ambassador, the Prussian minister, the Swiss minister, and the minister from Rome.*

According to Fordyce Hubbard, his "beauty of person and graceful manners, rendered more attractive perhaps by a slight *hauteur* which was natural to him, as well as the high rank in which he came, gained him a ready access to the most polished circles of that gay capital, and he soon became a favorite with those whose favor he most highly valued."[85]

And his own secretary, Joseph B. Littlejohn, wrote: "A man of his imposing appearance and dignified deportment could not fail to attract especial notice and respect, wherever he went. I could not but re-

---

*These mementos were presented to the Louis Round Wilson Library, Chapel Hill, by the children of William Richardson Davie Crockett, of Austin, Texas.

The French Mission

mark, that Bonaparte, in addressing the American legation at his levees, seemed for the time to forget that Governor Davie was *second* in the commission, his attention being more particularly directed to him." [86]

Once aboard the frigate *Portsmouth,* commanded by Captain McNeill, Davie no doubt pondered at length on the real significance of this so-called convention. Certainly the French were pleased with the dénouement. Napoleon Bonaparte and Talleyrand had both expressed their warm approval. In fact, the latter went so far as to describe it later as "a monument of justice, liberality, and common sense." [87] Moreover, Talleyrand had taken immediate steps to ensure French compliance with the spirit of the treaty. He promptly urged the French Council of Prizes to see that the principle of "free ships, free goods" was not violated. The minister of the navy and colonies was instructed to carry out at once the terms of the convention in the colonies. All American ships detained in French ports were to be released at once. Moreover, a copy of the convention was sent by the ship carrying Davie, to Letombe, the consul-general in the United States, with instructions to see that the French commercial agents in America resumed full commercial relations at once. Finally, to replace the aging Letombe, Talleyrand dispatched the energetic and experienced Pichon to serve as chargé d'affaires until a new minister should arrive.

The French press had hailed the convention as a striking achievement and loftily announced that it would be "delightful" to the First Consul "to evince himself anew, faithful to his principles by ratifying the treaty ... at a moment in which Europe resounds with the violation of neutral flags." The American ministers, it was thought, also "appreciated the advantages of being allied to a nation governed at length with wisdom and firmness." In fact, according to the press, "every thing announces that a strict and durable friendship is about to terminate the mutual commerce of the two nations." [88]

But what would be its reception in the United States? Especially, what would be its reception by the claimants against French depredations? Yet it must be admitted that it had definitely settled the question of neutral rights and had removed the causes of irritation arising under the treaties of 1778 and the consular convention of 1788. More important than that was the fact that the United States had been released from the one and only entangling alliance in her history.

In justifying their final action, the ministers had written the new Secretary of State, John Marshall, on October 4 that their only alternative would have been to have left the United States "involved in a contest, and, according to appearances, soon alone in a contest, which it might be as difficult for them to relinquish with honour as to pursue with a prospect of advantage." The most desirable features of the former treaties had been preserved; the embarrassing ones had been sloughed off.[89]

After a voyage of about six weeks, Davie finally landed at Norfolk, Virginia, the first week in December. He had been gone from his loved ones at Halifax for fifteen months. Although he was less than ninety miles from home, he dutifully proceeded to the Federal City of Washington,[90] after sending "a Waggon Load of Goods to Mrs. Davie" and a letter which contained "no Intelligence."[91]

Neither was any information as to the outcome of the mission revealed by him to the public, but a general optimism was reflected by the rise in the price of tobacco at Petersburg.[92]

Davie arrived in Washington December 11, an event which was revealed the following day by William Barry Grove in a letter to William Gaston of Newbern. He reported that, although he did not know the terms of the treaty, he had "no doubt they are the best, that our Divided Country could obtain, from a nation whose energy and Diplomatic Skill is acknowledged to be very great." He continued by a sarcastic reference to the radical change of the political picture, the so-called "Revolution of 1800," which had swept the Democratic-Republicans into office: "but on that score I suppose we may now be at ease, for if the Treaty does not please us, our new President can send Doc'r Logan with full powers to amend it." *

Having delivered the treaty and other papers of a confidential nature, Davie lost little time in setting out for Halifax, where he apparently arrived on December 23. The little town of Halifax indeed anticipated "great rejoicing" that Christmas season. In addition to the monthly ball on the twenty-sixth, there was the long-awaited arrival of General Davie, which was celebrated by "the firing of the

---

* Gaston Papers; S.H.C. Dr. Charles Logan was the self-appointed emissary who went to France to try to avert the war that threatened in 1798. As a result Congress passed the "Logan Act," which forbids a private citizen to undertake diplomatic negotiations without official sanction.

The French Mission

Cannon" and which would "give rise to some dinners, dances, &c, &c."[93]

Meanwhile the Convention with France was submitted to John Adams' lame duck Senate on December 16, where it was immediately attacked by the Jeffersonians. Their chief criticism was pointed out by Richard Dobbs Spaight, now in the Democratic-Republican camp, who reported to his friend and convert, John Gray Blount, that it would be "agreeable to the Anglo-feds"; but that it "barely makes peace between the two republics." More important, it "leaves to a future time the Settlement of all our real differences with france, the adjustment of which might have given umbrage to the rascally & Tyrannical Government of England & brought on a war between them & us." More venom emerged when he declared, "Yet such as it is the Essex Junto, or Anglo-feds, find great fault with it, & I am told censure Davie and Murray about it saying that if Elsworth had not had the Gout in his head, such a Treaty never had been made—would to God that Jno Jay had had the Gout in both head and stomach, if it could have prevented the British Treaty from being imposed on us."[94]

Yet eighteen days later Robert Williams wrote from Washington, "The Treaty this way is a popular thing—for the Situation of our Country and its disposition for peace (a few excepted) aided also by the weight of Characters, which...have much influence." As a result, "objections are founded more in principle, than from any defect in the instrument itself."[95]

The Senate continued its acrimonious debates upon the convention, against the backdrop of the tense contested election between Thomas Jefferson and Aaron Burr. Finally on January 23 the Senate rejected the convention by a vote of 16 for and 14 against ratification, thus failing to gain the two-thirds vote necessary for the ratification of a treaty.[96]

Commenting on the Senate action, Robert Williams, in a letter to the "Worshipful Court of Rockingham,"[97] said that it would "open the eyes of our Federal friends in No. Carolina," as it had done in Washington, and that it would "prove that this party never was sincere in Treating." As a result, he reported, "we are again afloat, on the political Sea of Uncertainty, and its perhaps more difficult to know what is best to be done now, than at any former period of our dispute."

But John Adams solved that dilemma by resubmitting the convention to the Senate, which, on February 3, ratified it with the exception of Article II which provided for further negotiation "at a convenient time" on the questions of indemnities and of the treaties of 1778 and the consular convention of 1788. In addition, the duration of the convention was to be fixed at eight years.

On March 2, Adams returned it with his signature to the Senate, along with the information that he had nominated Senator James Bayard to negotiate the exchange of ratification with Napoleon. Bayard, however, had declined the appointment, as a result of which Adams left the final exchange to his successor who could "proceed with them according to his wisdom." Thomas Jefferson commissioned Oliver Ellsworth to negotiate the final exchange, which was, at last, fully ratified—by Bonaparte on July 31 and by the United States Senate December 19, 1801.

Thus the famous French alliance was formally, bilaterally abrogated. Thus also American spoliation claims against France were abandoned. And thus, without loss to American honor, President Adams, through his ministers, Murray, Ellsworth, and Davie, had prevented his own party from rushing into war with France. It might be added that after over a century of delay the United States government partially indemnified its own citizens for their claims which had been sacrificed in the interests of diplomacy.[98]

CHAPTER XII

A Federalist Star Falls

DAVIE returned to a changed North Carolina. The political complexion of the nation, the state, and Davie's own bailiwick was colored predominantly by the Democratic-Republicanism brought forth by the "Revolution of 1800"—so called by Mr. Jefferson himself. The Federalist party had lost—irrevocably as it turned out—its political ascendancy in the national arena. On the state level it had felt keenly the absence of its titular leader, the arch-Federalist Davie. And with its waning, the entire temper and reactions of the populace had changed. Gone were most of the older aristocratic leaders whose Roman principles and attitudes refused to bend to the popular will. Gone were most of the statesmen and public servants of the *noblesse oblige* variety. Gone from the political scene was the venerable Samuel Johnston, who had retired from politics. James Iredell and Archibald Maclaine were dead. Richard Dobbs Spaight had apostatized to the Republicans. And Benjamin Hawkins and John Steele were soon to accept Federal appointments, thereby giving tacit support to Jefferson. Acutely present were the new politicians, such as Nathaniel Macon, who made a great ado of their democratic, simple virtues and austere economy and who scoffed at any display of aristocracy or refinement.

No one was more sensitively aware of this shift than Davie, who soon after his return from France wrote John Steele, on leave from Washington, that he congratulated him "upon being again 'once more under your own *humble* roof' which, by the by, is the most decent chateau in the neighborhood, ornamented too with no little taste, enough I am afraid to mark you soon as an Aristocrat." [1]

Not only was Davie aware of this change, but he also was alarmed by the crisis in government resulting from the disputed election between Jefferson and Aaron Burr for the presidency. Along with other Federalists he deemed "the destruction of the Constitution as an event certain under the administration of Mr. Jefferson, and as to the administration of Mr. B. altho' it may be energetic, no man *knows* what course it may take." [2]

During the first month of his return to Halifax he was "visited by a great number of the most enlightened friends of Government" in that part of the country. All expressed "an insuperable repugnance to the election of Burr, urging his want of character." Davie himself prophesied that it was "a measure that will sink the Federalists in the opinion of the Majority, and in its operation effect the entire destruction of the Federal party, by becoming *responsible* for an administration they can *neither control* nor influence, and consecrating beyond all doubt Mr. Jefferson in the eyes of the people." He considered the crisis "peculiarly gloomy." Under Jefferson, "every institution must crumble"; under Burr, "no one knows what to expect." He reported that "an alarming degree of discontent and disgust pervades every description of society"; that the "public spirit appears to be destroyed by party rage"; and that the public mind around Halifax was "haunted with apprehensions of a dissolution of the Union." The continued "uncertitude" had "produced the most disagreeable effects" around Halifax; the "violence of the antifederal party seems to have no bounds... and the wild frenzy of a demagogue is admired by the mass of the people in an effort of the sublimest patriotism." When Jefferson was finally chosen over Burr, Davie lamented that "the suspense served only to sour, agitate and almost convulse the public mind, and to prepare the way for more serious disasters at some future day." To Davie the future looked dim—so dim that "every man of reflection who has a family, must feel some unpleasant sensations when he looks forward on the future prospects of the American government, calculating that things will take their natural course and grow always worse and worse."

In such a situation he advised that "the true policy of the Federalists is to act an open and manly and decided part, by yielding at once to the public sentiment, with the best possible grace and placing the painful responsibility of the *future* where it ought to be, on the succeeding administration." ³

Yet Davie and his Federalist friends did not plan to sit idly by. When Davie paid his short visit to Washington he had found that the Federalists "were entirely occupied in forming some plans which might be best calculated to secure at some future period such an administration of our government as would promote what they conceived to be the real interests of our Country." It was therefore decided that it was of "considerable importance to undeceive the people of the state" as to "the misrepresentations" which had been circulated with "inconceivable industry." To effect this plan they decided that letters should be addressed to the most influential men and the "firm Federalists" in different parts of the state, and Davie was requested "to procure the information necessary & name such characters as it might be safe and proper to open a correspondence with." ⁴

In addition to this movement, the Federalists undertook to undo or outdo the exertions of Joseph Gales, the liberal editor of the *Raleigh Register*. This so-called Radical had been forced to flee from England because of his championship, along with Thomas Paine, of the French Revolution. After a brilliant display of liberal journalistic talent in Philadelphia, he had been induced by Nathaniel Macon and other North Carolina Democratic-Republicans in Congress to undertake the publication of a Democratic mouthpiece in the new capital village. And here, championed by Willie Jones and Macon and other leaders of their party, he had established, October 22, 1799, their official organ and what became "the best newspaper in the state for the next half century." ⁵

To combat this influence, Davie and his friends turned to their old spokesman, Abraham Hodge. Hodge, a native New Yorker and a personal friend of George Washington, had come to North Carolina in 1785. He soon became state printer, set up printing presses in Edenton, Halifax, Fayetteville, and Newbern, and operated three newspapers. In the Fayetteville office of his *Minerva*, he was ably assisted by his nephew, William Boylan, who was induced to transfer his paper to Raleigh. And here Boylan set as his goal, according to Davie's friend, Duncan Cameron, "the noble objects of suppressing falsehood and disseminating truth, of subverting the will and visionary projects of opinions of Democracy." [6]

As also reported by Cameron, the leading Federalists of the state proposed to set on foot a subscription in each district "to raise money sufficient to furnish about ten newspapers for each county" to be sent to "men of democratic principles of a moderate kind." The scheme was to be communicated to William Boylan for Newbern, William Barry Grove for Fayetteville, Colonel John Ashe for Wilmington, Colonel John Moore (of Lincoln County) for the Morgan District, Archibald Henderson for Salisbury, Duncan Cameron for Hillsborough, and Davie for Halifax and Edenton districts.[7]

But, with all their concerted efforts, Federalism could not be revived in North Carolina. None of the state's four Federalists in Congress, Archibald Henderson, William Barry Grove, John Stanly, and William H. Hill, was to be re-elected. They had, in accordance with a position taken by Federalists since the adoption of the Constitution, refused to be instructed by the Republican legislature to support the plan for the repeal of the Judiciary Act of 1801 passed under John Adams.[8]

Davie of course reacted violently to this repeal, writing that, "as the avowed object of this man [Jefferson] is to eventuate the removal of the Judges, the Constitution is no longer considered by Congress in any other light, than that in which Dr. Swift represents the Holy Scriptures, when he likens them to a loose pair of trousers, which any man with a little tugging may draw over his backside." Indeed, it appeared to him that "all Constitutions are useless... and that celebrated instrument vaunted as 'the world's best hope' is no more than an old woman's story—What course will things take? How long will the Lilliputian ties of the public debt &c &c hold us together?" [9]

After less than a year of the Jeffersonian administration, Davie foresaw a gloomy and alarming prospect. Although he claimed that his temperament was "not of the melancholy kind" and that he was not "hypocondriacal," he predicted that *"we shall never see one clear day"* and that "the highest graduation of our happiness will be marked by the observation, that 'these are only flying clouds'." He wrote Steele * that "the last violent struggle between the parties left the

---

* John Steele resigned his post as Comptroller General of the U.S. Treasury in 1802.

A Federalist Star Falls

public nerves in a state of morbid irritation, and it will be long before they will again resume a firm and healthy tone." His very real alarm over Jefferson's retrenchments induced him to continue: "Pray let me know something about the proposed financial reforms—is everything to be reduced to the simple trash!! Where will this business end—!" [10]

And yet Davie must not have been as publicly or as avowedly opposed to the Jeffersonian administration as his private correspondence would lead one to believe. His chance meeting in June, 1802, with Nathaniel Macon was reported by the latter: "I saw General Davie there, had some conversation with him, from which I hope he is inclined to give the present administration his support. I only mention this because very different reports were circulated at Washington last winter." [11]

Not only were political affairs in a distressing plight, according to Davie, but his personal financial affairs had suffered from his many years of public service. His autobiographical summary of his finances, in a letter to Steele, is revealing:

"While I was engaged in the business of my profession * my time and attention were exclusively devoted to that business, and my own affairs altogether neglected; my property it is true increased but it was not only unproductive but even expensive to me, under the pressure of professional business I had scarcely time to perceive their circumstance, and it was not an object to be felt; some unexpected accounts and charges from my plantations now and then put me in an ill humor, but they were paid and forgotten. When I was appointed Governor of the State, I supposed that the usual course of office of three years would give me leisure to bestow order and arrangement on the affairs of my estate; however before any thing was effected, I was obliged to go to Europe, our mission was prolonged there far beyond my expectations, and my directions were not predicated on an absence of such length; my overseers, as is usual, were contented with having an excuse, and my affairs fell back into the same state of neglect and confusion that they were in when I quitted my profession: my time since my return or rather since the spring has been entirely devoted to this important object... and thus my personal

---

* Apparently Davie considered himself primarily a military man.

engagements oblige me to be stationery here [in Halifax] till the 15th. of October, excepting a journey to Edenton and Petersburg, and from the 15th. of October till the last of November I had engaged to be in Chatham and South Carolina." [12]

Davie had hardly become re-acclimated in Halifax when his successor as governor, Benjamin Williams, asked him to take up again the onerous burden of the North Carolina-South Carolina boundary. In Davie's absence the legislature had passed a resolution requesting the governor to take measures to bring the matter before the United States Supreme Court for determination and to appoint an agent or "sole manager" to handle the case for the State. It was this position which Williams foisted on Davie.[13]

Davie, a true public servant, replied: "nothing could give me more satisfaction than to serve the State in any business in which her interests and her reputation & dignity were so much concerned." [14] And, characteristically, he immediately set to work. He began by collecting all documents on the question, even contemplating sending to Great Britain for further documents. His plan for getting at the truth of the entire boundary line has been described as "logical, scientific, and thorough." In carrying out this policy, he proposed, inasmuch as there was some doubt in regard to the trueness of the line, that two of the North Carolina commissioners should take observations at three places: at the eastern end of the survey of 1764, at its termination near the Waxhaws on the Salisbury-Camden road, and at the forks of the Yadkin, where the 1772 survey was begun. He thought (erroneously) that they "had inclined considerably to the Southward" in the 1764 survey, but he thought (correctly) that they had gone "much too far North, when they ascended the Catawba River as far as what is usually called the fork" in the 1772 survey. He reported that he planned to set out on April 2 for his estate on the Catawba only five miles from the termination of the 1764 line and hoped the observations could be made there while he "could attend and be convinced of their accuracy." [15]

Governor Williams, as determined as Davie to bring the matter to a successful conclusion, ordered the commissioners, Price and Alexander, to meet on May 1 at the first point suggested by Davie. This would coincide with Davie's trip to "Tivoli," his South Carolina estate. Williams also informed Governor John Drayton of South

A Federalist Star Falls

Carolina of the projected undertaking in case he felt disposed to send his own commissioners to join them.[16] These plans could not be carried out. Price, who, Davie thought, was at Nixonton and who had "the necessary Mathematical Instruments," was in Philadelphia.[17]

Meanwhile Davie was trying to build up a strong case for North Carolina, based on documentary evidence. He sought to establish the fact that the King in Council had approved the agreement or "convention" of 1735 which provided for the initial survey, an assumption based on the fact that the province tried to carry it out as late as 1764.* He also sought documentation of the official appointments of the commissioners for the survey of 1764 and also the proceedings of the survey of 1772. None of these documents was found; yet upon such proofs the state's claim to the line of 1764 rested.[18] And needless to say, North Carolina, through Davie, was contesting the proceedings of the survey of 1772 on the grounds of illegality.

Meanwhile, Governor Drayton, who had at first agreed to co-operate with Davie's and Williams' proposal to appoint commissioners to determine the true latitude, reversed himself. On July 16, he wrote Williams that his state would not co-operate in the proposed survey and would not be bound by the findings of the North Carolina commissioners. Instead, he urged that Williams "take the most speedy measures" to bring the matter before the Supreme Court.[19]

Despite this unfortunate turn of events, Davie still recommended proceeding with the survey. With Williams' approval he ordered the necessary instruments from Philadelphia and secured the appointment of Charles W. Harris, his legal assistant, in lieu of Price.[20] As late as October 26 Davie was still hopeful that the necessary documents could be unearthed. On that date he set out from Raleigh for South Carolina, informing the governor he planned to return about the first of December. He suggested that at that time, armed with these documents, he should inform a confidential committee of the legislature "of the real state of that business" in order to obtain their sanction.[21] The legislature, at the governor's request, complied.[22]

Davie returned from South Carolina with documentary sources which completely reversed North Carolina's position and showed

---

* His assumption was correct.—C.R., IV, 17.

that Davie and North Carolina had been wrong. These documents he manfully laid before the legislative committee and convinced them that, by the convention of April, 1735, all the lands claimed by the Catawba and Cherokee Indians had been ceded to South Carolina, thus depriving North Carolina of this disputed area. He also laid before the committee the orders of the King in Council of June 7, 1771, which provided for the running of the line of 1772. These orders he considered "peremptory and conclusive" and maintained that the line was accordingly run "in strict compliance with the letter of these instructions." But it was "under this very order" that we "were entitled alone to claim heretofore the whole of the State of Tennessee." It followed that "if the order of '71 could be set aside ... the State of South Carolina was entitled to claim under the convention of April 1735 the whole of the territory heretofore claimed by the Catawbas and Cherokees."

The committee also considered these royal orders as "conclusive" and that "it was the interest of the State of North Carolina not only to abide by it but to support it." Accordingly, they decided on two objectives: "to disembarrass" the State from its plan of appealing to the Supreme Court and thereby avoid "immense and unnecessary expence"; and to conclude the boundary dispute as soon as possible by substituting the Catawba River as the line from the Waxhaws to its forks instead of the old Salisbury road. They should then extend the line of 1772 to the Cherokee boundary—a distance of about seventy miles which ran through "a tract of Country which has already become the asylum of a number of Lawless men, on whom no process can be served, and who set the Laws of both States at defiance." [23]

In line with these recommendations, the legislature courageously adopted Davie's stand and, in a conciliatory mood, repealed the first section of the act of 1796 which had referred the matter to the Supreme Court.[24]

When these steps were reported to Governor Drayton—at Davie's suggestion [25]—he laid the matter before the legislature, suggesting that it refuse to compromise. In a letter to Governor Williams informing him that the legislature had taken no action, Drayton again urged that North Carolina proceed to submit it to the Supreme Court, and adamantly declared that his state would "have nothing to do with" any compromise, "for it knows its rights ... and is prepared to support the same...."[26]

On the basis of this uncompromising letter, Williams was ready to drop the controversy for a time, but Davie advised that Drayton's letter should not bother him, that it was "perfectly of a piece with his former correspondence on that subject." Moreover, South Carolina's refusal to act was probably a delaying action until the legislature could sound out "the real views" of its constituents.[27]

Affairs dragged along until the fall of 1803, when the South Carolina legislature adopted a more conciliatory attitude. It instructed its new governor, James B. Richardson, to reopen the boundary question with North Carolina's new governor, James Turner, and assure him of the "ardent desire of the former to have the affair amicably adjusted." On the basis of this turn of events, the North Carolina legislature passed an act for the appointment of three commissioners who could have "all power to settle all disputes, differences, and claims existing between the two States, and to establish permanently and mark their mutual boundary line to the eastern border of the territory ceded by North Carolina to the United States."[28] It further repealed the Acts of 1791 and 1796 and was silent regarding Section XXV of the Bill of Rights.

Governor Turner dispatched a copy to Governor Richardson, urging immediate action and announcing the appointment of William R. Davie, James Wellborn, and John Moore as commissioners.[29]

After a series of harassing delays, complicated by Georgia's claim to part of the disputed territory, a meeting of the joint commissioners was finally agreed to by the two states, which scheduled the meeting for October 28, 1805, at Lancaster Courthouse in South Carolina.[30]

At this very propitious and long-awaited time, North Carolina lost its most able and best informed agent on the dispute. General Davie resigned. His resignation was induced by the fact that he planned to reside permanently at "Tivoli," his South Carolina estate near Lancaster, after the first of November, 1805. Thus he would become a citizen of the latter state and could not represent North Carolina. He regretted having to resign "more particularly because I know that the origin and nature of our boundary disputes with South Carolina are not generally understood, and that the state of our unitorial claims has been heretofore altogether mistaken."[31]

WILLIAM R. DAVIE

This great loss to the North Carolina commission was hastily and partially compensated for by the appointment of Davie's friend, John Steele, of Salisbury, who soon became the spokesman for this state in the later proceedings. The October meeting, which accomplished little, did lead to a later one to meet in Charlotte the following January. Davie, still interested in the dispute, sent from Landsford, South Carolina, every document he could lay his hands on for the use of the North Carolina commissioners at Charlotte.[32] But it was not until 1808 that the joint commissions, meeting in Columbia, South Carolina, recommended that the lines of 1735 and 1746 be accepted as far as the Salisbury Road and that a divergence be made here to the southeast corner of the Catawba lands, which should be followed as far as the Catawba River, thence along the river to its fork, thence westward along the line of 1772, and from its terminus westward along the 35th parallel. This report was adopted, but difficulties in establishing an accurate survey were again encountered in 1813, and it was not until 1815 that the matter was finally adjusted, with a slight variation in the former agreement.[33]

Significantly enough, Thomas Jefferson, either in appreciation of Davie's ability or in an effort to wean him from the Federalist fold, conferred upon him a responsible post. Perhaps this was at the instigation of the arch-Jeffersonian, Nathaniel Macon, who reported to his idol that "the feds. every where [are] trying to impress their principles upon the people," but that General Davie had not returned (from South Carolina). Macon would "endeavor to see him as soon as possible," and he sincerely hoped "that he may be willing to undertake the negotiation with the Indians."[34]

The instructions, issued by Jefferson June 24, 1801, provided for the appointment of Davie to head a commission composed of General James Wilkinson and former United States Senator Benjamin Hawkins, "to hold conferences, and sign a treaty, or treaties," with the Cherokee, Creek, Chickasaw, and Choctaw Indians on the east side of the Mississippi River and south of the Ohio. They were to negotiate with these Indians for further cessions of lands, for the opening of roads, and for the settlement of boundaries.[35]

Davie declined this commission because of the urgency of his business; or, as he related it to John Steele, it "would have furnished such a feast for a philosophic traveller, I was obliged to decline." There was, however, a "great difference of opinion" among his friends as to his reasons for declining. His Federalist friends "were generally violently opposed" to his acceptance, but "those, who are attached to the present administration discovered great anxiety" that he should accept the appointment.[36]

But Mr. Jefferson would not take no for an answer. Again, in November, 1801, he sought to enlist Davie's services. This time he was appointed as sole commissioner on the part of the United States to arbitrate a treaty to be made between North Carolina and the Tuscarora Indians.[37]

The circumstances were these: The larger part of the Tuscarora tribe had abandoned North Carolina in June, 1713, after the Tuscarora War, and had joined the great confederacy of the Five Nations in New York, thus making it the Six Nations. A fragment, however, under the leadership of King Tom Blunt, had aided the whites in the war and had been rewarded for their services by Governor Charles Eden, who in 1717 granted them a tract of land on the north side of the Roanoke River, in what is now Bertie County. Part of the tract is referred to today as Indian Woods.

As the years passed, the ranks of these Tuscaroras began to thin out, largely by migration to New York, and much of their unused land was leased to whites. But the collection of their rents from such a distance became very difficult, and so they sought the superintendence of the United States in a treaty between themselves and the state of North Carolina.[38]

Davie accordingly met with the chiefs of the nation and the representatives of the state at Raleigh, where on December 4, 1802, a treaty was signed. By its terms the Tuscaroras were allowed to extend their former leases and to make new ones to run until July 12, 1916. On this date their title would terminate and the lands would revert to the state.* The General Assembly itself was to facilitate, by all means in its power, the punctual collection of the rents. Being thus assured of their rights, the remainder of the tribe joined their New

---

* These lands were sold by the Tuscaroras in 1832, their agent receiving $3,220.71 for the lands. See Herbert R. Paschal, Jr., "The Tuscarora Indians in North Carolina" (U.N.C.: Unpublished M.A. thesis, 1953), p. 148. According to Dr. W. P. Jacocks, of Chapel Hill, their chief, Mr. Pleasant of New York, was in Bertie County in 1956 investigating their claim.

York brethren in June, 1803, leaving only one member to receive the dues.[39] As pointed out by his early biographer, Davie "seems to have acted with great discretion in the execution of his trust, and, while maintaining good faith with all parties, to have watched with considerable benevolence over the interests of the Indians."[40]

In the winter of 1802 the serenity of Halifax and the surrounding counties in both North Carolina and Virginia was broken by the threat of a serious slave plot, reminiscent of the successful one of Toussaint L'Ouverture in Santo Domingo. The plot to exterminate the whites and to establish "liberty and equality" was discovered by James Gee of Southampton County, Virginia, who chanced upon a secret letter, signed "J. L., true friend in liberty or death," addressed to the "Representative of the lower Company." The limited and veiled details of the plot were relayed at once to Governor Williams by Davie on February 10, 1802. Davie informed him that "frequent military patroles in each Captain's district" had been temporarily adopted as "the most effectual mode of ensuring the public safety." Despite several urgent requests for immediate assistance, the governor, wary of the legislature's reaction to the expenditure of money and skeptical of the gravity of the plot, did nothing. Perhaps his decision was judicious, because it was to be another thirty years before this same section was to be aroused by the Nat Turner insurrection in Southampton County, Virginia.[41]

That summer, on April 14, 1802,[42] Davie was saddened by the death of his wife, in the fortieth year of her life and the twentieth year of their married life. In addition to his personal loss, this meant that the entire care of his children devolved upon him.

Probably this sadness and this care were the cause of his complaint in August that his health had been "bad" ever since his return from his South Carolina plantation in the spring. He laid his plans, nevertheless, to "set out for Bethlehem [Pennsylvania] with one of my daughters about the first of October."[43] By September 15, Macon reported that he appeared "to be in good health."[44]

In the following November Davie wrote Calvin Jones that Eli Whitney, the inventor of the revolutionizing cotton gin in 1793, had paid him a visit in Halifax, where they no doubt discussed the great advantages of this new mechanical process.[45]

A Federalist Star Falls

By the following spring, Davie was toying with the idea of trying to correct what he considered to be the abuses of democracy by running for Congress. As early as April 3, 1803, he inquired of Duncan Cameron as to Federalist prospects to the westward and informed him that as yet they were "laying upon our case, endeavoring to collect the necessary information." He believed that "the events of the last Congress have considerably shaken their Chief in the public opinion; the party have always held him up as the Mammouth of Wisdom, and they begin to find it impossible to disguise his folly: they have serious thoughts of changing him for Madison, but they know that this would be as delicate a manoevre as to change your front in the face of a formed enemy." [46]

By May 2, Davie had offered himself as a candidate from the second district for Congress by issuing a printed circular in which he wanted it "clearly understood" that he had never and never would surrender his principles "to the opinions of any man, or description of men, either in or out of power" and that he wanted no man to vote for him who would not be willing for him "to pursue the good of my Country according to the best of my judgment, without respect either to party men or party views." In a postscript he also saw fit to deny that he favored "a monarchical form of government." [47]

Davie was opposed by the incumbent, Willis Alston, and by Charles Jacocks, both Republicans.[48] Alston had been elected to Congress from the Halifax District in 1799 as a Federalist and had been returned uncontested in 1801. Immediately thereafter he had begun to act with the Republican part in Congress and was thus condemned by the Federalists as a traitor.[49]

The ensuing campaign was acrimonious and was waged on a despicably low plane by Davie's opponents. Attacks were directed against his aristocratic habits, dress, and way of life which he had allegedly acquired during his sojourn abroad. And a story that will not down—though there is no contemporary evidence to substantiate it—is that when Davie returned from France he brought a quantity of very fine china, among which was a china bowl he kept under the bed. In the heat of the campaign, Alston is supposed to have carried the day by saying that Davie could not do like the ordinary men of that day when it became necessary to meet certain calls of nature, that is, proceed to the outdoors, but instead used his fine china bowl. His defeat was supposedly attributable to this accusation.

Various speculations were made as to the outcome. Charles W. Harris, who worked in Davie's law office, thought on May 22 that he could "safely pronounce that if Alston & Jacocks (republicans) both stand a poll, Gen. Davie will be elected."[50] In July the outcome was still undecided.[51] But by the last of July, the situation had been materially changed by the withdrawal of Jacocks, who circulated a handbill to that effect. Jacocks stated that it was the opinion of the majority "that two Candidates of the same Politics should not prevent their Will from having its due Weight."[52]

Perhaps the sentiments of the majority of the citizens of Halifax were appropriately expressed by one of their number, when he said: "Notwithstanding I hold myself to be of republican Principles, according to the common acceptation of the Word and prefer the Present, to the future Administration, I shall regret, that Genl. Davie should not be Elected, but at Present the Prospect is very gloomy, and believe it will end so."[53]

Davie himself reported Jacocks' withdrawal "for the purpose of uniting all their forces" and declared that "nothing can equal their activity but their fertility in falsehood—so there can be no doubt about the issue of the election."[54]

Yet "great exertions" were made, according to Macon, up to the day of elections, which occurred on the second Thursday and Friday of August.[55] But before all precincts had been reported the *Raleigh Register*, on August 22, conceded that there was "no doubt" of Alston's election. Its tabulation showed the following returns:

	Alston	Davie
Halifax County	799	341
Northampton	411	246
Bertie, upper election	54	89
Watsford's	78	00

It further reported that the "principal election" in Bertie had not been heard from. Nor had they heard "precisely" from Martin County, though it had heard that General Davie "had a majority upwards of 200 in it."

And so, for the first and last time, Davie met defeat at the polls.

A Federalist Star Falls

This event, coupled no doubt with the death of his wife the previous year, embittered him to such an extent that he began making his plans to retire from the state which he had served so nobly and which had, in a matter of speaking, rejected him.

Davie unbosomed his sentiments quite feelingly to John Steele. "Party spirit," he wrote, "which had been slumbering under the ashes of 1800 was again blown into a perfect flame and the whole country in this quarter has been in commotion for two months past." He continued:

"The Gentlemen who prevailed upon me 'to offer' as they call it, consisted principally of the moderate men of both parties, who readily agreed that I should have no trouble with the election and if elected that I should be free to follow my own judgment.... My election depended altogether upon keeping the people cool and rational, and the repression of party spirit; I told these Gentlemen that I was certain this was impracticable, they were all of a different opinion, and a few days showed how much they were mistaken: the moment I was named as a candidate, the Demos seemed to set up one general howl, the voice of these moderies was completely drowned, and I was immediately denounced as a monarchist, and the intended King of the Federalists to the Southward &c. &c., this story in some time grew stale, was too gross to impose upon the more sensible part of the republicans attached to my interest—They then declared me the personal enemy of their beloved Chief, that my situation in Congress would enable me to intrigue against him with effect, and prevent his reelection, this succeeded—the party became alarmed, Mr. Jacocks was prevailed upon to withdraw to unite their whole force, and there remained no doubt about the issue." [56]

Steele replied that had he known Davie's intentions, he would have "used some arguments" to have deterred him, but then he remembered "how determined" Davie had been the preceding winter " *'to die sword in hand in the last ditch'.*" Steele concluded that Davie's "late essay might be regarded as a part of your plan of general hostility to the administration." [57]

To Richard Bennehan, Davie wrote the same type of letter, accusing the "Demos" of "raising the spirit of party into a flame, and alarming the ignorant and credulous with frightful stories about Kings and aristocrats." As a result, he concluded, "thousands of these poor wretches sincerely believe they have saved their Country from these monsters by preventing my going to Congress." [58]

Soon afterwards, Davie reported to John Haywood that Halifax was reposing "in a kind of 'dead calm' after the battle." And then he indulged in "sour grapes." He said that he had insisted that he should not run for office because he was "obliged to be traveling for five months in the year" attending to his private affairs. But, he said, it would be difficult "to convince the Demos that in preventing my election, they have bestowed the greatest favor in their power upon me." [59]

Davie's second letter to Steele after the election was even more vitriolic than the first and contains his first vilification of his adopted state:

"I have long beheld in silent indignation the low degraded situation of No. Carolina, destitute of National character, self-respect, and all political importance, content with being a miserable appendage of the Ancient Dominion, and even so debased as to think herself honored with the permission 'to wallow in the mire of Virginia politics'." He continued his diatribe against Virginia by saying that "the real source of our divisions" of parties is not "a difference on abstract principles," but that it "originates in the question whether Virginia shall be every thing, and the other States *NOTHING*, whether the National Constitution is to be continually moulded to the progressing views of her Statesmen &c &c." [60]

The following year, apparently, Davie spent licking his wounds, attending to his holdings in Halifax and Chatham counties and in South Carolina, and in defending himself in the famous Granville case.

The acquisition and management of these holdings in themselves would have kept the average man busy. Year by year since his coming to Halifax Davie had added to his property in that county and elsewhere. In addition to lot number 12 in Halifax, the location of his home "Loretta," he had acquired 11,401 acres in District 9 in 1786 and listed 23 polls, which meant he owned 22 slaves at that time. The following year he listed 25 black polls. In 1801 he acquired 24 slaves for $4,400 from his friend, Stephen Cabarrus of Edenton. In 1789 he paid £300 for a tract of 300 additional acres of land and, according to the Census of 1790, he had 36 slaves at that time. In 1793 he acquired an additional acre of land from Willie Jones, presumably adjoining "Loretta." Also, his will, written in 1799 but later cancelled, referred to his "lands and plantation situate on Quankey" Creek, just south of Halifax and to "all my lands, tenements and plantations in North Carolina" (presumably a plantation in Chatham and a thousand-acre plantation in Craven County) and to "the lands I occupy in Oconechie neck" across the Roanoke River in Northampton County. Finally in 1802 he added 287 acres to his Quankey Creek plantation.[61]

Davie also held vast tracts of land elsewhere. In 1784 he, his father-in-law, Allen Jones, and five other gentlemen petitioned the Assembly for "public encouragement to drain the lake of Scupperlong [sic] in the County of Tyrrell," in eastern North Carolina. The Assembly generously granted them "all the lands lying below the low water mark of the said lake of Scupperlong, which they . . . shall drain within the term of seven years."[62]

Apparently they were highly successful in their efforts, because in 1795 he and General Jones decided to sell 17,500 acres of these lands, "provided we can get one dollar per acre."[63]

Then too, for his services in the Revolution Davie was awarded 4,800 acres in the transmontane country of Tennessee, lying below Nashville in Dickinson County on both sides of Barton's Creek, which flowed into the Cumberland River. Among the "first locations of the Military Grant," they were "said to be of an excellent quality." From 1795 to 1804 Davie advertised these lands for sale.[64] This tract had been divided into eight 600-acre tracts and Davie asked "from one to two dollar according to the quality." He also had another tract of 1,000 acres which he offered to sell for 75 cents per acre. These lands he desired to exchange, at varying times, for cash, for Negro slaves, or lands "well situated in North Carolina."[65] Finally, in 1804, he sold 3,600 acres to William Sullivant for $5,400.[66]

Shortly after his return from France he became convinced he would never "enjoy my health" at Halifax and wrote Richard Bennehan that he was "extremely desirous of purchasing an agreeable situation in Orange or Chatham where I know a man may have health at least."[67]

WILLIAM R. DAVIE

Evidently by June, 1804, he had made up his mind to retire to South Carolina, because he began selling his North Carolina property. First he sold to James Hogg for £625 a valuable lot in Chapel Hill at the juncture of Franklin Street and Grand Avenue.[68] In January, 1805, he sold 1,222 acres on upper Reedy Branch to David Crawley for $3,050, another tract of 192 acres for £192, and a third tract of 400 acres for $600—all near Halifax. In August he sold two town lots in Halifax (lots 14 and 15) plus an adjoining acre for $350. And finally in November, just before his departure for "Tivoli," he gave his son, Allen Jones Davie, his 287-acre Quankey Creek plantation, his five-acre home place, and his thousand acres in Craven County. He granted to his father-in-law, Allen Jones, his half-share of the estimated 20,000 acres he held with Jones in Tyrrell County.[69]

It was these lands in Tyrrell that caused Davie, Josiah Collins, and Nathaniel Allen to become defendants in the famous Granville suit. This case, stated Governor David L. Swain in the mid-nineteenth century, was "a case involving most intricate legal questions, and title to property of greater value than any other ever litigated before an American tribunal." The facts in the case were strikingly similar to those in the Fairfax case involving Lord Fairfax's claims to the Northern Neck of Virginia.* When the seven other Lords Proprietors sold their Carolina territory to the King in 1729, the Earl of Granville had retained his one-eighth share, which comprised the upper half of North Carolina, two-thirds of the population, and approximately three-fourths of the wealth at the time of the Revolution.[70] During that war, of course, the new sovereign state passed confiscatory acts against all alien holdings. Under these statutes Davie, Allen, Collins, and many others obtained grants to parts of the Granville District. Finally in 1801 two actions of ejectment, with a view to try their titles to the lands, were brought against these three defendants by George William, Earl Coventry (who had succeeded to the title of Earl Granville), and other devisees. The plaintiffs were represented by Davie's friend and later Associate Justice of the United States Supreme Court, William Gaston, and Edward Harris. The defendants employed Judge Duncan Cameron, who had received

* For a comparison of these two cases see Albert J. Beveridge, *The Life of John Marshall* (Boston and New York: Houghton Mifflin Co., 1919), IV, 154-56.

much legal training from Davie, Blake Baker, the former Attorney General, and a Mr. M. Woods.[71]

The letter accompanying the declaration of the suit against Davie made it clear that the suit was not brought "with the intention to place the defendant in a worse situation than others claiming under the state ... but with a view only to bring the title of the claimants to a fair trial."[72] In fact, the state was chief defendant.

This being the case, Davie and Allen Jones immediately forwarded a copy of the proceedings to Governor Williams in order that he might take such measures as he deemed expedient for the defense of the state.[73]

A whispering campaign began against Davie, according to Duncan Cameron, in which "many Persons here [in Raleigh], who altho' they must feel a Conviction to the contrary, are still base enough to hazard an opinion that he is concerted in Interest in prosecuting the claim of Earl Granville's representatives." As a result, they decided not to assist in defending the suit, but to leave Davie "to support the whole Trouble & defray the whole Expence."[74]

Also, "a company of Gentlemen" in Raleigh, hostile to Davie and Duncan Cameron, noised abroad that Cameron had expressed a wish that the Granville devisees should recover their title. In addition it was reported that "the old story is revived about Genl. Davie's going to England and purchasing their claim on the State of N. C." They argued that "his being sued; and his defence, was nothing but a Juggle to impose on the ignorant, that his intention was to let judgment go against him." Otherwise, they continued, "why should he be singled out as an object to commence suit against?"[75] Such was the feeling and such were the manufactured lies disseminated throughout the state by Davie's enemies. Although it was not until 1805 that the suit was actually brought to trial, Davie had made a detailed study of the Granville claims and passed on to Cameron a detailed report of his defense arguments.

The plaintiffs, as he interpreted their argument, relied on three points: (1) that the lands were not confiscated at all because Lord Granville was not specifically mentioned in the confiscatory Revolutionary legislation, although others were; (2) that there was a saving of their rights in a proviso in the 25th article of the State Constitution;* and (3) that there has been "no escheat because Lord Granville was not an Alien."[76]

Davie took issue with each of these points. As to the first claim, that Granville was not specifically named, he argued that the state had the right to confiscate this property and the only question was "whether she used that right... Nothing was necessary but its execution." The act of April, 1777, he stated, "opened public offices in the several counties expressly for the sale of these lands," and it contained "all the essential features... of a confiscation act."[77]

As to their argument that they were excepted by the 25th Article of the Bill of Rights, he argued that, although the Lords Proprietors held their territory "with almost all the prerogatives of sovereignty," it was "a direct consequence of such a revolution as that of seventy-six that the new government succeeds to all the rights of the old whether royal or proprietary." In other words, by the terms of this provision, the Lords Proprietors were "placed on the same footing with George the third" and the persons referred to in the proviso were "plainly the persons holding under these two descriptions of sovereigns." Clearly this statement was "to operate also as a solemn investiture of the right of soil in the collective body of the people, the new sovereigns &c."

Finally, as to the non-applicability of the laws of escheat, Davie showed by cogent reasoning how there was "no similitude" between this case and Calvin's Case, upon which the plaintiffs rested their claims.†

The case was at last brought to trial before the Federal Circuit Court meeting in Raleigh in June, 1805, with Chief Justice John Marshall presiding with District Judge John Potter. Marshall, however, declined to take any part, because of his involvement in the Fairfax case in Virginia. Cameron followed in general the reasoning set forth

---

* The pertinent part of this proviso read as follows: "All the territory, seas, waters, harbors... lying between the lines above described (Virginia and South Carolina) are the right and property of the people of the State to be held by them in Sovereignty.... *Provided further,* that nothing herein contained shall affect the titles or possession of individuals holding, or claiming, under the laws heretofore in force, or grants heretofore made by the late King George II, or his predecessors, or the late Lords Proprietors, or any of them."

† For Davie's detailed argument, see Davie to Duncan Cameron, March 20, 1804.—Cameron Papers, S.H.C.

by Davie, that the jury decided against the plaintiffs, and that they appealed to the Supreme Court of the United States. The appeal was never prosecuted, perhaps because William Gaston had definite political aspirations which would have been jeopardized by this prosecution.

A great deal of Davie's time in this period was spent in the care of his children. In May, 1804, he visited the new Moravian Boarding School at Salem. Having had his eldest daughter, Mary Haynes, at the Moravian school in Bethlehem, Pennsylvania, he was "pleased with the beginning of a school here." [78] So pleased was he, in fact, that the following July he brought his daughter, Sarah Jones, "and three other daughters of relations and friends" to enroll in the Boarding School. For his special benefit the sermon that Sunday was delivered in English. Davie was "particularly glad to see Sr. Gambold, who had had one of his daughters in her care" at Bethlehem.[79]

The following May, 1806, General Davie, accompanied by Mary Haynes, brought his third daughter, Martha Rebecca, to join Sarah in the Boarding School.[80] And around the first of June, 1808, he spent several days at Salem, and then took Sarah home after three years of schooling.[81] In May, 1809, he, accompanied by a number of friends, attended the examination there. They all "noted with pleasure the progress made by the pupils," and "General Davie said, among other things: 'It is almost too beautiful to see so many children together,' adding: 'It reminds me of the word of our Saviour, "Of such is the kingdom of heaven"'." [82]

Such trips to Salem and to South Carolina were beginning to impair his health. In June, 1805, he wrote that he had been "two months on the road, and return perfectly worn down: my Constitution cannot now bear that degree of suffering, privation and incessant Toil, which when I enjoyed youth and health only gave me spirits and pleasure." He philosophically added that "Everything must yield to Time, and I have submitted with as good a Grace as possible." [83]

It was at this time he had definitely made up his mind to retire to "Tivoli" and to set out about the last week in November. Writing to John Haywood, June 9, 1805, he said that his "plan of life is to be completely changed, and those measures which are to lead me to a *Repose* I have long sighed for, and which is becoming every day more necessary for me are to commence this fall." This move, of course,

[379]

would involve "some painful sacrifices," the "most painful" being "a separation from friends to whom my Heart has been tenderly attached for many years." This separation he felt was to be "a prelude to that last separation to which the laws of our Nature compel us all to submit." [84]

A few weeks later Davie again wrote Haywood concerning his health and happiness. He stated that "a little Rest has in a great measure restored me the ordinary enjoyment of health, the other is buried in the grave, 'a bourne' from which nothing returns." He had "nothing before me but a dreary and joyless perspective, and no man on Earth has reason to think more highly of conjugal Happiness than I have, But I have children and should I marry again, I must commit their Happiness as well as my own." [85]

His real object in moving to "Tivoli," according to his account, was to "concentrate" his property, "to bring it within the constant reach of my own attention, and render it more productive, without that labor and fatigue, which I am now unable to bear; a duty I owe to myself and my fam[ily]." Yet, he continued, he left this state "with a thousand regrets," chiefly because "the friends of my youth and all the active part of my life are Here, and as a State, I feel towards her the attachment of gratitude for repeated marks of confidence and distinction." [86]

Upon his retirement to "Tivoli," his time for the next fifteen years was to be devoted to the reconstruction of his home, to agricultural pursuits, to keeping up a lively interest in the political situation, to a great deal of reading, and to writing voluminously to a number of old friends in the Old North State—especially John Haywood, John Steele, Duncan Cameron, and Richard Bennehan.

From the moment of his arrival he was in "a continual bustle," with "one vexatious job on the back of another." He was "constantly pestered with the clattering and hammering of carpenters," because he found his plantation "exceedingly out of order, no repairs done on my House, and every out-house wanting, no garden...." His first winter was mercifully mild—mercifully, because his "Hut which was weather boarded about sixteen years ago, and inhabited many years by the most negligent race of mortals, Overseers, was pervious to every blast." [87]

But in spite of these trials Davie adopted a definite routine. Each morning his horse was brought as soon as he had breakfasted and he rode around his plantation until dinner. In the afternoon he devoted himself "to little jobs" about his house or garden. The night was devoted to reading. "Thus," he reported, "exercise has kept my body in good health, while employment kept my mind alert and clear of Ennui." Then, too, he took occasional trips down to his plantation on the Wateree.[88]

Davie missed his children, who were "scattered" at Salem, Chapel Hill, and Halifax. He had, moreover, "left many of the comforts of life" at Halifax, "and these are not always easily assembled again." Then, too, he had had "to encounter the difficulties and inconveniences of a new settlement." But, he wrote Samuel Johnston, he hoped that "time and exertions, to which I have been all my life accustomed, will... enable me to enjoy something like your ease and calm tranquility in the descent of life."[89]

Though only fifty years old, Davie began to think and act as an old man. His melancholy and choleric complaints and outbursts at times suggest an involuntary melancholia. His letters frequently reflect this state of mind. Typical are such statements as: "It seems to be the lot of man that he has more to *suffer* than *enjoy* in this world, and no degree of prudence or experience can guarantee us against accidents and the effects of Time."[90] With a good deal of pathos he wrote John Haywood concerning domestic pleasures: "There is no pleasure on Earth equal to that of having that which is dearest to us always *near us* and *about us*," because "it then administers to our pleasures every moment."[91]

His loneliness and sadness were increased by the death of his father-in-law, General Allen Jones, in 1807. Referring to this loss, he wrote that "his parental affection was the solace of my misfortune, and the warmth of his friendship formed a great part of the happiness of my Life." He further eulogized Jones by saying that "his fine genius, cultivated mind, and the exalted virtues of his heart, made him at once an object of love, veneration and esteem; a polished scholar, with a refined taste, and universal information, a 'man of the world' with all the social virtues and the most active benevolence formed an extraordinary combination of character seldom to be met with in the most advanced stages of human society." A melancholy mood is again revealed in his statement that "The death of our friends being among the dispensations of Providence, our religion prescribes a cheerful submission to the Divine will; and as all grief for what in the course of nature cannot be helped, would be unavailing, it is therefore unwise, however correct all this may be in point of doctrine and reason, I could not deny myself the melancholy pleasure of mingling my regrets with a friend who is capable of appreciating loving and esteeming a man who was an honor to the age he lived in." [92]

Again, he lamented that his life had been "a series of incessant Toil which in the eye of philosophy could only be supportable by the end I propose to attain of compleat Independence of every Being but my God; and two or three years more of unremitted exertion, [I] hoped would enable me, to use the language of Bolingbroke, to bury myself from the world in an agreeable sepulchre, whose shrine none but my friends should approach." [93]

He felt "remarkably unfortunate" over the separation from his friends and felt "like a traveller who sojourns long enough at a stage to make some agreeable friends, then parts with them, to see them no more." [94] He found some solace in writing to his friends, if only to unburden his mind "from the melancholly pressure of the Times." Yet even here he was afraid to comment on politics, he wrote John Haywood, "lest under the fury, fanaticism, and political bigotry of the day" his letters "by some accidental exposure might injure the man I love most." [95]

His misery was further compounded, in the winter of 1809, by great suffering from "an obstinate attack of the rheumatism" which had confined him to his house for several weeks and with which he was to wage a battle the rest of his life. [96]

According to his correspondence, Davie's chief crops were cotton and corn. In the spring of 1806 he was having "a terrible struggle to save our crops from the grass," because of severe rains; [97] in August, as a result of "a dreadful drought," his cotton and corn had "suffered greatly"; [98] and in December he complained that the weather had been so inclement that he could not get his cotton out of the fields. [99]

The following July he was concerned over the grass which "has pushed us greatly in our cotton," but at present the latter had "an excellent appearance, where the cotton has not been destroyed by

A Federalist Star Falls

the hail."[100] By the next year, he did have serious cause for complaint as a result of Jefferson's embargo of all American products as an economic lever against France and England in their all-out war. This embargo, complained Davie, had "knocked the cotton Planters all stiff." When it became effective "a very small production of our crops had arrived at Market, and ... it is impossible to give you any idea of the distress of this country, and nothing except the pride of party spirit and the majic of Mr. Jeffersons popularity could muzzle the discontents of the *sovereign people* even at this moment. The Great Mass never reason, but the[y] can feel, and will soon begin to clamour."[101]

Two months later Davie complained that the "embargo has completely sunk our markets, so that the sale of produce is a dead sacrifice.... 'Gloomy' indeed are the Times dark and misterious are the ways of Providence, and so has been the course of our administration."[102]

From John Haywood Davie also received complaints against the embargo, which prompted the reply that "few men who had anything to lose have escaped from its baneful influence." He had been "a great sufferer" and had lost "twenty five hundred dollars at least,—a serious thing to an old man, who has not many crops to make, and who is anxious to place himself as speedily as possible out of the reach of the effects of a good or bad administration." He stated further that "this stroke of left-handed wisdom ... has made a compleat sacrifice of the planting interest of this country, and operated as a severer crisis, than any of the plagues of Egypt."[103]

Later he wrote Haywood, on what he called "coarse embargo paper," in the same vein: "Our crops Here (on the Catawba) ... are indifferent, my cotton suffered excessively by the drought, no rain of any consequence.... My corn which is made on a plantation joining ... is extremely good—On the Wateree my corn and cotton crops are both very good, so that I suppose I shall make about one hundred bags of cotton (our bags are 300 lb.) and some corn also for sale. This thank God would do very well, if it was not all blasted by the accursed policy of Mr. Jefferson, under which our property and industry all sink into nothing." He was particularly interested to know what North Carolina would do: "Will your Legislature remonstrate against the destructive policy of the General Government, or will they kiss the hand that crushes them, and be the humbled instrument of their own ruin?"[104]

Even after these hardships, he made "one hundred bags of cotton and some corn also for sale," and if business had "kept its ordinary course, such a crop would have produced all the money I wanted—At present it amounts to nothing."[105]

Davie believed that the embargo would lead "inevitably to war," that we could "not recede from this stand without sacrificing the honor and Independence of our Country," and that we were "on the verge of a War the course and Termination of which defy all political and military calculation." He felt that "we should not stand disputing *now, how* the national barque *got into* the dangers and perils," but that the question was "*how* shall we *get out* of these difficulties." He deplored the "violence, vacillation and distraction which prevail in our public councils" and stated that "no Country at any period ever stood more in need of the Union and exertion of its Citizens," that "the civil Tomahawk of party dissention should be buried," and that "the Administration should avail themselves of the best Talents of the republic."[106]

Although Davie made "a good crop of cotton" in the fall of 1809, he complained that the markets were "influenced altogether by political circumstances." As a result prime cotton was bringing 13¾ cents a pound, which was "still very low, however better than some time past."[107] By October, 1810, Davie reported that in Charleston "the cotton of the new crop" had been as high as 20 cents but had already fallen to 16 cents.[108]

With the approaching threat of the War of 1812, Davie reported that "we poor planters are much 'bothered' here to know what to do, [because] we depend entirely on foreign commerce and are now perfectly at a loss, what are you going to plant this year, what can we best do."[109]

Meanwhile Davie had been engaged for eighteen months in digging "a canal and building dams to erect a set of mills upon the river." He left all the planting to his overseer and "superintended the other business from day to day myself," which had "employed and amused" him. The canal—which still remains and which is three-quarters of a mile long—required digging through "several hundred yards... of piled or solid rock."[110]

A Federalist Star Falls

It was not until the year after the end of the War of 1812 that Davie's crops were not a cause of complaint. In May, 1816, he reported that he had "made a good crop of everything and the market has been good." [111]

That he was a progressive, scientific farmer of that era is attested to by his experimentation with new crops. In December, 1817, he sent "a little seed of that excellent grass the English call Cocksfoot" to Governor Andrew Pickens of South Carolina.[112] And to another friend in April, 1819, he sent "some of the Heligoland beans obtained from England lately by the Agricultural Society" of South Carolina. "These beans," he wrote, "are highly praised for their great produce (80 bushels to the acre) and they are said to be excellent food for man and beast." [113]

This Agricultural Society of South Carolina was founded in 1785 by a group of Low Country planters interested in agricultural experimentation and discoveries. Unfortunately the records of the Society do not antedate 1825, but the above reference to it by Davie, his known interest in such pursuits, and the claim of his ante-bellum biography all point to the fact that he was a member." [114]

Up to the last years of his life Davie maintained an alert interest in his crops. While seeking relief from his rheumatism in August, 1818, at Warm Springs in Madison County, North Carolina, he wrote his son, Frederick William, to know "the exact progress of my overseers work, and the exact progress of every field of corn and cotton on the plantation." He supposed that "the little wheat we made ... is now thrashed out, the seed must be carefully sunned, and kept from heating by being spread. How does the mill come on—Will anything be made this year by that. What about the dam? Write me particularly about everything." [115]

But Davie's retirement from active participation in politics did not preclude his continued interests in the affairs of North Carolina, the Union, and Europe. Naturally all of his writings reflected his Federalist proclivities and his deep and despondent distrust of the Democratic-Republicans. A sampling of his letters in this period reflects these sentiments.

In December, 1806, he was concerned over "how parties stand in Virga between Madison and Munroe and how far they have spread in N. C. Mr. [John] Randolph's plain truths were so unfashionable that I cant suppose they were well received by a people so abjectly devoted to the Idol of the day as my cidevant fellow citizens." [116]

Later, referring to the election of 1808, he feared that Monroe's friends would be discouraged "in consequence of the superior support Madison appears to have in the other States from the Congressional Caucus, and the prodigious weight of Jefferson's influence." Then Davie hit the nadir of despair: "The Federal Party is in fact *dead and buried*, and ought to be so considered even by the warmest friends. No good can arise from any attempts towards its resurrection, therefore the policy of Individuals of that description, for it is no longer a party, will, or ought, certainly to be what you mention, to take no active part, and give their votes to the least exceptionable of the republican candidates." [117]

By August of that year he wrote that never was the situation of our country "more critical or our prospects more pregnant with danger... war points to incalculable evils, and the Embargo, or Terrapin [to] hostilities... and the gradual but certain ruin of our financial resources." [118]

"What have we to hope from a feeble and timid administration," he lamented. And abroad, perhaps the holocaust in Europe was caused by the "imbecility and ignorance of their Princes, and the timidity and corruption of their ministers" and by "the devious temporizing policy of Prussia" and "the abject slavish condescensions of Spain." These mistaken policies he compared to the policy of the United States since 1800. "Mark their character and analogies," he wrote, "look at our interior arrangements... and the state of our foreign relations, and observe the presiding spirit of our Government, and tell me frankly if we are not directed in the same perilous track... to the same dreadful destiny." Again he asks, "has it not been the policy of our Government to lull us asleep with regard to the designs of this formidable Power [France];" "is it wise to wait with folded arms to see what good or rather *Evil* time may bring forth, or has not the crisis arrived which demands decision." [119]

Returning to this election of 1808 he felt that Madison would certainly be elected and that he was "the best choice that could be made among the present candidates." He was sure that Jefferson would "leave our affairs involved in the outmost confusion and difficulty." As to the Federalist candidates he felt that Rufus King "stands

A Federalist Star Falls

no chance" and that the Pinckneys * "with every thing that is virtuous and valuable, have sunk below the political horizon." [120]

A month later, however, Davie saw some faint hopes of their success, having been informed that General Pinckney had consented to run and that "our Eastern Brethren" favored him. He continued: "Delaware comes in also," and "hopes are entertained from Jersey, Pennsylvania & Maryland, but on what grounds I know not; much is expected from No. Carolina, but this must depend upon the combined and steady efforts of the friends of correct principles." He confessed that he did "not yet see clearly how this important object can be effected," but his friends seemed sanguine.[121]

On the same day Davie wrote Duncan Cameron that there was "at present 'a gleam,' and I hope not a fallacious dawning of a better state of things," according to his correspondents who stated that there was "a strong reaction of the public sentiment in all the New England States and in Delaware... and that sanguine hopes are indulged that a similar influence pervades a large part of Jersey, Pennsylvania and Maryland." [122]

He was pleased at the Federalist exertions in North Carolina and hoped that they would "serve at least to convince the Administration, that we are not all the passive slaves of power, and that a respectable portion of their fellow citizens still claim and exercise the right of thinking and judging for themselves." He could expect nothing from South Carolina, where "the People are literally chained down in darkness" and "their political creed is entirely taken from the Government papers... while these are their bibles, you will be at a loss to discover the Gods they worship." [123]

As the "Two Great Belligerent Powers," France and Britain, continued their great struggle for supremacy and their violation of American rights on the high seas, Davie in 1810 could see "no hope of any radical or material change of policy to be expected from either of them in regard to the U. States." He felt that their hope rested upon President Madison who, he "sincerely" believed, was "a man of great virtue," with "sense and the experience of many years in public life." It was also reported to Davie that he had "more promptitude and decision than any man who ever filled the Presidential chair." [124]

* Charles Cotesworth Pinckney was the Federalist candidate for president; Rufus King, for vice-president.

WILLIAM R. DAVIE

By January 10, 1812, Davie began to realize that we would be plunged into the war against England, especially after the government had been placed "in a situation from which they cannot retreat, without absolute disgrace... to their *popularity*." However, he thought that "if we can steer clear of an alliance with France... perhaps it will be better." After "two or three ratling fights, 30 or 40,000 men killed and a debt of as many millions," perhaps we would come to our senses.[125]

At this time, January, 1812, there was some talk of giving the command of the United States Army to Davie.[126] In reply to an enquiry about it from John Haywood he wrote: "As to the public, it would perhaps have been a great misfortune to the Army and the Country had I or any other Federalist been appointed to *the chief command*." This he based on the fact that "the immense sums of money necessary for military operations are always obtained with difficulty from any Government, and would certainly never be furnished by ours, unless to a Chief, who had popularity enough to manage both Congress and the Executive." Therefore, "a Federalist would have insuperable difficulties to struggle with, and nothing to expect but disaster and disgrace."[127]

He also implied that if the command were offered to him, he would refuse: "As to myself, altho' the war if it takes place cannot last long, the people will not support it, yet such a situation would have deranged the plan of my life, and abstracted my attention from my family who have now no parent but myself, and greatly injured my affairs; and nothing but the imperious sense of duty would induce me to embark again in public life in any manner." He maintained also that if war came, it would certainly not be the fault of the Federalists and predicted quite rightly that a war would "effect a complete change in the public sentiment and opinion"—away from the "degrading and ruinous" "diurnal expedients" of the present "wretched government."[128]

It was also at this crucial time that Davie was proposed for a number of important posts. A convention of delegates from eighteen Virginia counties met in Staunton in the fall and nominated Rufus King for president and General Davie as his running mate.[129] In December he was "spoken of" as secretary of war.[130] And in March, 1813, he was appointed a major general.[131] At least there were those who still remembered him.

Davie hoped that the War of 1812 might bring about the recrudescence of the Federalist party in North Carolina. Faced with the "melancholy issue of the invasion of Upper Canada, and the prospects of a disastrous war," he thought there must be a change of opinion in that state and that by exertion and the dissemination of information the "friends of Peace and commerce" might triumph. Then follows one of his diatribes against Virginia: "nothing is done while Virginia maintains her present ascendancy in the Confederacy, and ... our political liberties and our prosperity depend upon our raising up a competent rival to her ambitious pretentions." A Federalist victory "would insure us peace, commerce and prosperity," and in case of success of the Federalist candidate, George Clinton, "Peace would immediately take place, the Union be preserved, and the towering pretensions of Virginia be repressed perhaps forever."[132]

In February, 1814, Davie turned his mind to the peace commission then meeting in Ghent. To the original three-man commission, composed of John Quincy Adams, Albert Gallatin, and James A. Bayard, President Madison had added Henry Clay, speaker of the House and leading War Hawk, and Jonathan Russell, minister to Sweden. Davie feared that the "late addition to the mission augurs illy I think of its result." Clay he characterized as "a clamorous advocate for the continuance of the war and the conquest of the Canadas." Russell, he said, was "a time-serving wretch, added ... to effect the secret views of the Cabinet, by dividing the vote of the Commission, whenever it may be necessary for that purpose." In contrast to the usual appraisal of this mission, Davie thought that "a mission thus constituted will move awkwardly and always with embarrassment," that there would be "no affinity of principle or accordance of views, and of course no mutual confidence." Maybe he was right.[133]

In typical fashion, Davie launched into a condemnation of the maladministration of the army by Congress. He was "greatly surprised that no motion has been made by the minority in Congress to promote an enquiry into the abuses of expenditure in the army departments," because "they have certainly been enormous, and such an enquiry is necessary to prevent their continuance." He urged John

Steele, with the cry, "*This is the moment*," to get some of his friends to initiate such an enquiry.

And while he was anxiously awaiting the news of the outcome of the battle of New Orleans he argued that we have "not so much to fear from the enemy, as from the ignorance, want of foresight, and absolute incapacity of the administration to conduct the war." He felt that "the movement over the Niagara was foolish beyond all the calculations of human folly." Had we only ascended Lake Ontario, he said, "we had it in our power by *a direct* and well combined movement of our land and lake forces to have taken Kingston, and captured or destroyed the Enemy's fleet and all their naval and military stores at Lake Ontario, and this would have been but the affair of a week or ten days."[134]

Also in character was Davie's reaction to the Federalist threat of secession at the Hartford Convention: "The moderation and firmness displayed throughout their proceedings will, I hope, make some impression upon our wretched administration and the majority in Congress. Surely there must be some men of some sense and reflection among them, they cannot be all fools or madmen."[135]

Wrathful phrases continued to pepper his correspondence: "our mad and stupid Government," "our miserable Govern[ment] [re]sembles the convulsions of a maniac"; the "Tyranny of the Virginia Administration." He "could not help saying that without some great change the American confederacy will dissolve in its own weakness in less than two years and that Mr. Madison will end his long political career amidst the ruins of his country." So strongly did he feel that he wrote his old friend Colonel William Polk proposing some amendments to the Constitution which in his opinion were the only means of arresting "this downward progress" of our government.[136]

He began to view, with "the most lively anxiety," the "present alarming situation in the midst of a disastrous and ruinous war" and to fear a real revolution. This fear he based on the stand being taken by the Federalists in Massachusetts who were "weary of the Tyranny of Virginia, and disgusted with a Government in which they had no practical share and of course no influence," who had been at last "wrought up to the determination to secede from the Union." If this took place, Davie predicted that the separation would not stop at the southern boundary of New England. There was, he said, no hope for the situation "short of a constitutional regulation which will *wrest the sovereignty* of the *Union out of the hands of Virginia.*" He proposed as the only remedy for this evil a constitutional rotation in the election of the president, by which a president could not be chosen from the same state more than once in twelve or sixteen years.[137]

After the conclusion of the War of 1812, Davie turned his attention to the ordeal between Britain and France after Napoleon's return from Elba: "This struggle in Europe must decide whether the whole social order of the civilized community of man shall be subverted, and a stern military despotism established in its place: This dreadful result can only be prevented by 'the extermination' (to use Genl Jackson's phrase) of a corrupted army and their Chief."[138]

With the emergence of a new, ebullient spirit of American nationalism after the contest with Great Britain and the accompanying decline of the stigmatized Federalist party, the national government began, as John Randolph expressed it, to "out-Federalize the Federalists." Among the chief nationalistic courses embarked upon was the chartering in 1816 of the Second United States Bank, and Davie was "glad that the Bank Bill has passed the House of Representatives, even with all its objectionable parts," because "it is a measure of great importance to the Southern States."[139]

As to the presidential election of 1816, in which it was generally conceded that the Republicans would win, the contest revolved around Madison's choice, James Monroe, and William H. Crawford, Secretary of the Treasury and Georgia planter. Davie reported that he was "very anxious to learn whether the friends of Mr. Crawford will passively submit to the caucus nomination of Mr. Munroe, and anxiously hope they will not." He had been informed "that the interests of Mr. Crawford will be promoted by this proceeding in North Carolina and that the Federalists and 'Real Republicans' were extremely desirous that the Administration should adopt this unconstitutional mode of aiding Mr. Munroe's election, as it would probably furnish an opportunity of wrecking the Virginia Faction forever in that State." In South Carolina "implicit obedience to the will of the Administration" was the "leading article in the political creed of the Democrats." In fact, they were "the perfect slaves of the party, without any sense of independence or any pretention to any opinion whatever, except those sanctioned by the Holy See." [140]

In May, 1816, Davie delivered what amounts to his valedictory message in regard to the political situation. There is something pathetic and yet commendable in the bitterness and disillusionment of his words:

"As to our own Government it is progressing and must progress according to *the laws of our Nature,* and the principles of our political institutions, there is not a Government under the sun in which corruption is more completely organised or more generally ramified than in that of the United States—Power must be *obtained* by corruption, and *maintained* by it also, there is no help for this, there is nothing Here without alloy; I have been disappointed certainly in the moral character of this Government which I assisted to form, the consequence of the want of experience and sufficient reflection; I am now only surprised at the little time it has taken to effect so complete a change in the habits of thinking and feeling of seven or eight millions of people widely scattered over an immense surface.—The last Session of Congress flattens the hopes you have entertained, we have seen there an entire change in the principles of the Administration; with an adoption of all the leading principles of the Federal party when in power, only pushing them much farther than we ever contemplated; in general political principles there is therefore no difference between the parties and this should be proudly and publicly avowed by the Federalists; we may differ about the men we would choose to administer the Government, but that is to be expected, and will in effect eventuate in the public good, and keep alive that wholesome jealousy of power which is the best guarantee of the people's rights." [141]

Yet there was to be one final public honor to be bestowed on the aging Davie. In December, 1819, he accepted an appointment from Governor Joel R. Poinsett as a commissioner on the Board of Public Works. As such he planned to meet with the other commissioners in January when he hoped they would have "an opportunity of examining the ground at the Falls [of the Catawba River] near Rocky Mount." There he hoped they would be convinced "that it is by no means so formidable an undertaking to surmount those difficulties as it has generally been supposed." [142]

A Federalist Star Falls

Davie beguiled many a long winter's evening at "Tivoli" by reading. Occasional and acute references to books appear in his correspondence. One which he particularly enjoyed was Sir John Carr's *Stranger in France*. Carr impressed him as an "agreeable writer," whom he read "with pleasure," because "he furnishes both entertainment and information." Dr. Hugh Williamson's *History of North Carolina*, which sold for $4.50, he considered "a hard bargain."[143]

In his last years Davie began to assume something of a patriarchal status and was frequently appealed to for advice. Shortly after Andrew Jackson's great victory at New Orleans, a group of Charlestonians began discussing whether Andrew Jackson was born in North or South Carolina. They appealed to Davie, who had known Jackson from adolescence. Davie affirmed the fact that he was born in Lancaster District, now Lancaster County, South Carolina.[144]

And as late as November, 1819, a member of the Board of Trustees of the College of South Carolina appealed to him to try to induce Joseph Caldwell, President of the University of North Carolina, to accept the office of Professor of Mathematics and Astronomy in the South Carolina College. Davie accordingly wrote Caldwell of the offer of the position, which carried a salary of $2,000 and a comfortable house.[145] Of course the offer was declined. It might also be added that Davie still continued his interest in the University of North Carolina.

By this time Davie's children were fairly well settled: Allen Jones had married, had two sons, and had moved to the Mississippi territory. Hyder Ali had married, had one daughter, and was "extremely well settled within three miles" of Davie. Sarah had married William DeSaussure, the son of Chancellor DeSaussure, and lived at Columbia, where she had one daughter. His other two daughters, Mary Haynes and Rebecca, were living with him, and Frederick William, his youngest, was at school at Dr. Waddell's Academy at Abbeville, about 135 miles from "Tivoli."[146]

Davie wrote Haywood that he intended sending the boy to the College of South Carolina in the fall of 1816. He did not have "a very exalted opinion of that institution," but he was "extremely desirous that he should become early acquainted with those men among whom he is destined to live, if it should please God to prolong his Days: a knowledge of the World, that is of men and business is of more consequence to our Standing and Wellfare in Life than all the Latin and Greek which has been taught since the days of Cicero and Aristotle."[147]

From 1815 until his death five years later, Davie began to be plagued with various ailments. His rheumatism, of which he had complained periodically for several years, finally prompted him in July, 1815, to seek relief at Warm Springs (now Hot Springs), in Buncombe (now Madison) County, North Carolina. Here he hoped to achieve "even a year or two of exemption from pain."[148]

Here assembled each summer about fifty to seventy-five visitors from the "most respectable families" from North and South Carolina and Georgia. The hostelry had recently been greatly improved for the "Comfort & convenience of its visitors quite in Virginia Style." In addition to the medicinal waters, "blanket sweats" were provided for the guests.[149]

Among Davie's old friends who frequented this fashionable resort on the French Broad River were the Camerons and Bennehans of Hillsborough, Joseph Caldwell, the Pearsons of Salisbury, and the Izards of Charleston. In this delightful company Davie could "review a great deal of the past, reflect upon the Present, and compare... ideas and opinions of the Future."[150]

Perhaps the springs were not too efficacious, for in a fragmentary letter he wrote: "I have been otherwise as much exempt as most men from the physical ills of life, I am thankful for it, and should this attack continue shall endeavour to bear it with proper resignation and fortitude."[151]

In April, 1817, he wrote John Haywood that he had "suffered very much ever since about the 10th of January from my old inmate the Rheumatism, which contrary to all the analogies of animal affinities grows fonder and more attached to my carcass as it grows older." He planned to make another "pilgrimage" to Warm Springs in July, where he hoped "to obtain some respite from pain." He would "chearfully compromise for this blessing although I might wish that they possessed all the medical powers of the fabled cauldron of Medea."[152]

Davie returned again the following summer accompanied by his daughter Betsy (apparently a nickname for Rebecca) and his sons, Hyder Ali (and his wife) and Allen Jones. From here he wrote his

A Federalist Star Falls

daughter Mary Haynes that he had been "generally well except a bad cold of which I am now better."[153]

The following summer, 1819, Davie was compelled to remain at home, because he had become "much indisposed in the month of June by an attack of pain in the lumbar region respecting the nature of which the Doctors differed." He supposed "the old machine is beginning to give way under the 'tear and wear' of sixty years."[154] By November of that year he was "just recovering from a severe attack of bilious fever" and was obliged to employ an amanuensis.[155] This attack he further described as "a dreadful attack of fever... which reduced me to the verge of the grave [and which] has left me greatly debilitated, but my Health and strength now improve every day."[156]

His last extant letter—written May 24, 1820, to his old friend, John Haywood—deals exclusively with his health. His attack the previous October had severely shattered his constitution, since which he had suffered "two severe attacks of inflamation of the Liver." As medicinal relief he was administered mercury, as a result of which he suffered from "salivation or even Tylolism," * which in themselves were diseases. Still very weak, he planned to set out for Warm Springs on June 10, "where I hope with the blessing of God to get entirely freed from the affections of the liver, as I have known those waters operate effectually in removing biliary obstructions, and the ordinary disorders of this viscus."[157]

Although he "was nearly skinned alive by blisters and cataplasms" during his illness in October, he had "not suffered so much as usual from the rheumatism," but he had been "almost constantly confined to the house." Philosophically, however, he felt it was his "duty to be grateful to that kind providence of that God who disposes of all things, and I may say with the Arab, 'God is mercifull;' for notwithstanding my constant exposure for so many years during the war and in the practice and drudgery of my profession, I have experienced as few of the physical evils of life as most men, who have been so long on the road of life."[158]

He optimistically wound up by promising to write Haywood when

---

* No doubt Davie meant "ptyalism," which is excessive salivation.

he reached Warm Springs, though there is no record that he was able to make the trip. Finally, he assured him of his "warm attachment and that I know how to appreciate a friend, who to use the language of the English painter of Nature 'I have worn in my hearts core' for near forty years." [159]

Perhaps as a result of his liver disorder, Davie died November 5, 1820. Interment was just across the Catawba from "Tivoli" at the Old Waxhaw Presbyterian Churchyard, where he could join his parents and many of his Revolutionary comrades.

Davie left a considerable estate, which was valued at $46,989.37½. The value of his 116 slaves, whom he bequeathed to his six children, amounted to $32,050. Perhaps the most interesting features of his detailed will, drawn up in September, 1819, were the manumission of two of his faithful slaves and the bequest of his "arms and military accoutrement" to his son, Frederick William, with the admonition that he should "never forget that these arms were honorably employed in establishing the Liberties of their country...." In addition to a vast variety of possessions, he owned a "bathing tub," a pianoforte, a great deal of valuable china, glassware, and silver, a library valued at $2,500, a cotton gin, and a threshing machine.[160]

Upon hearing the news of his death, the Grand Lodge of North Carolina passed a resolution of respect, in testimony of which the brethren wore crepe on the left arm for thirty days.[161]

For the "last and melancholy service of writing his epitaph," Frederick William Davie appealed to Judge William Gaston, of Newbern. Gaston undertook the task because of the "high respect which I entertained for him, when in life, and my fond recollection ... of his many acts of kindness to me." Frederick William later assured Gaston of his "perfect satisfaction with the inscription," which reads as follows: [162]

> The Soldier, Jurist, Statesman, and Patriot,
> In the glorious war for American Independence,
> He fought among the foremost of the brave.
>   As an Advocate at the Bar,
> He was diligent, sagacious, learned, zealous,
> Incorruptibly honest and of commanding eloquence,
>   In the Legislative Hall,

A Federalist Star Falls

He had no superior in enlarged views and profound
     plans of Policy;
Single in his end, varied in his means, and inde-
     fatigable in his exertions,
Representing his nation in an important foreign embassy,
He evinced his characteristic devotion to her interests
And manifested a peculiar fitness for Diplomacy.
Polished in his manners, firm in act,
Candid without imprudence, Wise above Deceit.
          A true lover of his country.
Always preferring the People's good to the People's favour
     Though he disdained to faun for Office,
He filled most of the stations to which Ambition
          might aspire,
     And declining no public Trust
     Ennobled whatever he accepted,
     By the dignity and Talent,
Which he brought into the discharge of its functions.
     —A great man in an age of Great men.—
In life he was admired and loved by the virtuous
     and the Wise,
In death, he has silenced Calumny and caused Envy to
     mourn.

APPENDICES

NOTES

BIBLIOGRAPHY

INDEX

APPENDIX A

The Date of the Family's Arrival in America

THE YEAR of Archibald Davie's arrival in America is corroborated by the inscription on his tomb. That he brought his entire family with him in 1764 is an assumption which may or may not be correct. In fact, there are two accounts to the contrary—neither very reliable and both full of errors on other points relating to Davie. The oft-quoted Howe contended that William Richardson Davie had been brought over, at the instance of his uncle, in 1761, "when only five years old, in company with Robert Carr, the nephew of Mr. Archibald Davie" (*The Presbyterian Church in S. C.*, I, 331). Though this, on its face, seems unlikely, and though the boy was five years old in 1761, yet there is another source which cannot be completely ignored, in the form of a letter written by W. R. Davie's daughter-in-law, Mary Fraser Davie, to Sarah [(?) Davie's granddaughter], August, 1853, in the Mary DeSaussure Fraser Papers, a portion of which reads as follows:

"After he [William Richardson] had been here some time he wrote to his sister Mrs. Davie, requesting her to send him her eldest son, William Richardson Davie (your grandfather) and he would educate him and leave him all his property. She consented but at the same time told her husband that she would not send the child (who was but six years old) unless he would take him, himself, and deliver him into his Uncle's hands. The childs father consented. He left his business [a "manufactory of damask" at Whitehaven, according to an earlier portion of the letter] in the hands of his partner, in whom he had the most perfect confidence, and brought the child to his uncle. Before he left this state, he received a letter from his wife, stating that his partner had collected all the money he could in every possible way, and had absconded. That she had consulted lawyers and they advised that he should not return, as he would be put into prison for the debts that were left behind—and that she would sell all that was in her possession and join him as quickly as possible. She did so, and sailed for Charleston with her other two children. When she arrived in Charleston the yellow fever was raging in the place. She staid there only two days, came up with her husband & two children to Lancaster District, and died the third day after she had reached her brothers house, of yellow fever."

APPENDIX B

Davie's Revolutionary Sketches

OF PARTICULAR interest is the fact that parts of Davie's two Revolutionary Sketches have been followed, either *literatim* (with the usual amount of errors) or in substance, by a great number of later writers, some of whom gave due credit to Davie and some of whom did not. In fact, the local history of the Revolution in North Carolina and parts of South Carolina, as well as a number of biographical contributions, has been greatly influenced by these accounts. Conspicuous among those who have leaned heavily on them were the South Carolinians, Edward McCrady (who, incidentally, married Davie's granddaughter) and William Johnson; the North Carolinians, John H. Wheeler, John W. Moore, David Schenck, and C. L. Hunter; and such biographers as George Washington Greene in his *Life of Nathanael Greene* and Fordyce M. Hubbard in his *Life of William R. Davie*.

Also of interest is the provenance of these two accounts. The first was written sometime before January 7, 1810—probably in the latter part of the first decade of the nineteenth century. This account, along with other manuscripts, was in the hands of Davie's eldest son, Allen Jones Davie, until he moved to Tennessee, in the early 1840's, at which time they were left with his brother, Frederick William. These papers were the subject of several letters from Allen Jones Davie to John Haywood (state treasurer of North Carolina), William Gaston (Associate Justice of the Supreme Court of the United States), and Archibald De Bow Murphey, the last of whom wanted to use them in

APPENDICES

his projected history of the state. It was largely through the medium of Davie's ante-bellum biographer, Hubbard, whose *Life* appeared in Sparks's *Library of American Biography*, that this first account, after having been used by Hubbard, was, with Frederick William Davie's consent, deposited with the Historical Society of North Carolina at Chapel Hill in 1846. Nine years later, President David L. Swain, of the University of North Carolina, sent it to former Governor William A. Graham for use in an article in the *North Carolina University Magazine* on "The Revolutionary History of North Carolina: British Invasion of 1780-1781." In 1873 Lyman C. Draper found that it was still in Graham's hands. How it came back to the Southern Historical Collection at Chapel Hill is unknown, but there it is, under the label "Davie-Weems Historical Notes." The hyphenated title may be attributed to the fact that on the fly-leaf are the following words, inscribed by Parson Weems:

If Genl Davie will please to have transcribd in a round legible hand the followg valuable documents, and forward them to me to care of Doct. Dalco [Dr. Frederick Dalcho, editor of the *Charleston Courier*], Charleston, he will confer a very great favor on
his much oblgd M L Weems

NB. The sooner the better; at any rate by the 15th Feby 1810
Jany 7. 1810.

And well might he have made such a request! Written in a copy-book (12⅜ by 8 inches), containing sixty-eight written pages, now yellowed and mutilated, the script is scratchy and infinitesimal, and at times illegible.

The provenance of the second part is somewhat more difficult to trace. Written on twenty-two pages of regular writing paper (10⅜ by 8⅜ inches) the script is about the same as that of the first, though this part was written later—somewhere between 1816 and 1820—as proved by the content. According to George Washington Greene, it was prepared by Davie a few years before his death at the request of General Greene's youngest daughter. In all probability, a copy, rather than the original, was sent. As to the original, the recent donor of it to the Southern Historical Collection, Colonel Preston Davie, of New York, a collateral descendant, believes that it was given to him,

[404]

Appendices

together with a considerable number of other papers, by the late William Richardson Davie, a grandson of the first William Richardson Davie. The younger man lived for some time at "Tivoli," his grandfather's plantation near Landsford, South Carolina, and then moved to Austin, Texas, where he became Secretary of State.

APPENDIX C

Davie's Plan of Education

PLAN OF THE PREPARATORY SCHOOL.

The English Language to be taught Gramatically on the plan of Webster's & Lowth's Grammars *

Writing in a neat and correct manner.

Arithmetic, the four first rules with the Rule of Three—

English Additional exercises.—

Reading and pronouncing select passages from the present English Authors.

Copying in a fair and correct manner select English Essays.

When they can read English with fluency and write fairly and legibly. Students shall begin to learn the Latin language on the following plan, to Wit. Ruddiman's Rudiments, Cordery, Erasmus, Eutropius, Cornelius, Nepos, with translations; Caesar's Commentaries &

---

* These are two interesting old books, with typical eighteenth-century titles:

a. Noah Webster, *A Grammatical Institute of the English Language: Comprising An Easy, Concise and Systematical Method of Education. Designed for the Use of English Schools in America. In Three Parts. Part Second. Containing a Plain and Comprehensive Grammar, Grounded on the Principles and Idioms of the Language.* Printed at Boston, by Isaiah Thomas & Ebenezer T. Andrews, 1794.

b. Robert Lowth, *A Short Introduction to English Grammar: With Critical Notes.... A New Edition. To Which Is Now Added, An Essay on Rhetorical Tropes and Figures.* New York: Printed for Rogers and Berry, Anno 1795. Written by the Lord Bishop of Oxford (1710-1787), it was first published in 1762 and was reprinted six times up to this 1795 edition.

APPENDICES

Salust without translations; but when the Parent or Guardian shall choose it the whole of these Authors shall be read with translations—Kenneth's Roman Antiquities to be studied at the same time.—When they can render Eutropius & explain the Government and connection of the words; then the Students shall commence the Study of the French Language on the following plan, to Wit,—

    Grammar—Telamachus—Cyrus—Gil-blas.—If the Student is to be taught the Greek Language he will read—The Greek Grammar—The Gospels in Greek—The Rudiments of Geography on the plan of Guthrie.—

After the Student commences the Study of the French Language, the Study of the French & Latin Language Shall be associated, and the time so appropriated to each, that the course in both may be finished nearly at the same time.

When the Greek Languge [sic] is Studied with out the French the Studient [sic] will commence it at the time prescribed for the French.—

When the Latin, Greek, and French are all directed to be studied, the Study of Greek shall then commence so that the Student may be able to Read the Gospels in Greek and Translate them correctly when he finishes his course in the Preparatory School.

The English exercises shall be regularly continued, this Language being always considered as a primary object, and the other languages but auxiliaries.—

Any of the Languages (the English excepted) may be omitted if the Parent or Guardian of the Student shall so direct.

The Plan of Education under the Professorships of the University.—

                First—The President

Rhetoric & Belles lettres.
Rhetoric on the plan of Sheridan
Belles lettres, on the plan of Blair & Rollin

                Professorships.

First—Professor of Moral and political Philosophy and History.

    Moral and political Philosophy by the Study of the following Authors.—

APPENDICES

Paley's Moral & political Philosophy—
Montesquieu's Spirit of Laws—Civil Government & political Constitutions—
Adams' Defence & De Lolme
The Constitutions of the United States.
The Modern Constitutions of Europe.
        The Law of Nations.—
Vattell's Law of Nations
Burlamaquis Principals of Natural and political law—
        History
Priestley's Lectures on History and General Policy—
Millots Ancient and Modern History
Hume's History of England with Smolletts continuation
Chronology on the most approved plan—

Second—Professor of Natural philosophy, Astronomy and Geography.
    Natural Philosophy under the following heads—
        General properties of Matter

Laws of Motion	Geography
Mechanical Powers	The Use of the Globes
Hydrostatics	The Geometrical, Political & Commercial relations of the different nations of the Earth
Hydraulics	
Pneumatics	
Optics	
Electricity	Astronomy on the plan of Ferguson
Magnitism	

Third—Professor of Mathematics

Arithmetic in a Scientific manner

Thus far shall be the regular course of Study,—the remainder may be taught if requested.

Algebra, and the application of Algebra to Geometry
Euclid's Elements
Trigonometry and the application of Trigonometry to the Mensuration of heights and distances, of Surfaces & Solids, and Surveying and Navigation
Conic Section
The Doctrine of the Sphere & Sylinder

Appendices

The Projection of the Sphere
Spherical Trigonometry
The doctrine of fluxions
The doctrine of chances & Annuities

Fourth—Professor of Chymistry & the Philosophy of Medicine.
    Agriculture and the Mechanical Arts. Chymestry upon the most approved plan

Fifth—Professor of Languages.
    The English language
Elegant Extracts in prose and verse
Scott's Collection
    Latin Language
Virgil—Cicero's Orations—Horace's Epistles including his Art of Poetry.

    Greek Languge [sic]
Lucian. Xenophon

The Professor of Languages to attend when required, the Reading of Cicero de officiis, and Horace & Livy in the Latin language Longinus on the Sublime and the Orations of Demosthenes & Homer's Iliad in Greek.—

The Rudiments of Language are still to be attended to; the different forms and the figure of Speech will be noticed by the Professor, and Comments made on the Sentiments and beauties of the Authors.— parallel Sentences quoted—particular idioms observed; and all allusions to distant Customs and manners explained.

The Students under the 5th. Professorship shall deliver twice a Week, to the Professor of Languages an English translation from some of the Latin or Greek Classics, in which, after expressing the sence of the Author, the Spirit and eligance of the translation are principally to be regarded.—

The Students of the other Classes shall every Saturday deliver to the President an English composition on a subject of their own chusing, and he shall correct the Errors in Orthography, Grammar, Style or Sentiment, and make the necessary Observations thereon when he returns the Composition to the Writer.

Appendices

A Student who shall pass an approved examination upon the Exercises of the Preparatory School shall be admitted upon the general establishment of the University

Any candidate shall be admitted into the University to attend the Classes of Rhetoric and Belles-lettres or as a Student under any of the three first Professorships who shall pass an approved examination upon the English language, the four first rules of Arithmetic; and the Rule of Three.—

Any person may also be admitted as a Student under the fifth Professorship who can pass an approved Caesars Commentaries & Salust into English & explain the Government & connection of the words.—

No specific qualifications are required for a Student under the fourth Professorship alone.

The Preparatory School shall be considered as a branch of the Institution, and in all respects under the direction and regulation of the Trustees.—

That the present Students who are not qualified to be entered on the General Establishment of the University, shall be arranged to the Preparatory School & placed under the direction of the Tutors appointed to that part of the Institution.

That the Studies and exercises of these Students be so arranged after the next vacation as to remedy the defects of their past education, & come as nearly and as early as possible to the plan prescribed by the Board.*

---

* T. M., pp. 203-207. This was also published, with a number of errors, in *N.C.J.*, Feb. 22, 1796; it may also be found in Hugh T. Lefler (ed.), *North Carolina History Told by Contemporaries* (Chapel Hill: The University of North Carolina Press, 1948), pp. 160-62.

NOTES

CHAPTER I

1. Preston Davie, "The Story of Governor William Richardson Davie and His Times." Typescript sketch of Maryland branch of the family. Copy in possession of the writer.
2. Mary Fraser Davie to Sarah [?], Aug., 1853.—Mary DeSaussure Fraser Papers, Manuscript Room, Duke University, Durham, N.C.
3. Mary Richardson's Bible was recently presented to the Louis Round Wilson Library, University of North Carolina, Chapel Hill, N.C., by the children of William R. Davie Crockett, of Austin, Texas.
4. The Rev. John L. Dinwiddie, *The Ruthwell Cross and the Ruthwell Savings Bank: A Handbook for Tourists and Students* (Dumfries: Robert Dinwiddie, 1933), pp. 135-36.
5. F. W. Davie to William Gaston, Feb. 19, 1822; William Gaston to F. W. Davie, March 26, 1822; F. W. Davie to William Gaston, May 28, 1822.—The Gaston Papers in the H. G. Connor Collection, Southern Historical Collection, University of North Carolina, Chapel Hill, N.C. (hereafter cited as S.H.C.).
6. Tombstone of Davie; Mary Richardson Davie's Bible; Preston Davie, "The Early Years and Antecedents of Davie, 1756-1820," unfinished typescript sketch, a copy of which is in the possession of the writer; E. Alfred Jones to R. D. W. Connor, Oct. 31 and Nov. 2 [?], in the possession of the writer.
7. George Howe, *History of the Presbyterian Church in South Carolina*, 2 vols. (Columbia, S.C.: Duffie & Chapman, 1870), I, 291-92.
8. Samuel Cole Williams, *The Dawn of the Tennessee Valley and Tennessee History* (Johnson City, Tenn.: The Watauga Press, 1937), pp. 207-9. For biographical sketches of Samuel Davies, see Henry Alexander White, *Southern Presbyterian Leaders* (New York: The Neale Publishing Company, 1911), pp. 44-57; John E. Pomfret, "Davies, Samuel," *Dictionary of American Biography*, V, 102-3 (hereafter cited as *D.A.B.*).

Notes

9. William Henry Foote, *Sketches of North Carolina, Historical and Biographical*.... (New York: R. Carter, 1846), p. 245; William L. Saunders (ed.), *The Colonial Records of North Carolina* (Raleigh: Josephus Daniels, 1890), V, 1225 (hereafter cited as *C.R.*); Howe, *The Presbyterian Church in S.C.*, I, 292. For a biographical sketch of Pattillo, see White, *Southern Presbyterian Leaders*, pp. 95-97.

10. Alice M. Baldwin, "Sowers of Sedition: The Political Theories of Some of the New Light Presbyterian Clergy of Virginia and North Carolina," *William and Mary Quarterly*, Third Series, V (Jan., 1948), 64-68; Foote, *Sketches*, pp. 183-92; White, *Southern Presbyterian Leaders*, pp. 73-78; Guy S. Klett, *Presbyterianism in Colonial Pennsylvania* (Philadelphia: University of Pennsylvania, 1937), pp. 157-58.

11. Richardson's manuscript report on his mission to the Cherokees sent to the Reverend Samuel Davies. In the Wilberforce Eames Collection, MS Division, New York Public Library. Photostatic copy in S.H.C.

12. White, *Southern Presbyterian Leaders*, pp. 86-89.

13. Quoted in Howe, *The Presbyterian Church in S.C.*, I, 292.

14. *Ibid.*, pp. 291-92.

15. Preston Davie, "The Story of Governor William Richardson Davie and His Times"; R. T. Jaynes, "The Old Waxhaws" (n.p., n.pub., n.d.), p. 3; James Parton, *The Life of Andrew Jackson* (New York: Mason Brothers, 1860), I, 48-49; John S. Bassett, *The Life of Andrew Jackson* (New York: Doubleday, 1911), p. 4.

16. Howe, *The Presbyterian Church in S.C.*, I, 285-86; Marquis James, *The Life of Andrew Jackson, Complete in One Volume* (Indianapolis and New York: The Bobbs-Merrill Company, 1938), p. 6.

17. Richard J. Hooker (ed.), *The Carolina Backcountry on the Eve of the American Revolution: The Journal and Other Writings of Charles Woodmason, Anglican Itinerant* (Chapel Hill: Published for the Institute of Early American History and Culture at Williamsburg, Virginia, by the University of North Carolina Press, 1953), pp. 13-14.

18. *Ibid.*, p. 14.

19. See Carl Bridenbaugh, *Myths and Realities: Societies of the Colonial South* (Baton Rouge: Louisiana State University Press, 1952), pp. 169-71, for a discussion of the gentry of the Back Settlements.

20. Howe, *The Presbyterian Church in S.C.*, I, 288-89; James, *Andrew Jackson*, p. 8.

21. Howe, *The Presbyterian Church in S.C.*, I, 293, 330; James, *Andrew Jackson*, p. 12; White, *Southern Presbyterian Leaders*, p. 91.

22. Preston Davie, "The Early Years and Antecedents of William Richardson Davie."

23. Howe, *The Presbyterian Church in S.C.*, I, 330.

24. *Ibid.*, pp. 330, 421.

25. Information concerning these grants is found in later conveyances of

NOTES

these same tracts in which the descent of title is traced.—Old Deed Book H, p. 7, Clerk of Courts Office, Lancaster, S.C.

26. Preston Davie, "The Early Years and Antecedents of Davie."

27. Charles W. Wiltse, *John C. Calhoun, Nationalist, 1782-1828* (Indianapolis and New York: Bobbs-Merrill Company, 1944), pp. 17-18.

28. Williams, *The Dawn of the Tennessee Valley*, p. 209; John H. Wheeler, *Historical Sketches of North Carolina, From 1584 to 1851* (Philadelphia: Lippincott, Grambo and Co., 1851), II, 181; The Rev. E. W. Caruthers, *A Sketch of the Life and Character of the Rev. David Caldwell, D.D.* (Greensborough, N.C.: Printed by Swaim and Sherwood, 1842), p. 26 et seq.

29. James, *Andrew Jackson*, p. 7.

30. Howe, *The Presbyterian Church in S.C.*, I, 416.

31. *Ibid.*, p. 331.

CHAPTER II

1. Bridenbaugh, *Myths and Realities*, pp. 129-30.

2. Janie Revill (comp.), *A Compilation of the Original Lists of Protestant Immigrants to South Carolina, 1763-1773* (Columbia, S.C.: The State Co., 1939), p. 3.

3. Council Journal for South Carolina, in the office of the Historical Commission of South Carolina, Columbia, S.C. (hereafter cited as H.C.S.C.), XXXII, 505.

4. Duplicates of these two plats and surveyor's descriptions were annexed to the grants themselves, which were executed in the name of George III, through Governor Lord Charles Greville Montague, and were recorded in Grant Book, Vol. 14, pp. 405, 441, H.C.S.C.

5. Bond of Archibald Davie to William Richardson, witnessed by the latter's wife, Agnes.—W.R.D. Papers, No. 2, S.H.C.

6. Declaration for Pension by John Taylor, Senior (Granville County). —Walter Clark (ed.), *The State Records of North Carolina* (Goldsboro, N.C.: Nash Brothers, 1907), XXII, 156 (hereafter cited as *S.R.*).

7. Howe, *The Presbyterian Church in S.C.*, I, 417.

8. Hooker (ed.), *Carolina Backcountry*, p. 134.

9. Howe, *The Presbyterian Church in S.C.*, I, 17-18.

10. *Ibid.*, p. 18.

11. This account, reprinted in Howe, *The Presbyterian Church in S.C.*, I, 418, is there cited in a footnote (p. 293) as follows: "MS account of the Waxhaw Church, prepared at the request of Presbytery under the order of the General Assembly, signed John Davis, session clerk, Waxhaw, April 5th, 1794." An extensive search has failed to locate the original.

12. Quoted in *ibid.*, pp. 418-19.

13. Caruthers, *Sketch of David Caldwell*, p. 28.

14. *C.R.*, VIII, 429; *S.R.*, XXV, 519e.

[413]

NOTES

15. R. D. W. Connor, *History of North Carolina: The Colonial and Revolutionary Periods, 1584-1783* (Chicago and New York: The Lewis Publishing Company, 1919), I, 198 (hereafter cited as Connor, *Hist. of N.C.*).

16. *Ibid.*, pp. 204-5.

17. The original of this certificate is in the W. R. Davie Papers, North Carolina Department of Archives and History, Raleigh, North Carolina (hereafter cited as A.H.); W. H. Clemons [Reference Librarian, Princeton] to R. D. W. Connor, Sept. 17, 1909. In writer's possession.

18. John Rogers Williams (ed.), *Philip Vickers Fithian: Journals and Letters, 1767-1774: Student at Princeton College 1770-1772, Tutor at Nomini Hall in Virginia 1773-74.* Edited for The Princeton Historical Association (Princeton: The University Library, 1900), I, 287.

19. Alexander Garden, *Anecdotes of the Revolutionary War in America* (Charleston: Printed for the author, by A. E. Miller, 1822), pp. 37-38.

20. Howe, *The Presbyterian Church in S.C.*, I, 420.

21. Davie to Spruce Macay, Sept. 3, 1793. W.R.D. Papers, No. 1, S.H.C. Typed copy.

CHAPTER III

1. *C.R.*, X, 1024-26.

2. James, *Andrew Jackson*, p. 35; *C.R.*, V, 355; *S.R.*, XXIII, 810; R. D. W. Connor (comp.), *A Manual of North Carolina* (Raleigh: E. M. Uzzell & Co., State Printers, 1913), p. 381; Samuel James Ervin, "A Colonial History of Rowan County," *James Sprunt Historical Publications*, XVI (Chapel Hill: The University of North Carolina Press, 1917), 20-23; Bridenbaugh, *Myths and Realities*, pp. 149-50; James S. Brawley, *The Rowan Story, 1753-1953* (Salisbury, N.C.: Rowan Printing Co., 1953), *passim.*

3. Wheeler, *Sketches of N.C.*, II, 384.

4. James, *Andrew Jackson*, p. 34.

5. Robert E. Lee (ed.), *Memoirs of the War in the Southern Department of the United States By Henry Lee....* (New York: University Publishing Company, 1869), p. 577 (hereafter cited as Lee, *Memoirs*).

6. Wheeler, *Sketches of N.C.*, II, 296.

7. Fordyce M. Hubbard, *Life of William Richardson Davie*, Jared Sparks (ed.), *The Library of American Biography*, Second Series (Boston: Charles G. Little and James Brown, 1848), p. 5 (hereafter cited as Hubbard, *Davie*).

8. Lee, *Memoirs*, p. 577; Hubbard, *Davie*, p. 48; Wheeler, *Sketches of N.C.*, II, 189.

9. This commission is in the W.R.D. Papers, No. 1, S.H.C.

10. Lee, *Memoirs*, p. 577.

11. Hubbard, *Davie*, p. 5.

12. Lee, *Memoirs*, p. 577; Hubbard, *Davie*, p. 6; Wheeler, *Sketches of N.C.*, II, 189.

13. "Order Book of John Faucheraud Grimké," *South Carolina Historical and Genealogical Magazine*, XVI (Jan., 1915), 46.

Notes

14. Lee, *Memoirs*, pp. 118-22.
15. The Hon. J. W. Fortescue, *A History of the British Army* (London: Macmillan and Co., Limited, 1902), III, 273-75; David Ramsay, *The History of the Revolution of South Carolina* (Trenton: Printed by Isaac Collins, 1785), II, 16 (hereafter cited as Ramsay, *Rev. of S.C.*); William Moultrie, *Memoirs of the American Revolution* (New York: Printed by David Longworth for the author, 1802), I, 322-26 (hereafter cited as Moultrie, *Memoirs*); Connor, *Hist. of N.C.*, I, 456.
16. Edward McCrady, *The History of South Carolina in the Revolution, 1775-1780* (New York: The Macmillan Company, 1901), pp. 354-76 (hereafter cited as McCrady, *S.C. in the Rev., 1775-1780*).
17. Lee, *Memoirs*, pp. 577-78.
18. Hubbard, *Davie*, pp. 10-11. This story is also repeated in Wheeler, *Sketches of N.C.*, II, 186; in C. L. Hunter, *Sketches of Western North Carolina, Historical and Biographical* (Raleigh: The Raleigh News Steam Job Press, 1887), pp. 100-1; in McCrady, *S.C. in the Rev. 1775-1780*, pp. 390-91; and in Samuel A'Court Ashe (ed.), *Biographical History of North Carolina from Colonial Times to the Present* (Greensboro, N.C.: Charles L. Van Noppen, 1907), VI, 190.
19. Amos Kendall, *Life of Andrew Jackson, Private, Military, and Civil* (New York: Harper & Bros., 1843), p. 14; Augustus C. Buell, *History of Andrew Jackson: Pioneer, Patriot, Soldier, Politician, President* (New York: Charles Scribner's Sons, 1904), I, 43; James, *Andrew Jackson*, pp. 18-19.
20. Rowan County Court Minutes (1779).
21. Hubbard, *Davie*, pp. 11-12.
22. *S.R.*, XV, 385-86.
23. Lee, *Memoirs*, p. 578; Charles Caldwell, M.D., *Memoirs of the Campaigns of the Hon. Nathaniel Greene* (Philadelphia: Published by Robert Desilver, 1819), p. 114; Wheeler, *Sketches of N.C.*, II, 188; Ashe, *Biog. Hist. of N.C.*, VI, 189-90; McCrady, *S.C. in the Rev., 1775-1780*, p. 574.

CHAPTER IV

1. Davie's MS "Sketches," W.R.D. Papers, No. 2, S.H.C.
2. Greene to Sumter, Jan. 8, 1781. Quoted in Anne King Gregorie, *Thomas Sumter* (Columbia, S.C.: Press of The R. L. Bryan Company, 1931), p. 130.
3. Lynn Montross, *Rag, Tag and Bobtail: The Story of the Continental Army, 1775-1783* (New York: Harper and Brothers, 1952), p. 457.
4. "Notes of the Editor," *Magazine of American History*, VII (Oct., 1881), 293.
5. Robert O. DeMond, *The Loyalists in North Carolina during the Revolution* (Durham, N.C.: Duke University Press, 1940), *passim*.
6. Caldwell, *Memoirs of the Campaigns*, pp. 99, 101, 103.
7. *Ibid.*, pp. 113-14.
8. Garden, *Anecdotes of the Rev.*, p. 39.

NOTES

9. Kendall, *Andrew Jackson*, pp. 19-20.
10. Lee, *Memoirs*, p. 178; Hubbard, *Davie*, pp. 12-13.
11. William Gordon, *The History of the Rise, Progress, and Establishment of the Independence of the United States of America* (London: Printed for the Author; and Sold by Charles Dilly, 1788), III, 360-61; *Clinton-Cornwallis Controversy* (London: 4 Trafalgar Square, Charing Cross, 1888), II, 444 (hereafter cited as C.C.C.); for a detailed account of the battle, setting forth the British and American accounts, see McCrady, *S.C. in the Rev., 1775-1780*, pp. 519-24.
12. Howe, *The Presbyterian Church in S.C.*, I, 536; McCrady, *S.C. in the Rev., 1775-1780*, p. 523; James, *Andrew Jackson*, pp. 19-20; Parton, *Andrew Jackson*, I, 70.
13. Parton, *Andrew Jackson*, I, 70; James, *Andrew Jackson*, p. 20.
14. Clinton to Germain, June 4, 1780. Quoted in Lieutenant Colonel Banastre Tarleton, *A History of the Campaigns of 1780 and 1781 in the Southern Provinces of North America* (London: Printed for T. Cadell, in the Strand, 1787), p. 94.
15. Gregorie, *Sumter*, p. 76.
16. McCrady, *S.C. in the Rev., 1775-1780*, p. 580; Hunter, *Sketches*, p. 215.
17. McCrady gives the number embodied as "nearly thirteen hundred." —*S.C. in the Rev., 1775-1780*, p. 582.
18. This officer is erroneously called "Morgan" Bryan in John Richard Alden (ed.), *The War of the Revolution*, by Christopher Ward (New York: The Macmillan Company, 1952), II, 70.
19. This paragraph is taken from Davie's "Sketches" and from the narrative of another officer under the immediate command of Rutherford—Adjutant Joseph Graham. The latter's sketch, entitled "General Joseph Graham's Narrative of the Revolutionary War in North Carolina in 1780-1781," is reprinted in William H. Hoyt (ed.), *The Papers of Archibald D. Murphey* (Raleigh: Publications of the North Carolina Historical Commission, 1914), II, 212-311 (hereafter cited as Hoyt [ed.], *Murphey Papers*).
20. *Ibid.*; Chalmers G. Davidson, *Piedmont Partisan: The Life and Times of General William Lee Davidson* (Davidson, N.C.: Davidson College, 1951), p. 59.
21. Davie's "Sketches"; Hoyt (ed.), *Murphey Papers*, II, 217-21.
22. James, *Andrew Jackson*, p. 14.
23. This officer was listed as Colonel William Hagins by Hunter, *Sketches*, pp. 105, 112; as Colonel Higgins by Wheeler, *Sketches of N.C.*, II, 191; and as Heaggins by Lee, *Memoirs*, p. 176.
24. Buell, *Andrew Jackson*, p. 52.
25. Parton, *Andrew Jackson*, I, 72.
26. Hoyt (ed.), *Murphey Papers*, II, 230-31.
27. William Dobein James, *A Sketch of the Life of Brig. Gen. Francis Marion* (Charleston: Printed by Gould and Riley, 41 Broad Street, 1821), p. 74.

Notes

28. Tarleton, *Campaigns*, p. 94; Lee, *Memoirs*, p. 176.
29. Hubbard, *Davie*, p. 24.
30. Lee, *Memoirs*, p. 187.
31. Charles Stedman, *The History of the Origin, Progress, and Termination of the American War* (Dublin: Printed for Messrs. F. Wogan, P. Byne, J. Moore, and W. Jones, 1794), II, 224.
32. Gregorie, *Sumter*, p. 91.
33. For the killed and wounded officers, see Davie's "Sketches."
34. Tarleton, *Campaigns*, p. 95.
35. See Frank Monoghan, "Kalb, Johánn," *D.A.B.*, X, 253-54; Friedrich Kapp, *The Life of John Kalb* (New York: Privately printed, 1884).
36. Connor, *Hist. of N.C.*, I, 462-63.
37. Lee, *Memoirs*, p. 188.
38. *Ibid.*
39. Hubbard, *Davie*, pp. 32-33; Wheeler, *Sketches of N.C.*, I, 194; David Schenck, *North Carolina, 1780-1781* (Raleigh: Edwards and Broughton, 1889), p. 96; McCrady, *S.C. in the Rev., 1775-1780*, pp. 679-80.
40. *S.R.*, XXII, 94-95.
41. Davie's "Sketches"; Lee, *Memoirs*, p. 188.
42. McCrady, *S.C. in the Rev., 1775-1780*, p. 680. Caution should be used in following this author too closely as his connection with Davie inclined him on occasions to be too eulogistic. McCrady married Davie's granddaughter.
43. Lee, *Memoirs*, p. 188.
44. Hubbard, *Davie*, pp. 33-34.
45. Garden, *Anecdotes of the Rev.*, p. 38.
46. Gordon, *Hist. of Indep. of U.S.*, III, 444.
47. *C.C.C.*, II, 409-10.
48. This is at variance with the figures of Dr. Gregorie, whose figures are based on those of D. G. Stinson, who interviewed some of the survivors and who carried on a voluminous correspondence with Lyman C. Draper. Her figures listed as captured 310 Americans, 800 horses, 1000 stand of arms, 44 loaded wagons of stores, 2 ammunition wagons, and 2 cannons, with only 150 Americans killed and wounded.—Gregorie, *Sumter*, p. 102.
49. Fortescue, *Hist. of the British Army*, III, 320.
50. *Ibid.*
51. Hoyt (ed.), *Murphey Papers*, II, 235.
52. *S.R.*, XV, vi.
53. *Ibid.*, XIV, xvi.
54. Ramsay, *Rev. of S.C.*, II, 178.
55. *S.R.*, XV, vi.
56. Smallwood to Gates, Aug. 22, 1780, *S.R.*, XIV, 570.
57. *S.R.*, XV, 368-70; repeated in *ibid.*, XXII, 776-77; reprinted in *North Carolina University Magazine*, V (May, 1856), 184.
58. Hoyt (ed.), *Murphey Papers*, II, 236-37.
59. *Ibid.*, p. 237.

Notes

60. *Ibid.*, p. 238.
61. North Carolina Legislative Papers, House of Commons, Aug.-Sept., 1780. A.H.
62. The original commission is in the W. R. Davie Papers, A.H.
63. Hoyt (ed.), *Murphey Papers*, II, 238.
64. *Ibid.*
65. Kendall, *Andrew Jackson*, p. 28; Samuel H. Walkup (Monroe, N.C.) to D. L. Swain, Sept. 25, 1857, David L. Swain Papers, S.H.C.
66. Garden, *Anecdotes of the Rev.*, p. 39; also see Kendall, *Andrew Jackson*, pp. 28-29; Lee, *Memoirs*, pp. 195-96; James, *Andrew Jackson*, pp. 22-23.
67. *S.R.*, XIV, 647. This excerpt is repeated, with minor changes, in *ibid.*, p. 776.
68. *Ibid.*, p. 614.
69. Hoyt (ed.), *Murphey Papers*, II, 239.
70. W.R.D. Papers, No. 2, S.H.C.
71. Davie to Sumner, Sept. 26, 1780, "N.C. Letters from the Emmett Collection, 1757-1847," A.H. (typed bound copy).
72. Hoyt (ed.), *Murphey Papers*, II, 240.
73. Tarleton, *Campaigns*, p. 159.
74. Roderick Mackenzie, *Strictures on Lt. Col. Tarleton's History "Of The Campaigns of 1780 and 1781, in the Southern Provinces of North America"* (London: Printed for the Author; and Sold by R. Jameson, Strand; R. Faulder, New Bond-Street; T. and J. Egerton, Charing Cross, and T. Sewell, Cornhill, M DCC LXXXVIII), pp. 47-48.
75. Tarleton, *Campaigns*, p. 159.
76. *S.R.*, XXII, 123; *ibid.*, XIX, 958-59; Hoyt (ed.), *Murphey Papers*, I, 369.
77. Hoyt (ed.), *Murphey Papers*, I, 244.
78. Davidson, *Piedmont Partisan*, pp. 77, 150, n.20.
79. Stedman, *Hist. of the Amer. War*, II, 216.
80. Hoyt (ed.), *Murphey Papers*, II, 244.
81. Photostat in writer's possession. Original in The Papers of the Continental Congress, Vol. 2, no. 154, Library of Congress.
82. McCrady, *S.C. in the Rev., 1775-1780*, p. 446.
83. Hoyt (ed.), *Murphey Papers*, II, 251.
84. Tarleton, *Campaigns*, pp. 159-60.
85. *Ibid.*
86. Sumner to John Penn [no date or place but written Sept. 28 or 29, 1780, on the basis of the content]. *S.R.*, XIV, 777.
87. *Ibid.*
88. *Ibid.*, p. 778.
89. Gates to Sumner, Sept. 30, 1780.—Letter Copy-Book of Major General Horatio Gates, 1780-1781, p. 59. New York Public Library.
90. Gates to Sumner, Oct. 1, 1780.—*Ibid.*, p. 60.
91. Davie to Sumner, Oct. 1, 1780.—Gates Papers, New York Historical Society, New York.

Notes

92. Letter Copy-Book of Major General Horatio Gates, 1780-1781, p. 60. New York Public Library.
93. Davidson to Sumner, Oct. 5, 1780.—W.R.D. Papers, No. 2, S.H.C.
94. Davie to Sumner, Oct. 6, 1780.—*Ibid*. Hand-written copy. Original in Soldiers of the American Revolution, I, Historical Society of Pennsylvania, Philadelphia.
95. Davidson to Sumner, Oct. 7, 1780.—*S.R.*, XIV, 677.
96. James Iredell to Mrs. Iredell, Oct. 8, 1780.—Griffith J. McRee, *Life and Correspondence of James Iredell, One of the Justices of the Supreme Court of the United States* (New York: D. Appleton and Company, 1857), I, 465 (hereafter cited as McRee, *Iredell*).
97. Davie to Sumner, Oct. 6, 1780.—W.R.D. Papers, No. 2, S.H.C.
98. Davie to Sumner, Oct. 2, 1780.—*S.R.*, XIV, 791.
99. Tarleton, *Campaigns*, p. 192.
100. Lyman C. Draper, *King's Mountain and Its Heroes* (Cincinnati: Peter G. Thompson, 1881), p. 207.
101. Board of War to Governor Nash, Oct. 25, 1780.—MS Journal of the Board of War of North Carolina, 1780-1781. This Journal is bound with the Journals of the Fourth and Fifth Continental Congress, A.H.
102. Hoyt (ed.), *Murphey Papers*, II, 252, followed by Schenck, *N.C., 1780-1781*, p. 180.
103. Tarleton, *Campaigns*, p. 167; Stedman, *Hist. of the Amer. War*, II, 247; Lee, *Memoirs*, p. 201; Davie's "Sketches," followed by McCrady, *S.C. in the Rev., 1775-1780*, p. 808; McRee, *Iredell*, I, 463.
104. Hoyt (ed.), *Murphey Papers*, II, 250-51.
105. Davidson to Sumner, Oct. 9, 1780.—W.R.D. Papers, No. 2, S.H.C.
106. Davidson to Sumner, Oct. 13, 1780.—Papers of the Cont. Cong., L.C.; reprinted in *S.R.*, XIV, 694-95.
107. McCrady, *S.C. in the Rev., 1775-1780*, p. 808.
108. Hoyt (ed.) *Murphey Papers*, II, 252.
109. Mackenzie, *Strictures*, p. 49.
110. Davidson to Sumner, Oct. 13, 1780, 7 A.M.—Papers of the Cont. Cong., L.C.; reprinted in *S.R.*, XIV, 694-95.
111. Mackenzie, *Strictures*, p. 49.
112. Hoyt (ed.), *Murphey Papers*, II, 253.
113. Sumner to Gates, Oct. 13, 1780, 9 P.M.—Papers of the Cont. Cong., L.C.
114. Davidson to Sumner, Oct. 14, 1780.—Papers of the Cont. Cong., Vol. 2, No. 154, 307; *idem* to *idem*, Oct. 13, 1780, 7 A.M.—*Loc. cit*.
115. Hoyt (ed.), *Murphey Papers*, II, 253.
116. Davie to Sumner, n.d., n.p.—*S.R.*, XIV, 789. Content of next letter shows it to have been written Oct 15, 1780.
117. *Idem* to *idem*, Oct. 16, 1780.—*S.R.*, XIV, 789-90.
118. Sumner to Davie, n.d., n.p.—*Ibid.*, p. 791.
119. Davie to Sumner, Oct. 17, 1780.—Jethro Sumner Papers, S.H.C.; reprinted in *S.R.*, XV, 111.

NOTES

120. Hubbard, *Davie*, p. 51.
121. See Chap. X of the Laws of North Carolina, passed at Hillsborough, 1780, second session.—*S.R.*, XXIV, 355-57; Connor, *Hist. of N.C.*, I, 467.
122. A. R. Newsome, "Martin, Alexander," *D.A.B.*, XII, 333-34.
123. J. G. de R. Hamilton, "Penn, John," *D.A.B.*, XIV, 431.
124. *C.R.*, IX, 1102; X, 337, 584; *S.R.*, XII, 549; Wheeler, *Sketches of N.C.*, II, 203; W. C. Allen, *History of Halifax County* (Boston: The Cornhill Company, 1918), pp. 171-72.
125. Connor, *Hist. of N.C.*, I, 467.
126. Davie's "Sketches"; Lee, *Memoirs*, p. 200.
127. Lee, *Memoirs*, pp. 208-9; Hoyt (ed.), *Murphey Papers*, II, 254.
128. Lee, *Memoirs*, p. 209.
129. Smallwood to Gates, Oct. 27, 1780.—*S.R.*, XIV, 712; Hubbard, *Davie*, p. 51.
130. McCrady, *S.C. in the Rev., 1775-1780*, pp. 810-11.
131. Davie to Smallwood, Nov. 7, 1780.—Thomas Balch (ed.), *Papers Relating Chiefly to the Maryland Line During the Revolution* (Philadelphia: Printed for the Seventy-Six Society, 1857), pp. 120-21.
132. Lee, *Memoirs*, p. 203; McCrady, *S.C. in the Rev., 1775-1780*, p. 815.
133. Gordon, *Hist. of the Indep. of the U. S.*, III, 467; Lee, *Memoirs*, p. 204.
134. Balch (ed.), *Maryland Papers*, pp. 123-24.
135. This entire story is reprinted in Emily Ellsworth Skeel (ed.), *Mason Locke Weems, His Works and Ways. In Three Volumes. A Bibliography Left Unfinished by Paul Leicester Ford* (New York: Emily E. Skeel, 1929), III, 353-55.
136. Davie to Smallwood, Nov. 11, 1780.—Balch (ed.), *Maryland Papers*, pp. 164-65.
137. Smallwood to Gates, Nov. 16, 1780.—*S.R.*, XIV, 742.
138. Davie to Smallwood, Nov. 10, 1780.—Balch (ed.), *Maryland Papers*, pp. 124-25.
139. Davie to Smallwood, Nov. 15, 1780.—*Ibid.*, p. 130.
140. Cornwallis to Clinton, Dec. 3, 1780.—*S.R.*, XV, 306-7. Also reprinted in *C.C.C.*, I, 307-8.
141. John Rutledge to the Delegates of S.C. at the Cont. Cong., Nov. 23, 1780. Joseph W. Barnwell (annotator), "Letters of John Rutledge," *S.C. Hist. and Gen. Mag.*, XVII (Oct., 1916), 145.
142. Hubbard, *Davie*, pp. 52-53.
143. The Board of War to Governor Nash, Dec. 2, 1780.—*S.R.*, XIV, 471-72.

CHAPTER V

1. Victor Leroy Johnson, *The Administration of the American Commissariat During the Revolutionary War* (Philadelphia: University of Pennsylvania Press, 1941), pp. 25-27, 42-44.
2. *Ibid.*, pp. 72-73; Gaillard Hunt, Worthington C. Ford, John C. Fitz-

Notes

patrick, and Roscoe R. Hill (eds.), *Journals of the Continental Congress, 1774-1789* (Washington: Government Printing Office, 1907), VIII, 443. June 10, 1777.

3. Johnson, *American Commissariat*, pp. 161-64.
4. *Ibid.*, p. 183.
5. *S.R.*, XXIV, 345.
6. Alexander Martin to Governor Abner Nash, Nov. 10, 1780.–*S.R.*, XV, 150.
7. Johnson, *American Commissariat*, p. 186.
8. Davie's "Sketches."
9. *Ibid.*
10. *Ibid.*
11. Lee, *Memoirs*, pp. 219-20.
12. Greene to Lafayette, Dec. 29, 1780. Quoted in George Washington Greene, *The Life of Nathanael Greene,...* (New York: Published by Hurd and Houghton, 1871), III, 70.
13. Lee, *Memoirs*, p. 220; Greene, *Greene*, III, 72.
14. Greene, *Greene*, III, 86.
15. Iredell to Mrs. Iredell, May 18, 1780.–McRee, *Iredell*, I, 446.
16. Quoted in Greene, *Greene*, III, 86.
17. Locke to Greene, Nov. 30, 1780. Quoted in *ibid.*
18. Quoted in *ibid.*, p. 87.
19. Greene to Polk, Dec. 9, 1780. Quoted in *ibid.*, p. 88.
20. William Johnson, *Sketches of the Life and Correspondence of Nathanael Greene....* (Charleston: Printed for the Author, by A. E. Miller, 1822), I, 351.
21. Quoted in *ibid.*, I, 340.
22. Davie's "Sketches."
23. Winslow C. Watson (ed.), *Men and Times of the Revolution: Or, Memoirs of Elkanah Watson* (New York: Dana and Company, 1856), p. 297.
24. Johnson, *Greene*, I, 340.
25. Greene to the Board of War, Dec. 14, 1780.–W.R.D. Papers, No. 2, S.H.C.; Gates to the Board of War, Nov. 17, 1780.–Jethro Sumner Papers, S.H.C.; D. L. Swain to Benson J. Lossing, July 20, 1852.–D. L. Swain Papers, S.H.C.; A. R. Newsome, "Polk, Thomas," *D.A.B.*, XV, 42-43; Greene, *Greene*, III, 75-76.
26. Quoted in Greene, *Greene*, III, 75-76.
27. W.R.D. Papers, No. 2, S.H.C.
28. Quoted in Hubbard, *Davie*, p. 56.
29. Davie's "Sketches."
30. *Ibid.*
31. *Ibid.*
32. Hubbard, *Davie*, pp. 57-58.
33. Davie to Greene, Jan. 6, 1781.–W.R.D. Papers, No. 2, S.H.C.
34. The N.C. Board of War to Greene, Jan. 5, 1781.–*S.R.*, XIV, 486.
35. *Ibid.*, XVI, v.

Notes

36. *Ibid.*, XIV, 490-91.
37. *S.R.*, XXIV, 6-9; 390-94; 184-87; 320-22.
38. *Ibid.*, pp. 344-47; Johnson, *Greene*, I, 343.
39. *S.R.*, XXIV, 390-94; 434-37.
40. Hubbard, *Davie*, pp. 66-67.
41. Johnson, *Greene*, I, 343.
42. Hubbard, *Davie*, p. 63.
43. Johnson, *Greene*, I, 343.
44. *S.R.*, XVI, 171-72; Davie to Greene, Jan. 6, 1781.—W.R.D. Papers, No. 2, S.H.C.; Hubbard, *Davie*, p. 58.
45. Jan. 26, 1781. N.C. Legislative Papers, House of Commons, A.H.
46. *S.R.*, XVII, 663.
47. *Ibid.*, p. 958.
48. Davie's "Sketches."
49. Greene, *Greene*, III, 83-84, 91-92.
50. *Ibid.*, pp. 137-51.
51. Johnson, *Greene*, I, 391-92.
52. Davie's "Sketches"; Johnson, *Greene*, I, 428.
53. Lee, *Memoirs*, pp. 277-78; Greene, *Greene*, III, 198.
54. Davie's "Sketches."
55. Stedman, *Hist. of the Amer. War*, II, 373.
56. R. Lamb, *An Original and Authentic Journal of Occurrences During the Late American War, From Its Commencement to the Year 1783* (Dublin: Printed by Wilkinson and Courtney, 6 Wood Street, 1809), p. 343.
57. Johnson, *Greene*, I, 428.
58. Lee, *Memoirs*, pp. 248, 288-89.
59. Major Charles Magill to Governor Jefferson, March 8, 1781.—William P. Palmer (ed.), *Calendar of Virginia State Papers and Other Manuscripts, 1652-1781* (Richmond: R. F. Walker, Superintendent of Public Printing, 1875), I, 563.
60. W.R.D. Papers, No. 2, S.H.C.
61. Greene, *Greene*, III, 210-12.
62. Lee, *Memoirs*, p. 296.
63. *Ibid.*, p. 291.
64. Greene to Governor Nash, March 29, 1781. Quoted in Greene, *Greene*, III, 213.
65. Johnson, *Greene*, II, 67.
66. Davie to [?], Apr. 9, 1781.—W.R.D. Papers, No. 2, S.H.C. The content of the letter establishes the addressee as Greene; Hoyt (ed.), *Murphey Papers*, II, 295.
67. Greene to Polk, Apr. 3, 1780.—W.R.D. Papers, No. 2, S.H.C. For Polk's command, see Newsome, "Polk, Thomas," *D.A.B.*, XV, 43.
68. Davie in his "Sketches" gave this date, in which Lee agreed (*Memoirs*, pp. 325, 333). Gordon gave the date as the 5th, while George Washington Greene maintained it was the 6th, although Nathanael Greene in writing to

the President of Congress said the 7th. The latter, basing his contention on Greene's order book, said that the order was first given for the 5th but was changed to the 6th because of doubtful intelligence in regard to Cornwallis. —Greene, *Greene*, III, 230, n. 2.

69. Davie to [?], Apr. 9, 1781.—W.R.D. Papers, No. 2, S.H.C. The content of the letter establishes the addressee as Greene.

70. Thomas Wade to Greene, Apr 10, 1781.—*Ibid*.

71. Davie to Greene, Apr. 11, 1781.—*Ibid*.

72. Greene to Davie, Apr. 14, 1781.—*Ibid*.

73. Davie to Greene, Apr. 23, 1781.—*Ibid*.

74. *Idem* to *idem*, Apr. 26, 1781.—*Ibid*.

75. Davie's "Sketches"; Lee, *Memoirs*, p. 333; Greene, *Greene*, III, 233, 240-41.

76. Quoted in *Greene*, Greene, III, 245.

77. For his corrections of these two accounts, see Davie's "Sketches." For a more detailed picture, see his account reprinted in Johnson, *Greene*, II, 93-95. Johnson erroneously stated that Davie was at that time with the army. Instead, he was in Charlotte. See his letter to Greene from Charlotte, dated Apr. 26, 1781.—*Loc. cit.*

78. Johnson, *Greene*, II, 95.

79. Davie's "Sketches." This interview is also reprinted in Johnson, *Greene*, II, 116-18; Greene, *Greene*, III, 265-66; McCrady, *S.C. in the Rev., 1780-1783*, pp. 216-18.

80. McCrady, *S.C. in the Rev., 1780-1783*, pp. 229, 278.

81. Davie's "Sketches."

82. *Ibid.*; Davie to Greene, Dec. 2, 1783.—W.R.D. Papers, No. 2, S.H.C.; Lee, *Memoirs*, pp. 577-78.

83. S.R., XV, vii-viii; XVIII, 707.

84. Governor Burke to Davie, July 1, 1781.—Governors' Papers. Thomas Burke, III, June 7, 1781–February 17, 1782, A.H.

85. S.R., XVIII, 920.

86. *Ibid.*, XIV, 571-72.

87. Drayton and Davie to Burke, July 2, 1781.—W. R. Davie Papers, A.H.

88. Davie to the General Assembly, July 7, 1781.—N.C. Legislative Papers, Senate, June–July, 1781, A.H.

89. Jane Blair to her daughter, Nelly Blair, Aug. 14, 1781.—Charles E. Johnston Collection, A.H.

90. James Iredell to Mrs. Iredell, Aug. 25, 1781.—*Ibid*.

91. Davie to Governor Burke, Aug. 22, 1781.—Governor Burke's Letter Book, A.H.

92. Governor Burke to Davie, Aug. 23, 1781.—*Ibid*.

93. Davie to Governor Burke, Aug. 30, 1781.—*Ibid.*; reprinted in S.R., XV, 628-29.

94. Governor Burke to Davie, Aug. 31, 1781.—*Ibid*.

95. *Ibid*.

96. Governor Burke to Davie, Sept. 1, 1781.—*Ibid*.

Notes

97. James Read, Aide-de-camp to Governor Burke, to Davie, Aug. 30, 1781; Governor Burke to Davie, Sept. 1, 1781; J. Huske, Secretary to Governor Burke, to Davie, Sept. 2, 1781.—*Ibid.*

98. Davie to Governor Burke, Sept. 4, 1781.—*Ibid.*

99. Governor Burke to Davie, Sept. 4, 1781.—Governors' Papers. Thomas Burke, A.H.

100. *Idem* to *idem*, Sept. 7, 1781.—*Ibid.*

101. Davie to James Winn, Sept. 28, 1781.—W. R. Davie Papers, A.H.

102. Connor, *Hist. of N.C.*, I, 493.

103. Davie to Winn, *loc. cit.*

104. Johnson, *Greene*, II, 66-67.

105. Davie to Greene, W.R.D. Papers, No. 2, S.H.C.

106. Connor, *Hist. of N.C.*, I, 485.

107. Davie to Sumner, Nov. 1, 1781.—Jethro Sumner Papers, S.H.C.; also reprinted in *S.R.*, XV, 659.

108. Davie to Greene, Nov. 12, 1781.—W.R.D. Papers, No. 2, S.H.C.

109. W.R.D. Papers, No. 2, S.H.C.

110. Davie to Greene, Dec. 10, 1781.—*Ibid.*

111. Greene to Davie, Dec. 27, 1781.—*Ibid.*

112. Quoted in Hubbard, *Davie*, p. 73.

113. William Henry Smith (ed.), *The St. Clair Papers: The Life and Public Services of Arthur St. Clair* (Cincinnati: Robert Clarke and Co., 1882), I, 567.

114. Robert Fenner to Brigadier General Sumner, Jan. 24, 1782.—Jethro Sumner Papers, S.H.C. Also reprinted in *S.R.*, XVI, 488-89.

115. R. Bignall to Governor Martin, Dec. 4, 1781.—*S.R.*, XXII, 601-2; Robert Fenner to Sumner, Jan. 24, 1782.—Jethro Sumner Papers, S.H.C.; Governor Martin to Governor Burke, Jan. 31, 1782.—*S.R.*, XVI, 493-94.

116. *S.R.*, XVI, 513, 523.

117. Governor Martin to Governor Burke, Jan. 31, 1782.—*S.R.*, XVI, 493-94.

118. Governor Martin to Greene, Feb. 10, 1782.—W.R.D. Papers, No. 2, S.H.C.

119. Davie to Governor Benjamin Harrison, Feb. 17, 1782.—Palmer (ed.), *Calendar of Virginia State Papers*, III, 66.

120. Davie to Greene, Feb. 17, 1782.—W.R.D. Papers, No. 2, S.H.C.

121. Greene to Davie, March 5, 1782.—Greene's Letter Book. Vol. 2, pp. 109-10. New York Public Library.

122. Fragment of a letter, Governor Burke to Davie, Feb. 22, 1782.—W. R. Davie Papers, A.H.

123. Davie to Greene, Dec. 10, 1781; Allen Jones to Greene, Dec. 28, 1781. —*Ibid.*

124. J. G. de R. Hamilton, "Governor Thomas Burke," *North Carolina Booklet*, VI (Oct., 1906), 112; Elisha P. Douglass, "Thomas Burke, Disillusioned Democrat," *N.C.H.R.*, XXVI (Apr., 1949), 150-86.

125. Davie to Burke, Feb. 23, 1782.—W. R. Davie Papers, A.H.; also reprinted imperfectly in *S.R.*, XVI, 202.

Notes

126. O. H. Williams to Davie, Feb. 24, 1782.—W.R.D. Papers, No. 2, S.H.C.
127. Burke to Davie, Feb. 26, 1782.—Thomas Burke Papers, S.H.C. Also reprinted in *S.R.*, XVI, 561, under the incorrect date of March 26, 1782.
128. Captain Thomas Steele to Captain Martin, March 4, 1782.—*S.R.*, XVI, 531-32.
129. Davie to [?], Apr. 9, 1782.—W.R.D. Papers, No. 2, S.H.C. Content of letter identifies addressee as Burke.
130. Davie to Governor Burke, Apr. 14, 1782.—Governors' Papers, Thomas Burke, A.H.; also reprinted in *S.R.*, XVI, 284.
131. Governor Burke to the General Assembly, Apr. 22, 1782.—Thomas Burke Papers, S.H.C.
132. Davie to Governor Burke, Apr. 14, 1782.—*Loc. cit.*
133. *S.R.*, XVI, 107-8.
134. *Ibid.*, XVI, 170; XIX, 124.
135. Governor Martin to Major General Greene, May 12, 1782.—*Ibid.*, XVI, 683.
136. Governor Martin to Davie, [?], 1782.—*Ibid.*, p. 691. This letter was probably written a few days after May 17, when the department was abolished.
137. Quoted in Hubbard, *Davie*, p. 76.
138. Governor Martin to General Bryan, Aug. 16, 1782.—*S.R.*, XVI, 702-5.
139. Governor Martin to Greene, Aug. 29, 1782.—*Ibid.*, pp. 707-8.
140. Greene, *Greene*, III, 488.
141. Davie to Greene, Dec. 2, 1783.—W.R.D. Papers, No. 2, S.H.C. In other parts of this letter, Davie defended Greene in his unfortunate entanglement with John Banks, of the firm of Hunter and Banks of Fredericksburg, Va.
142. *Ibid.*
143. Davie to Greene, June 27, 1784, and Dec. 4, 1785.—W.R.D. Papers, No. 2, S.H.C.
144. Davie to Greene, Dec. 10, 1785.—*Ibid.* Copied from N.C. MS, Vol. 1, Lanier Bequest, Historical Society of Pennsylvania, Philadelphia. The date on the copy is 1783, but it obviously should be 1785.
145. Allen Jones Davie to A. D. Murphey, July 25, 1826. Quoted in Hoyt (ed.), *Murphey Papers*, I, 333.
146. Governor Martin to the General Assembly, May 10, 1783.—*S.R.*, XVI, 788-89; also reprinted in *ibid.*, XIX, 336-37.
147. *S.R.*, XIX, 665-66.
148. Hunt *et al.* (eds.), *Journals of the Cont. Cong.*, XVI, 5-6.
149. *S.R.*, XVI, 171-72.
150. Hubbard, *Davie*, p. 77; Wheeler, *Historical Sketches of N.C.*, II, 197.

CHAPTER VI

1. Halifax County, Record of Deeds, No. XIV, 1777, pp. 473-74; Commission of Joseph Montfort, preserved in the Halifax County Court House; tombstone of Joseph Montfort, Royal Hart Masonic Temple, Halifax, N.C.; J. Bryan

NOTES

Grimes, *North Carolina Wills and Inventories. Copied from original and recorded wills and inventories in the office of the Secretary of State* (Raleigh: Edwards and Broughton, 1912), pp. 514-22; James S. Purcell, Jr., "Literary Culture in North Carolina before 1820" (Duke University: unpublished doctoral dissertation, 1950), pp. 38-39. Incidentally, one of Milner's books, with his book-plate, is in the Carolina Room, U.N.C.: Arthur Young, *Political Essays Concerning the Present State of the British Empire* (London: Printed for W. Strahan and T. Cadell, MDCCLXXII).

2. Halifax County, Record of Deeds, No. XIV, 1778-1783, pp. 679-80.
3. *S.R.*, XXV, 354.
4. *Ibid.*, XXIII, 496.
5. *Ibid.*, XXV, 354-55.
6. *Ibid.*, p. 355.
7. J. Kelly Turner and John L. Bridgers, Jr., *History of Edgecombe County, North Carolina* (Raleigh: Edwards and Broughton Co., 1920), p. 32; Francis Nash, "The Borough Towns of North Carolina," *North Carolina Booklet*, VI (Oct. 1906), 93-94.
8. Watson (ed.), *Memoirs of Elkanah Watson*, p. 52.
9. John Clement Fitzpatrick (ed.), *The Diary of George Washington, 1748-1799* (New York: Houghton Mifflin Co., 1925), IV, 162-63.
10. *Ibid.*, p. 163.
11. Samuel Johnston to James Iredell, May 23, 1791.—Charles E. Johnson Collection, A.H.
12. Smyth, *A Tour in the U. S.*, I, 52, 55-56.
13. Turner and Bridgers, *Hist. of Edgecombe County*, pp. 32-33.
14. *C.R.*, VI, 333; *S.R.*, XXIII, 73-79.
15. *C.R.*, VI, 364-65; *N. C. Manual*, p. 366.
16. *C.R.*, VI, 752.
17. Nash, "The Borough Towns of North Carolina," pp. 93-94.
18. *S.R.*, XXIII, 490-92.
19. *Ibid.*, p. 484.
20. *Ibid.*, p. 512.
21. *Ibid.*, XIV, 17.
22. *Ibid.*, XXIII, 496.
23. *Ibid.*, XVIII, iii, 433.
24. *North-Carolina University Magazine*, IV (Aug., 1855), 249.
25. Ella Lonn, *The Colonial Agents of the Southern Colonies* (Chapel Hill: The University of North Carolina Press, 1945), p. 371.
26. Smyth, *A Tour in the U. S.*, I, 52, 54-55.
27. Watson (ed.), *Memoirs of Elkanah Watson*, p. 72.
28. T. Lowther to James Iredell, July 4, 1785.—Iredell Papers, Manuscript Room, Duke University.
29. Thomas Iredell to Mrs. James Iredell (his sister-in-law), [July or August], 1790.—Charles E. Johnson Collection, A.H.

NOTES

30. July 9, 1805.

31. Will Blair to James Iredell, Apr. 23, 1790.–Charles E. Johnson Collection, A.H.

32. James Iredell to Mrs. Iredell, Apr. 21, 1786.–Charles E. Johnson Collection, A.H.

33. Davie to John Haywood, Dec. 29, 1795.–Ernest Haywood Collection, S.H.C.

34. Turner and Bridgers, *Hist. of Edgecombe County*, p. 33.

35. Smyth, *A Tour in the U. S.*, I, 14.

36. Samuel Johnston to Mrs. Johnston, May 31, 1776.–Charles E. Johnson Collection, A.H.

37. Fairfax Harrison, *The Background of the American Stud Book* (Richmond: Old Dominion Press, 1933), pp. 19-20.

38. Allen Jones Davie to Thomas Bennehan, Apr. 30, [?].–Cameron Papers, S.H.C.

39. R.D.W. Connor, *North Carolina: Rebuilding an Ancient Commonwealth* (Chicago: American Historical Society, 1929), I, 217; Blackwell Pierce Robinson, "Willie Jones of Halifax," *N.C.H.R.*, XVIII (Jan., 1941), 3-4.

40. Henry M. Wagstaff (ed.), *The Papers of John Steele* (Raleigh: Publications of the North Carolina Historical Commission, 1924), I, 422-23.

41. Patrick Nisbett Edgar, *The American Race-Turf Register,...* (New York: Press of Henry Mason, 1833), I, 364.

42. John W. Moore, *The History of North Carolina: From the Earliest Discoveries to the Present Time* (Raleigh: Alfred Williams & Co., 1880), I, 410.

43. W. J. Peale (ed.), *Lives of Distinguished North Carolinians, With Illustrations and Speeches* (Raleigh: North Carolina Publishing Company, 1898), p. 80.

44. *Ibid*.

45. Printed handbill, Feb. 12, 1827.–Cameron Papers, S.H.C.

46. *North-Carolina Journal* (published weekly in Halifax, beginning July 18, 1792, and continuing until 1814), March 12, 1798; see other issues of this paper for other notices of cockfights, Apr. 30, 1794, May 1, 1797. Hereafter cited as *N.C.J.*

47. George W. Long to Thomas D. Bennehan, Apr. 10, 1798.–Cameron Papers, S.H.C.

48. Advertisement in the *Virginia Gazette*, July 9, 1772. Reprinted in David Leroy Corbett (ed.), "Historical Notes," *N.C.H.R.*, IV (Jan., 1927), 108-9.

49. *N.C.J.*, Feb. 12, Feb. 19, Apr. 9, 1798.

50. McRee, *Iredell*, II, 96.

51. Brigham, *Amer. Newspapers*, II, 764.

52. Stephen Beauregard Weeks, *The Press of North Carolina in the Eighteenth Century* (Brooklyn: Historical Printing Club, 1891), p. 40.

53. James Iredell to Hannah Iredell, Apr. 22, 1787.–Charles E. Johnson Collection, A.H.

NOTES

54. Quoted in Guion Griffis Johnson, *Ante-Bellum North Carolina: A Social History* (Chapel Hill: The University of North Carolina Press, 1937), p. 175.

55. *N.C.J.*, Oct. 26, 1795; Apr. 17, 1797; Jan. 15, Feb. 5, 1798.

56. Thomas Perkins Abernethy, *From Frontier to Plantation in Tennessee: A Study in Frontier Democracy* (Chapel Hill: The University of North Carolina Press, 1932), p. 44; Henry M. Wagstaff, "Federalism in North Carolina," *James Sprunt Historical Publications*, IX (Chapel Hill: Published by the University, 1910), No. 2, pp. 5, 19.

57. Bridenbaugh, *Myths and Realities*, pp. 1-2.

58. Connor, *Hist. of N.C.*, I, 302; William E. Dodd, *The Life of Nathaniel Macon* (Raleigh: Edwards and Broughton, 1903), pp. 16-17; Charles Christopher Crittenden, *The Commerce of North Carolina, 1763-1789* (New Haven: Yale University Press, 1936), pp. 87-88; Johnson, *Ante-Bellum North Carolina*, p. 33.

59. William Kenneth Boyd, *History of North Carolina*, Vol. II, *The Federal Period, 1783-1860* (Chicago and New York: The Lewis Publishing Company, 1919), pp. 147-49; Fletcher Melvin Green, *Constitutional Development in the South Atlantic States*... (Chapel Hill: The University of North Carolina Press, 1930), pp. 176-79, 204-33. For a brief resumé of sectionalism in North Carolina in this period, see Johnson, *Ante-Bellum North Carolina*, pp. 31-36.

60. Wheeler, *Sketches of N.C.*, II, 91-95; Abernethy, *From Frontier to Plantation in Tenn.*, pp. 44-45; Delbert Harold Gilpatrick, *Jeffersonian Democracy in North Carolina, 1789-1816* (New York: Columbia University Press, 1931), pp. 40, 128.

61. Wheeler, *Sketches of N.C.*, II, 131, 282-90, 402; McRee, *Iredell*, I, 194-95, 395; Abernethy, *From Frontier to Plantation in Tenn.*, p. 45; Connor, *Hist. of N.C.*, I, 167-69; Moore, *Hist. of N.C.*, I, 359n; Elisha P. Douglass, *Rebels and Democrats* (Chapel Hill: The University of North Carolina Press, 1955), pp. 123-24.

62. Wheeler, *Sketches of N.C.*, I, 119-20; McRee, *Iredell*, II, 333.

63. Wheeler, *Sketches of N.C.*, II, 122, 219-20, 272-73.

64. United States Bureau of the Census, *Heads of Families at the First Census of the United States in the Year 1790: North Carolina* (Washington: Government Printing Office, 1908), p. 608 (hereafter cited as *Census of 1790*); Gilpatrick, *Jeffersonian Democracy in N.C.*, p. 40.

65. Alice Barnwell Keith (ed.), *The John Gray Blount Papers* (Raleigh: State Department of Archives and History, 1952), I, xviii-xxvii; Wheeler, *Sketches of N.C.*, II, 111-12, 216, 382-83, 426-32; for a recent scholarly biography, see William H. Masterson, *William Blount* (Baton Rouge: Louisiana State University Press, 1954).

66. Clement Eaton, *Freedom of Thought in the Old South* (Durham: Duke University Press, 1940), p. 3.

67. Henry M. Wagstaff, "William Richardson Davie and Federalism," *Proceedings of the Twentieth and Twenty-First Annual Sessions of the State Literary and Historical Association of North Carolina* (Raleigh: Publications

Notes

of the North Carolina Historical Commission, Dec. 2-3, 1920; Dec. 1-2, 1921), pp. 47-48.

68. See Blackwell Pierce Robinson, "Willie Jones of Halifax," *N.C.H.R.*, XVIII (Jan. and Apr., 1941), 1-26, 133-70.

69. Wheeler, *Sketches of N.C.*, II, 24-25, 146, 181; Louise Irby Trenholme, *The Ratification of the Federal Constitution in North Carolina* (New York: Columbia University Press, 1932), pp. 22-23, 168-69.

70. Wheeler, *Sketches of N.C.*, II, 162-63; Nevins, *The American States*, p. 361; List of Taxables and Taxable Property for Granville County, 1782.—A.H. Quoted in James Roy Caldwell, Jr., "A History of Granville County, North Carolina: The Preliminary Phase, 1746-1800" (University of North Carolina: Unpublished doctoral dissertation, 1950), p. 93.

71. Wheeler, *Sketches of N.C.*, II, 290, 383-84, 398; McRee, *Iredell*, I, 456; II, 100, 233; Trenholme, *Fed. Const. in N.C.*, p. 32n.

72. Wheeler, *Sketches of N.C.*, II, 57-60, 62, 268-69, 384, 398, 462-66; William C. Pool, "An Economic Interpretation of the Ratification of the Federal Constitution in North Carolina," Part II, *N.C.H.R.*, XXVII (July, 1950), 291, 308, 313; McRee, *Iredell*, II, 233.

73. Nevins, *The Amer. States*, p. 362; Trenholme, *Fed. Const. in N.C.*, p. 111; Connor, *Hist. of N.C.*, I, 419-22; Wheeler, *Sketches of N.C.*, I, 87-90; Gilpatrick, *Jeffersonian Democracy in N.C.*, p. 21.

74. Wheeler, *Sketches of N.C.*, II, 181-83; Trenholme, *Fed. Const. in N.C.*, pp. 69-70; Newsome, "Martin, Alexander," *D.A.B.*, XII, 333-34.

75. Wheeler, *Sketches of N.C.*, II, 111; Nevins, *The Amer. States*, pp. 138, 362, 387; Connor, *Hist. of N.C.*, I, 424.

76. H. E. Colter, "Towns of the Revolution—Hillsboro, N.C.," *Southern Literary Messenger*, XXIII (Sept., 1856), 174-76.

77. Hawks *et al.*, *Rev. Hist. of N.C.*, pp. 27-28.

78. *Ibid.*, pp. 225-26.

79. *Ibid.*, p. 224.

80. Governors' Papers. Thomas Burke, March 28, 1782, A.H.; also printed in *S.R.*, XVI, 523; XX, 614.

81. Hawks *et al.*, *Rev. Hist. of N.C.*, p. 229; Hunter, *Sketches*, p. 183.

82. *S.R.*, XIX, 222, 227, 256, 307.

83. *S.R.*, XXIV, 48-75; Boyd, *Hist. of N.C.*, II, 60; Moore, *Hist. of N.C.*, I, 240.

84. Wheeler, *Sketches of N.C.*, II, 29.

85. Davie to [J. C. Blount], Oct. 10, 1789.—John Gray Blount Papers, A.H.

86. Boyd, *Hist. of N.C.*, II, 67-69.

87. Dec. 2, 1783.—W.R.D. Papers, No. 2, S.H.C.

88. *S.R.*, XIX, 489, 513.

89. *Ibid.*, pp. 489-90; Moore, *Hist. of N.C.*, I, 359.

90. Charles Jesse Bullock, *Essays on the Monetary History of the United States* (New York: The Macmillan Company, 1900), pp. 186-90; Trenholme, *Fed. Const. in N.C.*, pp. 30-31.

NOTES

91. July 13, 1785.—Macay-McNeely Papers, S.H.C.
92. S.R., XIX, 494-99.
93. *Ibid.*, pp. 210, 332, 340.
94. Henry Steele Commager (ed.), *Documents of American History* (New York and London: Appleton-Century-Crofts, Inc., 1948), pp. 118-19.
95. Henry M. Wagstaff, *State Rights and Political Parties in North Carolina, 1776-1861, Johns Hopkins University Studies in Historical and Political Science* (Baltimore: The Johns Hopkins Press, July-Aug., 1906), p. 12.
96. DeMond, *Loyalists in N.C.*, p. vii; Nevins, *The Amer. States*, p. 385.
97. S.R., XIII, 668.
98. *Ibid.*, pp. 688-89; XXIV, 123-24.
99. *Ibid.*, XXIV, 263-68.
100. *Ibid.*, XIII, 991-92.
101. Connor, *Hist. of N.C.*, I, 431.
102. McRee, *Iredell*, II, 81-82.
103. Moore, *Hist. of N.C.*, I, 373n.
104. March 15, 1784.—McRee, *Iredell*, II, 95.
105. S.R., XIX, 516.
106. *Ibid.*, pp. 530-31.
107. Johnston to Iredell, May 1, 1784.—McRee, *Iredell*, II, 99. Further details of this debate were reported by Hooper to Iredell and Iredell to McCulloh, *ibid.*, pp. 100, 103. See also DeMond, *Loyalists in N.C.*, pp. 163-64.
108. S.R., XIX, 671-73.
109. *Ibid.*, XXIV, 661-64.
110. *Ibid.*, p. 730.
111. Quoted in DeMond, *Loyalists in N.C.*, p. 176.
112. This case is reported in Walter Clark (annotator), *North Carolina Reports: 1 and 2 Martin, Taylor, and Conference Reports* (Raleigh: Bynum Printing Co., Printers to the State, 1937), 1 Martin, 5-10.
113. S.R., XVIII, 482.
114. *Ibid.*, p. 362.
115. Boyd, *Hist. of N.C.*, II, 9-10.
116. S.R., XVIII, 428.
117. McMurtrie, *Eighteenth Century N.C. Imprints*, p. 102.
118. 1 Martin, 10.
119. *Ibid.*
120. Boyd, *Hist. of N.C.*, II, 12.
121. *Ibid.*, pp. 12-13.
122. S.R., XIX, 641-44.
123. See below, p. 375.
124. S.R., XIX, 712-14.
125. *Ibid.*, XVII, 94.
126. *Ibid.*, XIX, 459-60, 804.
127. Trenholme, *Fed. Const. in N.C.*, p. 57.
128. S.R., XIX, 516, 575-76, 588, 594, 601, 603-4, 650.

Notes

129. *Ibid.*, pp. 748, 755, 758, 802.
130. *Ibid.*, XVII, 310-11, 330.
131. *Ibid.*, XVIII, 228.
132. *Ibid.*, p. 534.
133. McRee, *Iredell*, II, 150-51.
134. *Ibid.*, p. 151.
135. *S.R.*, XVIII, 228.
136. *Ibid.*, XIX, 603.
137. *Ibid.*, XXIV, 567, 734-35.
138. McRee, *Iredell*, II, 155.
139. *S.R.*, XVIII, iv.
140. *Ibid.*, pp. 231-33.
141. *Ibid.*, pp. 250-53.
142. *Ibid.*, pp. iv, v, 303, 307, 322, 371, 413.
143. McRee, *Iredell*, II, 155-56.
144. *Ibid.*, p. 156.
145. James Iredell to his wife, Jan. 31, 1787.—Johnson Collection, A.H.
146. *Idem* to *idem*, Feb. 13, 1787.—Johnson Collection, A.H.
147. *Idem* to *idem*, Feb. 19, 1787.—Johnson Collection, A.H.
148. McRee, *Iredell*, II, 156. The Halifax Gaol, in which he was confined, has recently been converted into a museum.
149. *Ibid.*, pp. 95-96; Nevins, *The Amer. States*, p. 364; Trenholme, *Fed. Const. in N.C.*, pp. 153, 154n.
150. *S.R.*, XVIII, 212-17, 420-25.
151. McRee, *Iredell*, II, 145; *S.R.*, XVIII, 213, 428.
152. *S.R.*, XVIII, 213, 428-29, 477.
153. McRee, *Iredell*, II, 145.
154. *S.R.*, XVIII, 230, 242, 279, 280-83, 449, 458; XXIV, 832-36.
155. *Ibid.*, p. 462.

CHAPTER VII

1. *S.R.*, XVIII, 650.
2. Boyd, *Hist. of N.C.*, II, 24.
3. *S.R.*, XXIV, 791.
4. McRee, *Iredell*, II, 151.
5. *S.R.*, XVIII, 462; McRee, *Iredell*, II, 151.
6. Williamson to John Gray Blount, March 19, 1787.—J. G. Blount Papers, A.H.
7. *S.R.*, XX, 6-11.
8. *Ibid.*, pp. 627-28.
9. *Ibid.*, p. 637.
10. *Ibid.*, p. 627.
11. *Ibid.*, p. 683.
12. J. G. Blount Papers, A.H.

Notes

13. *S.R.*, XVIII, 470; XX, 600, 634.
14. *Ibid.*, p. 607.
15. *Ibid.*, p. 608.
16. *Ibid.*, pp. 634-35.
17. Davie to Iredell, May 30, 1787.—McRee, *Iredell*, II, 161; Max Farrand (ed.), *The Records of the Federal Convention of 1787* (New Haven: Yale University Press, 1911), I, 1 (hereafter cited as Farrand, *Records*).
18. Davie to Iredell, May 30, 1787.—McRee, *Iredell*, II, 161.
19. *Ibid.*
20. Farrand, *Records*, III, 95-96.
21. *Ibid.*, I, 386, 568; II, 127.
22. *Ibid.*, II, 15, 450-51.
23. *S.R.*, XX, 724.
24. Davie to Caswell, June 19, 1787.—*Ibid.*, pp. 725-26. The second quotation which varies slightly from that in the *State Records* is found in the W. R. Davie Papers, A.H., copied from the George C. Thomas Collection, Philadelphia.
25. Farrand, *Records*, I, 78, 88.
26. *Ibid.*, pp. 487-88. The angle brackets indicate a later addition by Madison.—*Ibid.*, p. xix.
27. *Ibid.*, p. 498.
28. *Ibid.*, p. 511.
29. Andrew C. McLaughlin, *A Constitutional History of the United States* (New York: D. Appleton-Century Company, 1935), p. 175 and 175n.
30. Farrand, *Records*, I, 509-520.
31. McLaughlin, *Const. Hist. of U.S.*, p. 175.
32. Farrand, *Records*, I, 522.
33. *Ibid.*, p. 523.
34. *Ibid.*, pp. 524, 526.
35. The older historians, especially John Fiske, attributed the outcome of the vote to Massachusetts by virtue of the split in votes between Gerry and Strong on one side and King and Gorham on the other. However, Massachusetts' action was negativistic, whereas North Carolina's was positive, effective, and dynamic. See Hannis Taylor, *The Origin and Growth of the American Constitution: An Historical Interpretation...* (Boston and New York: Houghton Mifflin Company, 1911), pp. 45, 199; Charles Warren, *The Making of the Constitution* (Boston: Little, Brown and Company, 1937), p. 309.
36. Farrand, *Records*, III, 587.
37. *S.R.*, XX, 765-66; Farrand, *Records*, III, 70-71.
38. Farrand, *Records*, I, 542.
39. *Ibid.*, pp. 557-58.
40. *Ibid.*, pp. 564, 570.
41. *Ibid.*, p. 571.
42. *Ibid.*, pp. 575, 579.
43. *Ibid.*, p. 581.
44. *Census of 1790*, p. 608.

Notes

45. Farrand, *Records*, I, 593.
46. Boyd, *Hist. of N.C.*, II, 27-28.
47. Farrand, *Records*, I, 78.
48. *Ibid.*, II, 64.
49. *Ibid.*, p. 102.
50. *Ibid.*, p. 120.
51. McRee, *Iredell*, II, 161.
52. *Ibid.*, p. 163.
53. *Ibid.*, p. 165.
54. *Ibid.*, p. 167.
55. *Ibid.*, p. 168.
56. Farrand, *Records*, III, 587.
57. S.R., XX, 765.
58. *Ibid.*, pp. 764-65.
59. *Ibid.*, p. 766.
60. McRee, *Iredell*, II, 170; Boyd, *Hist. of N.C.*, II, 31.
61. McRee, *Iredell*, II, 167.
62. July 8, 1787, July 22, 1787.–*Ibid.*, pp. 163, 167.
63. *Ibid.*, pp. 170-71.
64. Trenholme, *Fed. Const. in N.C.*, p. 101.
65. McRee, *Iredell*, II, 170.
66. S.R., XX, 121, 301-2.
67. *Ibid.*, p. 225.
68. McRee, *Iredell*, II, 180; Boyd, *Hist. of N.C.*, II, 31; Wagstaff, "William Richardson Davie and Federalism," pp. 50-51.
69. S.R., XX, 186.
70. Lida Tunstall Rodman (ed.), *Journal of a Tour to North Carolina By William Attmore, 1787, James Sprunt Historical Publications*, XVII, No. 2 (Chapel Hill: The University of North Carolina Press, 1922), I, 19.
71. S.R., XX, 188, 256-58.
72. *Ibid.*, pp. 250-51.
73. *Ibid.*, pp. 247-48.
74. *Ibid.*, pp. 204, 265, 270, 273.
75. *Ibid.*, pp. 200, 212; XXIV, 885-86.
76. *Ibid.*, pp. 274, 280.
77. *Ibid.*, pp. 229-30, 245-46.
78. *Ibid.*, pp. 128-29.
79. *Ibid.*, pp. 133, 186.
80. *Ibid.*, pp. 193-94, 369.
81. *Ibid.*, pp. 194, 370.
82. *Ibid.*, 196-97, 370-71.
83. A. R. Newsome, "North Carolina's Ratification of the Federal Constitution," *N.C.H.R.*, XVII (Oct., 1940), 289.
84. McRee, *Iredell*, II, 180.
85. *Ibid.*, pp. 180-81.

NOTES

86. *Ibid.*, p. 181.
87. *Ibid.*, p. 186. The publication is reprinted in *ibid.*, pp. 186-215, and in Paul Leicester Ford, *Pamphlets on the Constitution, Published During Its Discussion by the People* (Brooklyn: No publisher, 1888), pp. 333-70.
88. Davie to Iredell, Jan. 11, 1788.—McRee, *Iredell*, II, 215-16.
89. *Ibid.*
90. Davie to Iredell, Jan. 22, 1788.—*Ibid.*, p. 217.
91. *Ibid.*, pp. 217-18.
92. *Ibid.*, p. 218.
93. Davie to Francis Child, Feb. 6, 1788.—W. R. Davie Papers, A.H. Handwritten copy from the original in the George C. Thomas Collection, Philadelphia.
94. McRee, *Iredell*, II, 232; Boyd, *Hist. of N.C.*, II, 33.
95. McRee, *Iredell*, II, 223.
96. *Ibid.*, pp. 223-24.
97. Newsome, "North Carolina's Ratification of the Fed. Const.," pp. 290, 292.
98. Davie to Iredell, July 9, 1788.—McRee, *Iredell*, II, 230.
99. *Ibid.*, pp. 230-31.
100. *Ibid.*, p. 230.
101. Jonathan Elliott (ed.), *The Debates in the Several State Conventions, on the Adoption of the Federal Constitution* ... (Washington: Printed for the Editor, 1836), IV, 250-51 (hereafter cited as Elliott, *Debates*).
102. Newsome, "North Carolina's Ratification of the Fed. Const.," p. 293.
103. *S.R.*, XXII, 6-7. The journals of the Hillsborough and Fayetteville Conventions are printed in *ibid.*, pp. 1-53.
104. Elliott, *Debates*, IV, 1-4.
105. *Ibid.*, pp. 4-7.
106. *Ibid.*, p. 8.
107. Newsome, "North Carolina's Ratification of the Fed. Const.," pp. 293-94.
108. Boyd, *Hist. of N.C.*, II, 37.
109. Elliott, *Debates*, IV, 7, 9.
110. *Ibid.*, pp. 13-15.
111. *Ibid.*, pp. 16-23.
112. *Ibid.*, pp. 30-31.
113. *Ibid.*, pp. 58-62.
114. *Ibid.*, pp. 102-4.
115. *Ibid.*, pp. 116-24.
116. *Ibid.*, pp. 152-60.
117. *Ibid.*, pp. 178-84.
118. *Ibid.*, p. 201.
119. *Ibid.*, p. 216.
120. *Ibid.*, pp. 225-26.
121. *Ibid.*, pp. 236-38.

Notes

122. *Ibid.*, p. 240.
123. *Ibid.*, pp. 240-41.
124. *Ibid.*, p. 242.
125. *Ibid.*
126. *Ibid.*
127. Trenholme, *Fed. Const. in N.C.*, pp. 183-84.
128. Elliott, *Debates*, IV, 247-51.
129. *Ibid.*, p. 251.
130. S.R., XXII, 26-28.
131. *Ibid.*, pp. 28, 33-34; Trenholme, *Fed. Const. in N.C.*, p. 190.
132. Elliott, *Debates*, IV, 251; S.R., XXII, 31-32.
133. S.R., XXII, pp. 30, 216-17.
134. McRee, *Iredell*, II, 235.
135. Iredell to Williamson, Jan. 22, 1789.—Johnson Collection, A.H.
136. Davie to Iredell, Jan. 23, 1789.—W.R.D. Papers, No. 2, S.H.C. Typescript, from original in the Emmett Collection, *loc. cit.*
137. Wagstaff, *Papers of John Steele*, I, 33.
138. McRee, *Iredell*, II, 235; G. J. McRee to D. L. Swain, Jan. [?], 1856.—D. L. Swain Papers, S.H.C.
139. Trenholme, *Fed. Const. in N.C.*, p. 197.
140. *State Gazette of South Carolina*, Dec. 1, 1788.
141. Davie to Iredell, Sept. 8, 1788.—McRee, *Iredell*, II, 239.
142. *Ibid.*
143. *Norwich Packet*, Dec. 19, 1788. This newsletter is taken from a typewritten volume, "North Carolina Items from New England Papers, 1754-1806," A.H.
144. The first part of this pamphlet, no copy of which is known to exist, was published in the *State Gazette of North-Carolina* (Edenton), Sept. 22, 1788.—Duke University Library, photostat; the quoted part is found in Trenholme, *Fed. Const, in N.C.*, pp. 201-2.
145. *State Gazette of N.C.*, Oct. 20, 1788.—Duke University Library, photostat.
146. [William Blount] to [John Gray Blount], Nov. 6, 1788.—J. G. Blount Papers, A.H.
147. Johnston to Iredell, Nov. 8, 1788.—Johnson Collection, A.H.
148. *Idem* to *idem*, Nov. 20, 1788.—Johnson Collection, A.H.
149. S.R., XX, 66, 129, 514-16, 526.
150. Newsome, "North Carolina's Ratification of the Fed. Const.," pp. 296-98.
151. McRee, *Iredell*, II, 260.
152. Davie to James Madison, June 10, 1789.—Madison Papers, L.C., reprinted in *Documentary History of the Constitution of the United States of America, 1786-1870* (Washington: Department of State, 1894-1905), V, 176-77.
153. *Norwich Packet*, Sept. 18, 1789.—Taken from "N.C. Items from N. Eng. Newspapers," A.H.

NOTES

154. S.R., XXII, 36, 39; XXI, 210, 244-50, 600-11.
155. Ibid., XXII, 36-39.
156. Ibid.; McRee, Iredell, II, 272.
157. McRee, Iredell, II, 271.
158. S.R., XII, 39-43.
159. Ibid., p. 43.
160. Ibid., pp. 43-45.
161. Ibid., pp. 45-46.
162. Ibid., pp. 46-47.
163. Ibid., pp. 48-49.
164. Ibid., pp. 50-51.
165. Ibid., pp. 51-53.
166. Newsome, "North Carolina's Ratification of the Fed. Const.," pp. 300-1.
167. S.R., XXI, 193, 210.
168. Ibid., pp. 221-249; McRee, Iredell, II, 270.
169. McRee, Iredell, II, 270.
170. S.R., XXI, 228, 332.
171. Ibid., pp. 216-17, 219, 221, 222, 225, 228, 229, 241, 247, 251, 252.
172. Ibid., pp. 210-12, 215, 223, 253, 268, 311.
173. Ibid., pp. 233-34, 288, 294, 304-5, 344-46.
174. Ibid., pp. 221, 225, 237, 255, 259, 285, 332.
175. Ibid., XXV, 7-9, 26-27, 57-58, 60.
176. Samuel Johnston to Iredell.—Johnson Collection, A.H.; McRee, Iredell, II, 274-75; Evarts B. Greene, "Johnson, William Samuel," D.A.B., X, 131-34.

CHAPTER VIII

1. S.R., XXV, 519 e.
2. See dedicatory page, Henry Pattillo, *A Geographical Catechism, To assist those who have neither Maps nor Gazetteers, To Read News-Papers, History, or Travels; With as much of The Science of Astronomy, and the Doctrine of the Air, As is judged sufficient for the Farmer, who wishes to understand something of The Works of God, around him; And for the studious Youth, who have or have not a prospect of further prosecuting those Sublime Sciences* (Halifax: Printed by Abraham Hodge, 1796).
3. C.R., X, 918.
4. Ibid.
5. Reprinted in Francis Newton Thorpe (ed.), *The Federal and State Constitutions, Colonial Charters, and Other Organic Laws of the States, Territories, and Colonies, Now or Heretofore Forming the United States of America* (Washington: Government Printing Office, 1909), V, 3091.
6. C.R., X, 1012.
7. S.R., XIX, 726.
8. Ibid., p. 765.

Notes

9. Davie to Spruce Macay, Sept. 3, 1793.—W.R.D. Papers, No. 1, S.H.C. Typed copy.
10. *S.R.*, XIX, 479, 822.
11. *Ibid.*, p. 781.
12. *Ibid.*, p. 447.
13. Archibald Henderson, Forty-Sixth Annual Phi Beta Kappa Address: "The Undying Flame: The Story of Its Lighting." Pamphlet (Chapel Hill: University of North Carolina, 1950), no page numbers.
14. *S.R.*, XXIV, 863; Walter Clark, "William Richardson Davie," in W. J. Peele (ed.), *Lives of Distinguished North Carolinians with Illustrations and Speeches* (Raleigh: North Carolina Publishing Society, 1898), p. 72.
15. Henderson, "The Undying Flame."
16. *S.R.*, XXII, 48-49.
17. McRee, *Iredell*, II, 270.
18. Archibald D. Murphey, *An Oration Delivered in Person Hall, Chapel Hill; On the 27th of June, 1827, the Day Previous to the Commencement under the Appointment of the Dialectic Society* (Raleigh: Printed by J. Gales & Son, 1827), p. 9.
19. *Ibid.*, p. 10.
20. *S.R.*, XXI, 228.
21. McRee, *Iredell*, II, 271.
22. *S.R.*, XXV, 21-24.
23. Hubbard, *Davie*, pp. 106-7.
24. *Ibid.*, p. 107.
25. Blackwell P. Robinson, *The History of Escheats* (Chapel Hill: The University of North Carolina, 1955), pp. 7-8.
26. *Ibid.*, p. 8.
27. *Ibid.*
28. *Ibid.*
29. University of North Carolina, Trustee Minutes, 1789-1791, p. 1. Bound manuscript volume in Carolina Room, Louis Round Wilson Library, Chapel Hill (hereafter cited as T.M.). This first meeting was also reported in *The State Gazette of North-Carolina* (Edenton), Dec. 31, 1789; see also University Papers, S.H.C., for the same account in Davie's handwriting.
30. *Ibid.*
31. Governors' Papers: State Series, Alexander Martin, A.H.
32. T.M., pp. 31-32.
33. *Ibid.*, pp. 35, 47.
34. Archibald D. Murphey, *Oration*, pp. 9-10.
35. Journal of House of Commons, 1791, p. 29; Journal of Senate, p. 24.—W. S. Jenkins Microfilm Collection, Louis Round Wilson Library, Chapel Hill.
36. T.M., pp. 60-62.
37. *Ibid.*, p. 64; Kemp Plummer Battle, *History of the University of North Carolina* (Raleigh: Edwards and Broughton Printing Co., 1907), I, 20.

Notes

38. T.M., pp. 74-75.
39. *Ibid.*, p, 79; Battle, *University*, I, 21.
40. T.M., pp. 79-83.
41. Battle, *University*, I, 24-25.
42. *N.C.J.*, Sept. 25, 1793.
43. T.M., pp. 84, 87.
44. *Ibid.*, pp. 87-95.
45. *Ibid.*, 92-94.
46. Frederick Hargett to James Hogg, Dec. 22, 1792. History of the University of North Carolina: Letters, 1791-1867. Carolina Room, Louis Round Wilson Library, Chapel Hill. Bound manuscript volume (hereafter cited as Univ. Letters).
47. *Ibid.*
48. Battle, *University*, I, 122-23.
49. *N.C.J.*, Jan. 9, 1793.
50. An article, signed, "A Friend of the University," *N.C.J.*, Dec. 19 and 26, 1792.
51. *N.C.J.*, Jan. 16, 1793.
52. Richard Walser, "The North Carolina Sojourn of the First American Novelist," *N.C.H.R.*, XXVIII (Apr., 1951), No. 2, pp. 138-49. Also see James S. Purcell, Jr., "Literary Culture in North Carolina Before 1820" (Duke University: unpublished doctoral dissertation, 1950), p. 296.
53. *Ibid.*, p. 149.
54. *Ibid.*, July 24, 1793.
55. T.M., pp. 105, 107-8.
56. *N.C.J.*, Aug. 7, 1793; also Sept. 18 and Sept. 25, 1793; *State Gazette of North-Carolina* (Edenton), Sept. 21, 1793.
57. T.M., p. 106.
58. Sept. 3, 1793.—W.R.D. Papers, No. 1, S.H.C. Typed copy, from original owned by Dr. Archibald Henderson, Chapel Hill, N.C.
59. *N.C.J.*, Sept. 25, 1793.
60. It is undoubtedly to this account that Battle refers in his *History of the University*, I, 35.
61. *N.C.J.*, Oct. 30, 1793.
62. Murphey, *Oration*, p. 10.
63. Battle, *University*, I, 21, 36.
64. *Ibid.*, pp. 36-37.
65. *Ibid.*, pp. 21, 36-37.
66. *N.C.J.*, Oct. 30, 1783.
67. *Ibid.*
68. T.M., pp. 108-9.
69. *Ibid.*, p. 123.
70. *Ibid.*, pp. 123-30.
71. *Ibid.*, p. 131; Battle, *University*, I, 59-60.
72. Hamilton, "W. R. D.," p. 30.

Notes

73. Davie to John Haywood, Nov. 6, 1794.—Ernest Haywood Collection, S.H.C.
74. *Ibid.*
75. T.M., p. 139. For a faithful summary of them, see Battle, *University*, I, 54-57.
76. T.M., p. 141.
77. Univ. Letters, 1791-1867, pp. 184-85, 201; Stephen B. Weeks, "Libraries and Literature in North Carolina," *Annual Report of the American Historical Association for 1895* (Washington: Government Printing Office, 1896), p. 223; Battle, *University*, I, 54.
78. He and his brother, Gavin, were sons of James Hogg, merchant and trustee. The father petitioned the legislature to change their surname to Alves when his wife's brother was lost at sea and the name had become extinct. See Archibald Henderson, *The Campus*, p. 12.
79. Cameron Papers, Feb. 21, 1795, S.H.C.
80. Davie to John Haywood, July 22, 1795.—Univ. Letters, 1796-1835. This is the other bound volume of manuscript letters dealing with the early history of the University, in the Carolina Room, Louis Round Wilson Library, Chapel Hill.
81. James Patterson to Davie, Oct. 17, 1795.—Univ. Papers, S.H.C.
82. *Ibid.*
83. Daniel Lindsey Grant (ed.), *Alumni History of the University of North Carolina* (Durham: Published and Distributed by the General Alumni Association of the University of North Carolina, 1924), p. 153.
84. Davie to John Haywood, July 22, 1795.—Univ. Letters, 1796-1835.
85. T.M., p. 193.
86. Davie to John Haywood, Nov. 6, 1794.—Ernest Haywood Collection, S.H.C.
87. T.M., pp. 139-41; R. D. W. Connor, "A State Experiment in Higher Education: An Address delivered at a Convocation of the University of North Carolina, Wednesday, December 4, 1946" (Chapel Hill: The Committee on Convocations and Lectures of the University of North Carolina, 1947), p. 8.
88. Quoted in Connor, "State Experiment," p. 8.
89. T.M., pp. 193, 208.
90. Connor, "State Experiment," p. 9.
91. Quoted in Battle, *University*, I, 97, as being from the *N.C.J.* "of that date," but a careful check of the years 1795-1796 does not reveal this quotation.
92. Univ. Letters, 1796-1835.
93. Battle, *University*, I, 98.
94. *Ibid.*
95. T.M., pp. 208, 212.
96. Davie to John Haywood, July 22, 1795.—Univ. Letters, 1796-1835.
97. *Ibid.*, p. 213.
98. *Ibid.*
99. *Ibid.*, p. 245; T.M., 1798-1801, p. 13.

Notes

100. Battle, *University*, I, 100-1.
101. T.M., pp. 215-19.
102. These two letters are referred to and the latter partially quoted in Battle, *University*, I, 100. A diligent search has failed to reveal the originals.
103. Jan. 4, 1796. U.N.C. photostat.
104. Weeks, "Libraries and Literature in North Carolina in the Eighteenth Century," p. 259.
105. Pattillo, *Geographical Catechism*, pp. 60-61.
106. Davie to John Haywood, March 7, 1796.—Ernest Haywood Collection, S.H.C.; *N.C.J.*, Apr. 4 and 11, 1796. See Battle, *University*, I, 826 (Appendix), for the cost of this and other early University buildings.
107. Trustee Minutes from November, A.D. 1801 to December A.D. 1810, inclusive, p. 212. December 7, 1810 (hereafter cited as T.M., III).
108. Davie to James Hogg, Aug. 21, 1796.—Univ. Letters, 1796-1835.
109. *Ibid.*
110. Sept. 10, 1796.—Cameron Papers, S.H.C.
111. Battle, *University*, I, 63, 113; Gladys Hall Coates, "The Story of Person Hall," *Bulletin of Person Hall Art Gallery*, III (Apr., 1943), No. 2, no page numbers.
112. Davie to John Haywood, Feb. 9, 1797.—Ernest Haywood Collection, S.H.C.
113. Battle, *University*, I, 113.
114. Ernest Haywood Collection, S.H.C.
115. Coates, "The Story of Person Hall"; Henderson, *The Campus*, p. 69.
116. Feb. 9, 1797.—Ernest Haywood Papers, S.H.C.
117. *N.C.J.*, May 7, 1798.
118. Davie to Haywood, Apr. 25, 1799.—Ernest Haywood Collection, S.H.C.
119. March 13, 1801.—Ernest Haywood Collection, S.H.C.
120. June 28, 1801.—Univ. Papers, S.H.C.
121. Quoted in Battle, *University*, I, 142. A careful search of all available newspapers of the period has failed to disclose this article, which Battle said appeared "in the public prints... two or three years after this" [Feb. 22, 1800].
122. *Ibid.*
123. T.M., 195, 247; Battle, *University*, I, 142-43; Henderson, *The Campus*, pp. 74-75.
124. Cornelia Phillips Spencer, "Pen and Ink Sketches of the University of North Carolina," *Daily Sentinel*, Apr. 26—July 6, 1869. Transcript copy in the Carolina Room, Louis Round Wilson Library, Chapel Hill.
125. Quoted in Battle, *University*, I, 108.
126. Davie to John Steele, Nov. 6, 1795.—Steele Papers, S.H.C.
127. Caldwell to Davie, Aug. 25 [1796].—Univ. Letters, 1796-1835.
128. *Ibid.*
129. T.M., pp. 225-43.
130. Quoted in Battle, *University*, I, 113.
131. Quoted in *ibid.*, I, 113-14.

Notes

132. *Ibid.*, p. 71; Hamilton, "W.R.D.," p. 29.
133. July 22, 1795.—Univ. Letters, 1796-1835.
134. Quoted in Battle, *University*, I, 60.
135. *Ibid.*, I, 84, 153-55.
136. Quoted in Henderson, *North Carolina*, I, 650.
137. Quoted in Battle, *University*, I, 154.
138. Journal of the House of Commons, 1794, p. 44.—W. S. Jenkins Microfilm Collection, Louis Round Wilson Library, Chapel Hill.
139. Davie to Caldwell, Feb. 26, 1797.—Univ. Letters, 1796-1835; also reprinted in Hamilton, "W.R.D.," pp. 31-33.
140. Richard Dobbs Spaight to Mr. Caldwell, Principal Professor, July 5, 1797.—Univ. Letters, 1796-1835.
141. [Joseph Caldwell] to [Davie], Jan. 24, 1797.—Univ. Letters, 1796-1835.
142. June [?], 1797, James Hogg to Davie.—Univ. Letters, 1791-1867, pp. 10-12. This is a manuscript copy in David L. Swain's handwriting. Also reprinted in Hamilton, "W.R.D.," pp. 33-36.
143. Univ. Papers, 1796-1835; also reprinted in Hamilton, "W.R.D.," pp. 36-38.
144. Davie to John Haywood, Aug. 20, 1797.—Ernest Haywood Collection, S.H.C.
145. Battle, *University*, I, 116, 118.
146. Nov. 5, Nov. 26, Dec. 3, and Dec. 17, 1798.
147. Nov. 5 and Nov. 19, 1798.
148. *N.C. Minerva*, Oct. 8 and Oct. 29, 1799.
149. For a list of the presidents of the Board of Trustees, see Battle, *University*, I, 826.
150. *Ibid.*, p. 279.
151. *Ibid.*, p. 155.
152. Willie Jones to Trustees of the University at Raleigh, Nov. 23, 1799.—Ernest Haywood Collection, S.H.C.
153. T.M., III, p. 118.
154. Battle, *University*, I, 155.
155. *Ibid.*, p. 124; Henderson, *The Campus*, p. 8.
156. T.M., Dec., 1798, to June, 1801, p. 9 (hereafter cited as T.M., II).
157. Howell Tatum to Davie, June 30, 1798.—Univ. Papers, S.H.C.
158. Univ. Papers, May [?], 1799, S.H.C.
159. Battle, *University*, I, 351.
160. *Ibid.*, p. 136.
161. Jan. 25, 1800.—Univ. Papers, S.H.C.
162. Davie to John Haywood, May 31, 1801.—Ernest Haywood Collection, S.H.C.
163. T.M., II, pp. 58-60.
164. Davie to John Eaton, Dec. 27, 1801.—John R. Eaton Papers, S.H.C.
165. T.M., III, p. 19.
166. *Ibid.*, pp. 17-29.

NOTES

167. Battle, *University*, I, 198.
168. T.M., III, pp. 31-33.
169. Oct. 1, 1803.—Cameron Papers, S.H.C.
170. *Minerva; or Anti-Jacobin* (Raleigh), July 18, 1803.
171. June 9, 1805. Duplicate of original in Univ. Papers, 1796-1835; also printed in Hamilton, "W.R.D.," p. 57.
172. *Ibid.*
173. Univ. Letters, 1796-1835; Hamilton, "W.R.D.," pp. 58-62.
174. T.M., III, pp. 220-21.
175. Rough draft of a letter to Davie conferring degree of LL.D., A.D. 1811. —Univ. Papers, S.H.C.
176. *Catalogus Universitatis Carolinae Septentrionalis* (Raleigh: E. Tysis, J. Gales, 1817).—Univ. Papers, S.H.C.
177. Reports from the Faculty to the Trustees of the Univ. of N.C. (1809 to 1829), p. 84. This citation was also repeated *literatim* in the Raleigh *Minerva*, Dec. 6, 1811.—U.N.C. original.
178. Univ. Letters, 1796-1836; Hamilton, "W.R.D.," pp. 65-66.

CHAPTER IX

1. *S.R.*, XX, 1055.
2. McRee, *Iredell*, II, 281.
3. Davie to Alexander Hamilton, Nov. 17, 1791.—Hamilton Papers, L.C.
4. Davie to Iredell, Aug. 2, 1791.—McRee, *Iredell*, II, 335.
5. *State Gazette of N. C.* (Edenton), July 30, 1790.
6. Maclaine to Iredell, Oct. 18, 1790.—McRee, *Iredell*, II, 298.
7. Davie to *idem*, Dec. 2, 1780. "N. C. Letters from Emmett Collection," A.H.
8. *Idem* to *idem*, Aug. 2, 1791.—McRee, *Iredell*, II, 335.
9. Davie to Martin, Nov. 1, 1790.—Governors' Papers: Alexander Martin, A.H.
10. Davie to Haywood, Jan. 15, 1791.—Ernest Haywood Collection, S.H.C.
11. *Ibid.*
12. Hugh T. Lefler and Albert Ray Newsome, *North Carolina: The History of a Southern State* (Chapel Hill: The University of North Carolina Press, 1954), pp. 291-92.
13. Davie to Haywood, Jan. 15, 1791, *loc. cit.*
14. Samuel Johnston to James Iredell, Apr. 15, 1791.—Charles E. Johnson Collection, A.H.
15. James Iredell to [?], Jan. 5, 1791. Charles E. Johnson Collection, A.H.
16. Thomas Blount to John Gray Blount, Nov. 16, 1790.—John Gray Blount Papers, A.H.
17. Journal of the House of Commons, 1791-1792, p. 6.
18. Thomas Iredell to James Iredell, Feb. 10, 1792.—Charles E. Johnson Collection, A.H.
19. Journal of the House of Commons, 1791-1792, pp. 11-12, 14.

Notes

20. *Ibid.*, p. 19.
21. *Ibid.*, pp. 43, 45-46.
22. *Ibid.*, p. 34.
23. *Ibid.*, p. 44.
24. *Ibid.*, p. 15.
25. *Ibid.*, pp. 31, 38.
26. Davie to Richard Bennehan, Feb. 4, 1792.—Cameron Papers, S.H.C.
27. *Ibid.*
28. See p. 230-31, *supra.*
29. Adelaide Fries (ed.), *Records of the Moravians in North Carolina* (Raleigh: North Carolina Historical Commission, 1941), V, 2364.
30. Davie to Steele, Dec. 16, 1792.—John Steele Papers, S.H.C.
31. *Ibid.*
32. *Ibid.*
33. *Ibid.*
34. Minutes of the Grand Lodge of N.C.—Steele Collection, S.H.C.; *N.C.J.*, Aug. 29, 1796, July 24, and Oct. 30, 1797.
35. *N.C.J.*, Jan. 2, 1797.
36. W. R. Davie Papers, A.H.
37. Josiah Collins to J. G. Blount, Feb. 27, 1793. John Gray Blount Papers, A.H.
38. 2 Dallas 419 (1793).
39. *Hans v. Louisiana*, 134 U. S. 1, 16 (1890).
40. Lefler and Newsome, *North Carolina*, p. 274; Henry McGilbert Wagstaff, *Federalism in North Carolina, James Sprunt Historical Publications* (Chapel Hill: N.C. Historical Society, 1910), Vol. IX, No. 2, p. 25.
41. McRee, *Iredell*, II, 382-83.
42. June 16, 1793.—Mary DeSaussure Fraser Papers, Manuscript Room, Duke University.
43. Journal of the House of Commons, 1793-1794, pp. 12-15, 21, 25, 35-36, 43.
44. *Ibid.*, pp. 20, 21, 29, 32, 45, 48, 52.
45. *Ibid.*, pp. 45, 50, 52. Original commission in W. R. Davie Papers, A.H.
46. Davie to Spaight, April 26, 1794, and Spaight to Davie, May 2, 1794.—Governor Spaight's Letter Book, 1792-1795, A.H.; *N.C.J.*, Sept. 17 and Nov. 10, 1794.
47. Journal of the House of Commons, July, 1794, pp. 1-3.
48. Ashe, *History of N. C.*, II, 144.
49. Journal of the House of Commons, 1794-1795, pp. 1-3, 12, 18, 30, 37.
50. *Ibid.*, pp. 7, 11.
51. *Ibid.*, pp. 8, 12, 15, 18, 44, 47.
52. Davie to Iredell, Dec. 15, 1794.—McRee, *Iredell*, II, 431; Ashe, *History of N. C.*, II, 144.
53. Davie to Richard Bennehan, Feb. 21, 1795.—Cameron Papers, S.H.C.
54. Davie to James Iredell, Sept. 4, 1795.—Marshall DeLancy Haywood Papers, A.H. Imperfectly reprinted in McRee, *Iredell*, II, 454.

Notes

55. R. D. W. Connor, *North Carolina: Rebuilding An Ancient Commonwealth, 1584-1925* (Chicago: The American Historical Society, 1929), I, 429.
56. *Ibid.*
57. McRee, *Iredell*, II, 450.
58. Davie to John Haywood, Dec. 29, 1795.—Ernest Haywood Papers, S.H.C.
59. Connor, *North Carolina*, I, 429.
60. Davie to John Haywood, March 7, 1796.—Ernest Haywood Papers, S.H.C.
61. Wagstaff, *Federalism in N. C.*, p. 28.
62. McRee, *Iredell*, II, 480.
63. *Ibid.*; Alice B. Keith, "Three North Carolina Blount Brothers in Business and Politics, 1783-1812," pp. 371-380.
64. Journal of the House of Commons, 1796, pp. 1, 3-4, 15, 20; Davie to Iredell, Feb. 1, 1797.—McRee, *Iredell*, II, 490.
65. Journal of the House of Commons, 1796, pp. 5-6.
66. *N.C.J.*, Sept. 7 and 28, 1795.
67. *Ibid.*, Oct. 2, 9, 16, 30, Dec. 4, 1797; June 4, 11, 18, 25, July 2, 23, 1798.
68. Journal of the House of Commons, 1796, pp. 29, 36, 40.
69. *Ibid.*, p. 32.
70. McRee, *Iredell*, II, 491.
71. *N.C.J.*, Sept. 18, 1797; *Hall's Wilmington Gazette*, Oct. 26, Nov. 3 and 13, 1797.
72. Original in W. R. Davie Papers, A.H.; reprint in *N.C.J.*, July 2, 1798.
73. Aug. 6 and Aug. 13, 1798.
74. W. R. Davie Papers, A.H. Davie's commission is also there.
75. William B. Grove to James McHenry, August 20, 1798.—W.R.D. Papers, No. 2, S.H.C.
76. McHenry to Davie, Aug. 31 and Sept. 12, 1798.—W. R. Davie Papers, A.H.
77. Davie to Major Gen. Smith *et al.*, Sept. 27, 1798.—W. R. Davie Papers, A.H.
78. George Washington to James McHenry, Oct. 15, 1798.—Fitzpatrick (ed.), *Writings of Washington*, XXXVI, 490; *idem* to *idem*, Oct. 21, 1798.—*Ibid.*, pp. 504-505; the letter is also reprinted in Ford (ed.), *Writings of Washington*, XIV, 117-118.
79. George Washington to Davie, Oct. 24, 1798.—William L. Saunders Papers, S.H.C.
80. Davie to George Washington, Nov. 14, 1794. Copy.—W. R. Davie Papers, A.H.
81. Washington to Davie, Dec. 28, 1798.—W. R. Davie Papers, A.H.
82. Davie to Washington, Jan. 7, 1799.—W. R. Davie Papers, A.H. The original draft was dated Dec. 3, 1798 [1799].
83. Davie to John Gray Blount, July 4, 1799.—John Gray Blount Papers, A.H.
84. Journal of the House of Commons, 1798, p. 71.

NOTES

85. McRee, *Iredell*, II, 532.
86. Davie to Thomas Pickering, Aug. [?], 1798.–Pickering Papers, XXIII, 3, Massachusetts Historical Society; William Polk to Davie, Nov. 30, 1798.–W. R. Davie Papers, A.H.
87. W. B. Grove to James McHenry, Aug. 20, 1798.–Bernard C. Steiner [ed.], *McHenry Papers, Publications of the Southern History Association*, IX (March, 1905), 102.
88. Lefler and Newsome, *North Carolina*, p. 280; Wagstaff, *Federalism in N. C.*, p. 30.
89. James McHenry to Davie, Aug. 31, 1798.–W. R. Davie Papers, A.H.
90. Nov. 28, 1798.–Charles E. Johnson Collection, A.H.
91. Samuel Johnston to Iredell, Nov. 21, 1798.–*Ibid.*
92. Johnston to Iredell, Nov. 28, 1798.–*Ibid.*
93. Journal of the House of Commons, 1798, pp. 18, 24-25.
94. *Ibid.*, p. 31.
95. *Ibid.*, pp. 35-38.

CHAPTER X

1. *N.C.J.*, Jan. 7 and March 4, 1799; Davie to Duncan Cameron, Jan. 29 and Mar. 12, 1799, and Thomas Read to Duncan Cameron, May 2, 1799.–Cameron Papers, S.H.C.; Davie to Ernest Haywood, Apr. 25 and May 27, 1799.–Ernest Haywood Papers, S.H.C.
2. Samuel Johnston to Iredell, Nov. 28, 1798.–Charles E. Johnson Collection, A.H.; Richard D. Spaight to John Haywood, Jan. 6, 1799.–Ernest Haywood Papers, S.H.C.
3. Ashe, *History of N. C.*, II, 155.
4. Samuel Johnston to Iredell, Dec. 23, 1798.–Charles E. Johnson Collection, A.H.
5. Samuel Johnston to Iredell, Dec. 30, 1798.–McRee, *Iredell*, II, 542.
6. Journal of the House of Commons, 1798, pp. 75-77.
7. Johnston to Iredell, Nov. 28, 1798.–Charles E. Johnson Collection, A.H.
8. *Idem* to *idem*, Dec. 23, 1798.–McRee, *Iredell*, II, 542.
9. Ashe, *History of N. C.*, II, 155.
10. Davie to John Adams, Jan. 4, 1799. Copy.–Governors' Papers, A.H.
11. *Ibid.*
12. *Ibid.*
13. John Adams to Davie, Jan. 11, 1799.–Governors' Papers, A.H.
14. Wagstaff, *Federalism in N. C.*, pp. 33-34.
15. Ashe, *History of N. C.*, II, 157.
16. Journal of the House of Commons, 1798, pp. 50-51.
17. Davie to Maj. Gen. Thomas Brown and Davie to Griffith J. McRee, May 1, 1799; Thomas Brown to Davie, May 29, 1799; Davie to Josiah Collins, June 9, 1799.–Governors' Papers, A.H.
18. See Governors' Papers, A.H.

NOTES

19. July 4, 1799. Also Davie to Maj. Gen. C. C. Pinckney, July 18, 1799.—Governors' Papers, A.H.
20. Davie to Maj. Gen. C. C. Pinckney, July 17, 1799.—Governors' Papers, A.H.
21. Legislative Papers, 1797, *passim;* Governors' Papers. Samuel Ashe, A.H.; Thomas P. Abernethy, *From Frontier to Plantation in Tennessee,* pp. 171-72; William H. Masterson, *William Blount,* p. 332.
22. *State Gazette of North Carolina,* Feb. 1, 1798; Abernethy, *Frontier to Plantation,* pp. 172-73; Masterson, *William Blount,* pp. 332-33.
23. Davie to B. Gaither and to Elija Law, Jan. 2, 1799.—Governors' Papers, A.H.
24. Davie to Martin Armstrong, Mar. 1, 1799.—Governors' Papers, A.H.
25. Davie to John Willis and Francis Locke, and Davie to Governor Sevier, Mar. 1, 1799.—Governors' Papers, A.H.
26. John Willis to Governor Davie, May 24, 1799.—Governors' Papers, A.H.
27. *Ibid.*
28. *Ibid.*
29. J. Willis and Francis Locke to Gov. Davie, Aug. 2, 1799.—Governors' Papers, A.H.
30. Davie to William White, Sept. 5, 1799.—Governors' Papers, A.H.
31. Journal of the House of Commons, p. 6; reprinted in *Raleigh Register,* Dec. 3, 1799.
32. Davie to Blake Baker and Davie to Edward Jones, Apr. 22, 1799.—Governors' Papers, A.H.; Journal of Council of State during Davie's Administration, A.H.
33. *Raleigh Register,* Dec. 24, 1799.
34. *Ibid.*
35. *Ibid.*
36. *Ibid.*
37. Davie to Samuel D. Purviance, June 11, 1799, and Blake Baker to Davie, August 15, 1799.—Governors' Papers, A.H.
38. Blake Baker to Davie and Edward Jones to Davie, August 15, 1799; Journal of Council of State.—Governors' Papers, A.H.
39. Journal of the House of Commons, 1799, pp. 5-6; also reprinted in *Raleigh Register,* Dec. 3, 1799.
40. Journal of the House of Commons, 1799, p. 3.
41. Ashe, *History of N. C.,* II, 176.
42. *Reports and Cases Ruled and Determined by the Court of Conference of North Carolina* (Raleigh: Printed by J. Gales, 1805), pp. 37-54.
43. Boyd, *Hist. of N. C.,* II, 73.
44. Davie to Mussendine Matthews, Joseph McDowell, and Col. David Vance, March 1, 1799; Davie to Governor Sevier, March 2, 1799.—Governors' Papers, A.H.
45. McDowell, Matthews, and Vance to Davie, May 26, 1799.—Governors' Papers, A.H.

NOTES

46. Mussendine Matthews to Davie, July 10, 1799; Joseph McDowell to Davie, July 29, 1799; Journal of the Council of State.—Governors' Papers, A.H.; *Raleigh Register*, Dec. 3, 1799.

47. Marvin Lucian Skaggs, *North Carolina Boundary Disputes Involving Her Southern Line, James Sprunt Studies in History and Political Science* (Chapel Hill: University of North Carolina Press, 1941), pp. 87-89; Lefler and Newsome, *North Carolina*, pp. 149-52.

48. Skaggs, *N. C. Boundary Disputes*, pp. 87-88.

49. *Ibid.*, pp. 93-94.

50. N.C. Legislative Papers, Jan. 16, 1792; Skaggs, *N. C. Boundary Disputes*, pp. 95-100.

51. Skaggs, *N. C. Boundary Disputes*, pp. 101-3.

52. Davie to the Governor of South Carolina, March 22, 1799.—Executive Letter Book, XIII, 41; N.C. Legislative Papers, 1798, Box No. 154; Davie's Message to the Legislature, reprinted in *Raleigh Register*, Dec. 3, 1799.

53. Davie to the Council of State, Aug. 15, 1799.—Journal of the Council of State, A.H.; Davie to Wallace Alexander.—Executive Letter Book, XIII, 159-60, A.H.

54. *N.C. Minerva and Fayetteville Advertizer*, July 9, 1799.

CHAPTER XI

1. Samuel Flagg Bemis, *A Diplomatic History of the United States* (New York: Henry Holt and Co., 1950), pp. 114-15.

2. *Ibid.*, p. 118.

3. *Ibid.*, p. 121.

4. *Ibid.*, pp. 121-23.

5. *Ibid.*, p. 123; George Gibbs, *Memoirs of the Administrations of Washington and John Adams* (New York: Printed for the Subscribers, 1846), II, 188-89, 196-97; Charles Francis Adams (ed.), *The Works of John Adams* (Boston: Little, Brown and Co., 1856), I, 542-45; IX, 251.

6. Gibbs, *Memoirs*, II, 204-5; Adams (ed.), *Life of John Adams*, I, 546-49; Charles W. Harris to Robert W. Harris, Apr. 19, 1799.—Walter Clark Papers, A.H.

7. Patrick Henry to the Secretary of State, Apr. 16, 1799.—*N. C. Minerva and Raleigh Advertiser*, Dec. 31, 1799. Davie's original commission is in the W. R. Davie Papers, A.H.

8. Adams (ed.), *Adams*, IX, 549-50.

9. Thomas to James Iredell, Feb. 2, 1799.—Charles E. Johnson Collection, A.H.

10. W. R. Davie Papers, A.H. Copy.

11. Timothy Pickering to John Adams, May 15, 1799.—W. R. Davie Papers, A.H. Typed copy; also reprinted in part in Adams (ed.), *Adams*, VIII, 651 n. 2.

12. Thomas Pickering to Davie, June 1, 1799.—W. R. Davie Papers, A.H.

Notes

13. W. R. Davie to Timothy Pickering, June 17, 1799.—Timothy Pickering Papers, XXIV, 330, Mass. Hist. Society.
14. Wm. V. Murray to Talleyrand, May 5, 1799; Talleyrand to Murray, May 12, 1799. *N.C. Minerva and Raleigh Advertiser*, Dec. 31, 1799.
15. Bernard Steiner, *The Life and Correspondence of James McHenry* (Cleveland: The Burrows Brothers Company, 1907), pp. 416-17.
16. Gen. Steele to James Iredell, Aug. 5, 1799. Charles E. Johnson Collection, A.H.
17. Timothy Pickering to W. R. Davie, Aug. 12, 1799.—W. R. Davie Papers, A.H.
18. Oliver Ellsworth to W. R. Davie and Timothy Pickering to *idem*, Aug. 13, 1799.—W. R. Davie Papers, A.H.
19. Pickering to Davie, Sept. 5, 1799.—W. R. Davie Papers, A.H.
20. *Raleigh Register*, Nov. 26, 1799.
21. *N.C. Minerva and Raleigh Advertiser*, Sept. 17, 1799; *Wilmington Gazette*, Oct. 3, 1799.
22. *Ibid.*
23. *Ibid.*
24. Davie to Iredell, Sept. 18, 1799.—McRee, *Iredell*, II, 584.
25. *N.C. Minerva*, Sept. 24, 1799.
26. Davie to John Steele, Aug. 25, 1799.—W.R.D. Papers, No. 2, S.H.C.; Charles W. Harris to Robert W. Harris, Sept. 29, 1799.—Walter Clark Papers, A.H.
27. Charles W. Harris to Robert W. Harris, Sept. 29, 1799.—Walter Clark Papers, A.H.
28. Davie to Iredell, Sept. 24, 1799.—Charles E. Johnson Collection, A.H.; *N.C. Minerva*, Oct. 1, 1799.
29. Fitzpatrick (ed.), *The Diary of George Washington, 1748-1799*, IV, 313-14.
30. *Raleigh Register*, Oct. 22, 1799.
31. Adams, *Adams*, IX, 251.
32. *Ibid.*, pp. 251-52.
33. *Ibid.*, pp. 25-26, 252.
34. Henry Cabot Lodge, *Life and Letters of George Cabot* (Boston: Little, Brown and Company, 1877), p. 237.
35. Adams, *Adams*, IX, 36.
36. *Ibid.*, pp. 252-53.
37. *Ibid.*, pp. 37-38.
38. *N.C. Minerva*, Oct. 29, 1799.
39. Walter Clark Papers, A.H.
40. Adams, *Adams*, IX, 253.
41. *Ibid.*, pp. 253-54.
42. *Ibid.*, p. 254.
43. *Ibid.*, pp. 254-55.
44. *Ibid.*, p. 255.

Notes

45. *Ibid.*, p. 39.
46. Ernest Haywood Papers, S.H.C.
47. *Ibid.*
48. Timothy Pickering to Jonathan Burrall, Oct. 21, 1799. W.R.D. Papers, No. 2, S.H.C.
49. W. R. Davie Papers, A.H. Typed copy.
50. *Ibid.*
51. Gibbs, *Memoirs*, II, 284-85.
52. W. R. Davie Papers, A.H.
53. John Steele to Mrs. Davie, December 14, 1799.—John Steele Papers, S.H.C.
54. *N.C. Minerva*, Nov. 12, 1799.
55. Proceedings of Envoys, A.H. For the remainder of this chapter, all references and citations not otherwise cited refer to this source. If cited, the abbreviation "P. of E." will be used.
56. *Raleigh Register*, Nov. 26, 1799; "Journal of Oliver Ellsworth, William R. Davie, and William Vans Murray, Envoys Extraordinary and Ministers Plenipotentiary to the court of France, containing their correspondence and negotiations from the 17th of January, 1800, to the 3d of October, in the same year; and terminating in the convention with France, of the 30th September, 1800" in "Proceedings of the American and French Commissioners for the Negotiation of a Treaty between France and the United States, 1799-1800," Lowrie and Clark (eds.), *American State Papers*. Class I. Foreign Relations, II, 295-345 (hereafter this will be cited as "Journal").
57. Nov. 19, 1799.
58. Reprinted in *N.C. Minerva*, Feb. 18, 1800.
59. Ellsworth and Davie to Timothy Pickering, Dec. 7, 1799, "Journal."
60. *Idem* to *idem*, Dec. 7, 1799, *ibid.*
61. *Idem* to *idem*, Feb. 10, 1800.—P. of E., A.H.; *Raleigh Register*, Apr. 22, 1800.
62. Ellsworth and Davie to Pickering, Feb. 10, 1800.—P. of E., A.H.; *Raleigh Register*, Apr. 22, 1800.
63. Jan. 30, 1800.
64. P. of E., A.H.; *Raleigh Register*, Apr. 22, 1800.
65. Ernest Haywood Papers, S.H.C.
66. Apr. 29, 1800. University Letters, 1796-1835, U.N.C.
67. *N.C. Minerva*, May 13, 1800.
68. *Ibid.*, May 20, 1800.
69. *Ibid.*, May 6, 1800.
70. Reprinted in the *Newbern Gazette*, May 23, 1800.
71. Davie to W. V. Murray, Aug. 16, 1800.—W. R. Davie Papers, A.H.
72. Instructions for the French ministers treating with the United States, March 22-April 20, 1800, Archives des Ministères des Affaires Étrangères, Correspondance Politique, États-Unis, Vol. 51, fols. 381-95v (Photostats in Library of Congress). Hereafter these will be cited as Archives, États-Unis.
73. W. R. Davie Papers, A.H.

Notes

74. E. Wilson Lyon, "The Franco-American Convention of 1800," *Journal of Modern History*, XII (Sept., 1940), 311.

75. Talleyrand's Report to the First Consul [undated], Archives, États-Unis, fols. 130-39.

76. Talleyrand's Report to the First Consul, *ibid.*, fols. 147-155v.

77. Lyon, "The Franco-American Convention of 1800," *loc. cit.*, p. 325.

78. *Ibid.*

79. Statements concerning the fête represent a composite of information derived from *Gazette Nationale ou Le Moniteur Universel* (original in L.C.) and from an extract from an unpublished memoir of Oliver Ellsworth, by his son-in-law (transcribed in 1880), N. Y. Public Library.

80. *Ibid.*

81. Various letters in the W. R. Davie Papers, A.H.

82. Gaven Mountflorence to Davie, Apr. 29, 1800.—W. R. Davie Papers, A.H.

83. *Idem* to *idem*, Sept. 29, 1800. Mary DeSaussure Fraser Papers, Duke University.

84. F. Peyrismans to Mrs. Davie, Oct. 23, 1800.—*Ibid.*

85. Hubbard, *Davie*, p. 124.

86. Reprinted in *ibid.*, pp. 124-25.

87. Talleyrand to Joseph Bonaparte, Roederer and Fleurieu, Nov. 17, 1800.—Archives, États-Unis, fol. 419.

88. Reprinted in *Raleigh Register*, Nov. 18, 1800, and the *N. C. Mercury and Salisbury Advertiser*, Nov. 27, 1800.

89. Lyon, "Franco-American Convention," *loc. cit.*, pp. 327-29.

90. *N. C. Minerva*, Dec. 16, 1800.

91. Willie Jones to John Haywood, Dec. 11, 1800.—Haywood Papers, S.H.C.

92. *Raleigh Register*, Dec. 16, 1800.

93. T. G. Amis to Thomas D. Bennehan, Dec. 24, 1800.—Cameron Papers, S.H.C.

94. Dec. 22, 1800.—John Gray Blount Papers, A.H.

95. Robert Williams to Duncan Cameron, Jan. 10, 1801.—Cameron Papers, S.H.C.

96. Richard Dobbs Spaight to John Gray Blount, Jan. 24, 1801.—J. G. Blount Papers, A.H.

97. Jan. 28, 1801.—Cameron Papers.

98. Bemis, *Diplomatic Hist. of U. S.*, p. 125.

CHAPTER XII

1. Davie to John Steele, Aug. 3, 1801.—John Steele Papers, I, S.H.C.

2. *Idem* to *idem*, Feb. 2, 1801.—John Steele Papers, I, S.H.C.

3. *Ibid.*; also letter of February 21, 1801 in *ibid.*; Davie to Richard Bennehan, March 9, 1801.—Cameron Papers, S.H.C.

4. Charles W. Harris to Duncan Cameron, Jan. 9, 1801.—Cameron Papers, S.H.C. Written at Davie's request.

Notes

5. W. G. Briggs, "Joseph Gales, Editor of Raleigh's First Newspaper," *N.C. Booklet*, VII (Oct., 1907), No. 2, pp. 107-15; W. E. Smith, "Gales, Joseph," *D.A.B.*, VII, 99-100; Lefler and Newsome, *North Carolina*, p. 282.
6. Duncan Cameron to Col. John Moore, Sept. 1, 1802.—W. E. Dodd (ed.), *Macon Papers, Branch Historical Papers*, III, No. 1. p. 38.
7. *Ibid.*, pp. 36-38.
8. Archibald Henderson, "A Federalist of the Old School," *N.C. Booklet*, XVII, No. 1, pp. 28-29.
9. Davie to John Steele, March 13, 1802.—John Steele Papers, I, S.H.C.
10. *Idem* to *idem*, Jan. 17, 1802.—John Steele Papers, I, S.H.C.
11. Dodd (ed.), *Macon Papers, loc. cit.*, p. 35.
12. Davie to John Steele, Aug. 3, 1801.—John Steele Papers, I, S.H.C.
13. Williams to Davie, Jan. 22, 1801.—Governor Williams' Letter Book, 1799-1802, A.H.
14. Davie to Williams, Feb. 2, 1801.—*Ibid.*
15. *Idem* to *idem*, Governor Williams' Papers, A.H.; Skaggs, *N. C. Boundary Disputes*, p. 111.
16. Williams to Davie, March 20, 1801.—Governor Williams' Letter Book, A.H.
17. Davie to Williams, March 25, 1801.—*Ibid.*
18. *Ibid.*
19. Drayton to Williams, July 16, 1801.—Governor Williams' Letter Book, A.H.
20. Davie to Williams, Sept. 5, 1801.—*Ibid.*
21. *Idem* to *idem*, Oct. 26, 1801.—*Ibid.*
22. Legislative Papers, 1801. Box No. 182, A.H.
23. Davie to Williams, Feb. 4, 1802.—*Ibid.;* Davie to Turner, Oct. 1, 1805.—Governor Turner's Letter Book, A.H.
24. N. C. Legislative Papers, 1801. Box No. 184, A.H.
25. Davie to Williams, Feb. 4, 1802.—*Loc. cit.*
26. Drayton to Williams, Jan. 9, 1802.—Governor Williams' Letter Book, A.H.
27. Williams to Davie, Jan. 22, 1802; Davie to Williams, Feb. 4, 1802.—*Loc. cit.*
28. Francis Xavier Martin (rep.), *The Public Acts of the General Assembly of North Carolina* (Newbern: Martin & Ogden, 1804), II, 214-15; Skaggs, *N. C. Boundary Disputes*, pp. 117-19.
29. Turner to Richardson, Dec. 18, 1803.—Governor Turner's Letter Book, A.H. Davie's commission is in the W. R. Davie Papers, A.H.
30. Turner to Davie, Sept. 23, 1805.—Governor Turner's Letter Book, A.H.; Skaggs, *N. C. Boundary Disputes*, pp. 119-21.
31. Davie to Turner, Oct. 1, 1805.—Governor Turner's Letter Book, A.H.
32. Davie to John Steele, Jan. 22, 1806.—John Steele Papers, I, S.H.C.
33. For the details of the controversy, see Skaggs, *N. C. Boundary Disputes*, pp. 123-57.

Notes

34. Macon to Thomas Jefferson, May 24, 1801. Dodd (ed.), *Branch Historical Papers*, III (June, 1909), No. 1, pp. 33-34.
35. *American State Papers*, I, 649 et seq.
36. Davie to John Steele, Aug. 3, 1801.—John Steele Papers, I, S.H.C.
37. The original commission from Jefferson is in the Davie Collection, A.H.
38. Hubbard, *Davie*, pp. 128-29.
39. Legislative Papers, A.H.; Hubbard, *Davie*, pp. 129-30.
40. Hubbard, *Davie*, p. 129.
41. Governor Williams' Letter Book, A.H., Feb.-May 1802.
42. Tombstone, Halifax Colonial Cemetery; *N.C.J.*, Apr. 19, 1802.
43. Davie to John Steele, Aug. 20, 1802.—John Steele Papers, I, S.H.C.
44. Nathaniel Macon to John Steele, Sept. 15, 1802.—Battle, *Sprunt Monograph No. 3*, p. 22.
45. Davie to Calvin Jones, Nov. 17, 1802.—Calvin Jones Papers, S.H.C.
46. Davie to Duncan Cameron, Apr. 3, 1803.—Cameron Papers, S.H.C.
47. Copy in Davie's handwriting in W.R.D. Papers, S.H.C.
48. *Minerva; or Anti-Jacobin* (Raleigh), July 18, 1803.
49. Wagstaff (ed.), *Steele Papers*, I, 403 n.
50. Charles W. Harris to Robert W. Harris, May 22, 1803.—Charles W. Harris Papers, S.H.C.
51. Peter Browne to Duncan Cameron, July 5, 1803.—Cameron Papers, S.H.C.
52. John Lockhart to Duncan Cameron, July 29, 1803.—Cameron Papers, S.H.C.; *Raleigh Register*, Aug. 8, 1803.
53. John Lockhart to Duncan Cameron, July 29, 1803.—*Loc. cit.*
54. Davie to Richard Bennehan, Aug. 2, 1803.—Cameron Papers, S.H.C.
55. Nathaniel Macon to Joseph H. Nicholson, Aug. 6, 1803.—Dodd (ed.), *Branch Historical Papers*, III, No. 1, p. 41; *idem* to John Steele, Aug. 7, 1803.—Wagstaff (ed.), *Steele Papers*, I, 403-4.
56. Davie to Steele, Aug. 20, 1803.—John Steele Papers, I, A.H.
57. Written by Steele's hand, across the bottom of the above letter.
58. Davie to Richard Bennehan, August 28, 1803.—Cameron Papers, S.H.C.
59. Davie to John Haywood, Sept. 2, 1803.—Ernest Haywood Papers, S.H.C.
60. Davie to John Steele, Sept. 25, 1803.—John Steele Papers, I, A.H.
61. Halifax County Records, List of Taxables, Books I and II for the years 1784-1789, A.H.; Halifax County Record Book, XVII, 125-26, 522, XVIII, 178, 827, 941-42, XXI, 22-33; Will, October 21, 1799.—Mary DeS. Fraser Papers, Duke MS Room.
62. *S.R.*, XXIV, 639-40.
63. Davie to John Gray Blount, March 9, 1795.—John Gray Blount Papers, A.H.
64. *N.C.J.*, Aug. 10, 17, 24, 31, May 30, June 6, 13, 1796; Apr. 15, 22, May 13, 1799.
65. Davie to John Steele, Jan. 10, 1804.—Wagstaff (ed.), *Steele Papers*, I, 422-24.
66. Halifax County, Record of Deeds, XXI, 99-100.

Notes

67. Davie to Richard Bennehan, Feb. 2, 1801.—Cameron Papers, S.H.C.
68. Deeds, A.H.
69. Halifax County, Record of Deeds, XX, 113, 125, 133-134, 153, XXI, 22-23; Indenture, Nov. 1, 1805.—W. R. Davie Papers, A.H.
70. Lefler and Newsome, *North Carolina*, p. 145; Henry G. Connor, "The Granville Estate and North Carolina," *University of Pennsylvania Law Review*, LXII (Oct., 1914), 677. This is a detailed and scholarly report of the entire proceedings.
71. Connor, "The Granville Estate," *loc. cit.*, 676-77.
72. *N.C.J.*, May 31, 1802.
73. Aug. 22, 1802.—Governor Williams' Letter Book; *N.C.J.*, Oct. 4, 1802.
74. Duncan Cameron to Richard Bennehan, Nov. 24, 1802.—Cameron Papers, A.H.
75. James Webb to Duncan Cameron, Dec. 8, 1802.—Cameron Papers, A.H.
76. Davie to Duncan Cameron, March 20, 1804.—Cameron Papers, S.H.C.
77. *Ibid.*
78. Fries (ed.), *Moravian Records*, VI, 2766.
79. *Ibid.*, p. 2810.
80. *Ibid.*, p. 2849.
81. *Ibid.*, p. 2919.
82. *Ibid.*, VII, 3079, 3090.
83. Davie to John Haywood, June 9, 1805.—University Letters, 1796-1835, U.N.C.
84. *Ibid.*
85. *Idem* to *idem*, July 1, 1805.—Ernest Haywood Collection, S.H.C.
86. *Ibid.*
87. Davie to John Haywood, March 19, 1806.—Ernest Haywood Collection, S.H.C.
88. *Ibid.*
89. Davie to Samuel Johnston, Feb. 20, 1806.—Hayes Collection, Edenton, N.C.
90. Davie to Richard Bennehan, Dec. 16, 1806.—Cameron Papers, S.H.C.
91. Davie to John Haywood, March 19, 1806.—Ernest Haywood Collection, S.H.C.
92. *Idem* to *idem*, Jan. 10, 1808.—*Ibid.*
93. *Idem* to *idem*, May 24, 1808.—*Ibid.*
94. *Idem* to *idem*, Oct. 20, 1808.—*Ibid.*
95. *Idem* to *idem*, Feb. 15, 1809.—*Ibid.*
96. *Ibid.*
97. Davie to General S. W. Carney, July 7, 1806.—W. R. Davie Collection, A.H.
98. Davie to Duncan Cameron, Aug. 20, 1806.—Cameron Papers, S.H.C.
99. Davie to Richard Bennehan, Dec. 16, 1806.—*Loc. cit.*
100. Davie to Duncan Cameron, July 20, 1807.—Cameron Papers, S.H.C.
101. *Idem* to *idem*, Feb. 29, 1808.—*Ibid.*

Notes

102. *Idem* to *idem*, Apr. 30, 1808.–*Ibid.*
103. Davie to John Haywood, May 24, 1808.–Ernest Haywood Papers, S.H.C.
104. *Idem* to *idem*, Oct. 20, 1808.–*Ibid.*
105. *Idem* to *idem*, Feb. 15, 1809.–*Ibid.*
106. *Ibid.*
107. *Idem* to *idem*, Feb. 1, 1810.–*Ibid.*
108. Davie to Richard Bennehan, Oct. 31, 1810.–Cameron Papers, S.H.C.
109. Davie to John Steele, Jan. 10, 1812.–John Steele Papers, S.H.C.
110. Davie to John Haywood, Apr. 8, 1812.–Ernest Haywood Collection, S.H.C.
111. *Idem* to *idem*, May 14, 1816.–*Ibid.*
112. Davie to Andrew Pickens, Dec. 9, 1817.–Francis Wilkinson Pickens Papers, Duke University.
113. Davie to [?], Apr. 16, 1819.–W.R.D. Papers, S.H.C.
114. Chalmers S. Murray, *This Our Land: The Story of the Agricultural Society of South Carolina* (Charleston: Carolina Art Ass'n, 1949), pp. 13, 28, 38, 54 n.
115. Davie to Mary H. Davie, Aug. 13, 1818 (postscript to F. W. Davie).–W.R.D. Papers, S.H.C.
116. Davie to Duncan Cameron, Dec. 16, 1806.–Cameron Papers, S.H.C.
117. *Idem* to *idem*, Feb. 29, 1808.–*Ibid.*
118. Davie to John Steele, Aug. 15, 1808.–John Steele Papers, S.H.C.
119. *Ibid.*
120. *Ibid.*
121. *Idem* to *idem*, Sept. 20, 1808.–*Ibid.*
122. Davie to Duncan Cameron, Sept. 20, 1808.–Cameron Papers, S.H.C.
123. *Idem* to *idem*, Nov. 22, 1808.–*Ibid.*
124. Davie to Steele, Jan. 4, 1810.–John Steele Papers, S.H.C.
125. *Idem* to *idem*, Jan. 10, 1812.–*Ibid.*
126. *Raleigh Star*, Jan. 31, 1812.
127. Davie to John Haywood, Apr. 8, 1812.–Ernest Haywood Collection, A.H.
128. *Ibid.*
129. *Raleigh Star*, Oct. 9 and 16, 1812.
130. *Ibid.*, December 18, 1812.
131. *Ibid.*, March 12, 1813.
132. Davie to Steele, Oct. 15, 1812.–John Steele Papers, S.H.C.
133. *Idem* to *idem*, Feb. 4, 1814.–*Ibid.*
134. Davie to William Gaston, Feb. 4, 1814.–Gaston Papers, S.H.C. The year is obviously wrong; it should have been 1815.
135. *Ibid.*
136. Davie to John Haywood, Nov. 13, 1814.–Ernest Haywood Collection, A.H.; Davie to John Steele, Nov. 29, 1814.–John Steele Papers, A.H.

Notes

137. Davie to William Gaston, Nov. 27, 1814.—William Gaston Papers, S.H.C.; Davie to John Steele, Nov. 29, 1814.—John Steele Papers, S.H.C.
138. Davie to John Haywood, June 27, 1815.—Ernest Haywood Collection, S.H.C.
139. Davie to William Gaston, Apr. 7, 1816.—William Gaston Papers, S.H.C.
140. *Ibid.*
141. Davie to John Haywood, May 14, 1816.—Ernest Haywood Collection, S.H.C.
142. Davie to J. R. Poinsett, Dec. 30, 1819.—W.R.D. Papers, S.H.C.
143. Davie to John Haywood, Jan. 22, 1807, and Jan. 10, 1808.—Ernest Haywood Collection, S.H.C.; Davie to Duncan Cameron, Sept. 5, 1813.—Cameron Papers, S.H.C.
144. James, *The Life of Andrew Jackson*, Part I, p. 793, n. 17.
145. Davie to Joseph Caldwell, Nov. 1, 1819.—W.R.D. Papers, S.H.C.
146. Davie to John Haywood, May 14, 1816.—Ernest Haywood Collection, S.H.C.
147. *Ibid.*
148. *Idem* to *idem*, June 27, 1815.—Ernest Haywood Collection, S.H.C.
149. Richard Bennehan to Thomas Bennehan, July 22, 1813, and Davie to Thomas D. Bennehan, June 24, 1815.—Cameron Papers, S.H.C.
150. Davie to Thomas D. Bennehan, June 24, 1815.—*Loc. cit.*
151. Davie to John Haywood, June 12, 1816.—Ernest Haywood Collection, S.H.C.
152. *Idem* to *idem*, Apr. 22, 1817.—*Ibid.;* Davie to Richard Bennehan, June 21, 1817.—Cameron Papers, S.H.C.
153. Davie to Mary Haynes Davie, Aug. 13, 1818.—W.R.D. Papers, S.H.C.; Richard Bennehan to his son, Aug. 26, 1818.—Cameron Papers, S.H.C.
154. Davie to John Haywood, Aug. 20, 1819.—Ernest Haywood Collection, S.H.C.
155. Davie to Joseph Caldwell, Nov. 1, 1819.—W.R.D. Papers, S.H.C.
156. Davie to J. R. Poinsett, Dec 30, 1819.—*Ibid.*
157. Ernest Haywood Collection, S.H.C.
158. *Ibid.*
159. *Ibid.*
160. Chester County, S.C., Office of Probate Court. Appraise Bill and Inventory of Estate, Book G, pp. 230-232; Last Will and Testament, Record Book G, pp. 225-29.
161. *Raleigh Minerva*, Dec. 15, 1820.
162. Frederick William Davie to William Gaston, Feb. 19, 1822; William Gaston to F. W. Davie, March 26, 1822; F. W. Davie to William Gaston, May 28, 1822.—William Gaston Papers, S.H.C.

BIBLIOGRAPHY

I. PRIMARY SOURCES

A. PHYSICAL SURVIVALS

Colonial Cemetery, Halifax, North Carolina.

"Loretta," home of William Richardson Davie from c. 1785-1805, Halifax, North Carolina.

Old Waxhaw Presbyterian Cemetery, eight miles from Lancaster, South Carolina. Here are the tombstones of Archibald Davie, Mary Richardson Davie, William Richardson Davie, William Richardson, and other members of the family.

Old Waxhaw Presbyterian Church, in which is hung a replica of the hatchment bearing the Davie Arms.

Royal Hart Masonic Temple Yard, containing tombstone of Joseph Montfort. Halifax, North Carolina.

Presbyterian Churchyard, Ruthwell Parish, Dumfriesshire, Scotland. Tombstone of David Richardson I and David Richardson II. The writer is indebted to Colonel Preston Davie for the inscriptions on these tombs.

Davie Family Bible, presented by the children of William Richardson Davie Crockett, of Austin, Texas, to the Louis Round Wilson Library, Chapel Hill, North Carolina.

B. MANUSCRIPTS

1. *Public Archives*

Charleston, South Carolina. Probate Court, Will Book, 1771-1774.

Chester County, South Carolina. Office of Probate Court. Appraise Bill and Inventory of Estate, Book G, pp. 230-32; Last Will and Testament of William R. Davie, Record Book G, pp. 225-29.

Bibliography

Halifax County, North Carolina. List of Taxables, 1784-1834 (Part I, 1784-1786; Part II, 1787-1834), North Carolina Department of Archives and History, Raleigh.

———. Record of Deeds, Book No. XIV, 1778-1783, Office of the Register of Deeds, Halifax.

Instructions for the French ministers treating with the United States, March 22–April 20, 1800. Archives des Ministères des Affaires Étrangères, Correspondance Politique, États-Unis, Vol. 51, fols. 381-95v (Photostats in Library of Congress).

Lancaster County, South Carolina. Old Deed Book H, Office of the Clerk of the Superior Court, Lancaster.

Northampton County, North Carolina. Record of Deeds, Office of the Register of Deeds, Jackson.

North Carolina. Governors' Letter Books and Governors' Papers, MS bound volumes, North Carolina Department of Archives and History, Raleigh. The volumes used were those covering the administrations from Governor Thomas Burke to Governor James Turner, for the period 1781-1805.

———. Journal of the Board of War, 1780-1781. North Carolina Department of Archives and History, Raleigh. This MS journal is bound with the Journals of the Fourth and Fifth Continental Congress.

———. Journal of Council of State during Davie's Administration, North Carolina Department of Archives and History, Raleigh.

———. Journals of the House of Commons, 1791-1805, North Carolina Department of Archives and History, Raleigh.

———. Journals of the Senate, 1791-1805, North Carolina Department of Archives and History, Raleigh.

———. Legislative Papers, House of Commons and Senate, for the years 1781-1805. North Carolina Department of Archives and History, Raleigh.

Rowan County, N.C. Court Minutes. Office of Register of Deeds, Salisbury.

South Carolina. Grant Book, XIV, Historical Commission of South Carolina, Columbia.

———. His Majesty's Council Journal for South Carolina, Historical Commission of South Carolina, Columbia.

———. Plat Book, No. 9, Historical Commission of South Carolina, Columbia.

Bibliography

2. Unofficial Collections

All papers or collections not cited are deposited in the Southern Historical Collection, Chapel Hill, North Carolina, while those in the North Carolina Department of Archives and History are designated as A.H.

John Gray Blount Papers, 1706-1828. A.H.

Thomas Burke Papers, 1744-1789.

Cameron Papers, 1700-1921. A particularly valuable collection for material on the University of North Carolina and for the manuscripts dealing with the social and economic background of the period.

Walter Clark Papers. A.H.

Papers of the Continental Congress. Vol. 2. Division of Manuscripts, Library of Congress.

William R. Davie Papers, No. 1, 1779-1819. This contains a few scattered items, including Davie's appointment as a lieutenant, April 5, 1779, a letter from Davie to David Caldwell, November 1, 1819, and the "Davie-Weems Historical Notes."

William R. Davie Papers, No. 2, 1758-1852. This represents 118 items, consisting of original manuscripts, photocopies, and typescripts, presented by Colonel Preston Davie of New York. Especially valuable is Davie's MS "Sketches" of the Southern Campaign after General Nathanael Greene's arrival.

William R. Davie Papers, 1778-1817. A.H. This consists of 3 volumes of mounted papers and 1 box of manuscripts. Two of these volumes deal with proceedings of the American and French peace commissioners 1799-1800, while one volume and the box contain a great many originals and typescripts.

John Rust Eaton Papers, 1794-1815.

Oliver Ellsworth. Unpublished Memoir. New York Public Library.

Mary DeSaussure Fraser Papers, 1800-1886. Manuscript Room, Duke University.

William Gaston Papers, 1744-1914, in Henry Groves Connor Collection, 1746-1934.

Horatio Gates Papers. New York Historical Society.

Horatio Gates Letter Copy-Book, 1780-1781. New York Public Library.

William Barry Grove Papers, 1792-1803.

Charles W. Harris Papers, 1777-1803.

Hayes Collection, 1748-1806. Typescript, bound volume. A.H.

Ernest Haywood Collection, 1752-1946. The correspondence of John Haywood in this collection has been an invaluable source of information.

BIBLIOGRAPHY

James Hogg Papers, 1772-1835.
James Iredell Papers, 1767-1856. Manuscript Room, Duke University.
Charles E. Johnson Collection, 1755-1875. A.H. This contains a great deal of the correspondence of James Iredell, much of which McRee included in his *Life and Correspondence*.
Calvin Jones Papers.
Macay-McNeely Papers, 1746-1918.
Griffith John McRee Papers, 1772-1908.
Joseph Montfort. Commission as Grand Master of Masons, framed in Halifax County Courthouse.
North Carolina Letters from the Emmett Collection, 1757-1847. Typescript. A.H.
Francis Wilkinson Pickens Papers. Manuscript Room, Duke University.
Pickering Papers. Massachusetts Historical Society.
Proceedings of the American and French Commissioners for the Negotiation of a Treaty between France and the United States, 1799-1800. A.H.
William Richardson. MS Report of Mission to the Cherokees, 1758-1759. William R. Davie Papers, No. 2, photocopy.
William L. Saunders Papers.
Soldiers of the American Revolution. Vol. 1. Historical Society of Pennsylvania, Philadelphia.
John Steele Papers, 1716-1859, Nos. 1, 2, and 3. These three collections contain a number of Davie-Steele and Steele-Davie letters.
John Steele Papers, 1777-1831. A.H.
Jethro Sumner Papers, 1775-1784.
David L. Swain Papers, 1740-1896.

3. *University of North Carolina Archives*

Dialectic Society Minutes, 1795-1798. MS volume.
Faculty Record, 1799-1814. MS volume.
Reports From the Faculty to the Board of Trustees of North Carolina, 1809-1829. MS volume.
Trustee Minutes, From December 18, 1789-December 6, 1797. MS volume.
Trustee Minutes, From December A. D. 1798, to June, 1801, inclusive. MS volume.
Trustee Minutes, From November, A. D. 1801, to December, A. D. 1810, inclusive. MS volume.
University Letters, 1791-1867. MS volume.
University Letters, 1796-1835. MS volume.
University Papers, 1792-1918. Unbound MS.

BIBLIOGRAPHY

C. PRINTED MATERIALS

1. *Public Documents*

Clark, Walter (ed.). *The State Records of North Carolina.* Vols. XI-XXVI. Winston and Goldsboro, North Carolina: M. I. and J. C. Stewart, and Nash Brothers, State Printers, 1895-1905.

Documentary History of the Constitution of the United States of America, 1786-1870. Deposited in the Bureau of Rolls and Library of the Department of State. 5 vols. Washington: Department of State, 1894-1905.

Hunt, Gaillard, Ford, Worthington C., Fitzpatrick, John C., and Hill, Roscoe R. (eds.). *Journals of the Continental Congress, 1774-1789.* 34 vols. Washington: Government Printing Office, 1904-1937.

Martin, Francis Xavier (rep.). *The Public Acts of the General Assembly of North Carolina.* New Bern: Martin & Ogden, 1804.

North Carolina Law Reports. Various volumes, variously printed.

Palmer, William P., *et al.* (eds.). *Calendar of Virginia State Papers and Other Manuscripts, 1652-1781.* 11 vols. Richmond: R. F. Walker, Superintendent of Public Printing, and various others, 1875-1893.

Saunders, William Lawrence (ed.). *The Colonial Records of North Carolina.* 10 vols. Raleigh: P. M. Hale, 1886; Josephus Daniels, 1887-1890.

Thorpe, Francis Newton (ed.). *The Federal and State Constitutions, Colonial Charters, and Other Organic Laws of the States, Territories, and Colonies, Now or Heretofore Forming the United States of America.* Vol. V. Washington: Government Printing Office, 1909.

United States, Bureau of the Census. *Heads of Families at the First Census of the United States Taken in the Year 1790: North Carolina.* Washington: Government Printing Office, 1908.

2. *Collected Documents, Contemporary Writings, and Travel Accounts*

Adams, Charles Francis. *The Works of John Adams, Second President of the United States: With a Life of the Author, Notes and Illustrations.* Boston: Little, Brown and Company, 1856. Vols. I and IX.

Balch, Thomas (ed.). *Papers Relating Chiefly to the Maryland Line During the Revolution.* Philadelphia: Printed for the Seventy-Six Society, 1857.

Barnwell, Joseph W. (annotator). "Letters of John Rutledge," *South Carolina Historical and Genealogical Magazine,* XVII (October, 1916), 131-146.

Battle, Kemp P. "Letters of Nathaniel Macon, John Steele, and William Barry Grove, with Sketches and Notes," *James Sprunt Historical Monograph,* No. 3. Chapel Hill: Published by the University, 1902.

Bibliography

Caldwell, Charles, M. D. *Memoirs of the Life and Correspondence of the Hon. Nathaniel Greene, Major General in the Army of the United States, and Commander of the Southern Department, in the War of the Revolution.* Philadelphia: Published by Robert Desilver, No. 110 Walnut Street, and Thomas Desilver, No. 2 Decatur Street, 1819.

Catalogus Universitatis Caroliniae Septentrionales. Raleigh: E. Typis and J. Gales, 1817.

Commager, Henry Steele (ed.). *Documents of American History.* New York and London: Appleton-Century-Crofts, Inc., 1948.

Dodd, William E. (ed.). *Macon Papers, The John P. Branch Historical Papers of Randolph Macon College.* Vol. III (June, 1909), No. 1, pp. 27-93.

Edgar, Patrick Nisbett. *The American Race-Turf Register, Sportsman's Herald, and General Stud Book: Containing the Pedigrees Of The Most Celebrated Horses, Mares, And Geldings, That Have Distinguished Themselves As Racers On The American Turf, From One Quarter Of A Mile Race Up To Four Miles And Repeat; Also, Such As Have Been Kept In The Stud—As Stallions And Mares For Breeding, From The Earliest Period To The Present Time: And From Which Have Descended The Most Valuable Blooded Stock At Present In The United States. The Whole Calculated For The Use and Information Of Amateurs, Breeders, And Trainers Of That Most Noble And Useful Animal, The Horse. Compiled from the Papers, Letters, Memorandums, Studbooks, and Newspapers, of the Most Celebrated and Distinguished Sportsmen; also, from other sources of the most correct information. In Two Vols.* Vol. I. New York: Press of Henry Mason, 76 Maiden Lane, 1833. A copy of Vol. I is in the possession of Henry Wilkins Lewis, Chapel Hill and Jackson, North Carolina. Vol. II was never published.

Elliot, Jonathan (ed.). *The Debates in the Several State Conventions, on the Adoption of the Federal Constitution, as Recommended by the General Convention at Philadelphia, in 1787.* Vol. IV. Washington: Printed for the Editor, 1836.

Farrand, Max (ed.). *The Records of the Federal Convention of 1787.* 4 vols. New Haven: Yale University Press, 1911.

Fitzpatrick, John C. (ed.). *The Diary of George Washington, 1748-1799.* 4 vols. New York: Houghton Mifflin Company, 1925.

———. *The Writings of George Washington from the Original Manuscript Sources, 1745-1799.* Washington: United States Government Printing Office, 1941, Vol. XXXVI (August 4, 1797–October 28, 1798) and Vol. XXXVII (November 1, 1798–December 13, 1799).

BIBLIOGRAPHY

Ford, Paul Leicester. *Pamphlets on the Constitution, Published During Its Discussion by the People.* Brooklyn: No Publisher, 1888.

Ford, Worthington Chauncey (ed.). *The Writings of George Washington.* New York: G. P. Putnam's Sons, 1893. Vol. 14. 1798-1799.

Fries, Adelaide L. (ed.). *Records of the Moravians in North Carolina.* Raleigh: The North Carolina Historical Commission, 1922-1947. 7 vols.

Garden, Alexander. *Anecdotes of the Revolutionary War in America with Sketches of Character of Persons the Most Distinguished, in the Southern States, For Civil and Military Services.* Charleston: Printed for the Author, by A. E. Miller, 1822.

Gordon, William. *The History of the Rise, Progress, and Establishment, of the Independence of the United States of America: Including An Account of the Late War; and of the Thirteen Colonies, From Their Origin to That Period.* 4 vols. London: Printed for the Author; and sold by Charles Dilly, 1788.

Hooker, Richard J. (ed.). *The Carolina Backcountry on the Eve of the Revolution: The Journal and Other Writings of Charles Woodmason, Anglican Itinerant.* Published for the Institute of Early American History and Culture at Williamsburg, Virginia, by the University of North Carolina Press, Chapel Hill, 1953.

Hoyt, William Henry (ed.). *The Papers of Archibald D. Murphey.* 2 vols. Raleigh: Publications of the North Carolina Historical Commission, 1914.

James, William Dobein. *A Sketch of the Life of Brig. Gen. Francis Marion, and A History of His Brigade, From Its Rise in June, 1780, Until Disbanded in December, 1782; With Descriptions of Characters and Scenes, Not Heretofore Published. Containing Also An Appendix, With Copies of Letters Which Passed Between Several of the Leading Characters of That Day; Principally From Gen. Greene to Gen. Marion.* Charleston: Printed by Gould and Riley, 41 Broad Street, 1821.

Johnson, William. *Sketches of the Life and Correspondence of Nathanael Greene, Major General of the Armies of the United States, in the War of the Revolution. Compiled Chiefly from Original Materials.* 2 vols. Charleston: A. E. Miller, 1822. This work was written before Davie's death.

Keith, Alice Barnwell (ed.). *The John Gray Blount Papers.* Vol. I. Raleigh: State Department of Archives and History, 1952.

Lamb, R. *An Original and Authentic Journal of the Occurrences During the Late American War, From Its Commencement To the Year 1783.* Dublin: Printed by Williams & Courtney, 6, Wood-Street, 1809.

BIBLIOGRAPHY

Lee, Henry. *The Campaign of 1781 in The Carolinas; With Remarks Historical and Critical on Johnson's Life of Greene. To Which Is Added An Appendix Of Original Documents, Relating to the History of the Revolution.* Philadelphia: Published by E. Littell, 1824.

———. *Memoirs of the War in the Southern Department of the United States.* 2 vols. Philadelphia: Published by Bradford and Inskeep; New York: Inskeep and Bradford, 1812.

Lee, Robert Edward (ed.). *Memoirs of the War in the Southern Department of the United States. By Henry Lee, Lieutenant-Colonel Commandant of the Partisan Legion During the American War. A New Edition, With Revisions, and A Biography of the Author.* New York: University Publishing Company, 1869.

Lefler, Hugh T. (ed.). *A Plea for Federal Union. A Reprint of Two Pamphlets.* Charlottesville: The Tracy W. McGregor Library, 1947.

——— (ed.). *North Carolina History Told by Contemporaries.* Chapel Hill: The University of North Carolina Press, 1934.

Lodge, Henry Cabot. *Life and Letters of George Cabot.* Boston: Little, Brown, and Company, 1877.

Mackenzie, Roderick. *Strictures on Lt. Col. Tarleton's History "Of The Campaigns of 1780 and 1781, In The Southern Provinces of North America"... Wherein Military Characters and Corps Are Vindicated From Injurious Aspersions, And Several Important Transactions Placed In Their Proper Point of View. In A Series Of Letters To A Friend... To Which Is Added, A Detail Of The Seige Of Ninety-Six, And The Re-Capture Of The Island of New-Providence.* London: Printed For the Author; And Sold By R. Jameson, Strand; R. Faulder, New Bond-Street; T. and J. Egerton, Charing Cross, and T. Sewell, Cornhill, M DCC LXXXVIII.

McMurtrie, Douglas C. *Eighteenth Century North Carolina Imprints, 1749-1800.* Chapel Hill: The University of North Carolina Press, 1938.

McRee, Griffith John. *Life and Correspondence of James Iredell, One of the Associate Justices of the Supreme Court of the United States.* 2 vols. New York: D. Appleton, 1857. A micro-offset has recently been published: New York: Peter Smith, 1949. Limited edition, 200 copies.

Marshall, John. *The Life of George Washington, Commander in Chief of the American Forces, During the War Which Established the Independence of His Country, and First President of the United States. Compiled Under the Inspection of The Honourable Bushrod Washington, From Original Papers Bequeathed To Him By His Deceased Relative, and Now In Possession of the Author. To Which Is Prefixed, An*

Bibliography

Introduction, Containing A Compendious View of the Colonies Planted By the English on the Continent of North America, From Their Settlement To The Commencement of That War Which Terminated in Their Independence. 5 vols. Philadelphia: Printed and Published By C. P. Wayne, 1805.

Moultrie, William. *Memoirs of the American Revolution, So Far As It Related to the States of North and South Carolina, and Georgia. Compiled from the Most Authentic Materials, the Author's Personal Knowledge of the Various Events, and Including an Epistolary Correspondence on Public Affairs, With Civil and Military Officers, at that Period.* 2 vols. New York: Printed by David Longworth for the Author, 1802.

Murphey, Archibald D. *An Oration Delivered in Person Hall, Chapel Hill; On the 27th of June, 1827, The Day Previous To The Commencement, Under The Appointment of The Dialectic Society.* Raleigh: Printed by J. Gales & Son, 1827.

North-Carolina University Magazine, V (May, 1856), No. 4, pp. 145-163.

"Order Book of John Faucheraud Grimké," *South Carolina Historical and Genealogical Magazine*, XVI (January, 1915), 39-48 (and continued in many succeeding issues).

Pattillo, Henry. *A Geographical Catechism, To assist those Who have neither Maps nor Gazetteers, To Read News-Papers, History, or Travels; With as much of The Science of Astronomy, and the Doctrine of the Air, As is judged sufficient for the Farmer, who wishes to understand something of The Works of God, around him; And for the studious Youth, Who have or have not a prospect of further prosecuting those Sublime Sciences.* Halifax: Printed by Abraham Hodge, 1796.

Ramsay, David, M. D. *The History of the Revolution of South Carolina, From a British Province To an Independent State.* 2 vols. Trenton: Printed by Isaac Collins, 1785.

Rodman, Lila Tunstall (ed.). *Journal of a Tour of North Carolina by William Attmore, 1787,* in *James Sprunt Historical Publications*, XVII, No. 2. Chapel Hill: The University of North Carolina Press, 1922.

Smith, William Henry (arranger and annotator). *The St. Clair Papers: The Life and Public Services of Arthur St. Clair, Soldier of the Revolutionary War; President of the Continental Congress; and Governor of the North-Western Territory, With His Correspondence and other Papers.* 2 vols. Cincinnati: Robert Clarke & Company, 1882.

Smyth, John Ferdinand Dalziel. *A Tour in the United States of America: Containing an Account of the Present Situation of that Country; the Population, Agriculture, Commerce, Customs and Manners of the In-*

Bibliography

habitants. 2 vols. Dublin, Ireland: Printed by G. Perrin, for Messrs. Price, Moncrieffe, etc., 1784.

Stedman, Charles. *The History of the Origin, Progress, and Termination of the American War.* 2 vols. Dublin, Ireland: Printed for Messrs. P. Wogan, P. Byne, J. Moore, and W. Jones, 1794.

Steiner, Bernard C. *The Life and Correspondence of James McHenry, Secretary of War Under Washington and Adams.* Cleveland: The Burrows Brothers Co., 1907.

Tarleton, Lieutenant-Colonel Banastre. *A History of the Campaigns of 1780 and 1781 in the Southern Provinces of North America.* London: Printed for T. Cadell, in the Strand, 1787.

Turner, Joseph Brown (ed.). "The Journal and Order Book of Captain Robert Kirkland of the Delaware Regiment of the Continental Line. Part I: A Journal of the Southern Campaign 1780-1782. Part II: An Order Book of the Campaign in New Jersey, 1777," *Papers of the Historical Society of Delaware,* LVI. Wilmington: The Historical Society of Delaware, 1910, pp. 1-277.

Wagstaff, Henry McGilbert (ed.). *The Harris Papers,* in *James Sprunt Historical Publications,* XIV, No. 1. Chapel Hill: The North Carolina Historical Society, 1916.

——— (ed.). *The Papers of John Steele.* 2 vols. Raleigh: Publications of the North Carolina Historical Commission, 1924.

Watson, Winslow C. (ed.). *Men and Times of the Revolution; or Memoirs of Elkanah Watson, including Journals of Travels in Europe and America, From 1777 to 1842, with His Correspondence with Public Men and Reminiscences and Incidents of the Revolution.* New York: Dana and Company, 1856.

Williams, John Rogers (ed.). *Philip Vickers Fithian: Journals and Letters, 1767-1774. Student At Princeton College 1770-72. Tutor At Nomini Hall in Virginia 1773-74.* 2 vols. Princeton: The University Library, 1900.

Williams, Samuel Cole (ed.). "General Richard Winn's Notes—1780," *South Carolina Historical and Genealogical Magazine,* XLIII (1942), 201-212; XLIV (1943), 1-10.

3. *Contemporary Newspapers*

The newspapers searched are all the available North Carolina eighteenth-century originals or photostats, deposited in the Library of the University of North Carolina, Duke University Library, and the North Carolina State Department of Archives and History. They are all weeklies.

Bibliography

For further information on these newspapers, see Clarence S. Brigham, *History and Bibliography of American Newspapers, 1690-1820* (Worcester, Massachusetts: American Antiquarian Society, 1947), II, 758-782. The newspapers listed are those which proved of value on this particular subject.

[Edenton] *State Gazette of North-Carolina*, 1789-1799. Fairly complete file.

[Fayetteville] *North-Carolina Centinel and Fayetteville Gazette*, 1795. A few issues.

Fayetteville Gazette, 1789-1790; 1792-1794. Only scattered issues available.

[Fayetteville] *North-Carolina Chronicle; or Fayetteville Gazette*, 1790-1791. A few issues.

[Fayetteville] *North-Carolina Minerva and Fayetteville Advertiser*, 1796-1799. In April, 1799, this paper was moved to Raleigh. Scattered issues.

[Halifax] *North-Carolina Journal*, August 1, 1792-May 13, 1799. Complete except for a few issues. This is an invaluable source of information on Davie, the founding of the University of North Carolina, and the economic, social, and political conditions of the period. There are also scattered issues from 1800-1807.

[New Bern] *North-Carolina Gazette*, 1787-1798. File incomplete.

[New Bern] *State Gazette of North-Carolina*, 1785-1788. In the summer of 1788 this paper, published by Hodge & Wills, was moved to Edenton. Scattered issues.

[Paris] *Publicisse*, February 8, 1800.

[Raleigh] *North-Carolina Minerva and Raleigh Advertiser*, May 28, 1799-1803. Fairly complete file.

Raleigh Register, and North-Carolina Weekly Advertiser, December, 1799-1820. File incomplete.

[Salisbury] *North-Carolina Mercury and Salisbury Advertiser*, June, 1799-1801. Scattered issues.

Wilmington Gazette, 1797-1799. Scattered issues.

4. *Maps*

[Graham, Major Joseph]. "A plan of Mclenburg and portions of joining Counties as laid down by a Scale of 5 miles to an inch. January 16th 1789," MS map, North Carolina State Department of Archives and History, Raleigh [This map is also reprinted in John Brevard Alexander. *The History of Mecklenburg County from 1740 to 1900*. Charlotte: Observer Printing House, 1902].

Mills, Robert. *Atlas of the State of South Carolina. A New Facsimile Edition of the Original Published in 1825. With An Introduction by*

BIBLIOGRAPHY

Francis Marion Hutson of the Historical Commission of South Carolina. Columbia, S. C.: Lucy Hampton Bostick and Fant H. Thornley, 1937.

Mouzon, Henry. *An Accurate Map of North and South Carolina, with Their Indian Frontiers, Shewing in a Distinct Manner All the Mountains, Rivers, Swamps, Marshes, Bays, Creeks, Harbors, Sandbanks, and Soundings on the Coasts, with the Roads and Indian Paths as Well as the Boundary or Provincial Lines, the Several Townships and Other Divisions of the Land in Both the Provinces; the Whole from Actual Surveys by Henry Mouzon and Others.* London, England: Robert Sayer and J. Bennett, 1775. Carolina Room, Louis Round Wilson Library, Chapel Hill.

Reprint of anonymous 1785 map appearing as the frontispiece in David Ramsay. *The History of the Revolution of South Carolina, From a British Province To an Independent State.* 2 vols. Trenton: Printed by Isaac Collins, 1785.

II. SECONDARY SOURCES

A. Biography

Ashe, Samuel A'Court (ed.). *Biographical History of North Carolina from Colonial Times to the Present.* 8 vols. Greensboro: Charles L. Van Noppen, Publisher, 1905-1917.

Bassett, John Spencer. *The Life of Andrew Jackson.* New York: The Macmillan Company, 1925.

Beveridge, Albert J. *The Life of John Marshall.* Boston and New York: Houghton Mifflin Co., 1919. Vol. IV.

Blythe, LeGette. *William Henry Belk: Merchant of the South.* Chapel Hill: The University of North Carolina Press, 1950.

Buell, Augustus C. *History of Andrew Jackson: Pioneer, Patriot, Soldier, Politician, President.* 2 vols. New York: Charles Scribner's Sons, 1904.

Carrington, Henry B. *Battles of the American Revolution, 1775-1781. Historical and Military Criticism, with Topographical Illustrations.* New York, Chicago, New Orleans: A. S. Barnes & Company, 1876. Fourth Edition.

Caruthers, E. W. *A Sketch of the Life and Character of the Rev. David Caldwell, D. D., Near Sixty Years Pastor of the Churches of Buffalo and Alamance. Including Two of His Sermons; Some Account of the Regulation, Together With the Revolutionary Transactions and Incidents In Which He Was Concerned; And a Very Brief Notice of the Ecclesiastical and Moral Condition of North-Carolina While in Its*

Bibliography

Colonial Status. Greensborough, N. C.: Printed by Swaim and Sherwood, 1842.

Craighead, James Geddes. *The Craighead Family: A Genealogical Memoir of the Descendants of Rev. Thomas and Margaret Craighead, 1658-1876*. Philadelphia: Printed for the Descendants, 1876.

Davidson, Chalmers G. *Piedmont Partisan: The Life and Times of General William Lee Davidson*. Davidson, N. C.: Davidson College, 1951.

Dodd, William E. *The Life of Nathaniel Macon*. Raleigh: Edwards and Broughton, 1903.

Graham, Major William Alexander. *General Joseph Graham and His Papers on North Carolina Revolutionary History, with Appendix: An Epitome of North Carolina's Military Services in the Revolutionary War and of the Laws Enacted for Raising Troops*. Raleigh: Published for the Author, By Edwards & Broughton, 1904.

Greene, George Washington. *The Life of Nathanael Greene, Major General in the Army of the Revolution*. 3 vols. New York: Hurd & Houghton, 1871.

Gregorie, Anne King. *Thomas Sumter*. Columbia, S. C.: Press of the R. L. Bryan Company, 1931.

Hamilton, Joseph Gregoire de Roulhac. "William Richardson Davie: A Memoir, Followed by His Letters with Notes," *James Sprunt Historical Monograph*, No. 7. Chapel Hill: Published by the University, 1907.

Hubbard, Fordyce M. *Life of William Richardson Davie, Governor of North Carolina*, Jared Sparks (ed.). *The Library of American Biography*. Vol. XV. Second Series. Boston: Charles C. Little and James Brown, 1848.

James, Marquis. *The Life of Andrew Jackson*. Complete in One Volume. Indianapolis and New York: The Bobbs-Merrill Company, 1938.

Kapp, Friedrich. *The Life of John Kalb*. New York: Privately printed, 1884.

Kendall, Amos. *Life of Andrew Jackson, Private, Military, and Civil*. New York: Harper & Bros., 1843.

Masterson, William H. *William Blount*. Baton Rouge: Louisiana State University Press, 1954.

Parton, James. *Life of Andrew Jackson*. 3 vols. New York: Mason Brothers, 1860.

Peele, W. J. (ed.). *Lives of Distinguished North Carolinians. With Illustrations and Speeches*. Raleigh: North Carolina Publishing Society, 1898.

Sabine, Lorenzo. *Biographical Sketches of the Loyalists of the American Revolution*. 2 vols. Boston: Little, Brown and Company, 1864.

BIBLIOGRAPHY

Skeel, Emily Ellsworth Ford (ed.). *Mason Locke Weems, His Works and Ways. In Three Volumes. A Bibliography Left Unfinished By Paul Leicester Ford.* New York: Emily E. F. Skeel, 1929.

Wagstaff, Henry McGilbert. "William Richardson Davie and Federalism," *Proceedings of the Twentieth and Twenty-First Annual Sessions of the State Literary and Historical Association of North Carolina.* Raleigh: Publications of the North Carolina Historical Commission, December 2-3, 1920; December 1-2, 1921, pp. 46-57.

Wiltse, Charles W. *John C. Calhoun: Nationalist, 1782-1828.* Indianapolis and New York: The Bobbs-Merrill Company, 1944.

B. GENERAL, STATE, AND LOCAL HISTORIES

Abernethy, Thomas Perkins. *From Frontier To Plantation in Tennessee: A Study in Frontier Democracy.* Chapel Hill: The University of North Carolina Press, 1932.

Alexander, John Brevard. *The History of Mecklenburg County From 1740 to 1900.* Charlotte: Observer Printing House, 1902.

Allen, William Cicero. *The History of Halifax County.* Boston: The Cornhill Company, 1919.

Ashe, Samuel A'Court. *History of North Carolina, 1584-1925.* 2 vols. Greensboro and Raleigh: Charles L. Van Noppen and Edwards & Broughton Printing Company, 1908 and 1925.

Boyd, William Kenneth. *History of North Carolina:* Vol. II, *The Federal Period, 1783-1860.* Chicago and New York: The Lewis Publishing Company, 1919.

Brawley, James Shober. *The Rowan Story.* Salisbury: Published by the Author, 1953.

Connor, Robert Diggs Wimberley. *History of North Carolina:* Vol. I, *The Colonial and Revolutionary Periods, 1584-1783.* Chicago and New York: The Lewis Publishing Company, 1919.

——. *North Carolina: Rebuilding An Ancient Commonwealth, 1584-1925.* 4 vols. Chicago: American Historical Society, 1929. North Carolina Biography by a special staff of writers, Vols. 3-4.

Ervin, Samuel James. "A Colonial History of Rowan County," *James Sprunt Historical Studies*, XVI, No. 1. Chapel Hill: The University of North Carolina Press, 1917.

Foote, William Henry. *Sketches of North Carolina, Historical and Biographical, Illustrative of the Principles of a Portion of Her Early Settlers.* New York: Robt. Carter, 1846.

Henderson, Archibald. *North Carolina: The Old North State and the New.* 5 vols. Chicago: The Lewis Publishing Company, 1941.

Bibliography

Hunter, Cyrus Lee. *Sketches of Western North Carolina, Historical and Biographical. Illustrating Principally The Revolutionary Period of Mecklenburg, Rowan, Lincoln and Adjoining Counties, Accompanied With Miscellaneous Information, Much Of It Never Before Published.* Raleigh: The Raleigh News Steam Job Press, 1877.

Jensen, Merrill. *The New Nation: A History of the United States During the Confederation, 1781-1789.* New York: Alfred A. Knopf, 1950.

Johnson, Guion Griffis. *Ante-Bellum North Carolina: A Social History.* Chapel Hill: The University of North Carolina Press, 1937.

Lefler, Hugh T., and Newsome, Albert Ray. *North Carolina: The History of a Southern State.* Chapel Hill: The University of North Carolina Press, 1953.

McCrady, Edward. *The History of South Carolina in the Revolution, 1775-1780.* New York: The Macmillan Company, 1901.

———. *The History of South Carolina in the Revolution, 1780-1783.* New York: The Macmillan Company, 1902.

McSherry, James. *History of Maryland; From Its First Settlement in 1634 to the Year 1848.* Baltimore: Printed and Published By John Murphy, 1849.

Moore, John W. *History of North Carolina; From the Earliest Discoveries to the Present Time.* 2 vols. Raleigh: Alfred Williams & Co., 1880.

Scharf, J. Thomas. *History of Maryland, From the Earliest Period to the Present Day.* 2 vols. Baltimore: Published by John B. Pret, 1879.

Turner, J. Kelly, and Bridgers, John L., Jr. *History of Edgecombe County, North Carolina.* Raleigh: Edwards & Broughton Printing Co., 1920.

Wheeler, John H. *Historical Sketches of North Carolina, From 1584 to 1851. Compiled from Original Records, Official Documents, and Traditional Statements. With Biographical Sketches of Her Distinguished Statesmen, Jurists, Lawyers, Soldiers, Divines, etc.* Philadelphia: Lippincott, Grambo & Co., 1851.

Williams, Samuel Cole. *The Dawn of Tennessee Valley and Tennessee History.* Johnson City, Tennessee: The Watauga Press, 1937.

C. Monographs and Special Studies

Alden, John Richard (ed.). *The War of the Revolution*, by Christopher Ward. 2 vols. New York: The Macmillan Co., 1952.

Battle, Kemp Plummer. *History of the University of North Carolina, From Its Beginning To the Death of President Swain, 1789-1868.* Vol. I. Raleigh: Edwards & Broughton Company, 1907.

Bibliography

Bemis, Samuel Flagg. *A Diplomatic History of the United States.* New York: Henry Holt and Co., 1950.

Bridenbaugh, Carl. *Myths and Realities: Societies of the Colonial South.* Baton Rouge: Louisiana State University Press, 1952.

Crittenden, Charles Christopher. *The Commerce of North Carolina, 1763-1789.* New Haven: Yale University Press, 1936.

Cutten, George Barton. *The Silversmiths of North Carolina.* Raleigh: State Department of Archives and History, 1948.

DeMond, Robert O. *Loyalists in North Carolina During the Revolution.* Durham: Duke University Press, 1940.

Dill, Alonzo Thomas. *Governor Tryon and His Palace.* Chapel Hill: The University of North Carolina Press, 1955.

Dinwiddie, The Reverend John L. *The Ruthwell Cross and The Ruthwell Savings Bank: A Handbook For Tourists and Students.* Dumfries, Scotland: Robert Dinwiddie, 1933.

Douglass, Elisha P. *Rebels and Democrats.* Chapel Hill: The University of North Carolina Press, 1955.

Draper, Lyman C. *King's Mountain and Its Heroes: History of the Battle of King's Mountain, October 7th, 1780, and the Events Which Led to It.* Cincinnati: Peter G. Thompson, 1881.

Eaton, Clement. *Freedom of Thought In the Old South.* Durham: Duke University Press, 1940.

Fortescue, J. W. *A History of the British Army.* Vol. III, 1763-1793. London: Macmillan and Co., Limited, 1902.

Gibbs, George. *Memoirs of the Administrations of Washington and John Adams, Edited from the Papers of Oliver Wolcott, Secretary of the Treasury.* New York: William Van Norden, 1846. 2 vols.

Gilpatrick, Delbert Harold. *Jeffersonian Democracy in North Carolina, 1789-1816.* New York: Columbia University Press, 1931.

Green, Fletcher Melvin. *Constitutional Development in the South Atlantic States, A Study in the Evolution of Democracy, 1776-1860.* Chapel Hill: The University of North Carolina Press, 1930.

Harrison, Fairfax. *The Background of the American Stud Book.* Richmond: Old Dominion Press, 1933.

Hawks, Francis L., Swain, David L., and Graham, William A. *Revolutionary History of North Carolina in Three Lectures.* Raleigh: William D. Cooke, 1853.

Henderson, Archibald. *The Campus of the First State University.* Chapel Hill: The University of North Carolina Press, 1949.

Howe, George. *History of the Presbyterian Church in South Carolina.* 2 vols. Columbia: Duffie & Chapman, 1870.

BIBLIOGRAPHY

Johnson, Victor Leroy. *The Administration of the American Commissariat During the Revolutionary War*. Philadelphia: University of Pennsylvania, 1941.

Johnston, Frances Benjamin, and Waterman, Thomas Tileston. *The Early Architecture of North Carolina: A Pictorial Survey with An Architectural History*. Chapel Hill: The University of North Carolina Press, 1947.

Klett, Guy S. *Presbyterianism in Colonial Pennsylvania*. Philadelphia: University of Pennsylvania, 1937.

Lonn, Ella. *The Colonial Agents of the Southern Colonies*. Chapel Hill: The University of North Carolina Press, 1945.

Lossing, Benson J. *The Pictorial Field-Book of the Revolution; Or, Illustrations, By Pen and Pencil, Of the History, Biography, Scenery, Relics, and Traditions of the War for Independence*. 2 vols. New York: Harper & Bros., 1860.

McLaughlin, Andrew C. *A Constitutional History of the United States*. New York: D. Appleton-Century Company, 1935.

Montross, Lynn. *Rag, Tag and Bobtail: The Story of the Continental Army, 1775-1783*. New York: Harper and Brothers, 1952.

Murray, Chalmers S. *This Our Land: The Story of the Agricultural Society of South Carolina*. Charleston: Carolina Art Association, 1949.

Nevins, Allan. *The American States During and After the Revolution 1775-1789*. New York: The Macmillan Company, 1924.

Robinson, Blackwell P. *The History of Escheats*. Chapel Hill: The University of North Carolina, 1955.

Schenck, David. *North Carolina, 1780-1781: Being a History of the Invasion of the Carolinas By the British Army Under Lord Cornwallis in 1780-'81, with the Particular Design of Showing the Part Borne by North Carolina in that Struggle for Liberty and Indep., & to Correct Some of the Errors of History in Regard to that State and Its People*. Raleigh: Edwards & Broughton, 1889.

Skaggs, Marvin Lucian. *North Carolina Boundary Disputes Involving Her Southern Line, James Sprunt Studies in History and Political Science*. Chapel Hill: The University of North Carolina Press, 1941.

Stevens, Benjamin Franklin (ed.). *Clinton-Cornwallis Controversy*. 2 vols. London: 4 Trafalgar Square, Charing Cross, 1888.

Taylor, Hannis. *The Origin and Growth of the American Constitution: An Historical Interpretation*.... Boston and New York: Houghton Mifflin Company, 1911.

Trenholme, Louise Irby. *The Ratification of the Federal Constitution in North Carolina*. New York: Columbia University Press, 1932.

BIBLIOGRAPHY

Wagstaff, Henry McGilbert. *Federalism in North Carolina, James Sprunt Historical Publications,* VI, No. 2. Chapel Hill: Published by the University, 1910.

———. *State Rights and Political Parties in North Carolina—1776-1861, Johns Hopkins University Studies in Historical and Political Science.* Baltimore: The Johns Hopkins Press, July-August, 1906.

Warren, Charles. *The Making of the Constitution.* Boston: Little, Brown and Company, 1937.

Weeks, Stephen Beauregard. *The Press of North Carolina in the Eighteenth Century.* Brooklyn: Historical Printing Club, 1891.

White, Henry Alexander. *Southern Presbyterian Leaders.* New York: The Neale Publishing Company, 1911.

D. ARTICLES IN PERIODICALS AND PAMPHLETS

Baldwin, Alice M. "Sowers of Sedition: The Political Theories of Some of the New Light Presbyterian Clergy of Virginia and North Carolina," *William and Mary Quarterly,* Third Series, V (January, 1948), 52-76.

"Biographical Sketch of Waightstill Avery, With Illustrative Manuscripts," *North-Carolina University Magazine,* IV (August, 1855), 242-64.

Briggs, Willis G. "Joseph Gales, Editor of Raleigh's First Newspaper," *North Carolina Booklet,* VII (October, 1907), 105-30.

Clark, Walter. "An Address Upon the Life and Services of General William Richardson Davie, at the Guilford Battle Ground, July 4, 1892." Greensboro: Reece, 1892. Pamphlet.

Coates, Gladys Hall. "The Story of Person Hall," *Bulletin of Person Hall Art Gallery,* III (April, 1943), No. 2. Pamphlet.

Cobb, Collier. "Governor Benjamin Smith," *N. C. Booklet,* Vol. XI (January, 1912), 158-68.

Colter, H. E. "Towns of the Revolution—Hillsborough, N. C.," *Southern Literary Messenger,* XXIII (September, 1856), 161-76.

Connor, Henry Groves. "The Granville Estate and North Carolina," *University of Pennsylvania Law Review,* LXII (October, 1914), 671-98.

Connor, Robert Diggs Wimberley. "A State Experiment in Higher Education: An Address delivered at a Convocation of the University of North Carolina, Wednesday, December 4, 1946." Chapel Hill: The Committee on Convocations and Lectures of the University of North Carolina, 1947. Pamphlet.

Corbitt, David Leroy (ed.). "Historical Notes," *North Carolina Historical Review,* IV (January, 1927), 95-114.

Bibliography

Douglass, Elisha P. "Thomas Burke, Disillusioned Democrat," *North Carolina Historical Review*, XXVI (April, 1949), 150-86.

Hamilton, Joseph Gregoire de Roulhac. "Governor Thomas Burke," *North Carolina Booklet*, VI (October, 1906), 103-22.

Henderson, Archibald. "A Federalist of the Old School," *North Carolina Booklet*, XVII (July, 1917), 3-38.

———. Forty-Sixth Annual Phi Beta Kappa Address. Alpha Chapter of North Carolina: "The Undying Flame: The Story of Its Lighting." Chapel Hill: University of North Carolina, 1950. Pamphlet.

Jaynes, R. T. "The Old Waxhaws." N.p., n.pub., n.d. Pamphlet in Carolina Room, Louis Round Wilson Library, Chapel Hill.

Lyon, E. Wilson. "The Franco-American Convention of 1800," *Journal of Modern History*, XII (September, 1940), 305-33.

Nash, Francis. "The Borough Towns of North Carolina," *North Carolina Booklet*, VI (October, 1906), 83-102.

Newsome, Albert Ray. "North Carolina's Ratification of the Federal Constitution," *North Carolina Historical Review*, XVII (October, 1940), 287-301.

"Notes of the Editor," *Magazine of American History*, VII (October, 1881), 293.

Olds, Fred A. "Sketch of Willie Jones," *The* [Oxford, North Carolina] *Orphan's Friend and Masonic Journal*, February 15, 1924.

Pool, William C. "An Economic Interpretation of the Ratification of the Federal Constitution in North Carolina," *North Carolina Historical Review*, XXVII (April, July, October, 1950), 119-41, 289-313, 437-61.

"The Presentation of the Plate," University of North Carolina *Alumni Review*, V (November, 1916), 38-41.

Review of Fordyce M. Hubbard, *The Life of William Richardson Davie, Governor of North Carolina*. *Southern Literary Messenger*, XIV (August, 1848), 510-17.

Robinson, Blackwell Pierce. "Willie Jones of Halifax," *North Carolina Historical Review*, XVIII (January and April, 1941), 1-26, 133-70.

Spencer, Cornelia Phillips. "Pen and Ink Sketches of the University of North Carolina," *Daily Sentinel*, April 26-July 6, 1869. Typescript copy in the Carolina Room of the Louis Round Wilson Library, Chapel Hill.

Spruill, Julia Cherry. "Virginia and Carolina Homes before the Revolution," *North Carolina Historical Review*, XII (January, 1935), 320-40.

Van Tyne, Claude H. "Influence of the Clergy, and of Religious and Sectarian Forces, on the American Revolution," *American Historical Review*, XIX (October, 1913), 44-64.

Bibliography

Wagstaff, Henry McGilbert. "State Rights in North Carolina Through Half a Century," *North Carolina Booklet*, IX (October, 1909), 79-97.

Walser, Richard. "The North Carolina Sojourn of the First American Novelist," *North Carolina Historical Review*, XXVIII (April, 1951), 138-49.

Weeks, Stephen Beauregard. "Libraries and Literature in North Carolina in the Eighteenth Century," *Annual Report of the American Historical Association for 1895*. Washington: Government Printing Office, 1896, pp. 171-267.

E. Unpublished Works

Caldwell, James Roy, Jr. "A History of Granville County, North Carolina: The Preliminary Phase, 1746-1800." University of North Carolina: unpublished doctoral dissertation, 1950.

Davie, Preston. "A Biographical Sketch of Mary Richardson (1723-67), Her Early Environments and Some of Her Antecessors." Typescript in writer's possession.

———. "The Early Years and Antecedents of William Richardson Davie (1756-1820)." Typescript in writer's possession.

———. "The Story of Governor William Richardson Davie and His Times." Typescript in writer's possession.

Keith, Alice Barnwell. "Three North Carolina Blount Brothers in Business and Politics, 1783-1812." University of North Carolina: unpublished doctoral dissertation, 1940.

Paschal, Herbert R., Jr. "The Tuscarora Indians in North Carolina." University of North Carolina: unpublished M.A. thesis, 1953.

Purcell, James S., Jr. "Literary Culture in North Carolina before 1820." Duke University: unpublished doctoral dissertation, 1950.

F. Miscellaneous Aids

Brigham, Clarence S. *History and Bibliography of American Newspapers, 1690-1820*. 2 vols. Worcester, Massachusetts: American Antiquarian Society, 1947.

Connor, Robert Diggs Wimberley (Compiler). *A Manual of North Carolina, Issued by the North Carolina Historical Commission For the Use of the Members of the General Assembly*, Session 1913. Raleigh: E. M. Uzzell & Co., State Printers, 1913.

Grant, Daniel Lindsey (ed.). *Alumni History of the University of North Carolina*. Published and Distributed by General Alumni Association of the University of North Carolina. Printed by Christian & King Printing Co., Durham, N. C., 1924.

BIBLIOGRAPHY

Heitman, Francis Bernard. *Historical Register of Officers of the Continental Army During the War of the Revolution, April, 1775, to December, 1783.* Washington: F. B. Heitman, 1893.
Johnson, Allen, and Malone, Dumas (eds.). *Dictionary of American Biography.* 22 vols. New York: Charles Scribner's Sons, 1937. The following biographical entries were used:
Alden, Edmund Kimball. "Campbell, William," III, 465-66.
Curtis, Edward E. "Williams, Otho," XX, 284-85.
Gregorie, Anne King. "Winn, Richard," XX, 390-91.
Hamilton, Joseph Gregoire de Roulhac. "Penn, John," XIV, 431.
Haskell, Daniel C. "Morgan, Daniel," XIII, 166-67.
Meriwether, Robert L. "Moultrie, William," XIII, 293-94.
Monaghan, Frank. "Kalb, Johann," X, 253-54.
―――. "Pulaski, Casimir," XV, 259-60.
Morris, Richard B. "Reed, Joseph," XV, 451-53.
Newsome, Albert Ray. "Jones, Allen," X, 159-60.
―――. "Martin, Alexander," XII, 333-34.
―――. "Nash, Abner," XIII, 383-84.
―――. "Polk, Thomas," XV, 42-43.
Pomfret, John E. "Davies, Samuel," V, 102-3.
Ross, Frank Edward. "Cleveland, Benjamin," IV, 202-3.
―――. "McDowell, Charles," XII, 23-24.
Smith, W. E. "Gales, Joseph," VII, 99-100.
Van Deusen, John G. "Huger, Isaac," IX, 344-45.
Whitaker, Arthur P. "Sevier, John," XVI, 602-4.
Wilson, Samuel M. "Shelby, Isaac," XVII, 60-62.
National Society of the Daughters of the American Revolution. *Lineage Book.* 166 vols. Harrisburg, Pennsylvania, and Washington, D. C.: Variously published, 1895-1935.
North Carolina Daughters of the American Revolution. *Roster of Soldiers from North Carolina in the American Revolution.* No place: Published by the North Carolina Daughters of the American Revolution, 1937.
Revill, Janie (compiler). *A Compilation of the Original Lists of Protestant Immigrants to South Carolina, 1763-1773.* Columbia, S. C.: The State Co., 1939.
Swem, Earl Gregg. *Virginia Historical Index.* 2 vols. Roanoke, Va.: Designed, printed, and bound by the Stone Printing and Manufacturing Co., 1934-1936.
Wilson, James Grant, and Fiske, John (eds.). *Appleton's Cyclopedia of American Biography.* 11 vols. New York: D. Appleton & Company, 1887.

INDEX

Adams, Charles Francis, 321
Adams, John, writes a defense of the Constitution, 188; defense measures against France, 294-301, *passim;* appoints Davie a brigadier general, 295; popular after "X.Y.Z." Affair, 299; Assembly sends address to, 304-5; sends mission to France, 319-30; in Trenton, 326-8; visits Ellsworth, 327; invites Davie and Ellsworth to dine, 329; instructions to envoys, 330, 340-2; submits French Convention to Senate, 357-8; mentioned, 362
Agricultural Society of S.C., 385
Albemarle section, 151
Alden, John R., cited, 60 n
Alexander, Daniel, 56-7
Alexander, Wallace, 317, 364
Alien and Sedition Acts, 300, 303-4
Alston, Willis, 371-2
Alves, Walter, 245
Amendments to Constitution, 213-5, 217-8
Amis, William, 147
Anderson, Archibald, 58, 62-3
Andrews, A. B., Jr., 239
"Anglo-feds," 357
Annapolis Convention, 178
Anti-Federalists, 149-56, 177 n, 189-218, 200
Archibald, Mr., 266
Aristocracy, in Eastern N.C., 153; defined, 153
Armour's Ford, 80
Armstrong, John, 307, 310-11
Armstrong, Martin, 295, 307-9
Articles of Confederation, 177
Ashe, John Baptiste, at Charleston, 31; invites Washington to dinner, 140; marries Elizabeth Montfort, 152; Federalist leader, joins opposition, 152; in 1784 House of Commons, 161; nominated by Davie for Speaker of House, 172-3; at Fayetteville Convention, 216; U.S. Congressman, 277, 285
Ashe, Samuel, elected Superior Court judge, 159; refuses to try *Bayard* v. *Singleton*, 166-7; effort to drive from bench, 175-6; elected governor, 292; calls out Davie's division, 295; and land frauds, 307, 313; and Tenn. line, 314; mentioned, 292-3
Ashe, Samuel A'Court, cited, 35 n
Ashley Ferry, S.C., 32
Assembly, creates Board of War, 82-3; sets up commissary system, 92-3; abolishes commissary and quartermaster departments, 132; appoints Polk colonel, 108; criticized by Greene, 123; Davie petitions for military expenses, 103, 114, 134-6; appoints Davie commissary general of purchases, 115; Davie pleads to, 116; dominated by Eastern N.C., 151; first meeting in Raleigh, 283; grants loan to University, 230-1; repeals Escheats Act, 269; sends address to John Adams, 304
Assembly (of 1784), 160-72; (of 1787), 190-3; Davie's activities at, 190-3; calls Hillsborough ratification convention, 193; (of 1788), calls second ratification convention, 212-3; (of 1789), 218-21; Davie at, 218-21; (of 1791), 281-3; Davie unpopular in, 281-3; (of 1798), 300-1. *See also* House of Commons and Senate
Assumption Act, 278
Atkins, Rhody, 289, 302
"Atticus," 164
Attmore, William, 191
Augusta, Ga., 31, 93, 114

[477]

INDEX

Austin-Leigh, Mr., cited, 223 n
Avery, Waightstill, 142

Bacon's Bridge, S.C., 32
Baker, Blake, 311, 377
Baldwin, Abraham, 184-5
Baldwin, Alice M., quoted, 9 n
Bancroft, George, cited, 184 n
Barker, Thomas, 139
Barnett, William, 29-30
Barnett's Creek, 79-80
Barras, 326
Barron, James, 335
Barry, John, 330, 332-5
Bath, 141
Battle, Elisha, 154, 193, 201
Battle, Kemp Plummer, quoted, 229, 232, 241, 265, 271 n, 272; cited, 247 n, 258, 260 n
Bayard, James, 358
Bayard v. *Singleton*, 166-9, 175
Bayard, William, Jr., 166
Beaufort, Duke of, 137
Beccaria, 241
Beggar's Ferry, 79
Belk, William Henry, cited, 67 n
Bennehan, Richard, 245, 271, 282-3, 291, 373
Bennehan, Thomas, 146, 161, 255
Bentham, Jeremy, 241
Benton, Samuel, 301
Bertie County, 120
Bethlehem, Pa., 370
Beveridge, Albert, Jr., quoted, 376 n
Bill of Rights. *See* Amendments
Blackguard Hall, 156
Black Swamp, Ga., 31-2
Blaine, Ephraim, 91-3
Blair, Will, 144
Bloodworth, Timothy, sides with conservatives on Loyalist issue, 150; Radical leader, 155; opposes Federal Constitution, 196, 198; at Hillsborough Convention, 204; at Fayetteville Convention, 216; U.S. Congressman, 277; chosen U.S. Senator, 290, 292
Blount, John Gray, Federalist leader, joins opposition, 152-3, 292, 357; Davie writes to, 158-9; letter from William Blount, 179; and coastal defense, 306; and land frauds, 307-8, 311; mentioned, 174, 209, 298
Blount, Thomas, Federalist leader, 152-3; defeated for U.S. Senator, 284; becomes Jeffersonian, 292; and land frauds, 307-8, 311; mentioned, 241, 253
Blount, William, Federalist leader, 152-3; favors paper money, 159; sketch of by William Pierce, 181; at Federal Convention, 179, 186; regarding Davie's rôle at Federal Convention, 189; at Assembly of 1788, 212; becomes Jeffersonian, 292; and land frauds, 307
Blunt, King Tom, 369
Board of War. *See* N.C. Board of War
Bolingbroke, Lord, 226
Bonaparte, Joseph, chosen as French minister to treat with Americans, 337; indisposed, 338; receives American envoys, 338-9; joins Napoleon, 346; dines American envoys, 346-7; confers with Talleyrand, 347-8; heated words of, 348-9; gives fête for Americans, 351-3
Bonaparte, Napoleon, made First Consul, 333; honors Washington, 336; receives envoys, 337; in Italy, 344-5; American proposals submitted to, 346; at fête, 351-3; converses with Davie, 352-3; approves of French Convention, 355; and regard for Davie, 355; mentioned, 38, 115, 347, 358
Boot, B. B., 64
Bordeaux, 335
Boundary lines. *See* Tennessee Line, South Carolina Line
Bourbon restoration, 329-30
Boyd, William Kenneth, cited 210 n
Boylan, William, 328, 361-2
Bradley, John, 95
Brandon, Capt., 43
Bretigny, Marquis of, 125
Briar Creek, Ga., 31
Brice, Francis, 176
Brickell, William, 301
Brown, Thomas, 306
Brown, William Hill, 235-6
Browne, Col., 50-4
Bryan, John, 133
Bryan, Samuel, 43, 44, 49, 51, 156-8
Buchanan, William, 91
Buford, Abraham, 40-1
Burgos, 334-5
Burke County, 43
Burke, Edmund, 280
Burke, Thomas, succeeds Gov. Nash, 115; instructs Davie regarding supplies, 115-21; visits Edenton with Davie, 117; captured by Fanning, 121; breaks parole, 126, 129; works with Davie, 128-30; de-

[478]

INDEX

fended, 129; Davie writes of marriage to, 131; pardons Bryan *et al.*, 157 n, 158; mentioned, 122
Burkett, Lemuel, 154, 196
Burn-Coat road, 117
Burnet, Major, 95
Burr, Aaron, 360
Butler, John, 33, 55, 105, 121, 135

Cabarrus, Stephen, Federalist leader 151; joins opposition, 152; in 1784 House of Commons, 161; defeats Iredell for Assembly of 1787, 190; at Hillsborough Convention, 206; at Fayetteville Convention, 218; speaker of House, 218; Davie buys slaves from, 374
Cabot, George, 326
Caldwell, David, marries Rachel Craighead, 14; beneficiary in William Richardson's will, 23; Radical, Anti-Federalist leader, 154; opposes Federal Constitution, 196; at Hillsborough Convention, 201; mentioned, 27, 28
Caldwell, Joseph, Davie writes about his "Plan of Education," 248-50; and University, 254 n; arrives from Princeton, 255; selected presiding professor, 258-61; praises Davie, 259-60; decides to resign, 264-5; re-elected "presiding professor," 267; proposed as president of College of S.C., 393; mentioned, 263, 271
Calvin's Case, 378
Cambacérès, 352
Camden, battle of, 55-6; Davie's account of Gates's retreat from, 55-8; fugitives from, 62-3; after battle, 65; Cornwallis leaves, 66; Tarleton at, 84-5; British post at, 93; Rawdon at, 107; Greene sets out for, 108; Rawdon evacuates, 113-4; mentioned, 64, 82, 83, 87, 109, 125
Cameron, Duncan, and University, 254 n; handles Gov. Davie's law cases, 302; efforts to raise money for Federalists, 362; defends Davie in Granville Case, 376-9; writes about Federalist party, 387; mentioned, 361, 371
Campbell, Archibald, 31
Campbell, Charles, 59
Campbell, William, 83
Cape Fear section, 121, 151, 306
Capital, 282-3
Capitol, 289-90
Carney, Stephen, 301
Carr, John, 393

Carr, Robert, 13
Carrington, Edward, 96, 99, 104, 110
Carruth, William Richardson, 22
Caswell County, 282
Caswell, Richard, commissions Davie a lieutenant, 29; grants law license to Davie, 35; under Kalb's command, 55; "pop" call at Charlotte, 60-1; reputation impaired after Camden, 83; on Council Extraordinary, 115; pursues enemy in Duplin County, 117; collects stores, 119-20; supplied, 126; Moderate leader, 155-6; speaker of 1784 Senate, 161; reports frauds in army accounts, 173; appoints additional delegates to Federal Convention, 178-9; chosen as delegate to Federal Convention, 178-9; decides not to go, 179; Davie's animosity towards lessens, 180; presents papers concerning Federal Constitution, 193; criticized by Davie, 195; death of, 218-9; mentioned, 189
"Castle, The," home of Allen Jones, 138, 144-5 n
Catawba Indians, 44, 366, 368
Chapel Hill, description of by Davie, 233-4; mentioned, 255, 257, 258, 263, 269. *See also* University of North Carolina
Charleston, Parker's repulse at, 1776, 31; battle of, 32; surrender of, 40, 54; British in, 93; British evacuate, 121, 133; lures western N.C. trade, 150; mentioned, 35, 112
Charlotte, Gates and Caswell at, 60-1; after Camden, 62-3; Davidson takes over at, 65; Sumner takes over at, 66; Cornwallis's first approach to, 69-70; defended by Davie against Cornwallis, 69-74; described by Davie, 70; Davie hovers around, 75-9; Cornwallis leaves, 78-80; Davidson returns to, 80; Davie returns to, 81; Gates moves to, 84; Greene relieves Gates at, 89, 93; Gates's army at, 94; Greene leaves, 104; Davie at, 109-10; hospital at, 118; scarcity of supplies in, 127; mentioned, 42, 45, 56, 58, 88, 97, 368
Cherokee Reservation, 315; Indians, 366
Cheraw Hills, S.C., 44, 104
Chisholm v. *Georgia*, 285-7, 290
Chowan County, 194
Cipritz Bridge, 231-2
"Citizen, The," 164
Clark, Elliott, cited, 137 n
Clark, Thomas, 97 n

[479]

INDEX

Clay, Henry, 389
Cleveland, Benjamin, 83
Clinton, Henry, 33, 40-1, 80, 88, 389
Coastal defense, 305-7
Cobb, Collier, quoted, 230 n
Cockfights, 144-5, 261
College of New Jersey (later Princeton), 24-6, 226
College of South Carolina, 393
Collins, Josiah, 264, 306
Colonel's Creek, 111
Colson's Ferry, N.C., 108-9
Colson's Mill, 65
Columbia, S.C., 368
"Columbus," pen name of William Hill Brown, 236
Commissariat, 94-7, 101
Commissary department, 90-3, 96-7, 131, 132
Commissary general, state, Davie appointed, 150-1; difficulties, 101-2
"Compromise, Great," 182-7
Compromise, Three-Fifths, 187-8
Confiscation laws. *See* Tories
Congress, loses sight of Southern states, 112; Davie and Greene plead to, 112-3; Davie's defeat for, 371-4
Connecticut Compromise. *See* "Great Compromise"
Connor, R. D. W., cited, 61 n; quoted, 228-9
Conservatives, 149-56, 161-6, 172, 172 n
Constitution of 1776 (N.C.), 138, 139, 151, 281, 316
Constitution (U.S.), N.C.'s fight over ratification, 194-218; amendments to, 204-6; N.C. refuses to ratify, 206-7; ratified by N.C., 217-8; proposed amendments to, 217-8
Continental Congress, 90-3, 135-6
Continentals, 83-4, 88, 94-5
Cooley, Doctor, 126
Corn, 382-5
Cornell, Samuel, 166
Corunna, Spain, 334
Cornwallis, Charles, Lord, takes Charleston, 40; moves up from Camden to Waxhaws, 66-7; at Waxhaws, 69; at Charlotte, 69-78; leaves Charlotte after King's Mountain, 78-82; informs Ferguson of Davie, 78; crosses Catawba at Landsford, 84; harassed by Sumter, 85; condemns Davie's cruelties, 88; at Winnsborough, 93; second invasion of N.C., 104-6; at Guilford Court House, 105-7; retreats to Ramsay's Mill, Cross Creek, and Wilmington, 107; threatens to cut off Southern states, 112; at Yorktown, 121; mentioned, 83, 88
Cotton, 382-5
Court reform, 159-60, 294; system, 220
Court of Conference, 313
Court of Patents, 312
Courts of chancery, 290
Council Extraordinary, 135
Coventry, Earl, 376
Cowan's Ford, 108
Cowpens, 104
Craig, James H., 107, 117, 118 n, 121, 123
Craighead, Agnes. *See* Richardson, Agnes Craighead
Craighead, Alexander, 8-10, 9 n, 14, 27
Craighead, Thomas, 23
Crawford, James, 44
Crawford, Robert, 44, 67
Crawford, William H., 391
Crawley, David, 376
Crockett, William R. Davie, 2 n, 353 n, 354 n
Cross Creek. *See* Fayetteville
Cruger, Major, 112
Currency, scarcity of, 122-3
"Cusatti," 164

Dancing, 262-3
Daniel, George, 236
Davidson, Chalmers G., quoted, 37-8 n
Davidson County, Tenn., 192
Davidson, George, 66-7
Davidson, William Lee, as partisan leader, 37-8; appointed brigadier general, 65; writes about Davie at Wauchopes, 69; retreats to Salisbury, 70; praises Davie, 74; retreats beyond Salisbury, 75-6; at Phifer's, 78; hovers around Charlotte, 79; concerning Cornwallis' departure, 79-80; marches to Charlotte, 80; troops under, 83; joined by Morgan and Washington, 84; discharges riflemen, 87; killed at Cowan's Ford, 108; mentioned, 43
Davie, Allen Jones (son), 145-6; 246, 262-3, 393, 394
Davie, Archibald (father), arrival in America, 1-15; early life of, 1-4; acquires land grants, 17-8, 17 n, 18 n; death of wife, 18; mentioned, 19
Davie, Frederick William (son), 385, 393, 396

[480]

INDEX

Davie, Hyder Ali (son), 246, 262-3, 291, 393, 394
Davie, Joseph (brother), 1, 22, 23 n
Davie, Mary (sister), 1, 7, 22, 23 n
Davie, Mary Richardson (mother), 1, 3, 5-7, 8
Davie, Mary Haynes (daughter), 379, 393, 395
Davie, Martha Rebecca (daughter), 379
Davie, Preston (collateral descendant), 2-3 n, 4-5 n, 8 n
Davie, Rebecca (daughter), 393-4
Davie, Sarah (daughter), 273, 379, 393
Davie, Sarah Jones (wife), 130-1, 252, 356
Davie, William Richardson, ancestry and birth of, 1-7; Arms of, 2 n; childhood, 18; mother's death, 18; educated for ministry, 19; beneficiary in uncle's will, 22-3; attends Queen's College, 23-5; attends College of New Jersey, 25-6; first volunteer service in Revolution, 25, 27; studies law, 26, 29; influence of Presbyterian clergy on, 27; second volunteer service in Revolution, 29; commissioned lieutenant, 29; third volunteer service in Revolution, 30; promoted to brigade major, 30; in Pulaski's Legion, 30-2; writes two accounts or sketches of his participation in Revolution, 30; at battle of Stono, 32-5; confined to Charleston hospital, 35; license to practice law, 35; fourth volunteer service in Revolution, 35-6; raises cavalry troop, 36; ranks with Sumter, Marion, and Pickens, 36-9; appraisals of as military leader, 39-40; re-enters army as major, 40; joins Rutherford after Buford's defeat, 42-3; reconnoitres, 43; pursues Tories after Ramsour's Mill, 43; ordered to Waxhaws, 44; appraisal of by Andrew Jackson, 44-5; before Hanging Rock, 45; at Flat Rock, 46-8; his cavalry called "the bloody corps," 50; account of battle of Hanging Rock, 50-4; sets up hospital at Charlotte, 54-5; encounters Gates after Camden, 55-6; Davie's critique of battle of Camden, 57-8; warns and censures Sumter, 56, 58, 59-61; censures Gates and Caswell, 61; leads only active corps, 62-3; first available letter, 63-4; reconnoitres after Camden, 62-7; promoted to colonel, 65; Wauchope's affair, 67-9; defends Charlotte against Cornwallis, 69-75; hovers around Charlotte, 75-80; Cornwallis warns Ferguson of, 78-9; returns to Charlotte, 81; pursues Cornwallis, 82; opinion of N.C. Board of War, 82-3; advances to Landsford, 84; account of Sumter at Fish Dam Ford, 85-7; quoted by Parson Weems, 86-7; complains of desertions, 88; at Salisbury, 88-9; cruelties condemned by Cornwallis, 88; is promised a legion by Smallwood, 89; his corps discharged, 89; Greene urges him as Commissary General, 89, 97-9; censures Whigs and Tories for pillage, 93-94; supplies Southern army at Charlotte, 94; Polk recommends as Greene's commissary general, 97; accepts job, 99; prepares sketches, 99 n; appeals to Board of War, 100; appointed state commissary general, 100-1; problems of supply, 102-3, 106-10; petitions Assembly for salary, 103; rejoins Greene at Guilford Court House, 103-5; establishes depot at Oliphants's Mill, 107; rejoins Greene in S.C., 111; his critique of Hobkirk's Hill, 111; Greene reports great despondency to, 112-3; pleas to Congress, 112-3; dispatched to N.C. Assembly, 114-5; appraisal of Greene, 114-5; appointed state commissary general of purchases, 115; makes plea to Assembly, 116; problems of supply, 115-22; reprimanded by Greene, 123; pressed for supplies, 124-8; urges Greene to effect Burke's release, 129; supplies French troops, 130; marriage, 130-1, 137; supplies to Greene, 132-3; writes Greene for certificate of services, 133-4; final military accounts of, 133-6; appraisal of as commissary general, 136; settles in Halifax, 137-9, 149; builds "Loretta," 137-8; in House of Commons, 1784, 138-9, 160-72; owns "Sir Archy," 146-7; defends Fanning's Tories, 156; defends Bryan et al., 156-8; opposes paper money, 158-62; favors court reform, 159-60; favors stronger Union, 161; favors Tory claims, 162-6; and *Bayard* v. *Singleton*, 166-7; pamphlet dedicated to, 167-9; opposes cession of Western lands, 169-71; nominated for governor, 1785, 172; serves in House of Commons, 1785, 172-6; and Warrenton trials, 174-5; protests against judges, 176; at Federal Convention, 176-89; animosity towards Caswell lessens, 180; writes Iredell three letters, 180; sketch by William Pierce, 181;

[481]

INDEX

ranks second to Williamson, 181; Davie's rôle in the "Great Compromise," 182-7; speech of, 183-4; favors "Three-Fifths Compromise," 188; leaves Federal Convention, 188-9; serves in House of Commons, 1787, 190-3; efforts for ratification of Federal Constitution, 194-218, *passim;* at Hillsborough Convention, 194-207; prepares pamphlet on Federal Constitution with Iredell, 197; and publication of Hillsborough Debates, 208-10; called a scoundrel, 212; at Fayetteville Convention, 215-8; writes Madison regarding N.C.'s adoption of Constitution, 213-4; serves in House of Commons, 1789, 215, 218-21; introduces bill to ratify Constitution of U.S., 217, 277; introduces bill to charter University, 219, 221, 225-8, 277; charters and supports University, 222-76; Pattillo dedicates *Geographical Catechism* to, 223; secures charter for Warrenton Academy, 224-5; Murphey describes, 225-7, 230-1; on University Board of Trustees, 229-76, *passim;* secures loan from Assembly, 230-1; and Davie Poplar, 232; describes Chapel Hill, 233-4; University building commissioner, 234-7; appeals for subscriptions for University, 235-6; donates to University, 235, 244-5; attacked by "Ignoramus," 235; defended by Brown, 235-6; ceremonies at laying of cornerstone of Old East, 237-42; and South Building, 243-4, 256; presents his "Plan of Education" for University, 247-51, Appendix C; and faculty, 250-1, 258-61; and problems of University buildings, 253-8; considered founder of University, 254 n; attacked as a "demigod," 256-7; praised by Joseph Caldwell, 259; deism of, 260-1; vetoes dramatics and gambling at University, 261-2; encourages dancing at University, 262-3; concerned over son's education, 263; elected president of University Board of Trustees, 265; retires to go on French mission, 266; resumes University activities, 268-74; contrasts education in North and South Carolina, 273; decides to move to S.C., 273; parting advice to University, 273-5; Trustees refer to as founder and award him first degree of Doctor of Laws, 275-6; opposes Assumption Act, 279; writes Hamilton regarding Excise Tax, 278-9; and U.S. Bank, 279; attacks Judiciary Act of 1789, 279; declines Federal judgeship, 279; endorses Edmund Burke, 280; favors court reform, 280-1; rated as lawyer by Iredell, 281; serves in House of Commons, 1790, 281-3; John Hamilton threatens duel with, 281; favors return of Tory property, 281-2; opposes new Western counties, 282; favors new Eastern counties, 282; favors internal improvements, 282; and location of capital at Raleigh, 282-3; and his growing family, 283; visits Salem, 283; deplores Martin's victory over Steele for U.S. Senator, 284-5; elected Grand Master of N.C. Masons, 285; upholds Iredell's dissent in *Chisholm* v. *Georgia,* 285-7; writes wife, 287-8; serves in House of Commons, 1793, 288-9; appointed major general of state militia, 288-9; serves in House of Commons, 1794, 289-90; and Eleventh Amendment, 290; suffers attack of pleurisy, 290-1; favors Jay Treaty, 291-2; and sick family, 291; son dies, 291; serves in House of Commons, 1796, 292-4; proposed for Speaker, 292; and address to George Washington, 293; and Roanoke Navigation Company charter, 293-4; appointed brigadier general of U.S. Army, 295-6; proposed for governor, 295-6; aids Washington in selecting officers, 296-8; writes *Instructions to the Cavalry,* 298-9; serves in House of Commons, 1798, 300-1; directs Federalist policy in Commons, 300; as governor, 301-18; and legal practice, 302; influences Assembly to address John Adams, 304; describes N.C.'s reaction to France, 304-5; and military defenses against France, 305-7; prosecutes N.C. and Tenn. land frauds, 307-13; and running of Tenn. line, 313-5; and running of S. C. line, 315-8; resigns as governor to go on French mission, 318; appraisal of his governorship, 318; Raleigh celebration for, 318; French mission of, 319-62; Adams appoints to French mission, 321-2; journey to Trenton, 324-7; dines with Washington, 325; in Trenton, 327-33; dines with Adams, 329; observations regarding France, 331; and instructions from Pickering, Stoddart, and Wolcott, 331-2; and trip to Paris, 332-5; described by

[482]

INDEX

Paris paper, 336; received by Napoleon, 337; received by Joseph Bonaparte, 338; negotiates with French minister, 339-50; dines with Joseph Bonaparte, 346-7; signs French Convention, 351-2; at Joseph Bonaparte's fête, 351-3; and episode with Napoleon, 352-3; sails for home, 353-4; and private affairs in Paris, 354; described by Hubbard and Littlejohn, 354-5; and Napoleon, 354-5; arrives in Washington, 356; arrives in Halifax, 356-7; encounters a changed political situation, 359-60; deplores decline of Federalists, 359-63; meets Macon, 363; and financial affairs, 363-4; serves as commissioner to settle S.C. line, 364-8; refuses Jefferson's appointment to treat with Indians, 368-9; serves as Jefferson's commissioner to treat with Tuscaroras, 369-70; and death of wife, 370, 380; visited by Eli Whitney, 370; and defeat for Congress, 371-4; accused of aristocracy, 371-4; vilifies N.C., 374; property and slaves of 374-6; decides to leave Halifax, 375-6; chief defendant in Granville case, 376-9; takes daughters to Salem, 379; and poor health, 379; retires to Tivoli, 379-81; children scattered, 381; and death of Allen Jones, 381-2; writes Haywood of retirement, sadness, and crops, 379-83; and rheumatism, 382, 385, 394; and crops, 382-5; and Embargo, 383-4; summers at Warm Springs, 385 394-5; continues interest in N.C. politics 385-9; mourns death of Federalist party, 386-7; and hope for revival of Federalist party, 387-90; and opinion of James Madison, 387; criticises War of 1812, 388-91; talk of his commanding U.S. army, 388; proposed for vice president and secretary of war, 388; appointed a major general, 389; criticizes Ghent peace commission, 389; endorses Hartford Convention, 390; criticizes government, 390-2; appointed to S.C. Board of Public Works, 392; and reading, 393; says Jackson born in S.C., 393; and children, 393; last illness, death, and epitaph of, 395-7; estate and will of, 396

Davie Collection, 354

Davie Family, various spellings of name, hatchment, Arms, 1, 2 n, 3, 3 n, arrival in America, 16-7

Davie Poplar, 232
Davies, Samuel, 7-9
Davis, Thomas, 148
Davis, Orondates, 82-3, 89, 100
DeKalb, Baron. *See* Kalb, Johann
Delaware troops, 54, 83-4
Delvaux, Mr., 263-5
de Medici, Cosimo, 138
Democratic-Republicans, 291-3, 320, 347, 356-7, 359-62
DeMond, Robert O., quoted, 50-1 n
"Demos," 373-4
De Saussure, William, 393
Dewey, Stephen, 141
Dialectic Society, 262
Dill, Alonzo T., cited, 192 n
Dobbs, Arthur, 141
Dobbs County, 282
Donelson, Stockley, 308, 311-2
Dorchester, S.C., 32
Drama, 148-9, 261-2
Draper, Lyman C., estimate of Davie, 78-9
Drayton, John, 364-7
Drayton, Stephen, 116
Dukinfield, Nathaniel, 164
Duels, 269, 271
Dunk, George Montagu, 139
Duplin County, 117

Eagle Tavern, Halifax, 148
Eaton, Clement, cited, 153
Eaton, John R., 312
Eaton, Thomas, 105
Edenton, magazines stored at, 102; visited by Davie and Burke, 117; supplies at, 120, 122, 126, 130; social mecca, 139; more politically-minded than Halifax, 145; political center of Albemarle, 151; favors ratification of Constitution, 211, 214-5
Edgecombe County, 139, 142
Edgecombe County, The History of, quoted, 144
Edwards, Isaac, 152
Eleventh Amendment, 285, 290
Elliot, Capt., 47
Elliot, Jonathan, cited, 199, 210 n
Ellsworth, Oliver, at Federal Convention, 185; appointed to French mission, 321; suggests Davie for mission, 322, 323; ready to embark, 324; dreads mission, 326; visited by Adams, 327; in Trenton, 328-33; Pickering, Wolcott, and Stoddert instruct, 331-2; sails for France,

INDEX

332-3; Paris paper describes, 336; received by Napoleon, 337; ill, 353; remains in England, 353-4; resigns as chief justice, 354; mentioned, 220, 351, 358
Elmsley, Alexander, 142
Embargo Act, 383, 386
Enfield, N.C., 141
English settlers, 150
Escheats, 228-9, 230, 256-7, 269
Essex Junto, 357
Established Church, 150
Excise Tax, 278-9

Fairfax case, 376
Falls, Capt., 43
Fanning, David, 121, 156
Fanning, Edmund, 24
Farrand, Max, cited, 186 n
Fauchet, 339
Fayetteville, Cornwallis at, 107; Assembly meets at, 212-3, 218-21, 288; ratification convention at, 215-8; University trustees at, 229, 242-4; judicial district created, 281; Davie in, 287; compared to Raleigh, 289
Federal Constitution, N.C.'s fight over ratification of, 189-218
Federal Convention, N.C.'s rôle in, 177-89; and "Great Compromise," 185-6; Davie's important votes at, 185-8
Federalists, fight for N.C.'s ratification of Federal Constitution, 189-218; riding high, 277; suffer as result of Jay Treaty, 291-3; gain as result of "X.Y.Z." affair, 299-300, 304-5, 319-20; decline of, 359-62; plans for recovery, 360-2; accused of aristocracy, 373-4; refuse to be instructed by Assembly, 362, party dead, 386-7; hope of revival of, 387, 389-91; mentioned, 149-56, 177 n, 283-4, 371, 388-9
Federalist, The, 194, 196
Ferguson, Patrick, 74, 78-9, 85
Fenner, Robert, 125-6
Fifer, Martin, 56
Fish Dam Ford, S.C., 85
Fishing Creek, 59-60
Flat Rock, S.C., 47-8
Flennikin, David, 49
Fleurieu, Charles P. C., 337, 350
Forsyth, Robert, 93, 99, 114
Fort Granby, S.C., 114
Fort Johnston, 306

Fort Motte, S.C., 112, 114
Foster, William Richardson, 22
Foust, Thomas B., 239 n
France, undeclared Naval war with, 294-301, *passim;* N.C.'s reaction to, 304-5; Davie's mission to, 319-62; naval war with, 319-20; invites a second mission, 320; political situation in, 333; commercial relations with, 344
Franklin, Benjamin, 185-6
Franklin, Jesse, 302-3
"Franklin, Lost State of," 171
Frauds, by military commissioners liquidating army accounts, 173-5. See also North Carolina, land frauds; Tennessee, land frauds
Frederick the Great, 115
French Alliance of 1778, 319, 338, 343-4, 346-50, 355
French Convention, title of, 350; signed, 351; Napoleon requests changes in, 351; French and American reaction to, 355-8; submitted to Senate, 357-8; passed, 358
French Directory, 320-1, 326, 333
French mission, and departure of, 327; and procrastination, 338-9; French envoys set out rules, 339-40; Adams' instructions to, 340-2; Americans submit their proposals, 342-5; French reply, 343; at a standstill, 345-6; American proposals sent to Napoleon, 346; Americans make concessions, 347; change in American attitude, 347; and heated words, 348-50; Americans make overtures, 349. See also French Convention
French troops, 130
Frithian, Philip, 24
Funding Act, 278

Gaither, Basil, 308, 311
Gales, Joseph, 328, 361
Galloway, James, 200, 216-7
Garden, Alexander, 30, 39-40, 58, 69
Garden, Major, 50
Gary, Nannie, 148 n
Gaston, William, 6, 139, 152, 356, 376-79, 396
Gates, Horatio, at Rugeley's Mill, 54; arrives at Hillsborough, 55; at Camden, 55; writes Davie, 55; flees from Camden, 55-6; encounters Davie, 55-8; Davie's censure of, 57-8; "pop" call at Charlotte, 60-1; at Hillsborough, 66; upbraids

INDEX

Sumner, 76-7; letters to regarding Cornwallis, 79; Sumner to, 80; reputation gone, 83; army reorganized, 83-4; moves up to Charlotte, 84; relieved by Greene, 89; impresses supplies, 93; at Charlotte, 94; complains of Thomas Polk, 96-7; mentioned, 64, 69, 74, 102, 104, 112

Geddy, John, 195

Gee, James, 370

General Assembly. *See* Assembly

Geographical Catechism, dedicated to Davie, 223, 253

George, Marcus, 262

George Washington (ship), 332

Georgia, 31

Germain, George 41

German settlers, 150

Gerrard, Charles, 267-8

Gerrard Hall, 256, 268

Gerry, Elbridge, 185

Ghent, Treaty of, 389

Gibson, John, 139

Gilberttown, S.C., 79

Gillaspie, James Smiley, 264-5, 267

Gimghoul Castle, 233 n

Gist, Mordecai, 61-2

Glasgow, James, 307, 310-1, 313

Gordon, William, cited, 85, 111, mentioned, 30

Gorham, Nathaniel, 187

Goudy, William, 202

Greene, George Washington, cited, 113 n; quoted, 99 n

Greene, Nathanael, and partisans, 38; arrives in Charlotte, 89; recognizes urgency of army's subsistence, 90; assumes command of Southern Army, 90; purchaser of salt for army, 91; reviews army at Charlotte, 94; finds subsistence deplorable, 95-6; letter to Lafayette, 95; reports destitution of Va. troops to Jefferson, 96; urges Board of War to appoint Davie, 97-9; recommends Davie as commissary general, 100-1; Davie supplies, 102; Davie rejoins at Guilford Court House, 104; leaves Charlotte for Hicks Creek, 104; quoted, 104; strategic retreat of, 104-5; at Guilford Court House, 105-7; en route to Camden, 107-9; at Hobkirk's Hill, 111; reports great despondency to Davie, 112-3; at Eutaw Springs, 121; condition of army, 122-3; reprimands Davie, 122; requisitions of, 126-7; complains of Rutherford, 128; writes Davie regarding supplies, 128; Davie supplies, 132-3; Davie tries to collect from, 133-4; Davie writes to, 161; mentioned, 30, 93, 103, 109, 129

Grady, Henry A., cited, 117

Graham, Joseph, cited, 63, 65; petitions Assembly for Davidson, 65; aids in defense of Charlotte, 70-5; wounded, 74; condemns Davie, 74; quoted, 80; Radical leader, 155; mentioned, 61

Granville County, 66

Granville case, 168, 376-9, 374

Great Britain, 288-92, 347, 388-91

Great Wagon Road, 150

Gregorie, Anne King, quoted, 42 n; cited, 51 n, 52 n

Gregory, Isaac, 55, 126

Grove, William Barry, 151-2, 291, 296, 300, 356

"Groves, The," home of Willie Jones, 138, 153

Guilford County, 66

Guilford Court House, 96, 104-7

"Guilford runaways," 122-3

Hague, The, 320

Halifax, N.C. Board of War at, 89; Davie visits, 100; military stores at, 102, 125-6, 130; Assembly at, 103; Iredell at, 117; Greene passes through, 133; Davie settles in, 137-8, 172, 222; description and history of, 139-49; fairs at, 141-2; cockfights at, 144-5, 261; horseracing at, 145-7; taverns in, 147-8; the drama in, 148-9; political center, 152; heated campaign over Federal Constitution in, 195-6; Constitution of 1776 adopted at, 222-3; Halifax Resolves, 222; Charles Harris in, 261; Davie represents in House of Commons, 281; Masonic celebration in, 285; Gov. Davie's visits to, 302; C. C. Pinckney visits Davie at, 321; and celebration for Davie, 325; Davie returns to, 356-7; celebration, 356-7; haunted by political fears, 360; Davie in, 364; Whitney visits Davie in, 370; Davie decides to leave, 375-6; mentioned, 210; 226, 293, 381

Halifax Division, Davie commanding officer of, 288-9

Halifax, Earl of, 139

Hamilton, Alexander, 158, 277-9, 284, 298, 327, 330

Hamilton, Archibald, 143, 282

[485]

Index

Hamilton, John (Tory), 42, 50-4, 64, 143, 281-2
Hamilton, John (Edenton), 281
Hamilton, J. G. de R., cited, 247 n, 266 n
Hampton, John, defended by Davie, 157-8
Haywood Hall, 302
Haywood, John (Judge), 313
Haywood, John (Treasurer), becomes state treasurer, 173; at laying of Old East cornerstone, 240-1; and University, 243, 252, 253, 255, 256-7, 265, 268, 272-3; death of wife, 260; home of, 302; letter from Davie, 330-1; Davie explains defeat to, 374; Davie writes of retirement, sadness, and crops to, 379-83; Davie writes regarding his possible choice as commander of U.S. army, 388; last letter from Davie, 395-6; mentioned, 136, 250, 281, 292, 303, 313, 335, 393-4
Hanger, George, 71, 72, 73
Hanging Rock, S.C., British establish post at, 41; Davie at, 49; Davie's account of skirmish at, 49-50; battle of, 50-4; mentioned, 44-5, 48, 62, 157
Hannon's Tavern, 325
Hargett, Frederick, 241
Harper, Dr., 45
Harris, Edward, 376
Harris, Charles W., at University, 246, 250-1, 258-9; enters Davie's law office, 261, 325; and letter from Davie, 328; mentioned, 365, 372
Harrisburgh, 110
Harrison, Benjamin, 127
Harrison, William Henry, 115
Hartford Convention, 390
Havre de Grace, 332, 345, 353
Hawkins, Benjamin, 152, 153, 218, 277, 290, 359, 368
Hawkins, John W., 269-71
Hawkins, Philemon, 193, 197
Hay, John, 151-2, 161, 175-6
Heaggins, William, 44
Heitman, F. B., cited, 97 n
Henderson, Archibald (author), cited, 247 n
Henderson, Archibald (lawyer), 232 n, 233 n
Henderson, Richard, 157-8
Henderson, William, 33, 33-4 n
Henry, Patrick, 321-2
Hertford County, 120
Hicks Creek, S.C., 104
Hill, William, 50, 52
Hill, William H., 240

Higgins, William, 44
Hillsborough, Kalb at, 54-5; Gates at, 55, 66, 83-4; rendezvous at after Camden, 63; Continental troops collecting at, 77; Davie's prisoners taken to, 78; Assembly meets at, 82, 130, 161; Davie at, 100; supplies at, 104; Cornwallis retires to, 106; bacon sent to, 110; Burke captured at, 121; Fanning's Tories tried at, 156; ratification convention at, 193-208; University Trustees meet at, 231; land office at, 307, 310; mentioned, 61, 236, 262
Hobkirk's Hill, 111
Hodge, Abraham, 114 n, 148, 208-9, 361-2
Hodge, Philemon, 255
Hogg, James, 234, 255, 262-5, 376
Holmes, Samuel, 263
Hooper, George, 151, 165, 172
Hooper, William, 129, 151, 164-5, 190, 225
Hopkins, Samuel, 246, 256, 269-71
Horry, Daniel, 32
Horse-racing, 145-7
Hôtel Casa Nova, 337
Hôtel des Oiseaux, 337, 351
Hot Springs. See Warm Springs
House of Commons, 172-6, 281-3. See also Assembly
Howe, Robert, 31
Hubbard, Fordyce M., describes Davie, 354; cited, 56, 157 n, 385; quoted, 24 n, 88-9, 102, 136, 227, 370
Huger, General, 56
Hunt, Memucan, 173
Hunter, Isaac, 207
Hunter, Theophilus, 318
Huske, John, 215

"Ignoramus," 235
Indemnities, and France, 347-50
"Independent Citizen, An," 167-9
Industry (ship), 125
Inflation. See Paper money
Instructions to the Cavalry, by Davie, 298-9
Internal improvements, 282, 293
Iredell, James, has high opinion of Davie, 117; Burke maintains confidence of, 129; disgruntled with Halifax, 144; Federalist leader, 151; drafts court reform bill, 159; elected Superior Court judge, 159; favors Tory claims, 164; and *Bayard* v. *Singleton*, 166-9; and Warrenton trials, 174-5; and elections to Federal Convention, 178; letters from Davie, 180, 188-9;

[486]

INDEX

defeated for Assembly, 190; identified as "Marcus," 194; at Hillsborough Convention, 194-207; efforts for ratification of Federal Constitution, 194-218, *passim;* prepares pamphlet on Federal Constitution with Davie, 197; responsible, with Davie, for publication of Hillsborough Debates, 208-10; interest in University, 225; appointed Associate Justice of U.S. Supreme Court, 277; rates Davie as lawyer, 281; dissents in *Chisholm* v. *Georgia,* 285-7; death of, 359; mentioned, 140, 143, 148, 216, 220, 227, 279, 281, 290, 292, 293, 299, 300, 323, 325

Iredell, Thomas, 143

Irwin, Robert, 48-9, 50-2, 65

Jackson, Andrew, 28, 44-5, 307, 393
Jackson, Hugh, 35
Jackson, Robert, 44
Jacocks, Charles, 371-3
Jacocks, W. P., cited, 369 n
James Island, S.C., 133
James, William D., cited, 52 n
Jay, John, 285-6, 291-2
Jay Treaty, 291-2, 319
Jefferson, Thomas, Greene reports destitution of Va. troops to, 96; Davie asks for supplies, 106; accuses Hooper of Toryism, 151; Willie Jones cites as authority, 204-5; N.C. votes for, 1796, 292; and Alien and Sedition Acts, 303; and presidential election, 347; commissions Ellsworth, 358; election of, 359-62; appoints Davie to treat with Indians, 368-9; appoints Davie to treat with Tuscarora Indians, 369; mentioned, 152, 248, 293, 320, 383, 386
Jenifer, Daniel, 184
Jensen, Merrill, cited, 177 n
Johnson, Charles, 216, 218, 229
Johnson, Victor Leroy, cited, 90-1 n
Johnson, William, cited, 99 n, 113 n; quoted 102-3, 106
Johnson, William Samuel, 220
Johnston, Frances Benjamin, cited, 138 n
Johnston, Gabriel, 152
Johnston, John, 136, 218
Johnston, Samuel, describes specific tax, 102; has high opinion of Davie, 117; Burke maintains confidence of, 129; describes Washington's reception, 140; on horse-racing in Halifax, 145; Federalist leader, 151; favors Tory claims, 164-5; and *Bayard* v. *Singleton,* 166-9; elected governor, 190-1; efforts for ratification of Federal Constitution, 194-218, *passim;* at Hillsborough Convention, 194-207; at Fayetteville Convention, 215-8; re-elected Governor, 218; elected first U.S. Senator, 218, 277; interest in education and University, 225; resigns as U.S. Senator, 284; denounces Jay Treaty, 291; directs Federalist policy, 300-1; describes reaction to Va. and Ky. Resolutions, 303; retires, 359; mentioned, 122, 153, 209, 220

Jones, Allen (father-in-law), Davie serves under, 29; 900 men under, 83; at Providence, 84; on Council Extraordinary, 115; Burke maintains confidence of, 129; daughter marries Davie, 130-1; home of, 138, 142, 144-5 n; opposes Tory confiscations, 166; Federalist leader, 152; marries Miss Edwards, 152; on committee to draft Constitution of 1776, 223; interest in education, 225; and Davie buy lands, 375; Davie sells lands to, 376; Davie's grief at death of, 381; mentioned, 139, 252 n, 332, 377

Jones, Calvin, 370
Jones, Edward, 311
Jones, John Paul, 330
Jones, Robert, 139, 152
Jones, Willie, and Burke, 129; uncle of Sarah Jones Davie, 131; sells lot to Davie, 137; home of, 138; a deist, 139; private race track of, 146; sides with Conservatives on Loyalist issue, 150; Radical, Anti-Federalist leader, 153-4; protests Tory treatment, 163-5; military commissioner to liquidate army accounts, 173; chosen delegate to Federal Convention, 178; declines, 178-9; efforts to prevent ratification of Federal Constitution, 195-218; proposes site for capital, 207; effigy of burned, 211; pamphlet attacks, 211-2; his reply, 212; at Hillsborough Convention, 194-207; at Fayetteville Convention, 215-8; on committee to draft Constitution of 1776, 222; interest in education, 225; and University, 231-2, 235-6, 259, 263-4, 266; defended by Brown, 235-6; George Washington writes to regarding University, 266; resigns as Trustee, 267; visits Salem with Davie, 283; influence on Macon, 293; chosen president of Roanoke

[487]

INDEX

Navigation Co., 294; champions Gales, 361; mentioned, 144, 152, 155, 292
Jones, Willie William, 267
Judicial review, 166-9
Judiciary Act of 1789, 279
Judiciary Act of 1801, 362
Judges, 175-6, 220

Kalb, Johann, 54-5
Keith, Alice B., cited, 159 n, 209 n
Kendall, Amos, 40, 48 n
Ker, David, 243, 246, 250-1
Kerr, Mr., 64
Kinchen, John, 157-8
King, James, 311
King, Rufus, 386-7, 388
King's Mountain, 78-9
Kingston (Kinston), 83, 117, 121, 125
Knoxville, 308

Lacey, Edward, 50
Lafayette, 38, 119, 351
Lam, Elija, 308
Lamb, John, 198
Lamb, Sergeant, quoted, 106
Lancaster Courthouse, 367
Land frauds. *See* North Carolina, Tennessee
Landsford, S.C., 50, 82, 84, 94
Lane, Joel, 283
Lee, Arthur, 326
Lee, Charles, 328
Lee, "Light Horse Harry," writes *Memoirs*, 30; tells of Davie after Camden, 58; eluded by Watson, 111; retreat of, 112; cited, 33 n, 35 n, 50, 52 n, 69 n, 70, 85, 111, 113 n, quoted, 29-30, 54, 84, 94, 106
Lefler, Hugh T., cited, 198 n
Leigh, John, 284, 292
Lenoir, William, 155, 283
Leslie, James, 139
Leslie, Alexander, 104
Letombe, 355
Liberty Hall. *See* Queen's College
Lillington, Alexander, 117, 126
Lincoln, Benjamin, 31-4, 40, 54
Lincoln County, 43
Lisbon, 333
Littlejohn, Joseph B., 325, 354-5
Locke, Francis, 43, 65, 95, 108, 308-9
Locke, George, 72
Locke, Matthew, 155

Logan, Charles, 356
Logtown, S.C., 111
Long, George W., 147
Long, Nicholas, 125, 126, 142-3
Long, Polly, 143
"Loretta," 137-8, 374-5
L'Orient, France, 332-3
Lorimer, Mr., 208, 210
Louis XVIII, 328-9
Louisiana, 320
L'Ouverture, Toussaint, 370
Loyalists. *See* Tories
Lutherans, 150
Lutrell, John, 103
Lynch's Creek, S.C., 84, 87, 109

Macay, Spruce, 28-9, 224, 237, 238-41
McAlpine's Creek, 69-70
McArthur, Archibald, 44, 74
McCafferty, William, 79-80
McCauley, fight with Hooper, 190
McCorkle, Samuel Eusebius, drafts earlier bill to charter University, 224; given credit by Davie, 237; at laying of Old East cornerstone, 240; address of 241-2; not chosen "Presiding Professor" of University, 243; draws up University by-laws, 244; his plan of education for University, 247; professor at University, 250-1; ousted from faculty, 251-2; mentioned, 323 n
McCrady, Edward, cited, 52 n, 113 n
McCullock, Capt., 54 n
McCulloh, Alexander, 139, 143, 173
McCulloh, Henry, 164, 268
McCulloh, Benjamin, 173-5
McDonald, Donald, 41
McDowell, Charles, 83
McDowell, Joseph, 155, 196, 202-3, 205-6
McHenry, James, 295-7, 300, 323 n, 326
McJunkin, Joseph, 51 n
Mackinzie, Roderick, 30, 70
Maclaine, Archibald, Conservative leader, 151; favors Tory claims, 164-5; and pamphlet dedicated to Davie, 166-7; writes George Hooper regarding Davie, 172; prefers charges against judges, 176; efforts to ratify Federal Constitution, 194; identified as "Publicola," 194; at Hillsborough Convention, 204; efforts for second ratifying convention, 210; at Fayetteville Convention, 217; death of, 359; mentioned, 197, 209

[488]

INDEX

McLaughlin, Andrew C., cited, 184 n, 186 n
McLean, John, 259
McNairy, John, 308
MacNeal, Capt., 64
McNeill, Capt, 345-6, 355
McNeill, Daniel, 176
Macon, John, 173-5
Macon, Nathaniel, votes against address to Washington, 293; scoffs at aristocracy, 359; invites Gales to Raleigh, 361; meets Davie, 363; tries to see Davie, 368; reports Davie in good health, 370; quoted, 155-6, 372
McRee, Griffith J., quoted, 172, 174, 175, 194, 210; cited, 218 n, 219, 306
McWhorter, Alexander, 42
Madison, James, report of Davie's speech, 183; regarding Davie, 187; receives letter from Jefferson regarding amendments to Constitution, 205; leads movement for Bill of Rights, 213-4; and Alien and Sedition Acts, 303; Davie's opinion of, 387; mentioned, 371, 385-6
Main Building. *See* South Building
Maitland, Lieutenant Colonel, 33-4
Malmedy, Francis, 33-4
Mangum, Willie P., quoted, 156
Marbury v. *Madison*, 167
"Marcus," 194
Marengo, 346
Marion, Francis, 36-7, 39-40, 85, 88, 111
Marshall, John, 61 n, 167, 347, 348, 356, 378-9
Martignor, Mr., 306
Martin, Alexander, appointed to N.C. Board of War, 82; Davie's opinion of, 82-3; Davie visits, 100; on Council Extraordinary, 115; succeeds Burke, 121; Davie criticizes, 122; and supplies, 125, 132-3; aids Greene, 126-7; and Davie's pay as commissary general, 135; Moderate leader, 155-6; suspected of being "Cusatti," 164; chosen delegate to Federal Convention, 178-9; sketch of by William Pierce, 181; at Federal Convention, 186; elected Governor, 218; urges education, 223; retires as governor, 283; chosen U.S. Senator, 284; Davie's ridicule of, 299; "wonderfully Federal," 300-1; loses U.S. Senate race, 302-3; mentioned, 130, 164, 170, 188, 230, 280
Martin, Capt., 43, 56, 58-9
Martin, Luther, 184

Martinique, 125
Maryland troops, 54, 58, 83-4
Mason, David, 33-4
Mason, George, 194
Masons, 137, 239, 285, 396
Massena, General, 344
Matthews, Mussendine, 300
May's Mill, 109
Mebane, Alexander, 241
Mecklenburg County, 62, 64-5, 75, 94, 110
Merchant marine, 319
Mifflin, Thomas, 91
Miller, Robert, 12-3
Milner, James, 137
Money, scarcity of, 124
Monroe, James, 385-6, 391
Monroe Doctrine, 344
Montfort, Elizabeth, 152
Montfort, Henry, 173-5
Montfort, Joseph, 137
Montford, Mary, 137
Moore, Alfred, prosecutes Fanning's Tories, 156; prosecutes Bryan *et al.*, 157-8; and *Bayard* v. *Singleton*, 166-9; prosecutes in Warrenton trials, 174-5; favors Federal Constitution, 197; compared with Davie, 225-6; and University, 225-6, 240, 254; Iredell rates as lawyer, 281; defeated for U.S. Senator, 290, 292, 302-3; becomes Superior Court Judge, 302-3; Adams appoints to U.S. Supreme Court, 303 n; a commissioner to run S.C. line, 316-8; mentioned, 301
Moore, James, 42
Moore, John, 367
Moore, Stephen, 295
Moore's Creek Bridge, battle of, 41
Moore's Plantation, N.C., 121
Moravians, 288
Morfontaine, 351-3. *See also* French Convention
Morgan, Daniel, 76-7, 79, 84-5, 88-9, 104
Morganton, 281
Morris, Gouvernour, 187
Morris, Robert, 128
Moseley, William D., 232
Most-favored-nation clause, 348-50
Moultrie, William, 30, 32, 316
Mountflorence, Gaven C., 354
Mountflorence, James Cole, 89, 125, 134, 216-7
"Mount Gallant," 144-5 n
Mount Vernon, 325
"Mowfield," 147

Index

Murfreesborough, 236
Murphey, Archibald D., 226-7, 230-1, 337 n
Murray, William Vans, 320-3, 333, 336-7, 351, 358

Napoleon. *See* Bonaparte, Napoleon
Nash, Abner, and Gates's defeat, 61; appoints Davie colonel, 65; recommends creation of Board of War, 82; and Davie's legion, 89; issues warrants to Davie, 103; letter from Greene, 107; Davie criticizes, 122; Moderate leader, 155-6; and *Bayard* v. *Singleton*, 166-9; mentioned, 24, 115, 136
Nashville, Tenn., land, office at, 307
Naval war with France, 294-301, *passim*
Navy Department, 295, 319
Neel, Andrew, 42, 48
Neilson, A., 117
"New Acquisition," 315
Newbern, Craig's march to, 118-9; Davie attends court at, 191; Academy, 224; dancing teacher at, 262-3; Davie attends court at, 283; Davie made Grand Master of N.C. Masons in, 285; last Assembly meets at, 289; compared to Raleigh, 289; mentioned, 118, 120, 125-6, 133, 209, 211, 282
New Currituck, 118
New Hope Chapel Hill, 232-3
New Orleans, battle of, 390
Newport, envoys sail from, 332
New River, General, 44
Newsome, Albert Ray, 210 n
New York, Davie in, 332
Ninety-Six, S.C., 82, 93, 111, 114, 134
North Carolina, militia, 55, 63; political scene in 1776-83, 149-56; sectionalism in, 150-1, rôle in Federal Convention, 177-89; and fight over ratification of Federal Constitution, 194-218, *passim;* religion in, 260; reaction to Hamilton's financial measures, 277-9; rejects Va. and Ky. Resolutions, 303; land frauds, 307-13; Davie vilified, 374; Davie's continued interest in politics in, 385-9
North Carolina, University of. *See* University of North Carolina
North Carolina Board of War, 82-3, 93, 97-8, 100-1, 103, 115, 118
North Carolina Board of Trade, 119
North Carolina Council Extraordinary, 115

North Carolina General Assembly. *See* Assembly
North-Carolina Gazette, 148
North-Carolina Journal, quoted, 144
North-Carolina Minerva, quoted, 333
North East Bridge, 121
Norfolk, Virginia, 140-1
Nut-bush, N.C., 121, 164
Nunn, Hugh, 269

Occoneechee Neck, 138
Ocracock, 306-7
Old Chapel. *See* Person Hall
Old East Building, 236-7, 237-42, 246
Old Nation Ford, 80-2
Olds, Fred A., cited, 223 n
Oliphant's Mill, 102, 107-8, 118
Orange County, 66
Orangeburgh, S.C., 114
Osborn, Adlai, 153
Over-mountain men, 79

Painted Rock, 314
Pamphlets, 164, 167-8, 194, 197-8, 211
Paper money, 94-5, 158-62, 280
Paris, 332, 355-6. *See also* Treaty of Paris
Parker, Peter, 31
Partisans, 37-8
Party organization, 149-56
Paschal, Herbert R., cited, 369 n
Patterson, James, 235-6, 238, 246, 253
Pattillo, Henry, 8, 27, 222-3, 225
Pendleton, Edmund, 154
Penn, John, 76, 82-3, 100, 154, 157-8
Perrin, Mr., 263
Person Hall, 226, 246, 254-6
Person, Thomas, complains of commissary department, 131-2; Radical leader, 154-5; opposes Constitution, 193, 196, 198, 200, 207; holds out against ratification, 211; effigy of burned, 211; tries to prevent second ratification convention, 212; gift to University, 254-6
Petersburg, Va., 150, 325
Petit, Capt., 46-7
Phifer, Caleb, 155
Phifer's plantation, 70-4, 77, 78
Philadelphia Wagon Road, 16-7
Philadelphia, yellow fever in, 325
Philanthropic Society, 262
Pichon, Louis André, 320, 339, 355
Pickens, Andrew, 36-7, 39-40, 68, 385

INDEX

Pickering, Timothy, Davie writes concerning "X.Y.Z." affair, 300; writes Davie of French mission, 322-4; urges suspension of French mission, 326-7; instructions to envoys, 330-1; envoys write to, 333-4, 344; sends ship for envoys' return, 345-6; replaced by John Marshall, 347
Pierce, William, 181
Pinckney, Charles Cotesworth, 184, 296-8, 306-7, 321, 387
Pitt, William, 330
Playmaker's Theater, 230 n
Poinsett, Joel R., 392
Political scene in North Carolina, 1776-83, 149-56
Political parties, nomenclature of, 177 n
Polk, Thomas, 60, 65, 96-7, 108
Polk, William, 46-7, 390
Ponton, Doctor, 149
Pool, William C., cited, 199
"Poplar Spring," 17
Porterfield, William, 55
Portsmouth (ship), 345, 353-4
Potter, John, 378-9
Potts, Joshua, 110
Presbyterians, 27, 150, 222-3
Prevost, Augustine, 31-2
Prevost, Mark, 31
Price, Jonathan, 316, 364-5
Prince's Bridge, 231
Providence, N.C., 66, 84, 88, 94
Princeton, 255, 258. *See also* College of New Jersey
Publicisse (Paris newspaper), 336
"Publicola" (Archibald Maclaine), 194
Puente d'Eume, 334
Pulaski, Casimir, 30, 32-3
Purviance, Samuel D., 311-2
Purysburg, Ga., 31-2

Quankey, 375-6
Quartermaster department, 95-6, 109-10, 130-2
Queen's College (also called Queen's Museum and Liberty Hall), 23-5, 222-4, 226
Quincy, 326-7

Radicals, 149-56, 161-6, 169-71, 177 n
Raleigh, site for chosen, 207; University Trustees meet at, 244, Caldwell meets Davie in, 259-60; location of capital at, 282-3; 1794 Assembly meets there, 288-90; compared to New Bern and Fayetteville, 289; Assembly of 1796 meets in, 292-4; attempt to burn capitol, 308; celebration honoring Davie, 318, 324-5; Davie meets Tuscaroras at, 369; Granville case tried at, 378-9
Raleigh Register, 361
Ramsay, Alexander, 30
Ramsay's Mill, 107
Ramsour's Mill, 40-1, 41-4
Randolph, Edmund, 187
Randolph, John, 385-6, 391
Randolph Plan, 180
Randolph-Semple house, 138
Ratification conventions. *See* Hillsborough, ratification convention at; Fayetteville, ratification convention at
Rawdon, Lord, 43, 107, 111-4
Read, James, 97 n
Religion in N.C., 260
"Revolution of 1800," 356-7, 359
Richards, William Augustus, 262-5
Richardson, Agnes Craighead, 8, 14, 19-21
Richardson, James B., 367
Richardson, William (maternal uncle), education and early life of, 5, 6; early ministry of, 7-11; minister at Waxhaw Presbyterian church, 11-5; description of by Woodmason, 12; marriage, 14; resides at "Poplar Spring," 16; care and education of Davie, 18; strange death of, 19-22; will of, 22-3; trustee of Queen's College, 222-3; mentioned, 27, 154
Roanoke River and Valley, 140, 144-7, 152
Roanoke Navigation Company, 293-4
Robbins, William M., cited, 108 n
Robinson, Blackwell P., cited, 257 n
Robinson, Mr., 208
Rockfish Creek, 121
Rocky Mount, S.C., 41, 44, 48-50, 59, 110
Roederer, Pierre Louis, 337, 347-8, 350
Rowan County, 27-8, 43, 64-5, 75, 110
Rowan, Matthew, 152
Royal White Hart Lodge, 285
Rugeley's Mill, 54, 64
Rum, 122-3, 125-6, 172
Russell, Jonathan, 389
Rutgers v. *Waddington*, 158
Rutherford, Griffith, as partisan leader, 37-8; orders out militia after Buford's defeat, 42-3, late at battle of Ramseur's Mill, 43; orders Davie below Charlotte,

[491]

INDEX

44; brigade at Camden, 57-8; after Camden, 64; supplies for, 121; criticizes Davie, 124-5; Greene complains of, 128; Radical leader, 155; opposes Tory claims, 164; mentioned, 65

Rutledge, John, 41, 85, 88

St. Clair, Arthur, 125, 129
St. Mary (parish of), 142
Salem College, 156, 273, 283, 379
Salisbury, description of, 27-8; Davie studies law in, 27-9; used as hospital after Camden, 62-3; Sumner and Davidson retreat towards, 70; Davie at, 75, 77, 88-9, 108, 127; Morgan and Washington reach, 84; and supplies at, 104, 110, 116, 127, 130; trial of Bryan *et al.* at, 156-8; Academy, 224; mentioned, 211
Salt, 95, 118-20, 122, 126-7
Saura Town, 118
Savannah, 31-2
Schenck, David M., quoted, 107-8 n
Schism Act, 6
Scotland-Neck Volunteer Company, 295
Scots, Highland, 107
Scots, Ulster, 150, 222-3
Scuppernong Lake, 375
Sectionalism, in N.C., 150-1
Senate, approves French Convention, 357-8
Senf, Colonel, 60
Seven Creeks, 121
Sevier, John, 83, 277, 307-9, 314
Sharpe, William, 223-4, 237
Shelby, Isaac, 83
Sherman, Roger, 184 n
Simmons, Capt., 43
Simpson, Archibald, 5, 5 n, 7, 10-1, 21-2
Sitgreaves, John, 152, 190-1, 197, 209, 263, 279-80, 335
Sitgreaves, Sallie, 191
Six Mile Creek, 84
Slaves, 290, 294, 370, 374-5
Smallwood, William, 61-3, 76-7, 83-4, 87-9, 94, 96
Smith, Benjamin, 190, 217, 229-30, 300
Smith Hall, 230 n
Smith, Samuel Stanhope, 259
Smyth, J. F. D., quoted, 138; cited, 144-5 n, mentioned, 140, 142-3
South Building, 243-4, 253-4, 256-8
South Carolina, 32, 33, 41, 56, 61-2, 273
South Carolina, Agricultural Society of, 385

South Carolina, College of, 393
South Carolina Line, running of, 315-8, 364-8
Specie, 95
Specific Provision Act, 101-2, 130
Spaight, Richard Dobbs, Federalist leader, 153; delegate to Federal Convention, 178-9; sketch of by William Pierce, 181; votes against "Great Compromise," 186; memorial of, 192; and University, 255, 258; elected governor, 283; appoints Davie a major general, 288-9; calls special Assembly, 289; and coastal defense, 306; and S.C. line, 316; joins Jeffersonians, 300, 357
Spencer, Cornelia Phillips, 232
Spencer, Samuel, signs Davie's law license, 35; Radical, Anti-Federalist leader, 154; presides over Bryan's trial, 157-8; elected Superior Court judge, 159; presides over *Bayard v. Singleton*, 166-9; attacked as judge, 176; opposes Federal Constitution, 196; at Hillsborough Convention, 203-6; effigy of burned, 211; at Fayetteville Convention, 216; and federal judgeship, 220-1
State House. See Capitol
Stedman, Charles, quoted, 74, 106; cited, 71 n; mentioned, 30
Steele, John, Federalist leader, 153; at Hillsborough Convention, 206; at Fayetteville Convention, 216; and McCorkle's ousting from University, 251-2; U.S. Congressman, 277; defeated for U.S. Senate, 284; appointed Comptroller General of U.S. Treasury, 285; and French mission, 323; and Davie reconciled, 330-1, 332; accepts Federal appointment, 359; letters from Davie, 359-60, 363-4, 373; replaces Davie as commissioner on S.C. line, 368; mentioned, 146, 209
Stephenson, Turner, 138 n
Stevens, Edward, 55
Stewart, David, 266
Stoddert, Benjamin, 326, 335
Stokes, John, 152, 164, 280
Stokes, Montfort, 164, 284
Stone, David, 300
Stone Mountain, 313-4
Stono, battle of, 32-5
Suffolk, Va., 140-1
Sugar Creek, 70, 81-2
Sullivant, William, 375
"Sully," suspected of being Davie, 164

INDEX

Sumner County, Tenn., 192
Sumner, Jethro, at Charleston, 31; at Stono, 33-4; as partisan leader, 37-8; at Charlotte, 61, 66; below Charlotte, 69; writes about Davie at Wauchopes, 69; retreats to Salisbury, 70; retreats beyond Salisbury, 75-6; upbraided by Gates, 76-7; reports to, 78-9; and Cornwallis's leaving Charlotte, 79-82; troops under, 83; at Providence, 84; commands "Guilford runaways," 122-3; presses Davie for supplies, 125
Sumter, S.C., 64
Sumter, Thomas, as partisan leader, 36-40; joins Rutherford's militia, 42; at Charlotte, 45, 61-2; council with Davie, 48; at Rocky Mount, 48; at Hanging Rock, 50-4; warned by Davie, 56, 58-9; at Fishing Creek, 59-60; defeat of, 66; pursues Tarleton, 81-2; harasses Cornwallis, 85; promoted to brigadier general, 85; rendezvous at Fish Dam Ford, 85; skirmish, with Wemyss, 85-7; refuses to obey Greene, 112
Supplies, in Revolution, 93-7, 105-7, 123-4, 130, 132-3
Supreme Court, of Conference, 160; of N.C., 160
Surry County, 110
Sutherland, Ransom, 337 n
Suvarov, 329 n
Swain, David L., quoted, 376
Swift, Dean, 262

Tagus River, 333
Talleyrand, invites a second mission to France, 320; advised of envoys' appointments, 322; assures proper reception, 323; envoys write to, 334, 336, 339; instructs French ministers, 337-8; ill, 344; sends courier to Napoleon, 345; delivers French Convention to Napoleon, 352; presents American envoys to Napoleon, 353; approves of French Convention, 355; mentioned, 333, 347-8
Tarborough, 102, 121, 190, 211
Tarleton, Banastre, writes history of campaigns, 30; defeats Buford, 40-1; "Tarleton's quarter," 40-1; swings back to Camden, 42; legion at Hanging Rock, 50-4; legion of, 56, 59-60, 63-4; attacked by Davie at Wauchopes, 67-9; at Charlotte, 70-5; describes hostility of Mecklenburg and Rowan counties, 75; crosses Old Nation Ford, 81; withdraws to Winnsborough, 84; pursues Marion, 85, 88; at Camden, 87; pursues Morgan, 104
Tatum, Howell, 268, 308
Taverns, 147-8
Taxes, state, 101-2
Taylor, John, 75-7, 246
Tennent, William, 9
Tennessee, lands of Davie, 375; land frauds, 307-13
Tennessee Line, running of, 313-5
Tennessee. See Western lands
Tillery, Junius, 138
"Tivoli," 364, 367, 376, 379-80, 396
Tories, at Moore's Creek Bridge, 41; at Ramsour's Mill, 41-4; cleared west of Catawba River, 44-5; after Camden, 63; in Cornwallis' army, 67; Davie's prisoners sent to Hillsborough, 78; in Duplin, 17-8; feeling towards, 143; trials of, 156-8; claims of, 162-6; sale of property, 165-6; and return of property, 281-2; mentioned, 31, 112
"To the People of the State of North Carolina," 197-8
Tracy, Uriah, 323
Treaty of Paris, 162-6
Trenton, N.J., 252, 325-7
Trevett v. *Weeden*, 167
Trumbull, Joseph, 91
Tryon, William, 24, 152, 156, 164
Tryon's Palace, 192, 289
Tuckasegie Ford, 77
Tuileries, 337
Tulifinny Bridge, S.C., 32
Turnbull, Col., 64
Turner, James, 367
Turner, Nat, 370
Tuscarora Indians, 369-70
Tyrrell County, 376
Tyrell, William, 308, 311-2
Tyson, Thomas, 228

United States Bank, 279, 391
United States Constitution. See Constitution (U.S.)
United States (ship), 330, 332
University of North Carolina, Davie introduces bill to charter, 219, 221, 225-8; founding and early history of, 222-76; accused of being aristocratic, 228, 257; arrearages and escheats awarded to, 228-9; donation of land to, 229-30;

[493]

INDEX

escheats, 230; loan of £5000 to 230-1; subscriptions for, 235-6; laying of cornerstone, 237-42; sale of lots, 237-8, 240, 242; "Presiding Professor" of chosen, 243; books and curios presented to by Davie, 244-5; complaints against food, 246-7; Davie's "Plan of Education" for, 247-51, Appendix C; curriculum, 247-51; described by Pattillo, 253; opening of, 255; faculty and staff, 258-61; dramatics at, 261-2; no gambling at, 262; dancing at, 262-3; student rebellion at, 265-6, 272-4; duels at, 269-71; expenses at, 270; student regulations at, 270-1; Davie's parting advice to, 273-5; refers to Davie as "Founder" and confers first honorary degree on him, 275-6; Davie's continued interest in, 393. *See also* Chapel Hill, University Trustees

University Trustees, provided for in charter, 227; state arrearages vested in, 228-9; escheats vested in, 228-9; Board meets, 229-30, 231, 242-4; finance committee, 230; choose site of University, 231-3; building committee, 234-7, 243-6; faculty committee, 243; approve Davie's "Plan of Education," 250; ballot for faculty, 250-1; building committee and its problems, 253-8; Davie president of, 265

Van Schellebeck and Marshall, Newbern merchants, 125
Vattel, 348
Virginia troops, 55, 84
Virginia, N.C. a slave to, 140-1, 374; Davie anxiety over Federal Constitution in, 196, 198; University of, 248; politics in, 385-6; mentioned, 389, 391
Virginia and Kentucky Resolutions, 303
Virginia Plan, 180, 183

Wahab. *See* Wauchope
Wahub. *See* Wauchope
Waddell's Academy, 393-4
Wade, Thomas, 109
Wadsworth, Jeremiah, 91
Wagstaff, Henry McGilbert, 261 n
Walkup. *See* Wauchope
War of 1812, 388-91
Warren County, 110
Warrenton Academy, 224-5, 262
Warrenton trials, 174-5

Warm Springs (now Hot Springs), 283, 385, 394-6
Washington, Bushrod, 296-8
Washington, N.C., 209
Washington, George, describes Halifax, 140; attacked in pamphlet, 212; writes Willie Jones regarding University, 266; appoints Iredell Associate Justice of U.S. Supreme Court, 277; Assembly addresses, 293; commands new army against France, 295-8; Davie sends *Instructions to the Cavalry* to, 299; Davie dines with, 325; Paris fête honoring death of, 335-6; and neutrality, 344; mentioned, 91, 122
Washington, William, 84, 88
Waterman, Thomas T., cited, 138 n
Watson, Elkanah, quoted, 140
Watson, John, 111
Watters, Henry, 264
Wauchope, James, 67-9
Wauchope, Margaret Pickens, 68
Waxhaw Presbyterian Church, 11-13, 41, 396. *See also* Woodmason, Charles
Waxhaws (S.C.), 1, 11-2, 40-1, 44, 62, 66-7, 84, 87, 110-1
Weeks, Stephen Beauregard, cited, 299
Weems, Parson Mason L., 86-7
Wellborn, James, 367
Wemyss, James, 85-7
Western counties, division of, 282
Western lands, cession of, 169-71
Whiskey, 120. *See also* Rum
Whitaker, John, 268
White, Nicholas, 157-8
White, William, 310
Whitefield, George, 9
Whitney, Eli, 370
Wilkes County, 110, 282
Wilkinson, James, 368
Williams, Benjamin, 152, 301, 364-8, 370, 377
Williams, John, 156, 157-8, 164, 166-9, 176, 241, 243-4, 258
Williams, Otho, 83-4, 129
Williams, Robert, 275-6, 357
Williams, Samuel C., quoted, 51
Williamsborough, 125, 267
Williamson, Hugh, Federalist leader, 151; opposes cession of Western lands, 170-1; arrives at Annapolis Convention too late, 178; at Federal Convention, 179-81, 186; regarding Davie's rôle at Federal Convention, 188-9; hopes Federalist win election, 190; efforts in ratification

[494]

Index

of Federal Constitution, 194; at Fayetteville Convention, 216; education of, 225; U.S. Congressman, 277; and University, 258; history of N.C., 393; mentioned, 174, 187, 209
Willis, John, 308-9
Wills, Henry, 144 n, 148, 208-9
Wilmington, 107, 117, 121, 123, 126, 209, 306
Wilson, James, 285-6
Wilson, Robert, 43, 64
Winn, James, 121
Winn, Richard, 51

Winnsborough, S.C., 82, 84, 88, 93, 104
Winton, 120
Witherspoon, John, 25, 27
Wolcott, Oliver, 326, 332
Woodmason, Charles, 20

"X.Y.Z." affair, 294, 299-300, 319, 347

Yates, Robert, 183-4, 185
Yeamans, John, 240
Yorktown, 121

www.ingramcontent.com/pod-product-compliance
Lightning Source LLC
Chambersburg PA
CBHW020727160426
43192CB00006B/138